THE CAMBRIDGE SOCIAL HISTORY
OF BRITAIN 1750–1950

VOLUME 3
Social agencies and institutions

THE CAMBRIDGE SOCIAL HISTORY OF BRITAIN 1750–1950

VOLUME 3

Social agencies and institutions

Edited by

F. M. L. THOMPSON

Director of the Institute of Historical Research
and Professor of History, University of London

CAMBRIDGE
UNIVERSITY PRESS

Published by the Press Syndicate of the University of Cambridge
The Pitt Building, Trumpington Street, Cambridge CB2 1RP
40 West 20th Street, New York, NY 10011–4211, USA
10 Stamford Road, Oakleigh, Victoria 3166, Australia

© Cambridge University Press 1990

First published 1990
First paperback edition 1993

Printed in Great Britain by The Bath Press, Avon

British Library cataloguing in publication data

The Cambridge social history of Britain 1750–1950.
Vol. 3. Social agencies and institutions.
1. Great Britain. Social conditions, 1714–
I. Thompson, F. M. L. (Francis Michael Longstreth)
941.07

Library of Congress cataloguing in publication data

The Cambridge social history of Britain, 1750–1950.
Includes bibliographies and indexes.
Contents: v. 1. Regions and communities –
v. 2. People and their environment –
v. 3. Social agencies and institutions.
1. Great Britain – Social conditions.   2. Social
institutions – Great Britain – History.   3. Associations,
institutions, etc. – Great Britain – History.
I. Thompson, F. M. L. (Francis Michael Longstreth)
HN385.C14   1990   306′.0941   89-9840
ISBN 0 521 25788 3 (v. 1)
ISBN 0 521 25789 1 (v. 2)
ISBN 0 521 25790 5 (v. 3)

ISBN 0 521 25790 5 hardback
ISBN 0 521 43814 4 paperback

Contents

Contributors

VIRGINIA BERRIDGE is co-director of the recently established unit for the social history of AIDS at the London School of Hygiene and Tropical Medicine, University of London. Her work on the social history of medicine includes (with J. G. Edwards) *Opium and the People: Opiate Use in Nineteenth-Century England* (1981), and many articles on the history of addiction.

V. A. C. GATRELL is Fellow of Gonville and Caius College, Cambridge. He has worked on the history of the cotton industry as well as on the history of crime and policing. He edited, with B. Lenman and G. Parker, *Crime and the Law: The Social History of Crime in Western Europe since 1500* (1980).

JOSÉ HARRIS is Fellow of St Catherine's College, Oxford. Her publications on the formation of social policy include *Unemployment and Politics: A Study of English Social Policy, 1886–1914* (1972), and *William Beveridge: A Biography* (1977).

R. J. MORRIS is Senior Lecturer in Economic and Social History, University of Edinburgh. He is the author of *Class and Class Consciousness in the Industrial Revolution, 1780–1850* (1979), and editor, with J. Langton, of *Atlas of Industrializing Britain, 1780–1914* (1986), and contributor of many articles on the middle classes.

JAMES OBELKEVICH is Lecturer in Social History, University of Warwick. His contributions to the social history of religion include *Religion and Rural Society: South Lindsey 1825–1875* (1976), and, with L. Roper and R. Samuel, *Disciplines of Faith: Studies in Religion, Politics and Patriarchy* (1987).

F. K. PROCHASKA is Research Fellow at the Wellcome Institute, London, working on the history of the King's Hospital Fund. His many works on Victorian and twentieth-century philanthropy include *Women and Philanthropy in Nineteenth-Century England* (1980), and *The Voluntary Impulse* (1988).

GILLIAN SUTHERLAND is Fellow of Newnham College, Cambridge, and historian of education. Her books include *Policy-Making in Elementary Education 1870–1895* (1973), and *Ability, Merit and Measurement: Mental Testing and English Education 1880–1940* (1984).

PAT THANE is Principal Lecturer in Social and Political Theory, Goldsmiths' College, University of London. She edited *The Origins of British Social Policy* (1978), and her many other contributions in the field include *The Foundations of the Welfare State* (1982).

Editorial preface

The historian's job is to find out about the past and make it intelligible and accessible to the present. Such an apparently straightforward task is by no means as simple as it may sound. Finding out what happened and interpreting it in patterns and designs which make sense of the past are complicated and demanding processes, requiring scholarship and expertise of a high order, but their value remains limited unless the results are communicated in a language and form which reach beyond the restricted circle of fellow-specialists. Communication is particularly important for social history, a field whose contours and boundaries have altered out of all recognition in the last generation, a subject which is bubbling with the vitality of an outpouring of monographs and journal articles, and a young discipline which lacks the settled framework of a conventional orthodoxy or a received interpretation within which or against which new departures or open rebellions can be placed or assessed. The old stand-bys – constitutional history, political history, diplomatic history, ecclesiastical history, for example – all have these established frameworks which define their subject matters and enshrine explanations of the course of history. These are widely familiar, although often misleading or mistaken; this means that the terms of debate are well understood, that revisions are easily recognised as revisions, and that the iconoclasm of overturning entrenched views does not go unnoticed. Economic history, while much younger than these other subjects, has nevertheless established its rules of enquiry, its methodologies, and its canons of debate, even if it has never succeeded in staking out a territory with sharply defined and stable boundaries. Some might say that it has dug a groove for itself which succeeds in shutting out adequate consideration of factors of central importance, for example the nature and operation of demand and of consumption, in which social history can be illuminating and supportive.

Social history derives its appeal and fascination in no small measure from its open-endedness, its freedom from the constraints of a formal tradition, its eclectic habits, and stands in no need of being rendered into an authorised version. This is just as well, for orthodoxies are not created by editorial decree and if perchance they are fashioned by bands of disciples then the three volumes of this series are in little danger of becoming a Cambridge gospel, for the authors do not belong to any one single camp and do not have a common axe to grind. That is not to say that they are a particularly disputatious or dogmatic bunch, but simply that they are a team of individualists each of whom has been invited to bring their own scholarly judgment to bear on the task in hand. That task is to communicate the fruits of recent writing and the most recent research in social history to the wider audience of students who are curious to know what the specialists have been doing and how their work fits into a general picture of the whole process of social change and development. There are two ways of producing a synthesis: single-handed combat, in which one author takes on the whole field and produces a digest and interpretation of a large slice of history; or a team effort, in which the field is sliced up among contributors according to their expertise and the overview is a co-ordinated package of separate authoritative elements. As with individual sports and team games, tennis and cricket or golf and football, each approach has its own attractions and disadvantages, for players and spectators alike, and each has its partisans. There are several examples of solo syntheses on offer in the field of modern social history, notably from Penguin, Fontana–Collins, and Hutchinson. As the author of one of these it is not my purpose to decry their merits. No doubt their main strength comes from the coherence and unity which a picture of an entire landscape may have when seen through one pair of eyes and painted by one hand, and their main weakness from the inability of a single pair of eyes to see everything or to be well educated and well informed about the structure and meaning of all the features in that landscape.

Such virtues and vices are neatly balanced by the collaborative synthesis, in which each major feature is given critical appraisal by a leading specialist, while the landscape as a whole is left to look after itself in the expectation that an impression will form in the mind of the beholder. It would be unwise to try to compensate for this by raising an overarching superstructure over the individual contributions in these volumes, for that would come close to courting a disaster akin to those which customarily visit university buildings designed in committee. The design of this, the first enterprise to marshal the resources of the multi-author technique to view the entire sweep of modern British social history, does, however, call for explanatory comment and description.

In the last generation or so social historians have been casting their nets wider and wider, into waters previously unnoticed and unexplored by historians as well as into those formerly fished with the conventional equipment of the political, administrative, or trade-union historian. So far has this gone that it is sometimes said that all history which is not concerned with the technicalities of high politics, diplomacy, or econometrics has become a kind of social history. This social history has moved a long way, in its intellectual approach as well as in its subject matter, from the 'history with the politics left out' which still served as a definition of social history in the 1940s. There may not be a 'new' social history in the same way that there is a 'new' economic history as a school of thought applying econometrics and models drawn from economic theory to the understanding of historical economic phenomena; but social historians draw widely on concepts from historical demography, social anthropology, sociology, social geography, and political science, as well as from economics, and are well aware of the importance of quantification. Social historians operating in this conceptually eclectic and experimental fashion do not have the methodological certainty, unity, or rigidity of 'new' economic history, and deal in conclusions which are probable and plausible rather than directly verifiable.

This social history has generated many vigorous controversies and debates on topics within the period covered by this series: on the standard of living, class formation, the labour aristocracy, or social control, for example, and more recently on gender roles and women's emancipation. These issues have not been picked out for separate treatment in these volumes. The debates are best followed in the original exchanges, or in the several admirable surveys which are available, and references can be found in the bibliographies here. The issues, moreover, are best understood when placed within the framework of the conditions, customs, and institutions that shaped the way in which the people lived. Hence questions of class, social relationships, gender differences and roles, and social conflict are discussed in the context of a series of particular themes which constitute the main elements in that framework. The thematic structure means that much matter of interest is left out, because it chances to fall into one of the oubliettes between themes; but while there is no attempt at a literally complete coverage, taken together the chapters add up to a comprehensive and balanced account of the complexity, and diversity, of the interactions between continuity and change which have determined the development of British society in the two centuries since 1750.

The series, indeed, provides three social histories of these two centuries, each one complete in itself at a level of partial coverage. That is to say, the volumes themselves are not divided chronologically, but into three broad thematic clusters: regional communities; social environment; and social institutions. Much of the recent pioneering work in social history has advanced through intensive study of particular localities and communities, and Volume 1, *Regions and Communities*, draws on this approach by presenting a series of chapters on the social histories of distinctive regions. This is not an attempt to parcel up the whole of Britain into a number of regions, which could run the risk of reducing social history to a sub-branch of local history. It is, rather, a collection of studies of regions – if Scotland and Wales can forgive the label – whose separate identity is clearly established by their distinctive national, institutional, legal, and administrative histories, and of those of undisputed significance as examples of immense social and economic change (the north-west), concentration of power and wealth (the metropolis), and violent changes in fortune (the north-east). The obvious geographical gaps in this disposition are bridged by two chapters, on the countryside and on the city, whose 'regions' are not localities with fixed boundaries but shifting social territories defined by environmental, occupational, and cultural criteria. Regional communities, their social cohesion, disintegration, and reformation, are strongly influenced by regional economies, and this volume, therefore, is more directly concerned than the following two with the links between economic history and social history, and with explicit confrontation of the interaction of economy and society.

Where questions of social structure and class relations are raised in the setting of specific localities in Volume 1, in Volume 2, *People and their Environment*, they are approached, using national data and national patterns, through a collection of studies of the living and working environment. The family and household, the social implications of demographic change, domesticity and the separation of home and workplace, housing and the changing meaning of the home, the working environment and employer–worker relationships, nutrition and patterns of food and drink consumption, and leisure and popular culture are the themes of this volume. Together they show how the social order was shaped, reproduced, and changed through the processes of getting, spending, and staying alive, through family, marriage, home, work, consumption, and leisure. These agencies both generated and mediated social tensions, but the more explicit, institutionalised, efforts to protect the social order, to control or suppress conflicts, to influence attitudes and behaviour, and to manipulate social conditions are reserved for Volume 3, *Social Agencies and Institutions*. Much of the running was made by those in power and authority, and the chapters on government and society which explain the changing impact of government on people's lives and the changes in popular expectations of what government could and should provide, as well as the chapter on crime and policing, are central to this theme. Most socialisation, however, took place through voluntary and non-official institutions that were largely generated from within a social group and not imposed upon it. These are the subject of chapters on philanthropy and voluntary associations; while education, religion, and health were in a half-way position, partly the province of official and often coercive action, partly a sphere of voluntaryism, self-help, and self-determination.

Each volume is self-contained, with its own set of bibliographies, and with each chapter carrying its own chronology of the 200 years. Together the three volumes, with their three different and complementary angles of approach, are designed to offer an integrated and well-rounded social history that is exciting and challenging, as well as being as up-to-date as the contributors, who have written at different times within the last five years, can make it.

F. M. L. THOMPSON

CHAPTER 1

Government and society in England and Wales, 1750–1914

PAT THANE

The theme of this chapter is the manner in which Government influenced the lives of citizens of England and Wales, their behaviour and conditions of life according to which principles and with what effects. A central assumption – widely shared for a substantial portion of the period, most fully developed in the ideas and actions of Peel and Gladstone, though with earlier roots, and most dominant from the 1840s to the 1870s – was that the government's role was at most strictly limited, that it not only should not but could not determine the structure and working of society. Rather its role was to provide a firmly established and clearly understood framework within which society could very largely run itself.

Even in the mid-Victorian period the reality of government action did not wholly match this ideal, but it was widely enough shared at all social levels for government transgression of it long to require justification against challenges. It had distinctive institutional effects. In contrast with most other societies of the period in England and Wales, many of the functions performed by central government else-where were, throughout the period, performed by groups of self-governing citizens either on an elective, but unpaid, official basis, as in the various institutions of local government, or through voluntary associations. Though Britain certainly possessed highly effective central government institutions, unlike other European countries she did not develop in the nineteenth century a strong bureaucratic stratum with powerful interests of its own, a strong set of popular expectations of the role of the state or a sense of popular identification with it. Victorian central government involved itself in the lives of its citizens in many ways and had a clear vision of its role, but its methods of, for example, taxing and policing the population were, compared with other societies of the time, indirect and discreet. A range of buffer institutions, both official and voluntary, developed between this

1

central state and the citizen such that by the 1880s the only agent of the central state whom the provincial citizen could regularly expect to encounter was the benign post office clerk.

Such a system of government was both a product and a reinforcement of a relatively homogeneous and stable society. England in the later eighteenth century had the advantage of being linguistically and geographically far more homogeneous than other European states. After the Act of Union Scotland was increasingly integrated into the British whole. Improved roads, postal communications, an expanding press furthered this integration. The system of government did not emerge without challenge and Victorian society was by no means free from conflict, though compared with much of continental Europe tensions were muted and contained. The flexibility provided by a system of government which was not rigidly centralised or bureaucratised left space for negotiation and rapid adaptation, within limits, in periods of conflict or crisis, such as war.

This approach to government emerged from the somewhat different circumstances of the eighteenth century, and from the 1880s the visible power of the central state grew, as did demands for further growth, although the dominant ideas of the immediately preceding period retained significant force until at least 1914. The state in the late eighteenth and nineteenth centuries went, as it had in previous times, through a continuing process of change and adaptation, not usefully characterised as progress. What was the nature of these changes and how did they come about?

I

Characterisation of the eighteenth-century state is taking on a new but yet not wholly distinct shape in a period which historians are at last bringing excitingly to life. Current interpretations range from its description as: 'an *ancien régime* state, dominated politically, culturally and ideologically by the three pillars of an early modern social order: monarchy, aristocracy, church'[1] to emphasis not only upon its decidedly powerful character but also upon its increasing accommodation to structural change (including rapid population growth, the capitalisation of agriculture and industrialisation) and to the

---

[1] Publicity handout for J. C. D. Clark, *English Society, 1688–1832* (Cambridge, 1985), quoted in Linda Colley, 'The Politics of Eighteenth-Century British History', *Journal of British Studies*, 25 (1986), p. 369 n. 26.

associated, changing needs and demands of assertive social groups among the prosperous and confident gentry, financiers and other business people, and among the lower orders.

New interpretations are reactions against an older perception of the eighteenth-century state as limited in ambitions and activities, such that 'the work of the British government was virtually restricted to preserving the constitution (which meant doing nothing in home affairs) and conducting foreign policy';[2] domestic affairs (such as maintenance of law and order, relief of the poor) being seen, in this view, as largely delegated to the local responsibility of landowning elites, in contrast to their conduct by armies, police forces and bureaucracies as in continental autocracies.

It has long been hard to understand how so modest a state could so effectively have achieved victory in a succession of eighteenth-century wars, extended its empire (if with a major loss in North America), acquired extraordinary economic and political power in international terms and maintained domestic harmony in a period of considerable structural change. Assessing the exact nature and extent of the activities of the eighteenth-century state is complicated by the lack of good institutional histories, for example of the influence of the crown or of the House of Lords. But it is clear that in the eighteenth century Parliaments met more frequently and for longer periods than before 1688 and were increasingly, as the century went on, considering more items of national domestic legislation than before, in addition to the local and private bills with which its time has previously been assumed to have been absorbed; that the army was trained and dispersed with the maintenance of order at home at least as much in mind as winning victory abroad (with considerable success on both counts); and (an important indicator and reinforcement of its power) the British state could extract more taxation, more regressive in its incidence, whilst arousing less opposition from its citizens than could its more openly authoritarian European peers. In the 1760s Britain succeeded in appropriating about 20 per cent of the nation's output in taxation, almost twice the comparable French figure.[3]

The amount of revenue which a government can raise through taxation strongly influences the range of activities it can undertake without risking debilitating debt. The means whereby the British government maximised its revenue through taxation, in comparison with its major

[2]   Colley, 'The Politics of Eighteenth-Century British History', pp. 372–3.
[3]   *Ibid.*, p. 359.

European rival, is instructive about its methods of government and its relationship with society more generally. Between the mid-eighteenth century and 1810 Britain was able more effectively and flexibly to appropriate an increasing share of rising national income even than Napoleon following his administrative and institutional modernisation of the French state. Yet taxation was a cause of major political crisis in France as it was not in Britain. In Britain direct taxes, including land taxes, were paid by all social groups with no privileged exemptions; they were paid by landowners who passed them on to tenant farmers, labourers, artisans and other tenants in rents and other charges, a form of tax payment which was 'invisible' to the lower orders as direct taxes were not to the independent, *taille*-paying French peasantry. They were levied and assessments made locally by unpaid representatives of the taxpaying gentry and magistracy. This amateur administration minimised corruption and evaded the resentment aroused by the professional collectors backed by the more openly severe legal powers prevalent in France. It was a method of amateur, decentralised but effective administration widely employed by the British state.

Indirect taxes were levied on a wider range of goods in France, directly upon the household by officials with strict powers of enforcement, at levels of incidence which varied regionally. In Britain also officials with strict enforcement powers levied customs and excise duties, which provoked skirmishes on occasion and frequent evasion. But the tax was upon a narrower range of goods, was nationally uniform and levied not upon the purchaser but upon the manufacturer or importer, who passed it on to the consumer for whom, again, the tax was 'invisible' and involved no direct contact with officialdom. The result was a higher tax yield in Britain than in France, efficiently collected by means which strictly contained potential points of conflict.[4]

Nor did British governments risk trouble over matters of taxation by overstepping the limits of consent in this highly sensitive area. The income tax, introduced in 1799, to help pay for the war, which evolved during the war into a reasonably efficient and equitable tax, was summarily ended by Parliament in 1816, against the preference

---

[4] P. Mathias and P. O'Brien, 'Taxation in Britain and France, 1715–1810: A Comparison of the Social and Economic Incidence of Taxes Collected for the Central Government', *Journal of European Economic History*, 5 (1976), pp. 601–50.

of the Treasury and of government leaders, but following pressure from landed and other monied taxpayers. It obliged all with incomes above £200 p.a. to declare their income and was regarded as a serious encroachment upon liberty, acceptable in time of war but not of peace.

By the mid-eighteenth century, indeed, England had developed an apparatus of central government comparable with most European states. In addition to the effectiveness of the standing army and of the fiscal system, though it acknowledged no regulatory role over the economy, through the legal system it was the enforcer of business contracts and through private acts of Parliament sanctioned enclosures, dock building, turnpike trusts and canal companies. The mercantilist inheritance remained powerful: British overseas trade was protected and promoted. A complex range of tariffs and prohibitions protected production, notably of corn, timber and sugar. Under a series of ancient statutes labour mobility might be curtailed, wages fixed and crafts protected through regulation of apprenticeship. Unlike in most other European countries the indigent were relieved within the framework of a national poor law, financed through local taxes (rates) and administered very largely in accordance with local needs and preferences.

There are strong indications, then, that the eighteenth-century British state had the will and the capacity to influence the lives of its citizens in a variety of ways, which may explain the increased appetite of members of the landed elite for official employment later in the century. However, it did so by methods markedly less visible than those of its European counterparts, operating through channels which were decentralised though closely linked with central government, and it showed some sensitivity to the dangers of overstepping too far the limits of consent. Compared with other eighteenth-century states, England was unusual in the combination of strength and liberality of its government, the two qualities being mutually reinforcing. The roots of this combination lay in England's long tradition of unusually strong royal government and, compared with much of continental Europe, somewhat weaker feudal nobility, combined with an equally strong indigenous tradition of attachment to 'liberty', popularly believed to be embodied and upheld above all in the common law and by Parliament.

This strong central state was associated with an unusual range of 'free institutions', official and voluntary, enabling local communities to achieve a high degree of self-government within the broad framework of the law and their representatives to influence the activities of central government. Parliament could and did act as a check upon the actions of crown, ministers (normally resident in the House of Lords) and civil service. Chartered municipalities had considerable independence in the conduct of their local affairs including, often (their exact powers varied with the terms of their charters), extensive judicial powers, both civil and criminal. Unpaid justices of the peace (*ex officio* members of municipal corporations, in the counties nominees of the Lords Lieutenant, approved by the crown, of varied background) had a wide range of powers at the local level. They could arrest and punish offenders for drunkenness, vagrancy, profanity, poaching and much else. They supervised ale-houses, decided bastardy cases and exercised jurisdiction over runaway servants or apprentices. They might fix prices and wages, regulate apprenticeships, order highway maintenance, decide poor law policy (as authorities above the parishes), suppress nuisances, oversee markets, license or ban fairs and amusements, appoint constables, assess rates.

Even in the area of policing the English householder constable system may well have been a more effective force than its professional French equivalent. Poor relief policy was effectively made at parish level by local ratepayers, and administered normally also by ratepayers taking up in rotation the post of overseer of the poor. The practice of poor law administration varied from place to place and over time according to local conditions and pressures. The magistrates' bench could intervene but was not necessarily attended to. Through the eighteenth and early nineteenth centuries, however, Parliament recurrently paid close attention to poor law policy, and changes in the framework of national policy were proposed and discussed, though it felt unable to make major changes before 1834.[5]

Central government had long provided a framework within which local communities provided for their poor. Space also existed for new community institutions to emerge in response to new needs and to obtain government sanction. A striking example is 'the remarkable flowering of initiative in the provision of civic amenities which took place in the late eighteenth and early nineteenth centuries'.[6]

[5]   P. Mandler, 'The Making of the New Poor Law *Redivivus*', *Past & Present*, 117 (1987).
[6]   E. P. Hennock, 'The Creation of an Urban Local Government System in England and Wales', in Helmut Naunin, ed., *Stadteordnungen des 19 Jahrhunderts* (Köln, 1984), p. 22.

Municipal corporations had no tradition of responsibility for regulating and improving the urban environment. As towns grew in the later eighteenth century and environmental problems multiplied, better off citizens did not turn to the existing corporations for improvement measures but established free associations of their own to obtain from Parliament, by means of a petition or local bill, powers to levy a local rate to provide urban areas with street-lighting, stone paving, watchmen, refuse removal and much else. These 'improvement commissioners' existed in urban areas with and without municipal corporations, sometimes in corporate boroughs overlapping in membership with the corporation, but legally distinct.

The belief in local responsibility for local needs was strong, sanctioned, supervised, but not intrusively controlled by central government. Closely associated with it was the conviction that all members of the community possessed certain rights, enforceable at law, including that of subsistence, if not from labour at a fair rate of pay then through poor relief. However weakly, burgesses and landowners felt it their responsibility to uphold these rights and primarily through the agency of the magistracy could do so. Individuals could believe in, and defend, the rights of 'free born Englishmen' – in particular the rights to basic material security, protection from violence, theft and extreme oppression – because the authorities paid sufficient, if far from complete, attention to them to invest them with reality. The courts tended to favour the rich against the poor, but not so invariably as to make freedom before the law a myth. Though the penalties available to the criminal law became more severe during the eighteenth century (many more offences became liable to capital punishment) they were not necessarily more frequently invoked, but rather developed as part of a system of deterrence, in an exemplary manner possible only in a society which broadly accepted the need to protect property and to restrain violence.[7]

Those holding governing responsibility generally did not try to exclude the mass of the population from all participation in the regulation of their own lives. Through the courts, through petition to those in authority, attendance at parish meetings – where even non-ratepayers could influence decisions, on such matters as policing and poor relief policy, customarily reached by acclamation rather than

---

[7] J. Brewer and J. Styles, eds., *An Ungovernable People: The English and their Law in the Seventeenth and Eighteenth Centuries* (1980).

the vote – through the similar intervention of non-voters in parliamentary elections in which voting was not secret, even the lower orders could express their views and exert some influence. As, still more effectively, could disaffected sections of the gentry and the middling classes aided by their capacity to use an expanding press, to organise public meetings, to vote for and to petition Parliament.

The country was governed through a process of negotiation in which, of course, the sides were strictly unequal and the poorest played least part, but which could avoid severe conflict because the rulers were not wholly cut off from popular aspirations nor the population at any level without hope of redress or the capacity to express grievances. Eighteenth-century society was not 'democratic' in any meaningful sense, but nor was that of the 1900s; what is not plain is that those outside the limited circles directly able to influence government were necessarily or always *more* excluded from negotiation over matters of crucial importance to their lives than they were to become, although major changes occurred in the channels and processes of negotiation.

The combination of strength and overall control by central government linked with decentralised liberal institutions enshrining a strong sense of local community and of the duty to safeguard individual rights within that community created a distinctive type of *ancien régime* state, which was neither a simple expression of social relations, nor an accidental product of historical accumulation, but a partially autonomous creation operating according to clear and widely understood principles.

II

In the last quarter of the eighteenth century, largely in response to the pressures of demographic and economic change and of war, successive governments set about the task of making central government more professional, more efficient and, in relation to the economy, in particular under Pitt, more liberal. Steps were taken to reduce the role of influence and patronage in the civil service. The Treasury was reorganised, sinecures reduced, a new career structure initiated. The first moves were made towards a new conception of 'service' which gave salience to responsibility and efficiency. Government placed more reliance upon expertise and greater specialisation of work in departments. The Treasury began to emerge as the department crucial to central control of administrative efficiency and financial accountability. The civil service remained small and change was gradual but it became better suited to carrying greater power and responsibility delegated by Parliament.

Associated with the changes was the belief on the part of government that political liberalisation and constitutional reform were unnecessary and undesirable. Rather it was thought that efficient, clear-sighted central government promoting equitable and expedient laws could best promote the nation's prosperity, international position and internal stability. It might effectively and justifiably be led by men of landed background since land, though increasingly diversified and commercialised, stood at the core of capitalist expansion and landowners recognised that governing responsibility lay with them.

The period of the French wars, from 1793, demonstrated the effectiveness of the central state apparatus in its successful conduct of the war administration and of war finance. The costs of war, its organisational demands and, not least, the fear in elite circles of the spread of the revolutionary contagion from France brought about changes in the structure and activities of government, difficult though these influences are to disentangle from those of the significant economic, demographic and social changes of the twenty-two years of war. Most clearly, fears of political upheaval drew the government into a more overtly interventionist role than was customary in peacetime with the suspension of Habeas Corpus in 1794 and 1798, the Treason and Sedition Act, 1795, the Unlawful Oaths Act, 1797, the Corresponding Societies Act, 1799, the Stamp Duties Act, 1796, restricting circulation of the press, all designed to prevent or silence organised opposition. In the absence of systematic comparisons with other eighteenth-century wars, however, it is not clear that the government did impose stricter controls in this war. It was, for example, standard practice to suspend Habeas Corpus in wartime.

Social questions continued to be addressed at central and local level in wartime. Demographic pressure combined with rising food prices caused a crisis for the rural poor law, for which parishes and justices devised a variety of responses in accordance with local pressures and needs, most commonly parochial employment of paupers, or a labour rate, or variants on the Speenhamland provision (initiated in 1795) of relief in proportion to size of family and the price of bread. In the prosperous war years landowners could, more willingly than they were always inclined, afford to acknowledge the rights of the poor to subsistence.[8]

At parliamentary level investigative select committees proliferated, some in response to organised pressures, producing some legislation, notably the abolition of the slave trade in 1807 and the Health and Morals of Apprentices Act in 1802. Equally notable was the inability to enforce the latter attempt to improve the conditions of cotton factory children. Enforcement was placed in the hands of local magistrates and clergy, provided that they were not themselves mill owners, with exiguous effects. Effective enforcement was impossible through existing machinery in the absence of consent from powerful groups materially affected by the legislation. Government was unwilling to incur disapprobation by developing new machinery for enforcement except under urgent pressure, which was, in this case, absent.

Public order remained a problem after the war, from the Pentridge rising of 1815 to Peterloo in 1819, fuelled by postwar unemployment, demographic pressure, the ebbs and flows of a still unstable industrialism, fluctuations in the economically dominant agricultural sector and the effects of a rapid, government-guided deflation which appeared unduly to favour the rich. Habeas Corpus was once more suspended in 1817; the Six Acts followed Peterloo. At the local level justices mollified expressions of discontent where they could, applied summary punishment where they could not; maintained, with the parishes, a flexible if never generous poor relief policy; encouraged the increased use of imprisonment of offenders; and sought to pacify or to destroy the centres where the lower orders made the associational links which could turn to discussion of grievances: beer places, fairs, Guy Fawkes celebrations, prize fights, footraces, cockfights were more strictly policed, controlled, pacified or banned, though not everywhere or without opposition.[9] The other side of the controls was the further official and unofficial encouragement of virtue through, for example, the formation by local social leaders of voluntary institutions (such as Sunday schools or friendly societies) for those below them, attempting, not always successfully, to substitute 'rational' for turbulent recreation, channels for exhortation to stability, responsibility, sobriety and hard work.

Against this background, following the temporary derangement brought about by the war, the moves of Pitt and his contemporaries

[8] Mandler, 'Poor Law', pp. 134–5.
[9] R. D. Storch, ed., *Popular Culture and Custom in Nineteenth-Century England* (1982).

towards more professional, and economically liberal, if politically authoritarian, government were carried forward by the 'liberal Tory' governments of the years after 1815. Underlying and promoting change in this direction was a changing approach to the role and theory of government which achieved increasing support in aristocratic, gentry, government and business circles in and out of Parliament. Its theme was further reconstruction of the powers of Parliament, executive and party with the aim of reducing them to the provision of a framework within which individuals and free institutions could operate with maximum safety and freedom. Government should maintain but modernise and streamline its irreducible public order and foreign policy functions whilst stripping away the great pre-modern weight of intrusive legislation, custom and regulation especially in relation to economic activity and the remaining bureaucratic inefficiency and corruption. In their place should be constructed mechanisms which would emulate and assist, or at least not impede, the automatic mechanism of the 'natural order' which was believed to lie beneath and to be impeded in its beneficial working by the unnecessary superstructure created over the centuries. Thus liberated individuals and the economy would be freed to achieve optimal fulfilment of their potential. Society would be freed from the shackles of customary rights, the elite of their responsibility for enforcing them. In this view the maximisation of the freedom of the individual to enjoy his property and the development of his intellect and aptitudes in a framework provided by minimal, efficient and undemocratic government was more important, a more certain guarantor of 'liberty', than the extension of political rights currently being demanded by constitutional reformers.

The theory of government could be and was sustained by selective reading of political economy and utilitarian thought. Equally importantly in a period when political and religious thought were a unity in most minds and evangelicalism was becoming a major medium through which members of powerful social groups constructed their understanding of a changing world (as Methodism was for many of the lower orders), evangelicals could equate the 'natural order' with the workings of Providence.[10] Moral and material rewards would come to individuals and to society as a whole in return for the exercise

---

[10] Boyd Hilton, 'The Role of Providence in Evangelical Social Thought', in D. Beales and G. Best, eds., *History, Society and the Churches* (Cambridge, 1985).

of responsible independent activity. Human constructs like constitutions risked interference with this natural order which provided the only secure basis for social stability and progress. Such a theory competed with older ideas of rights and responsibilities and even those who embraced it were not in agreement as to the desirable role of central government. Hence the boundaries between the permissible activities of the strong central state and those of free institutions and individuals, between public and private spheres of activity, were at the core of political contention throughout the nineteenth century as the state went through the long process of adaptation.

The repeal in 1815 of the ancient Assize of Bread, whereby prices of bread and ale could be controlled through the courts, following a select committee recommendation that 'more benefit is likely to result from the effects of free competition',[11] was accompanied by the introduction of the Corn Law in the same year, protecting a powerful economic interest. Interest in constitutional reform was limited in government circles, but the Sturges Bourne Select Vestries Acts of 1818 and 1819 were moves towards the equation of political participation with property rights. Whereas previously all ratepayers had held votes of equal weight, where select vestries were formed ratepayers were granted between one and six votes according to weight of property.

It was in the 1820s that a strategy of constructing a minimal but firm regulatory state within which a free economy and free individuals could flourish clearly took precedence in government circles. The movement towards liberalisation of the economy was most evident under the Tory governments of the mid to late 1820s. Huskisson, Peel and their colleagues operated in the belief that it was both useless and immoral for governments to try to rescue economic victims whether they were bankrupt capitalists or unemployed handweavers (in 1826 Peel refused financial relief to companies which had crashed). It was useless because the government's effective powers of intervention were extremely limited; immoral because economic actors who failed were deemed not to have exercised conscience in their commercial dealings. Rather, by dismantling ancient restrictions on trade, reducing the range of protective duties, beginning the construction of a system for regulating the conduct of banking and the supply of money, enabling joint stock companies to be formed by, in 1825,

---

[11] Quoted in John Burnett, *Plenty and Want: a Social History of Diet from 1815 to the Present Day* (Harmondsworth, 1968), p. 111.

repealing the Bubble Act, the government could provide a framework which more effectively supported and facilitated hard work and fair dealing.

In home affairs Peel at the Home Office (1822–7, 1828–30) initiated the reconstruction of the government's public order role, substituting the strict interventionism of his Tory predecessors and their use of espionage and *agents provocateurs* with 'preventative police' designed not to impose blanket controls upon all citizens but to identify and punish actual transgressors, combining maximum freedom where possible with strict force where necessary. The Metropolitan Police Force was founded in 1829 under the direct control of the Home Secretary; the strength of hostility to central authority and of support for local autonomy was such that a national force could not be created for the remainder of the country, which for the time being retained established systems of policing. Peel also reduced the number of capital and other offences, but encouraged more rigorous enforcement of penalties for those which remained.

The right to form trade unions (in the eyes of this government an acceptable means whereby men protected their property in their labour, provided that they did so peaceably) was restored in 1824 and 1825 following its withdrawal in the panic years of the war, and other wartime restrictions upon freedom of speech and association were lifted.

But the Tories set their faces against 'useless' constitutional reform and such social intervention as factory reform. 'Peel's objective, indeed, was to show that fiscal liberalism was possible without political reform; equality of opportunity should be the gradual result of fiscal measures not the result of deliberately pursued programmes of social and political reform.'[12] They had, however, underestimated popular support for customary rights and the reality of fears of the consequences of their withdrawal without provision of convincing safeguards for individuals liberated into the marketplace. The Tory approach strengthened demands for constitutional reform, above all reform of a Parliament which was seen as abandoning its role as guardian of popular liberties and, rather, sanctioning retrenchment upon them. The outcome was the upheavals of 1830–2, the return of the Whigs and the Reform Act of 1832.

[12] H. C. G. Matthew, *Gladstone, 1809–1874* (Oxford, 1986), p. 172.

III

The chief thrust of pre-1830 Whiggery was defence of political and civil liberty against arbitrary rule by the executive and support for moderate constitutional reform. The Whig tradition of judicious intervention in social questions, stemming from Fox, was muted, but it revived in office under the younger generation which gradually took over after 1830. The Whigs in the 1830s were more interventionist than their predecessors though they differed among themselves as to the nature and degree of desirable interventionism, indeed appeared to be searching for an acceptable social policy. They were, in any case, severely constrained by social and political pressures as to what they could reasonably hope to achieve. Their stance can broadly be characterised as standing with the Peelites on economic liberalism; on social issues – essentially questions of state intervention in public health, safety and morals – they took an independent line. 'They exhibited great impatience with endless debates over the *abstract* question of state intervention. They preferred a case-by-case judgment on the merits. If they agreed that the nation's weal was wedded to wealth, they would never go so far as to subordinate completely the former to the latter. They preferred an even-handed approach to securing both.'[13]

The religious inspiration was weaker upon the Whigs and the tradition of aristocratic paternal obligation stronger. It was not, however, overwhelming; they were too thoroughly imbued with notions of individualism. They 'favoured a society which was hierarchic but not authoritarian; pluralist but not organic'.[14] Yet though they might accept the liberal vision of a self-regulating society populated by economic free agents as an ideal, they recognised its limitations in the real world. Labouring men and women still required protection if they were to be materially and morally equipped for the responsibilities to be thrust upon them. Individuals needed positive assistance to attain and use freedom.

'Thus the guiding role of the noble paternalist remained but the ends to which subordinates were to be guided had changed and with them the style of rule.' The moral dicta of the old society – obedience, humility, sobriety and right conduct – had begun to yield to the liberal

[13]   P. Mandler, 'Cain and Abel: Two Aristocrats and the Early Victorian Factory Acts', *Historical Journal*, 27 (1984), p. 96. This section owes a considerable debt to an unpublished paper by Peter Mandler, 'The Strange Birth of Liberal England'.
[14]   Mandler, 'Cain and Abel', p. 107.

ideals of self-determination, advancement, improvement, innovation. Though not hostile to the liberal preference that such guidance should be by voluntary means, they instinctively preferred extension of the sphere of government: 'The times required a bold lead from the liberal aristocracy to march all the classes together along the road of spiritual and material improvement.'[15] But the Whigs were as divided as everyone else as to how extensive the sphere of government should be and constrained by the strength of liberal forces.

Within these broad principles they promoted constitutional reform in 1832. The Act of 1832 defined more clearly than ever before the distinction between those who were and were not sanctioned to wield power and did so entirely in terms of property ownership, entrenching the power of landed wealth whilst acknowledging new sources of power. They further promoted reconstruction of essential institutions of government. In particular the serious delays in the higher courts, due to confusions over procedure and a chaotic appeals system, were dealt with by restructuring the Privy Council and House of Lords appeals procedures; and legislation in 1832 and 1833 sought to establish clear and simplified rules of pleading at common law.

Althorp at the Treasury until 1835 pursued policies of economic liberalism indistinguishable from those of the Tories. However, it has been convincingly argued that the positive commitment of the Whigs to social intervention has been underestimated.[16] Social questions were investigated with unprecedented thoroughness. The Royal Commission overtook the select committee as the chief method of official investigation. Forty-one were established between 1832 and 1841. They were chosen and appointed by ministers and not, like select committees, by proponents of parliamentary bills, and they could include members from outside Parliament. They could investigate in greater depth than a select committee; sittings were not confined to parliamentary terms and staff could be appointed for investigations additional to the oral evidence of witnesses.

What remains unclear is the precise role of the Whigs in relation to members of Royal Commissions, pressure groups, energetic reformers of the kind of Edwin Chadwick – to all of the forces commonly given greater credit for the social measures of the 1830s. Who influenced whom? The Whigs appointed the Royal Commission, used

---

[15] *Ibid.*, p. 108.   [16] *Ibid.*, pp. 107–8.

their patronage to appoint Chadwick and others to administrative posts and the Whig leadership supported most of the social reforms enacted before 1841. Whig ambitions almost certainly went beyond the rather limited outcomes. Two areas of action illustrate the limitations they faced.

State entry into the field of working-class education was a Whig ambition, but it was unprecedented, encroached upon the entrenched interests of Anglicans and Nonconformists and was controversial both on grounds of cost and of its presumed social effects. A succession of Whig bills to foster national education failed to pass both Houses of Parliament. The most that could be achieved was from 1833 an annual grant of £20,000, for school building alone, administered by the religious voluntary societies who continued to take responsibility for the content of education without subordination to government control. The Factory Act of 1833, hastily put together and much influenced by the recommendations of Edwin Chadwick, was much modified in Parliament by mill owner pressure. It restricted the hours of work and attempted to enforce school attendance among mill workers under the age of fourteen. It was largely ineffective, but probably the most that could have been achieved in the climate of the 1830s. It was notable for introducing a new species of agent of the central state and a new method of enforcement: the inspectorate. The inspectors were centrally appointed, specialist, professional civil servants, responsible to the Home Office with, initially, the powers of justices to enter factory premises and enforce the law. Their appointment was an attempt to create an enforcement mechanism independent of customary institutions. It was a cumbersome mechanism – another brainchild of Chadwick – and there were only four of them, covering vast districts (one for the whole of Lancashire and Yorkshire), with too few and poorly paid assistants and the act was widely evaded. The inspectors were reluctant to use their judicial powers due to the opposition they aroused, hence their withdrawal in 1844. More effective enforcement would have faced opposition on grounds of costs, and opposition in principle to state intrusion in industry and upon the liberty of mill owners, if in the interest of that of their workers. Inspection was a method of enforcement and supervision of state legislation which continued to be employed with gradually increasing effectiveness into the twentieth century. Inspectorates with varying powers were appointed to supervise or enforce regulation of the poor law, public health, prisons, mines, public health and schools over the following twenty years. They were an important growth point in the civil service, providing Whitehall with its first provincial arms of administration.

Education and factory reform were new areas of state action. In 1834 the Whigs sought to reconstruct an older one with the Poor Law Amendment Act. This they could do more effectively in view of the closer congruence of the principles underlying the reform with the ideas coming to dominate thinking in ruling circles. It was a further step in ensuring the primacy of property over customary rights and enforcing individual self-responsibility, withdrawing in principle the right of the able-bodied labourer to sustenance and the responsibility of the propertied for him or her. The indigent and helpless retained such rights provided that their pauperisation was indeed judged to be no fault of their own, due to drink or other misbehaviour, and that they had no immediate family able to support them. Along with new (if long proposed and debated) principles of relief was introduced a new administrative structure. The role of magistrates in the poor relief system was reduced, enabling them thereafter to concentrate their efforts more fully upon maintenance of public order. The vestries were replaced with 'unions' of parishes presided over by Boards of Guardians who were elected triennially by ratepayers, allowed multiple votes on the property-related scale introduced in the Sturges Bourne Acts. The act introduced the first nationally uniform and nationwide system of elected local government in Britain.

The guardians appointed the paid officials of the poor law and were responsible for local administration within guidelines established by legislation and administrative orders from a new Central Poor Law Commission composed of three administrators whose membership included Chadwick (who had again been largely responsible for the proposals on which the act was based) and supervised by a regional inspectorate.

The new poor law faced opposition from some landowners still supportive of customary rights and stronger opposition from defenders of local autonomy. The latter became muted as it became clear that a certain local flexibility was permissible, indeed unavoidable if serious crisis was to be avoided. Local poor law practice indeed remained highly variable for the remainder of the century. Labouring people opposed it more fiercely, especially in the north, where implementation, from 1837, coincided with economic downturn. This further loss of customary rights, sanctioned by a reformed Parliament, was an important contributor to the demands for more wholesale reform of Parliament embodied in Chartism.[17]

In the eyes of many (though not all, there were acute divisions of opinion on all of them) of their supporters the education, factory and poor law measures were complementary means of providing a framework within which individuals could become self-supporting actors within the natural order. Educated people freed from degraded work lives and without expectation of community support except for reasons beyond their personal control would become independent contributors to and beneficiaries of increasing abundance. In the cases both of elementary education and factory reform central supervision became somewhat more effective over time. By 1850 the education grant totalled £189,000 p.a., by 1860, £724,000 p.a., supervised from 1839 by a new department, the education committee of the Privy Council. It was not, however, a history of smooth administrative growth.

This enlargement of the public sphere which gathered pace in the 1830s has been described as a 'revolution in government',[18] carried forward by a new type of bureaucrat, brought in from outside the civil service, often from a professional, middle-class, provincial background, said often to have been inspired by the ideas of Jeremy Bentham. Such new men were indeed prominent. Edwin Chadwick, lawyer by training, influential in the construction of the new poor law and of the Factory Act of 1833, public health activist in the 1840s and thereafter a tireless if less influential supporter of reforming causes until his death, was the archetype. At least as influential was James Kay-Shuttleworth (originally James Phillips Kay) initially a medical man, from 1840 secretary to the Privy Council committee for education and until 1849 a remarkable force behind the expansion of state provision for education; Leonard Horner, one of the first factory inspectors; William Farr, another medical man, from 1837 the first Registrar General of Births, Marriages and Deaths, who used his role to investigate the major causes of disease and death and to stress the importance of healthy 'human capital' for a thriving economy.

These men, and others like them, were indeed different in experience and, generally, age from other recruits to the civil service, though like others they were appointed by patronage. Their approach to their role was specialist and professional and also more assertive than was

---

[17]   Mandler, 'Poor Law', p. 157.
[18]   O. Macdonagh, 'The Nineteenth-Century Revolution in Government: A Reappraisal', *Historical Journal*, 1 (1958).

civil service custom. They assumed, and were allowed by ministers to do so, a role of advising on policy, where possible making as well as administering it and of advocating it publicly – theirs was a very public role. They had an historically unique opportunity due to the demand in the 1830s for new areas of expertise in new spheres of government action which the existing service could not provide at the level required, at a time when ministers could still appoint by patronage the advisers they wished. They flourished in a temporary atmosphere of encouragement of such initiatives; though, as already suggested, their precise relationship with the Whigs remains unclear.

They were neither rigid dogmatists seeking to implement a prescribed and unified set of theories, Benthamite or otherwise, though selected elements of Benthamism as of other contemporary theoretical currents plainly influenced them to varying degrees as they did most of those actively concerned about social and economic issues in this period. Nor have historians interpreted them in such crude terms, whatever some commentaries might imply. As Macdonagh and others have recognised, they were influenced in their fields of action by a blend of ideals, ideas and imperatives previously held or pressed on them by discoveries in the course of their professional and subsequent administrative experience.[19] They have been, however, described as initiating a 'self-expanding administrative process',[20] which, acquiring its own momentum, carried state intervention forward despite ideological and political resistance through the middle years of the nineteenth century. Macdonagh proposed a five stage model of such growth: first, public exposure of an intolerable social evil; secondly, legislation to deal with it, which due to inexperience was ineffective; thirdly, the introduction of more effective procedures of enforcement or detection, which continually revealed new problems; fourthly, recognition that occasional parliamentary legislation was inadequate and continuous regulation was required in the light of growing and changing experience; finally, discretionary initiative was given to executive officers to deal with problems as they were continually revealed.[21]

Plainly, administration and government have independent dynamics broadly of this kind, though equally plainly they do not operate

[19] O. Macdonagh, *Early Victorian Government* (1977). U. R. Q. Henriques, *Before the Welfare State: Social Administration in Early Victorian England* (1979), pp. 259–66.

[20] R. Lambert, 'Central and Local Relations in Mid-Victorian England: The Local Government Act Office, 1853–1871', *Victorian Studies*, 6 (1962).

[21] Macdonagh, 'Revolution in Government'.

wholly autonomously of other ideological, social and political forces
but intersect with them. What was or was not judged 'intolerable'
enough to necessitate reform was not simply self-evident but partly
determined by ideology and by structures of power. Bad water
acquired greater salience as a social evil in the 1840s over the at least
as appalling state of housing partly because reluctance to intrude upon
the rights of property ownership made the former more amenable
to solution. Underlying Chadwick's influential proposals to the Factories Inquiry Commission of 1833 was the conviction that the conditions and lack of education of children in the textile factories were
intolerable, whereas he judged the long hours and conditions experienced by adult males less intolerable than the losses he assumed
manufacturers would bear due to a reduction in adult hours of work.
Others disagreed. His was not simple, objective judgment of intolera-
bility. Similarly, the form of action to be taken in response to a range
of perceived evils – punitive or reformative penitentiaries, routinised
or intellectually rewarding elementary education, a supportive or a
deterrent poor law – required choices to be made among the variety
of prescriptions available at the time, which were not determined
simply by administrative imperatives. Only in rare cases, such as the
improvement of the terrible conditions on immigrant ships, was the
solution fairly obvious and relatively simply undertaken.[22] More frequently choices had to be made among competing solutions arising
from differing ideological assumptions, and they were influenced by
sets of social ideas which were not necessarily explicitly theorised,
by social and political pressures and by awareness of what was possible within existing structures of power and of available administrative resources.

The broad framework of ideas within which Chadwick and his peers
operated were clear enough. They shared, to varying degrees with
Bentham and many others, a commitment to honest, efficient and
not excessive government; to institutions which maximised equality
of opportunity to operate freely in the marketplace; they sought a
moralised free enterprise capable of minimising deprivation and
degradation and were prepared, where it was possible and unavoidable, to override the self-interest of employers and property owners
to achieve it. Within such a framework a wide variety of action was
possible and courses of action were chosen amid a variety of

22   O. Macdonagh, *A Pattern of Government Growth, 1800–1960: The Passenger Acts and
their Enforcement* (1961).

constraints which changed over time in no unilinear direction. Macdonagh's progressive model allows too little space for the setbacks experienced to administrative momentum in the 1840s and, still more, in the 1850s. The momentum of growth was checked in the 1840s and its direction altered in important respects in the 1850s for ideological and political motives which do not easily fit the model of self-sustaining growth. The independent Poor Law Commission, proposed by Chadwick, acquired so bad a reputation for tyrannous imposition (assisted by Chadwick's own undiplomatic style) that he was dismissed in 1847, the Commission was wound up and the poor law was brought under closer ministerial control. In the 1850s the civil service was reorganised on principles partially designed to restrain public and innovatory activities in the style of Chadwick and his peers on the part of bureaucrats.

A further limitation on effective government intervention in social questions on lines compatible with customary approaches was the absence of reformed local institutions capable of administering new social measures in the tradition of central government delegation to the locality. The 1834 Act had taken a step towards such reform in respect of the poor law. The Municipal Corporations Act of the following year was a further step. The Whigs had a number of reasons for wishing to reform the ancient corporations. Largely Tory, most had used their powers of patronage to have Tory members returned to Parliament in 1832. Liberal nonconformist burgesses felt that the corporations were failing in their customary duty to represent the interests of their communities to Parliament and felt excluded from local influence. Additionally, the corporations were criticised for failing to use their power as magistrates to maintain law and order throughout the troubled years since 1815 and especially in the riots of 1831. An Act of 1832 prevented municipal corporations from using their funds to influence parliamentary elections. A Royal Commission appointed in 1833, with substantial liberal radical representation, carried out a detailed investigation of the corporations. It recommended elected local government in existing corporate boroughs and other sizeable towns as a further step in the construction of an effective liberal constitution. The legislation which followed was more limited. It laid down a uniform constitution for only 178 existing corporations. Others were deemed too small, with the exception of the City of London which was too large. It was assumed that separate legislation for London would follow, but the power of the City of London Corporation was employed effectively to resist this. Hence London government remained largely an unreformed assortment of vestries, plus the City of London, increasingly reinforced by *ad hoc*, London-wide bodies, until 1888. Unincorporated large towns (such as Birmingham and Manchester) were enabled to seek incorporation and proceeded to do so, Birmingham in 1837, Manchester in 1838; by 1851 the number of municipal boroughs had risen to 196; in 1871 there were 224, by 1891, 295.

For each borough the act established a town council composed three-quarters of councillors elected by male ratepayers (on a one person one vote basis) and one quarter of aldermen chosen by the councillors. There was a property qualification for councillors. The council's accounts were to be audited annually by elected auditors. In theory, every head of household was eligible to pay rates but in practice rates were only levied on those occupying property valuable enough to make the rate worth the trouble of collecting. Hence, poorer householders often did not qualify for the municipal vote. The many single women and widows who did pay rates as heads of households were also excluded until 1869 when Parliament quietly gave them the municipal vote, two years after refusing women the parliamentary vote. The value of a property deemed worth rating was a matter for local discretion and varied widely. In many boroughs the local franchise at least until the 1850s was more limited than the parliamentary franchise.

The principle behind the changes was that of making the corporation more truly responsible to the local community. Whereas members of the former corporations had not infrequently been resident elsewhere, the new municipal franchise was restricted to those residing within 7 miles of the borough, as was council membership. The role of the corporations was not initially seen as primarily governmental or administrative. Indeed they lost one major source of power the unreformed corporations had possessed: that to appoint magistrates, who were thereafter appointed by the crown, i.e. the Lord Chancellor. They acquired only one new function, though a significant one: that of setting up a watch committee responsible for the establishment and conduct of a police force, establishing a framework whereby police forces on the model pioneered by Peel in London could be extended through the country without arousing antagonism against centrally controlled policing. By 1842, 125 boroughs had established a police force, though by 1853 six still had not.

Some corporations carried on functions they had previously

performed where no other body existed to perform them, e.g. Hull and Plymouth supplied water, Leeds and Nottingham did not; Bristol provided street-lighting, Nottingham owned a market. Elsewhere improvement commissions continued their separate existence, although increasingly over the following decade the corporations took over and extended their powers, especially in the 1840s when environmental health issues took on a new prominence. Under the 1848 Public Health Act they were to constitute the local Board of Health, where this was required. By the end of the 1850s in most boroughs the municipal corporation had become the recognised sanitary authority. This was primarily because the extensive environmental improvements which localities were under increasing popular and central pressure to provide, such as comprehensive drainage systems, necessitated a degree of ratepayer consent and resources available only to elected local government. This led on to a widening range of responsibilities as the century went on and councils increasingly became significant governing institutions.

But their chief function in the 1830s was seen as the representation of local opinion on national and local issues to Parliament, through resolutions and petitions, and it was not uncommon for them to do so on a wide range of issues. Local urban elites often regarded the solution of social problems as the role of voluntary rather than municipal action. The extent and form of the activities of the municipalities for the remainder of the century depended to a great extent upon the outcome of power struggles among ratepayers, crucial to which was the level and disposition of the rates themselves. For many tax-payers local rates were the most substantial direct tax leaving their pockets and lower middle-class ratepayers, for whom rates were a substantial burden, were often especially reluctant to pay for local improvements until crisis (such as an epidemic arising from water pollution) made them inescapable. Manchester, Birmingham, Leeds and Sheffield among others fell in the middle decades of the nineteenth century into the hands of 'shopocracies' reluctant to innovate or spend.

But if municipal corporations with governmental and administrative potential were established in most sizeable towns, government in the counties and in London remained unreformed and non-elective until 1888. This continued to limit the capacity of central government to extend social intervention, or necessitated cumbersome innovations, generally the creation of *ad hoc*, elected or non-elected, bodies. The poor law guardians as the only elected authorities covering the whole country acquired a miscellaneous collection of further tasks over the following decades. For expensive, extensive and specialised tasks concerning the entire country, separately elected authorities had to be established, with powers to levy separate rates and generally with distinct boundaries, such as Public Health Boards from 1848 and School Boards under the 1870 Education Act. As a result by the 1880s the picture of local government in England and Wales was one of some chaos.

The Whigs' ambitions to satisfy a variety of conflicting constituencies aroused more opposition than support by the later 1830s. Popular expectations had been raised, then dashed by parliamentary reform and its outcome, by education and factory reform followed by a widely disliked poor law. The outcome was both Chartism and the election of Peel's Tory government in 1841.

IV

Peel's fundamental approach to government was unchanged since 1830; however, he and his colleagues had learned the necessity to take some account of the effects of that approach upon subordinate groups, that whatever the abstract desirability of self-improvement and individual moral responsibility the mass of the population could not achieve these ideals without assistance. Peel remained unconvinced of the importance of constitutional matters – his 1841–6 Ministry notably neglected them – or of party. He was prepared to smash his own party in 1846 over corn law repeal, in pursuit of the higher goal of economic liberalism.

Peel returned to his pre-1830 trajectory in a position of enhanced power, above all devoted to further liberalisation of the economy. Tariffs were further reduced, culminating in corn law repeal; the income tax was reintroduced in 1842 to replace revenue lost due to the abolition of tariffs. The annual Budget began to take on a central political role. The Ministry also moved further towards the construction of a framework of government designed to enhance business efficiency and reward fair dealing, providing a more reliable banking system and money supply and moving towards an enforceable commercial law which safeguarded contracts and provided adequate protection against fraud. It also sought to establish a more efficient set of institutions through which the law could operate. In 1842 district bankruptcy courts were established, to provide speedy redress for creditors and hence to increase the availability of credit. The Railways Act, 1844, protected the public and business users against the abuse of local monopoly by enabling government to control charges, inspect companies and impose safety regulations, whilst holding back from the opportunity to control their erratic development more firmly.

Peel carried on the reconstruction of the regulatory state on principles designed to minimise intervention in personal life, whilst establishing a clear and as far as possible unambiguous economic policy designed to facilitate free and fair economic activity. He had, however, learned from the experience of the preceding decade that the mass of the population could not be pushed unsupported into the free market, for reasons both of humanity and of the practicalities of maintaining social stability, though he viewed social intervention with no favour. He was hostile to the ten hours factory movement. The, very limited, 1844 Factory Act was a remodelled Whig measure; it closed some enforcement loopholes and placed greater emphasis upon safety in the workplace than had earlier legislation. It was left to the Whigs to introduce ten hours legislation in 1847. The Tories resisted Chadwick's pressure for public health reform; the first major Public Health Act was passed by the Whigs in 1848. The 1842 Mines Act was slow to take effect, with just a single inspector appointed to enforce it. At the Privy Council committee Kay-Shuttleworth gradually increased government subsidy, supervision to schools and teacher education though with an overextended and understaffed department.[23]

The Ministry remained unresponsive to demands for further constitutional reform. Its main response to the continued force of Chartism was the extension of the machinery of public order. With Home Office encouragement increasing numbers of local police forces were established during the 1840s.[24] Peel's approach to government, however, modified or redirected many of the grievances which fuelled Chartism. His Ministry did not conspicuously intrude further upon customary liberties and did not appear indifferent to popular needs and causes. The Mines and Factory Acts and corn law repeal were popular and felt to be beneficial and the Tories' explicit disapproval of the grosser, more irresponsible or fraudulent capitalist activities further mollified radical criticism.

[23] R. Johnson, 'Administrators in Education before 1870: Patronage, Social Position and Role', in G. Sutherland, ed., *Studies in the Growth of Nineteenth-Century Government* (1972).

[24] J. Saville, *1848: The British State and the Chartist Movement* (Cambridge, 1987).

The minimal regulatory state was not widely experienced as intrusive or oppressive and government presented itself as working for a common good, for a national interest above that of party or of sectional interest, with improved living standards as its aim. Popular radicalism was not imbued with hostility to economic liberalism (rather the reverse) provided that it did not lead to the undermining of living standards. Effectively Peel obtained a significant degree of popular consent to an approach to government on which Gladstone was to build. The conjuncture which had built Chartism as a mass movement in defence of constitutional liberty passed. Popular radicalism did not die after 1848, nor the desire to defend customary liberties, though the latter was somewhat weakened. Rather it was diffused and channelled into a range of spheres of activity tolerated by the state: local government, public health and poor law matters, trade unionism, friendly societies and other forms of voluntarism.[25]

V

Against this background in the 1850s constitutional questions lost their prominence and government growth was slowed, after another brief flowering under the Whigs in 1846–52. Their coalition with the Peelites thereafter gave the *coup de grâce* to Whig interventionism in pursuit of social progress. Evasion and insufficiencies in factory regulation remained and abuses tended to overtake remedies. The General Board of Health, established in 1848 was wound up in 1858, due to local hostility to central direction, especially as implemented by Chadwick, who had been forced to resign, following bitter parliamentary criticism in 1854. The initiative in public health matters was left largely to the localities who, unevenly, gradually and contentiously, extended their powers.

The Peelite ideal of government reached its zenith after 1853 in the hands, pre-eminently, of Gladstone, whose political and intellectual position had reached maturity during his period of office under Peel in the 1840s; though in Gladstone's hands it was politicised and dramatised. As Chancellor of the Exchequer he restored fiscal policy to its pre-1846 trajectory, progressively dismantling duties and tariffs and reconstructing the income tax, until by 1860 the fiscal system was as open as it would ever be and considerably more so than that

25 G. Stedman Jones, 'Rethinking Chartism', in G. Stedman Jones, *Languages of Class* (Cambridge, 1983), pp. 90–178.

of any other major nation. Equally central was his determination to minimise government expenditure. He kept the proportion of government spending to national wealth at a low level at a time when it was rising in other countries. Acting with a high degree of independence, he made the post of Chancellor of the Exchequer, and the annual drama of the Budget, central to politics, whilst encouraging the Treasury to assert control over the activities and personnel of the entire civil service. This process had gradual, if slow, success, aided by the civil service reforms initiated in the 1850s. Treasury primacy was recognised in 1867 when its permanent secretary was granted seniority over heads of other departments.

A dominant feature of Gladstonian finance was 'positive retrenchment'. The underlying principle was that the direct relationship between government and the economy should be minimal but the indirect relationship, through the setting up of a self-sustaining economy, would be considerable. Gladstone saw this as a process of influencing the politics and the morals of the country as much as their economic activity. A government and Parliament freed from responsibility for economic intervention would also be freed from pressure from economic interest groups and hence could act fairly and dispassionately towards all classes. This approach would bring, he announced in his Budget speech of 1860, blessings to all:

In legislation of this kind you are not forging mechanical supports and helps for men, nor endeavouring to do for them what they ought to do for themselves; but you are enlarging their means without narrowing their freedom, you are giving value to their labour, you are appealing to their sense of responsibility, you are not impairing their temper of honourable self-dependence.[26]

In the mind of this profoundly religious man, economic progress was linked with religion as paths to moral and social development and a central function of government was to facilitate this. Though he was predominantly an economic individualist, as with most of his contemporaries it was individualism premised not upon greed and self-regard but conditioned by probity, self-control, a sense of duty and Christian morality. Even the objectives underlying his reconstruction of the tax system united the moral and the political with the fiscal. His aim (achieved at least temporarily by 1860) was to bring the yield of direct taxation (mainly the income tax) paid by the better-off gradually into equilibrium with that of indirect taxation, which by 1860 had been reduced to fifteen items of consumption bought

[26] Matthew, *Gladstone*, p. 116.

mainly by the less well-off (tea, sugar, etc.). By this means, he believed, all groups in society would come to recognise their equal responsibility for sanctioning and financing government activity and hence would have an incentive to keep it under control. Furthermore, the rich would not feel that they were subsidising the poor, nor the poor expect to gain from redistribution, so an important source of class disharmony would be removed. In 1853 he reduced the income level at which income tax was paid from £150 to £100 p.a. This increased the yield and also put the tax threshold roughly at the income level which qualified for the parliamentary vote, as a reminder that taxpaying and property ownership equated with political duty. He exempted from taxation savings in the form of life insurance or deferred annuities, in order to relieve and encourage 'intelligence and skill as compared with property'. Whatever the actual moral and political effects, the outcome was a highly efficient fiscal system, high in yield and cheap to administer, which stood the test of financing the, fortunately brief, war in the Crimea (1854–6).[27]

The conduct of the war in other respects, however, led to demands for further administrative and army reforms.[28] Gladstone was indeed committed to the continued overhaul of governing institutions. He was closely involved in the reform of Oxford University in the 1850s. Since Oxford was an important source of civil service recruits the reform was in part aimed to improve the intellectual and moral quality of recruits to the government service; it was designed to promote a liberal education, one of whose purposes was believed to be to produce morally good subjects. It was one means to the moral regeneration of an elite and of recruits to it, their transformation into the ideal 'man required for the coming generation' whom Lord Ashley had described in 1844 (as a model for his own son) in contrast to what he saw as the careless upper-class style of his time: 'We must have nobler, deeper, sterner stuff; less of refinement and more of truth; more of the inward and not so much of the outward gentleman; a rigid sense of duty, not a delicate sense of honour.'[29]

If Gladstone and his peers sought to moralise and control the behaviour of the masses, as they did, they sought a similar transformation of the rest of society. Gladstone's support of Cardwell's army reforms

[27] H. C. G. Matthew, 'Disraeli, Gladstone and the Politics of Mid-Victorian Budgets', *Historical Journal*, 22 (1979), pp. 629–30.
[28] O. Anderson, *A Liberal State at War* (1967).
[29] Mandler, 'Cain and Abel', p. 84.

under his premiership in 1871 was partly rooted in a desire for the creation of a professional service comparable with that of the Prussians; but he also saw it as a further step in the reconstruction of the mores of the 'vast, leisured and wealthy class' which officered it, to enhance their sense of duty by, among other things, introducing promotion by merit rather than by purchase. He wanted 'court and country to follow the middle class values of efficiency, application, economy'.[30]

Gladstone's approach to the reconstruction of leading institutions was, however, cautious, and designed to minimise the tensions that might be caused. In reforming Oxford he rejected radical Liberal proposals for overthrowing tradition and replacing the collegiate system with a faculty structure, on 'the principle of working with the materials which we possess, endeavouring to improve our institutions through the agency they themselves supply and giving to reform in cases where there is a choice the character of return and restoration'.[31] The role of Parliament, that is, was 'to permit regeneration rather than to impose novelty, to work from within a set of historic institutions rather than from an *a priori* plan'.[32]

Gladstone's work on the reform of Oxford led him directly to reform of the institution which Oxford was expected to feed. In 1853 he asked Sir Stafford Northcote and Sir Charles Trevelyan, of the Treasury, to investigate and report on the civil service. The purpose was to take further the moves towards a more efficient service. Corruption, though it still occurred, was no longer the main criticism. Greater pressure of government business was changing the role of the service, demanding more work and more responsibility delegated from ministers. In addition a certain tension had built up between the zealous public men of the type of Chadwick and the increasing numbers of professional civil servants entering directly from Oxford or Cambridge, more discreet, less public or openly political, pioneers of the classical nineteenth- and twentieth-century service. Gradually, they were already replacing the 'new men'. When the General Board of Health was wound up its work went partly to the Local Government Act office of the Home Office, under the career civil servant Tom Taylor, who urged local authorities forward in the public health field less contentiously than had his predecessors. The medical work of the General Board, concerned with epidemic disease and the causes

---

[30] Matthew, *Gladstone*, p. 210.   [31] *Ibid.*, p. 84.   [32] *Ibid.*, p. 84.

and prevention of ill-health, was directed from 1858 at the medical department of the Privy Council by a medical man closer to the Chadwick mould, John Simon, until his replacement in 1871 by John Lambert, a career civil servant, determined to separate administration and policy formulation from the research and propaganda which had been Simon's main interest. In 1849 Kay-Shuttleworth was replaced at the education committee by Robert Lingen, one of a group of Balliol educated men who came in the 1840s to dominate the department and amongst whom Kay-Shuttleworth felt insecure and 'uneducated'. Under Lingen, at least until 1861, the department continued to expand, but its initiatives were less exclusively concerned with popular education and were directed also to such issues as the reform of Oxford.

The Northcote–Trevelyan report (1854) recommended means to recruit an efficient, professional, apolitical service. They made three main proposals: the service would be divided into two categories, a higher or 'intellectual' grade, concerned with key decisions, and a lower or 'mechanical' grade, concerned with routine copying. Both were to be recruited through open competition rather than through patronage, the higher grade via examinations which were effectively a repeat of Oxford and Cambridge degree examinations and largely impenetrable from any other source. The exam would yield for the service the cream of high-minded, liberally educated men. 'It was a means of extending, confirming, cleansing and legitimising an existing elite.'[33] Thirdly, promotion was to be by merit, not by seniority; and pensions were to be instituted to facilitate removal of those rendered inefficient by ill-health or advancing age. A unified system of recruitment, grading and pay was intended gradually to break down the autonomy of the departments of the service.

The changes spread slowly through the service, especially in the more elite departments, jealous of their independence. Theoretically the reform was completed by Orders in Council under Gladstone's premiership in 1870, whereby all departments, except the Foreign Office, were to observe the new norms. However, the Treasury avoided appointing anyone by open competition until 1878 and few even in the 1880s and 1890s.

Other institutional reforms were carried forward by the Coalition and Liberal governments of the 1850s and 1860s. The Common Law

[33] Ibid., p. 85.

Procedure Acts, 1854 and 1860, sought further to simplify and speed proceedings; the Court of Chancery Acts, 1852 and 1858, to speed up the notorious slowness pilloried by Charles Dickens. They showed less interest in constitutional reform. The role of Parliament in the Gladstonian state was to check the excesses of government, to maintain stability, rather than to initiate; to debate and give sanction to the actions of the executive. Gladstone kept the all-important planning of expenditure firmly in ministerial hands rather than in those of Parliament; the parliamentary Public Accounts Committee (established in 1862) was introduced with power only to check abuses of expenditure retrospectively. Big bills and big Budgets represented a means of regular renewal of the legitimacy of Parliament and of the political system. Unlike Peel, Gladstone did not risk appearing to underestimate the importance of gaining parliamentary sanction for executive action; he recognised the need to maintain popular consent.

He shared Peel's belief in a strong, initiating executive and his lack of conviction that fiscal need by accompanied by political liberalism. Though he was the most effective promoter of the minimal state in modern history it was no mere 'nightwatchman state', with its connotation of largely inert guardianship. It was to be a strong, decisive and efficient state, firmly moulding the framework within which the moralised citizenry would enjoy their freedom. It was 'an almost corporatist view of the state'.[34] It was designed to foster social stability, by being seen to deal evenly with all classes, to imbue all with the sense of political responsibility and probity; the citizenry were the guardians of the probity of the state and the state reciprocated by safeguarding their well-being. For all the 'People's William's' unprecedented (for a Victorian politician) and calculated wooing of all classes especially in the 1860s, he was no democrat in any conventional modern sense. Constitutional reform had as an abstract principle as little appeal for him as for Peel. Pragmatically, in the 1860s he became increasingly convinced, due to his contacts with trade unionists, that moderate artisans if allowed the vote would strengthen the economical wing of Liberalism. They possessed the intelligence, probity and sense of responsibility which in his view should be the prime qualification for active membership of the constitution. His 1866 proposals for parliamentary reform were designed to extend the vote to such eminently worthy men, and of course to palliate discontent arising from their

[34] *Ibid.*, p. 117.

exclusion. He believed that the 1867 household franchise, introduced by Disraeli, went too far, risking upsetting the delicate balance he had erected by bringing too many indirect taxpayers into the electorate; they might be tempted to try to push government into excessively redistributive measures bringing 'class politics' to the fore. He viewed the introduction of the secret ballot as a regrettable necessity.

Yet Gladstone's view of the minimal state did not, at least by the 1860s, incorporate total conviction that market forces alone could produce a just society. Some interference was acceptable and necessary, at least at the margins, on grounds of social justice. As he put it:

Once security has been taken that an entire society shall not be forced to pay an artificial price to some of its members for their production, we may safely commit the question [of cheapness of goods] to the action of competition among manufacturers and of what we term the laws of supply and demand. As to the condition of the workpeople, experience has shown, especially in the case of the Factory Acts, that we should do wrong in laying down any abstract maxim as an invariable rule.[35]

Absence of an 'abstract maxim' allowed a certain flexibility, enabling him, for example, to introduce a Post Office Savings Bank and Post Office annuities, despite the hostility of friendly societies to this competition in the field of self-help. His government accepted and consolidated the Tory nationalisation of the telegraphs immediately upon coming into office in 1868.

Nevertheless, 'no industrial society can ever have existed in which the state played a smaller role than that of the United Kingdom in the 1860s'.[36] The government had foresworn responsibility for economic management. It had abolished virtually all tariffs save for those non-protective duties required for revenue purposes. Government responsibility for education was confined to its limited relations with the established church and the universities and through small grants to non-established denominations. Despite growing fears of the economic ill-effects of Britain's apparent educational backwardness, especially in relation to Prussia and especially in the technical sphere, Gladstone's attachment to the classical curriculum was such that he and his colleagues refused a government grant to Owen's College (Manchester) or aid for the establishment of the University College at Aberystwyth. He deplored 'the *low* utilitarian argument ... for giving [education] what is termed a practical direction'.[37]

---

[35] *Ibid.*, p. 118.   [36] *Ibid.*, p. 169.   [37] *Ibid.*, p. 201

Government involvement in industrial relations was non-existent outside the royal dockyards. Factory legislation remained in place but was not significantly pushed forward. In the field of social welfare, government accepted overall responsibility for public health and the poor law, but in both cases left a high degree of discretion to the localities. The minimal state was, indeed, premised upon the capacity of a vast network of voluntary organisations, in co-operation with local government, to superintend most moral, charitable, education and welfare services. The limited extent of initiative by central government in these areas was premised on the vigorous involvement of its citizens, of the kind Gladstone himself undertook throughout his life. How effective and extensive were such local initiatives?

VI

Devotion to local autonomy against central state intervention in what were perceived as local affairs remained powerful and the powers and activities of local authorities expanded in the mid-Victorian period. Throughout the period the most direct experience of most people of government was of local government; it affected their lives more visibly than did central government. But the energy of local citizens and the speed and direction of local government expansion varied considerably from place to place for reasons not always easy to explain. In Rochdale (Lancashire) a secure employer elite of Liberal nonconformists created 'one of the most alert and socially creative towns in England'.[38] In Bradford (Yorkshire) a similar elite, after an initial burst of energy following incorporation in 1847, fell into an 'almighty stillness'[39] running a police force and sanitation efficiently, but resisting innovation in any other field.

For the municipalities the period was one of local battles over incorporation and associated struggles for control of guardians, vestries, police, improvement and highways commissioners and over church rates; struggles as much, or more, about which social group or party achieved local status and influence as about administration and reform. Still in 1861 towns as large as Bury (pop. 87,563), Merthyr Tydfil (83,875) and Birkenhead (41,649) had no municipal corporation.

[38] J. Vincent, *The Formation of the Liberal Party, 1857–68* (1966), p. 96.
[39] A. Elliot, 'Municipal Government in Bradford in the Mid-Nineteenth Century', in D. Fraser, ed., *Municipal Reform and the Industrial City* (Leicester, 1982), p. 122.

Even the most reluctant corporations, however, expanded their powers by local statute, transforming their purpose, increasingly becoming administrative bodies. They were not left entirely to their own devices by central government. Above all it persistently encouraged local action in the two areas of policing and public health, which were seen as particularly essential to the maintenance of public order and social stability. From 1856 central government was prepared to pay a 25 per cent subsidy to local police forces on condition that a Home Office inspectorate recognised them as efficient; though several authorities refused it, preferring to retain wholly independent control of their police.

Local sanitary improvements were chivvied along until 1871 by Tom Taylor at the Local Government Act Office. Where local initiative was taken it was less often a response to recognition of intolerable evils, which local elites were generally slower to perceive than were the inhabitants of some of the appalling urban areas of the period, than to dramatic crisis with wide social impact. In 1852 an acute water shortage in Leeds forced a reluctant Liberal-controlled corporation to buy the local waterworks. The bursting of the Dale Dyke dam in Sheffield in 1864, killing 240 people and destroying 800 dwellings, revealed the shortcomings of the local water company and of the Liberal corporation's previous refusal to take it over.[40]

In general, local authorities were more willing to accept central government advice on the technical problems with which public health administration was riddled (concerning, for example, the purification of water) than central involvement with their policing. Opposition to a national police force still went deep. In general, corporations were satisfied with the capacity of local forces to keep order in the relatively quiescent mid-Victorian era. The military had to be called out in reinforcement of the police only twice in the mid-century, on both occasions in the Home Office-controlled Metropolitan Police district: in response to the successful riots against the ban on Sunday Trading in 1855 and during the parliamentary reform agitation of 1866–7.

A range of general permissive statutes potentially widened the scope of local authority activities: the Baths and Washhouses Act, 1846, the Lodging Houses Acts, 1851 and 1853, the Public Libraries Acts, 1855

---

[40]   D. Smith, *Conflict and Compromise: Class Formation in English Society, 1830–1914* (1982), p. 163. E. P. Hennock, *Fit and Proper Persons: Ideal and Reality in Nineteenth Century Urban Government* (1973), p. 231.

and 1856, the Labourers' Dwellings Act, 1855, further permissive housing legislation in the 1850s and 1860s and the Industrial Schools Acts, 1857 and 1862. Their local implementation was predictably patchy and riddled with dispute.

In the mid-century, sections of the urban middle class felt secure in their status and power in the larger towns. They celebrated with building and ritual. Great town halls were built, and museums and concert halls. By nine local statutes between 1858 and 1863, Liverpool Corporation dignified its city centre by driving spacious new streets through previously congested areas. But non-urban areas still had no all-purpose elected authority. The Poor Law Boards accumulated a wide range of responsibilities in the effort to avoid proliferation of government agencies and to minimise costs, providing a kind of embryo-elected local government in the countryside. They acquired some public health functions, administered the Vaccination Acts (and faced the enormous opposition to this compulsory medical treatment at the behest of the central state), became civil registrars of births, marriages and deaths from 1837, were responsible for registering voters and administering elections and were involved with rural police and highways administration. Between 1844 and 1874 'poor law' expenditure for these non-poor law purposes rose from 27 per cent to 40 per cent of the total, mostly arising from expenditure on police.

Some wished the Poor Law Boards to become all-purpose local authorities. But stronger was the conviction that specific authorities should be established to carry out important specialised tasks which were believed to be easily defined and mutually exclusive. Hence Boards of Health were separately established, separately elected (on a property-weighted franchise identical with that for Boards of Guardians) with separate rating powers; from 1852 Burial Boards could be established to provide cemeteries, from 1862 Highway Boards to maintain roads and from 1870 School Boards, on a householder franchise which included women, who successfully asserted their right to be elected;[41] shortly afterwards women put to the test their right to be elected to Boards of Guardians, from 1875 the number of female guardians steadily increased. Often local authorities had different and overlapping boundaries.

One reason for the unevenness of local government activity was the belief that social responsibility should to the maximum amount

---

[41] P. Hollis, *Ladies Elect: Women in English Local Government 1865–1914* (Oxford, 1987), pp. 71–194.

possible be borne by voluntary organisations. The mid-Victorian period indeed saw a proliferation of voluntary effort directed towards almost every conceivable type of social casualty. Its total receipts and expenditure can never be fully quantified since so much charity was ephemeral and ill-recorded, but it must at least have equalled the social expenditure of central and local government throughout the period up to 1914. But its extent and direction was locally uneven, dependent upon the capacity and will of individuals to give money and effort and their inclinations as to the desirable direction philanthropy should take.[42]

Another important reason for the variety of local activity was the reluctance of ratepayers to pay the growing costs of local government. In 1868 national taxation raised £67,800,000 and local rates in England and Wales £19,800,000. Local expenditure amounted to £30,140,000, the gap being made up of loans, government subventions and the rents on property owned by local authorities. The incidence and levels of assessment of rates varied from place to place according to local needs and policies and fell unevenly on different forms of property. It was a persistent source of dispute that land was more heavily rated than manufacturing business, since rates were levied only upon the value of real estate and not upon moveables, such as stock in trade. In London nominal rates in the pound varied from 2s. 1d. in the wealthy parish of St George's, Hanover Square, to 6s. 9d. in the much poorer St George the Martyr, Southwark. Moves to equalise London rates began in 1855, largely as a result of the need to meet the cost of Metropolitan Board of Works capital projects, such as the building of the Thames Embankment. A Metropolitan Common Poor Fund was established in 1865 to equalise part of the burden (above all the costs of workhouses) of this major item of rate expenditure. The Board and the Fund were two of the *ad hoc* bodies which had to be established to overcome the lack of unitary government in mid-Victorian London.

In the 1860s rating was a national political issue. Leading Tories argued that where local authorities had to deal with essentially national issues, the cost should be borne by the Exchequer. Gladstone was hostile to the notion of using the Exchequer for local purposes, in keeping with his belief in local responsibility and the moral and

[42] F. K. Prochaska, *Women and Philanthropy in Nineteenth-Century England* (Oxford, 1980). D. Owen, *English Philanthropy, 1660–1960* (1964).

political functions of taxation. It was an issue of which he and his colleagues were acutely aware, but to which they found no solution, though by constraining the willingness of citizens to promote active local government it risked undermining one of the pillars of the minimal state.

Concern about the complexity and cost of local government – George Goschen complained that one of his suburban properties, assessed at £1,100, attracted eighty-seven separate rate demands in a year – was such that in 1869 Gladstone's government appointed a Royal Commission to undertake a drastic reconsideration of the structure of local government in England and Wales. Its report, in 1871, recommended principles which were gradually to be implemented over the next half-century. In particular, it discredited the policy of establishing separate local authorities for each major task. It proposed the consolidation of local powers in the hands of single local authorities, to be established throughout the country. It failed to find a solution to the rating problem. Whilst it was sitting the last new single purpose authorities, the School Boards, were established in 1870. They survived until 1902, when their powers were merged with those of local councils. Until elected local government could be established in the counties and in London there was little option in the case of such an expensive and specialised task as education. Once county councils were established, in 1888, including in London, special purpose authorities were gradually assimilated to municipal and county councils, though the oldest established, the Board of Guardians, survived until 1929.

The government did, however, immediately take steps to impose greater uniformity of practice upon local authorities by, in 1871, consolidating in a new department, the Local Government Board, responsibility for public health, the poor law and miscellaneous other local activities. If this seemed to run counter to Gladstone's belief in local self-responsibility it illustrates the flexibility of his principles in respect of social needs and his preference for strong executive action to provide a clear framework for action of national and highly political importance when local initiative failed to do what was expected of it.

The new department immediately set about trying to achieve greater uniformity. In a memorandum to poor law authorities, Goschen (the first President of the Board) initiated a policy of striving to systematise and co-ordinate with publicly funded poor relief the mass of voluntary effort directed at the poor. Outdoor relief was to be reduced, and ideally abolished, the deserving poor to be directed to local charities with whom Poor Law Boards were expected to work closely. Ideally also the disparate mass of charitable effort would be co-ordinated and assimilated to operate on common principles under the guidance of the Charity Organisation Society (founded 1869, with Gladstone among its early supporters). The poor law authorities could then concentrate their efforts upon punishment of the feckless in the workhouse and the provision of improved institutional care for those for whom this was appropriate: children, the sick, the helpless elderly, the mentally ill. The outcome was steady but uneven improvement in such institutional provision and a serious reduction in aid especially to the elderly and to single mothers who had been the chief recipients of outdoor relief. Few had families able to support them and voluntary action proved to be neither extensive enough to take the burden nor willing to be organised and controlled by either the Charity Organisation Society or the Local Government Board. Such proposals conflicted with ideals of the independence of voluntarism from outside control.[43]

The Public Health Act, 1872, compelled local authorities to act, whereas the new poor law policy was in principle merely advice to local Boards, though advice very firmly relayed by the inspectorate. From 1872 local health authorities were compulsory throughout the country, the responsibilities to lie with municipal councils, elected Boards in non-corporate towns and Boards of Guardians in the counties. The appointment of Medical Officers of Health became compulsory and half their salaries were met by the Local Government Board – the third central government subsidy to local government following those in respect of police (increased to 50 per cent in 1874) and education.

Variability in local government practice in these and other spheres, however, continued and central government was well aware that there were limits to the control that could be exerted without incurring opposition. And the problem remained that more active local government necessitated either higher rates, to which there was strong resistance, or larger government subsidies, which would increase the national tax burden. Disraeli, who did not wholly share Gladstone's principles as regards taxation or central/local government relations, increased the total Exchequer grant to local authorities from £1.15m

---

[43]   M. E. Rose, 'The Crisis of Poor Relief in England, 1860–1880', in W. J. Mommsen, ed., *The Emergence of the Welfare State in Britain and Germany* (1981).

to £2.24m in his first two years in office following Gladstone's defeat in 1874, but this was far from sufficient to remove the problem.

Municipalisation of services was the form of local self-help adopted by increasing numbers of urban authorities, either as a means of limiting rate rises by using the profits from municipal services partially to finance their further development, or of subsidising ratepayers by providing cheaper gas and water supplies. Manchester was first to municipalise its gas supplies; Leeds followed, disastrously, in 1870, Glasgow at too high a price in 1869; forty-seven other authorities followed by 1870, sanctioned by Parliament by local statute. From 1875 it was permitted on Local Government Board sanction alone.

Joseph Chamberlain, as Liberal mayor, proposed buying the Birmingham gas companies in 1873, when the city was at the peak of its nonconformist-inspired period of civic improvement and ratepayers were showing signs of rebellion. Chamberlain indeed erected municipalisation into a – distinctly non-socialist – principle of local government. For him it was the application of good business principles to government. Services should be bought at a good price, efficiently run and the profits devoted to town improvement – to make Birmingham the Paris of Midland England. In the boom of the mid-1870s, he was able to use the profits of municipally built city centre shops and offices to finance slum clearance, improved sanitation and house building.

By the time Chamberlain left the Birmingham council chamber for national politics in the late 1870s this new approach was firmly established. It asserted that elected authorities could achieve for their communities what voluntary organisations could not. Chamberlain proclaimed: 'Private charity is powerless, religious organisations can do nothing to remedy the evils which are so deep-seated in our system ... I venture to say that it is only the community acting as a whole that can possibly deal with evils so deep seated.'[44]

The local government problem points up especially clearly some of the limitations to the possibility of the minimal state's fulfilling Gladstone's ambition as to its effects, or his hopes for its permanency. Local and voluntary bodies did not, even in the 1870s, appear able to bear the full weight of social responsibility placed upon them.

Another major premise on which the theory of the Gladstonian state was built was that a free economy would employ capital and

[44] Hennock, *Fit and Proper Persons*, p. 174.

labour at the optimum. Continuing evidence of underemployment and pay inadequate for basic needs suggested that it could not and that the outcome would be further pressures for central government intervention. The willingness of Gladstone and his contemporaries to accept, at least in principle, that market forces alone would not necessarily create a good society left the door ajar for the disintegration of the minimal regulatory state. As Gladstone's biographer puts it:

There were always substantial qualifications both in Gladstone's view and in the minds of most mid-Victorians to the view that minimal 'interference' was the best government. It is probably the case that although the minimalist state was achieved in Victorian Britain in the fullest form compatible with the social requirements of an industrialised population, nonetheless, in these qualifications were contained the assumptions which were to lead to its gradual disintegration.[45]

This was, however, hardly perceived in the 1870s. Gladstone and his colleagues continued to pursue retrenchment and the minimal state with the greatest earnestness.

VII

The Liberal hegemony of the mid-Victorian period was followed by a period in which Conservative governments held office for twenty-three of the years from 1874 to 1906. This did not imply a fundamental change in attitudes to government at any level, not surprisingly given the common origins of Disraeli and Gladstone in the Tory party of Peel's day. Disraeli and most of his colleagues shared Toryism's traditional stress upon the role and responsibilities of established authority, associated with disbelief in social views based on individualism or a doctrine of natural rights. More important than recognition of any particular or personal claims was the achievement of stability and well-being through properly constituted control. They saw society as an organic hierarchy in which a sort of natural aristocracy must rule; levelling was not so much undesirable as impossible. But it was not a leadership attained through property and inheritance alone, but one justified by talent, probity, experience, service and a sense of duty. Devotion to public service and the general welfare was a matter of the greatest significance. They believed in leadership and strong executive authority, legitimated by popular consent secured through Parliament and the gradual extension of the parliamentary

---

[45] Matthew, *Gladstone*, p. 170.

franchise as the respectable and educated section of the population expanded, and of elected local government.

Just as the character of leadership favoured by prominent Tories would have been acceptable to Gladstone, so would the limited role envisaged for it: providing a firm framework within which individuals would be free and self-governing. And no more than in Gladstone's moral scheme was this a freedom to give rein to acquisitiveness and self-interest. Indeed, an important component of the need for authority, as Burke had stressed, was to curb such natural human passions. 'Society', said Burke, 'cannot exist unless a controlling power upon will and appetite be placed somewhere.'[46] Responsible use of power by leaders of the utmost probity, directed in large part towards the moral ends of curbing greed, aggression and lack of responsibility and care for the community as a whole were the core of the values shared by leading politicians throughout the mid- and late-Victorian periods. Anyone who fails to understand this grossly fails to appreciate the true nature of Victorian values.

Also like Gladstone, Disraeli recognised the need for the constant adaptation of institutions, rather than their radical transformation, as the structure of society changed:

In a progressive country change is constant and the great question is not whether you should resist change which is inevitable but whether change should be carried out in deference to the manners, the customs, the laws and the traditions of a people or whether it should be carried out in deference to abstract principles and arbitrary and general doctrines – the programme of the Conservative party is to maintain the constitution of the country.[47]

The Conservative interpretation of the proper role of the state in respect of social intervention was somewhat, though not radically, more flexible than that of Gladstone. To economic liberalism they remained, despite Joseph Chamberlain's tariff reform challenge from 1903, wedded until the First World War and beyond. But Toryism had never been averse in principle to the use of power as a means to enhance social welfare. Disraeli's second government (1874–80) was prepared to take social intervention further than Gladstone had done, not least in order to win votes. Disraeli came into office with no concrete plans. The government did produce an unusually large concentration of reforming legislation: the Sale of Drugs Act, another Public

[46] Quoted in W. H. Greenleaf, *The British Political Tradition*, vol. 2: *The Ideological Heritage*, (1983), p. 197.
[47] Quoted in F. O'Gorman, *British Conservatism: Conservative Thought from Burke to Thatcher* (1986), p. 33.

Health Act, the Artisans' Dwelling Act, the Rivers Pollution Act, Factory Acts in 1874 and 1875 and the labour legislation of 1875. But much of it either continued existing trajectories (e.g. the Public Health and Factory Acts) or had very limited effects (e.g. the housing legislation). The practical significance of the legislation was limited and there is little sign that Disraeli wished to go further or was motivated by any Conservative philosophy of paternalism. Anti-interventionism was still the predominant approach of the Ministry and of the party, in line with the Earl of Derby's warning in 1872:

I don't tell you in so many words that the State should take on itself no functions except those which it actually performs; but I do tell you that the tendency to enlarge indefinitely the scope of the operations is one to be watched with great jealousy. There is risk of extravagance and jobbery; there is discouragement of individual self-reliance; there is the inevitable discontent caused by the disappointment of unreasonable expectations.[48]

Nor were the Conservatives of the mid-Victorian period any more wedded than the Liberals to centralisation. Disraeli's conception of government required a stress on the diffusion of initiative and responsibility. Local institutions created and safeguarded liberty: 'by the bulwark which they offer to the insidious encroachments of a convenient yet enervating system of centralisation, which if left unchecked will prove fatal to the national character. I have ever endeavoured to cherish our happy habit of self-government, as sustained by a prudent distribution of local authority.'[49]

VIII

Lord Salisbury, Disraeli's successor as Conservative leader entirely shared the Victorian commitment to the importance of leadership, strong but minimal central government, combined with decentralisation, to economic liberalism and limited social interventionism, probity and a sense of duty in public life, underpinned by profound religious conviction. He commented in 1891: 'The Conservative Party has always leaned, perhaps somewhat unduly leaned, to the use of the State, so far as it could properly be used for improving the physical, moral and intellectual condition of our people and I hope that mission in the Conservative Party will never be renounced.'[50] His inclination,

[48] Greenleaf, *The Ideological Heritage*, p. 215.
[49] *Ibid.*, p. 209.   [50] *Ibid.*, p. 228.

however, was to use the state in this fashion only with the utmost caution and, despite the important and continuing undercurrent of preference for more decisive social intervention (combined with continuing commitment to economic liberalism) represented in the 1880s by Lord Randolph Churchill and his 'Tory democratic' associates, this was the dominant view in the party.

The major structural changes which Britain was undergoing in the later nineteenth century, however, increased pressure upon government to adapt constitutional mechanisms and extend the social role of the state. The growth of industry and of urbanisation, in a situation in which the country's economic stability and economic and political position in international terms seemed less assured and international rivalries were intensifying; the decline of land as a primary contributor to wealth and employment and the associated rural disturbances in the 1880s; the spread of mass communications; the existence of a more prosperous, better educated working population, potentially and increasingly actually more assertive in defence of their interests, all necessitated steps to maintain internal stability, to integrate all who safely could be into the constitution, to secure a sense of national cohesiveness overriding sectional interests. Hence Disraeli's, largely successful, use of nationalist and imperialist rhetoric and the successive extensions of the national and local franchise. In a period of intensified awareness of nationhood, and of race, in most advanced countries and urgent international rivalries, British governments also, more than before, were comparing their performances in all respects, not always unfavourably, with those of their major rivals, above all newly unified Germany. If some looked to Germany as a model of efficient organisation, others deplored what they perceived as its excessive bureaucratisation, which stifled individual freedom and initiative. France, already formally more democratic than Britain, having introduced universal manhood suffrage, with a more developed system of popular education and a distinctly more meritocratic administrative structure, was no longer seen as the chief enemy and aroused less interest than did Germany.

In 1884 rural householders were granted the vote, by Gladstone's second ministry, on the same terms as voters in the boroughs, with especially dramatic effects in rural Ireland and Wales. Equally important, in 1885 the long overdue redrawing of constituency boundaries gave something closer to equal representation for each voter by creating constituencies of approximately equal size. With an electorate of about 5 million, all women and in practice about 40 per cent of adult males still lay outside the official definition of citizenship by 1914.

The absence of elected local government in the counties, other than for *ad hoc* bodies, appeared the more anomalous when rural householders acquired the parliamentary vote. The ancient system of non-elected landowner authority seemed antiquated as agriculture lost its economic predominance and it presented a definite barrier to any extension of rational and efficient social intervention. Also the multiple problems of the sprawling capital of the Empire could evidently no longer be left to the Corporation of the City of London and an assortment of vestries and *ad hoc* bodies.[51] Hence in 1888, the Tories introduced elected county councils, firmly overriding landlord opposition,[52] and a council for London, to be elected on a householder franchise. Initially, the functions of these county councils were confined to policing and the control of highways and bridges. The new units were deemed too large to administer other social welfare activities. In 1894 lower tier urban and rural district councils were created, with responsibility for the range of public health duties by now imposed or permitted by legislation, and in whose hands were gradually consolidated the remaining functions of local authorities, other than for poor relief. In 1899 second tier authorities, the boroughs, were also established in London with similar powers (including for housing and libraries). The property qualification for membership of these authorities was at first minimal and then (in 1895) opened to all householders, increasing the numbers of women and workingmen eligible to stand. Women in particular were playing an increasingly significant role in extending and humanising the social functions of local authorities, especially Poor Law and School Boards. They were debarred until 1907 from seats on county and municipal councils, though if they were independent ratepayers, as very large numbers of widows and single women were, they might vote for both. As their participation in local government grew, their exclusion from the national vote was ever more visibly absurd; their success in local government contributed to the growing women's suffrage movement.

The numbers of workingmen elected to local authorities were fewer (86 were elected in 1907, 196 in 1913) due partly to the lack of time

[51]   John Davis, *Reforming London: The London Government Problem 1855–1900* (Oxford, 1988), pp. 1–67.
[52]   J. Dunbabin, 'The Politics of the Establishment of County Councils', *Historical Journal*, 5 (1963).

and capacity to forgo income of most of them, especially since most authorities held daytime meetings and did not pay expenses. Those who stood mainly had trade-union or independent labour support. The involvement of workingmen and women in local social politics on issues which directly affected their lives (housing, education, health, poor relief) in which state involvement was growing was one of the roots of the organisational development of the political labour movement. This did not imply that their demands for state intervention were necessarily far in advance of those of radical Liberalism or Toryism. Suspicion of the central state and attachment to independence and voluntary effort was strong among working people, though the more politically active tended to favour more state action in such fields as housing and unemployment, provided that it did not undermine aspirations to independence and remained, so far as possible, under local control.[53] Also, as central government showed signs of intervening more directly in their lives, their desire for more active participation in the decision-making process and administrative apparatus of the state was, understandably, strengthened. Working people nowhere obtained a majority in local elections until a trade-union and socialist alliance captured West Ham municipal council in 1898. Nor could they assume that workers would vote for independent labour candidates even when they were eligible and registered to vote, as many of their potential electorate were not. However, in a number of localities in alliance with progressive Liberals representatives of labour were able to bring about changes in the relief of the unemployed (as in Poplar, East London, from the mid-1890s), promote municipal ownership and improve municipal working conditions, and extend housing and infant care, as in Bradford, also from the 1890s. The increasing number of manual workers employed by local authorities (e.g. as gas or water workers) on occasion translated dissatisfaction with work conditions into political opposition to the ruling parties, as in Leeds in 1890 and several London boroughs in the 1900s.[54]

All of these changes stimulated further the still uneven growth of local government activity, though it left unresolved the problem of the rates. Local government expenditure in England and Wales almost

---

[53] P. Thane, 'The Working Class and State "Welfare" in Britain, 1880–1914', *Historical Journal*, 27 (1984), pp. 877–900.
[54] Hennock, *Fit and Proper Persons*, p. 326.

doubled between 1870 and 1890 (from £27.3m to £48.2m), a period of falling prices; and rose to £125.8m in 1910. Goschen, as Liberal Unionist Chancellor from 1886 returned to the issue, recognising the need for central subsidies to local government of a type which did not undermine their sense of autonomy, and aiming also to equalise the incidence of rating between real and personal property which remained a source of political contention. In 1888 the plethora of separate central grants to local government (then amounting to £2.8m p.a.) were abolished. In their place local authorities were 'assigned' revenues totalling £4.8m (which rose to £6.4m in 1891–2). Local authorities were free to choose on what these revenues should be spent. The source of the assigned revenues was that part of probate duty which fell on realised personalty, plus the revenues from excise licences.

This did not solve the problem. Ratepayers continued into the 1900s to resist the cost of the decentralisation which they in principle defended. Further municipalisation was one solution. In 1882 Huddersfield was granted permission to run its own trams because no private company would operate in its steep streets. Plymouth and Blackpool shortly received similar sanction. Many other authorities, including the London County Council, began to run their own services after 1891 when the leases of private companies expired. They estimated that they could run them more efficiently and profitably than private enterprise. Also, increasingly, city corporations tackled the problem by borrowing on the money markets, beginning with Liverpool in 1888. By 1910 local government in the UK was £600m in debt.

The energy and range of activities of local authorities continued to vary, in no clear relationship with the party politics of their control. Unionist Birmingham in the 1880s had passed its great innovatory stage, though it was less inert than Liberal-controlled Leeds. A cholera epidemic in Leeds in 1889 which exposed the poor state of public health provision, combined with the council's inept handling of the gas workers' strike in 1890, brought the Conservatives back to control, businessmen back to local leadership and Leeds into a period in which closely balanced party competition proved highly productive of innovation.[55]

London by 1888 had fallen behind the major provincial cities even in the provision of basic amenities. The Lib-Lab progressive alliance,

[55] *Ibid.*

led by Lord Rosebery, and the focus of much radical and philanthropic idealism, which controlled the London County Council from its formation until 1907, quickly acquired a reforming reputation. It especially promoted working-class education, cultural and leisure facilities, in close association with voluntary organisations such as the settlement houses, and established a reputation for providing favourable conditions for its employees.

Increased capital expenditure (facilitated by falling interest rates), especially on housing, hospital building (authorised by the 1875 Public Health Act) and transport, and further municipalisation of services characterised the activities of the more energetic local authorities in the 1890s. But not all were energetic. The conflicting trends in municipal action indeed became more stark due to two opposing forces: reforming pressure for more action versus resistance to rate rises, an episode in the more general political and social polarisation of the 1890s. Rates rose by between 30 and 50 per cent in London between 1891 and 1906. Organisations of ratepayers grew and blamed municipalisation as the cause rather than the cure of rate rises.

Opposition to municipalisation as an undesirable and ineffective intrusion upon the free market built up in the later 1890s, in response both to its actual extension and to proposals, however improbable of outcome, for more of it, of a more socialist character, from Fabians, the Independent Labour party and some radical Liberals for, among other things, municipal workshops, bakeries, pawnshops and pubs. The struggle culminated in the inconclusive Select Committees on Municipal Trading of 1900 and 1903. In the 1900s enthusiasm even among supporters of municipalisation was, in any case declining. It was not evident that it actually provided better or cheaper services, except for water supplies, or even better working conditions, than private enterprise. The considerable local variation in the quality of provision led many of its previous supporters to advocate national provision and national minimum standards for essential services. Growing Lib-Lab demands for rate redistribution between rich and poor districts contributed to a very gradual decline in the attachment to local autonomy.

Local government by 1914 was more active in social and occasionally economic intervention, somewhat more uniform in its activities and somewhat less independent of central government than fifty years earlier. Its activities were guided until its abolition in 1918 by an increasingly burdened and cumbersome Local Government Board.

IX

The problem that was increasingly evident by the 1890s was that, for all the high-minded principles underlying the Victorian consensus on the minimal state, the liberal economy, decentralisation, probity in public life and the responsible involvement of the citizenry, serious social problems visibly remained. They had diminished over the years of consensus but remained substantial and there were signs and fears that unless action was taken by the central state, as the only body with adequate resources and powers, the social stability which had been one of the main aims and achievements of the mid-Victorian years would be broken. The signs were not excessively alarming – riots in Trafalgar Square, more militant statements and actions by a minority of trade unionists, the formation of the small Independent Labour party – but they suggested the need for a response if social divisions were not to be exacerbated.

The philanthropically inclined in all social groups expressed disturbance at the material and moral condition of a substantial minority of the population who were not sharing the general rise in living standards, indeed were probably falling behind because, due to age, youth, infirmity or other misfortune, they could not enter an overstocked labour market, surviving only precariously on its fringes. It seemed increasingly clear that the liberal economy had produced no mechanism for distributing to the deprived a desirable share of the gains of economic growth. The producers and consumers of a growing polemical, descriptive and quantitative literature on this under-class, members of a generation which had forgotten older fears of a coercive, corrupt and exclusive state since they had never experienced it, no longer persuaded by any conception of a 'natural order', encouraged by the *étatist* element visible in the Victorian conception of the state, increasingly looked to central government to provide this mechanism. They did not necessarily relinquish commitment to the virtues of voluntarism and decentralisation, but called in question more forcefully the boundaries between public and private, central and local action. On an intellectual level, liberal theorists from T. H. Green and his Oxford associates in the 1880s to Hobhouse in the 1900s proposed changing conceptions of the state, as the embodiment rather than the antithesis of communal responsibility.

It was Joseph Chamberlain who most clearly sought an alternative practical approach to government designed to ward off what he saw as the otherwise unavoidable rise of labour and of pressures for an unacceptable degree of state intervention, to reconcile Victorian impulses with the pressing need to diminish poverty and promote economic expansion and a wider share in its benefits. He first expounded a national policy in his 'unauthorised programme' of the 1880s. The Third Reform Act convinced him that 'The centre of power has shifted and the old order is giving place to the new.'[56] In consequence, policy would have to be shifted much more than in the past towards 'social subjects': 'Property must recognise its obligations to those whom it has exploited and pay its "ransom" or "insurance" to secure the necessary improvement in the general conditions of life.'[57] The owners of property should act through the medium of the government acting on behalf of the community as a whole. 'Government is the organised expression of the wishes and wants of the people and under these circumstances let us cease to regard it with suspicion . . . now it is our business to extend its functions and to see in what way its operations can be usefully enlarged.'[58] This involved a new conception of public duty, reflecting an explicitly non-libertarian attitude to the state:

They sound the death-knell of the *laissez-faire* system . . . the goal towards which the advance will probably be made at an accelerated pace is that in the direction of which the legislation of the last quarter of a century has been tending – the intervention . . . of the State on behalf of the weak against the strong, in the interests of labour against capital, of want and suffering against luxury and ease.[59]

But Chamberlain did not envisage increasing centralisation. Rather, desirable action initiated by central government should be administered by elected local authorities in association with voluntary organisations rather than directly through the agency of central government. His ideas were developed first within the Liberal party. He made minor steps towards their implementation during his brief tenure of the Presidency of the Local Government Board in the Liberal government of 1886, permitting local authorities to establish public works to provide employment rather than poor relief for the unemployed, with minimal effects; and removing the stigma of exclusion from the vote from those receiving poor relief for medical purposes only.

[56] Greenleaf, *The Ideological Heritage*, p. 227.
[57] *Ibid.*   [58] *Ibid.*
[59] *Ibid.*, pp. 227–8.

Significantly, he was able to take his ideas intact, and to develop them further, into the Conservative party as a Liberal Unionist from the 1890s. It is equally significant that his far-reaching programmes of social reform made little discernible impact upon party policy. The Conservatives in the 1880s and 1890s initiated exhaustive Royal Commissions into a wide range of social problems – housing, 'sweated' labour, the condition of the aged poor among others – and reform proposals proliferated. The legislative outcome, however, was slight and taxpayer resistance to legislation favouring the working classes remained considerable and highly influential within the Conservative party. It acted more positively in the field of industrial relations, acting to strengthen 'responsible' trade unionism. Following the Conciliation Act, 1896, central government took on the entirely new role of conciliation and arbitration in labour disputes. The Labour Department of the Board of Trade, formed to administer the act and more generally to investigate labour conditions, appointed officials with trade-union experience in a conscious attempt to promote and institutionalise Gladstonian notions of a community of interest between capital and labour. The Workmen's Compensation Act, 1897, followed trade-union criticism of previous, ineffective legislation. It dealt with the serious problem of occupational injury, made employers liable for accidents at work and obliged them to insure and to compensate the injured, at no cost to the state; the obligation was until 1906 limited to certain dangerous occupations.

Yet simultaneously a series of legal decisions, culminating in the House of Lords decision in the Taff Vale case in 1901, appeared severely to restrict the legal rights which unions believed that they had gained in the 1870s and the Conservative Lord Chancellor, Halsbury, was believed to have played a role in bringing them about. The failure of Parliament to reverse these decisions played an important role in disillusioning respectable trade unionists with the party and constitutional system as it stood, whilst the further involvement of the central state in matters which so directly concerned them made them increasingly aware of the need to participate in that constitution.

When Chamberlain went further, entrenching upon economic liberalism with his tariff reform programme from 1903, he seriously divided the Conservative and Unionist party, but lost. Into the 1900s the mid-Victorian consensus retained its hegemony in both parties; social tensions and crises were still believed to be containable within a slightly modified liberal framework.

x

This framework was put to a further test by the Boer War (1899–1902). This found the government unprepared in particular for the level and cost of weaponry required for this first modern war. The Treasury calculated initially that the war would cost not more than £10m and that most of this would be recouped from a swift annexation of the Transvaal goldmines. This was perhaps understandable in view of the apparent puniness of the Boer opposition to the might of the British Empire. In the event it cost £250m to send almost half a million British and colonial soldiers against an enemy the total population of whose country was scarcely one fifth of that number. It was mainly financed by loans and tariffs (notably the contentious corn tariff introduced in 1902) which imposed considerable pressure upon postwar government finance.

It might have been a little less costly, or at least more cost efficient, had it not also been Britain's last free enterprise war. It required an unparalleled commitment of industrial resources which were given inadequate state support. These resources had to be expanded very rapidly in view of the low level of military supplies stockpiled at the outbreak. Defence expenditure had risen in the 1890s, but by the least amount possible because of opposition in Parliament, among taxpayers and from the Treasury. The War Office had seen little need to build up reserve supplies, apparently in the belief that British free enterprise could achieve the impossible: produce large quantities of supplies quickly, in response to haphazard orders, without government subsidy or guarantees for future use of expanded plant to supplement the limited production of government ordnance factories. With all due effort neither source of supplies could comply with the required immediacy.[60]

The military setbacks of the early period of the war, the cost, together with revelations of the physical unfitness of volunteer recruits (there was no conscription and liberal opposition to enforced recruitment delayed its introduction even in the First World War), gave new urgency and new sources of support to fears of relative national decline. The machinery and competence of government and administration as well as methods of finance were called in question. More 'businesslike' administration, 'efficiency' – this time 'national

[60]   C. Trebilcock, 'War and the Failure of Industrial Mobilization: 1899 and 1914', in J. M. Winter, ed., *War and Economic Development* (Cambridge, 1975).

efficiency' – were called for. Demands of this kind came, in particular, from a shifting, cross-party alliance which included the Liberal leader Lord Rosebery, the imperial administrator Alfred Milner and the Webbs, loosely united by varying degrees of commitment to the desirability of efficient, expert administration and strong leadership, ideally on a non-party basis. They did not appear to achieve extensive support but such ideas remained an undercurrent in British politics at least until 1914, some again pointing to Germany as the model to be observed.[61]

The war did not last long enough or make such extensive demands upon the administrative apparatus or upon society more generally (it was not a 'total war') as to enforce significant changes upon the state. The most obvious legacies were the government revenue problem and the pressure for increased state action to improve the health of children, to build (as some had been demanding since at least the 1860s) a stronger race to meet the military and economic needs of the future. The main outcome was the introduction of school meals and medical inspection and treatment for schoolchildren under the post-1906 Liberal government, and some increased local and voluntary activity in the field of child and maternal welfare.

In other respects the lessons of the war were forgotten, to be recalled in 1914–18. Pressures to minimise defence and other government expenditure, against state action to build up military supplies, or to expand the army reserve, remained strong until the eve of the First World War. The Conservatives, who remained in office until 1905, responded by keeping further social intervention to a minimum but could not be wholly unresponsive to the demands for change which had been building up in the 1890s and revived after the war. The major Education Act of 1902 was their most decisive step, though it antagonised nonconformists and also ratepayers by further increasing their commitments. The Unemployed Workmen Act, 1905, was a minimal response to a problem of increasingly pressing urgency, which, classically, placed the main burden of administration and finance on voluntary agencies in association with local government within a framework of central government supervision. The equally urgent problem of reforming a poor law whose principles and practices were increasingly perceived as inappropriate for needs as they were defined in the early years of the twentieth century, and which were

---

[61]   G. Searle, *The Quest for National Efficiency* (Oxford, 1971). E. P. Hennock, *British Social Reform and German Precedents* (Oxford, 1986).

increasingly the focus of labour and radical Liberal criticism, was met by the establishment of a Royal Commission in 1905.

XI

Shortly afterwards the Conservatives were succeeded by a Liberal government, brought in on a landslide propelled by disillusion at Conservative inactivity and nonconformist revolt. Since the later nineteenth century the balance within the Liberal party had shifted somewhat towards preference for a more constructive role for the state in minimising social problems, but it remained acutely divided as to how far such intervention should go and was still strongly defensive of voluntarism as embodying a desirable personal commitment to furthering the good of the community and to the need to protect private life from official intervention; a range of views which were almost identically apparent in the strengthened but still small Labour party. The Liberal commitment to economic liberalism had hardly shifted, indeed its commitment to free trade was strengthened by the furore over tariff reform in the Conservative party, set off by Joseph Chamberlain from 1903. There had been a shift of emphasis in the Liberal party rather than a quantum leap from Gladstonianism.

Indeed, the Liberals came into office in 1906 offering few promises of social legislation. Much of its electoral appeal lay rather in its promises of economy by free trade, though minor members of the new government (such as C. F. G. Masterman) were advocating comprehensive programmes of social reform. The Liberals' actions in their first two years in office were either redemptions of their pact with Labour (the Trade Disputes Act, 1906) or initiated from outside the cabinet (the introduction of school meals, by a Labour backbencher in 1906, or school medical inspection in 1907 largely on the initiative of two civil servants, Robert Morant, the force behind the 1902 Education Act, and George Newman). Any desire on the part of the government to go further was constrained by the hostility of the Conservative-dominated Lords (who rejected the Education Bill of 1906 and less important measures) and by the shortage of government revenue.

The revenue problem was compounded by rising prices which raised the costs of day-to-day government activity, and the commitment to free trade limited the available sources of additional income. The unpopularity of the rates and the gains made by Conservatives from mobilising around ratepayer discontent (they won control of the LCC in 1907, of Sheffield, Nottingham and Leicester in 1908) removed one means of financing social measures. Hence the Liberal legislation which followed was either very cheap or funded from new sources, such as the national insurance contributions introduced in 1911. But a more fundamental solution was needed to the problem. Asquith, as Chancellor, chose to move cautiously towards a graduated income tax.

Such theorists as J. A. Hobson and Sidney Webb provided intellectual reassurance that increased and more equitable direct taxation, an income tax graduated according to income, in place of the flat-rate basis always previously employed, was a means of increasing revenue compatible with free trade. Following a favourable report by the Select Committee on the Income Tax in 1906, Asquith's 1907 Budget took the first step, in the most painless way available, by distinguishing for tax purposes between earned and unearned income and reducing the rate of tax for the former from 1s. to 9d. in the pound. He also introduced compulsory returns for all classes of taxable income, a response to the revelation of widespread tax evasion by a departmental committee in 1905. The yield to the Exchequer was small, but the move opened the way to Lloyd George's more dramatic Budgets to come and to an important break with Gladstonian principles. Higher rates of taxation of the rich would alienate a social group a high proportion of which seemed already disposed to vote for the Conservatives; lower income taxpayers would not be adversely affected and those below the income tax threshold would be encouraged by hopes of redistribution. These were the groups whose support the Liberal party needed to hold. The 'class politics' which the Gladstonian tax policy had been designed to keep at bay was now inescapable.

Asquith also took the first step towards innovative and popular social reform. He was responsible for the Old Age Pensions Act, 1908, though it was guided through the Commons by Lloyd George when Asquith was elevated to the premiership in 1908. On Treasury insistence the amount of the pension was small. It was paid, on a means-tested basis, to the very elderly and very poor who could also pass tests of respectability not dissimilar to those imposed by the poor law. The administration was cheap. The pensions were paid through the Post Office. Local administration was supervised by voluntary committees appointed by local councils and drawn from institutions with relevant experience such as friendly societies, and carried out day to day by paid officials appointed by the Treasury and briefed to restrain excessive generosity on the part of the local committees. However, the measure was popular and the Lords dared not reject it (though they contemplated doing so) in view of the evidence of thirty years of growing support for non-stigmatising relief to a manifestly deserving group. Due to the political problem posed by the rates, previous proposals to finance pensions by this means were rejected; they were the first cash benefit to be financed entirely by the central state.[62]

The social legislation of the following four years was above all the work of Winston Churchill, who entered the cabinet in 1908, and Lloyd George, who became Chancellor of the Exchequer. Neither possessed any philosophy of resistance to central state action, if indeed Lloyd George can be said to have owned a political philosophy at all. He responded, rather, to a gut concern for social justice, tempered by a shrewd eye for combining the politically popular with the politically attainable. Churchill, of very different social origins from the lower middle-class Welshman, was living testimony to the continuing fluidity of party boundaries and philosophies. The Tory in him sustained a preference for active ministerial leadership and innovation, where this was needed to palliate pressing social deprivation and to quell the class disharmony which flowed from its neglect; or (when he moved to the Home Office in 1910) to repress the manifestations of disharmony, in the shape of industrial militancy, where indirect measures failed. As he put it in 1908:

It is false and base to say that these evils [of unemployment, the malnourishment of children, among others] are inherent in the nature of things, that their remedy is beyond the wit of man, that experiment is foolhardy, that all is for the best in 'merrie England'. No one will believe it any more ... the Nation demands the application of drastic corrective and curative processes.[63]

Yet neither he nor Lloyd George could have been as effective as they were without the support of the cabinet and of Asquith – Churchill in introducing Labour exchanges, minimum wages and protection of working conditions for 'sweated' female labour and unemployment insurance, and Lloyd George for his Budgets and national health insurance. Indeed, measures as important as theirs came also from

[62] P. Thane, 'Contributory vs Non-Contributory Old Age Pensions, 1878–1908', in P. Thane, ed., *The Origins of British Social Policy* (1978).
[63] Greenleaf, *The Ideological Heritage*, pp. 152–3.

the Home Office in 1908, in the shape of the great Children Act, consolidating, extending and making more effective existing legislation concerning the welfare and judicial treatment of children, and from the Local Government Board, under the Presidency of the retired socialist and industrial militant John Burns, in the shape of the Housing and Town Planning Act, 1908.

The National Insurance Act, 1911, to which Lloyd George contributed Part I (health insurance) and Churchill Part II (unemployment insurance), as the chapter to follow points out, institutionalised the fusion of and tension between the conflicting philosophies and political imperatives and trends of the time: the central state provided a firm framework within which workers were to practise self-help by means of compulsory weekly contributions, for the purpose of enhancing both their sense of security and their welfare. The entirely new state benefits, in principle payable as a right to contributors by virtue of their contributions, would be subsidised by further contributions from the employer and the taxpayer. The latter were designed to promote, also by compulsion, the sense of social responsibility of the higher classes, whilst promoting among workers the sense of belonging in an organic community bonded by a network of reciprocal rights and responsibilities. The measure was as much moral and political in intent as social and rooted in older values; but the state no longer left it to the self-responsibility of individuals to act upon these values, but exercised compulsion. The legislation was administered largely by voluntary institutions, mainly trade unions and friendly societies, in the interests both of economy and of winning the support of bodies suspicious of the intrusion of the state into the territory of self-help; this approach upheld the voluntary principle whilst partially incorporating it into the state apparatus.

The Liberal social legislation left many problems unsolved, not surprisingly in view of their magnitude. There was no attempt to reconstruct the poor law despite the recommendations of the two reports (minority and majority) delivered by the Royal Commission on the Poor Laws in 1909, though the Liberals had, rather vague, plans to do so which were aborted by the onset of war; and an important effect of their legislation was to withdraw large groups of the deserving poor (the elderly, children, the sick and unemployed) from the poor law as their only publicly funded resource.

The measures were also economical, and not, or intended to be, significantly redistributive. 'Class politics' was a force in the 1900s to a degree which would have alarmed Gladstone, but it was still not dominant and the Liberals did not propose that it should become so, nor that the obligation to self-help should be diminished. Rather they recognised the limits to self-help and voluntarism as solutions to deprivation when it was not the fault of the individual, and sought to supplement them whilst upholding and where possible extending them. The 5s. old age pension was fixed at 2s. per week below the amount calculated by Seebohm Rowntree as sufficient for individual subsistence; the gap was to be filled by self-help or philanthropy. To a high degree working people shared this approach, regarding state welfare as a poor substitute for full employment, a 'fair' wage and independence, other than to meet the needs of the undeservedly deprived who lacked other resources.[64]

The most striking characteristic of the Liberal social legislation com- pared with what had gone before was the effectiveness with which it was implemented. Whereas, for example, the considerable amount of legislation passed since the 1860s concerning the care and protection of children had been left to patchy and far from comprehensive imple- mentation by voluntary organisations and local authorities, the intent of the Children Act was largely carried out, in part by these same bodies, but under closer central supervision. The effectiveness of implementation, for example of the Education and Public Health Acts, had gradually increased in the later nineteenth century; but, more than before, the major Liberal measures largely did what they were intended to do. This was partly due to the larger and more efficient bureaucratic resources of central and local government (though the latter are much under-researched). In 1851 there had been 39,100 civil servants, in 1881, 50,900, in 1901, 116,400; in 1911 there were 172,000. The civil service had undergone further gradual transformation, with the introduction by the 1900s of reasonably efficient techniques of recruitment and organisation, and with uniformity of pay, grades and conditions of work close to becoming fully established. The pace of work was still leisurely by later twentieth-century standards and ten- sions remained among departments and between most of them and the Treasury. Some, like the Local Government Board were seriously overstretched.[65] The service was controlled by administrators of the

---

[64] Thane, 'Working Class and "Welfare"'. H. Pelling, 'The Working Class and the Welfare State', in H. Pelling, *Popular Politics and Society in Late Victorian Britain* (1968).
[65] R. McLeod, *Treasury Control and Social Administration* (1968).

type Gladstone had envisaged; men of liberal education from Oxford and Cambridge (though a very few women had now entered as, for example, factory inspectors), subscribing to an ethos of impartial service, though quite capable, as in the case of Robert Morant, of taking a strong initiating role. The effectiveness of a machine still small and unobtrusive by continental European standards was to be demonstrated by its conduct in the coming war.

At least as important in bringing about the effective implementation of legislation was the will on the part of ministers to bring this about, impelled, presumably, by recognition that more serious gestures were needed than before to palliate evident if not uncontainable social disharmony (the National Insurance Act passed in the midst of a strike wave). They worked hard to ensure implementation of the measures and to pacify opposition potentially capable of subverting it. Officials visited and persuaded trade-union officials and employers who were dubious about the Insurance Act and won many of them over by incorporating them into local insurance committees.

The Liberal government sought, like its predecessors, to present itself as standing above social divisions and for the national interest. To achieve this successfully necessitated real if not excessive enhancement of the welfare of the bulk of working people and some, if not dramatic, entrenchment upon wealth. Hence Lloyd George's controversial Budget of 1909. Following Asquith's first steps he raised the tax on unearned income from 1s. to 1s.2d. in the pound; raised death duties to a maximum 15 per cent on inheritances of over £1m; imposed a super-tax of 6d. in the pound on incomes over £5,000 p.a.; introduced an allowance in respect of every child under the age of sixteen against incomes under £500 p.a.; raised duties on spirits and tobacco and imposed the first taxes on petrol and on land. Of these, the small tax on the unearned increment of land values was of greater social and political than revenue significance, in view of the distress it caused to landlords, not least due to the national land valuation which it necessitated. The Budget also established a £1m Development Fund, to provide state funding for improvements in rural transport, afforestation and agricultural education and research, all designed to assist the revival of the rural economy. Overall the Budget marked a shift from indirect to direct taxation, especially of the better off, and towards marginally greater state intervention in the economy. Its significance is evident from the fact that it provoked two general elections and a permanent curbing of the power of the

Lords, who lost, as a result, their power of veto over financial legislation.

Lloyd George went further in the Budget of 1914. This projected a record national expenditure of over £200m, introduced a graduated scale of tax on incomes of £1,000 p.a. and above and lowered the super-tax threshold to £3,000 p.a. Death duties were increased and tax relief in respect of children doubled. In seven years maximum rates of direct taxation had risen from 9d. to 2s.8d. in respect of earned income and from 8 per cent to 20 per cent in respect of death duties. The proportion of government revenue obtained from direct taxation was 60 per cent, having been 44 per cent in 1888.

The Liberals were seeking to promote a politics of social harmony in increasingly difficult circumstances in the years before 1914, amid the militancy of the Irish, trade unionists and unenfranchised women. In quelling the more extreme manifestations of militancy, like past governments, they did not hold back from overt interventionism. In the case of industrial militancy they sought where possible to build upon existing preventive mechanisms. The militant suffragists introduced a new kind of social disharmony, initiated by women bewildered and infuriated by their continued exclusion from active participation in national politics. Their fierce treatment of the militant suffragettes won the government some support but also growing criticism and by 1914, due in large measure to the subtler, pressure group tactics of constitutionalist suffragists, government leaders were accepting that they could not for much longer refuse to concede the vote to most, if not all, adult women. Women's wartime service was to offer them a face-saving excuse for doing so.[66]

With industrial militancy the government was on more familiar territory. The government sought to restrain the more extreme tendencies on the part of both employers and workers by accustomed, discreet, methods. The Labour Department of the Board of Trade carried on its role of encouraging a middle course between extremists among both employers and workers, against the intense suspicion of both, seeking channels for the minimisation of conflict and outcomes which disturbed the workings of the market least, facilitated by the fact that neither employers, labour nor the cabinet had united views about how industrial relations should be conducted. When it was suggested to the Home Office that Tom Mann should be arrested during the

---

[66] S. Holton, *Feminism and Democracy: Women's Suffrage and Reform Politics in Britain, 1900–1918* (1986), pp. 116–50.

1911 railway strike the permanent secretary replied, 'If Tom Mann is to be arrested there are one or two ship-owners who should go with him to prison.'[67] He showed similar impatience with the pleas of manufacturers for police protection from strikers. Churchill as Home Secretary tried initially, contrary to myth, to avoid coercive action against strikers, including the South Wales miners. His limited patience broke during the 1911 railway strike. He marched soldiers into twenty-four towns, convinced that continuation of the strike would lead to a breakdown of the economy and of public order. The more politically sensitive Lloyd George intervened and brought the strike to a negotiated end.

In other disputes of the period the conciliators appointed by the Labour Department under the terms of the Conciliation Act were generally individuals not directly involved in industrial relations or with state institutions. They were usually professional men, though increasing numbers of workingmen were appointed after 1906. Most of them were not entirely neutral arbitrators between the opposing factions but nor were they simply spokesmen for the employers' interest. Nor were they always successful. Effective conciliation depended upon achieving the consent and co-operation of both sides and in these years of rising costs of living, relatively full employment and strengthened labour willingness to oppose even hard-line employers, this was not always forthcoming.[68] Hence the government felt forced to take the unprecedented step of regulating by legislation miners' hours and wages in 1912 as the only apparent means to achieve industrial peace in a situation in which conciliation was ineffective; though it was taken reluctantly because it appeared to favour one class over another and presented the government as intervening directly rather than, as it still preferred, through the encouragement of voluntary agreements.

In the years before 1914 the government increasingly felt forced to resort to an interventionist role. The practice, successful since the 1840s, of firmly governing an unequal but stable society through a process of negotiation among the major social factions, by an apparently neutral state by means, as Maurice Cowling has put it, of 'manipulation of the electorate to want leadership rather than participation

[67]   Jill Pellew, *The Home Office, 1848–1914: From Clerks to Bureaucrats* (1982), p. 91.
[68]   Roger Davidson, 'The Board of Trade and Industrial Relations, 1896–1914', *Historical Journal*, 21 (1978).

and to protect the classes by persuading the masses to support the parliamentary conflict through which inequality was sustained'[69] was under pressure; though it was very far from clear that the Victorian liberal consensus had collapsed.

[69] M. Cowling, *The Impact of Labour 1920–1924* (Cambridge, 1971), pp. 6–7.

CHAPTER 2

Society and the state in twentieth-century Britain

JOSÉ HARRIS

I

In the chapter on 'Social Movements' in Volume 12 of the old Cambridge Modern History published in 1910, Sidney Webb predicted that one of the main characteristics of twentieth-century society would be that it would consist *only* of government and of private citizens. As democratic rights were extended and as public authorities acquired increasingly extensive powers over social and economic affairs, the great ramshackle mass of private, pluralistic and voluntary institutions that had constituted the fabric of past societies would be progressively displaced by a streamlined, simplified, rationalised two-way relationship between the individual and the state. Seventy years later a distinguished American political scientist, Samuel Beer, diagnosed the relationship between British government and society in the latter half of the twentieth century in diametrically opposite terms: government *had* acquired greater powers and citizens *had* acquired greater democratic rights, but these trends had been accompanied by a proliferation of pluralistic interest groups unprecedented in British history. The upshot was that both government and individuals were in many ways more impotent than they had been under the traditional, restricted, imperfectly democratic system that had prevailed earlier in the century.[1]

Curiously enough, though apparently the antithesis of each other, both the predictions of Sidney Webb and the historical diagnosis of Professor Beer contain important elements of historical truth. They both capture genuine elements in the immensely complex and con-

[1] Sidney Webb, 'Social Movements', in *Cambridge Modern History*, vol. 12: *The Latest Age* (Cambridge, 1910), pp. 730–65; Samuel H. Beer, *Britain Against Itself: The Political Contradictions of Collectivism* (1982).

tinually changing relationship between British government and society in the twentieth century. This pattern of change to a certain extent reflects global rather than purely national history – the pressures of war, industrialisation, ideological dissent and demographic growth that have remodelled government institutions in all advanced countries. But the history of the twentieth-century British state cannot be explained purely in terms of cross-national convergence. No other state has experienced quite the same degree of rapid imperial expansion and withdrawal. No other major European country in the twentieth century has avoided both a violent overthrow of central government and invasion by a foreign power. These facts alone suggest a political culture of exceptional stability and continuity, and an unusual relationship between government and people. Yet paradoxically the powers and functions of the state have changed more dramatically since the beginning of the twentieth century than in any comparable span of years in earlier history. Though the pace of change varied at different times and there were some impulses towards contraction as well as expansion, nevertheless the British state after the Second World War occupied a very different position both in the lives and in the minds of men from that which it had occupied before 1914. Whereas the nineteenth-century 'revolution in government' had been an elusive and essentially limited phenomenon, that of the twentieth century pressed tangibly on nearly every facet of human life. The boundaries of what constituted the 'public' and the 'private' domain were radically redefined. Expressed in crudely quantitative terms, public authorities in the 1900s spent less than 8 per cent, in the 1960s more than 50 per cent, of gross domestic product; and, perhaps even more important, by the latter date, government had become the single most important customer for producers in the private sector. Expressed in more subjective terms, Englishmen in the 1900s greatly admired their country's system of government, but on the whole expected it to do very little. By the 1960s they were much more critical of the whole range of governmental institutions; but their expectations of and demands upon government were incomparably more ambitious than they had been half a century before.

Such a profound change in political culture has not passed without scholarly comment, and numerous academic and official monographs supply us with detailed profiles of the state's role in fiscal, monetary, commercial, social and industrial affairs. The *dramatis personae* of political society – ministers and MPs, officials and experts, interest and promotional groups, producers and consumers – have all been the objects of detailed sociological scrutiny. Ambitious attempts have been made to discover the hidden motors of change and to fit them within various patterns of general explanation – such as the revival of 'corporatism', the contest between individualism and collectivism, the displacement of a Ricardian by a Keynesian paradigm, the changing character of 'civic culture', the entrenchment of capitalism by crisis-management, the growth of humanitarianism and changing perceptions of citizen rights.[2] Yet, unsurprisingly perhaps in the face of such a complex phenomenon, the exact nature of the changing relationship between 'government' and 'society' remains obscure. Most of the general explanations advanced can be supported up to a point with empirical evidence, yet remain in the last resort disappointingly tautological; they merely redescribe in more abstract terms the trends whose existence they are trying to explain. 'Corporatism' in particular offers an unsatisfactory tool to the analytic historian, because the term is often used to refer to two diametrically opposite processes (on the one hand the delegation of state functions to private institutions, on the other hand the absorption of private functions by the state). This brief essay cannot hope to unravel such complexity: but an attempt will be made to map the social history of the state since the First World War and to identify the nodal points of change and continuity.

I I

The relationship between government and society in Britain in the early years of the twentieth century was hedged around by a network of assumptions and conventions that were well understood within

---

[2] See, e.g., R. K. Middlemas, *Politics in Industrial Society: The Experience of the British System since 1911* (1979); Walter Greenleaf, *The British Political Tradition*, 2 vols. (1983); Gabriel Almond and Sidney Verba, eds., *The Civic Culture: Political Attitudes and Democracy in Five Nations* (Princeton, 1963); Dennis Kavanagh, 'Political Culture in Britain: the Decline of the Civic Culture', in Gabriel Almond and Sidney Verba, eds., *The Civic Culture Revisited* (Boston, Mass., 1980), pp. 124–76; Trevor Smith, *The Politics of the Corporate Economy* (Oxford, 1979); T. H. Marshall, *Citizenship and Social Class and Other Essays* (Cambridge, 1950), pp. 1–85.

the political community.[3] One of the most important of these assumptions was that the political community itself was limited to those capable of such tacit understanding. The traditional equation between political participation and property rights, though marginally eroded by the nineteenth-century reform acts, had not yet given way to a purely capitational notion of democracy. Between the Franchise Acts of 1867 and 1884, which gave the vote to male heads of households, and those of 1918 and 1929, which effectively introduced universal suffrage, lay the assumption clearly articulated by Gladstone: that active membership of the constitution was not a birthright but a prize. It was a prize awarded to those with sufficient education, intelligence, experience and responsibility to enable them to comprehend what the working of the constitution was all about. The constitutional rules that participants were meant to endorse were nowhere codified, but consisted of a series of principles formulated with varying degrees of precision and formality. Those most clearly articulated by early twentieth-century constitutional theorists were the notions of parliamentary sovereignty and the rule of law. Buttressing these twin pillars of constitutional theory were a host of lesser principles, some embodied in statutes, some plucked from the air of everyday political practice: some of long-standing, others recently enunciated to meet the changing needs and constitutional environment of the nineteenth century. These concerned such diverse issues as the powers of the monarch, the independence of the judiciary, the autonomy of MPs, the relationship between Lords and Commons, the frequency of parliamentary elections and the circumstances under which ministers were required to resign. Outside this inner core of constitutional rules was a wide penumbral region of principles and practices which fell short of full constitutional status but which it was widely believed public servants should observe. Much of this informal code of conduct was of relatively recent (Peelite and Gladstonian) origin: it included

[3] It is difficult to offer precise references to such imprecise phenomena as assumptions and conventions, but I found the following works useful and suggestive: Henry Sidgwick, *The Principles of Political Economy*, Book 3: *The Art of Political Economy* (3rd edn, 1901), pp. 395–592; A. V. Dicey, *Law and Public Opinion in England during the Nineteenth Century* (2nd edn, 1914); A. V. Dicey, *Introduction to the Study of the Law of the Constitution* (8th edn, 1924); A. Laurence Lowell, *The Government of England*, 2 vols. (New York, 1908); Maurice Cowling, *1867: Disraeli, Gladstone and Revolution. The Passing of the Second Reform Bill* (Cambridge, 1967); Robert Currie, *Industrial Politics* (Oxford, 1979); H. C. G. Matthew, ed., *The Gladstone Diaries*, vol. 7 (Oxford, 1982), pp. xxv–ciii; Martin Pugh, *The Making of Modern British Politics* (Oxford, 1982), Parts 1 and 2.

such principles as the impropriety of approaching electorates with 'promises' and 'programmes', the desirability of balanced budgets, the need for 'evenhandedness' in dealing with competing interest groups, and the iniquity of 'class legislation'. Above all there was a belief among politicians of all complexions that the relationship between government and society was essentially a limited one; it was a marriage of convenience rather than a marriage of true minds. The aim of the government even at its most ambitious was not to determine the structure and working of society; such an aim would have been seen as not so much undesirable as inherently unattainable. Rather, it was to provide a framework of rules and guidelines designed to enable society very largely to run itself.

Behind these constitutional rules lay something more intangible: a widely diffused popular political philosophy, often ignored by historians who see social history as by its nature a materialist enterprise, but which constituted one of the most enduring and powerful facts in the life of English society. Because of its very diffuseness this popular philosophy is not easy to define. In contradistinction to much continental political thought, it saw 'civil society' (business, work, culture, leisure, family life, religion) as the highest sphere of human existence and the arena in which men enjoyed some form of absolute rights. 'The State', by contrast, was an institution of secondary importance and dubious linguistic status (Englishmen generally preferred the concept 'government') which existed mainly to serve the convenience and protect the rights of individuals in private life. This is not to deny that there was always a tradition of English theorists who saw the state in more transcendental or sacramental terms, but for most of the nineteenth century this was the view of a dwindling and dissentient minority. An instrumental view of the state did not necessarily add up to a mere atomistic individualism: but the corporate life of society was seen as expressed through voluntary association and the local community, rather than through the persona of the state. Similarly, the state was rarely seen as an indispensable vehicle of collective national identity. The institutions of the state (crown, Parliament, the established church) might in certain respects and at certain times enhance and symbolise such a sense of identity, and Parliament in particular was seen as closely linked with national history. But for most Englishmen, Scotsmen and Welshmen a sense of belonging to their country was very remote from any sense of belonging to its governing institutions (only among the Irish was there a lurking belief that national identity was somehow inextricably mixed up with institutional separateness and sovereign power).

The practical expression of such beliefs was not the oft-cited but largely imaginary 'nightwatchman state'. Victorian government did involve itself in the life of its citizens in many visible and invisible ways; but such involvement had to be justified in strictly functional and expedient terms. In the few areas where the state laid down a systematic framework for social life (as in the poor law, support for free trade, and management of currency) this was thought to be merely an institutional enforcement of certain universally valid behavioural laws. This is not, of course, to claim that practice always corresponded with principle and theory: interest groups never abandoned the quest for state support, and Victorian politicians never wholly ceased to use state resources to placate their own supporters. But, as a matter of general policy, the state was deemed to be above particular interests. More extensive government was widely viewed as not merely undesirable but unnecessary, in the sense that most of the functions performed by government in other societies were in Britain performed by coteries of citizens governing themselves. The full extent of such informal collectivism is incalculable: but sources such as the Annual Charities Register and the annual reports of the Registrar of Friendly Societies bear witness to the dense network of self-governing social institutions that encircled the citizen at every level. As late as 1911 the gross annual receipts of registered charities exceeded national public expenditure on the poor law – a figure that takes no account of unregistered charities, nor of such bastions of voluntarism as friendly societies, trade unions and other forms of institutional self-help.[4]

This bundle of political ideals and institutional practices found powerful expression in English public life right down to 1914. Since the 1880s, however, there had been gradually accumulating signs of change:[5] change which some contemporaries viewed as a necessary adaptation to modern conditions, others as a reversion to the era of 'old corruption', or to the even earlier period of arbitrary executive power. Politics grew noticeably more programmatic; market forces

---

[4]   A. R. Prest and A. A. Adams, *Consumers' Expenditure in the United Kingdom 1900–1919* (Cambridge, 1954), p. 162; B. R. Mitchell and Phyllis Deane, *Abstract of British Historical Statistics* (Cambridge, 1962), p. 148.

[5]   See, e.g., Pugh, *The Making of Modern British Politics*, chaps. 4–7; Harold Emy, *Liberals, Radicals and Social Politics* (Cambridge, 1973), *passim*; George Dangerfield, *The Strange Death of Liberal England* (1936), esp. Part 2.

began to erode the independent viability of local communities, charity and self-help; social and economic dislocation forced central government to extend its responsibility into certain traditionally local and private spheres. Politicians who could not impose their will through established channels began to toy with heretical notions about constituency sovereignty and the doctrine of the mandate. Interest groups on both right and left of the political spectrum began increasingly to look to the state for protection and financial support. Professional 'activists' and practitioners of 'politics as a vocation' made their appearance in all political parties. Disenchanted intellectuals, critical of Britain's loss of economic leadership and poor showing in the Boer War, pressed for the remodelling of public institutions and the replacement of an amateur 'customary' style of government by professionalism and rationality. Social and political theorists questioned the optimality of a 'natural' distribution of material goods and criticised the poor law's purely negative role in protecting individuals against destitution. The emergence of 'class politics' posed an implicit threat to the theory of the even-handed impartial state. And, perhaps more fundamentally, in the years immediately before 1914 syndicalists, suffragettes and Irish intransigents posed violent challenges to parliamentary sovereignty and the rule of law. All these pressures suggest that the liberal constitutional consensus of the mid-Victorian era was winding down: the very vehemence with which Edwardian constitutional theorists tried to rationalise and defend that consensus indicates that it was no longer so universally binding as it had been when less clearly spelt out some decades before.

Nevertheless, what is perhaps most surprising about the Edwardian period is, not that traditional notions of government and society were challenged, but – given the social, economic and international pressures of the period – the extraordinary tenacity with which mid-nineteenth-century principles and practices survived. The most outstanding example of this was the successful battle for free trade: a battle in which protection was denounced not merely as economically indefensible, but as the epitome of that 'hand in the till' approach to politics which the era of reform was supposed to have stamped out. Among Edwardian public administrators there was a handful of zealots who preached centralism and rationalisation as ends in themselves, but the vast majority continued to see local government as the rightful locus of public life, centralisation as an occasional and regrettable economic necessity. On the eve of the First World War

what is perhaps most striking about attitudes to government is not
the eclipse of an older by a newer philosophy, but the way in which
individuals and political groups found themselves pulled in several
contrary directions at once. The major piece of social legislation of
the period, the National Insurance Act of 1911 was a classic attempt
to reconcile advanced bureaucratic rationality with market forces, compulsion and uniformity with voluntarism and pluralism, the 'impartial' with the 'patronage' state. Nowhere were the constitutional
tensions of the period more clearly exemplified than in the labour
movement, torn between its commitment to the interests of the working class and its commitment to a liberal definition of the political
'rules of the game'.[6] The unpopularity with many workers of government social policies suggests that dislike of state intervention was
in no sense confined to the taxpaying upper and middle classes. The
labour movement's greatest prewar triumph, the 1906 Trade Disputes
Act, exhibited like the National Insurance Act profoundly contradictory principles: on the one hand it was an illiberal piece of sectarian
'class' legislation; on the other hand it enshrined an ancient liberal
principle that there was a sacrosanct sphere of 'natural liberty' ante-
cedent to and outside the purview of the law and the state.

III

Historians remain undecided about whether the tensions of the pre-
1914 period were merely transient difficulties which could ultimately
have been contained within a predominantly liberal framework or
whether they were building up towards a radical social explosion.
The outbreak of war rendered such a question purely academic. Britain
declared war on Germany in August 1914 almost totally unprepared
both mentally and institutionally for the four years that were to follow.
Public and political opinion at the start of the war was divided into
three camps: a tiny minority opposed to war on principle, an equally
tiny minority who wanted to seize the opportunity to remodel British
institutions on the lines of 'national efficiency' and a large majority
who supported the war but had no idea that it might present a challenge to established social structures and constitutional principles.
The military defeats, production failures, shell shortages, manpower
mismanagement, beer dilution and food queues of the first two years

---

[6]   Ross McKibbin, 'Why Was there no Marxism in Britain?', *English Historical Review*,
99 (1984), esp. pp. 311–20.

of war led to increasingly bitter conflict between the second and third of these alternatives, and to the gradual displacement of the old style of government by a much more dynamic and arbitrary system geared not to constitutional niceties but to winning the war.[7] Traditional approaches were symbolised by the Chancellor of the Exchequer, Reginald McKenna, who clung to free trade and sterling convertibility; and by the Governor of the Bank of England, Lord Cunliffe, who even as late as 1917 spent financial missions to North America on fishing trips to Florida, convinced that no human action could modify relations between the dollar and the pound.[8] The new model of government first began to emerge with the setting-up of the Ministry of Munitions in 1915. The next seventeen months saw a series of running battles within government, Parliament and society at large over such issues as military conscription, direction of civilian manpower, regulation of wages, prices and profits, and the scope and content of government emergency powers. The most crucial and symbolic of these battles was that over conscription: no other issue so trenchantly challenged the mid-nineteenth-century vision of a citizen's autonomy and detachment from the institutions of the state. Conflict between these rival conceptions of government led at the end of 1916 to a crucial change of Prime Ministers: the cautious constitutionalist Asquith was replaced by his more dynamic, more pragmatic, more *étatist* colleague, David Lloyd George.

Lloyd George's wartime premiership may be seen as a crucial turning point in the evolution of modern politics and the modern British state. Though Lloyd George himself had no clear-cut constitutional ideas (and indeed lacked anything resembling a coherent political philosophy), nevertheless he became the catalyst and animator of many of the new political forces already stirring before 1914 and now unleashed by the crisis of war. Indeed, his very lack of principle, combined with his restless innovatory energy, made him a resonant sounding board for fashionable ideas. His move to the premiership was accompanied by radical changes in the structure, personnel and ethos of British government, and in the impact that it made on citizens' private lives. The traditional cabinet of senior ministers (an institution that had evolved over 200 years without acquiring a regular status

[7] A. J. P. Taylor, *English History 1914–45* (Oxford, 1965), chaps. 1 and 2; Cameron Hazlehurst, *Politicians at War July 1914 to May 1915* (1971); Kathleen Burk, ed., *War and the State: The Transformation of British Government, 1914–19* (1982).
[8] Kathleen Burk, *Britain, America and the Sinews of War* (1985), p. 129.

and procedures) was replaced by a much smaller, more formalised war cabinet, concerned not with rubber-stamping departmental business but with formulating and co-ordinating high policy. Cabinet business, previously recorded only in a few lines penned by the Prime Minister to the monarch, was now managed and minuted by a professional secretariat.[9] At the same time a whole range of new Whitehall departments was set up, to deal with expanding areas of government responsibility, such as Labour, Food, Shipping, Pensions and (somewhat later) Health. The new ministries were staffed partly by professional civil servants, partly by a large body of businessmen recruited into Whitehall for the duration of the war: 'men of push and go', whose proclaimed purpose was to galvanise British government into entrepreneurial standards of speed and efficiency. By 1917 the wartime emergency had propelled these departments into a degree of regulation of civilian life never dreamt of in the prewar era: food rationing, price controls, compulsory purchase and requisitioning of raw materials, bulk importation of essential supplies, control of rents and housebuilding, registration and direction of labour – all the paraphernalia of what a mid-nineteenth-century liberal would have regarded as a classic authoritarian state. In addition to new ministries Lloyd George also set up a range of advisory and policy-making institutions without precedent in British constitutional history; such as his own personal secretariat of policy advisers (the famous 'Garden Suburb') and a Directorate of National Service, whose head was neither a civil servant nor a Member of Parliament but a businessman administrator responsible only to the war cabinet. Finally, the later years of the war also produced an upsurge of what can only be described as 'planning', though the term was not current at the time. In several Whitehall departments groups of ambitious administrators formed themselves into 'think-tanks' to plot long-term policy objectives, and a series of 'reconstruction' committees culminated in the setting-up of a full-blown Ministry of Reconstruction charged with rebuilding British society and institutions in the postwar world.[10]

This explosion of institutional change was accompanied by widespread flouting of long-established norms of public administration. Treasury and parliamentary control over public spending were swept

[9]   Stephen Roskill, *Hankey: Man of Secrets*, vol. 1: *1877–1918* (1970), chap. 12; John Turner, 'Cabinets, Committees and Secretariats: The Higher Direction of War', in Burk, ed., *War and the State*, pp. 57–83.

[10] José Harris, *William Beveridge: A Biography* (Oxford, 1977), pp. 250–62; Burk, ed., *War and the State*, pp. 157–81.

away in the monsoon of war finance. Businessmen – administrators, often unfamiliar with or contemptuous of established Whitehall rules, shocked their civil service counterparts by simply by-passing the normal channels of authority. Permanent secretaries would find their decisions overturned by determined temporary subordinates who got their way by appealing direct to the minister. Civil servants themselves were not averse to using the cloak of the Defence of the Realm regulations to extend the scope of administrative tribunals and delegated legislation. The importation into Whitehall of specialists in particular fields may have enhanced administrative efficiency but it also gave a foothold in government to vested interest groups in a way that horrified protagonists of the prewar 'impartial state'.[11] Indeed, an overt purpose of the creation of new ministries was precisely to placate and incorporate the demands of such interest groups: the Ministry of Labour and Ministry of Food were cases in point. The pressures of war also provoked a widespread questioning of the traditional purposes and structures of government at a more speculative level: some of which, at least, offered a fundamental challenge to established constitutional thought. Within the business community and to a certain extent within Whitehall there was some enthusiasm for a permanent reconstruction of government on more 'corporatist' lines, with industrial relations and wage levels being permanently regulated by an enforceable framework of law.[12] At the opposite end of the spectrum, syndicalist guild socialists and militant shop-stewards pressed for the partial or total dismantling of the sovereign state and its replacement by various forms of workers' control.[13] In all parties there were voices raised in favour of retaining some aspects of wartime emergency powers after the return of peace. At a more modest level, but still presenting a radical challenge to traditional ideas and structures, the Haldane Committee on the Machinery of Government proposed a far-reaching rationalisation of the whole system of public administration. Historic divisions between departments were to be replaced by functional specialisation, *ad hoc* decisions by long-term policy programmes, gentleman administrators by experts; 'in all departments

[11] José Harris, 'Bureaucrats and Businessmen in British Food Control', in Burk, ed., *War and the State*, p. 148; Harris, *William Beveridge*, pp. 244 5.
[12] John Turner, 'The Politics of "Organised Business" in the First World War', in John Turner, ed., *Businessmen and Politics: Studies in Business Activity in British Politics, 1900–1945* (1984), pp. 33–49; Harris, *William Beveridge*, pp. 251–3.
[13] G. D. H. Cole, *Self-Government in Industry* (1917), esp. pp. 71–123; James Hinton, *The First Shop Stewards' Movement* (1973), pp. 275–329.

better provision should be made for enquiry, research and reflection before policy is defined and put into operation'.[14] Perhaps most fundamentally of all, the late Victorian ideal of limited democracy gave way before the Representation of the People Act of 1918, which tripled the size of the electorate and gave the vote to women over thirty and to all adult males other than peers, criminals and lunatics. The enfranchisement of paupers cut the age-old constitutional link between voting and property rights, and put an end to the formerly sacrosanct principle that recipients of public money should have no say in how that money was spent.

IV

Relations between government and people at the end of the First World War were therefore in a highly fluid and contingent state.[15] The constitutional certainties of the prewar period appeared to have collapsed in the face of unconventional ideas and demands at all points of the political spectrum. The erosion of old landmarks seemed to be symbolised by Lloyd George's decision to fight the 1918 election on a coalition platform, and by the emergence of the Labour party as the main party of opposition. The dwindling of the Liberals signified more than the displacement of one radical party by another: it involved the squeezing out of that section of the political community in which Victorian constitutional principles – particularly dislike of 'class politics' and idealisation of the impartial state – had been most strongly held. The Easter rising and emergence of Sinn Fein in Ireland meant that the Irish question – always the Achilles heel of the Victorian political consensus – could no longer be contained by traditional constitutional means. The abandonment of the gold standard in 1919 meant yielding up a principle that many constitutional purists saw as an indispensable component of the impartial state. The wave of armed uprisings that swept central and Eastern Europe at the end of the war aroused fears in many quarters, and hopes in a few, that civil conflict would soon extend to Britain: fears that were compounded by rent strikes, police strikes, passive resistance towards 'paternalist' social policies, and widespread industrial unrest. A

---

[14]   *Ministry of Reconstruction, Report of the Machinery of Government Committee*, PP 1918, XII, *passim*.
[15]   Kenneth O. Morgan, *Consensus and Disunity: The Lloyd George Coalition Government, 1918–22* (Oxford, 1979), *passim*; Maurice Cowling, *The Impact of Labour 1920–1924* (Cambridge, 1971), introduction and chap. 1.

detached observer looking at the state of Britain in 1919 might well have predicted a prolonged period of class war culminating in the emergence of economic autarchy and a much more powerful, central-ised, rationalised, autocratic, modern state.

In fact this did not happen. For a variety of reasons governmental and social change after the First World War was much more limited and incremental than seemed probable in the short term. What emerged was not a new form of government but a system in which old and new ideas interlocked with and to a certain extent neutralised each other. One important cause of this was that those who wanted radical change were profoundly divided in their ambitions. Those who supported a perpetuation of wartime socio-economic controls, for example, differed widely about which controls should be dis-pensed with and which retained. Followers of Lord Milner and the 'national efficiency' school of government favoured external protec-tionism and permanent curtailment of trade-union and civil liberties, combined with a return to an internal free-market economy; whereas leaders of the Labour party wanted continuing controls over prices and production in combination with a return to prewar trade-union autonomy. By contrast, those who favoured a return to more limited government – strongly represented among professional civil servants and in the City – were much clearer and more united about their long-term aims. Another factor was the rapid collapse of the postwar economic boom, the harsh reality of Britain's war debt to America and the financial disintegration of most of her European creditors: all of which meant that end-of-war promises of postwar reconstruction were rapidly overtaken by severe financial restraint.[16] A third import-ant though less tangible factor was that the example of continental revolutions proved to be negative rather than positive: avoidance of bolshevism and all that it entailed became a primary aim not merely of Conservative but of Labour leaders and socialists committed to change by parliamentary means. A further more long-term pressure but perhaps in the last resort the most crucial one was the unexpec-tedly moderate character of mass electoral democracy. Though man-hood suffrage produced a handful of 'little Moscows' in local government, and a few revolutionary MPs for individual constituen-cies, the single most striking fact about the extended franchise was

---

[16] R. H. Tawney, 'The Abolition of Economic Controls 1918–21', *Economic History Review*, 1st ser., 13 (1943), pp. 1–30; Susan Howson, 'The Origins of Dear Money 1919–20', *Economic History Review*, 2nd ser., 27 (1974), pp. 88–107.

that more people voted Conservative than for any other party at every single election throughout the interwar years. The new voters and their representatives showed some signs, initially at least, of being more concerned with narrowly sectional interests than their Victorian counterparts had been;[17] but they evinced very little concerted desire for radical change in wider social or governmental institutions.

This widespread organic resistance to change, coming after an intensely compressed period (1916–19) in which traditional ideas and institutions seemed on the brink of the melting pot, has often been misinterpreted by analysts of twentieth-century institutions. The reversion to prewar governmental norms and procedures has often been portrayed in terms of bureaucratic conspiracy, tacitly reinforced by financial interests, to hold in check the forces of innovation and progress. Higher civil servants, recruited even more exclusively than before 1914 from an elite Oxbridge educated class and now for the first time united into a single administrative corps, used their power in a consistently negative fashion to sustain class privilege and outmoded values. Such a framework has been invoked to explain the reassertion of Treasury control in 1919, the return to the gold standard in 1925, the public expenditure cutbacks of 1922 and 1931, the policy-making impotence of the 1924 and 1929 Labour governments, and official resistance to new approaches to planning and deficit finance.[18] This pattern of explanation is, however, inadequate on several different levels. At the most obvious level it is analytically redundant, in that it ascribes to bureaucratic conspiracy something that can much more simply be ascribed to the general political culture of the period. This is not to deny that interwar civil servants were powerful and cautious (clearly they were both); but there was nothing essentially conspiratorial in their continual reference to the fact that public expenditure was inherently limited by electoral pressures.[19] If civil servants preferred to keep taxes low, to encourage voluntary effort and to confine public administration so far as possible to the sphere of local

---

[17] Morgan, *Consensus and Disunity*, chaps. 3 and 4.
[18] See, e.g., Bentley B. Gilbert, *British Social Policy, 1914–39* (1970); Royden Harrison, 'Labour Government: Then and Now', *Political Quarterly*, 41 (1970), pp. 71–3. For critical discussion of this approach, see Max Beloff, 'The Whitehall Factor: The Role of the Higher Civil Service 1919–39', in Gillian Peele and Chris Cook, eds., *The Politics of Reappraisal 1918–1939* (1975), pp. 209–31; and R. Davidson and R. Lowe, 'Bureaucracy and Innovation in British Welfare Policy 1870–1945', in W. J. Mommsen, ed., *The Emergence of the Welfare State in Britain and Germany* (1981), pp. 263–95.
[19] See, e.g., Rodney Lowe, *Adjusting to Democracy: The Role of the Ministry of Labour in British Politics 1916–1939* (Oxford, 1986), p. 97.

government, so on the whole did the majority of the British public – who, after a brief hiccup during the early years of the First World War, rapidly resumed their Victorian habits of voluntary action and self-help.[20] Such was the power and caprice of public opinion that Stanley Baldwin at the election of 1935 felt bound to conceal the degree of his government's commitment to rearmament[21] – only to be blamed by a fickle posterity for not having pursued rearmament more firmly. (If there was a conspiracy here, as arguably there was, it was one in which ministers and officials conspired to promote rather than retard policy innovation.) The conspiracy approach is also misleading in that it greatly exaggerates the uniformity of the official mind. It is true that the idea of being 'above politics' was probably even more deeply entrenched in Whitehall in the 1920s than it had been in the Edwardian period and probably few questioned its dubious ontological status. But, as a number of recent studies have shown, it by no means led to automatic official consensus. Throughout the interwar years government was fraught with inter- and intra-departmental disagreements over the proper sphere and direction of policy on such issues as unemployment, health, rearmament, defence priorities and colonial affairs.[22] All departments to a greater or lesser degree resisted Treasury control, and within the Treasury itself there were many voices promoting different nuances of economic and fiscal policy.[23] A third objection to the conspiracy thesis is that it tends to exaggerate the range of historical options that was open to ministers and their advisers in the interwar years. Historians remain divided about how far Keynesianism was intellectually and practically available to policy-makers in the economic sphere,[24] and many have compared British

---

[20] Prest and Adams, *Consumers' Expenditure in the United Kingdom*, p. 148; Mitchell and Deane, *Abstract of British Historical Statistics*, p. 454.

[21] Taylor, *English History*, pp. 382–3, 387.

[22] See Lowe, *Adjusting to Democracy*; Ian Drummond, *Imperial Economic Policy 1917–1939* (1974); Stephen Stacey, 'The Ministry of Health 1919–29: Ideas and Practice in a Government Department' (unpublished PhD thesis, Cambridge University, 1984); George Peden, *British Rearmament and the Treasury* (Edinburgh, 1979).

[23] Susan Howson, *Domestic Monetary Management in Britain 1919–1938* (Cambridge, 1975), p. 42; Donald Winch, 'Britain in the Thirties: A Managed Economy?', in Charles Feinstein, ed., *The Managed Economy: Essays in British Economic Policy and Performance since 1939* (Oxford, 1983), pp. 47–67; George Peden, 'Keynes, the Treasury and Unemployment in the later 1930s', *Oxford Economic Papers*, n.s., 32 (1980), pp. 3–4; George Peden, 'Sir Richard Hopkins and the "Keynesian Revolution" in Employment Policy', *Economic History Review*, 2nd ser., 36 (1983), pp. 281–96.

[24] Robert Skidelsky, *Politicians and the Slump* (1970 edn), pp. 426–7; Ross McKibbin, 'The Economic Policy of the Second Labour Government 1929–1931', *Past & Present*, 68 (1975), pp. 95–123.

unemployment policies unfavourably with more expansionist programmes adopted in Sweden and America. But it has been plausibly
argued that the whole of British public expenditure in the early thirties
was too limited a base from which to generate a Keynesian-style 'mul-
tiplier' effect sufficient to absorb 2 million unemployed; and in any
case the institutional division of expenditure between hundreds of
separate local government institutions was a major barrier to fiscal
regulation based on techniques of national accounting. Moreover,
what was possible in terms of centralised economic planning for a
viable autarchy like the USA or for an exporter of raw materials like
Sweden was much more problematic for an economy like that of Britain, caught in the crossfire of being both a major creditor and major
debtor nation and heavily dependent on overseas services and international trade.[25]

Perhaps the major obstacle to a 'bureaucratic' explanation of resistance to change, however, is that widespread governmental and policy
change did in fact occur at many levels, both within the limits imposed
by the political culture and to a certain extent in defiance of it. In
spite of the 'dismantling of controls' that occurred after 1919, many
wartime innovations did in fact survive the war – most notably the
streamlined cabinet system and the Ministries of Labour, Pensions
and Health. Pressure for statutory containment of industrial relations
survived in the form of Whitley Councils, which regulated wages
in the public sector. Although the 'functionalist' model of government
proposed by Haldane proved unacceptable, many of the ideas floated
by the Haldane committee – notably on research and long-term thinking about policy – did gradually seep into conventional wisdom. (Interwar governments were surprisingly well informed about 'social'
trends, though the same cannot be said about their 'economic' fore-
casts.) For all the familiar portrayal of the interwar years as a time
of severe retrenchment, public expenditure over the whole period
grew at a faster rate (2.1 per cent p.a. from 1924 to 1937) than in
any other peacetime period of the twentieth century.[26] For all the
emphasis on detachment from private interests, governments worked
much more closely than before the war with representative industrial

[25] Roger Middleton, 'The Treasury and Public Investment: A Perspective on Interwar
      Economic Management', *Public Administration*, 61 (1983), pp. 351–70; T. Thomas,
      'Aggregate Demand in the United Kingdom 1918–45', in Roderick Floud and Donald
      McCloskey, eds., *The Economic History of Britain since 1700*, 2 vols. (Cambridge, 1981),
      vol. 2, pp. 337–8.
[26] Middleton, 'The Treasury and Public Investment', p. 352.

bodies such as the FBI (on economic policy) and the NCEO (on social welfare).[27] For all the strength of official attachment to classical economics, Britain did come off the gold standard in 1931, and the National Government did introduce a limited measure of protection and imperial preference under the Ottawa Agreement of 1932. There was nothing in Britain approaching the formal 'corporatism' of many continental regimes of the period; but a latent enthusiasm for various 'corporatist' modes may be seen in the Ministry of Labour's encouragement of 'home rule for industry', in the Board of Trade's support for sectoral 'rationalisation', and in the Baldwin government's sponsorship of the Mond–Turner talks on worker–employer cooperation.[28] Only rationalisation bore practical fruit, but official patronage of such schemes suggests a degree of government involvement in day-to-day industrial concerns that would have been virtually unthinkable before the First World War. Similar 'modernising' impulses can be seen in many other areas of government: in reform of central-local finance, in the absorption of the poor law by county councils, and in attempts to extend and harmonise different aspects of contributory social insurance.[29] In no branch of public administration were changing relationships between government and society more succinctly epitomised than in the interwar system of support for the unemployed. When in 1916 reconstruction-minded civil servants had tried to extend the very limited prewar coverage of unemployment insurance to a majority of the labour force, they had met with massive resistance and refusal to pay contributions from both employers and employed. When the extension was eventually achieved, in the teeth of the rising unemployment of the early 1920s, administration of the system was fraught with crisis and conflict over such issues as individual entitlement for benefit and how far beneficiaries had to prove that they were 'genuinely seeking work'. For several years policy lurched violently in contrary directions: first in

---

[27]   T. W. Rodgers, 'Work and Welfare: The National Confederation of Employers' Organizations and the Unemployment Problem 1919–36' (unpublished PhD thesis, Edinburgh University, 1982), *passim*.

[28]   Rodney Lowe, 'The Failure of Consensus in Britain: The National Industrial Conference 1919–21', *Historical Journal*, 21 (1978), pp. 649–75; M. W. Kirby, *The British Coalmining Industry 1870–1946* (1977), pp. 108–37, 201–8; G. W. Donald and Howard F. Gospel, 'The Mond–Turner Talks 1927–1933: A Study in Industrial Cooperation', *Historical Journal*, 16 (1973), pp. 807–9.

[29]   Stacey, 'The Ministry of Health', chaps. 3 and 4; P. M. Williams, 'The Development of Old-Age Pensions Policy in Great Britain 1878–1925' (unpublished PhD thesis, London University, 1970), chap. 14.

the direction of detaching benefits from contributions and making the former of unlimited duration, and then to returning to a strictly actuarial self-financing scheme of the kind originally envisaged in 1911.[30] Not surprisingly, the system generated much overt conflict, at parliamentary, local and street-demonstration level. In August 1931 unemployment benefit was largely responsible for the flight from sterling and public expenditure cuts that led to the collapse of the second Labour government. Three years later it again provoked a major political uproar when the new Unemployment Assistance Board tried to introduce a uniform national scale of relief that in some areas was lower than that paid by local unemployment committees and poor law guardians. However, the Unemployment Act of 1934, which separated off the two spheres of contributory unemployment insurance and non-contributory unemployment relief proved within a few years to be surprisingly popular. For the first time there appears to have been an upsurge of popular enthusiasm for the compulsory insurance principle – in marked contrast to the widespread hostilities and fears of a 'servile state' that it had provoked a quarter of a century before. This transformation of the image of social insurance was to be of crucial significance in converting popular attitudes to the state from one of negative to one of positive social expectation. It helps to explain the overwhelming preference for 'rights' rather than 'discretion', fixed benefits rather than means tests, contributions rather than state charity that Beveridge was to find when writing his Social Insurance Report of 1942.[31]

V

The relationship between government and society in the interwar years was therefore considerably less static than has often been claimed. Into the old bottle of the late Victorian constitution much new wine was poured in the form of government intervention in industry, extension of social welfare schemes and general administrative rationalisation. Subsidised migration (in the 1920s and early 1930s) and financial support for regional development (in the late 1930s) made only a marginal impact on mass unemployment, but nevertheless

---

[30]   Alan Deacon, *In Search of the Scrounger* (Occasional Papers in Social Administration, No. 60, 1976), *passim*.
[31]   Harris, *William Beveridge*, chap. 16. This theme is more fully developed in a thesis in progress on state insurance and the working class by Ann Gross of Nuffield College. I am grateful to Ms Gross for permission to refer to her unpublished work.

involved a substantial effort by the state to modify and streamline imperfect market forces.[32] Civil servants and public officials were largely oblivious of the kind of 'scientific management' theories so popular during this period in the United States;[33] but nevertheless in the world-view of Whitehall, precedent and custom perceptibly declined in importance, rationalisation and criteria of cost-effectiveness increasingly came to the fore. 'Reason alone can now correct what instinct has created', wrote a distinguished ex-civil servant in a widely read polemical work advocating state control of the economy in 1932.[34] It is notable that, despite many historians' perceptions to the contrary, few people at the time believed that they were living in an era of contracting government power. Sir Josiah Stamp, addressing a meeting of the newly founded Institute of Public Administration in 1924, observed that the residual Victorian state had been replaced by 'the state as nurse, doctor, chemist, benefactor, guide, philosopher and friend'.[35] The same phenomenon was described a few years later in more menacing terms by the Lord Chancellor, Lord Hewart, who claimed that civil liberties and the rule of law were being progressively undermined by administrative discretion, delegated legislation and the protracted use by government of what had originally been acquired as temporary wartime powers. The trade-union movement – no friend of Lord Hewart – interpreted the Conservative trade-union legislation after the General Strike in very similar terms, as a governmental encroachment upon basic civil liberties. Lord Hewart's outburst precipitated the setting-up of a committee of enquiry into ministerial powers, which concluded that wide executive discretion and 'quasi-judicial' processes had become an indispensable feature of modern government.[36] But though groups and individuals often complained about administrative invasion of their own personal concerns, there was little popular response to Lord Hewart's more generalised, principled attack on the growth of overall governmental power. Among

---

[32] Lowe, *Adjusting to Democracy*, pp. 176ff; Gavin McCrone, *Regional Policy in Britain* (1969), pp. 91–105.

[33] Rosamund M. Thomas, *The British Philosophy of Administration 1900–39: A Comparison of British and American Ideas* (1978), pp. 20–32.

[34] Arthur Salter, *Recovery* (1933 edn), chap. 6.

[35] J. Stamp, 'Recent Tendencies towards the Devolution of Legislative Functions to the Administration', *Public Administration*, 2 (1924), p. 25.

[36] Lord Hewart, *The New Despotism* (1929); Arthur Henderson, *The Government's Attack on Trade Union Law* (Trade Union Defence Committee, 1927); D. G. T. Williams, 'The Donoughmore Report in Perspective', *Public Administration*, 60 (1982), pp. 273–92.

interest groups generally, there was an acceleration of the trend towards looking to the state for material support that had already been
apparent before 1914: to such an extent that officials sometimes complained that one of their main tasks had become to foster and stimulate
the private initiative that they were often accused of repressing.[37]
There was perhaps a hint in such complaints of a shift away from
an Anglo-Saxon perception of liberty to a more 'idealist' or Rous-
seauesque setting in which citizens had in some sense to be 'forced
to be free'.

Nevertheless, as with the Edwardian period, what is most striking
about the interwar years is not the extent of governmental change,
but the very high degree of institutional continuity in an era when
governments all over Europe were being subverted by political violence feeding upon economic recession. Britain was more exposed than
most countries to world trading conditions, and had her own peculiar
problem of long-drawn-out structural decline in her staple industries.
Though she was still ostensibly one of the world's great imperial
powers, it is clear in retrospect that this power was rooted in a very
fragile and overextended base. Britain's large manufacturing sector,
well-organised trade-union movement and highly stratified class system might have been expected to make her peculiarly vulnerable to
class conflict and violent upheaval. Yet no country proved more
immune to revolutionary pressure from both right and left. The hiving-
off of Ireland in 1922 – which Unionists for half a century had feared
would cause the collapse of the British state – passed with scarcely
a ripple in domestic politics and no immediate repercussions in the
rest of the Empire. The recurrent threat of a general strike in the
early twenties seemed to presage a more widespread breakdown, and
constitutionalists like Dicey deplored the 'singular decline among
modern Englishmen in their respect or reverence for the rule of law';[38]
but when the General Strike came in 1926 it mobilised only 11 per
cent of the male workforce. The TUC participated in the strike with
marked lack of enthusiasm and, in spite of much rhetoric to the contrary, most trade-union leaders seized the opportunity of the strike's
collapse to retreat into more narrowly 'industrial' concerns.[39] Though

---

[37] Lowe, *Adjusting to Democracy*, pp. 75, 83.
[38] Dicey, *The Law of the Constitution*, xxxvii–xxxviii.
[39] John Lovell, 'The TUC Special Industrial Committee January–April 1926', in Asa
      Briggs and John Saville, eds., *Essays in Labour History 1918–1939*, 3 vols. (1960–77),
      vol. 3, pp. 36–56; Currie, *Industrial Politics*, pp. 117–32.

the strike caused much bitterness in many close-knit working-class communities, in large cities it provoked an unexpected wave of social camaraderie, similar to that experienced in Zeppelin raids and later in the Blitz.[40] Though the map of mass unemployment reflected profound divisions in British society, class relationships were never again as fraught as they had been in the early and mid-1920s. The message of social harmony preached by Stanley Baldwin found an echo not merely in the shires and suburbs but among all social groups – as witnessed when Jarrow, famous as the 'town that was murdered', returned a Conservative candidate in the National Government election of 1931. In the 1930s, as in the 1900s, most Britons continued to observe – and on the whole found that it paid to observe – the rules of an unwritten but widely acknowledged constitutional code.[41]

The causes of this unusual social tranquillity must be to a certain extent conjectural. One factor that may have been important was that regional and sectoral divisions in the economy tended to muffle or divert the kind of direct class confrontation that might have discredited a constitutionalist position (though it should be noted that regional and sectoral divisions were also present in countries such as Germany, Spain and Italy where constitutionalism did break down). Such divisions existed not merely between different groups within the working-class but between different sectors of capital: one of the major perceived structural problems of the period was the so-called Macmillan gap between industry and high finance. Another relevant factor was the underrated prosperity of the period: the fact that for people in work it was a time of rising real wages and burgeoning consumerism, and that even for people out of work average unemployment benefit in the 1930s was higher than unskilled real wages twenty-five years before. Equally significant was the surprising degree of social integration into family, community and society at large: surprising because social theorists earlier in the century had predicted that advancing industrialisation would produce exactly the opposite effect – the increasing estrangement of individuals from social institutions. Throughout the 1920s and 1930s crime rates were low, family breakdown rare, participation in voluntary institutions high: and it was

[40] M. V. Hughes, *A London Family between the Wars* (Oxford, 1940), pp. 101–3.
[41] John Stevenson, 'The Politics of Violence', in Peele and Cook, eds., *The Politics of Reappraisal*, pp. 161–4.

the golden age of the supposedly 'traditional' close-knit working-class family and community (whose traditionality in many cases dated only from the beginning of the twentieth century).[42]

Behind all these material points lay a long-standing ideological tradition of political scepticism and social self-sufficiency, a continuing belief that, for better or worse, there were limits to what governments could do to alter the state of the world. Though the state was increasingly seen as a source of material support, the embodiment of corporate life remained for most men and women in Britain something much more mundane and immediate – his or her voluntary association, trade union, family, local community, church, place of work, public house. An early Mass-Observation survey found that membership of a football pools syndicate was the most rapidly growing form of communal life for men in northern towns.[43] A characteristic institution of the interwar years, and one that in some sense embodied the transitional forces of the period was the 'approved society' – the non-profitmaking organisations set up by friendly societies, trade unions and insurance companies to administer national health insurance. Approved societies were sternly criticised by a later generation on the (not altogether consistent) grounds that they were inegalitarian, financially inefficient, administratively expensive and infected by market criteria, but the historical reality was somewhat different. It was true that some approved societies had become impersonal business organisations; but many of them retained a strongly democratic structure and face-to-face friendly society spirit. In many of them members actively participated in a wide variety of activities, ranging from management of benefits and running of convalescent homes to care of widows and orphans and visiting the sick. Their administrative running-costs compared very favourably with those of the National Health Service later in the century. The varying levels of benefit paid by different societies were in a sense a price that had to be paid for their small-scale pluralistic democratic structure – though the large societies were by no means always the most cost-effective. As a recent study of their history points out, the major constraint upon approved society expansion was not smallness of scale nor amateur methods

---

42   Michael Anderson, *Family Structure in Nineteenth-Century Lancashire* (Cambridge, 1971), pp. 178–9.
43   Mass-Observation, *The First Year's Work 1937–38* (1938), pp. 32–45.

of management but the spending limits imposed on the national health insurance system by the government actuary and Treasury control.[44]

VI

Though the electorate as a whole might be happy with the unheroic gradualism of the interwar years, many groups and individuals were less so; and the 1930s saw a build-up of political disaffection and social criticism in many quarters. The British constitution and its attendant economic system was a 'Heath Robinson contrivance composed of the clutter of past generations and tied together with rotten bits of string', complained the progressive *Weekend Review*.[45] 'What looms before us is a battle for the possession of state power', predicted Professor Harold Laski. 'The class relations of our society have become incompatible with the maintenance of social peace.'[46] For the first time in British history, the continental phenomenon of the deracinated intellectual became a recognisable figure on the political scene. An uncertain number of mainly upper-class British citizens transferred their allegiance to a foreign power (some of them while continuing to be employed in the British civil and espionage services). Many more, disgusted with the inequity and inefficiency of capitalism or the muddles of democracy were attracted by the examples of totalitarian governments on the continent. Russia in particular in the 1930s exerted a powerful magnetic field. The famines, purges and treason trials were reported with horror in the British press, but by the later 1930s even people of impeccable liberal credentials were writing favourably of the Soviet government's success in reaching production targets and abolishing unemployment.[47] In particular, Russia was seen as the crucible of experiments in social and economic 'planning' – a key word in the political vocabulary of the era. Ideas about planning came from many quarters; from Sir Oswald Mosley and his New party, from socialist intellectuals in the ILP, from modernising businessmen

[44] Noelle Whiteside, 'Private Agencies for Public Purposes: Some New Perspectives on Policy-Making in Health Insurance between the Wars', *Journal of Social Policy*, 12 (1983), pp. 165–83.

[45] I owe this quotation to Daniel Ritschel of St Antony's College; my account of the planning movement in this paragraph is derived from his thesis on 'The Non-Socialist Movement for a Planned Economy in Britain in the 1930s' (unpublished PhD, Oxford University, 1987). I am grateful to Mr Ritschel for permission to cite his material. See also Smith, *The Politics of the Corporate Economy*, pp. 28–49.

[46] Harold J. Laski, *The State in Theory and Practice* (1935), p. 274.

[47] E.g. William Beveridge, 'Soviet Communism', *Political Quarterly*, 2 (1936), pp. 346–67.

in the Federation of British Industries, from progressive Conservatives like Harold Macmillan, and from advanced Liberals like the authors of the 1929 Liberal Yellow Book. There were very many different perceptions of what planning entailed, some seeing it as a means of refurbishing capitalism, others as a means of replacing capitalism by a socialist or 'corporatist' state. Some believed that planning should be undertaken directly by government, others by cartels of businessmen or by tripartite Industrial Councils of shareholders, workers and consumers. Some thought that planning was a logical corollary of protectionism, others that it was compatible with international free trade; some that it involved a mere reallocation of existing resources, others that it should be fuelled by a programme of deficit finance. But planners all were agreed that market mechanisms could no longer be relied upon to modernise British industry and to lift the economy out of the slump.

For a time it seemed that the planning movement, or at least the non-socialist elements in it, might find a political focus in Political and Economic Planning (PEP), a research and publicity organisation founded in 1931 with the eventual aim of setting up a new Planning party. But planners were too divided among themselves to form a real power base, and most of them were confused about how collective command over resources was to be translated into practical reality. Moreover, many who despaired of the efficient working of the market nevertheless feared the authoritarian state apparatus and constraints on freedom that planning might entail. (Aldous Huxley, a founder-member of PEP's radical off-shoot, TEC Plan, rapidly withdrew to write his novel *Brave New World*.[48]) Few were convinced by Harold Macmillan's argument that planning could be pursued without state control by self-regulating Industrial Councils and that functional corporatism was merely a resurrection of the 'old organic conception of our society'.[49] A possible way out of both the practical and the political impasse was offered by J. M. Keynes's *General Theory of Employment, Interest and Money* (1936), which as well as being an economic classic, was one of the most ingenious essays in political philosophy of the twentieth century. Keynes showed how government manipulation of aggregate incomes might be used to determine levels of investment and hence of employment without reliance (or without exclusive reliance) upon the private saver. His account of the

[48] Ritschel, 'The Non-Socialist Movement', pp. 112–13.
[49] Harold Macmillan, *Reconstruction: A Plea for a National Policy* (1933).

behaviour patterns of investors and workers rejected the notion that private economic decisions could be assumed to add up to collective rationality. He also argued that there was no necessary antithesis between a sphere of firm state action pursuing politically defined goals and a sphere of private behaviour conforming to the norms of classical economics. All classical theorists had in fact agreed that there were two such spheres: but in Keynes's view most of them had erred in consigning consumption and investment to the latter sphere, whereas they more properly belonged to the former. Viewed as an exercise in politics as well as economics, these arguments offered a fascinating gloss upon the orthodox tradition of English constitutional theory. Keynes's downgrading of the role of private rationality and responsibility seems very remote both from Victorian liberalism and from the progressive 'New Liberalism' of the Edwardian era; indeed there was a vein of high Toryism in his vision of governments pursuing desirable goals that people could not be trusted to pursue for themselves. Yet the notion of government intervening in certain spheres in order to buttress freedom and privacy everywhere else might have appealed to orthodox constitutionalists in the tradition of Sir Robert Peel. For all its interventionism and its contempt for conventional wisdom, Keynes's *General Theory* in its political aspects was and was meant to be a reasoned defence of the limited, instrumental and mundane view of government enshrined in the legacy of the Victorian state.[50]

Neither the grand visions of the planners nor the technical nostrums of Keynes initially made much impact on government policy. Indeed, as was pointed out above, the institutional barriers to Keynesianism – let alone to the much more ambitious conception of centralised planning envisaged by bodies like TEC Plan – were immense. Far from being boosted by Keynesianism the planning movement in the late 1930s seems temporarily at least to have lost some of its momentum. Businessmen planners were largely satisfied by the enabling legislation of the National Government, while the more radical wing of the planning movement was diverted away from macro-economics into schemes for improving social services and national health.[51] By many policy-makers in Whitehall, Keynes's advocacy of budget deficits was

---

[50] J. M. Keynes, *the General Theory of Employment, Interest and Money* (1936), esp. chap. 24.

[51] PEP, *Report on the British Social Services* (1937) and *Report on the British Health Services* (1937).

viewed not merely as analytically unsound but as fiscally and consti-
tutionally subversive.[52] Greater government involvement in economic issues came in the late 1930s not as a result of intellectual
influences but as a response to the threat of Hitler. Rearmament, the
shortage of skilled manpower, fear of bomber attacks on civilian targets, anxiety about food supplies in the event of war: all these pressures induced ministers and government departments to engage in
long-term planning, to interfere in the labour market, to negotiate
with prominent trade unionists and to acquire contingency powers
in a way that had been thought inconceivable during the economic
crises of 1929 and 1931.[53] The late 1930s also witnessed a profound
bouleversement in the ideology and public image of the Labour party
that was to have important long-term repercussions on the development of the British state. After 1931 Labour had figured for some
years in national politics as an idealistic but largely ineffectual body,
dominated by the pacifism of George Lansbury and the impossibilism
of the Socialist League. By the late 1930s, however, a new Labour
party had emerged that was committed both to rearmament against
dictators and to piecemeal but far-reaching socio-economic planning.
In marked contrast to the ill-defined utopianism of some years earlier
Labour's Immediate Programme of 1937 set out detailed proposals on
such questions as old age pensions, extension of health services,
nationalisation of key industries and the setting-up of a National
Investment Board 'to mobilize our financial resources . . . and to advise
the Government on a financial plan for the full employment of our
people'. For the first time in its history, it was possible for Labour
to challenge the Conservatives not merely as the party of social justice
but as the party of tough foreign policy and radical economics: a package that seemed to please the electorate, if one may judge by the
flurry of Labour by-election successes between 1937 and the summer
of 1939.[54]

---

[52] R. Middleton, 'The Treasury in the 1930s: Political and Administrative Constraints
to Acceptance of the "New" Economics', *Oxford Economic Papers*, 34 (1982), pp.
48–77.

[53] R. A. C. Parker, 'British Rearmament 1936–9: Treasury, Trade Unions and Skilled
Labour', *English Historical Review*, 96 (1981), pp. 306–43.

[54] Paul Addison, *The Road to 1945: British Politics and the Second World War* (1975),
pp. 53–74; Maurice Cowling, *The Impact of Hitler: British Politics and British Policy
1933–1940* (Cambridge, 1975), pp. 218–21, 248.

VII

Nevertheless, it was the outbreak of war that precipitated many of the latent forces for change in British government that had been slowly building up over the interwar years. For all the opprobrium that has been heaped upon the National Government's mismanagement of the first year of war, practical commitment to total war policies in the form of conscription, rationing, requisitioning and an excess profits tax came much more swiftly than in 1914. After Dunkirk when Churchill became Prime Minister and Labour entered the coalition, the pressure for change became yet more powerful. Plans for a constitutional amalgamation of the United Kingdom and France proved instantly abortive: but the very fact that such an improbable proposal was mooted at all is indicative of the unusual temper of the time.[55] As in 1916 the functional imperatives of war were expressed in new institutional arrangements – a small co-ordinating war cabinet, specialist cabinet committees to supervise key areas of non-military policy, and a series of new ministries responsible for Supply, Information, Aircraft Production, Economic Warfare and Reconstruction.[56] Churchill himself combined the role of Prime Minister with that of Minister of Defence and worked in close daily contact with military chiefs. He had no garden suburb, but chose as his chief personal adviser an Oxford Professor of Theoretical Physics. Large numbers of academics, businessmen and trade unionists were imported into Whitehall departments, and their relationship with permanent civil servants proved markedly more harmonious than in 1914–18 (a fruit perhaps of the growing inter-relationship between government and private interest groups during the interwar years). The appointment of Ernest Bevin, general secretary of the largest trade union in Britain, as Minister of Labour and National Service with a seat in the war cabinet symbolised an 'equal partnership' between government and working people that had been almost wholly absent during the First World War. Bevin's dynamic transformation of his ministry rapidly disabused those who imagined that bureaucrats had largely superseded politicians in the hierarchy of power; and his combination of implacable patriotism with unyielding devotion to working-class sectional interests puzzled and confounded orthodox devotees of the ideal of

[55]   Taylor, *English History*, pp. 487–8.
[56]   D. N. Chester, ed., *Lessons of the British War Economy* (Cambridge, 1951), esp. chap. 2.

the 'impartial state'.[57] No less significant was the appointment of Kingsley Wood, insurance expert and leading representative of 'business' Conservatism, as Chancellor of the Exchequer. It was Kingsley Wood who imported Keynes into the Treasury and in 1941 introduced the first 'Keynesian' budget, based on centralised regulation of national levels of consumption and investment via the mechanisms of low interest rates, high taxation, cost-of-living subsidies for those with low incomes and compulsory saving for the better off.[58] Financial controls were accompanied by a massive extension of physical controls over manpower, food and raw materials, going far beyond the scope of such policies in 1916–19 – though planners were careful to harmonise controls with 'normal incentives so far as they were practicable'.[59] Planned production brought about a degree of day-to-day contact and interpenetration between ministerial officials and managers of private industry (and from 1942 onwards with representatives of American government and business) that would have been inconceivable even to the most ardent prewar supporters of the corporatist state. Strategic intervention in the economy was reinforced by *ad hoc* measures to meet recurrent crises: the German bomber offensive forced public authorities to set up an emergency hospital service, to provide communal feeding arrangements, to requisition surplus housing, to organise mass evacuation and to provide foster-homes for millions of urban children.[60] Finally, for the first time for many centuries, local authorities ceased to be the main intermediaries of power between the citizen and the state. Preparations for invasion, coping with emergencies and practical enforcement of wartime controls were all entrusted to regional commissioners and their subordinate staffs, appointed by central government and vested with far-reaching discretionary powers.[61] Centralised control over people and resources far exceeded that of any other combatant power, with the possible exception of Russia.[62] By a strange irony of history, the United Kingdom, with her tradition of scepticism and hostility towards state power, generated

[57]   *Ibid.*, pp. 24–5; Harris, *William Beveridge*, pp. 373–6.
[58]   R. S. Sayers, '1941 – The First Keynesian Budget', in Feinstein, ed., *The Managed Economy*, pp. 107–17.
[59]   E. A. G. Robinson, 'The Overall Allocation of Resources', in Chester, ed., *Lessons of the British War Economy*, pp. 34–57; Margaret Gowing, 'The Organisation of Manpower in Britain during the Second World War', *Journal of Contemporary History*, 7 (1972), pp. 147–67.
[60]   Richard M. Titmuss, *Problems of Social Policy* (1950), *passim*.
[61]   Taylor, *English History*, p. 569.
[62]   Alan S. Milward, *War, Economy and Society 1939-1945* (1977), chaps. 4, 7 and 8.

a far more powerful centralised wartime state than any of her more metaphysically minded, state-exalting continental enemies.

All these developments profoundly affected the daily lives of the British people and have often been portrayed as generating the climate of opinion that led to the emergence of the postwar welfare state. R. S. Sayers described the 1941 budget as 'the manifestation in the financial sphere of the national change of heart that marked the summer of 1940'.[63] Similarly Richard Titmuss in his official history of wartime social policy portrayed the war and particularly Dunkirk and the Blitz as bringing about a revolution in popular expectations about the role of the state. Government was seen no longer merely as the guarantor of private freedom and the prop of the very poor: 'instead, it was increasingly regarded as a proper function or even obligation of Government to ward off distress and strain among not only the poor but almost all classes of society ... the mood of the people changed, and in sympathetic response values changed as well'.[64]

Whether such a transformation actually occurred at the level of ordinary citizens remains a matter of doubt. Support for the war and acceptance of the need for overall controls was almost certainly more general than in the First World War; but an unpretentious popular patriotism in no way precluded widespread resentment against 'red tape', 'bull', 'snoopers' and other manifestations of official interference. Illegal swapping of ration coupons and mass participation in the black market may have been at least as important media of social solidarity as the Dunkirk spirit: and though many citizens engaged in extensive community action it was not necessarily of the kind that looked to the state for support.[65] Days lost in strikes throughout the war were fewer than in 1914–18, but were still sufficiently numerous to indicate considerable industrial discontent; and among conscripted men and their families there was much resentment of the wide gap between high civilian wages and the allowances paid by the armed forces. Surveys of consumer opinion (albeit unreliable) found an unsurprising desire for higher levels of financial assistance from the state, combined with a general dislike of state officialdom.[66] Popular humour of the period portrayed the prevalent attitude to authority as one of

[63] Sayers, '1941 – The First Keynesian Budget', p. 108.
[64] Titmuss, *Problems of Social Policy*, pp. 506–8.
[65] E. Smithies, *The Black Economy in Britain since 1914* (Dublin, 1984), pp. 64–84.
[66] José Harris, 'Did British Workers Want the Welfare State? G. D. H. Cole's Survey of 1942', in Jay Winter, ed., *The Working Class in Modern British History: Essays in Honour of Henry Pelling* (Cambridge, 1983), pp. 200–14.

'much binding in the marsh'. The transformation of popular attitudes towards the state remains therefore an open question: it is by no means certain that attitudes changed, nor, if they did, that they changed in the direction of greater state involvement in civilian life.

Nevertheless, Titmuss was undoubtedly right in portraying the war as a golden opportunity for intellectual and reformist groups committed to various forms of social and governmental reconstruction. Almost from the start of the war, reformers in all parties were pressing for measures of redistributive social policy, not merely as desirable ends in themselves but as an essential means of 'giving the British people something worth fighting for' and of maintaining popular morale.[67] Similarly, the government was urged to treat the management of the war economy not merely as a means of meeting a military crisis, but as a model for a new relationship between government and society after the return of peace. Such demands came from trade unionists, academics, even groups of businessmen; from liberals like Keynes, socialists like R. H. Tawney and imperialist conservatives like L. S. Amery.[68] Popular journals like *Picture Post* published graphic portrayals of the social misery of the past and the social splendour of the future; contrasting the unplanned towns and higgledy-piggledy cottages of yesteryear, with the high-rise flats, geometrically designed boulevards, and hygienic separation of work, home and leisure that would characterise the coming millennium.[69] In protest against the by-election truce among the major parties, a new political party was formed, the Commonwealth party, committed to replacing competitive individualism by altruism and human fellowship.[70] The reformist mood infected many permanent civil servants, and from 1940 onwards plans were being laid within Whitehall for far-reaching extension of health, education and social insurance services. In 1942 a cabinet committee was appointed to advise on the permanent remodelling of the 'machinery of government' on more professional and managerial lines.[71] Late in 1942, however, modest behind-the-scenes reformism was overtaken by the publication of the Beveridge Plan, which

[67] Harris, *William Beveridge*, pp. 380–1.
[68] J. M. Keynes, *How to Pay for the War* (1940); Tawney, 'The Abolition of Economic Controls'; L. S. Amery, *The Framework of the Future* (Oxford, 1944), pp. 94–8, 121–59.
[69] 'A Plan for Britain', *Picture Post*, 10, No. 1 (1941), pp. 7–40.
[70] Addison, *The Road to 1945*, pp. 159–60.
[71] Harris, *William Beveridge*, pp. 380–3; P. H. J. H. Gosden, *Education in the Second World War: A Study in Policy and Administration* (1976), pp. 237–67; J. M. Lee, *Reviewing the Machinery of Government 1942–1952: An Essay on the Anderson Committee and its Successors* (SSRC Report, 1977), chap. 1.

catapulted social reform into the arena of mass media. Originally commissioned by the government as a purely technical exercise in harmonising the different branches of social security, Beveridge's report proved to be a dramatic and ambitious document that called for far-reaching state action to abolish unemployment, to set up a free national health service and to secure people against poverty by means of contributory social insurance covering all social groups. The government was urged to seize the historic moment presented by the war to sweep away vested interests and to commit itself to permanent economic and social planning. The result, declaimed Beveridge, would be a uniquely 'British revolution', which would preserve traditional liberties and freedom of choice, but at the same time do away with status differences between rich and poor and inaugurate a wholly new relationship between the state and the private citizen.[72]

Beveridge's Plan received extensive coverage in the press and was widely portrayed as a social Magna Carta. Beveridge himself – previously a largely unknown academic administrator – became something of a popular folk hero, and his mingled tone of patriotism and pragmatic utopianism pervaded public discussion of social issues throughout the war. The Beveridge Report, and indeed the reform movement generally, met with little initial enthusiasm among senior ministers, but in the spring of 1943 a revolt of back-bench MPs forced the government to commit itself to detailed postwar planning. A committee of civil servants was set up to consider the practical implementation of Beveridge, and academic economists in the Economic Section of the war cabinet were instructed to produce a detailed analysis of Keynesian techniques of demand management. Within the Ministry of Reconstruction discussions on social and economic themes were held with businessmen, trade unionists and social scientists – and revealed a surprising degree of support for 'community planning', for 'state ownership of developmental rights' and for state involvement in the management of private industry.[73] The next two years saw the publication of a series of white papers on full employment, a national health service, town and country planning and comprehensive social insurance – all of which, while varying widely in administrative detail, envisaged a high degree of permanent centralised direction

[72]   *Social Insurance and Allied Services* (the Beveridge Report), PP 1942–3, VI, *passim*.
[73]   José Harris, 'Some Aspects of Social Policy in Britain during the Second World War', in Mommsen, ed., *The Emergence of the Welfare State*, pp. 252–4.

of economic and social affairs.[74] The Education Act of 1944, which provided for universal secondary education, and the Family Allowances Act of 1945, which introduced state subsidies for families of two or more children, were the first statutory embodiments of what was soon to become known as the 'welfare state'. More radical in tone than any official document was Beveridge's *Full Employment in a Free Society*, published in 1944 under private auspices but widely regarded as a logical extension of Beveridge's earlier report on social insurance. This second report, written with the help of Keynesian socialists like Joan Robinson, Barbara Wootton and Nicholas Kaldor, proposed to combat unemployment by a mixture of fiscal controls, manpower planning and the channelling of both public and private investment through a National Investment Board. Such policies it was argued were perfectly compatible with either a socialist or a capitalist society; and Beveridge himself made it clear in discussions with the Ministry of Reconstruction that he no longer saw 'the individual's right to control capital' as an essential liberal freedom. 'Ownership of Means of Production' was 'not one of the essential British liberties' and could not be allowed to obstruct the pursuit of social justice in the postwar world.[75] Such claims did not go entirely uncontested, and particularly in the last year of the war there was a growing stream of literature of the opposite kind: protests against the 'mechanistic' and impersonal nature of planning theory, criticism of the logical assumptions on which plans were framed and sceptical questioning of the applicability of war experience to the conduct of peace.[76] Most famous of such protests was F. A. Hayek's *The Road to Serfdom*, which claimed that the apparatus of planning, however benign, must inevitably lead to an authoritarian state. But such reservations made little impact on the tide of public opinion, and, in marked contrast to the mid-1930s, planning enthusiasts made little attempt at intellectual engagement with the reservations of their critics. For perhaps the first time in the history of British government the onus of proof lay on the proponents of muddling through.

Promises for the future reached a crescendo with the general election of July 1945, when all parties committed themselves to a National Health Service, full employment and extensive social security. The

---

[74]   *Employment Policy*, Cmnd. 6527 (1943–4); *Statement on a National Health Service*, PP 1943–4, VIII; *Report of the Committee on Compensation and Betterment*, PP 1941–2, IV.
[75]   Harris, *William Beveridge*, p. 433.
[76]   Smith, *The Politics of the Corporate Economy*, pp. 51–62.

election marked the end, however, of the wartime party truce. Labour hastened to link Conservatism with mass unemployment and appeasement of dictators, while Churchill portrayed his erstwhile Labour colleagues as the thin end of the wedge of a Gestapo state. Victory went to the Labour party, which promised not only full employment and social security, but nationalisation of certain key industries, continuing control over scarce resources and legislation to protect the interests of trade unions (in fact a more cautious programme than that of 1939 which had envisaged nationalisation of land and the joint stock banks). For the first time Labour got more votes than any other party, and won an absolute majority in the House of Commons. For the first time Labour successfully extended its appeal beyond the traditional working-class communities and coteries of intellectuals, and made substantial gains among the middle and lower middle class.

What did this victory signify? Was it a major turning point in relations between citizens and the state, or was the break with the past more apparent than real? Was Labour's triumph merely an organisational victory brought about by the fact that Labour constituency machinery had held up better during the war years than that of the Conservatives, or was it a delayed reaction against the privations of the 1930s? Was it a reflection of the sociological changes wrought by war, such as the massive expansion of the labour force, increased geographical and social mobility, and the erosion of an ethic of social deference? Or was it a symbol of a new corporate consciousness forged by war – the consciousness identified by Titmuss as the moral and philosophical basis of a new approach to society and the state? Historians remain profoundly divided on these issues, and it seems probable that no simple answer can be given to a question of such complexity.[77] As indicated above, the reasons and feelings which motivated ordinary people may have been widely different from those which motivated the leaders of public opinion. Even among the latter there is some evidence to suggest that the ideological changes brought about by war were somewhat artificial: the war induced a sense of fraternity, consensus and reckless indifference to practical obstacles that was unlikely to survive the return to peace. Such a key figure as Beveridge,

[77] Addison, *The Road to 1945*, esp. chap. 5; R. B. McCallum and Alison Readman, *The British General Election of 1945* (Oxford, 1947), pp. 266–71; Henry Pelling, *Britain and the Second World War* (1970), pp. 226–36; Henry Pelling, 'The 1945 Election Reconsidered', *Historical Journal*, 23 (1980), pp. 399–414.

for example, was incomparably more *étatist* in the middle of the war than he was a few years later when Labour was constructing a supposedly Beveridgean welfare state.[78] Within the Conservative party business groups who had enthused over planning in 1942 were in marked retreat after 1945. What is undoubtedly the case, however, is that public discussion of politics and society in the mid-1940s constituted a profound break with some of the major conventions of the previous hundred years. Promises, programmes and planning had become the norm: those who questioned their validity now occupied the eccentric minority position previously occupied by programmers and planners. This change was accompanied by an elusive but important change in perceptions of the mutual relationship between society and the state. The older view of politics had seen society as essentially 'given', as something which might change or evolve with the course of history or according to its own inner dynamics but which at any given moment in time was largely outside the control of its members. The new view of politics saw society as something that could be moulded and modified, made and un-made by acts of political will.[79]

VIII

This constructivist view of politics was one of the few common philosophical factors that linked together the disparate collection of democratic socialists, administrative collectivists, professional trade unionists, and ex-liberal progressivists, together with a small handful of fellow-travellers, who constituted the Labour majority of 1945. In marked contrast to the Labour governments of Ramsay MacDonald, Labour under the new Prime Minister Clement Attlee did not believe in waiting passively for history to bring about a long-term process of desired social change. For the first time Labour had a strong team of ministers with considerable government experience: Ernest Bevin at the Foreign Office, Herbert Morrison at the Home Office, Hugh Dalton at the Treasury; and Aneurin Bevan as Minister of Health. A month before the end of the war the King's speech to the new Parliament promised immediate action on nationalisation of coal and the Bank of England, creation of a National Health Service and implementation of the Beveridge Plan. The Supplies and Services (Transitional Powers)

[78] Harris, *William Beveridge*, pp. 458–9.
[79] The contrast between the old and new moods was captured by Aneurin Bevan, *In Place of Fear* (1952; Quartet Books edn, 1978), chap. 2.

Act extended wartime emergency powers until 1950 and indicated the government's intention of applying wartime precedents to the conditions of peace. Almost immediately, however, Labour's plans for social reconstruction came up against the realities of Britain's post-war economic plight. American aid and the 'lend-lease' programme came to an end, foreign debts had been incurred of more than £4,000 million, exports had shrunk to 40 per cent of their level for 1939. Income from overseas investments – since the mid-nineteenth century one of the bulwarks of British capitalism – had dwindled to £120 million. Raw materials for the rebuilding of damaged homes and for the resurrection of peacetime industries were in desperately short supply. In a memorandum warning that the nation faced a 'financial Dunkirk', the Treasury predicted a trade deficit for 1946 of £750 million.[80] Fears that the United States *might* withdraw, and the growing realisation that the Soviet Union would *not* withdraw, from a military presence in Europe made any rapid reduction in defence expenditure impossible. Massive civil disorder in India led inexorably to the granting of independence to India and Pakistan as the first step towards dismemberment of the Empire. It was a strange irony that a government so committed to seizing history by the horns took office at a moment when Britain appeared to have less autonomous control over her own destiny than had been the case for several centuries.

Balancing the demands of social reconstruction against those of the international situation became the *leitmotif* of Labour administration throughout its period of office. The initial crisis was warded off by a massive American loan in December 1945, granted on condition that Britain restored the pound to full convertibility. American dollars enabled Hugh Dalton to stimulate investment and expansion of exports by a period of 'cheap money', which tided Britain over the first eighteen months of peace. The relief, however, was short-lived. The snowbound winter of 1947 exacerbated an already chronic shortage of fuel; and over the next few months the rising world price of raw materials, the costs of feeding a starving Europe and the anxiety of bondholders to shift their holdings into dollars led to a growing trade deficit and a severe sterling crisis.[81] Convertibility was abandoned, an emergency Budget imposed severe cuts on consumer

---

[80] Taylor, *English History*, p. 599.
[81] P. M. Cottrell, 'The Convertibility Crisis', paper given to a seminar in All Souls College, Oxford 1983; C. C. S. Newton, 'The Sterling Crisis of 1947 and the British Response to the Marshall Plan', *Economic History Review*, 2nd ser., 37 (1984), pp. 391–401.

spending and – after a Budget leak – the expansionist Dalton was replaced by an iron Chancellor, Sir Stafford Cripps. Thereafter, defence of the pound, balanced Budgets and capital reinvestment in both public and private sectors were accorded stern priority over social and redistributive goals. The reluctant devaluation of the pound in September 1949 was a dramatic indicator of the economic straitjacket within which Labour ministers worked. Given the pressures of the international economic situation, however, what is more surprising is not that Labour's social programme was curtailed, but that so much of it was put into operation. The Bank of England was nationalised in 1946, coal in 1947, gas, electricity and railways in 1948 and steel in 1951. The Town and Country Planning Act of 1947 made all land subject to planning controls and imposed a 100 per cent levy on development values. Comprehensive social insurance for sickness, unemployment and old age was introduced in 1946 (though without the commitment, foreshadowed in the Beveridge Plan, to paying benefits at subsistence level); and in 1948 the National Health Service nationalised voluntary hospitals, united all the different branches of health care and made specialist and general practitioner treatment freely available to all citizens. The National Assistance Act of 1948 symbolically proclaimed the abolition of the Elizabethan poor law and renounced the centuries-old policy of attaching stigma to recipients of public relief. Local authorities – threatened with extinction during the war but revived because so many of them were strongholds for Labourism – began to develop wide-ranging social work services to cater for the ex-clients of the poor law (children under care orders, old people in institutions, the disabled and mentally ill). Local councils lost some of their functions to central government, but acquired others in the form of greatly expanded responsibility for council housing and secondary education. Local authorities in poor areas benefited particularly from the replacement of global exchequer subsidies by an Exchequer Equalisation Grant, designed to concentrate resources on areas of greatest need.[82] In the sphere of industrial relations, trade-union demands were met by a new Trades Disputes Act, which removed civil penalties for 'peaceful picketing' and restored the pre-1927 rules about 'contracting-out' of political funds. Social and industrial reforms were accompanied by some largely cosmetic political

---

[82]   Clive Martlew, 'The State and Local Government Finance', *Public Administration*, 61 (1983), p. 139.

reforms: university constituencies were abolished and the House of Lords's veto over parliamentary legislation reduced to one year.

As with Labour's election victory, historians have varied widely in their interpretations of Labour's six-year term of office, some seeing it as rooted in modest prewar reformism, others as the apotheosis of radical innovation. Clement Attlee as Prime Minister and party leader has been variously portrayed as an impassive Machiavellian, as a man of unobtrusive but unbending conviction and as a ridiculous mouse.[83] Attlee's merits as a leader cannot be fully discussed here; but one point that immediately strikes the historian is the extent to which the position of the Labour leadership was in certain respects strengthened rather than weakened by Britain's precarious foothold in the international economy. Throughout its earlier history the Labour party had been agitated by irreconcilable rivalries between strong leadership and grass-roots activism, between socialist purity and sectional interests, between visionary internationalism and belief that Britain was a self-contained planet composed of mining valleys. Such tensions continued to exist between 1945 and 1951 and at times irrupted into the forefront of politics; but they were incomparably more muted than might have been the case if Labour had taken office at a time of affluence and international tranquillity. Desperate scarcity may have clipped the wings of Labour's programme, but it also enabled Labour ministers to ride with a tight rein their own dissident supporters and to enact the central features of that programme with remarkable speed. It was the context of economic crisis that enabled Labour ministers largely to ignore left-wing demands for nationalisation of profitable industries (the exception being steel nationalisation, which was forced onto the government's agenda by a resolution of party conference). Even more crucially, it was the atmosphere of crisis which induced the unions to co-operate with Stafford Cripps's income pause thus avoiding the dangerous spiral of wage inflation that was to dog full employment policies over the next three decades. Desperate scarcity also helped to legitimise continued resort to emergency powers and to blunt the effectiveness of opposition demands for a more rapid return to a free market.

What impact did 1945–51 make upon the permanent structure of British government and society? At government level, one significant

---

[83] Kenneth Harris, *Attlee* (1982); Kenneth O. Morgan, *Labour in Power* (Oxford, 1984), pp. 47–9, 456; Janet Morgan, ed., *The Backbench Diaries of Richard Crossman* (1981), pp. 147–8.

factor was that the sheer size of bureaucracy was proportionately much larger than it had ever been in peacetime. The retention of controls meant that, although some wartime industries were dismantled, there was little contraction of personnel at the end of the war, and the total civil service establishment in 1950 was 70 per cent larger than in 1939.[84] An even greater number had become public employees by virtue of nationalisation. In the upper reaches of government Attlee favoured a small 'inner cabinet' on the wartime model, within a larger cabinet of senior departmental colleagues;[85] only a few of the latter were made aware of certain crucial items of strategy – such as the decision (taken in fear of renewed American isolationism) to manufacture an independent British nuclear deterrent. An important feature of cabinet business was that economic matters figured much more prominently than in the agenda of any previous government. Cabinet committees were appointed on major items of economic policy, the Chief Economic Adviser (a post formally in existence since the early 1920s) ceased to be a mere honorary figurehead, and resort to professional economic advice became a regular part of policy formation. Attempts to streamline the machinery of government, begun during the war, continued into peacetime. Committees of permanent secretaries met regularly to co-ordinate policies between departments and there was much discussion of a rather inconclusive kind on the managerial problems posed by civil service expansion and by economic planning.[86] There was some talk of separating the 'establishment' and 'economic policy' functions of the Treasury into two separate departments, but the experiment with setting-up a separate Ministry of Economic Affairs in the autumn of 1947 proved to be short-lived. The social character of central government was remarkably little changed by war and socialism. Attlee's ministry was conspicuously less working class than those of 1924 and 1929: ten members of his first cabinet were from public schools, as were nearly a quarter of Labour MPs. The administrative grade of the civil service included a slightly higher proportion from working-class backgrounds than in the 1920s, and the Oxbridge element had been slightly diluted by wartime

---

[84] David Butler and Anne Sloman, *British Political Facts 1900–1975* (4th edn, 1975), p. 239.

[85] Harris, *Attlee*, pp. 401–8. Attlee had formulated a plan for an inner cabinet of super-ministers, free from departmental responsibilities, as early as 1932. The model was not strictly adhered to, since all the members of his inner cabinet also held senior departmental posts.

[86] Lee, *Reviewing the Machinery of Government, passim.*

recruitment, but over 70 per cent of higher civil servants still came from a middle-class professional parental background.[87] The ethic of the 'Impartial State' was still strongly held, and there was little fore-shadowing during this period of the later Labour complaint that civil service neutrality was a form of covert bias towards the status quo.[88] Ministers made little use of specifically 'political' advisers, though outside experts from business and the trade unions were regularly consulted through joint Advisory Councils and often directly employed by government to man the new planning machinery.[89] The pursuit of a planned economy brought with it a further shift towards the interpenetration of public and private spheres already noticeable in the 1930s. Perceptions of 'planning', however, underwent some-thing of a change over the course of the period. 'Planning' continued to be a vogue word, and even free-market bodies like the Design for Freedom League portrayed themselves as in some sense 'plan-ners'.[90] But there was widespread retreat from the synoptic visions of 1944–5. The government's Official Steering Committee on Economic Policy set out to produce a 'national plan', but found the data required for such a plan more elusive and complex than had been imagined.[91] Trade-union, business and consumer groups who had enthused over planning in the middle of the war proved singularly unwilling to con-template permanent direction of civilian manpower and private invest-ment.[92] Manpower controls in particular were highly unpopular with the public and were increasingly replaced by less visible and therefore less overtly coercive fiscal techniques.[93] Harold Wilson's 'bonfire of controls' at the end of 1948 came at the beginning rather than the end of a period of intensified austerity, and signified a certain disen-chantment with physical controls as the best means of managing a civilian economy.

---

[87] R. K. Kelsall, *Higher Civil Servants in Britain from 1870 to the Present Day* (1955), pp. 146–60.

[88] For the subsequent emergence of the latter view, see Ralph Miliband, *The State in Capitalist Society* (1969; Quartet Books edn, 1973), p. 110.

[89] Roger Eatwell, *The 1945–1951 Labour Governments* (1979), p. 68.

[90] 'Design for Freedom', issued by the Design for Freedom Committee (? 1946), p. 19.

[91] Eatwell, *The 1945–1951 Labour Governments*, p. 67.

[92] Addison, *The Road to 1945*, p. 274. Some of the organisational difficulties unexpec-tedly encountered in peacetime planning were hinted at in Sir Oliver Franks, *Central Planning and Control in War and Peace* (1947).

[93] Samuel H. Beer, *Modern British Politics: A Study of Parties and Pressure Groups* (1965), pp. 194–202.

The impact of Labour on society in general is more difficult to assess. One obvious difference from the 1930s was that virtually everyone who wanted one had a job, and there was a chronic shortage of both skilled and unskilled labour. Economic historians remain unclear about how far full employment was due to specific government policy and how far simply to the continuance of high wartime levels of investment and production.[94] (Comparison with the post-1919 era, however, suggests that at the very least Labour's refusal to meet postwar difficulties by deflation must have had some direct effect on employment levels.) Another major departure, not merely from the 1930s but from all earlier periods of British history, was the persistence of conscription in peacetime. The 1947 National Service Act was introduced with reluctance, partly in response to an unsettled international situation and partly to speed up the demobilisation of disgruntled wartime conscripts. It had little or no ulterior purpose in the direction of character-building or civic virtue; and the experience of compulsory soldiering seems to have done little to dislodge and much to enhance the Englishman's habitual stance of lackadaisical irreverence towards the majesty of the state.[95] In the civilian sphere industrial relations were relatively harmonious. Days lost in strikes throughout the period were considerably less than in the last two years of war[96] (though the absorption of trade-union leaders into the councils of government led to some discontent at shop floor level that boded ill for future industrial peace). Shortage of labour brought substantial immigration from Eire, and some immigration from what was later to be known as the 'new commonwealth', though the census of 1951 made no distinction between entry of new ethnic groups and return of expatriates after Indian independence. (The Royal Commission on Population of 1949 clearly had not the faintest inkling that Britain was on the brink of a revolution in ethnic identity.[97]) There was much pride in the new social services. The National Health Service was flooded with the backlog of decades of untreated sickness, and many applicants came forward for national assistance who had previously been deterred by the stigma of poor relief. Continued reliance on means-tested benefits was seen, however, as a temporary and residual

---

[94] R. C. O. Matthews, 'Why Has Britain Had Full Employment since the War?', *Economic Journal*, 78 (1968), pp. 555–69.

[95] Trevor Royle, *The Best Years of their Lives: The National Service Experience 1945–63* (1986).

[96] B. R. Mitchell, *European Historical Statistics, 1750–1970* (1975), p. 182.

[97] *RC on Population*, PP 1948–9, XIX, paras. 328–30.

phase in welfare provision.[98] Labour, at least at the parliamentary level, wholly shared Beveridge's view that state welfare should be rooted in flat-rate contributory insurance, which was seen as embodying a large cluster of desirable social principles, such as egalitarianism, freedom from enquiry into personal behaviour, and maintenance of incentives to saving and work. There was criticism on Labour's left of the low level of insurance benefits, but little evidence of dissatisfaction among insurance beneficiaries. The concentration of building resources on local authority housebuilding, combined with stringent rent controls in the private sector, greatly accelerated the already existing migration from private to public rented accommodation.[99] The local authority housing estate became increasingly a central feature of working-class culture, aspiration and social frame of reference, and was to become much more so in the decades that followed: a paradoxical outcome, in view of the fact that the Housing Act of 1949 specifically renounced the requirement of earlier acts that public sector housing should be confined to members of the working class. Social debate of the period was, however, remarkably innocent of awareness of class divisions. There was a widespread belief that the new social services, combined with high levels of income tax and death duties, were rapidly leading to a more equal and integrated society and to the lopping-off of extremes of poverty and wealth. Nearly all Labour as well as most Conservative supporters shared the assumption of the 1944 Education Act that the selection of clever children for free places at grammar schools would not merely increase personal 'opportunity' but would achieve the withering away of status distinctions between middle and working class. A survey on social mobility conducted in 1949 found little modification of the long-established tendency for status to be determined by parental occupation; but few observers of the period shared the fears of the sociologist T. H. Marshall that 'tripartite' education might reinforce rather than erode barriers of social class.[100] Enthusiasm for the new social services was combined with much popular irritation with government controls. Disenchantment with planning in Whitehall mirrored a much more widespread feeling among the public at large, symbolised by the outcry against the ill-timed claim of a Labour minister that 'the

[98]   Phoebe Hall *et al.*, *Change, Choice and Conflict in Social Policy* (1975), pp. 410–12.
[99]   A. H. Halsey, ed., *Trends in British Society since 1900* (1972), p. 307.
[100] D. V. Glass, ed., *Social Mobility in Britain* (1954), p. 216; Marshall, *Citizenship and Social Class*, p. 63.

gentleman in Whitehall really does know better what is good for people than the people know themselves'.[101] The philosophical bases of planning (its bogus rationalism and lack of a sense of the processes of history) were subject to caustic academic attack.[102] William Beveridge, the high priest of the wartime planning movement, wrote his major postwar work as a critique of the government's failure to encourage social diversity and to support the traditional ethic of voluntary effort. It was significant, however, that Beveridge favoured, not what a mid-Victorian would have seen as voluntarism, but voluntarism working under the auspices of a 'Minister-Guardian of Voluntary Action'.[103] The very idea of such a ministry epitomises the blurring of the boundaries between the public and private spheres that has been such a marked feature of British history throughout the twentieth century.

IX

The Conservatives regained power in 1951 with an election manifesto based on the slogan 'Set the People Free', and much political debate of the 1950s centred upon the supposed antithesis between collectivism and individualism. Much of this debate was little more than shadow-boxing, for one of the most striking features of the 1950s was the extent to which Conservative ministries adopted and developed the policy framework laid down by the coalition and Labour governments of the 1940s. Physical controls over the economy were further dismantled, rationing was ended and subsidies to food were severely curtailed; but there was no retreat from centralised management of the economy through fiscal controls and regulation of the level of public expenditure. There was some shift in emphasis from income tax to purchase tax, but the concept of 'Butskellism' accurately reflected the practical common ground between Conservative and Labour budgetary policies (if not the differing philosophies on which these policies were based). Levels of investment and employment remained high, and the rate of economic growth exceeded that of

---

[101]   Douglas Jay, *The Socialist Case* (1948 edn), p. 258.
[102]   J. Jewkes, *Ordeal by Planning* (1948), chap. 3; M. Polanyi, *The Logic of Liberty* (1951), pp. 111–37; Michael Oakeshott, *Rationalism in Politics and Other Essays* (1962), p. 6.
[103]   William Beveridge, *Voluntary Action: A Report on Methods of Social Advance* (1948), p. 313.

any previous period of British history. Close relations were maintained with both sides of industry, culminating in 1961 with the setting up of a National Economic Development Council designed to involve both management and labour in decisions about 'the availability and use or misuse of our resources'.[104] In spite of protests from the Conservative right wing, withdrawal from Empire continued on the lines initiated by Labour, accelerated by Mau Mau and Cypriot terrorism and by the government's mismanagement of the Suez crisis in 1956. All branches of the welfare state were maintained, though recurrent inflation (not at first perceived as a major problem) made attainment of the goal of subsistence-level benefits more elusive than had been envisaged in 1942 or 1946. The proportion of GNP absorbed by public expenditure had fallen during the late 1940s but rose steadily throughout the 1950s.[105] The rise in local authority spending was particularly steep, causing some central government alarm and an attempt to reassert Treasury control over specific items of expenditure under the Local Government Act of 1958.[106] One of the major differences between Conservative and Labour administrations was not that Conservatives abandoned earlier policies, but that they added onto them or encouraged a range of options that had not been available in the late 1940s – such as the development of owner-occupied housing and occupational pension schemes and the licensing of commercial television. Currency controls were gradually relaxed, allowing some travel abroad and the resumption of foreign investment (though the latter was subject to the payment of a dollar premium). In the late 1950s there was much criticism by socialist academics of the failure of social insurance to abolish poverty; but such complaints were really objections to the Beveridgean scheme introduced by Labour rather than to policies introduced by the Conservatives. The remedy proposed – abolition of flat-rate insurance and substitution of an earnings-related scheme embodying an element of redistribution[107] – was rapidly borrowed by the government and incorporated in the National Insurance Act of 1959, which introduced graduated insurance in combination with 'contracting-out' into the private market. Such policies were strongly criticised by Labour, but whether Labour would have

[104] Francis Boyd, *British Politics in Transition* (1964), pp. 154–5.
[105] Alan T. Peacock and Jack Wiseman, *The Growth of Public Expenditure in the United Kingdom* (2nd edn, 1967), pp. 43–9.
[106] Martlew, 'The State and Local Government Finance', pp. 139–41.
[107] Labour party discussion paper on *National Superannuation* (1957).

pursued markedly different policies in the face of widening market opportunities remains unclear. As in the 1940s there was spasmodic discussion of the machinery of government and the training and re-cruitment of civil servants; but once again the problem was evaded of how to convert bureaucrats into the business managers of an advanced industrial economy. Early in the 1950s there was a flurry of administrative scandals, culminating in the Crichel Down Affair, which revived earlier fears about abuse of executive power. A subse-quent committee of enquiry under Sir Oliver Franks reasserted the importance of rules of natural justice and recommended legislation to strengthen the framework of administrative law.[108]

In general, however, the 1950s was a period of widespread content-ment with the quality of British government and its impact on national life. British stability was continually compared with the cavalcade of ministries in the French Fourth Republic. The most significant consti-tutional debates occurred not within government but within the Labour party, where constituency activists (not necessarily at this stage of a particularly left-wing complexion) challenged the right of the Parliamentary Labour party to control the formulation of party policy: hence the fraught debates in Labour party conferences over such issues as nuclear disarmament.[109] The Beveridge-based welfare state was believed to be unique (even though far more ambitious social insurance schemes had been or were in process of being set up in several continental countries). It was commonly assumed, not that total equality had been achieved or was even desirable, but that both groups and individuals were socially mobile: that 'class escalators' were transporting the working class into middle-class levels of affluence and that personal status was largely determined by personal effort and ability. A cross-national survey of *The Civic Culture* carried out in 1959 (and published in 1963) identified Britain as one of the classic homelands of 'civic culture', in contrast to societies character-ised by rootless instability, apathy or totalitarianism. The survey por-trayed typical British citizens as deferential but democratic. They were active participants in political processes, strong in their political con-victions but tolerant of those with opposing views (more than 80 per cent of both Conservative and Labour supporters did not mind if

---

[108]   *Report of the Committee on Administrative Tribunals and Enquiries*, PP 1956–7, VIII, esp. paras. 402–9.
[109]   Philip M. Williams, *Hugh Gaitskell* (Oxford, 1982 edn), pp. 198–213, 314–38.

their children married into the opposite political persuasion). They were active joiners of voluntary institutions and strong upholders of the rule of law, confident in the sensitivity of government to democratic pressures. Even the most passive respondents to the survey, though nervous of 'police and other government bureaus' were actively patriotic and 'proud of the fact that there is a welfare state'. The result was a political culture that was

neither traditional or modern but partaking of both: a pluralistic culture based on communication and persuasion, a culture of consensus and diversity, a culture that permitted change but moderated it. The participant role is highly developed. Exposure to politics, interest, involvement, and a sense of competence are relatively high ... attachment to the system is a balanced one: there is a general system of pride as well as satisfaction with specific governmental performance.[110]

Over the quarter of a century since it was published there have been many methodological criticisms of *The Civic Culture* survey. What is perhaps more significant is that at the time of its publication in 1963 it appears to have been generally accepted as an accurate account of prevailing attitudes and norms: it 'produced little reaction as a study of Britain largely because it told most British academics little that they did not think they already knew'.[111] That year was, however, probably the last point in recent British history when such a claim could have been confidently upheld. A few weeks after *The Civic Culture* was published, the choice of an earl as Conservative Prime Minister provided the spark for a conflagration of public values that was to last for several decades. Labour returned to power a year later making much of the archaic and reactionary character of its opponents, but soon found itself scorched by the same critical fire. Satisfaction with Britain's (historically high) rate of growth collapsed in the face of her (relatively poor) performance when measured against resurgent foreign competitors. Instead of being upheld as a model for the rest of the world, Britain's 'generalist' civil service was increasingly compared unfavourably with the managerial technocrats who staffed General de Gaulle's Fifth Republic.[112] Satisfaction with the country's educational processes was challenged by the view that selective

[110] 'Almond and Verba, *The Civic Culture*, pp. 455–69.
[111] Kavanagh, 'Political Culture in Britain', p. 127.
[112] Brian Chapman, *British Government Observed: Some European Reflections* (1963), *passim*.

secondary schooling merely reinforced class differences, and by the discovery of the Robbins Committee that Britain's ratio of university graduates was the lowest of any advanced country.[113] There was a wave of public enquiries into administrative recruitment and organisation and a feverish attempt to inject both central and local government with managerial science.[114] A Royal Commission on Local Government found, confusingly, that the ideal 'local authority' size for purposes of maximum efficiency varied considerably between different social services.[115] Lack of confidence in Whitehall values was signalled by the increasing importation into ministries of political advisers and private cabinets. In marked contrast to the late 1940s, shop floor trade unionists widely rebelled against the absorption of their leaders into the government embrace – leading to waves of often unofficial industrial disputes. Spiralling wages led to balance-of-payments problems, which led to desperate attempts to defend the pound by high interest rates – which in turn depressed domestic investment and further undermined Britain's industrial competitiveness. Labour's attempts to purge the welfare state of the legacy of 'less-eligibility', by raising benefit levels close to average wages, provoked further wage demands from workers who complained that they were 'better off on the dole'.[116] Welfare beneficiaries and their sponsors learned the lesson of trade-union militancy and formed claimants' unions to enforce 'welfare rights'. For the first time for several decades political debate became suffused with the language of class conflict – paradoxically, just at a moment when traditional class identities were crumbling in society at large. Popular diffusion of the 'sociology of knowledge' led to a widespread collapse of belief in objective standards and in the putative neutrality of public and legal institutions. The problem of integrating widely diverse immigrant communities

---

[113]   A. H. Halsey, Jean Floud and C. Arnold Anderson, *Education, Economy and Society* (1965 edn), Parts 2, 3 and 4; *Report of the Committee on Higher Education* (The Robbins Report), PP 1962–3, XI.

[114]   Ironically this occurred at a moment when the validity and effectiveness of a scientific approach to public administration were being questioned in countries where it had long held sway (Thomas, *The British Philosophy of Administration*, pp. 241–2).

[115]   *RC on Local Government in England*, PP 1968–9, XXXVIII, pp. 37–40.

[116]   In 1968 the net income of a national insurance claimant with a wife and two children was 74.5 per cent that of the average wage earner, compared with 36.2 per cent in 1951 and 44.6 per cent in 1964 (B. Abel-Smith, 'Public Expenditure on the Social Services', *Social Trends*, 1 (1970), pp. 12–19). The argument of V. N. George, *Social Security: Beveridge and After* (1968), pp. 35–6, exemplifies the political and academic pressures behind these trends.

(5.26 per cent of the population of England and Wales in 1966),[117] the eruption of civil violence in Ulster and – slightly later – the rise of Scots and Welsh nationalism, all threatened the traditional constitutional view that a variety of norms and national identities could be contained and harmonised within an impartial, secular, instrumental state. The revival of political feminism after fifty years of quiescence challenged the assumption that the democratic interests of women could be adequately subsumed under those of men. The issue of British entry into the common market posed questions relating to Britain's national, imperial and European character that little in her traditional stock of social and political theory enabled her to face.

The result in the late 1960s and throughout the 1970s was a transmutation of political culture and norms of political behaviour at two levels. At the level of government policy there was a disintegration of the Keynesian-cum-welfare state consensus that had dominated all parties to a greater or lesser extent since the Second World War. The model of the 'mixed economy' was increasingly under pressure from groups on the left who wanted Keynes's 'euthanasia of the rentier' carried towards its logical conclusion, and from groups on the right who blamed governmental Keynesianism for inflation, erosion of competitive incentives and the bloating of public expenditure. A low rate of economic growth was increasingly ascribed to the financial albatross of the welfare state – even though by the 1970s Britain's expenditure on social services in relation to GDP was among the lowest in Europe.[118] The National Health Service was simultaneously accused of extravagance, parsimony and misdirection of resources; and it was revealed that after thirty years of state medicine class differentials in morbidity and mortality were actually wider than they had been before the Second World War.[119]

At a deeper and less immediately detectable level there were seismic

---

[117] This bald and rather misleading figure from the 1966 sample census says little about the ethnic composition of the immigrant population. About one third of immigrants came from the New Commonwealth, one third from Eire, one third from elsewhere. But the census data gave no indication of the ethnic origin of children of immigrant parents born in Britain. Halsey, ed., *Trends in British Society*, pp. 458–9.

[118] E. James and André Laurent, 'Social Security: The European Experience', *Social Trends*, 5 (1974), p. 268. Peter Flora, *State, Economy and Society in Western Europe 1815–1975*, vol. 1 (Frankfurt, 1983), p. 465.

[119] David J. Hunter, 'Back to Black', *Public Administration*, 61 (1983), pp. 209–15. This conclusion, however, took little account of the twin factors of upward mobility and immigration from countries with only rudimentary health care.

shifts in the kind of constitutional values that had invisibly pervaded all sections of political society over a much longer period. Political violence and direct action markedly increased, whilst active participation in representative politics markedly declined.[120] Even among the vast majority who continued to favour the 'rule of law', there was a growing belief (in marked contrast to the views of the 1930s) that people who resorted to violence and intransigence usually got their way.[121] Confidence in the efficacy of the 'rules of the game' (that phrase constantly reiterated by historians writing of the earlier twentieth century) was replaced by the 'isolation paradox' or the 'paradox of first performance' (i.e. refusal by citizens to pursue policies which they believed to be in the public good until everyone else was seen to have done the same).[122] Pursuit of sectional self-interest was perhaps no more intrinsically avid than it had been in earlier eras, but collapse of belief in an objective 'common good' gave sectionalism a moral legitimacy that it had not enjoyed for over a century. The first nationwide civil service strike of 1973 marked a symbolic turning point in the philosophy and day-to-day practice of public administration.[123] Logical anomalies within the system of political representation which had earlier attracted little comment now became major sources of grievance: such as the fact that most MPs were not the most-favoured candidates of a majority of their constituents, and that parliamentary majorities returned by general elections always distorted and sometimes (as in 1951 and February 1974) actually negated the popular vote. Cornerstones of constitutional theory were also called in question, by the actual or threatened dilution of sovereignty stemming from entry to the EEC and by proposals for an 'Irish condominium' or a 'bill of rights'. The appointment of an Ombudsman – a parliamentary commissioner for administration – was interpreted as an implicit admission of parliament's failure to fulfil its traditional function of preventing governmental encroachment upon citizens'

---

[120] Kavanagh, 'Political Culture in Britain', p. 150.
[121] E.g. a survey of 1974 found that only 2 per cent of people approved of personal violence and damaging property as means of achieving political ends, but 11 per cent (10 per cent in the case of damaging property) thought such methods effective (Alan Marsh, *Protest and Political Consciousness* (Beverly Hills and London, 1977), p. 45).
[122] McKibbin, 'Why was there no Marxism in Britain?', pp. 313–14; Stevenson, 'The Politics of Violence', p. 163; Alan T. Peacock and Martin Ricketts, 'The Growth of the Public Sector and Inflation', in Fred Hirsch and John H. Goldthorpe, eds., *The Political Economy of Inflation* (1978), pp. 126–8.
[123] Sir Douglas Wass, 'The Public Service in Modern Society', *Public Administration*, 61 (1983), p. 15.

rights.[124] A Royal Commission on the constitution found that 45 per cent of the population favoured substantial constitutional reforms and only 5 per cent thought that existing arrangements could not be improved.[125] Rapid social and economic change continually eroded the already ill-fitting relationship between local government and local communities, while the remodelling of local government institutions in 1974 appeared to mark the final triumph of managerial rationality in its long-drawn-out battle with local identity, custom and history. Symbolic modes of political expression lost their meaning: politicians in the mid-1970s, for example, who wished to make use of the Union Jack (for centuries a visual embodiment of Britain's historic pluralism) found that they could not do so because the flag had been cornered (or was thought to have been cornered) by the National Front.[126] Informed political discussion of relations between government and society in the late 1970s and early 1980s was characterised, not merely by the breakdown of consensus, but by the breakdown of a common political language and theoretical frame of reference: the common constitutional culture based on tacit acceptance of a common history and unspoken assumptions about the nature of political behaviour which had been so pervasive earlier in the century had virtually ceased to exist.[127]

X

The above discussion has attempted to provide an Ariadne's thread through the institutional and ideological maze that enmeshes the history of government in the twentieth century. Many important themes have been ignored or relatively neglected: monarchs, schools, churches, financial institutions, soldiers, parties, mass media, the political emergence of women. A perhaps undue emphasis has been laid on changing nuances of constitutional thought, on developments within the structure and theory of government, and on shifting perceptions of the role of the state: all of which might plausibly be seen as lying outside the sphere of 'social history'. Even historians who share my view that social history and high politics are more closely

---

[124] Gillian Peele, 'The Developing Constitution', in Chris Cook and John Ramsden, eds., *Trends in British Politics since 1945* (1978), p. 14.
[125] Cited in Kavanagh, 'Political Culture in Britain', p. 141.
[126] John Ramsden, 'The Changing Basis of British Conservatism', in Cook and Ramsden, eds., *Trends in British Politics*, p. 41.
[127] E.g. Hirsch and Goldthorpe, eds., *The Political Economy of Inflation*, passim, and esp. chaps. 5, 7, 8 and 9.

related than is often supposed are unlikely to endorse all my points of interpretation. Some will object that I have greatly underrated the structural significance of social class. If I have done so, this is not because I discount the existence of 'class' in British society, but because characterisations of government as the stronghold of a ruling class seem to me unhelpfully tautological. Moreover, for all its importance in society at large, class *per se* raised its head within the context of government with surprising infrequency. Radical critiques of the character of government were far more often concerned with its cultural bias (Oxbridge humanism) than with its class component; and most proposals for reform of government structure and personnel were much more concerned with substituting a hierarchy of scientific expertise than with abolishing the hierarchy altogether.[128] In other words, struggles for control of the government machine took the form of a horizontal contest between different sectors of the professional middle class rather than a vertical struggle between two different social classes. Other historians concerned with the social roots of high politics may take issue with my portrayal of the modern British state in terms that are primarily secular, utilitarian and mechanistic. This I have done, not because I necessarily share the values contained therein, but because such a portrayal seems to me to convey accurately the inexorable, if regrettable, facts of modern British government and political life.

Throughout my narrative I have attempted to engage in analysis and explanation of specific institutions and events; but (apart from the negative points made above) is it possible to identify any more synoptic themes which characterise and give meaning to the whole period? One striking point is the tendency of certain apparently long-resolved or long-forgotten issues to resurface in the *longue durée* of constitutional history. Labour activists who in the 1970s and 1980s tried to bind MPs by conference decisions had their predecessors in Lord Randolph Churchill and in Edmund Burke's electors of Bristol. Critics of sovereignty in the 1970s harked back, often unwittingly, to the arguments advanced by guild socialists earlier in the century – who in turn harked back to what they believed to have been the relationship between government and society in the Middle Ages. Throughout the period visions of the state as the champion of sectional interests wrestled with visions of the state as the guardian of the

---

[128]   D. Judge, 'Specialists and Generalists in British Central Government: A Political Debate', *Public Administration*, 59 (1981), pp. 1–12.

common good. A corollary of this was that there was no simple movement of history in a unilinear direction. Dicey's comments about collapse of belief in the rule of law in 1924 and a similar finding by
a popular television programme in 1976, must be compared with
Almond and Verba's finding of almost universal support for the rule
of law in 1959.[129] Impulses towards 'corporatism', in the sense both
of state encroachment upon private institutions and of private
encroachment upon the state, ebbed and flowed throughout the century. Certain moments, like the end of the First World War, seemed
to threaten or promise radical constitutional upheaval but in fact
proved to be the prelude to a prolonged period of containment and
stability. (The same may or may not be true of the present moment.)
Different principles and practices competed and co-existed with each
other, often appearing much more mutually antagonistic than was
in fact the case. This was true of the frequently cited antithesis between
collectivism and the free market. That these two principles sometimes
clashed head-on is undeniable: but more often and less obtrusively
they advanced in tandem at the expense of other more traditional
social arrangements, such as philanthropy, the family and the local
community. Together they came to dominate many spheres of
twentieth-century society which in Victorian times had been largely
contained within these older arrangements, spheres such as medicine,
leisure, social welfare and education. Indeed, it would not be implausible to argue that the growth of the collectivist state was largely facilitated by the advance of the market – by the latter's erosion of the
stable communities, charitable relationships and autonomous organisations upon which the Victorian constitution so heavily relied.

Another important point is that apparent continuity in social composition or behaviour of institutions could mask quite profound changes
in attitudes and expectations. This was so in the case of the voluntary
sector. Englishmen in the 1900s were energetic joiners of voluntary
societies and continued to be so (contrary to the predictions of Sidney
Webb in 1911 and of William Beveridge in 1947) right down to the
end of the period. But the ethos of voluntarism was, nevertheless,
subtly transformed over the course of the twentieth century. Voluntary institutions in the 1900s were (with certain exceptions such as
denominational primary schools) very remote from contact with the

[129] Dicey, *The Law of the Constitution*, p. xxxviii; John P. Mackintosh, 'The Declining
Respect for the Law', in Anthony King, ed., *Why is Britain Becoming Harder to
Govern?* (1976), pp. 74–95; Almond and Verba, *The Civic Culture*, pp. 455–69.

organs of the state: they expected no public financial support and were subject to little or no state regulation. They were the very sinews of autonomous 'civil society', supported by the state only through a general framework of law. This unpretentious and invisible private collectivism continued in some spheres throughout the period, largely falling through the meshes of the history of government. In many voluntary organisations, however, such autonomy progressively dwindled: they became increasingly the agents and clients of the state, holders of state licences, beneficiaries of state tax concessions, recipients of and competitors for state financial aid – or simply pressure groups urging government to change its policies on some deserving cause. The boundary between public and private spheres became much more confused than in the late nineteenth century: voluntary action became much less of an end in itself, much more of a means to an end – the end of manipulation or controlling or participating in the sphere of public provision. To this extent Sidney Webb was right in forecasting the decline of autonomous intermediate institutions standing between the state and the individual: in terms of social and political principle there was a world of difference between the private self-governing pluralism of Victorian society and the competitive client pluralism of the later twentieth century.

Was government more or less powerful at the beginning of the century than in the 1960s and 1970s? Clearly governments tried to do far more in the latter period than in the former, and had far more financial and bureaucratic resources at their disposal: totalitarianism was a technological possibility in the reign of Elizabeth II to a far greater degree than in the reign of Edward VII. The sheer growth of government business and of delegated legislation tended to weaken parliamentary control (though this was partly counteracted in the 1960s by the extension of standing committees). Other factors, however, placed severe constraints on government power – Britain's dwindling position in the world economy, her indebtedness to the United States, her historic commitments to defence. Democracy itself was a major constraint: the vote may have done little to enhance the power of individuals but it did a great deal to fetter the hands of government – particularly in dealing with unpopular or underprivileged minorities. Democracy and affluence in combination effectively ensured that the problems of relative (as opposed to absolute) poverty and deprivation would never be solved. Moreover, certain structural characteristics of British society virtually ruled out certain options from the practical agenda of British politics (though not out of public debate). Recurrent programmes for the regeneration of British industry always came up against the greater cultural attractions (and superior profitability) of landownership, property management and high finance. Britain's heavy dependence on overseas trade and in particular her reliance on a buoyant financial sector severely limited the possibilities for autarchic economic planning except in time of war. Similar constraints were imposed by entrenched trade-union liberties, and indeed by the whole libertarian tradition of which unincorporated trade unionism was merely a part. Moreover, the growth of a managed economy, whilst in some respects greatly enhancing the powers of government, also placed certain inherent limitations on those powers: it became increasingly difficult for governments to withdraw even from failed or undesirable policies in cases where new popular expectations had been created and new public responsibilities assumed. It is probable also that economic management greatly increased the power of both capitalist and labour 'producer' groups at the expense of responsible democratic institutions: the agenda of policy at both central and local level was increasingly 'predetermined' by professions, industries and organisations engaged in supplying goods and services to the public sector.[130] The rise of competitive interest groups created a situation in which it was ever more difficult for government to satisfy one client without pacifying all the others – the phenomenon of 'pluralistic stagnation' so graphically described by Samuel Beer.[131]

A final and perhaps paradoxical point that seems to emerge is that though expectations of the state massively expanded, basic assumptions about political obligation appeared to change very little. Apart from a largely unsuccessful attempt to develop an 'organic' theory of the state during the Edwardian period, discussion of public policy throughout the century continued to be conducted within a predominantly utilitarian framework of thought. Debates on the welfare state in the 1940s were often clothed in the language of altruism and duty, but reasoned analysis of these concepts was conspicuous by its absence.[132] Twenty years later Richard Titmuss tried to formulate a

---

[130] Patrick Dunleavy, *The Politics of Mass Housing in Britain 1945–1975: A Study of Corporate Power and Professional Influence in the Welfare State* (Oxford, 1981), esp. chap. 10.

[131] Beer, *Britain against Itself*, pp. 23–76.

[132] José Harris, 'Political Ideas and the Debate on State Welfare 1940–45', in Harold L. Smith, ed., *War and Social Change: British Society in the Second World War* (Manchester, 1986), pp. 252–7.

more systematic philosophy of altruism as a basis for state welfare, but even Titmuss ultimately rooted his claims in utilitarianism (i.e. public altruism was preferable to the market because in the last resort it was more efficient at delivering social goods).[133] No new theory of property legitimised high taxation, planning controls or appropriation of development rights. Protagonists of planning made a sharp distinction in principle between outmoded 'economic freedom' and inviolable 'individual freedom'; but how the two were to be differentiated in practice was never made clear.[134] The rise of academic Marxism in the 1950s injected a new and potent vocabulary into discussions of the state, and the widespread diffusion of sub-Marxian thought probably helped to erode confidence in an objective 'impartial' constitution. But in active politics groups and individuals influenced by Marxism were perennially torn between the theoretical belief that the state was a function of private capitalism and the pragmatic demand that the state should help the poor. The main practical impact of vulgar Marxian ideas was simply to compound a long-standing utilitarian disposition to get as much as possible out of the state while giving as little as possible in return. As in all industrialised countries, capitalist and socialist, liberal and totalitarian, there remained a continuing unresolved tension both in public policy and in social values between the competing claims of 'right', 'desert' and 'need'.[135]

At a more popular level political attitudes retained a strongly libertarian vein. Certain aspects of the welfare state – most notably the National Health Service – appear to have fostered a new sense of national corporate identity and moral solidarity: but this was not true of state services in general.[136] Citizens who in the 1930s or 1950s looked to the state for financial support were even less inclined than their self-helping forbears to accept official interference in their private lives: indeed one of the charms of state insurance was supposed to be that it substituted the impersonal 'magic of averages' for the intrusive discrimination of charity and poor relief. Within the labour movement the holistic claims of socialism were always potentially in conflict with the claims of trade unionists to be nothing more than unincorporated

[133]   Richard M. Titmuss, *The Gift Relationship: From Human Blood to Social Policy* (1973), pp. 274–7.
[134]   Jay, *The Socialist Case*, pp. 272–4; Smith, *The Politics of the Corporate Economy, passim*.
[135]   Marshall, *Citizenship and Social Class*, pp. 69–74. For the existence of such tensions in a variety of political cultures see Gaston Rimlinger, *Welfare Policy and Industrialization in Europe, America and Russia* (New York, 1971).
[136]   Ann Cartwright and Robert Anderson, *General Practice Revisited: A Second Study of Patients and their Doctors* (1981), pp. 178–9.

bundles of individuals exercising their private rights. In spite of the rise of large firms and nationalised industries, both workers and managers tended to view such institutions as at best an economic convenience (and at worst as a source of alienation and estrangement) rather than, as in Japan and certain continental countries, as the basis of new modes of social and political life.[137] Tawney's judgment on the First World War – that 'war collectivism had not been accompanied by an intellectual conversion on the subject of the proper relations between the state and economic life' – may legitimately be applied to all aspects of collectivism throughout the twentieth century.[138] An instinctive attachment to 'natural liberty' remained as strong in the days of centralised planning and giant corporations as in the days of governmental minimalism and economic laissez-faire.

[137] Sir Henry Phelps Brown, *The Origins of Trade Union Power* (Oxford, 1983), pp. 307–8. Currie, *Industrial Politics*, pp. 8–15, 223, 273–6.
[138] Tawney, 'The Abolition of Economic Controls', p. 7.

CHAPTER 3

Education

GILLIAN SUTHERLAND

Education is best defined as the 'methodical socialisation of the young generation'.[1] Thus family and kinship networks, apprenticeships, patterns of child employment all have a part to play in the educative process, alongside any provision of a formal or semi-formal kind for schooling. It would be impossible to treat all of these adequately in one chapter; and indeed family, kinship and work are all themselves subjects for separate extended treatment. This chapter will therefore focus primarily on the development of provision for formal schooling, but not to the exclusion of all other aspects of the process. For one of the chapter's most important themes is the rise of formal schooling. In 1750 this was a relatively insignificant and brief part of the educative process and one not necessarily encountered by all children. By 1950 it was central and it was what most people, adults and children alike, meant when they spoke of education.

1750–1850

I

In England in the seventeenth, eighteenth and early nineteenth centuries, the vast mass of the population did not see the basic skills of reading, writing and arithmetic as an integrated package – the 3Rs – and one to be acquired in a formal institutional setting, as a prelude to economic activity. These skills were seen as discrete, reading far outweighing the other two in importance. If acquired at all, they were acquired – and offered by teachers – in sequence: reading before

I am grateful to Robert Anderson, Peter Slee, Pat Thane and David Vincent for reading and commenting on a draft of this chapter. The errors, omissions and infelicities that remain are, of course, solely my responsibility.
[1] Emile Durkheim, *Education and Sociology*, trans. Sherwood D. Fox (Glencoe, Ill., 1956), p. 71.

writing, writing before arithmetic. A 'teacher' might be anyone more proficient than the pupil in the skill being sought; and the learning process was all too often interspersed with, interrupted or even terminated by the exigencies of economic survival and the necessity to acquire or to practise more immediately profitable skills. Not everyone displayed the doggedness of Thomas Tryon, born the son of a plasterer in Oxfordshire in 1643 and taken away from school after a year to card and spin wool. Subsequently he became a shepherd:

> All this while, tho'now about Thirteen Years Old, I could not Read; then thinking of the vast usefulness of Reading, I bought me a Primer, and got now one, then another, to teach me to Spell, and so learn'd to Read imperfectly, my Teachers themselves not being ready Readers: But in a little time having learn't to Read competently well, I was desirous to learn to Write, but was at a great loss for a Master, none of my Fellow-Shepherds being able to teach me. At last, I bethought myself of a lame young Man who taught some poor People's Children to Read and Write; and having by this time got two sheep of my own, I applied myself to him, and agreed to give him one of my Sheep to teach me to make the Letters, and Joyn them together.[2]

In the case of John Clare, born the son of a Northamptonshire day-labourer in 1793, the determination came at least initially from his mother:

> As my parents had the good fate to have but a small family, I being the eldest of 4, two of whom dyed in their Infancy, my mother's hopeful ambition ran high of being able to make me a good scholar ... but God help her, her hopeful and tender kindness was often cross'd with difficulty, for there was often enough to do to keep cart upon wheels, as the saying is, without incurring an extra expence of putting me to school ... I believe I was not older than 10 when my father took me to seek the rewards of industry ... [but] As to my schooling, I think never a year pass'd me till I was 11 or 12 but 3 months or more at the worst of times was luckily spared for my improvement.[3]

The schooling of William Heaton, whose father was a journeyman tanner, was similarly uncertain. His father managed to send him to a local reading school but could not then afford to send him on to a writing school. William Flewitt told one of the Children's Employment Commissioners in 1842 that he 'went to day-school afore I worked in the pit ... I can read (very well) and write but very little,

---

[2] Quoted in Margaret Spufford, 'First Steps in Literacy: The Reading and Writing Experiences of the Humblest Seventeenth-Century Autobiographers', *Social History*, 4 (1979), reprinted in Harvey J. Graff, ed., *Literacy and Social Development in the West: A Reader* (Cambridge, 1981), p. 132.

[3] Eric Robinson, ed., *John Clare's Autobiographical Writings* (Oxford, 1983), pp. 2–3.

I am learning now in a copy-book at home.' Their experience and that of many more children was summed up by Isaac May, a Bristol 'Haulier of Coals' who had the courage to reject the simple dichotomies of category offered by the 1851 census form and described his two children, James, aged nine, and Elizabeth, aged seven, as 'Schollor [*sic*] occasionally'.[4]

Such a pattern of experience has enormous implications for attempts to gauge the distribution of these skills amongst the population at large in the period before 1870. Attempts to do this have taken two main forms: a counting of institutions and a counting of signatures on marriage registers. Nineteenth-century attempts to count schools and their scholars were inaugurated by a select committee chaired by Henry Brougham in 1816. But this and all further attempts by central government agencies to count institutions before 1870, when the decision was taken to provide a national network of schools, were roundly criticised by contemporaries for all manner of deficiencies in their collection. In the twentieth century E. G. West has attempted to compensate for this by taking some of the better conducted local surveys and attempting to generalise from them. This, too, is open to criticism, both in the detailed interpretation of the data and more generally. How 'typical' were any urban areas – in West's case Bristol and Manchester – of nineteenth-century urban Britain? His assumptions about average attendance, length of the school year, average length of school life, are assumptions with very little evidential basis. Much as we would like to know about all these things, we simply do not have the data. In 1888, when the country was supposed to have had a functioning network of schools for at least ten years, a Royal Commission on Elementary Education noted that 'no trustworthy figures illustrating this point [length of school life] have been collected'.[5]

But assumptions about average attendance and length of school

[4] For Flewitt and May, see Phil Gardner, *The Lost Elementary Schools of Victorian England* (1984), pp. 99 and 47. For Heaton, see David Vincent, *Bread, Knowledge and Freedom: A Study of Nineteenth-Century Working Class Autobiography* (1981), p. 96.

[5] *RC on the Elementary Education Acts* (the Cross Commission), Part II, 51, PP 1888, XXXV, fo. 75. E. G. West, 'Resource Allocation and Growth in Early Nineteenth-Century British Education' *Economic History Review*, 2nd ser., 23 (1970), pp. 68–95; J. S. Hurt, 'Professor West on Early Nineteenth-Century Education', and E. G. West, 'The Interpretation of Early Nineteenth-Century Education Statistics', *ibid.*, 24 (1971), pp. 624–42; H. J. Kiesling, 'Nineteenth-Century Education According to West: A Comment', and E. G. West, 'Nineteenth-Century Educational History: The Kiesling Critique', *ibid.*, 36 (1983), pp. 416–34.

life look the more implausible set against the intermittent, informal or at best semi-formal encounters with opportunities to learn to read and sometimes to write which were all that most of the late eighteenth- and early nineteenth-century labouring poor managed.

Such implausibilities in turn prompt questions about the plausibility, indeed the reality, of the categories 'school' and 'scholar' when applied to such fragmentary and diverse experiences. These categories undoubtedly had meaning and reality for the earnest middle-class observers, whether commissioned by a select committee or a local statistical society. Their use and the determination to 'count' them tell us quite a lot about the attitudes of the elite groups in society towards education, both their own and that of the working class. But counts of 'schools' and 'scholars' will only give a very much more limited and partial picture of working-class attitudes towards, access to and acquisition of the skills of reading, writing and arithmetic.

The measure of the spread of these skills offered by marriage register signatures by-passes many of these problems. It focusses attention on the skills actually acquired rather than on the mechanisms, context or timing of the learning process. Under the provisions of Lord Hardwicke's Marriage Act of 1753 only those marriages recorded in the registers of Anglican churches, the record signed by both parties and two witnesses, were legal. Then in 1837 a system of secular state registration supplemented and reinforced this. There were those, of course, who never married; and, before 1838, those who, even to conform with the law, would not set foot in an Anglican church. But these were, relatively, a tiny minority. From the mid-eighteenth century onwards it is in principle possible to calculate annually what proportion of young adults, both male and female, were able to sign their names. From 1838 on the Registrar General did it for us. Roger Schofield has made a comparable calculation for the period 1754–1837, using data from a random sample of 274 parish registers. The resulting graphs are reproduced as Figures 3.1 and 3.2.

They show that by the mid-eighteenth century just over 60 per cent of women were unable to sign the marriage register; by 1840 the percentage had fallen to just under 50, the rate of decrease picking up at about 1800. The percentage of men unable to sign remained stable from mid-century to 1795 at just under 40; fell in the next five years; rose again and then fell steadily, but more slowly than in the case of the women, to 33 per cent in 1840. Thereafter the trend was ever

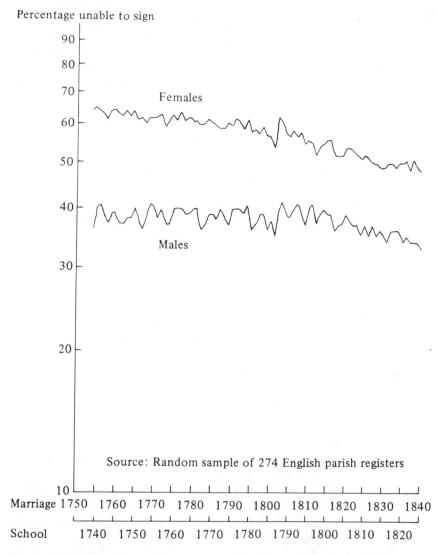

Percentage unable to sign

Source: Random sample of 274 English parish registers

Figure 3.1 Estimated annual percentages of males and females unable to sign at marriage, England, 1754–1840

Reproduced by permission from R. S. Schofield, 'Dimensions of Illiteracy, 1750–1850', *Explorations in Economic History*, 10 (1973), reprinted in Harvey J. Graff, ed., *Literacy and Social Development in the West: A Reader* (Cambridge, 1981), p. 207.

more steeply downwards, although again slightly steeper for women than for men.

These are the best figures we can get, far more soundly based than attempts to count schools or scholars. But even they are not without

Percentage unable to sign

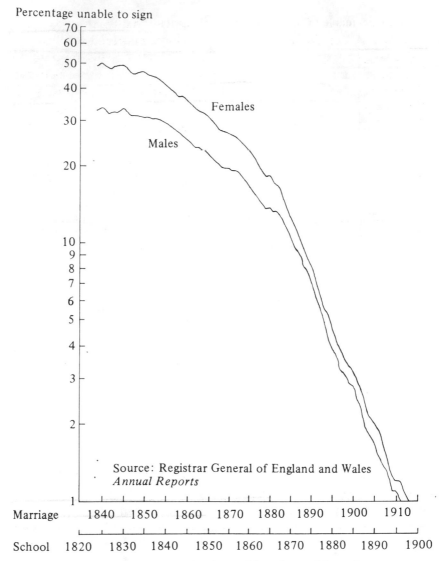

Figure 3.2 Annual percentages of males and females unable to sign at marriage, England and Wales, 1839–1912

Reproduced by permission from R. S. Schofield, 'Dimensions of Illiteracy, 1750–1850', *Explorations in Economic History*, 10 (1973), reprinted in Harvey J. Graff, ed., *Literacy and Social Development in the West: A Reader* (Cambridge, 1981), p. 205.

their limitations, all of which stem from the fact that they are indirect measures of the skill that did most to transform people's lives, the one that understandably mattered most to contemporaries, the ability to read. Given the sequential approach to the acquisition of skills already described, it is reasonable to suppose that those able to sign their names are likely to be those who have mastered reading and begun on writing. But to construct calculations on this supposition over time is to assume that the relationship and interval between the acquisition of the two skills is far more regular, stable and constant than the evidence will allow. The value of reading was pretty generally acknowledged. In the seventeenth and eighteenth centuries writing seems to have been of use only in a handful of occupations and very much a male preserve. Yet the activities of many seventeenth-century dissenting congregations suggest that a significant fraction of their female members could read. In the course of the nineteenth century the economic uses of writing became more generally apparent. All of this underlines the point that marriage register signatures at the end of the nineteenth century may stand in a relationship to the capacity to read which is different from that which they occupied a century or so earlier. In particular, part of the growth in 'literacy' among women in the nineteenth century may simply mean that more of them now added the writing skill to the reading skill.

One further caveat needs to be entered against too heavy or simplistic a reliance on literacy statistics. To say people can read tells you nothing about whether they do read, and if they do, what they read and what they make of it. As Natalie Zemon Davis observed of sixteenth-century French peasants: 'When a peasant read or was read to, it was not the stamping of a literal message on a blank sheet; it was the varied motion of a "strange top" (to use Jean-Paul Sartre's metaphor for the literary object) set to turning only by the combined effort of author and reader.'[6]

'Read or was read to': it is only in the course of the nineteenth century too that reading gradually became a private rather than a public act for the mass of the population. Until at least the early nineteenth century, if you could read, you were expected to read aloud and share your reading with family, neighbours, friends, workmates. Readership of the radical unstamped press in the 1820s and 1830s far exceeded sales, perhaps by as much as twenty times, the majority of 'readers' hearing the papers read aloud in their workplaces or in public house, coffee and reading rooms.[7] A population with a significant proportion of 'illiterates' may not be an ill-informed or stupid

[6] Natalie Zemon Davis, 'Printing and the People: Early Modern France', in Graff, ed., *Literacy and Social Development*, p. 71.
[7] Patricia Hollis, *The Pauper Press* (Oxford, 1970), p. 119.

one; it may be at least as well-informed as a population where the formal reading skill is widely diffused but seldom used.

To argue for the inappropriateness of 'schools' and 'scholars' as categories through which to measure the extent of educational activity and the diffusion of skills in the late eighteenth and early nineteenth centuries is not, however, to suggest that they were categories of no importance at all. Formal schooling was well on the way to becoming the dominant mode of education among the elite groups in the society, the aristocracy and the emergent middle classes, as we shall see. And those among the elite who concerned themselves with the education of the working classes expected to use similar mechanisms. For formal schooling is a mechanism not an end in itself; and many working-class enthusiasts for education, while they might look askance at what was actually offered by the elite, were not averse to all types of formal and systematic schooling. It is difficult to think of other mechanisms for providing teaching expeditiously for large numbers of children. Neither John Clare's mother nor William Heaton's father *chose* that their children should receive teaching in intermittent fragments. It was a necessity forced on them by the exigencies of economic survival.

In the late eighteenth and early nineteenth centuries working-class enthusiasts and middle-class reformers alike were much concerned with what might be done, in the face of such exigencies, to extend working-class children's encounters with schooling. Amongst the most successful enterprises were Sunday schools. Robert Raikes of Gloucester has traditionally featured as pioneering Sunday schools in the 1780s; in fact teaching Bible reading and basic skills on a Sunday was an established activity in a number of eighteenth-century Puritan and evangelical congregations. But the turn of the century did see a particularly rapid expansion and the best guess of their most recent historian, T. W. Laqueur, is that by the early 1830s over a million children and adolescents were attending Sunday school.[8] Samuel Bamford, the future Chartist, described the scene at one such Methodist Sunday school at Middleton:

Big collier lads and their sisters from Siddal Moor were regular in their attendance. From the borders of Whittle, from Bowlee, from the White Moss, from Jumbo and Chadderton and Thornham, came groups of boys and girls with their substantial dinners tied in clean napkins, and the little chapel was so

[8] T. W. Laqueur, *Religion and Respectability: Sunday Schools and Working Class Culture 1780–1850* (New Haven, 1976), p. xi.

crowded that when the teachers moved they had to wade, as it were, through the close ranked youngsters.[9]

Sunday schools fitted into the interstices of working-class struggles for economic survival peculiarly well. Sunday was the one day when schooling did not compete with any other more immediately gainful work. Chapel or church could be used as schoolroom; and teachers gave their services free, so that if fees were charged at all, they were very low, a penny or twopence. All Sunday schools taught reading and a minority taught writing and even, in some cases, arithmetic as well. From 1807 controversies raged, particularly within Methodist circles, as to the appropriateness of activities other than reading on the Sabbath; and the teaching of writing is usually a good guide to those Sunday schools under local and lay control.

In offering scope for local self-government, which undoubtedly appealed to some working-class parents, Sunday schools differed yet again from most day schools. Regular week-day school required some sort of building and paid teachers, which in turn required an initial capital outlay, either from endowment or charitable subscription, or both, as well as reasonably regular and sizeable fee income. Capital usually required the involvement of some of the more affluent members of the community. Earnest middle-class promoters of Sunday schools often became involved, too, in the promotion of day schools; and the early years of the nineteenth century saw the formation of two societies designed to co-ordinate effort and spread best practice nationally. The National Society for Promoting the Education of the Poor in the Principles of the Established Church in England and Wales was formed in 1811. In 1814 followed the British and Foreign School Society, which supported undenominational religious teaching of a temper more generally acceptable to nonconformists and dissenters.

Day schools, however, could not emulate the mushroom growth of Sunday schools. Not only were they more expensive to establish and run, an expense reflected in fees ranging typically from twopence to fivepence per week, they also competed directly with work, whether it be cotton factory, mine, delivering laundry, crow-scaring, pea-picking or simply minding the baby to free an adult or elder sibling. And work almost always won. Its competition made it difficult to get the child into the day school at all and even more so to keep him or her there.

[9] Samuel Bamford, *Passages in the Life of a Radical* and *Early Days*, ed. Henry Dunckley, 2 vols. (1893), vol. 1, p. 101.

National and British schools' attractiveness was not enhanced either by their teaching methods. Both favoured the monitorial or mutual system of teaching, by which a teacher taught the older children – monitors – who then passed on what they had learnt to groups of younger children. This was designed to enable a single teacher to cope with very large groups of children indeed. But the mechanical and economical aspects which so pleased contemporary adult observers did not appcal as much to the children actually in the system. At the same time, many monitorial schools were ambitious enough to try to teach reading, writing and arithmetic as an integrated, simultaneous package.

Altogether these early nineteenth-century day schools offered an experience significantly different from the pattern of schooling familiar to the working class and one which many of them chose to avoid. The numbers and persistence of what middle-class contemporaries disparagingly called dame or private adventure schools is striking. Phil Gardner's model analysis of the extremely intractable data for a single city, Bristol between the 1840s and 1870s, suggests that there were nearly 200 working-class private adventure schools there in the 1850s.[10] Their flexibility and informality – willingness to accept attendance on an intermittent basis, parents paying when they could, fetching a child out to run an errand, do a job – were part of their attraction, so it is difficult to generalise about them. But in size they seldom seem to have had more than thirty children on the books and there could be as few as ten. They met often in the teacher's home, in back kitchen, basement or living room. They might simply be reading schools, taught indeed by an elderly woman or dame; but writing, to be tackled after reading, and for an additional fee, might also be offered; and sometimes arithmetic ditto. They had no more in the way of resources than the voluntary societies' day schools, probably rather less. But they lacked the noise, the numbers, the barrack-room discipline; they functioned often as an extension of the child's familiar domestic environment, rather than a place separated from and often alien to it.

However, in competing for the custom of working-class parents and their children, the voluntary societies and the schools affiliated to them had one resource which the working-class private adventure

[10] Gardner, *Lost Elementary Schools*, pp. 10, 30.

schools signally lacked: access to central government and thus the possibility of mobilising its power and resources in their support.

By no means everyone was convinced either that the working class should be educated or that government should have a hand in the process. In the 1720s Mandeville had attacked charity schools on the ground that to secure the contentment of the poor with their lot, 'it is requisite that great numbers of them should be Ignorant as well as Poor',[11] and this view had its adherents well into the nineteenth century. But in the 1820s and 1830s the argument began to be heard that the working-class demand for education was too vigorous to be choked off; therefore it had better be guided and appropriately chan- nelled. Or, as the Chartist, William Lovett put it:

While a large portion of the hawks and owls of society were seeking to perpetu- ate that state of mental darkness most favourable to the securing of their prey, another portion, with more cunning, were for admitting a sufficient amount of mental glimmer to cause the multitude to walk quietly and conten- tedly in the paths they in their wisdom had prescribed for them.[12]

This kind of approach has been labelled 'social control'. But such a label is a crude one, covering a multitude of stances from the crudely manipulative and instrumental attitude of a man like Lord London- derry, building schools in his mining villages after the Chartist distur- bances, to the wholly sincere attempt to remake the working-class child in the middle-class image, of a man like Sir James Kay-Shuttle- worth, the first Secretary to the Committee of the Privy Council on Education, 1839–49. All education is social control – as Lovett himself acknowledged, as he went on to write of those few who:

had talked of education as a means of light, life, liberty, and enjoyment for the whole human family; but these were of course the *Utopians of the World*; men who failed to perceive that God had made one portion of mankind to rule and enjoy, and the other to toil for them, and reverentially obey them.

The interesting question is not *whether* a given educational scheme is designed as social control but *what* sort of society is it intended to produce? Lovett was right to suggest that the vast majority of the members of the middle and upper classes who made the case for action on working-class education in Parliament wished to make the existing social structure run more smoothly. Many of them saw the

[11] Quoted in Harold Silver, *The Concept of Popular Education* (1965), p. 23.
[12] *Life and Struggles of William Lovett* (1876; 1967 edn), p. 111.

working-class family, remade through education, as the key agent of cultural transmission.[13]

Initially, the two day school societies, National and British, allied with factory reformers in efforts to limit children's hours of work and to secure effective enforcement of that limitation. The idea was that if there was no work the children could lawfully do, they would go to school instead. The first major breakthrough came with the Factory Act of 1833, which banned children under eight from textile factories altogether, limited the hours worked by children between the ages of eight and thirteen to eight daily, and, most important, created an inspectorate to enforce its provisions. A further Factory Act of 1844 limited the work of children between eight and thirteen to six and a half hours daily, or ten hours daily for three days a week, and specifically required them to attend a school in between. Meanwhile the Mines Act of 1842 had banned all females, child and adult, and all boys under ten, from work underground and also created an inspectorate.

Factory and mines inspectors were expected only to see that the children were out of the workplace – and the first mines inspectors were not even required to go underground. Neither set of inspectors had responsibility for or jurisdiction over the schools. Effective enforcement of child labour legislation was a very much more intractable problem than getting legislation on to the statute book; and it is doubtful whether indirect legislation of this kind made any impact at all on school attendance, a question to which we shall return. But at least middle-class enthusiasts were at one in the view that working-class children should be in school, not at work. On the question of which school they should attend and whether government aid could be deployed to ensure that there were schools within reach of all working-class children, major divisions arose because of religion.

Everyone was agreed that any education worth the name had a moral and therefore a religious core. But if religious, whose denomination? Anglicans, as members of the established church, argued that any schools named in law and/or supported by government funds should be theirs. Dissenters and Roman Catholics hotly disputed this. It was for this reason that there were two voluntary day school societies (joined by a third, the Catholic Poor School Committee, in 1849) not one. As Lovett bitterly put it, they declared 'all light to be

---

[13] For an extended discussion of this, see David Vincent, *Literacy and Popular Culture in England 1750–1914* (Cambridge, 1990).

impious and godless, unless it were kindled at their particular altars'.

The Whig government of 1833 attempted to side-step the issue by making available a grant for which any voluntary school, of any or no denomination, which satisfied certain conditions of efficiency, could bid. This was a beginning, but it was a system of 'giving to them that hath'. Arguably, government initiatives and funding were most needed in the areas of so-called 'educational destitution', where there were no middle-class enthusiasts to start schools. In 1839, therefore, the Whigs attempted to grasp the nettle of the 'religious problem', with a scheme which included grants to districts according to need and government training schools for teachers, organised on a non-denominational basis. The Tories mobilised against it in both Commons and Lords; and the opposition of almost the entire bench of bishops brought most of the scheme down to defeat. In 1843 the Tories attempted to take the initiative with the education clauses of Graham's Factory Bill, creating Anglican-run factory schools. They faced a comparable storm of protest from dissenters and Catholics and likewise retreated. Thereafter there was stalemate: each side had demonstrated its power to block the other; neither was strong enough to break through to a new system. The amount of grant continued to rise: by the beginning of the 1860s the government grant to schools in England and Wales exceeded £800,000 a year; but still the money went only to localities already making an effort.

Traditionally, school provision in Scotland has been seen as the great exception to all this. John Knox's *First Book of Discipline* had laid great stress on education; and legislation of 1695 and 1803 placed responsibility for the provision of a school on each parish. The 'heritors' or substantial landowners of each parish were obliged to maintain a school and pay a schoolmaster. Funds were to be provided from a rate levied on landed property. The minister was to exercise day-to-day supervision of the school and the presbyteries were to inspect the schools and test the teachers' qualifications.

But parish rates were not always equal to the burden, particularly in the Highlands and Islands; and the need for the child's contribution to the family economy was as real in Scotland as in England and Wales. Recent work has suggested that although levels of literacy tended to be somewhat higher in Scotland than in some parts of England and Wales, the differences were not so great as to suggest a major cultural divide. And in those areas where industrial development brought a great increase of population in the early nineteenth century, the parish school system was nearing breakdown.

Even so, the difference of degree was a substantial one. When civil registration of marriages was introduced in Scotland in 1855 the male literacy rate was 89 per cent and the female 77 per cent, compared with figures of 70 per cent and 59 per cent respectively for England and Wales. The curriculum of the Scottish parish school also had pretensions and ambitions which were unheard of in English voluntary schools. A good parish school taught mathematics, Latin and maybe even a little Greek; and it was possible for a boy to go direct from the parish school to the university. For the Scottish universities admitted boys at fifteen or even younger and provided quite elementary instruction in the 'junior classes' which began their courses. How frequently the poor 'lad o' parts' actually travelled this route is difficult to assess; but the model of the Scottish parish school, if not always the reality, provided an emphatic comment on the limitations of English provision.[14]

II

Before 1850 no one seriously canvassed the need for the state to provide schools for middle- and upper-class children in England and Wales. Here it was thought the free market was functioning admirably. Certainly, it seems there was considerable activity and formal schooling appears to be becoming the norm for boys. This sense of activity has to remain an impressionistic one; its volume is impossible to quantify. When schools were private enterprises, without endowment, they could leave remarkably little trace on the written record unless successful over an exceptionally long period. Nor can we make precise enough statements about the size and rate of growth of their clientele, that section of the population which was not the labouring poor.

One strand in the activity of the period was provided by dissenters. The conformity legislation of the seventeenth century had cut Protestant nonconformists off from access to many endowed grammar schools, as well as from other institutions associated with the established church. In creating their own schools the nonconformists did not simply follow the classical humanist model which had dominated

---

[14]   R. A. Houston, *Scottish Literacy and the Scottish Identity* (Cambridge, 1985); R. D. Anderson, *Education and Opportunity in Victorian Scotland* (Oxford, 1983), chap. 1, and *idem*, 'Education and the State in Nineteenth-Century Scotland', *Economic History Review*, 2nd ser., 36 (1983), pp. 518–34.

the scene since Dean Colet's foundation of St Paul's in 1509. To a core of theological training many of them added work in new and 'useful' subjects, modern languages, literature, mathematics and natural sciences. As John Conder, tutor in Divinity at the King's Head Academy in London in the mid-eighteenth century, put it:

What is counted a polite education now is very different from what was esteemed a century ago. Then if a man was versed in the learned and dead languages and in Aristotle's logic and metaphysics and Master of the Distinctions of the School of Divinity, he passed for a considerable scholar and a divine whereas now 'tis the mathematical learning carries the Bell.[15]

Some of the dissenting academies were quite literally peripatetic, teacher or teachers moving to wherever there was a patron or group of patrons, and pupils following teachers. In this sense they resemble some of the informal or semi-formal educational activity amongst the working class. It also makes it exceedingly difficult to measure their impact; and even an intensive study of a particular area, like Margaret Bryant's admirable survey of London, is unable to do this. One may suspect that they have enjoyed attention from historians out of all proportion to their numbers because of their 'modern' curriculum.

Almost certainly quantitatively more significant was the very much less ambitious demand for 'modern' and 'useful' subjects which was beginning to be brought to bear upon the endowed grammar schools. Analysis of a sample of endowed grammar schools functioning in the eighteenth century, drawn from fourteen counties and London, has shown that almost 90 per cent of those actually founded during the century provided for the teaching not only of Latin and Greek but also of English, arithmetic and writing. Again, where there is evidence of curriculum change during the eighteenth century, the overwhelming bulk of changes, nearly 80 per cent, entailed the introduction of English and arithmetic.[16]

It might be argued that some of this demand could be working class: a well-run charity school would expect to teach writing and arithmetic as well as reading. But it is more likely that it came from parents who considered themselves to be a cut above the clients of ordinary charity schools. It is significant that the children of clerical workers were a steadily increasing group at Christ's Hospital during

---

[15] Quoted in Margaret Bryant, *The London Experience of Secondary Education* (1986), p. 115.

[16] Richard S. Tompson, *Classics or Charity? The Dilemma of the Eighteenth-Century Grammar School* (Manchester, 1971).

the course of the eighteenth century, while the children of unskilled workers disappeared. The trustees of Leeds Grammar School were in dispute over the scope of the curriculum with two successive head-masters between 1779 and 1805, a dispute which led eventually to proceedings in the Court of Chancery. In the course of the dispute they explained quite precisely whom they wished to attract as pupils:

The Parish of Leeds [they declared] contains upwards of sixty thousand inhabitants, is wholly mercantile and nine tenths of the boys are brought up to trade and commerce, in consequence they are taken from school about the age of fourteen years and put out [as] apprentices or are placed in the counting-houses of the merchants – To such boys arithmetic and low algebra may and will be of use and the Committee found so much difficulty in limiting the number of boys to be taught writing that they are of opinion writing should be wholly excluded, but that arithmetic should not be excluded – They conceive that a master appointed merely for algebra and mathematics will not be so useful to the inhabitants of the town of Leeds as a master to teach low algebra and arithmetic, as they conceive the boys in general are taken from school at too early an age to avail themselves of algebra and mathematics.[17]

They want nothing fancy like 'high' algebra – or Latin and Greek – but they do not want a writing school either: they did not think of themselves as an elementary school, doing the most basic work.

Judgment went against them: they were prevented from remodelling the curriculum of the grammar school. But they were not debarred from opening a commercial department beside the classical grammar school, which they promptly did. They were imitated by grammar school trustees in Wolverhampton, Norwich, Nottingham and Bury St Edmunds. The clergyman who devised the Wolverhampton scheme remarked that 'a large class unprovided with public education will remain between the Grammar School and the parochial and similar schools'.[18]

The trustees of the Harpur Trust at Bedford had taken this route as early as 1764, when they amended the terms of their trust by private act of Parliament, to enable them to open a modern school beside the grammar school. This grew and flourished, while the grammar school continued to languish. The revival of its fortunes was begun in 1811, when the trustees acceded to the request of the new head-master to be allowed to take boarders, 'as masters of other public schools are universally permitted to do' and he instanced Rugby and

[17]   *Ibid.*, p. 119.
[18]   Quoted in F. E. Balls, 'The Origins of the Endowed Schools Act 1869 and its Operation in England 1869–95' (unpublished PhD thesis, Cambridge University, 1964), pp. 42–3. I am grateful to Dr Balls for permission to refer to his thesis.

Harrow.[19] At Shrewsbury at this time Butler, the headmaster, was doing likewise.

If one could take boarders, one could develop a national rather than a purely local appeal. And if we are right to posit an increased demand for formal schooling amid the middle and upper classes in the century following 1750, a central feature of that demand was its increasingly sharp social differentiation. The traditional grammar school curriculum would no longer do for everyone with aspirations beyond the simple acquisition of basic skills. While small tradesmen and farmers might be interested in 'useful subjects', those who wanted their sons to become gentlemen seemed at least as much interested in the capacity of the school to provide a degree of social segregation and style, as in any curriculum content.

The decisions taken about the education of his sons by John Gladstone, the Liverpool merchant and founder of the family fortunes, show the range of possible choice as perceived by one ambitious and concerned parent. He himself had ended school in Leith at the age of thirteen, when he was apprenticed to a rope merchant. Initially he determined that all four boys should go to Eton, despite his wife's and daughters' (entirely justified) fears about its moral tone; and the family responded only with bracing encouragement to the miserable letters home of poor Tom, the first to go in 1817. Young John, by insisting on his determination to go into the navy from the age of thirteen onwards, escaped altogether. Robertson spent two years there; but when it was decided that he should follow his father in the business, he was taken away in 1821 and sent off to stay with an uncle in Glasgow, from whose house he could attend selected classes at the university and learn mathematics, physics and metaphysics, as well as the classics. Only William throve at Eton.[20]

In the first half of the nineteenth century in England, schools for gentlemen became sharply differentiated from schools providing 'useful' or clearly vocationally geared training; and no one expected the same institution to provide both. Sir John Romilly, Master of the Rolls, finally refusing the trustees of Bristol Grammar School permission to take boarders in 1860, summed up developments thus:

Either the school becomes a school for the rich, that is, for what may be termed the high branch of the middle classes, or it becomes a school from

[19] Quoted in Joyce Godber, *The Harpur Trust 1551–1973* (Bedford, 1973), p. 65.
[20] S. G. Checkland, *The Gladstones: A Family Biography 1764–1851* (Cambridge, 1971), pp. 10, 129–40.

which they are practically withdrawn. It is in the nature of things that it should be so. The regard paid to wealth in this country gives an unusual degree of importance to boys whose parents are supposed to possess it, over those whose parents are supposed to be wanting in that respect.[21]

As the need of the Bristol trustees to resort to the Court of Chancery suggests, local circumstances and the terms of the particular trust did not always make it possible or straightforward for grammar school trustees to respond clearly to one type of demand or the other, or, as at Bedford, to respond to both with two separate schools. The first half of the nineteenth century saw a series of sharp and prolonged conflicts over the use and remodelling of particular trusts, from which, often, only Chancery profited.

An alternative mode of response to the perceived demand for boarding education was to open a new private or joint stock – proprietary – boarding school. The figures compiled by T. W. Bamford, showing the number of boarding schools founded by decade in England and Wales, set out below, indicate a slowly gathering momentum.[22]

1800–9	2
1810–19	2
1820–9	2
1830–9	2
1840–9	13
1850–9	5
1860–9	13

The great surge of the 1840s included schools such as Cheltenham, Marlborough, Rossall and Radley.

Although the expansion of middle-class schooling in England 1750–1850 had its parallels in Scotland, class expectations and boundaries were much less sharply defined and demarcated. Insofar as there was boarding, it tended to be of the private enterprise variety favoured by the Gladstones for Robertson – a son sent to stay with relatives or friends in the neighbourhood of the chosen institution. The first school built explicitly on the English 'public school' model was Trinity College, Glenalmond, in 1847. For the most part, provision which went beyond the curriculum of the parish school took the form of the town day school.

The parish school legislation did not apply to towns. It was

---

[21] Quoted Balls, 'Origins of the Endowed Schools Act', pp. 14–15.
[22] T. W. Bamford, *The Rise of the Public Schools* (1967), p. 18.

customary for burghs to maintain a school, although in the smaller burghs there was little to choose between their schools and the neighbouring parochial ones. Larger towns, however, supported more ambitious enterprises. From the mid-eighteenth century these were complemented by, sometimes in competition with, schools teaching modern subjects and then the more ambitious 'academies'. The first of these, the Perth Academy, was founded in 1760 by the town council; but other 'proprietary' academies were run by non-profitmaking boards. In the early nineteenth century there was a move to amalgamate burgh schools and academies, coupled with the rebuilding and expansion of a number of burgh schools.

All of this suggests a sizeable increase in demand, although it is no more possible to quantify it for Scotland than it is for England. What remains distinctive, however, is the involvement of the local community in the management of the school, whether it be the town council direct, a board appointed by the subscribers, or a mixed board with representatives of both. As Sir John Sinclair commented in 1826, a school 'by its connection with such bodies is, in some measure, interwoven with the frame of the body politic, and a foundation is thus laid for its future durable prosperity'.[23]

III

As the foregoing sections might suggest, the universities occupied a very different place in Scottish life and culture from that occupied in England and Wales. There were more of them, they were more accessible and central government was already involved in their running. The four centres of university education had been explicitly safeguarded in the Act of Union. By the 1830s they were receiving between £5,000 and £6,000 a year in parliamentary grants; and appeals for more and collisions between the university administration and the city council in Edinburgh, and between professors and students at Marischal College in Aberdeen, had already brought one Royal Commission of Inquiry in 1826.

In 1825–6 the total student population of the four, Edinburgh, Glasgow, St Andrew's and Aberdeen (King's and Marischal together), was estimated at about 4,500. Some of these might be fifteen- or even fourteen-year-old 'lads o'parts' from the parish schools, others could be men in their twenties, thirties even, making major changes of

---

[23] Quoted in Anderson, *Education and Opportunity*, p. 17.

direction, or returning to education. Students paid for each class separately and there were no restrictions on entry. Thus while each university recommended a fixed curriculum, giving approximately equal weight to classics, philosophy, mathematics and physics, which was compulsory for those aiming at the ministry, students could be exceedingly eclectic and intermittent in their choices – and as their funds would allow. The university session ran from late October to Easter and it was not uncommon for the poorer students to work full time during the summer and indeed part to near full time when courses were in session. Such flexibility could make for an exceedingly diverse student body, perhaps most marked in Glasgow and Edinburgh, both of which reckoned themselves European cities in the late eighteenth century.

Many have seen the late eighteenth century as the golden age of the Scottish universities. By contrast, Oxford and Cambridge, the two English universities, were just beginning to emerge from a deep trough both in terms of intellectual vitality and of numbers. The verdict of Gibbon, who reckoned the fourteen months he spent at Oxford between 1752 and 1753 'the most idle and unprofitable' of his entire life, was a harsh one; but recent work has done little to soften this outline.[24] In the decade 1750–9 new entrants to Oxford and Cambridge annually averaged respectively about 180 and 150. By 1820–9 these totals had climbed back up to match the figures of the early seventeenth century: annual admissions to Oxford colleges averaged 400 and to Cambridge colleges, 440.[25] How long the average stay was, is unclear; but if we were to assume three years, this would still give a total student population only half that in Scotland at the same period.

There were other differences too. Oxford and Cambridge colleges required continuous residence of their students during term and formally a full-time commitment to either classics or mathematics respectively. In terms of age and social background their students were also a much more homogeneous group than the Scots. In the course of the eighteenth century, 'plebeians', those whose fathers were not

---

[24]   T. H. Aston, gen. ed., *The History of the University of Oxford*, vol. 5: *The Eighteenth Century*, ed. L. S. Sutherland and L. G. Mitchell (Oxford, 1986), esp. Mitchell's 'Introduction', pp. 1–8; M. M. Garland, *Cambridge before Darwin: The Ideal of a Liberal Education 1800–1860* (Cambridge, 1980), chap. 1.

[25]   Lawrence Stone, 'The Size and Composition of the Oxford Student Body 1580–1909', Appendix IV, Tables 1a and 1b, in Lawrence Stone, ed., *The University in Society*, 2 vols. (Princeton, 1975), vol. 1, pp. 91–2.

gentlemen, disappeared altogether. At the same time the median age of matriculants rose gradually, to eighteen and a half.

The coincidence between the decline in Oxbridge numbers from 1680 and the changing political scene and structure is a dramatic one; although which way – or ways – the arrows of causal connection might point is another matter. Likewise we can speculate on the reasons for the recovery in numbers which gets under way towards the end of the Napoleonic Wars. But we can only note its coincidence at a global level with the general intellectual and political ferment; and, more parochially, with the apparently increasing demand for formal schooling for a younger age group and the movements for reform within each university.

The great instrument of reform was the formal examination. Cambridge appears to have led the way. By 1800 the 'Senate House Examination' had emerged as the most important part of the Mathematical Tripos. As early as 1765 St John's College had established twice-yearly examinations for its own students. From 1786 Trinity began to award fellowships on the basis of competitive examinations and gradually followed St John's in regularly examining its own undergraduates. Oxford reformed its procedures with the Examination Statute of 1800 and Oxford colleges hastened to develop their own examinations. William Gladstone, who much gratified his father's ambition by proceeding from Eton to Christ Church, Oxford, secured First Classes in both the Classical and Mathematical Final Honour Schools in 1831.

But reform from within was a painfully slow process; and from the 1820s Oxford and Cambridge were faced with challenges far more fundamental. The first set out to by-pass them altogether; to found other universities. In 1828 'the godless institution of Gower Steet', which was to become University College, London, opened its doors. It was followed in 1831 by the firmly Anglican King's College in the Strand. In 1832 another Anglican University was established at Durham. In 1836 the Whig government created by charter a University of London which was simply an examining and degree-giving body, under whose umbrella University College and King's College – and any number of institutions and individuals – could gather. Already by 1850 the number of candidates successfully meeting its matriculation requirements was just short of 200 a year.[26]

The Whig government's preparedness to get involved in the debates

---

[26] Negley Harte, *The University of London, 1836–1986* (1986), p. 106.

about the existence and nature of a University of London was not an isolated occurrence, nor simply a function of Brougham's involvement with the foundation of University College, London. Others besides Brougham were sympathetic to criticisms of the intellectual narrowness and social and denominational, that is, Anglican, exclusiveness of Oxbridge. Lord John Russell, after all, had been sent to study in Edinburgh in 1809 because his father took the view that 'nothing was learned in the English universities'.[27] Moreover, like it or not, governments were already heavily involved in the affairs of the Scottish universities and the whole thorny question of higher education in Ireland. And in this decade the Anglican exclusiveness of Oxford at least came to look positively threatening. Keble, John Henry Newman and their supporters were beginning to question the basis of Establishment, the competence of Parliament to regulate the affairs of the Anglican church, launching upon a course which eventually took Newman, Henry Edward Manning, two of the sons of William Wilberforce and several others over to Rome. The Oxford Movement, more than any other single event, ensured the eventual appointment in 1850 of Royal Commissions of Inquiry into the affairs of both Oxford and Cambridge.

This decision and all changes in university provision in this period obviously affected only a minute fraction of the population. But the gradual increase in numbers attending and the increase in public scrutiny and discussion of the role of universities was significant. Demonstrably those attending universities were an elite group: were they the right elite? How were they recruited, how ought they to be recruited? What did they learn and in what manner; what ought they to learn? All these questions were now beginning to be asked.

In this period 1750–1850 full-time formal schooling emerged clearly as the preferred mode of education for males among the elite groups in society, the aristocracy and the emergent middle classes. The educational experience of the vast mass of the population was very different: intermittent, chancy, partial, often wholly informal or at most semi-formal. In the short term this development accentuated differences, contributed to the making of class. In the longer term the sheer success of the mechanism of formal schooling was to lead to efforts to extend its operation to the society as a whole.

[27] John Prest, Lord John Russell (1972), p. 11.

1850–1914

The period before 1850 had seen the involvement of central government both in the provision of elementary schools and in the regulation of the affairs of universities. The period 1850–1914 saw government drawn into educational provision at all levels, although not without much debate. Half a century after the rest of Western Europe, England at last took to system-building in education. By 1914 there could be identified a national structure for formal schooling, albeit a knobbly and curiously shapen one.

I

Until the 1850s and beyond, much of the schooling of the working class, elementary education as it was coming to be called, was still informal or semi-formal. Efforts to bring government resources to bear had so far been hampered by the 'religious problem' and it took another twenty years to hack through this Gordian knot. A first attempt was made at the end of the 1850s, in the report of a Royal Commission on Elementary Education, chaired by the Duke of Newcastle. This recommended involving local as well as central government in the provision of schools, allowing local government agencies to offer rate aid to supplement government grants. They suggested that this rate aid should be dependent on the school's results, in effect a series of incentive payments.

Local government involvement foundered amid denominational squabbles; but the payment by results principle was taken up and made the basis for a reconstruction of the government grant – the so-called Revised Code – in 1862–3. Henceforward, the bulk of a school's grant, roughly half its income, was to be dependent upon satisfactory performance by each child aged seven and over in examinations conducted by Her Majesty's Inspectors of Schools.

It was a move welcomed not by those who thought the government should be doing more but by those who thought educational expenditure was mushrooming out of control, who doubted whether governments were getting value for money. And its immediate effects were all they could have wished: grant aid to education immediately fell by almost a quarter and the levels of 1861 were not reached again until 1869.

It is impossible to judge whether greater efficiency was achieved in the sense that teachers spread their attention more evenly across their classes than they were supposed to have done before. Class sizes were so variable and classes often so big that it was no easier than it ever had been to give each child, the less able as well as the able, the amount of attention needed. But probably the most far-reaching changes wrought by the Revised Code were in the relationships between teachers and their paymasters, both school managers and government inspectors. In effect, payment by results was a piece-rate system, putting teachers in the position of factory hands. HM Inspectors, who hitherto had been advising, guiding, encouraging, now sat in judgment on the 'product', the more or less proficient child. All too many managers followed the logic of the situation through to the point where they made a part, or even the whole, of the teacher's salary dependent upon the school's grant earnings.

Payment by results did nothing, of course, for the so-called 'areas of educational destitution'; and efforts were resumed by Gladstone's administration of 1868–74, resulting in the Education Act of 1870, known as Forster's Act. This at last embodied a commitment to nation-wide provision; but the form it took showed the continuing power of the denominational vested interests. The act allowed voluntary schools to continue unchanged, with the same committees of managers. But where a proven deficiency of school accommodation existed, or where a majority of the ratepayers demanded it, a body called a School Board could be created. This was a triennially elected body, its size varying with the population of the town or civil parish, with powers to build and run schools, the prior right to supply any deficiency which existed or might develop, and power to draw on the rates for funding. An early draft of the bill had given voluntary schools access to rate aid too. But nonconformist opposition put a stop to that and in compensation the rates of government grant, for which both voluntary and board schools were eligible, were increased.

The religious problem left its mark in other ways. School Board members were directly elected by cumulative vote: that is to say, each voter had as many votes as there were seats and could distribute them as he wished, one for each of a number of candidates, all for one candidate or some votes for one candidate, some for another. This was expressly designed to allow the representation of minorities and thus the localisation of denominational conflict. Certainly it achieved this; although many in areas where denominational conflict waxed came to question whether the energies that went into this actually benefited the local schools. Not foreseen was the way in which the cumulative vote facilitated the election first of women and later of workingmen, bringing vital political and administrative experience for both groups.

Outside urban areas the School Board unit was the civil parish, a very small one. By the 1890s there were over 2,000 School Boards in existence in England and Wales. Besides these there were still the individual committees of management of voluntary schools, some 14,000 of them. They, like the School Boards, dealt directly with the Education Department in Whitehall and in this sense must be treated as quasi-local authorities. The administrative difficulties of dealing with all these small bodies were vastly exacerbated by the lop-sidedness of the financial arrangements. Board schools with rates as well as government grant to draw on had the resources to grow. Voluntary schools had no source of local income comparable to rates. There was no way they could keep pace.

In this sense if no other the settlement of 1870 carried within it the seeds of its own destruction from the very beginning. By the 1890s it was plain that provision for elementary education was uneven and annually growing more so. Nor was the structure one on to which any provision for secondary education, now beginning seriously to be discussed, could be grafted. Lord Salisbury's third administration tinkered with education throughout its life, finally with the Education Act of 1902 'putting the Church on the rates'. School Boards were abolished. In return for rate aid voluntary schools' committees of management came within the control of the new Local Education Authorities, county and county borough councils, a mere 140-odd of them. These LEAs also had powers and responsibilities in the secondary field, to which we will return.

The act of 1870 had at last created a mechanism to provide an elementary school wherever needed. It did not include a mechanism for getting the children into these schools, once built. All it contained was a permissive clause, allowing School Boards, if they chose, to frame bye-laws to compel attendance. And even this gesture towards direct compulsion, as it was called, was controversial, representing, as the *Edinburgh Review* put it in 1874, 'the principle of direct interference with individual liberty and parental authority'.[28] Yet indirect compulsion, provisions excluding children from work in mines or factories

---

[28] Quoted in Gillian Sutherland, *Policy-Making in Elementary Education 1870–1895* (Oxford, 1973), p. 123.

before a certain age, was patently not working. Mines and factory inspectors queried the activities of obviously under-age children when they noticed them. But this was less easy than it sounds. A glance at any twentieth-century primary school class will show you considerable variety in any given age group; and poverty and chronic undernourishment meant that working-class children in the nineteenth century were in general smaller, uglier, dirtier and smellier than their middle-class counterparts, confusing the issues further. And registration of births became compulsory only in 1874.

Problems of enforcement apart, there were whole areas of child employment not covered by factory acts. There was no regulation of child labour in agriculture at all before 1873. A first attempt to regulate smaller industrial enterprises was made in the Workshops Act of 1867. But the only secure way to regulate an industry was to name it specifically; and there were limits even to the effectiveness of this. So much of what children did was ancillary, supporting. How did you control a situation in which a child's mother took in washing and used the child or children to return the clean and collect the dirty? Moreover, even if a child was successfully prevented from working, there was no guarantee he was spending the time in school instead.

Reviewing the jumble of existing legislation in 1876 a Royal Commission on the Factory Acts at last came down firmly in favour of universal direct compulsion. Meanwhile, managers of voluntary schools worried that taking powers to compel attendance would enable School Boards to secure a larger and more regular fee income; and that such powers might be seen as an incentive for the creation of more Boards. The 1876 Education Act added yet another local authority to the fray: in non-School Board areas the local sanitary authority might make bye-laws to compel attendance. Only by the Education Act of 1880 were all School Boards and all sanitary authorities in non-School Board districts *required* to make attendance bye-laws. If they failed, the Education Department would step in and make them for them.

By 1880, therefore, the formal legal position was clear and unequivocal. Every parish was expected to have an elementary school and all the children of the labouring poor between the ages of five and ten were expected to attend it on a full-time basis. It took rather longer for the reality to approach this. Between 1870 and 1885 the number of children in regular attendance at inspected schools, expressed as a percentage of those whose names were on the registers, crept up from 68 per cent to 76 per cent. By 1895 it had only reached 82 per cent.[29] School managers grumbled perennially about the difficulties of prosecution and magistrates' reluctance to convict. But the real problems of enforcement were much more deep-rooted; how to change the habits of employers, parents, children, often unbalancing fragile household economies in the process. Or, as Flora Thompson put it, 'it was only the second generation to be forcibly fed with the fruit of the tree of knowledge; what wonder if it did not always agree with it'.[30]

The 'forcible feeding' metaphor is horribly apt. The framework of payment by results restricted the range of grant-earning subjects. All too often it bred a mechanical drilling in the classroom, a rehearsal every day for the examination that came once a year. Although the basis for grant was changed in the first half of the 1890s, the habits engendered took much longer to die. And until the Fees Act of 1891, parents were required to pay to keep their children out of work and subject them to a classroom regime little more attractive than that offered in the monitorial schools of the 1820s and 1830s. Gardner has surmised that the legislation of 1870–80 killed off the bulk of the working-class private adventure schools, whose flexibility and informality – 'user-friendly' in the argot of the 1980s – had competed so successfully with the government-endorsed enterprises earlier in the century. Only a detailed local study around the time of the censuses of 1891 and 1901 would really establish that beyond doubt. The persistence of some survivors, like the enterprise run in Walsall until 1937 by the redoubtable Miss Beetlestone, makes one wonder.[31]

It also tends to be assumed that the virtual collapse of the market for child labour coincided with, was even caused by, the arrival of direct compulsion. This assumption has never been adequately documented. It is possible that a great deal of children's work, ancillary, supporting, intermittent and seasonal as it was, was simply displaced, pushed to times outside school hours, early mornings, evenings, week-ends. An inter-departmental committee of 1901 estimated the number of children working outside school hours 'for wages or profit' at about 300,000. Besides these, there were the children between ten and twelve or ten and thirteen allowed by attendance authorities to

[29] *Special Reports on Educational Subjects*, PP 1897, XXV, p. 50.
[30] Flora Thompson, *Lark Rise* (1939; World Classics edn, 1954), p. 195.
[31] Gardner, *Lost Elementary Schools*, chaps. 6 and 7, esp. pp. 219–42.

work part time, recorded in 1909 as numbering 44,360.[32] They were minorities in an elementary school population by now numbering just over 5 million; but they formed a not insignificant fraction.

Having cut the Gordian knot in England in 1870, it was difficult for the Liberal government to go on ignoring the complaints about the limitations of the parish school system in Scotland; and legislation for Scottish elementary schools was carried in 1872. The long tradition of government concern for and involvement in the provision of schools, and the dominance of Presbyterianism, albeit in a variety of forms, made it possible to create universal, rate-aided School Boards. All were required to make bye-laws to compel attendance between the ages of five and thirteen, although until 1901 some partial exemptions after the age of ten were allowed. Payments by results had been operated in a somewhat dilute version in Scotland since 1864. The Act of 1872 brought a stronger version, but that lasted only until 1885, when control of the Scottish Education Department passed from the Privy Council Office to the new Scottish Office.

In its formal structures Scottish popular schooling was thus coming increasingly to resemble the English. But there was still a certain Scottish distinctiveness to boast about. By 1901 less than 1 per cent of Scots were unable to sign their names in the marriage register; for the English and the Welsh the figure was 3 per cent.

II

Up to the mid-nineteenth century government involvement with schools other than elementary had been confined to the regulation and remodelling of trusts, initially in the Court of Chancery, after 1853 through the Charity Commission. By the end of the 1850s something more general and co-ordinated was being sought. Brougham presented a petition with 40,000 signatures to the Commons, praying for the improvement of middle-class education, and the first of a series of letters signed 'Paterfamilias' in the *Cornhill* in May 1860 launched a vigorous debate in the periodicals, in which the terms 'middle-class' and 'secondary' came to be used with increasing interchangeability.

Palmerston's government's first gesture was a very modest one:

---

[32]   Jocelyn Dunlop and R. D. Denman, *English Apprenticeship and Child Labour: A History* (1912), pp. 310–17.

a Royal Commission under Lord Clarendon to look into the affairs of Eton and eight other schools of similar standing. As Matthew Arnold pointed out, it was not Eton and its 'eight co-respondents' which needed the spotlight of public enquiry so much as the decaying grammar schools and the proliferating mass of private and proprietary schools, claiming to offer a cheap but sound education for the children of 'the great mass of middling people, with middling incomes'.[33] In 1864 the government conceded another Royal Commission, under Lord Taunton, to investigate all schools not looked at by either Clarendon or Newcastle.

The two Commissions took as a given the stratification of schooling for the middle class as it had developed in the first half of the century and proposed to formalise and systematise it in an hierarchy. At the top were 'first grade schools', modelled on Eton and its eight co-respondents, mostly boarding, with a classical curriculum, sending boys to the universities. Next came 'second grade schools', mostly day, teaching Latin but not Greek, whose boys would leave at sixteen. Finally there were 'third grade schools', all day, teaching a little Latin, sending boys into employment at fourteen. The three grades were conceived as parallel, separate tracks, only the common study of Latin allowing mobility via scholarships from one track to another for the exceptionally bright boy.

Insofar as this stratification was a description of the differentiation already taking place, no action needed to follow the two reports. But as we have seen, seeking to remodel individual trust deeds could be an expensive, time-consuming and not always successful manoeuvre. Two pieces of legislation greatly expedited the process. The Public Schools Act of 1868 clarified the position of headmasters *vis-à-vis* both staff and governors, regulated the management of certain endowments at the nine Clarendon schools and – of great symbolic importance – removed the last vestiges of local connection and foundation rights from Harrow and Rugby. Harrow already had a commercial school, intended for the sons of local tradesmen. The 1868 Act enabled the creation of another such at Rugby; and foundation privileges for local boys were transmogrified into scholarships open to national competition.

[33] *A French Eton, or Middle-Class Education and the State*, first published 1863–4, reprinted in *Complete Prose Works of Matthew Arnold*, ed. R. H. Super, 11 vols. (Ann Arbor, Mich., 1960–77), vol. 2: *Democratic Education*, p. 281.

The Endowed Schools Act of 1869 created a fixed-term Statutory Commission, to last for three years, with extensive powers to remodel educational endowments throughout England and Wales. Efforts actually to embody the hierarchy of grades in the legislation and provide for a national examining scheme failed; but the Endowed Schools Commissioners treated the Taunton recommendations as binding guidelines in all their work. When the Commission's life came to an end in 1873, some of its powers were vested in the rather less energetic Charity Commission. But they, too, treated the Taunton guidelines as sacrosanct.

In aiming for three grades rather than two, the systematisation proposed by the Taunton Commissioners proved overelaborate. The differentiation of demand in the early nineteenth century had been essentially a bifurcation, an increasingly clear distinction between schools for gentlemen and schools for those who aimed at respectability rather than gentility; and this pattern of demand remained constant in the second half of the century. Much more work needs to be done on the detail of provision after 1870; but it looks as though those schools defined as second grade were the ones which found it most difficult to attract a clientele and survive.[34]

A twofold pattern of demand was particularly clear to see in the case of girls' schools. It was supposed to have been said of the Endowed Schools Commissioners that 'they could take a boys' school in Northumberland and turn it into a girls' school in Cornwall'. The power to make provision for girls, of all their powers, was the one with the most far-reaching implications; and one which they used. By the time of their demise in 1874 they had made schemes creating twenty-seven schools for girls; schemes for another twenty were in the pipe-line; and provision for girls 'when funds allow' had been built into a number of other schemes. The Charity Commissioners proceeded at a much slower pace; but a further forty-five girls' schools had been added by 1903.

Parallel with these developments went the creation of proprietary schools for girls. The pioneer establishments had been the North London Collegiate School and Cheltenham Ladies' College in the 1850s. But in 1872 a Girls' Public Day School Company was formed and

---

[34] Hilary Steedman, 'Defining Institutions: The Endowed Grammar Schools and the Systematisation of English Secondary Education', in Detlef K. Mueller, Fritz Ringer and Brian Simon, eds., *The Rise of the Modern Educational System* (Cambridge, 1987).

already by 1880 it had opened eleven schools in the London area and eleven elsewhere.[35]

A handful of the new girls' schools, such as Cheltenham, Wycombe Abbey, St Leonard's and Roedean, were boarding, modelling themselves more or less on boys' public schools; but the vast majority were day schools. On the face of it this grouped them with second and third grade boys' schools; although when the question of grades for girls' schools was raised with the Endowed Schools Commissioners they shied away from it. 'Upper' and 'lower' was the description they preferred; although Lyttelton, the Chief Commissioner, successfully prevented the inclusion of Greek in the subjects taught even in those 'upper' girls' schools with a leaving age of nineteen. But by the end of the century a handful of the most ambitious girls' schools, with a clear eye on university entrance, were teaching Greek as well; and 'upper' and 'lower' amongst girls' schools corresponded pretty well to Taunton's first and third grades.

The Bryce Commission, reviewing the stratification of schools by grade between 1893 and 1895, were somewhat coy, referring rather obliquely to the difficulties of grammar schools with small endowments in unfortunate locations. But in making recommendations for the future they envisaged essentially two types of school: 'local', meeting local needs, to be defined by the locality, and 'non-local' or boarding.

The efforts of Commissioners, trustees and proprietary enterprises appeared to be meeting the demand for 'upper' schools. By and large the parents could pay. But, as earlier, the demand that was much more difficult to meet, yet far more extensive, was for 'lower' schooling, going further – or having greater pretensions – than that supposed to be provided in the elementary school, but not aiming at university entrance.

Pressure for more extensive and ambitious work was already being felt within the elementary sector. Early in the life of the London School Board, T. H. Huxley had challenged the view that elementary and secondary should be separate and self-contained sectors. 'He should like', he said,

to have an arrangement considered by which a passage could be secured for children of superior ability to schools in which they could obtain a higher

[35] Sheila Fletcher, *Feminists and Bureaucrats: A Study in the Development of Girls' Education in the Nineteenth Century* (Cambridge, 1980), Appendix 3; Josephine Kamm, *Indicative Past: A Hundred Years of the Girls' Public Day School Trust* (1971), Appendix II.

instruction than in the ordinary ones. He believed that no educational system in the country would be worthy the name of a national system, or fulfil the great objects of education, unless it was one which established a great educational ladder, the bottom of which should be in the gutter and the top in the University and by which every child who had the strength to climb might, by using that strength, reach the place intended for him.[36]

His language was not unlike that used by members of the Taunton Commission, including the Rev. Frederick Temple, the future Archbishop of Canterbury, when they had argued that money originally set aside for local privileges should now be used to provide open scholarships and bursaries; but Huxley's 'scholarship ladder' was a much more extensive one. Huxley and others of like mind worked to secure endowments, remodelled and new, to allow movement from elementary to secondary schools, and to sustain the poorer child in a secondary school.

Huxley's formulation and initiative were of enormous symbolic importance. More significant, in terms of the numbers affected, were developments within the elementary schools themselves: the pupil–teacher system and higher grade schools. The pupil–teacher system had originated in a series of Minutes of 1846, part of central government's efforts to be as generous as possible, within the constraints of denominational deadlock. In schools of which HMI approved, children of thirteen and over could be apprenticed to the teacher for five years, taking on some teaching work and undertaking additional study. This earned the school extra grant. HMI examined the work of these teacher apprentices each year and they could also enter national examinations for the Normal Schools or training colleges. The best secured Queen's Scholarships to enable them to attend college; others might win Certificates of Merit which enabled them to command better salaries at the end of their apprenticeship.

This scheme spelled the end of the monitorial system – as its architect, James Kay-Shuttleworth, had intended. It also brought elementary teaching a status and a financial security which it had hitherto lacked, and one which even payment by results did not entirely erode. It offered a limited little career ladder by which the working-class child could move to white-collar respectability. Its opportunities were exploited by many. Already by 1859 there were 15,224 pupil teachers. Not all pupil teachers completed their apprenticeship successfully and uncertificated teachers did not disappear. But by 1899 there were

36 Quoted in Hugh B Philpott, *London at School: The Story of the London School Board 1870–1904* (1904), pp. 153–4.

62,085 certificated teachers, 30,233 provisionally or un-certificated teachers and 30,783 pupil teachers teaching in government-inspected schools in England and Wales.[37]

Higher grade schools meshed with the development of the pupil–teacher system. In the late 1870s a handful of the larger urban School Boards perceived the advantages and economies of bringing together in one institution those few children in their area wanting to tackle work under the higher Standards of the Code. Such a school could also then bid for grants from the Science and Art Department at South Kensington. In addition boards might require their pupil teachers to do some of their work at the higher grade schools. By the time the Bryce Commission surveyed the scene in the early 1890s some of these higher grade schools were secondary schools 'of the second (and not merely of the third) grade'[38] in all but name.

The establishment of the Royal Commission chaired by Lord Bryce was itself indicative of a different kind of demand: the concern of those who felt – like Matthew Arnold in the 1860s – that secondary education was too important to be left to the random distribution of endowments and the operations of the market. The argument that both government and society needed a properly educated middle class was being advanced with a new urgency. The Scottish Education Department, the SED, had, as we shall see, embarked upon intense activity in this area. The cry of 'national efficiency' was beginning to be heard.

Already before Bryce there had been some legislative initiatives. The Welsh MPs, exploiting the fact that there were very few endowed grammar schools in the Principality, had carried the Welsh Intermediate Education Act of 1889, allowing the newly created county councils to play a part in the establishment of 'intermediate' or lower secondary schools. By 1900 ninety such schools had come into existence.[39] County councils in both England and Wales were also empowered by the Technical Instruction Act of 1889 to encourage technical and scientific education; and the 1890 Budget brought them the windfall of the 'whisky money', the excise duty on spirits, to spend on it.

But all these new initiatives added further to the administrative muddle. The Education Act of 1902, which finally put the church

[37] A. Tropp, *The School Teachers* (1957), pp. 21, 117–18.

[38] *RC on Secondary Education* (the Bryce Commission), Part I, PP 1895, XLIII, para. 59, p. 53.

[39] E. L. Ellis, *The University College of Wales, Aberystwyth 1872–1972* (Cardiff 1972), p. 97.

schools 'on the rates' and abolished School Boards, rationalised the provision of post-elementary schooling in England and Wales at last. The new LEAs, county and county borough councils, were charged with the responsibility for provision of secondary as well as elementary schooling in their areas, with power to build schools where needed. Existing secondary schools had a choice of options. They could remain wholly separate; or, in return for full funding, they could put themselves under LEA control; or, by complying with certain conditions, they could be directly grant-aided by central government.

The result of this was a massive expansion in the physical provision for secondary schooling in the years up to 1914. Nor did the government neglect the question of access for the elementary school pupil to the new, fee-charging secondary schools. The Free Place Regulations of 1907 made available enhanced government grant to all secondary schools prepared to offer 25 per cent of their places without fees to ex-elementary school pupils. Would-be 'free-placers' were expected to sit a simple qualifying examination. Pressure of numbers soon made this as ferociously competitive as any of the existing scholarship tests.

Simultaneously, steps were taken to end the pupil–teacher system. Intending teachers were henceforward encouraged to attend a secondary school and then go on to a training college; and a system of bursaries was developed to support this. By 1912, 49,120 children, 32 per cent of the total population of maintained secondary schools, were ex-elementary school pupils, holding a scholarship, bursary or free place.[40] Some rungs were being supplied for Huxley's ladder.

The Scottish Education Act of 1872 had not restricted Scottish School Boards to the provision of elementary education. But there was no grant aid for secondary education and most ratepayers thought secondary schooling an expensive luxury. Moreover, given the Scottish tradition of advanced work in the parish school, the creation of separate public secondary schools, or even of post-elementary departments linked to but separate from elementary schools, was a highly controversial issue. For two decades fully public provision for secondary schooling languished; only a few Boards provided what were known as 'higher class' schools and a few more provided advanced classes for the older children in their elementary schools. As in England a decade earlier, the remodelling of endowments occupied the

---

[40]   Gillian Sutherland, *Ability, Merit and Measurement: Mental Testing and English Education 1880–1940* (Oxford, 1984), p. 111.

centre of the stage. The Endowed Institutions Acts of 1878 and 1882 allowed a remodelling even more ruthless than that conducted in England, sweeping away local charitable rights and privileges wholesale and requiring provision for girls to match that for boys.

From 1885, however, Scottish education was no longer amongst the responsibilities of the Privy Council Office in Whitehall; it was in the care of a separate department within the newly created Scottish Office. Almost immediately its officials began to demonstrate a clear commitment to the development of separate public secondary schooling. Despite controversy and opposition which made the course they pursued a somewhat crab-wise one, they pushed ahead; and their efforts, of course, added to the pressure for action in England. Unlike the English Education Department, the Scots were not hampered by the need to reconstruct the local government of education first. School Boards survived in Scotland until 1918, to be replaced first by directly elected, county-wide *ad hoc* authorities and then in 1929 by the county councils.

A first step towards public secondary schooling was taken with the institution of the Leaving Certificate in 1888, an examination designed both to achieve an appropriate curriculum and to raise standards in higher class – secondary – schools, both public and private. A grant in 1892, roughly equivalent to the 'whisky money', and to be administered by committees combining representatives of School Boards and county councils, enabled the expansion of post-elementary provision attached to elementary schools. They, too, were now allowed to present pupils for the Leaving Certificate.

Next came efforts to demarcate the elementary phase of schooling more clearly. A Merit Certificate, initially instituted in 1892 for children over thirteen in the elementary school, had by 1903 been metamorphosed into a Qualifying Examination to be taken by all children of twelve in the elementary school. Those who did best were eligible to go on to secondary schools providing a five-year course which culminated in the Leaving Certificate. The next best could pursue a three-year 'intermediate' course at a secondary school. The remainder stayed in the elementary schools, working at 'supplementary' courses, which lasted two years.

Between 1905 and 1907, too, the SED began to wind up pupil-teacher schemes in the elementary schools, directing intending teachers instead towards secondary schooling. Finally, the Education (Scotland) Act of 1908 consolidated the grant system, facilitating the development of a bursary scheme which made provision for ex-elementary school pupils at higher class schools at least as generous as that represented by the English Free Place regulations.

III

The second half of the nineteenth century had thus seen both a vast growth in and an attempt at systematisation of secondary schooling. There was likewise significant growth and innovation in the university sector, although the absolute scale of this was still so small that the changes can only be called 'vast' in a relative sense. Higher education was still accessible only to a tiny minority.

Admissions to Oxford and Cambridge began to move steadily upwards from the 1870s, but even by 1899 were averaging only around 820 and 930 a year respectively. In 1901 the male student populations of Oxford and Cambridge were 2,537 and 2,880.

Of at least equal moment were changes in the composition of the university population, in the structure of university government and in the curriculum. The 1870s saw the arrival at Oxford and Cambridge both of dissenters and of women. The legislation for the abolition of University Tests in 1871 untied both undergraduate places and fellowships and in the process allowed fellows of colleges to marry. Fellowship reforms combined with curriculum specialisation to pave the way for the development of an academic profession.

The growing regiment of dons' wives was augmented by a small file of women students. Emily Davies's College was founded at Hitchin in 1869 and moved to Girton, near Cambridge, in 1873. Henry Sidgwick and Anne Jemima Clough opened the residence which became Newnham College, in 1871. In Oxford, 1879 brought the foundation of Somerville, Lady Margaret Hall and the Society for Home Students, which eventually became St Anne's; followed in 1886 by St Hugh's and in 1892 by St Hilda's. But the numbers were tiny: in 1900–1, 296 women students at Cambridge and 239 at Oxford.[41] And women did not become full members of the university in Oxford until 1919 and in Cambridge until 1948.

The Royal and Statutory Commissions of the 1850s had begun the process of overhauling college statutes and strengthening the central

[41] Stone, 'Oxford Student Body', Appendix IV, Tables 1a and 1b; Janet Howarth and Mark Curthoys, 'The Political Economy of Women's Higher Education in Late-Nineteenth and Early-Twentieth Century Britain', *Historical Research*, 60 (1987), pp. 208–31, Table 1, pp. 210–11.

organs of university government. A second sequence of these in the 1870s proposed to continue the process, although their more ambitious plans were spoiled by the fall in colleges' income brought about by the agricultural depression. At the same time, a reassertion of control over teaching and pastoral responsibilities by many colleges counter-balanced such trends towards centralisation very powerfully.

As far as the formal curriculum went, the end of the 1840s had already seen the first breaches in the dominance of Classics and Mathematics, namely the creation of the Natural and Moral Sciences Triposes in Cambridge and of undergraduate courses in History and Law in both universities. In the early 1870s these were split, allowing the emergence of two separate courses in History and Law; and the 1890s saw the arrival of courses in English and Modern Languages.

In parallel, came the emergence of research as a systematic post-graduate activity. In Arts subjects the case for it had been argued as early as the 1840s by H. H. Vaughan; although in his tenure of the Regius Chair of Modern History at Oxford he had set a poor example. It was only really becoming an established feature by the end of the century. Systematic research in the sciences had established itself somewhat earlier, primarily through the sponsorship of a handful of wealthy colleges, in Cambridge notably Trinity and St John's. But Cambridge as a whole benefited from the munificent benefaction of the Duke of Devonshire in 1871, creating the Cavendish Laboratory. The somnolence of the eighteenth century had been decisively left behind.

Changes in Oxbridge, however, were only a pale reflection of the changes outside it. By 1900 there were more students, women as well as men, in higher education in Great Britain outside Oxford and Cambridge than within them. A variety of undergraduate and post-graduate courses were on offer; and other universities besides the Scottish ones were in receipt of state funds. The sequence of foundations was as follows:

1851	Owen's College, Manchester
1871	Newcastle
1872	University College of Wales, Aberystwyth
1874	Leeds
1874	Mason College, Birmingham
1876	Bristol
1879	Firth College, Sheffield

1881   Liverpool
1881   Nottingham
1883   Cardiff
1883   Bangor
1892   Reading
1902   Southampton

Many of these institutions began by taking external London degree examinations before seeking Royal Charters to enable them to grant their own degrees.

Other institutions, often likewise exploiting the London examining umbrella, proliferated in London itself; including the medical schools attached to the teaching hospitals; in South Kensington the Royal School of Mines, the Royal College of Science and the Central Technical College, which in 1907 were to form the giant Imperial College of Science and Technology; the London School of Economics and Political Science (1895); and the women's colleges, Bedford (1849), Westfield (1882) and Royal Holloway (1886). But the University of London only acquired a teaching as well as an examining function in 1899, following the University of London Act of 1898, which brought all these and other institutions together in a complex and uneasy federation.

By 1900–1 full-time students in England outside Oxford and Cambridge totalled 7,943; those in Wales a further 1,253 and those in Scotland another 5,151. Of this grand total of 14,347, 2,749 were women.[42] The University of London had admitted women to all its degrees since 1878.

Most of these establishments were operating on a shoe-string, especially compared to the endowments of Oxford and Cambridge. In individual cities like Birmingham, university colleges benefited from the generosity of wealthy local industrialists like the Chamberlain family. But the University College of Wales at Aberystwyth was so poor that the size of the chapel collections on the annual 'University Sunday' was of crucial importance. The Scottish universities, as we have seen, were already in receipt of some government funding; and from 1839 the University of London secured a small recurrent grant in recognition of the imperial and colonial as well as domestic function of its examining umbrella. In 1883–4 the Welsh parliamentary lobby succeeded in securing short-term grant aid for the three Welsh

---

[42] Howarth and Curthoys, 'Political Economy', Table 1.

colleges; and in 1889 the Treasury finally conceded the principle of grant aid to the English institutions outside Oxford and Cambridge. By 1906 persistent lobbying had forced direct Treasury grants to universities up to £100,000. From 1892 onwards the annual grant to the Scottish universities was running at £72,000 per annum.[43]

Thus by 1900 the state was irrevocably involved in the governance and funding of universities in Great Britain. But with a full-time student population, including Oxford and Cambridge, of 20,000, they catered still for an elite. By 1914 only 1 per cent of the age group were entering university. Our knowledge of their social background is so far patchy. But it looks as though the dominance of the landed gentry and clergy was gradually reduced by the advance of the new professional middle classes. And outside Oxford and Cambridge, by 1914, the children of the lower middle classes and skilled artisans were beginning to appear. Nearly a third of Cambridge men 1850–99 had fathers who were clergymen. The sons of landowners represented another fifth. But the sons of doctors and lawyers were yet another fifth. By 1910 at Oxford, the sons of the landed gentry and clergy had fallen to only 28 per cent of the student population and a scattering of the sons of janitors, servants, postal and transport workers had appeared. At Mason College, Birmingham, in 1893, the only year for which we have any data, the sons and daughters of professional men again were a sizeable group – nearly 37 per cent. But the children of the lower middle class accounted for another 37 per cent and those of artisans for almost 13 per cent.[44]

Oxford, Cambridge and Mason College apart, we know most about the composition of the Scottish student body, because of the controversy that has raged over the question of the 'anglicisation' of the Scottish universities. Did the changes in courses and entrance requirements that were the price of the continuation and increase in the government's financial support, culminating in the work of the Statutory Commission of 1889, amount to a reconstruction on the English model? Did they put an end to the possibility whereby 'the lad o' parts' might make his way from ploughtail to university?

The reality seems to be paler and less dramatic. Certainly at the end of the nineteenth century Scottish universities looked more like

---

[43] R. O. Berdahl, *British Universities and the State* (Berkeley, 1959), pp. 52–3; Anderson, *Education and Opportunity*, p. 286.

[44] Michael Sanderson, *Educational Opportunity and Social Change in England* (1987), pp. 42–3; Stone, 'Oxford Student Body', p. 67.

those in England and Wales than they had at the beginning. Highly specialised courses existed beside, and as an alternative to, the traditional general ones; and the matriculation qualifying requirements had been replaced by a single consolidated examination. But there were still large numbers of students who took no degree at the end of their courses; and only a minority took the specialised Honours courses. The general degree course, with its broad training, was still the norm. In Glasgow in 1913–14, for example, as many as 79 per cent of students were taking this. The age at matriculation gradually drifted upwards in the last quarter of the nineteenth century. But this seems to have owed at least as much to the expansion of the secondary schools as to the new matriculation examination; and in 1913–14 there was still a wider spread of ages among Scottish students than among those at Oxbridge. As for 'lads o'parts', there is no evidence that opportunities for the sons of unskilled workers, labourers, miners or crofters to get to the universities changed much – either decreasing or increasing – over the century as a whole. The expansion of secondary provision from the 1880s, both endowed and rate-aided, reinforced subsequently by the munificence of the Carnegie Trust and the national bursary policy developed by the SED, did, however, increase the opportunities for the children, daughters as well as sons, of the labour aristocrats and the lower middle class, skilled workers, shopkeepers and small farmers to get to university. By 1914 they were a more significant presence among Scottish students than those children of the service trades at Oxford.[45]

1914–50

By 1914 England, Wales and Scotland had something which could be called an educational system; and all members of the society were expected to have some encounter with formal schooling. For many, of them, however, that encounter might be a minimal one; and the categories into which this 'system' was organised, elementary, secondary, higher, were still recognisably associated with class. Secondary schools were now established as the royal routes to both gentility and respectability, routes which by definition only some could take. The great divide lay thus between elementary and

[45]   George Davie, The Democratic Intellect: Scotland and her Universities in the Nineteenth Century (Edinburgh, 1961), and Anderson, Education and Opportunity, chaps. 7 and 8 and Appendix II.

secondary schooling. Some mobility between these tracks was now possible; but it was the exception rather than the rule. The years 1914–50 saw a small extension of school life for everyone and the first systematic efforts to turn the elementary and secondary tracks into sequential stages, appropriate to age rather than to social groupings. Likewise, there was a parallel attempt to extend access to higher education. The limited extension that there was, however, owed at least as much to changes in the demographic balance, to the fall in the size of the five to fourteen age group between 1915 and 1945, as it did to the tinkering of central government. On the eve of the Second World War, access to secondary schooling and even more to higher education was still a function of social class.

I

The reappraisal of the social and political structure precipitated by the First World War included education. The plans made by H. A. L. Fisher, Lloyd George's President of the Board of Education, and his department for educational reconstruction were ambitious. But the rapidly deepening depression of the postwar years put paid to many of these; a number of sections of Fisher's Education Act of 1918 were never implemented.

One of the few pieces of reconstruction to be carried through – perhaps because the government was frightened of the electoral consequences of reneging – was an improvement in teachers' pay and conditions of service. Separate legislation in 1918 created a state-supported pension scheme for teachers in maintained schools. Fisher also lent his weight to the creation of a national standing joint negotiating committee, with representatives both of the LEAs – the employers – and of the teachers' unions, chaired by the newspaper magnate Lord Burnham. Their first report dealt with war bonuses, transfer payments and minimum scales. Because of wartime and immediate postwar inflation, teachers were only slightly better off in 1920 than they had been in 1914. But with the fall in prices from 1921 onwards they gained substantially; and the combination of this with the security brought by the pension scheme did much to eradicate the bitterness left over from the piece-rates of the payment by results era.

The habits and relationships derived from payment by results were also undermined in quite another way, that is, by a radical reappraisal of teaching methods in the infant school. This was already under way before the war, both triggered and represented by the work of the American John Dewey and the Italian Maria Montessori. Their arguments that education must be 'child-centred', that play had a central role in the learning processes of young children, found a ready audience among the English disciples of Froebel and ethical socialists like Margaret MacMillan.

Such an approach became the orthodoxy in the teaching of five- to seven-year-olds and began to affect approaches to the teaching of seven- to nine-year-olds in the interwar years. The classrooms gay with the children's own paintings, equipped with weighing scales, water-measuring jugs, modelling clay, building bricks, Wendy houses, toyshops, so familiar to mid- and late twentieth-century English children, first began to be seen and then to be widely copied in the years following 1920.

One of the few sections of Fisher's 1918 Education Act to come into effect was the abolition of all remaining English bye-laws allowing half-time exemptions from school attendance for children over ten. The act also raised the school leaving age to fourteen. It provided, indeed, for the raising of the age an additional year, to fifteen, in the very near future; but this was one of the provisions which kept on being postponed.

Extension of compulsory schooling into adolescence raised in an acute form questions about the nature of that schooling. Should yet another bit be tacked on to the elementary curriculum, allowed to grow out of it, rather as the old higher grade schools had done? Already eleven-plus had emerged as the preferred age for free-placers and scholarship winners to transfer to the secondary track and this underlined the need to reconsider provision for twelve-, thirteen- and fourteen-year-olds as an age group entire.

The SED, with scope for being far more *dirigiste* than ever the English Board of Education could be, had already begun to address this question in the years before the First World War. The Qualifying Examination at age twelve clearly marked the end of elementary schooling. The child's ranking in this determined what came next: full-scale secondary education, leading to the Leaving Certificate, usually taken at age seventeen, or various shorter courses, also certificated. In 1923 these were consolidated into two, the Day School (Higher) Certificate requiring three years' work and the Day School (Lower), requiring two. Both were to be offered in Advanced Divisions, which could be either separate schools or separately organised classes linked to elementary schools. The children in Advanced Divisions were expected to be the majority. The SED Circular inviting schemes from local authorities for the reorganisation of secondary education after 1918 had told them that, 'in every country only a relatively small percentage of the population will be endowed by nature with the mental equipment which they must possess if they are to profit by Secondary School or University study'.[46] The thinking was not very different in England; although the moves towards a similar model, given the scale and structure of local government, were more long-drawn-out and halting.

Given the movement of free-place-holders and scholarship winners at eleven in England, the logical step for those reviewing the education of the adolescent was to propose either a break or at least a punctuation point for all children at eleven. The Board of Education's Consultative Committee, chaired by Sir Henry Hadow, argued in 1926 that education up to eleven should be renamed 'primary'. 'Post-primary', or as they hoped it would come to be called, secondary, education should then be provided in three types of institutions, 'grammar schools' – existing maintained secondary schools – 'modern schools' and 'senior classes', the last housed with the elementary/primary school. Their successors, reporting in 1939 under the chairmanship of Sir Will Spens, went further: there should be three distinct types of secondary schools: grammar schools, technical schools and modern schools.

The Board of Education accepted these reports as providing appropriate guidelines. But they had no financial carrots to offer and implementation depended entirely upon the energy, resources, demographic situation and political configuration of the individual LEA. By 1938 only 64 per cent of those children over eleven in public elementary schools in England and Wales were in schools which had attempted some separation and reorganisation of provision for the older children. The remainder (some 600,000 children) were still in entirely un-reorganised schools.[47]

In parallel went efforts to define more clearly the nature of selective secondary education and to expand access to it. Some order had finally been established in the jungle of examinations on offer to English

---

[46] Quoted in T. R. Bone, *School Inspection in Scotland 1840–1966* (Scottish Council for Research in Education Publications, No. 57, Edinburgh, 1968), p. 183.

[47] Sutherland, *Ability, Merit and Measurement*, Appendix I, Table 2.

secondary schools in 1917, with the achievement of agreement amongst the examining boards as to the standards and core subjects of a School Certificate and a Higher School Certificate, to be taken at the age of sixteen and eighteen respectively. In 1920 a Departmental Committee of the Board of Education, chaired by Fisher's friend Edward Hilton Young, proposed a major expansion of free-place provision. But implementation of this fell victim to financial blight, as did the schemes of the Labour governments of 1924 and 1929–31. Finally in 1932 the National Government replaced free places with 'special' or means-tested places. The majority of LEAs retained two separate modes of entry to their secondary or 'grammar' schools, as, using the Hadow terminology, they were increasingly coming to be called: what had become a highly competitive examination for those from public elementary schools, aiming for scholarships or special places; and what was more like a qualifying examination for those whose parents were able to pay the full fee. But a handful of LEAs – rising to thirty-six by 1938 – responded by abolishing a separate examination for fee-payers and making all their grammar school places means-tested or special places.

At least as significant as any of this tinkering was the fall in the child population aged between five and fourteen by about one and one third of a million in England and Wales between 1921 and 1938. This improved the chances of access to a selective secondary school for children of all social classes. In 1938 about 50 per cent more of the thirteen-year-olds in the population were in grant-aided secondary education than had been in 1921.

But in absolute terms this was only 85,000 children, about 13 per cent of the whole age group.[48] Selective secondary schooling, still, in many people's eyes, the only true secondary schooling, was still the preserve of an elite, its primacy as the route to both respectability and gentility unchallenged. School Certificate, Higher School Certificate and the Scottish Leaving Certificate were indispensable preliminaries to university entrance. Leaving and School Certificates were also fast becoming the essential passports to non-graduate white-collar employment in banks, businesses and solicitors' firms.

Despite scholarships, bursaries, free-place and qualifying examinations, this elite continued to be as much a social as an intellectual one. The meritocracy was still some way off. At the end of the 1930s

---

[48] *Ibid.*, Appendix I, Commentary and Table 1.2.

in England and Wales, the boy with a professional or managerial father was four times as likely to go to grammar school as the boy whose father was a skilled manual worker, and five times as likely to do so as the boy whose father was an unskilléd manual worker. The girl whose father was in a professional or managerial occupation was seven times more likely to go to grammar school than the girl whose father was an unskilled manual worker.[49]

There were a cluster of interlocking reasons for this. Those parents who could pay the fees could still buy their children places at many selective secondary schools. Not all English LEAs examined their whole population of eleven-year-olds as a matter of course; and many working-class parents chose not to enter their children for free- or special-place examinations. Places might be free, or with reduced fees, but there were usually hidden costs of uniform, equipment and travel, as well as the opportunity cost of the child's earnings once the age for compulsory attendance was past. For similar reasons working-class parents in areas where the examination was taken by everyone declined places at grammar or higher class schools offered to their children.

Moreover, when working-class children did sit the examinations they tended, as a group, to do less well than their middle-class peers. Allegations of coaching and cramming aside, it became plain that the usual attainments tests in English and Arithmetic presented fewer problems for children from the better-equipped primary schools of suburbia, supported by comfortable, literate homes. A number of LEAs, both in England and Scotland, began to experiment with the use of group intelligence tests in attempts to identify and 'measure' abilities not susceptible to improvement/development by such influences. Even when working-class children did surmount all these hurdles and get to selective secondary schools, they figured in dispro-portionately large numbers among the 'early leavers', dropping out after, or even before, the School Certificate examination at sixteen. The pressures which operated to discourage some working-class parents from even contemplating a grammar school place for their child operated with full force on those families who gave it a try. And these were the material pressures. There were also cultural press-ures. As Richard Hoggart put it, the working-class scholarship boy

---

[49] Jean Floud, 'The Educational Experience of the Adult Population of England and Wales as at July 1949', in D. V. Glass, ed., *Social Mobility in Britain* (1954), p. 107.

'is between two worlds of school and home; and they meet at few points'.[50]

The reconstruction plans of the Second World War brought renewed efforts to complete the transformation of 'elementary' into 'primary' and to make clearly separate and different educational provision for all older children. The Scots had already begun on this process under legislation of 1936. Butler's Education Act of 1944 and the Education (Scotland) Act of 1945 finally redeemed the promise to raise the school leaving age to fifteen. The Butler Act also required all LEAs to produce plans for free and universal secondary schooling, in the process re-organising out of existence the remaining all-age elementary schools.

These plans were approved and implemented in the decade following the end of the war. One authority, Anglesey, took advantage of its thinly spread, predominantly rural population to create common or comprehensive secondary schools. Everyone else in England and Wales followed the Spens Report model, developing three distinct types of secondary school: grammar – their existing maintained secondary schools – technical schools and modern schools, some of these last with new buildings, some the 'higher tops' of the old elementary schools, now more carefully physically separated from 'junior' and primary schools. In Scotland the division was between senior secondary schools, whose pupils were expected to take the Leaving Certificate, and junior secondary schools, the old Advanced Divisions upgraded.

The Scottish Qualifying Examination at twelve-plus was already long established as the mechanism for allocating children to different types of post-elementary and secondary schooling. In England and Wales, the 'Eleven-Plus', the examination to select scholars and free- and special-place-holders, completed the transition to the same function. It became compulsory everywhere. Tests in English and Arithmetic, now almost invariably supplemented by an intelligence test, were used to classify the entire eleven-year-old population of each primary school, to determine to which schools they should go next.

'Classifying' is a neutral-sounding word. But this process was also a ranking process. The three types of secondary school were supposed to enjoy parity of esteem: in reality the status hierarchy was as clear

[50]   Richard Hoggart, *The Uses of Literacy* (1957; paperback edn. 1968), p. 296. For some experiences of scholarship *girls*, both in England and in Scotland, see Liz Heron, ed., *Truth, Dare or Promise: Girls Growing Up in the Fifties* (1985).

as that of the Taunton Commission's first, second and third grade schools had ever been. At the top came the grammar school, then the technical school, then the secondary modern school. Likewise, the Scottish senior secondary school clearly out-ranked the junior secondary school.

There were more grammar school places than there had been. In the process of reorganisation a number of LEAs in England and Wales tried to expand their provision; and by the early 1950s about 20 per cent of the age group nationally were securing grammar school places. But this average concealed gross variations in provision between one authority and another; and any general gains the postwar expansion might bring were soon to be negated by the impact of the postwar 'baby boom'. The supply of children grew even faster than the supply of grammar school places. The cohort born 1943–52 were to find their chances of getting to grammar school less good than those of the cohort born 1933–42 had been.

At the beginning of the 1950s, thus, selective secondary schooling was still for the few; and even fewer of these came from the working class. Of grammar school entrants in places as widely different as south-west Hertfordshire and Middlesbrough in 1953, only 9 per cent were the children of unskilled manual workers. Access to Scottish senior secondary schools in this immediate postwar period was less skewed by social class and more nearly meritocratic than anything in England.[51] But both north and south of the Border mechanisms of selection, and indeed the very principle, were to come under increasingly critical scrutiny in the course of the 1950s.

II

The pattern of development in higher education 1914–50 was not dissimilar from that in primary and secondary education. Financial stringency and interwar depression bit less deeply than in other sectors of education, perhaps because the sums involved were relatively small; and the contraction of the child population brought easement here too. Overall, there was an increase in the number of places provided and the state became ever more heavily involved in the funding, if not the direction, of higher education. But like the grammar schools,

[51] Sanderson, *Educational Opportunity*, pp. 45–7; Keith Hope, *As Others See Us: Schooling and Social Mobility in Scotland and the United States* (Cambridge, 1984).

the universities remained the preserve of an elite, social as much as intellectual.

H. A. L. Fisher was an academic historian before – and indeed after – he was a cabinet minister and he fought hard for the interests of universities between 1917 and 1922. He wrung a series of important financial contributions out of the Treasury; first there was a non-recurrent grant of £0.5m to replace at least some of the fee and other income lost during wartime; second, the level of recurrent grant was raised to £1m in 1919–20. He attempted also to establish a mechanism to maintain momentum in the pressure for funds. From 1904 a committee had advised the Treasury on grants to universities in England. Fisher in 1919 secured the reconstitution and formalisation of this committee, henceforward to advise on grants in aid of both recurrent and capital expenditure at all universities in the UK. Its first President, William McCormick, had appropriately been secretary to the Carnegie Trust, the great benefactor of the Scottish universities, and brought with him the system of quinquennial planning that the Trust had devised.[52]

Fisher fought also for financial support for students. In June 1919 the cabinet agreed to a grant to LEAs towards maintenance allowances to those in education above the elementary level; and in 1920 the Board of Education itself established 200 scholarships for students going from secondary education to university. These State Scholarships were to be divided equally between men and women and were to be awarded by the seven university-based examining boards who set examinations for secondary schools. In 1930 their numbers were increased to 300 and in 1936 to 360. These supplied a new rung to the educational ladder as important as that provided by the Free Place Regulations of 1907.

Oxford and Cambridge had for the first time joined the universities' deputation to ask for increased public subsidy in 1918. Interim awards were made to them but regular and recurrent state financial help was made dependent upon further enquiry into their structure of government and existing financial resources – another Royal Commission, which reported in 1922. The recommendations of this carried yet a little further the process of developing and strengthening the central organs of university government which had begun in the 1850s. Between 1924 and 1926 two Statutory Commissions did the detailed work on the universities' statutes needed to give effect to the Royal

---

[52] Geoffrey Sherington, *English Education, Social Change and War 1911–20* (Manchester, 1981), p. 131; Anderson, *Education and Opportunity*, p. 288.

Commission's recommendations; and thereafter the two universities came under the aegis of the University Grants Committee with all the others. In addition, four new university colleges joined the ranks of the clients of the UGC in the 1920s, Exeter in 1922, Swansea in 1923 and Hull and Leicester in 1927.

By the end of the 1920s, thus, central government had an established place in the funding of all higher education. But it is important not to overestimate this or the scope it might be thought to offer for policy direction. In absolute terms the grants were very small – about £2m a year in the mid-thirties – and represented only a third of total university income. Even outside Oxbridge, no university received as much as half its income from the UGC in 1935, St Andrew's being the most dependent, with 46 per cent of its income deriving from the UGC grant. Thus most universities retained considerable room for manoeuvre – and freedom from parliamentary audit.

They did not use this in any dramatic way. There were no major changes of direction or innovations in fields of study. At Oxford and Cambridge the majority of students – 80 per cent and 70 per cent respectively – were in the arts faculties; and only in London, Manchester, Leeds and Edinburgh did science dominate.[53]

State scholarships and the fall in the child population allowed some expansion of numbers and a little broadening of the social base. In 1938–9 there were 50,000 full-time students in universities in Great Britain. Just under a quarter of these were women. Almost all came from middle- and upper-class backgrounds. No child born to an unskilled or semi-skilled father before 1910 could expect to get to university at all. Of children born to an unskilled or semi-skilled father between 1920 and 1929, 0.5 per cent might expect to find their way there.[54]

The Second World War brought manpower planning on an unprecedented scale. It underlined especially the need for skilled manpower, preparing the ground for a radical review of the nature and extent of higher education. The undermining of university finances by war for the second time in thirty years made universities simultaneously much more dependent on the state. But the impact of these changes and of demographic pressure on demand for university places and

---

[53] John Carswell, *Government and the Universities in Britain: Programme and Performance 1960–1980* (Cambridge, 1985), pp. 8–9, 11.
[54] Sanderson, *Educational Opportunity*, pp. 42–4; *Report of the Committee on Higher Education* (the Robbins Report), PP 1962–3, XI, App. 2(A), para. 13.

expectations of the role of a higher education system began to be felt only in the second half of the 1950s. In the immediate postwar period the university scene seemed remarkably unchanged. A new university college opened its doors at Keele in Staffordshire in 1949. In the four years from 1945 student numbers were swelled sharply by demobilised servicemen and women. Thereafter they fell back. In 1954, 3.2 per cent of the age group were going to university, 3.8 per cent of boys and 1.5 per cent of girls. Of these 0.5 per cent were the children of semi-skilled or unskilled fathers.[55]

The primary school of the 1950s thus looked very different from the elementary school of a century earlier. The existence of the Eleven-Plus examination made for a continuing formality in the work of the older children, the nine- and ten-year-olds. But in general its atmosphere and style were relaxed, informal, an emphasis on creativity rather than on a barrack-room drilling. It was the school for the vast bulk of the child population of the appropriate age group, much closer to a common school than to a class school. The class origins of secondary schooling were, by contrast, much easier still to identify. Perhaps the survival of the name is no accident? Some of the curriculum content, institutional structures and teaching styles of the selective grammar school would have been recognisable to those who encountered a maintained secondary school of 1910, or even a remodelled endowed grammar school of the 1880s. Likewise, the universities were still the preserve of an elite; and both the social and the intellectual configurations of British universities between 1920 and 1950 would have been recognisable to earlier generations.

The institutions of formal schooling have come to dominate this chapter as they came increasingly to dominate the lives of British children in the two centuries 1750–1950. By 1950 central and local government spending on education was absorbing between 3 and 4 per cent of national income. But to examine the processes of formal schooling is not to exhaust the educational experiences and modes of socialisation to which both children and adults in the society were subject. Given limited space, the necessity to trace a path through the developing institutional labyrinth of schooling gets increasingly in the way of exploring all other modes of education. We might, for example, spend much more time on the shrinkage of the place occupied by paid employment in the lives of children and young

[55] Sanderson, *Educational Opportunity*, p. 72.

adolescents; begin to consider the emergence of specific youth organisations like Scouts and Guides; consider whether evening classes and adult education groups are heirs to the autodidact tradition or a very different kind of enterprise. Charting the rise of formal schooling must be the starting point of an examination of the processes of education in the period, not its end.

CHAPTER 4

Health and medicine

VIRGINIA BERRIDGE

I THE SOCIAL HISTORY OF MEDICINE

The social history of medicine, like most social history, is primarily a development of the last two decades, and arose out of the same congruence of interests which have transformed economic and labour history into social history in that period. The older tradition of the history of medicine, which it has by no means displaced, saw the discipline as essentially inward-looking. This was a doctor-oriented version of medicine, justifying medical history as an illumination of the internal history of the profession or of the discovery or development of technical medical procedures. It assumed a Whig framework of progress towards ever-superior forms of knowledge or organisation, culminating in the state of medical practice at the present day. It therefore had a strongly biographical emphasis; the lives of the 'great men' of medicine filled the shelves of the medical history sections. The scientific basis of medical practice was seen as a series of discoveries and of contributions or advances towards present understanding; the analysis of medical institutions was in terms of celebratory histories concentrating on internal milestones of development. 'The need for a knowledge of the origin and growth of one's profession is surely self-evident', said Sir Douglas Guthrie in his Presidential address to the History of Medicine section of the Royal Society of Medicine in 1957, 'it is obvious that history supplies an essential basis for medicine. It gives us ideals to follow, inspirations for our work and hope for the future.'[1] The 'graph of medical progress' could, he considered, be depicted as 'an ever-mounting curve'.

Social history of medicine has developed with a very different focus. As George Rosen, one of the earlier exponents of a new approach, wrote, 'medicine is an activity whose developments can be most fully

[1] D. Guthrie, 'Whither Medical History?', *Medical History*, 1 (1957), pp. 307–17.

understood only when considered in relation to the network of social interaction within which it occurs'.[2] George Rosen, Erwin Ackernecht and Richard Shryock were American-based historians of medicine, who followed the pattern set by Henry Sigerist's *History of Medicine* in assessing the cultural significance of medicine and disease. Their work formed the first stage in the development of the new social history of medicine.[3] Although informed by an understanding of the social relations of medicine, it concentrated on the field of public health, with which 'social medicine' came to be identified. In England, too, many of the earlier enthusiasts for the social history of medicine in the late 1960s were themselves Medical Officers of Health or had connections with the contemporary public health scene. At around the same time, traditional medical history also came under attack from a different direction. A radical sociological critique was developed by Ivan Illich, Michel Foucault, Peter Sedgwick and Thomas Szasz, most notably, who argued that medicine had 'expropriated' health and 'constructed normality'. Medicine, they argued, exercised sociopolitical strategies of power and control in the name of apparently objective and value-free scientific knowledge.[4] Historical work, in particular in the social history of insanity, was inspired by this revisionist approach.

More recently, this 'anti-history' has itself been modified and attacked in its turn as reductionist. The sociological critique, while pertinent, still does not do justice to past experience of health and health care. It is necessary to reconstruct how sickness was dealt with and health conceptualised in past societies. We should be aware of how, for instance, the range of medical practitioners operated rather than assuming a model based on a unified medical profession. Consequently, unlicensed midwives, unqualified practitioners and herbalists, even patients themselves, have been rescued from the

---

[2]   G. Rosen, 'The New History of Medicine: A Review', *Journal of the History of Medicine and Allied Sciences*, 6 (1951), pp. 516–22.

[3]   R. Shryock, *The Development of Modern Medicine* (Philadelphia, 1936; London, 1948); H. E. Sigerist, *Civilisation and Disease* (Ithaca, 1943); E. H. Ackernecht, *Medicine at the Paris Hospital, 1794–1848* (Baltimore, 1967); G. Rosen, *A History of Public Health* (New York, 1958). For further discussion, see C. Webster, 'The Historiography of Medicine' in P. Corsi and P. Weindling, eds., *Information Sources in the History of Science and Medicine* (1983), pp. 29–43.

[4]   I. Illich, *Medical Nemesis: The Expropriation of Health* (1975); M. Foucault, *The Birth of the Clinic: An Archaeology of Medical Perception* (1975); P. Sedgwick, *Psycho-Politics* (1982); T. Szasz, *The Manufacture of Madness: A Comparative Study of the Inquisition and the Mental Health Movement* (New York, 1970); I. Kennedy, *The Unmasking of Medicine* (1981).

'condescension of posterity'.[5] The area of interest is now what Charles Webster has called 'the total relationship of health and social forces'.[6] The concepts of health and disease are being used to examine general issues of social relations and popular belief. In this general area, approaches differ. The social history of medicine has in recent years drawn on approaches and concepts ranging through demography, gender studies to economics and ethnography.[7] But there is a more fundamental division. Paul Weindling has pointed to two forms of social history of medicine, one seeking to reconstruct collectivities, the role of health care in past communities, the other portraying individuals and their characteristics in order to establish their social relevance. In his view, the result of the latter approach is 'to exchange the Whig concept of professional advance for the Whiggery of historical individualism in the realm of patients and practitioners'.[8]

That such debates can occur is testimony to the current vigour of the social history of medicine. The question of function is part of the debate. The earlier social historians saw the discipline as contributing to an understanding of contemporary medical and public health problems. To Thomas McKeown 'the social history of medicine is medicine with the public interest put in'.[9] Yet this is too narrow, albeit a necessary perspective. The tensions in health care in the 1980s and the political willingness to invoke idealised 'Victorian values' have meant that historians cannot simply ignore contemporary relevance. But relevance cannot be the only function. Nor does the social history of medicine, as has been argued, simply add a dimension to the pre-existing history of medicine specialism. The social history of medicine is an integral part of, and structured by, the philosophical and theoretical perspectives of social history. It is, in its turn, the basic history of medicine.

[5] For example, see R. Porter, ed., *Patients and Practitioners: Lay Perceptions of Medicine in Pre-Industrial Society* (Cambridge, 1985); also R. Porter and A. Wear, eds., *Problems and Methods in the History of Medicine* (1987).
[6] C. Webster, 'Social History and Medical Science', *Bulletin of the Society for the Social History of Medicine* (hereafter *Bull. SSHM*), 19 (1976), pp. 1–3.
[7] For other influences on the social history of medicine, see M. MacDonald, 'Anthropological Perspectives on the History of Science and Medicine', and L. J. Jordanova, 'The Social Sciences and History of Science and Medicine', in Corsi and Weindling, eds., *Information Sources*, pp. 61–79, 81–95. The articles by Pelling, Corsi and Weindling in this volume should also be consulted.
[8] P. Weindling, 'Patients and Practitioners: Virtues and Vices of the New Social History of Medicine', *History Workshop*, 24 (1987), pp. 191–4.
[9] T. McKeown, 'A Sociological Approach to the History of Medicine', *Medical History*, 14 (1970), pp. 342–51.

II THE SETTING AND SOME THEMES

The changes in British society in this period easily lend themselves to some debate around the notion of progress in health and medicine. The rapid rise in population from nearly 9 million in 1781 to 20 million in 1851, the movement of rural workers into the rapidly industrialising cities and the lack of basic services and amenities all had clear consequences for health. John Aikin's verdict on Manchester in 1795 presents one side of the coin:

> the poor are crowded in offensive, dark, damp and incommodious habitations, cellars are so damp as to be unfit for habitation ... the poor often suffer from the shattered state of cellar windows. This is a trifling circumstance in appearance, but the consequences to the inhabitants are of the most serious kind. Fevers are among the most usual effects; and I have often known consumptions which could be traced to this cause. Inveterate rheumatic complaints, which disable the sufferer from every kind of employment, are often produced in the same manner.[10]

From this zenith of health, so it has been argued, came progress in health and in medical care. Declining mortality, increased access to medical services, the impact of new technologies and therapies on disease all came into play. Legislative milestones marked the way – the 1848 Public Health Act; the 1911 National Health Insurance Act; the establishment of the National Health Service in 1948. But the 'progressive' view of health and medicine has been seriously revised. Perhaps better nutrition rather than medical technology led to improved health in the nineteenth century.[11] In any case, mortality, and in particular infant mortality, did not decline very noticeably until just before the First World War. Infant mortality was still high enough at the time of the Boer War to cause concern about deterioration of the race. The National Health Service itself had serious structural flaws which have marked subsequent health service planning.

As this chapter will indicate, the language of progress is inadequate. We also need to consider among other questions how medicine consolidated itself as a profession, more prestigious in the 'health division of labour' than professions such as pharmacy or dentistry, or than the mainly gender-specific occupations of nursing and midwifery. Such a question is bound up, on the one hand, with the increasing

---

[10] Quoted in R. Porter, *English Society in the Eighteenth Century* (1982), p. 355.
[11] A view initially advanced by T. McKeown. See, for example, T. McKeown, *The Modern Rise of Population* (1976).

differentiation between orthodox and unorthodox medical practice, and, on the other, with medicine's growing involvement with the activities, and policies, of the state in the nineteenth century. The 'rise of the institution' – be it hospital or asylum – provided another potential source of power. What impact did such activities have in terms of the reduction of sickness and of mortality? We need to consider what 'scientific' medicine or 'public health' medicine effectively achieved, and to analyse the increasing division between the two approaches. The relationship between medicine and the state has taken new forms in the twentieth century. How and why was health policy formed? What was the rationale – and effectiveness – of the forms of health care organisation adopted? Across this range of issues, much research still remains to be done. The efflorescence of research into the social history of medicine in recent years has done much to open up the subject. But, for lack of evidence, it is still more difficult, for example, to delineate 'lay' than 'professional' medicine. Much research, too, has concentrated on the nineteenth century or on the development of health policy in the twentieth century. Until recently, the social history of eighteenth-century medicine was relatively neglected. The eighteenth century was seen either as the preface to nineteenth-century medical progress, or, conversely, as a period when the Enlightenment and medicine together engineered a new age of secular medicalised control.[12] But the concept of 'medical police', the recruitment of the medical profession to control social morals through public hygiene, is perhaps more appropriate for the Enlightened Absolutism of the German states than for England.[13] The Enlightenment did have a profound impact and health matters were secularised. The gentlemanly ethos of enlightened conspicuous philanthropy underpinned local institutional health provision by the rich for the poor. The Englightenment concern for bodily fulfilment rather than suffering and pain justified medical interventionism.[14] The eighteenth century also provided a wide range of social forms and alternatives in medicine preceding the more familiar formal structures of the next century. There was a well-developed critique among the literate laity

[12] Compare P. Gay, 'The Enlightenment as Medicine and as Cure', in W. H. Barber *et al.*, eds., *The Age of the Enlightenment: Studies Presented to Theodore Besterman* (Edinburgh, 1967); and, for example, M. Foucault, *Madness and Civilisation: A History of Insanity in the Age of Reason* (1967).

[13] G. Rosen, *From Medical Police to Social Medicine* (New York, 1974).

[14] For discussion of these points, see R. Porter, 'Was there a Medical Enlightenment in Eighteenth Century England?', *British Journal of Eighteenth Century Studies*, 5 (1982), pp. 49–63.

with practitioners joining in as equals rather than exclusive experts.[15] Medical entrepreneurship was the order of the day. Georgian quacks and orthodox medical men were united in their attachment to commercial imperatives at the time of the growth of a consumer society.[16]

III   1750–c.1900

The provision of medical care; the medical profession

One 'progressive' notion raised by eighteenth-century, and earlier, research is the idea that medical care was only adequately provided when the medical profession emerged in recognisably 'modern' form in the nineteenth century. Work on early modern and eighteenth-century medicine has stressed that traditional healers should be placed centre-stage rather than be relegated to the borderland of 'quacks' and charlatans.[17] The provision of medical care has, however, been dominated by discussions of the process of professionalisation, most notably in connection with medical practitioners but also for pharmacy, nursing and midwifery. For doctors in particular, there has been disagreement among historians because of different criteria adopted for the definition of the concept. As Margaret Pelling has pointed out, the process of professionalisation has both positive and negative aspects. On the positive side, high status, autonomy and institutionalisation are involved, with some relation to public interest. On the other hand, professionalisation can be seen as a middle-class conspiracy aimed at self-interested control of a particular market.[18] Clearly, both aspects are demonstrated in the history of professionalisation in medicine. The traditional view for doctors saw the years between 1794 and 1858 as the 'Age of Medical Reform'. During these years, so it was argued, the rank and file of the profession, the

---

[15] R. Porter, 'Lay Medical Knowledge in the Eighteenth Century: The Evidence of the Gentleman's Magazine', Medical History, 29 (1985), pp. 138–68.

[16] These points are discussed in R. Porter, ed., Patients and Practitioners; W. F. Bynum and R. Porter, eds., William Hunter and the Eighteenth-Century Medical World (Cambridge, 1985); W. F. Bynum, 'Health, Disease and Medical Care', in G. S. Rousseau and R. Porter, eds., The Ferment of Knowledge (Cambridge, 1980), pp. 211–54. See also R. Porter, Disease, Medicine and Society in England, 1550–1860 (1987), chap. 4.

[17] M. Pelling and C. Webster, 'Medical Practitioners', in C. Webster, ed., Health, Medicine and Mortality in the Sixteenth Century (Cambridge, 1979), pp. 165–235; also J. Barry, 'Publicity and the Public Good: Presenting Medicine in Eighteenth-Century Bristol', in W. F. Bynum and R. Porter, eds., Medical Fringe and Medical Orthodoxy (1987), pp. 29–39, and other contributions in this volume.

[18] M. Pelling, 'Medical Practice in the Early Modern Period: Trade or Profession?', in W. Prest, ed., The Professions in Early Modern England (1987).

surgeon-apothecaries, changed from an undifferentiated mass of lowly and ill-educated practitioners, barely distinguishable from the host of bone-setters, midwives, 'wise-women' and patent medicine vendors into a respectable, scientifically trained and professionally organised occupation with a considerable degree of public status and esteem. The basic division in English medicine, the consultant/general practitioner divide, was established during these years.[19]

This view does have something to recommend it. The tripartite structure of the medical profession, which defined the social structure of the profession and in theory the division of medical labour, was no longer operating well by the end of the eighteenth century. The hierarchical division between the Royal College of Physicians, the Company of Surgeons (speaking for the more lowly Barber Surgeons' Company in 1745 and becoming the Royal College of Surgeons of London in 1800) and the Society of Apothecaries, the organising body for those who dispensed drugs, no longer corresponded to the way in which medical practice actually worked. Apothecaries, as well as prescribing and dispensing, also performed minor surgical operations, while surgeons prescribed medicines as well as operating. The old corporate order was breaking down.[20] Medical organisations and societies cutting across established structures were established; and it was the reform movement led by one of these societies, the Association of Apothecaries and Surgeon Apothecaries, which led to the passing of the Apothecaries Act of 1815. After it, no one could legally enter on a career as an apothecary without a licence. The act was seen as a 'milestone' on the way to the 'modern' status of the general practitioner.

But some of these basic structures must now be subject to serious revision. Was there substantial discontinuity between eighteenth- and nineteenth-century rank-and-file practitioners? Medical care was growing rapidly in the eighteenth century. Georgian doctors operated in a medical marketplace based on rapidly expanding consumer demand. Geoffrey Holmes has argued that the modern doctor arrived in the period between 1680 and 1730. The tripartite system was already breaking down; and the education of doctors was improving through attendance at hospitals. The role of naval and military medicine in

[19] For the standard account of the rise of the medical profession written in the 'progressive' mode, see C. Newman, *The Evolution of Medical Education in the Nineteenth Century* (1957).

[20] G. N. Clark, *A History of the Royal College of Physicians of London*, vol. 2 (Oxford, 1966).

raising medicine's status was also important.[21] Revisionism has in addition centred on the question of substantial discontinuity between the eighteenth- and nineteenth-century rank-and-file practitioners.

Generally applicable conclusions have been prevented by lack of sustained research on the period before 1800. But there does seem to be some case for tracing elements of continuity both before and after 1800.[22] Irvine Loudon has turned the traditional interpretation on its head by showing that the eighteenth-century surgeon-apothecary was usually of good background and reasonably well trained; hospital training, in particular in the voluntary hospitals, was the norm by the end of the eighteenth century well before the passing of the 1815 act.[23] Medicine, at this level, was a profitable occupation; the surgeon-apothecaries' expansion into man midwifery in the mid-eighteenth century was an indication of a rise in status and a means to expand the boundaries of practice. It was the rise of the dispensing druggist in the 1780s and 1790s, offering cheaper medical care, which triggered off the reform movement of the early nineteenth century. The result was a medical marketplace which became increasingly over-crowded, and vicious competition for paying patients. The disparities between the general practitioners' expectations and the realities of his position were what really lay behind the campaign for reform.

So far as the 1815 act is concerned, Sidney Holloway's work has demolished any idea of it as a great reforming piece of legislation.[24] The act itself was muddled, and perpetuated the tripartite system. It degraded the general practitioner through the apprenticeship clause and failed to outlaw irregular practitioners. In fact, general

---

[21] G. Holmes, *Augustan England: Professions, State and Society, 1680–1730* (1982).

[22] I. Waddington, *The Medical Profession in the Industrial Revolution* (Dublin, 1984); see also his 'General Practitioners and Consultants in Early Nineteenth Century England: The Sociology of an Intra-Professional Conflict', in J. Woodward and D. Richards, eds., *Health Care and Popular Medicine: Essays on the Social History of Medicine* (1977), pp. 164–88; T. Gelfand, 'The Decline of the Ordinary Practitioner and the Rise of the Modern Medical Profession', in S. Statum and D. E. Larson, eds., *Doctors, Patients and Society: Power and Authority in Medical Care* (Ontario, 1981), presents the view which argues for discontinuity between eighteenth and nineteenth centuries.

[23] I. S. L. Loudon, *Medical Care and the General Practitioner, 1750–1850* (Oxford, 1987); see also his 'The Vile Race of Quacks with which this Country is Infested', in Bynum and Porter, eds., *Medical Fringe*, pp. 106–28, and J. Lane, 'The Medical Practitioners of Provincial England in 1783', *Medical History*, 28 (1984) 353–71.

[24] S. W. F. Holloway, 'The Apothecaries Act, 1815: A Reinterpretation', *Medical History*, 10 (1966), pp. 107–29 and 221–36; see also his 'Medical Education in England, 1830–58: A Sociological Analysis', *History*, 49 (1964), pp. 299–324.

practitioners were given no governing body of their own: their status was not raised but lowered. It was a compromise forced on them by the medical colleges in the struggle for power and status.

Although the general structure of the medical profession as it exists in present-day Britain was broadly in place by mid-century, the structure was confirmed by the 1858 Medical Act. The act created the single medical register and established the General Medical Council (GMC) to oversee education and licensing. There was no attempt to secure uniformity of training between the existing nineteen licensing bodies. No single basic qualification in medicine and surgery and midwifery was established, unlicensed practice was not outlawed and the GMC itself was dominated by representatives of the Royal Colleges and the Society of Apothecaries with no general practitioner representation.[25] But the act succeeded in defining the ranks of orthodox medical practitioners, at all levels, against the 'unorthodox', who were hitherto relegated from status and influence. The GMC's function of official authorisation confirmed the boundaries of the profession. The British Medical Association (BMA) developed from its earlier radical oppositional origins to become the profession's public voice.

Another vital period of professional unification and consolidation was, as Jeanne Peterson has argued, the years between 1858 and the Medical Act Amendment Act of 1886.[26] Although the bulk of the act dealt with medical licensing in the colonies, it also required that the examination of all three main branches of medicine – medicine, surgery and midwifery – be compulsory, too, so that the divisions of status both within the profession and in relation to their clientele became much clearer. In the eighteenth and early nineteenth centuries, physicians and surgeons were not consultants in the modern sense; specialisation in one organ of the body or one disease was regarded unfavourably. But changes in theory of disease and in demand for services brought developments in the structure and organisation of the profession. Specialisms multiplied in the last half of the century; this was the age of the Harley Street doctor and the consolidation of the 'new priesthood' of medical men.[27] Specialists

[25] C. Varlaam, 'The 1858 Medical Act: The Origins and the Aftermath', *Bull. SSHM*, 21 (1977), pp. 31–3.

[26] M. J. Peterson, 'Gentlemen and Medical Men: The Problem of Professional Recruitment', *Bulletin of the History of Medicine*, 58 (1984), pp. 457–73; also her *The Medical Profession in Mid-Victorian London* (Berkeley, 1978).

[27] R. Pound, *Harley Street* (1967).

were increasingly associated with hospital practice, and responded to the opportunities it afforded for teaching and for developing and exercising patronage. The general practitioner's authority over his patient, and social status, remained more indeterminate. N. D. Jewson's argument for a shift from patient-dominated medicine in the eighteenth century to a doctor-dominated system in the nineteenth broadly holds good.[28] But the changes in doctors' status which affected this position were slower to come. Medical men did not generally come from the upper ranks of society. They were the sons of 'men of the secondary professional classes or of tradesmen', of 'intelligent artisans' and sometimes tradesmen and domestic servants' families. Only 3 per cent of Fellows of the Royal College of Surgeons in the period 1800–89 could be classified as 'gentlemen' against 45 per cent of navy officers in the period 1814–49.[29]

The medical profession was increasingly overstocked in the nineteenth century as the medical teaching centres of Edinburgh, Glasgow, Oxford and Cambridge turned out their annual number of medical graduates. Medicine still suffered from a lack of independence. Interference was likely from hospital committees, patients and from sick-club committees. Many doctors had to take on uncongenial tasks such as Poor Law Medical Officer, to make ends meet. The concept of the 'family doctor' arose out of professional necessity in order to keep the support of patients and to provide confidence in the efficacy of the still limited aid a doctor could offer. But times were changing; across a variety of fronts, control within the doctor/patient relationship was shifting to the doctor around the turn of the nineteenth and twentieth centuries. The rising status of the profession was reflected in the moves by middle-class women to gain admittance. Elizabeth Garrett's success in the LSA examination in 1865 was a harbinger of the fall of the 'citadel of male monopoly' as women were enabled to qualify, in the late 1870s, through the Irish College of Physicians, Queen's University, Belfast, and the University of London. The coming of national health insurance and the National Health Service brought further changes in status and independence.

---

[28]   N. D. Jewson, 'Medical Knowledge and the Patronage System in Eighteenth Century England', *Sociology*, 8 (1974) pp. 369–85.

[29]   Peterson, *Medical Profession*; for lack of status and radicalism of the early doctors, see I. Inkster, 'Marginal Men: Aspects of the Social Role of the Medical Community in Sheffield, 1790–1850', in Woodward and Richards, eds., *Health Care and Popular Medicine*, pp. 128–63.

The other medical professions: pharmacy

Part of the pattern of tradesmen recruitment into the medical profession was the attraction it held for sons of pharmacists. Becoming a medical practitioner was a greater source of esteem than remaining in the parallel trading occupation. It was the rapid rise of the dispensing druggist that threatened the status and income of the surgeon-apothecary.[30] In 1775 in Bristol, for example, there were fifty-six surgeons and apothecaries and three druggists. By 1835, there were one hundred and four and forty-five respectively. The general ratio of medical practitioners to population was changing rapidly in the patients' favour. Some druggists were anxious to turn commercial success into professional consolidation. The process of institutional professionalism followed, and somewhat preceded that of the medical practitioners. The formation of the Pharmaceutical Society in 1841 and an initial Pharmacy Act in 1852 were followed by the 1868 Pharmacy Act – obtained against the opposition of the GMC, which wanted to register those connected with both medicine and pharmacy.[31] In a sense the 1868 act, with its regulated education system for 'pharmaceutical chemists', and its specific function of a schedule of poisons reserved for them alone to dispense, set up a tighter form of professional organisation than had the 1858 act for doctors. But, as Sidney Holloway has pointed out, the activities of Jacob Bell and the Pharmaceutical Society of Great Britain were not a response to strong demands from the chemists and druggists, who had little desire to become 'professional men'.[32] The professionalising process was an attempt by an influential sector to regulate and control the rest. The conflict between professionalism and trade was not solved by legislative control. The status of pharmacists has remained in general lower than that of doctors ever since. This had much to do – apart from the trading connection – with the pharmacist's clientele and his relationship with them. There were many levels of prosperity and graduations within the ranks. But the corner pharmacist had a predominantly working- and lower middle-class clientele. Counter-prescribing

---

[30] Loudon, *Medical Care and the General Practitioner*. Roy Porter has argued that this change came earlier and was in train by the earlier part of the eighteenth century.

[31] L. G. Matthews, *History of Pharmacy in Britain* (Edinburgh and London, 1962); J. K. Crellin, 'The Growth of Professionalism in Nineteenth Century British Pharmacy', *Medical History*, 11 (1967), pp. 215–27; also G. Trease, 'Introduction' in F. N. L. Poynter, ed., *The Evolution of Pharmacy in Britain* (1965), p. 16.

[32] S. W. F. Holloway, 'The Orthodox Fringe: The Origins of the Pharmaceutical Society of Great Britain', in Bynum and Porter, eds., *Medical Fringe*, pp. 129–57.

by the pharmacist was fruitfully combined with self-prescribing by customers; family recipes were made up. Most chemists and druggists rarely saw a doctor's prescription; before the introduction of national health insurance in 1911, 90 per cent of all dispensing took place in doctors' surgeries. But the corner druggist, diagnosing, prescribing, treating venereal diseases, practising dentistry, treating eye disorders throughout the nineteenth century and beyond, was in direct competition with the local GP. He also remained a product of the older tradition of folk medicine and self-medication.[33]

Dentistry, nursing and midwifery

Many other 'medical' groupings did not attain full professional status until the twentieth century. This was certainly the case for the dentists who remained largely unorganised in the first half of the nineteenth century. Despite some moves towards professionalisation in the 1840s and 1850s, and the establishment of the Licentiate of Dental Surgery (LDS), dentistry remained undifferentiated, and practised as a sideline.[34] In country districts, it was often an adjunct to a blacksmith's trade. Christine Hillam's work has, however, shown that it could sometimes be a profitable and high-status occupation.[35] When a preliminary but not exclusive form of professional control was established by the 1878 Dentists' Act, this was firmly under medical control and supervision. The dentists' register was kept by the GMC; and the rights of doctors to practise dentistry were safeguarded. The medical profession sought to protect its premier position in the health care division of labour. But unregistered dental practice was not outlawed; and full dental professionalisation had to wait until the 1920s.

The social history of dentistry and pharmacy remain largely unexplored; most attention has concentrated on their legislative and organisational histories. For the professions on the other side of the sexual division of labour, the position is better, thanks to the burgeoning

---

[33] For examples of corner shop counter-prescribing, see V. Berridge and J. G. Edwards, *Opium and the People: Opiate Use in Nineteenth-Century England* (1981).

[34] See D. Richards, 'Dentistry in England in the 1840s: The First Indications of a Movement towards Professionalisation', *Medical History*, 12 (1968), pp. 137–52; and his 'Final Chapters in the Campaign to Effect Dental Registration', *Bull. SSHM*, 23 (1978), pp. 23-6.

[35] C. Hillam, 'The Financial Attractions of being a Dentist in the Early Nineteenth Century', *Bull. SSHM*, 41 (1987), pp. 70–1.

both of professional self-awareness and of feminist history. At one level the 'progress' of nursing in the nineteenth and early twentieth centuries seems to provide a classic case of reform coupled with professionalisation. Dickens's portrayal of Sarah Gamp and Betsy Prig in *Martin Chuzzlewit* purports to show a low-grade occupation ripe for a few standards, where the patient was given his draught by 'the simple process of clutching the patient's windpipe to make him gasp, and immediately pouring it down his throat'.[36] Reforming work was initiated by religious sisterhoods.[37] The 'ministering angel' image expanded with the work of Florence Nightingale in the Crimea. The work of the Nightingale School, attached to St Thomas's in 1861, has been seen as important in establishing the image of nursing as a professional occupation suitable for middle- and upper-class women.[38] Nursing politics during the rise to full professional status were not gentle; a thirty-year 'nursing war' began in the late 1880s and specifically with the establishment in 1887 of the British Nurses' Association by Mrs Bedford Fenwick. Its emphasis on uniform and adequate training and a register of qualified nurses was entirely in the professional tradition. Its aims were opposed by Florence Nightingale – who argued that registration would limit numbers of nurses – and by sections of the medical profession. The London GPs and hospital doctors supported registration since relationships between doctors and nurses were already clearly delineated. But rural GPs, whose professional status was as yet uncertain, feared nurse competition as a source of rival and possibly cheaper professional competition.[39] The outcome of the 'battle for registration' including the eventual trouncing of the BMA came in the early decades of the twentieth century.[40]

But this concentration on London hospital developments and on the internal institutional arrangements and 'politics' of nursing professionalisation has tended to obscure wider structural changes in nursing. In particular, the time scale of change in nursing and the type of 'new nurse' recruited appear to have differed from the standard

---

[36] Quoted in C. Maggs, *The Origins of General Nursing* (1983), p. 153; see also B. Abel-Smith, *A History of the Nursing Profession* (1960), p. 24.

[37] S. W. F. Holloway, 'The All Saints' Sisterhood at University College Hospital, 1862–1899', *Medical History*, 3 (1959), pp. 146–56.

[38] M. Baly, *Florence Nightingale and the Nursing Legacy* (1986).

[39] Maggs, *Origins of General Nursing*.

[40] See below, p. 235.

reformist view.[41] The overall increase in hospital beds and hence the demand for nurses, came in the later part of the nineteenth century rather than in the oft-stressed 'Nightingale period' of 1850–75. The rapid expansion of the poor law sector after the 1897 Poor Law Order increased both numbers of infirmaries and numbers of nurses. There was a significant absolute increase in the numbers of women employed in nursing in any capacity from 35,216 in 1881 to 110,039 in 1921.[42]

Florence Nightingale, as nursing's equivalent to the 'great men' of medicine, has been brought under critical review and the 'Nightingale myth' of the earlier biographies undermined. The 'nursing revolution' was by no means her achievement alone, although F. B. Smith's assessment that she served nursing less than it served her is more iconoclastic than most.[43] The lady pupils were, as Christopher Maggs has pointed out, usually more trouble than they were worth. They were phased out and their place taken by the first generation of general hospital trained nurses.[44] Patterns of recruitment – to provincial as opposed to London hospitals – show not only that the nurse population was – in the twenty-one to twenty-five age group – younger than generally supposed, but that hospitals until well into the twentieth century were staffed overwhelmingly by inexperienced probationers with relatively few trained nurses.[45] Not until the First World War did even the proportion of probationers increase. Poor law nursing, generally regarded, with its emphasis on pauper nurses and a bare minimum of poorly trained staff, as very much the poor relation of nursing in the voluntary hospitals, was numerically more significant; and there the nurses themselves were not necessarily the drunken incompetents of medical iconography.[46]

The establishment of rigid distinctions between 'curing' and 'caring' functions allocated to male doctors and female nurses, appear to have been peculiarly a product of the nineteenth century. But more research

[41]   There are now a number of 'revisionist' histories of nursing and a flourishing nursing history group of the Royal College of Nursing. See, for example, C. Davies, ed., *Rewriting Nursing History* (1980); and C. Maggs, *Nursing History: The State of the Art* (1986).

[42]   C. Maggs, 'Nurse Recruitment to Four Provincial Hospitals, 1881–1921', in Davies, ed., *Rewriting Nursing History*, pp. 18–40.

[43]   F. B. Smith, *Florence Nightingale: Reputation and Power* (1982); for military nursing and concepts of 'genteel' nursing, see A. Summers, 'Pride and Prejudice: Ladies and Nurses in the Crimean War', *History Workshop*, 16 (1983), pp. 32–56.

[44]   Maggs, *Origins of General Nursing*.

[45]   Abel-Smith, *Nursing*, p. 50.

[46]   R. White, *Social Change and the Development of the Nursing Profession: A Study of the Poor Law Nursing Service, 1848–1948* (1978).

remains to be done both on pre-nineteenth-century traditions of heal-ing and care and on organisation of labour within the hospital between doctor, nurse and male medical orderlies, who still appear to have performed a great part of the work in some institutions.[47] Midwifery was the area of care where conflicts were at their sharpest. In the seventeenth century nearly all babies were delivered by female mid-wives. But from the 1720s more men came into this area. The distinc-tion of the great 'men-midwives' of the period – Richard Manningham, William Smellie, William Hunter – reflected credit on every male prac-titioner. Men began to compete for attendance at normal labours. An early form of technological change, the introduction of midwifery forceps, about 1720, accelerated the trend, further enhancing the pos-ition of men through the use of an instrument not available to mid-wives in their practice.[48] The image of female midwifery presented by the male medical protagonists in the struggle was encapsulated in the caricatures like the one by Rowlandson of drunken, blowsy old hags, or Dickens's Sairey Gamp. 'Ignorant midwives' were a per-sistent stereotype, so that by the 1850s midwives were virtually rele-gated to attendance on the poor, eking out a poor living with other work like washing and charing.[49]

The moves among middle-class women to gain admittance to the medical profession had their impact on the status of midwives. They led to the re-entry of a class of highly educated and vocal midwives capable of forming a pressure group to advance professional ends, and also to a confused succession of efforts over the next thirty years to bring about training and control. The battle was between medical pressure groups seeking legislation to control the midwives in their own interests and by the middle-class section of midwifery seeking independent professional status. The 1902 Midwives Act which brought these pressures to an end was to a great degree a compromise. The Central Midwives Board was removed from previously proposed GMC control; but unqualified practice was prohibited, although a

[47] There is some discussion of these issues in B. Ehrenreich and D. English, *Witches, Midwives and Nurses: A History of Women Healers* (1974); also in M. Versluysen, 'Old Wives Tales?: Women Healers in English History', in Davies, ed., *Rewriting Nursing History*, pp. 175–99.

[48] T. R. Forbes, 'The Regulation of English Midwives in the Eighteenth and Nineteenth Centuries', *Medical History*, 15 (1971), pp. 352–62; also A. Wilson, 'William Hunter and the Varieties of Man Midwifery', in Bynum and Porter, eds., *William Hunter*, pp. 343–69.

[49] J. Donnison, *Midwives and Medical Men: A History of Inter-Professional Rivalries and Women's Rights* (New York, 1977).

period of grace until 1910 was allowed. Significantly, from the point of view of the sexual division of labour, midwives were placed 'in a uniquely disadvantaged position among the professions'. The Central Midwives Board had a medical majority and local supervision was in the hands of Medical Officers of Health. The Board was not even required to include a midwife among its members.[50] The maternal death rate did not fall as much as had been expected once the untrained midwife was removed; many medical men practising obstetrics were equally inadequate.

Popular and commercial medicine

Throughout the professionalising battles, the medical profession had sought to maintain its pre-eminent position in the division of labour, in particular with regard to legal registration or licensing of other competitors.[51] But the extension of medical power did not mark the demise of older traditions of folk medicine and self-medication. In the eighteenth, nineteenth and into the twentieth centuries, most working-class medication was self-prescribed and self-administered. Outside advice came from the chemist, but rarely from a doctor. The free dispensaries, poor law infirmaries and out-patient departments of the voluntary hospitals provided a limited form of orthodox medical care. But the bulk of poor people dealt with everyday ailments themselves. Popular medicine was never a static or indeed an organic whole; nor was it always rigidly separate from and opposed to orthodox medical practice. It would be oversimplistic to see the areas as 'distinct and hermetically separate regions of cultural production', with overt opposition always between dominant medical and subordinate oppositional popular forms. Medical practices were combined in different relations at different stages. As William Bynum and Roy Porter have commented, 'regular and irregular medicine has dialectically interacted within the larger social whole'.[52]

In its simplest form, folk medicine was based on herbs, flowers and roots which could easily be grown or gathered in a rural setting and which were represented in standard texts such as Nicholas

[50]   Ibid., p. 190.
[51]   For discussion of these strategies, see G. Larkin, Occupational Monopoly and Modern Medicine (1983).
[52]   Bynum and Porter, eds., Medical Fringe, pp. 1–4; T. Bennett, 'Popular Culture: Divided Territory', Social History Society Newsletter, 6 (1981), pp. 5–6, addresses some of the issues involved in ideas of hegemony and the relationship with the formation and transmutation of cultural relations.

Culpeper's *Physicall Directory* of 1649 (Culpeper's Herbal) which continued to appear down to the nineteenth century. The use of these home-made preparations continued in rural areas where the ingredients (such as poppy heads for infusion for poppy head tea) were still easily available. The country traditions were carried on in urban settings also, as the character of Old Alice in Mrs Gaskell's *Mary Barton* (1848) demonstrates.

She had been out all day in the fields, gathering wild herbs for drinks and medicine, for in addition to her invaluable qualities as a sick nurse and her worldly occupation as a washer woman, she added a considerable knowledge of hedge and field simples; and on fine days, when no more profitable occupation offered itself, she used to ramble off into the lanes and meadows as far as her legs could carry her. This evening she had returned loaded with nettles and her first object was to light a candle and see to hang them up in bunches in every available place in her cellar room ... the cellar window ... was oddly festooned with all manner of hedgerow, ditch and field plants, which we are accustomed to call valueless, but which have a powerful effect either for good or for evil and consequently much used among the poor.[53]

Such practices were not simply 'the inertia of simple minds'; there was also a strong current of opposition to middle-class and medical professionalism. John Wesley's *Primitive Physic* which went through numerous editions after it first appeared in 1747, with its thousand self-help remedies for over 200 afflictions, represented this feeling that the profession was too academic and did not serve working-class needs. The status of the medical profession was generally not secure with the working class until well into the nineteenth century. Little, if any, working-class income could at this period be made available for medical attention and this was only available free to a limited extent. But there was more than an economic reason. Different working-class conceptions of disease and of death were, in particular in the eighteenth and early nineteenth centuries, in opposition to those advanced by the nascent profession. The riots at Tyburn in mid-eighteenth century against the use of hanged criminals for anatomical purposes demonstrated a clear opposition between arguments of medical utility and the importance and dignity of death to the labouring poor.[54] Similar feelings of hostility surfaced in opposition to the Anatomy Act of 1831 which legalised a cheap supply of pauper bodies

[53] E. Gaskell, *Mary Barton* (1848; Penguin edn 1970).
[54] P. Linebaugh, 'The Tyburn Riot against the Surgeons', in D. Hay, P. Linebaugh and E. P. Thompson, eds., *Albion's Fatal Tree: Crime and Society in Eighteenth-Century England* (1975), pp. 64–117.

for research, and by the riots against doctors and surgeons during the cholera epidemic of 1831–2.[55]

But we should be careful not to assume all popular or 'quack' medicine was necessarily oppositional. As Roy Porter has pointed out, Georgian quack medicine was not in opposition to orthodox medicine.[56] Many quacks had *bona fide* medical degrees; James Graham, who set up his Temple of Health at the Adelphi, had been a pupil of Cullen. The 'growth of a consumer society' which historians have recently located in the late eighteenth century, provided a golden opportunity for cultivating the business side of medicine; the marketing of medical products – many patented, like James's Fever Powders – came to the fore. There is perhaps a danger of constructing a Whiggish history of alternative medicine with late eighteenth-century 'quack' medicine seen as the ancestor of Victorian alternative medicine. Clearly the shifting boundaries between orthodox and unorthodox, together with the strong commercial and capitalist tendencies in both eighteenth- and nineteenth-century unorthodoxy, should be recognised.

But it was the oppositional tendency which was uppermost in the first half of the nineteenth century. A self-conscious radical 'fringe' emerged, aggressively repudiating medical orthodoxy. Herbalism was one example. The Coffinite variety of medical botany, for example, based on a democratic organisation of local societies with a strong Methodist and Primitive Methodist influence, and particularly strong in the industrial towns of Lancashire in the late 1840s, was a search for social reform as well as medical good health.[57] It had connections with post-Chartist popular politics – Coffinites were to be the forefront in petitioning against the 1858 Medical Act – and with the temperance and anti-professional feeling in the industrial working class. The specific appeal of Coffinism was on the wane after Coffin's death in 1866, but medical herbalism in general remained strong. As late as 1913,

---

[55]   M. J. Durey, 'Bodysnatchers and Benthamites: The "Dead Body Bill" and the Provision of Bodies to the London Anatomy Schools, 1820–42', *Bull. SSHM*, 19 (1976), pp. 10–11; R. Richardson, *Death, Dissection and the Destitute* (1987).

[56]   R. Porter, 'Before the Fringe' (paper given to the Conference on Medical Fringe and Medical Orthodoxy, Wellcome Institute, London, 1985). See also Porter, *Disease, Medicine and Society*, pp. 44–7.

[57]   For Coffinism and medical botany, see S. Chapman, *Jesse Boot of Boots the Chemists* (1974), pp. 20 and 34; J. V. Pickstone, 'Medical Botany (Self-Help Medicine in Victorian England)', *Memoirs of the Manchester Literary and Philosophical Society*, 119 (1976–7), pp. 85–95; E. Gaskell, 'The Coffinites', *Bull. SSHM*, 8 (1972), p. 12. Also L. Barrow, 'Democratic Epistemology: Mid Nineteenth-Century Plebeian Medicine', *Bull. SSHM*, 29 (1981), pp. 25–9.

Ashton-under-Lyne had 1,400 herbalists serving a working-class population.[58] They were part of a whole range of unqualified medical practitioners who flourished where medical aid was otherwise unobtainable. Bone-setters like the Taylors who practised in various Lancashire towns for over a century, leechmen, watercasters, aurists and others were to be found in most poor localities, often carrying on their medical occupation in conjunction with a number of other activities.[59] Women had a particular role to play in particular through assistance at childbirth and their work as abortionists. The 'local woman' would in any case usually go in to the family for a week or more after the birth, doing general housework and cooking as well as giving directly 'medical' help. Her other role as an abortionist was also widely accepted in working-class communities.[60]

Popular or unorthodox medicine was not confined to the working class. Other forms of non-professional treatment had their vogue within the middle class. Hydropathy, established by Dr James Wilson at Malvern in 1842, numbered Darwin, Tennyson and Carlyle among its devotees.[61] Homoeopathy, introduced to England in 1827 by Dr Frederick Harvey Quinn who had studied under Hahnemann, had reached its peak by his death in the 1870s.[62] Phrenology and mesmerism also had their middle-class following; in Edinburgh, for example, the former found its support among an 'outsider group' of professionals for which it was a symbolic expression of antipathy to the institutional thought of the local elite.[63] But it, like mesmerism, had working-class support, offering as it did a simple and logical scientific

---

[58]   E. M. Schofield, *Medical Care of the Working Class about 1900* (Lancaster, 1979), quoted in J. V. Pickstone, ed., *Health, Disease and Medicine in Lancashire, 1750–1950* (Manchester, 1980), p. 1.

[59]   J. L. West, *The Taylors of Lancashire: Bonesetters and Doctors, 1750–1890* (Eccles, 1977); E. Sigsworth and P. Swan, 'Para-Medical Provision in the West Riding', *Bull. SSHM*, 29 (1981), pp. 37–9; Berridge and Edwards, *Opium*, p. 227.

[60]   M. Chamberlain, *Old Wives' Tales: Their History, Remedies and Spells* (1981), pp. 111, 116; P. Knight, 'Women and Abortion in Victorian and Edwardian England', *History Workshop*, 4 (1977), pp. 57–69; A. McLaren, 'Women's Work and Regulation of Family Size: The Question of Abortion in the Nineteenth Century', *History Workshop*, 4 (1977), pp. 70–81. Also A. McLaren, *Birth Control in Nineteenth-Century England* (1978), pp. 231–53.

[61]   R. Price, 'Hydropathy in England, 1840–70', *Medical History*, 25 (1981), pp. 269–80. F. B. Smith, *The People's Health, 1830–1910* (1979), p. 342.

[62]   Smith, *People's Health*, pp. 342–3; B. Inglis, *Fringe Medicine* (1964), pp. 77–80; R. Cooter, 'Interpreting the Fringe', *Bull. SSHM*, 29 (1981), pp. 33–6, draws attention to the lack, for Britain, of the most basic accounts of homoeopathy, hydropathy and mesmerism.

[63]   S. Shapin, 'Phrenological Knowledge and the Social Structure of Early Nineteenth Century Edinburgh', *Annals of Science*, 32 (1975), pp. 219–43.

system which focussed again on the strong artisan tradition of self-help.[64]

By the end of the nineteenth century, working-class attitudes towards health care were changing. There was a shift away from the independent ideas of folk and herbal medicine towards a greater reliance on outside, 'expert' and professional help although such changes should not be overemphasised. The late nineteenth and early twentieth centuries in fact formed a transitional period when both official and unofficial medicine had their place in patterns of experience. Professional medicine became more of a possibility for working people through the spread of dispensaries in London and the provinces.[65] There were more opportunities for relatively cheap professional help, at least for emergencies or in exceptional circumstances. At the self-helping level, too, professional influence became stronger, and the two forms of knowledge intermingled in a way which has only recently begun to be studied. Various editions of *Aristotle's Works*, a popular work on conception and childbirth, show how advances made in professional science and medicine were incorporated and interpreted within the control of popular theories of generation.[66] A similar process was at work as manufactured ingredients began to be used in traditional remedies. The role of the chemist and counter-prescribing was important in this mediation of popular and professional. In Manchester in the 1940s, families brought their own private recipes for the chemist to make up. Later the balance of the drugseller/purchaser relationship inclined more to the vendor as home-made recipes were abandoned or forgotten in favour of a preparation recommended and made up by the pharmacist.[67]

The commercial tendency, the marketing of medicine already apparent in late eighteenth-century medicine, became more apparent. Patent medicines had begun to replace herbal and folk medicines by the end of the century. These were excluded both from the 1868 Pharmacy Act (which had given professional pharmacists control of certain

[64] A. McLaren, 'Phrenology: Medium and Message', *Journal of Modern History*, 46 (1974), pp. 86–97; and R. Cooter, *The Cultural Meaning of Popular Science* (Cambridge, 1985).

[65] I. S. L. Loudon, 'The Origins and Growth of the Dispensary Movement in England', *Bulletin of the History of Medicine*, 55 (1981), pp. 322–42; Smith, *People's Health*, pp. 31–2. For further discussion of dispensaries, see below, p. 206.

[66] J. Blackman, 'Popular Theories of Generation: The Evolution of *Aristotle's Works*. The Study of an Anachronism', in Woodward and D. Richards, eds., *Health Care and Popular Medicine*, pp. 56–88.

[67] Berridge and Edwards, *Opium*, p. 30; Chamberlain, *Old Wives' Tales*, p. 90.

preparations) and from the 1875 Sale of Food and Drugs Act. A fall in the price of drugs was part of a general decline in the cost of raw materials in the 1870s and was accompanied by a rise in real wages. Patent medicines took their share of increased working-class prosperity. The number of outlets from which they were available – chemists, grocers and general stores – multiplied from 10,000 in 1865 to 40,000 in 1905.[68] Newspaper advertising of such products, always a feature of the popular press, expanded; and the advertising expenditure of entrepreneurs like Holloway and Beecham reached unprecedented heights. Holloway's expenditure jumped from £5,000 a year in 1842 to £50,000 in 1883.[69] Several of the leading proprietors and sellers, like Beecham himself, who had been a noted herbalist in his youth, and Jesse Boot, who was expanding his cash chemists business in the Nottingham area in the 1870s, had strong connections with the earlier traditions of folk medicine and medical botany.[70] The abuses of patent medicine sale and advertisement, which undoubtedly existed, were attacked in a campaign promoted primarily by the medical and pharmaceutical professions in the 1890s and 1900s.[71] Earlier traditions remained strong, and it would be unwise to overstress the commercialisation of popular medicine at the turn of the century. In Barrow and Lancaster, for example, patent medicines were not widely purchased before the 1930s; they were more expensive than remedies made at home.[72]

Disease, medicine and public health

Analysis of the historical relations of orthodoxy and alternatives, and the renewal of interest in 'alternative' medicine, have been prompted by doubts about the efficacy of high-cost, technological medicine. One of the central areas involved and stimulated by these concerns has been the question of the transformation of health and increase of population since the eighteenth century. This has stimulated a debate which

---

[68] Chapman, *Jesse Boot*, pp. 23–8; R. Roberts, *The Classic Slum: Salford Life in the First Quarter of the Century* (Manchester, 1971), pp. 125–8.

[69] E. S. Turner, *The Shocking History of Advertising* (1952), pp. 66–8.

[70] Chapman, *Jesse Boot*, pp. 23, 34.

[71] British Medical Association, *Secret Remedies, What they Cost and What they Contain* (1909); British Medical Association, *More Secret Remedies, What they Cost and What they Contain* (1912): Turner, *Shocking History*, p. 172.

[72] C. Roberts, 'Oral History Investigations of Disease and its Management in the Lancashire Working Class, 1890–1939', in Pickstone, ed., *Health, Disease and Medicine in Lancashire*, pp. 33–51.

is in its turn underpinned by crucial divisions in the provision of health care – between preventive and curative medicine, between a public as opposed to an individual approach to health care.

The question which in fact concerned many Victorian observers in the 1830s and 1840s was not why health was improving and mortality rates declining, but why they were not. The health of large sections of the population was worse than it had been at the end of the eighteenth century. The crude death rate for the country as a whole had been declining from about 1780 to 1810. Thereafter, it began to rise and continued to do so until the 1840s. What Anthony Wohl has called the 'urban demographic revolution and its accompanying densities and pressures upon air, water and space' clearly had much to do with it.[73] Surveys, investigations and statistics revealed the extent of health problems – in the Reports of the Poor Law Commissioners in the 1830s, Edwin Chadwick's *Report on the Sanitary Condition of the Labouring Population* in 1842; and in the studies carried out for Sir John Simon as Medical Officer to the Privy Council in the 1860s.[74] A belief in numerical empiricism governed much Victorian social investigation. Surveys revealed dramatic variations in mortality rates according to class and area. William Farr, Registrar General, calculated that the mortality rate in country districts was 18.2/1,000 between 1831 and 1839 compared with 26.2/1,000 in urban areas.[75] Tables revealing the gulf in life expectancy according to class were common among Victorian sanitary reform publications. Victorian public health reform, founded on these statistical investigations, was fuelled by dual motives of guilt and fear. Epidemics could spread from working- to middle-class areas of a great city. But sanitary reform went further than this. It coloured the approach to a much wider compass of social indicators; 'the most widely held of Victorian social doctrines was that physical well-being and a pure environment were the essential foundation for all other areas of social progress'.[76] Public health reform was both a moral and a scientific crusade.

Such an awareness of the state of the public health was not new. The eighteenth century has also had its revelations of slum conditions,

---

[73]   A. Wohl, *Endangered Lives: Public Health in Victorian Britain* (1983), p. 4.

[74]   For Chadwick's report, see M. W. Flinn, 'Introduction', to E. Chadwick, *Report on the Sanitary Condition of the Labouring Population of Great Britain* (Edinburgh, 1965); for Simon, R. Lambert, *Sir John Simon 1816–1904 and English Social Administration* (1963).

[75]   J. Eyler, *Victorian Social Medicine: The Ideas and Methods of William Farr* (Baltimore and London, 1979).

[76]   Wohl, *Endangered Lives*, p. 6.

overcrowding and fever. But these were not considered to be appropriate areas for central government action. Action was left to local initiative, to local vestries and parishes, or to bodies or commissioners who undertook responsibility for certain local matters, such as street cleaning in return for the levying of a rate. While these did much to clean up towns in the late eighteenth century, such a patchwork of bodies could not cope with the vastly different scale of urban hygiene problems in the nineteenth century.[77]

In the nineteenth century, a more interventionist role was adopted, partly out of necessity, but partly also from a Benthamite and reforming perspective. The legislative development of state medicine in the nineteenth century is a well-known story.[78] Most attention has concentrated on the pioneering work of Edwin Chadwick and his surrounding group of statisticians, doctors and social reformers, sharing an underlying Benthamite ideology. Chadwick's 1842 *Report* was the model for many another and presented a compelling case for sanitary reform. The publicity generated by this first stage of public health reform culminated in the 1848 Public Health Act which established a central General Board of Health and empowered local authorities to establish local boards with powers, amongst other things, to manage sewers, provide water supplies and remove nuisances. But Chadwick, as Secretary of the Board, tried to do too much too soon. Centralisation aroused fear of despotic attempts to control local affairs. In 1858 the Board was dismantled. The absorption of the Board's functions by the Privy Council Office in the 1860s was not, however, a blow to centrally administered preventive medicine. The work of Sir John Simon and his investigators at the Privy Council Office in that decade was in many respects more productive. The piecemeal legislation of the 1850s and 1860s was extended in the 1866 Sanitary Act, the first public health act in which compulsory clauses were dominant. As a symbol of the power of central government to intervene in local affairs, it stimulated local authorities to greater activity on their own account. Simon's work was more extensive than this – in investigating industrial disease and occupational hazards and in generally publicising the sanitary idea more widely. The 1871 Local Government Act,

[77] J. C. Riley, *The Eighteenth-Century Campaign to Avoid Disease* (1986).
[78] There are many basic histories of particular aspects of public health, e.g., S. E. Finer, *The Life and Times of Sir Edwin Chadwick* (1952); C. Fraser Brockington, *Public Health in the Nineteenth Century* (London and Edinburgh, 1965); W. M. Frazer, *History of English Public Health, 1834–1939* (1950). Most have now been largely overtaken by Wohl, *Endangered Lives*.

which created a unified public health administration combined in one body, the Local Government Board, the Local Government Act Office, the Registrar General and Simon's Privy Council staff, and which undermined Simon's own personal position, in fact marked another significant expansion of effective public health action at the local level. The unifying Public Health Act of 1875 finally consolidated most of the existing sanitary legislation. The work of both the Privy Council Office and the Local Government Board was gradual and evolutionary, less showy but ultimately more effective than its Chadwickian predecessor. As Anthony Wohl has noted, together they 'must take much credit for the gradual acceptance, between 1860 and 1880, of the role of the central government as a supervisory power in public health'.[79] The role of the local authorities was important; the Infectious Disease (Notification) Act of 1889 had, by 1891, been adopted by 555 urban and 372 rural sanitary districts.[80]

Preventive medicine at this local level in its broadest sense was dependent on the appointment of a qualified Medical Officer. This was made possible by an Act of 1848; the first appointment was in Liverpool, followed by John Simon as Medical Officer of Health for the City of London in 1848. But only in 1872 did the Public Health Act make the appointment compulsory for all local sanitary authorities. As Dorothy Porter has shown, despite their importance at the local level and the institution of the Diploma in Public Health (DPH) in 1886, the Medical Officer of Health remained the Cinderella of the medical profession.[81] These 'medical police' were not accorded the status of the rest of the profession, and preventive medicine in general has continued to suffer from comparative medical neglect. Important, too, for the task of safeguarding the public health were the medical services set up under the new Poor Law of 1834. Alongside the workhouse was set up the poor law infirmary; these often expanded to encompass fever and isolation hospitals, and non-paupers suffering from contagious diseases were admitted. Ruth

[79] Wohl, *Endangered Lives*, p. 164. For interpretations of the post-Chadwick period, see also Lambert, *Sir John Simon*; R. M. MacLeod, 'The Anatomy of State Medicine, Concept and Application', in F. N. L. Poynter, ed., *Medicine and Science in the 1860s* (1968), pp. 226–7; and R. M. MacLeod, 'The Frustration of State Medicine', *Medical History*, 11 (1967), pp. 5–40.

[80] This rendered obligatory the notification of the Medical Officer of Health of a list of specified contagious diseases, including typhus, typhoid, smallpox and scarlet fever. The medical officer could remove the affected person to an isolation hospital.

[81] D. Watkins (now D. Porter), 'The English Revolution in Social Medicine, 1889–1911' (unpublished PhD thesis, London University, 1984).

Hodgkinson has seen in them the elements of a nineteenth-century National Health Service, but directed only at the poor and widely detested, along with the workhouse, for its harsh and authoritarian attitudes.[82]

The death rate dropped in the nineteenth century. It had been in decline from the 1740s, rising during the early decades of the nineteenth century, then slowly declining again from the 1830s. But the adult mortality rate began a noticeable decline only in the 1870s. The question remains, what part did medicine play in this? Historical demographers now attribute the rise in population from the 1740s to a rise in the birth rate as the result of earlier marriage rather than to declining mortality.[83] But medicine's contribution to the latter still needs examination. This is a debate which has concerned historians and others for more than thirty years. What can be termed the 'old orthodoxy' saw the conquest of disease, the decline of mortality between the eighteenth and twentieth centuries, as due to the advent of new scientific medical procedures and discoveries. The 'march of scientific medicine' appeared an adequate explanation. This version had a particular appeal in the 1950s, when the success of antibiotics appeared to demonstrate the validity of a bio-medical approach to health care.[84] It was at that time that Thomas McKeown, Professor of Social Medicine at Birmingham, introduced a defence of social medicine which has since become so widespread as to become the 'new orthodoxy'. He argued, most notably in *The Modern Rise of Population* published in 1976, but the fruit of over twenty years' work, that medical intervention had little to do with the lowering of the death rate.[85] Many of the most important diseases involved had already virtually disappeared before the relevant scientific medical

[82]   R. G. Hodgkinson, *The Origins of the National Health Service: The Medical Services of the New Poor Law, 1834–1871* (1967).

[83]   E. A. Wrigley and R. S. Schofield, *The Population History of England, 1541–1871: A Reconstruction* (1981).

[84]   Stephen Kunitz has pointed out that the concept of medical intervention and its impact on mortality was a product of the 1950s then back-projected into history. S. Kunitz, 'The History of Mortality' (Wellcome Institute seminar paper, September 1987).

[85]   For the McKeown argument, see T. McKeown, *Modern Rise of Population*; also T. McKeown and R. Brown, 'Medical Evidence Related to English Population Change in the Eighteenth Century', *Population Studies*, 9 (1955–6), pp. 110–51; G. McLachlan and T. McKeown, *Medical History and Medical Care* (1971); T. McKeown, R. G. Brown and R. G. Record, 'An Interpretation of the Rise of Population in Europe', *Population Studies*, 26 (1972), pp. 345–82; T. McKeown and R. G. Record, 'Reasons for the Decline in Mortality in England and Wales during the Nineteenth Century', in M. W. Flinn and T. C. Smout, eds., *Essays in Social History* (Oxford, 1974).

innovations occurred. The fall in mortality in fact resulted mainly from a decline in deaths due to infectious diseases, and also a lessening of the infant death rate and starvation. McKeown described how the decline in mortality from airborne diseases derived from changes in their character and the relation of the organisms to their host. The death rate from water- and vector-borne diseases declined because of sanitary improvements. Until the second quarter of the twentieth century the decline of mortality from infections owed little to specific measures of preventing or treating disease in the individual. Mortality had begun to fall before the identification of causal organisms and effective immunisation and treatment. The only exception was small-pox, whose contribution to the total reduction was small. McKeown saw as the main reasons hygienic measures taken from about 1870, and the prevention and treatment of disease in individuals, in particular after the discovery of the sulphonamides in 1936. But the crucial factor, in his view, for the nineteenth-century decline, was an improvement in nutrition, although his argument was one by exclusion rather than a specific demonstration of how this came about. McKeown's attack on scientific, 'high-tech' medicine also entailed an undermining of medicine in all its forms. The public health movement, sanitation and improvement in hygiene, were seen as a positive influence, but one of a secondary kind.

Many of McKeown's conclusions about the role of scientific medicine still hold good. The new medicine made its advances, and we should first consider what these were. Diseases, in the older conception, were manifestations of humoral imbalances; the different forces vital for life had to be kept in equilibrium. But in the new dispensation, they were real entities with specific causes, a view already adopted by Sydenham as early as the seventeenth century and by Cullen at Edinburgh in the eighteenth century. The 'new medicine' was most specifically associated with French and Scottish medicine – Xavier Bichat's theory of tissues contributing notably to localised theories. A battery of new technological devices – the stethoscope most notably – offered material support for a more specific model based on physical examination of the patient. Discoveries in anaesthesia rightly impressed contemporaries as advances; chloroform became more popular than ether by the late 1840s. Lister's use of antiseptics – based on Pasteur's germ theory of disease – in the 1860s and 1870s in Glasgow, Edinburgh and in London, demonstrated the superiority of the method. Germ theory developed further when in 1876 Robert Koch demonstrated that specific bacteria caused specific animal diseases. The function of bacteria in the disease process was now known, and in 1882 Koch isolated the tubercle bacillus. Finally, the cell theory of Rudolf Virchow of Berlin saw the body as a 'cell-state in which every cell is a citizen'. The body was a mass of cells with changes in cell structure or function at the basis of various diseases. The study of disease was based no longer on organs or tissues but on the basic components of organic structure. The doctor was joined in the examination of disease by the laboratory pathologist and the microscope.[86]

But of all the major epidemic diseases under consideration, only one, smallpox, was conquered by a medical discovery. Vaccination, as eventually established, was undoubtedly important in its decline. But even this is not the only explanation.[87] Opposition to compulsory vaccination, discussed below, made certain that vaccination was incomplete as late as 1885 when the downward turn in smallpox mortality became decisive. Isolation established after 1889 was probably more effective. This apart, there is little evidence that scientific medicine alone could counter lethal disease. What remains problematic is the relative roles of public health and of improved nutrition. Recent modifications to the McKeown thesis give equal weight to both rather than to nutrition alone; and in particular the role of interventionist public health activity has been stressed. The McKeown thesis saw cholera, often stressed as the engine of public health reform (a temporary Board of Health was set up to deal with the first epidemic) as less significant in terms of its impact on the death rate. Its significance was seen to lie more in its role in the larger controversy over the origin and spread of infectious disease. Sanitary reformers like Chadwick poured scorn on what they saw as medical commitment to 'contagionist' theory – the view that specific contagia were the sole cause of epidemic

---

[86] For general surveys of these developments, see L. S. King, *The Medical World of the Eighteenth Century* (New York, 1971); Ackernecht, *Medicine at the Paris Hospital*; S. J. Reiser, *Medicine and the Reign of Technology* (Cambridge, 1978); Shryock, *Development of Modern Medicine*; A. J. Youngson, *The Scientific Revolution in Victorian Medicine* (1979).

[87] The accepted view here was that Edward Jenner's cowpox vaccination, introduced in 1796, was the first safe method available. But Razzell's researches indicate that the vaccines used by Jenner and his contemporaries in fact derived from smallpox virus and hence the eighteenth-century practice of smallpox inoculation (variolation). P. E. Razzell, 'Edward Jenner: The History of a Medical Myth', *Medical History*, 9 (1965), pp. 216–29; also *idem*, 'Population Change in Eighteenth Century England: A Reappraisal', *Economic History Review*, 2nd ser., 18 (1965), pp. 312–32; A. Hardy, 'Smallpox in London: Factors in the Decline of Disease in the Nineteenth Century', *Medical History*, 27 (1983), pp. 111–38.

diseases like cholera. The sanitary view stressed 'miasmatic' or 'state of the atmosphere' theory which automatically led to a stress on engineering rather than medical means of intervention (in fact Margaret Pelling has shown that this traditional division is an oversimplification; medical men ranged diseases along a 'spectrum of contagiousness' aided by Liebig's chemical researches and his concept of contagious molecular action).[88] The decline in fevers (primarily typhus and typhoid) occurred, according to McKeown, primarily because of a change in the virulence of the micro-organism rather than because of the effects of better sewerage and water, whose effects had, in his views, yet to be felt when typhus began to decline in the 1870s. For typhoid, the provision of sewers may even have increased the number of deaths, for they often poured filth into rivers which were a source of drinking water.[89]

But more recent research has tended to cast doubt on the secondary role of public health. Turberculosis provided a major plank in the McKeown thesis. It was an airborne disease accounting for 13.3 per cent of all deaths between 1848 and 1854, and was, by his figures, in decline by the 1830s and 1840s. A decline in deaths from TB was bound to make a major contribution to any overall reduction in mortality. Neither clinical medicine nor municipal sanitation could account for its decline; the part played by nutritional improvement was thereby stressed. But Simon Szreter has recently shown that tuberculosis was not only associated with poor nutritional standards and that other risk factors such as poor living conditions were also important. More importantly, he has questioned the classification of tuberculosis and bronchitis mortality figures and shown that there is no good evidence for TB's chronological priority in mortality decline.[90] The significance of the airborne diseases in nineteenth-century mortality decline has

---

[88]   See M. Pelling, *Cholera, Fever and English Medicine* (Oxford, 1978); also *idem*, 'The Reality of Anticontagionism – Theories of Epidemic Disease in the Nineteenth Century', *Bull. SSHM*, 17 (1976), pp. 5–7. Pelling criticises a 'classic' article by E. H. Ackernecht, 'Anticontagionism between 1821 and 1867', *Bulletin of the History of Medicine*, 22 (1948), pp. 562–93, which argued for the association of anti-contagionism with economic liberalism and opposition to quarantines and loss of trade. For further comment on this point, see R. J. Morris, *Cholera, 1832* (1976).

[89]   Wohl, *Endangered Lives*, p. 126; W. Luckin, 'Evaluating the Sanitary Revolution: Typhus and Typhoid in London, 1851–1900', in R. Woods and J. Woodward, eds., *Urban Disease and Mortality in Nineteenth Century England* (1954), pp. 102–19.

[90]   S. Szreter, 'The Importance of Social Intervention in Britain's Mortality Decline, c. 1850–1914: A Re-interpretation of the Role of Public Health', *Social History of Medicine*, 1 (1988), pp. 1–37.

been downgraded; the 'classic sanitation and hygiene' diseases – cholera, typhus, typhoid – have returned to prominence. The extension of public health activity at the local level in the last three decades of the century thus becomes significant. Clean local water supplies were essential for the eradication of typhoid and cholera: and the establishment of Port Sanitary Authorities in the 1870s provided advance warning of outbreaks abroad. Problems of housing were also being tackled. Although, as John Kellett has shown, some of the slum clearance acts resulted in even worse overcrowding than before, since no provision was initially made for re-housing, the worst of the back-to-backs and cellar dwellings had been banned.[91] The Torrens and Cross Acts legitimised the need for municipal involvement in slum clearance, and uncertain steps were taken towards municipal housing. Where preventive legislation was not forthcoming, the consequences were obvious. In industry, industrial diseases, like miners' asthma or matchmakers' necrosis, remained part of working life (only in 1895 did the Factory and Workshop Act require the notification of industrial diseases for the first time).[92]

Despite the upgrading of public health, the nutritional case also remains important. McKeown's claims about improvements in agriculture and in food supply all derive from the early nineteenth century. That the provision of adequate or better nutrition is of fundamental importance in increasing resistance to disease is well known. The Victorian working-class diet, encapsulated in Dr Edward Smith's report on the labourers he visited in 1863 on behalf of the Privy Council, was, in country and in town, based on bread, potatoes and tea. There was a serious lack of green vegetables, low protein and vitamin intake, and very little fresh milk. Families, particularly mothers and children – for the best food always went to the breadwinner – were underfed and particularly so when the children were too young to contribute to the family income. The poorer classes also spent a disproportionate amount of income on drink, although the drink question, largely because of temperance influence, never became part of the

---

[91] J. R. Kellett, *The Impact of Railways on Victorian Cities* (1969); Wohl, *Endangered Lives*, p. 320; M. J. Daunton, *House and Home in the Victorian City* (1983); A. Wohl, *The Eternal Slum* (1977).

[92] For the social history of occupational health and an excellent bibliography, see P. Weindling, 'Linking Self Help and Medical Science: The Social History of Occupational Health', in P. Weindling, ed., *The Social History of Occupational Health* (1985), pp. 1–31.

public health movement in the nineteenth century.[93] How far general improvements in nutrition and the standard of living had progressed by the end of the century remains uncertain. The rise in real wages after 1850, declining expenditure on alcohol after the mid-1870s and increasing food supplies were important. From the 1870s, consumption of meat and fruit in particular rose dramatically. But the Food and Drug Acts were inadequately enforced; and bread and potatoes, as Derek Oddy has shown, remained staple foods in many families in the 1890s as they had been in the 1840s.[94] Our knowledge of food supply, quality and preparation, and, more important, the amounts eaten by particular classes and within families remains limited. A cautious but realistic conclusion, on the whole debate, is Anthony Wohl's – 'That death rates did decline is the result, among other things, of an improved diet; that they did not decline as sharply as the remarkable sanitary engineering of the Victorians merited was due to the low nutritional standards which, despite general improvements, still prevailed.'[95]

One comment on the inadequacy of diet, despite rising real wages, was the continuing and even rising rate of infant mortality at the end of the century. Infant mortality, at 150 per 1,000 live births in the years 1856–60, had, after a slight decline in the late 1870s and early 1880s, risen to 156/1,000 births in the years 1896–1900. Prematurity, characteristic of the 'culture of poverty' endemic among the Victorian working class, was a major cause of infant mortality. But respiratory and gastro-intestinal diseases were the most common causes of death, including scarlet fever, whooping cough and diphtheria. Throughout the nineteenth century scarlet fever was the main cause of childhood death (95 per cent of all cases were of children under ten). Between 1861 and 1891, scarlet fever deaths declined by 81 per cent; its decline (in part due to a decrease in potency of the streptococcus, but also because of notification and isolation of sufferers) was responsible for 19 per cent of the total decline in death rates in the second half of the century. But mortality was concentrated

---

[93] D. J. Oddy, 'Working Class Diets in Late Nineteenth Century Britain', *Economic History Review*, 2nd ser., 23 (1970), pp. 314–23; for drink, see B. Harrison, *Drink and the Victorians: The Temperance Question in England, 1815–1872* (1971); and A. E. Dingle, 'Drink and Working Class Living Standards in Britain, 1870–1914', in D. J. Oddy and D. Miller, eds., *The Making of the Modern British Diet* (1975), pp. 117–34.

[94] D. J. Oddy, 'A Nutritional Analysis of Historical Evidence: The Working Class Diet 1880–1914', in Oddy and Miller, eds., *Modern British Diet*, pp. 214–31.

[95] Wohl, *Endangered Lives*, p. 56.

in infants under one year. It was a cliché of Victorian social reform that the high death rates were the responsibility of individual working-class mothers; such views have often been uncritically accepted by later historians.[96] Working mothers, so it was argued, unhygienically bottle-fed rather than breast-fed their infants. The children were left with child-minders who drugged their charges with opiates to keep them quiet. The situation was more complex than this perspective allows.[97] More information about infant feeding practices and their variation is needed; it may indeed be the case that bottle feeding was the exception rather than the norm.

Why, then, did the infant death rate decline so markedly in the early years of the twentieth century? Between 1901 and 1905, the death rate fell to 138/1,000 births, between 1906 and 1910, to 117/1,000 live births, a rapid decline indeed from the 1899 figure of 163 deaths per 1,000, the highest ever recorded. This, it should be noted, was a decline which was not peculiar to England and Wales; it can be traced in many countries at the same time. Why this downturn occurred when it did is not easy to explain. Certainly, the worst abuses of baby-farming had been controlled by the Infant Life Protection Act of 1872, and opiates (but not opiate-based patent medicines) were under pharmaceutical control after 1868. Of considerable importance was a decline in the birth rate and the spread of knowledge and use of contraception.[98] Between 1876 and 1909 births fell in England and Wales from 36.3 to 25.8 per 1,000 population. Birth control, originating in middle-class families since at least the 1860s, was a practice, as J. A. Banks has argued, crucially determined by the costs of educating male children for entry to the professions rather than by feminism or secularist propaganda. The Bradlaugh–Besant trial (for republication of the *Fruits of Philosphy*) of 1877 accelerated, but did not initiate, the spread of birth-control practices. The working classes did not begin to use contraception on a large enough scale to influence the birth

[96] For example in I. Pinchbeck and M. Hewitt, *Children in English Society*, vol. 2 (1973).
[97] For discussion on this, see, for example, J. Lewis, 'The Social History of Social Policy: Infant Welfare in Edwardian England', *Journal of Social Policy*, 9 (1980), pp. 463–86, and Berridge and Edwards, *Opium*.
[98] For debates on birth control, see J. A. Banks, *Prosperity and Parenthood: A Study of Family Planning among the Victorian Middle Classes* (1954); J. A. and O. Banks, *Feminism and Family Planning in Victorian England* (Liverpool, 1964); J. A. Banks, *Victorian Values: Secularism and the Size of Families* (1981); R. A. Soloway, *Birth Control and the Population Question in England, 1877–1930* (Chapel Hill, 1982); Knight, 'Women and Abortion in Victorian and Edwardian England'; McLaren, 'Women's Work and the Regulation of Family Size'.

rate until the end of the century. A decline in the birth rate of illegitimate children, the population most at risk, may also have helped.[99]

The downturn in infectious epidemic disease in general marked a shift in the types of major killer disease at the turn of the century. The main causes of death were changing from the infections to the non-communicable diseases such as cancer, heart disease and accidents (although the incidence of heart disease in the nineteenth century was seriously under-registered).[100] Despite the successes of public health, there was a change in emphasis from preventive to curative medicine. With the development of Pasteur's germ theory of disease (similar to contagionism) in the late nineteenth century, the emphasis in medicine swung towards the individual case rather than the broader public health and sanitarian idea. The split between preventive and curative approaches widened and the social and health policies of the early years of the twentieth century provided the basis for the ultimate dominance of curative medicine. The starkness of the contrast may have been overemphasised, but many of the 'new diseases' of the last quarter of the nineteenth century were set, not within an environmentalist public health model, but predicted on an individualistic, hereditarian basis.

Alcoholic and later drug inebriety were seen very much in this way.[101] Post-Darwin, biological reductionism was the order of the day and states such as homosexuality were also defined and classified as diseases.[102] But the oversimplification of the preventive/curative divide obscures the developing relationship between medicine and the state in the Victorian period in matters of health and disease. The phrase 'medical police', so common among Enlightened Absolutism in Europe in the eighteenth century, was barely comprehended in England. There was no centralised system of state medicine on the lines envisaged by H. W. Rumsey. But throughout the nineteenth

[99]   J. Gillis, *For Better, for Worse: British Marriages 1600 to the Present* (Oxford, 1986).
[100]   M. Bartley, 'Coronary Heart Disease: A Disease of Affluence or a Disease of Industry?', in Weindling, ed., *Occupational Health*, pp. 137–53.
[101]   R. M. MacLeod, 'The Edge of Hope: Social Policy and Chronic Alcoholism 1870–1900', *Journal of the History of Medicine and Allied Sciences*, 22 (1967), pp. 215–45; Berridge and Edwards, *Opium*.
[102]   J. Weeks, '"Sins and Diseases": Some Notes on Homosexuality in the Nineteenth Century', *History Workshop*, 1 (1976), pp. 211–19. For aspects of the social construction of concepts of disease, see P. Wright and A. Treacher, 'Introduction' to P. Wright and A. Treacher, eds., *The Problem of Medical Knowledge: Examining the Social Construction of Medicine* (Edinburgh, 1982), pp. 1–22; and K. Figlio, 'Chlorosis and Chronic Disease in Nineteenth Century Britain: The Social Construction of Somatic Illness in a Capitalist Society', *Social History*, 3 (1978), pp. 167–97.

century the role of the state in health matters had gradually extended, often in the face of public hostility. In two cases, vaccination (made compulsory for children by legislation of 1853) and the control of prostitution and hence venereal disease by the Contagious Disease Acts of 1864, 1866 and 1869, public hostility to state and medical power was substantial. The incidence of vaccination had actually declined by the end of the century in the face of a well-organised popular movement centred on Leicester.[103] The Contagious Disease Acts, with their double-standard of morality (prostitutes, but not their clients were to be policed and medically examined) were repealed in 1886.[104] But by the end of the century the administrative state had been endowed with powers which, while falling short of the policing or criminalisation of disease, were considerable. As Anthony Wohl comments, 'it was not until the advent of compulsory education late in the century that the daily lives of Victorians were as widely affected by any government action as by state medicine'.[105]

Hospitals as social institutions

The role of the hospital in the provision of state medicine was to become crucial in the twentieth century. In the eighteenth and nineteenth centuries their role has been closely enmeshed in the debate on medical care and mortality decline. The perspectives of economic history have dominated. But issues such as the place of the hospital in medical care, shifts in authority within the hospital, the changing role of in-patient and out-patient care, or its importance within the developing medical professional career structure are now beginning to be investigated. The institutional aspect of hospitals has received less emphasis. The rich preferred to be treated at home, even in surgical cases, until quite late in the nineteenth century. Hospitals had both a controlling function and a differential impact.[106]

It is clear, however, that it was during the eighteenth century that the hospital as an institution began to enter into the area of health care. Few voluntary hospitals were old-established – Bart's (1123) and

[103] R. M. MacLeod, 'Law, Medicine and Public Opinion: The Resistance to Compulsory Health Legislation, 1870–1907', *Public Law*, 107 (1967), pp. 189–211.
[104] P. McHugh, *Prostitution and Victorian Social Reform* (1982); J. Walkowitz, *Prostitution and Victorian Society: Women, Class and the State* (Cambridge, 1980).
[105] Wohl, *Endangered Lives*, p. 42.
[106] Charles E. Rosenberg, 'Inward Vision and Outward Glance: The Shaping of the American Hospital, 1880–1914', *Bulletin of the History of Medicine*, 53 (1979), pp. 346–91, outlines some of the possibilities for future research.

St Thomas's (1207) were almost the only pre-eighteenth-century foundations. From the opening of the Westminster Infirmary in 1720, to 1760, five general hospitals, three lying-in institutions and two special hospitals were founded in London. This was the limit of expansion until the nineteenth century. In the provinces, there were no general hospitals in existence before 1735; by 1800 there were thirty-eight. The peak period of construction appears to have been the decades between 1735 and 1775, when twenty-one hospitals were established.[107] Lying-in, or maternity hospitals, and 'Lock Hospitals' for venereal cases, were also opened. This notable move towards hospital provision has traditionally been ascribed to an awakening spirit of charity and humanitarianism, Christian philanthropy providing for a previously neglected section of the population. Considerations of prestige and social status, along with the simple financial advantage gained through subscribing to a hospital, must also have weighed heavily in the balance. It was a mark of social status to subscribe to, or govern, a voluntary hospital. Subscribers had the right to bestow patronage, and admission to hospital, except in an emergency, could only be obtained by presentation of a subscriber's letter. Subscriptions also gave real power within the hospital itself. The governance and administration of hospitals was, at this stage, still under lay control.[108] Medical staff in eighteenth-century hospitals played a subordinate role. Mostly, they provided medical supervision without payment, partly as a means of making a contribution to the welfare of the poor, but also in order to retain the good will of patrons.

Whether these general hospitals did in fact contribute to the health of the population has lately been much disputed. It was long the conventional wisdom that general hospitals, in both eighteenth and nineteenth centuries, played a significant role in the reduction of mortality, thereby contributing to the population increase which marked the early stages of the industrial revolution. The impact of hospitals

[107]   These developments are dealt with in a number of histories, notably B. Abel-Smith, *The Hospitals, 1800–1948* (1964), pp. 4–16; W. Hartston, 'Medical Dispensaries in Eighteenth Century London', *Proceedings of the Royal Society of Medicine*, 56 (1963), pp. 753–8; W. H. McMenemy, 'The Hospital Movement of the Eighteenth Century and its Development', in F. N. L. Poynter, ed., *The Evolution of Hospitals in Britain* (1964), pp. 43–71; and J. Woodward, *To Do the Sick No Harm: A Study of the British Voluntary Hospital System to 1875* (1974), p. 36. See also G. McLoughlin, *A Short History of the First Liverpool Infirmary, 1749–1824* (Chichester, 1978).

[108]   For example in the Royal Salop Infirmary, see W. B. Howie, 'The Administration of an Eighteenth Century Provincial Hospital: The Royal Salop Infirmary 1747–1830', *Medical History*, 5 (1961), pp. 34–55; and *idem*, 'Finance and Supply in an Eighteenth Century Hospital', *Medical History*, 7 (1963), pp. 126–46.

was a small, but important, argument in the general debate amongst economic historians over birth and death rates and their relative contributions to population increase. The 'McKeown thesis' was revisionist here also. Hospitals' only useful contribution was seen as the isolation of infectious patients; but the likelihood of infection in hospital was also strong.[109] More detailed research – that of S. Cherry on the Norfolk and Norwich Hospital, or Eric Sigsworth on York County Hospital for example – has brought a more equivocal conclusion.[110] In-patient mortality was generally low – below 5 per cent in the Norfolk and Norwich, rarely exceeding 10 per cent in York. The number at York classified as 'cured and relieved' was always around 90 per cent in the century after 1742. John Woodward's findings also mitigate the picture drawn by the sceptics. If admission was limited to young people and adults with non-infectious ailments, at least these limitations made hospitals safer places for their inmates and improved their ability to help those particular patients. Amputations, reckoned to be an index of high mortality, were in fact few in number, at least before anaesthesia became common in the late 1840s. The conclusion at present must be that the contribution of the hospitals to the falling mortality rate 'must remain indeterminate'; they were not, in any case, 'gateways to death'.[111]

Hospitals were in fact catering for only a minute proportion of the population. If they were not 'gateways to death' it was mainly because so few people entered them. In 1800, at the main period of population growth, the general hospitals in England could, with around 4,000 beds, deal with only 30,000 patients a year out of the 10 million people in Great Britain. The impact on population change was minimal. Nor was every would-be patient dealt with, even with a subscriber's letter. Most hospitals excluded pregnant women, children under six, the insane, cases of smallpox, venereal disease, other infectious diseases and fevers (except where the hospital specifically catered for those types of case).[112] The section of the population for which hospital

---

[109] McKeown and Brown, 'Medical Evidence Related to English Population Change'.

[110] S. Cherry, 'The Role of a Provincial Hospital: The Norfolk and Norwich Hospital, 1771–1880', *Population Studies*, 26 (1972), pp. 291–306; E. Sigsworth, 'Gateways to Death? Medicine, Hospitals and Mortality, 1700–1850', in P. Mathias, ed., *Science and Society, 1600–1900* (Cambridge, 1972), pp. 97–110; also Woodward, *To Do the Sick No Harm*, pp. 123–44.

[111] 'Gateways to death' was coined by K. Helleiner, 'The Vital Revolution Reconsidered', in D. Glass and D. Eversley, eds., *Population in History* (1965), pp. 79–86.

[112] Howie, 'The Administration of an Eighteenth Century Provincial Hospital', p. 50, gives an example of the excluding regulations at the Royal Salop Infirmary.

medical care was available was thereby considerably narrowed. Hospitals in fact appear to have made, as Charles Webster has pointed out, only minimal concessions to the crisis of health of the industrial revolution.[113] In some cities, notably Manchester, where medical men like John Ferriar and Thomas Perceval were influential and the radicals and Unitarians associated in the literary and philosophical societies were dissatisfied with the traditional boundaries of Tory and Anglican philanthropy, changes were made.[114] But in most areas, opposition to the modernisation of hospitals, where it was even attempted, won the day.

The dispensaries, which dealt with all cases rather than only those of a less serious nature, supplied the needs not met by the voluntary hospitals. After 1770, dispensaries were founded in rapid succession, mostly on the plan of John Coakley Lettsom, leader of the dispensary movement which started with the establishment of the General Dispensary in Aldersgate Street in 1770. By 1800, there were sixteen general dispensaries in London and twenty-two outside. By the end of the eighteenth century, they were admitting at least 100,000 patients a year with total attendance usually three to four times that number. Although the voluntary hospitals always had greater prestige, between 1770 and 1850, the dispensary provided a more important institutional form of health care for the urban poor. Their decline in importance in the latter half of the nineteenth century came only when hospital out-patient departments expanded to take over most of their work.

The voluntary hospitals were also expanding in the first half of the nineteenth century. The average number of beds increased to around 11,000 by 1861, of which over 3,000 were in London. In London, three more general and eleven special hospitals had been established by 1840, by which date there were 114 provincial general hospitals in existence.[115] Many of this new wave of foundations were established to serve the needs of medical students and teachers as much as those of subscribers, or even patients. Their establishment coincided with the development of medical education as part of the process of

---

[113]   C. Webster, 'The Crisis of the Hospitals during the Industrial Revolution', in E. G. Forbes, ed., *Human Implications of Scientific Advance: Proceedings of the Fifteenth International Congress of the History of Science* (Edinburgh, 1978), pp. 214–23.

[114]   J. V. Pickstone, *Medicine and Industrial Society: A History of Hospital Development in Manchester and its Region, 1752–1946* (Manchester, 1985). For a history of one special hospital, see L. Granshaw, *St Mark's Hospital, London: A Social History of a Specialist Hospital* (1985).

[115]   Woodward, *To Do the Sick No Harm*, p. 36.

professionalisation; this period saw medical teaching firmly located in the hospitals. By 1858, there were twelve London hospitals which had medical schools.[116] This was accompanied by a shifting pattern of authority within the hospital overall from lay to medical control, or, at most, a bipartite system of administration. Increasingly, the control of the lay trustees was exercised indirectly, through bureaucratic channels symbolised by the appointment of house committees and senior lay administrators like hospital secretaries. The doctors, on the other hand, formed themselves into medical committees to ensure their interests were represented in management. By the 1860s, lay and medical committees were working in tandem with responsibility for their own areas; but the house committee had ultimate authority. In the latter half of the century, this process of shifting control was carried further; it was accompanied by change in the function of the hospital. Entry was widened and it became seen as a reparative, curative institution. From the late 1880s, as F. B. Smith has noted, this was taken a stage further, and 'the hospital began to be transformed into an expensive scientific clinical, highly mechanised, research organisation'.[117] This was of importance for the hospitals' predominant twentieth-century role. Such functional changes coincided with the declining power of the governors and transfer of power to doctors within the hospital. The hospital, by the end of the century, had come to take a central part in the medical career structure.

This took place, perhaps paradoxically, at a time of crisis for the hospitals. In the 1860s, the expansion of their facilities and the range of services they offered brought doubts about their effectiveness. The range of surgical operations attempted in the late eighteenth- and early nineteenth-century hospital had been very limited indeed. The introduction of surgical anaesthesia was therefore a not unmixed blessing. Eric Sigsworth suggests that, at York County Hospital, anaesthesia led to higher mortality because of the wider range of operations attempted. Surgery expressed as a proportion of total numbers of in-patients also increased. The resultant pressure on the physical resources of the hospital increased the dangers of sepsis.[118] Lister's antiseptic methods have the credit for saving the hospital from this crisis but evidence also suggests that better nutrition and overall health

---

[116]   Abel-Smith, *The Hospitals*, p. 16.
[117]   Smith, *People's Health*, p. 259.
[118]   Sigsworth, 'Gateways to Death?', p. 108.

among patients operated on could have a significant effect in producing improved host defence.[119]

By the 1860s, too, the hospitals had entered a period of financial crisis. Expanding services produced expanding costs. Money was raised through private charity and the introduction of pay beds. The Hospital Sunday and Hospital Saturday funds, the latter primarily a working- and lower middle-class charity, established themselves as sources of hospital finance in the 1870s. Hospitals, whose patients had previously been almost entirely working class, now began to admit paying patients. By 1890, patients' payment amounted to 5 per cent of the income of London hospitals.[120] The rich were beginning to enter hospitals; but this should not disguise the strong controlling function over working-class patients which the hospital still exercised. Changes in hospital design emphasised the virtues of hygiene and order. The 'slovenly army barracks' of the pre-1860 period gave way to the 'orderly barracks' of the pavilion plan in the 1870s. Many of the eighteenth-century hospitals were like private mansions; and until the 1870s, the characteristic hospital ward was usually square with one window, one fireplace and one door leading into a passage. 'Typical Victorian wards' were built only in the last three decades of the nineteenth century.[121] They enabled the nurse to exercise greater supervision and introduced a strong element of regimentation along with sanitary order. The foundation of hospitals themselves could also be used to secure working-class loyalty.[122]

The late nineteenth century was a period of hospital expansion. By the turn of the century, not only were there more hospitals, but they were also of a greater variety and type. To the voluntary hospitals were added the poor law infirmaries, set up in London in particular

[119]   D. Hamilton and M. Lamb, 'Surgeons and Surgery', in D. Checkland and M. Lamb, eds., *Health Care as Social History: The Glasgow Case* (Aberdeen, 1982), pp. 74–85.

[120]   Abel-Smith, *The Hospitals*, pp. 135–8.

[121]   On hospital design and its association with social order, see A. King, 'Hospital Planning: Revised Thoughts on the Origin of the Pavilion Principle in England', *Medical History*, 10 (1966), pp. 360–73; M. Millman, 'The Influence of the Social Science Association on Hospital Planning in Victorian England', *Medical History*, 18 (1974), pp. 122–37; J. Thompson and G. Goldin, *The Hospital, A Social and Architectural History* (New Haven and London, 1975), pp. 87, 118; and Youngson, *Scientific Revolution in Victorian Medicine*, pp. 186–7.

[122]   J. V. Pickstone, 'Comparative Studies of the Development of Medical Services in Lancashire Towns', in Pickstone, ed., *Health, Disease and Medicine in Lancashire*, pp. 7–32, makes the point that the notable increase in hospital foundations in the factory towns in the late nineteenth century was part of the reassertion of paternalistic values.

after the 1867 Metropolitan Poor Act as part of the Poor Law Board's crusade against outdoor relief. Nineteen London parishes were required to build new, separate infirmaries. There were also separate infectious disease hospitals which were under the control, in London, of the Metropolitan Asylums Board, empowered after 1889 to admit infectious persons who were not paupers. By 1908, 18.2 per cent of all deaths in England and Wales occurred in public institutions, a figure which had doubled over thirty years. It was this tripartite structure which expanded at the end of the century along with improvements in medicine and nursing and the campaign against outdoor relief. In 1861, voluntary hospitals had provided only 18.5 per cent of hospital beds in England and Wales; by 1911, they provided nearly 22 per cent. The relative importance of the poor law infirmaries thus declined, although they continued to expand in absolute terms. In 1861, workhouses provided around 50,000 beds for the sick; in 1911, 121,161.[123] These developments brought with them fundamental changes in the role of patients and in the relationship between doctors in and outside the hospital. The number of out-patients increased rapidly from about 1835, but the most dramatic rise occurred in the last decades of the century. Out-patients now outnumbered in-patients in many hospitals several times over.[124] Until the introduction of the principle of GP referral, hospital out-patient departments were providing primary health care.

Treatment of the abnormal

Most discussion of institutionalisation and social control has concentrated on the asylum, and not the hospital. The history of madness and of psychiatry has encapsulated the changes in the social history of medicine. Initially, it suffered from the overall shortcomings of Whig medical history, tending (as it was primarily compiled by practitioners) to be uncritically optimistic about medical progress; and regarding development in the treatment, control and conceptualisation of insanity as relatively autonomous products of clinical science, thereby ignoring the crucial connections between these developments

---

[123] M. A. Crowther, *The Workhouse System, 1834–1929* (1981), p. 57.
[124] I. S. L. Loudon, 'Historical Importance of Outpatients', *British Medical Journal*, 1 (1978), pp. 974–7.

and the broader socio-cultural features of society.[125] This approach has by no means been abandoned in some quarters, but much has also changed. The anti- and alternative psychiatry movement which had its origins in the 1960s brought in its train a sustained and extensive body of historical revision. Writers like Thomas Szasz denied that the history of insanity was a story of benign and progressive reform. Madness had, he claimed, been 'manufactured' in order to legitimise the emergent psychiatric profession. Michel Foucault interpreted reform as the reverse of humane, a 'gigantic moral imprisonment'.[126] These views were elaborated so that the treatment of the mad was no longer seen within a progressive framework, but in terms of the strategies of professionalisation, the labelling of social deviance, the elaboration of social control through medicalisation. Overtly penal and punitive approaches were replaced, in the modern capitalist state, by the social policing function of institutions and asylums. The historical work stimulated by these types of perspectives has enormously enriched the study of the insane.

Central to both 'old' and 'new' traditions in the history of insanity has been the concept of the eighteenth century as a decisive epistemological break in theories of insanity and attitudes towards the insane. Until the mid-seventeenth century, Bedlam was the only asylum in England and mad people were treated by medical, magical or religious means.[127] Lunatics and others were liable to be tried and executed as witches or possessed by the devil. Michel Foucault offered a contrasting 'optimistic' view of pre-Enlightenment Europe, whereby the 'holy fool' was seen as the embodiment of a type of higher wisdom. In England this was not the general rule; mad people were frequently neglected and reduced to begging. Michael MacDonald's study of the case books of a clergyman-doctor, Michael Napier, in early seventeenth-century England has suggested a number of

---

[125]   See, for example, R. Hunter and I. MacAlpine, *Three Hundred Years of Psychiatry, 1535–1860* (Oxford, 1963); also *idem, Psychiatry for the Poor, 1851. Colney Hatch Asylum, Friern Hospital, 1973: A Medical and Social History* (1974); D. Leigh, *The Historical Development of Psychiatry* (Oxford, 1961); and K. Jones, *A History of the Mental Health Services* (1972).

[126]   For an introduction to the debates in this area, see J. Busfield, *Managing Madness* (1986); Sedgwick, *Psycho-Politics*; also Szasz, *The Manufacture of Madness; idem, The Myth of Mental Illness* (1972); Foucault, *Madness and Civilisation*.

[127]   See, for example, B. Clarke, *Mental Disorder in Earlier Britain* (Cardiff, 1975); T. J. Schoeneman, 'The Role of Mental Illness in the European Witch Hunts of the Sixteenth and Seventeenth Centuries: An Assessment', *Journal of the History of the Behavioral Sciences*, 13 (1977), pp. 337–51.

conclusions relevant also to discussion of the eighteenth-century change. Whether the malady was physical or mental, and whether its cause was thought to be natural or supernatural, Napier's treatment was eclectic, with a mix of medication, religion and advice, and care in the family, not custody. MacDonald also clearly demonstrates the connection between politics and dominant images of health and disease. 'Medical science' triumphed over religious explanations and reactions not because it was any more effective at that time but because its attitudes better suited the establishment in its drive to political power. Religious and magical alternatives were not favoured because of their association with political radicalism.[128]

In MacDonald's view, the eighteenth century was 'a disaster for the insane'. How then are we to interpret the developments of this century? Traditionally it was seen as a pre-reform age of whips and beatings, culminating in a House of Commons committee in 1815 which exposed Bethlem's corruption in horrifying detail and thus inaugurated the reform era in psychiatry.[129] Foucault's revisionist interpretation fundamentally opposed this view. He argued that all over Europe from the mid-seventeenth century, the age of the 'great confinement' dawned. With the coming of the 'Age of Reason', the new rationalist mentalities associated with the Enlightenment and the bureaucratic and police powers associated with the modern absolutist state combined to sequester 'irrational' elements of society.[130] Madness had a threatening power and unreason was dealt with by total seclusion. The mad were threats to the dominant moral and political economy and had to be locked away. But Roy Porter has recently pointed out that there really was no 'great confinement' in eighteenth-century England. By 1800 no more than 5,000 people were confined in institutions (compared to 100,000 by 1900).[131] Most lunatics who were confined were put in special new institutions, but the majority were private rather than public, admitting middle- and upper-class patients in considerable numbers as well as the poor. Porter sees the rise of the madhouse from the late eighteenth century as an important historical phenomenon. It was not a state initiative, but part of the

---

[128] M. MacDonald, *Mystical Bedlam: Madness, Anxiety and Healing in Seventeenth Century England* (Cambridge, 1982).

[129] For a traditional view, see, K. Jones, *Lunacy, Law and Conscience, 1744–1845* (1955).

[130] Foucault, *Madness and Civilisation*.

[131] This is discussed in R. Porter, *Mind Forg'd Manacles: Madness and Psychiatry in England from the Restoration to the Regency* (1987), pp. 1–32, 110–68.

developing consumer society. Most of these institutions – about fifty were in existence by 1800 – were privately owned entrepreneurial ventures, part of what William Parry-Jones has called the 'trade in lunacy'. They were part of a booming market economy in which families handed over functions formerly dealt with in the family to newly developing service occupations.[132] Not all such asylums were run by medical men, but the ideology of humanity and curability was developed as part of the service, to appeal to 'respectable' families. There were also a small number of public asylums set up – the Manchester Lunatic Hospital was established in 1763 – as part of the wider philanthropic concerns of the age.

The question of treatment is part of the debate. The orthodox view argued that moral and humane treatment dates from when Pinel struck the chains from the mad at the Bicêtre in Paris, and, in England, when the Tuke family at the York Retreat initiated 'moral therapy'. These were attempts to influence insanity by moral example rather than physical force. Foucault has also emphasised the brutality of the eighteenth century. Brutal treatment was common, but also within an ideology of care and cure which increasingly emphasised the humanity of treating lunatics in a 'rational' manner. The 'psychiatric' approach to madness associated with the nineteenth century had its roots in the eighteenth. Locke's *Essay on Human Understanding*, aiming to give an account of false beliefs and consequently disorders of the mind, held out hopes of cure by a process of moral re-education.[133] Through Enlightenment rationalism developed therapeutic optimism and faith in the possibility of cure.[134] There are almost two eighteenth-century histories of psychiatry, dependent variously on reactions to middle-class 'vapours' and 'the spleen' and to those of 'Bedlam madness'.[135] But certainly some of the intellectual origins of nineteenth-century psychiatry lay in the previous century.

It is in the nineteenth century that controversies between rival interpretations have been most acute, in part because the nineteenth-century history so closely relates to contemporary concerns. The radical urge to 'decarcerate' the insane to community care (as distinct from

---

[132]   W. L. Parry-Jones, *The Trade in Lunacy: A Study of Private Madhouses in England and Wales in the Eighteenth and Nineteenth Centuries* (1971).
[133]   Porter, *Mind Forg'd Manacles*, pp. 169–228.
[134]   V. Skultans, *English Madness, Ideas on Insanity, 1580–1890* (1979), pp. 36, 56.
[135]   An observation made by W. Bynum at a Wellcome Institute research seminar, 1982.

its cost-containing reality in the 1980s) found historical justification in the operation and impact of the asylum in the nineteenth century.[136] The movement against orthodox psychiatry in the 1960s questioned, historically as well as currently, whether medical methods of treatment were indeed appropriate. The question of incarceration has been central to treatment. By the mid-nineteenth century, the large county asylums under central inspection became the norm for the treatment of the pauper insane. Earlier permissive or partial legislation – chiefly the County Asylum Acts of 1808 and 1828 and the Madhouse Act of the same year – had made possible the establishment of county asylums. A certain amount of administrative centralisation began, although the role of the visiting justices under the 1828 County Asylums Act and of the Metropolitan Commissioners in Lunacy who replaced the Visitors of the Royal College of Physicians under the 1828 Madhouse Act was relatively ineffectual. But the 1845 acts – associated with the work of Lord Shaftesbury – provided the Lunacy Commissioners on a permanent basis with national powers of inspection – and compelled the provision of asylums chargeable to the poor rate. By the end of 1847, thirty-six of the fifty-two counties had built asylums of their own. The pauper insane were moved out of the workhouses and private licensed houses and into the new asylums.[137] The more that were built, the more people were sent to them. Some, like Colney Hatch, were gigantic, holding up to 3,000 patients.

The asylum system can no longer be simply seen as a triumphant achievement of Victorian social concern. Like many other developments, it was far from being entirely new. There was already an extensive institutional network of private madhouses in the eighteenth century.[138] Its connection with industrialisation and social control remains problematic. Andrew Scull, for instance, has argued that lunacy as a problem and institutionalisation as its solution must be related to the creation of a society where mobility of labour and a wage economy had rapidly increased. Economically vulnerable families who were no longer able to support an unproductive and

---

[136] For the radical commitment to community care, see A. Scull, *Decarceration: Community Treatment and the Deviant: A Radical View* (Englewood Cliffs, 1977).

[137] Parry-Jones, *Trade in Lunacy*, p. 51; Skultans, *English Madness*, p. 119; R. G. Hodgkinson, 'Provision for Pauper Lunatics 1834–71', *Medical History*, 10 (1966), pp. 138–54.

[138] Parry-Jones, *Trade in Lunacy*, pp. 168, 221, 289–92. Parry-Jones argues that the abuses publicised in some private houses were untypical of general standards of care.

disruptive family member were only too willing to hand over responsibility to the asylum doctors.[139] Klaus Doerner's argument is that the extension of the asylum had its origins in the bourgeois state's need for labour power; asylums were the means of integrating economically useless members of society into the factories and armies.[140] The low cure rate in asylums makes this explanation doubtful; and it does not explain the 'birth of the asylum' in countries such as Ireland, where a public asylum system was established without the necessary industrialisation preconditions.[141]

The connection between industrialisation and insanity was not a simple one. Olive Anderson's work on suicide shows the highest incidence in non-industrial areas and particularly in London.[142] John Walton's study of asylum admissions in Lancashire between 1848 and 1850 shows that the emerging large urban conurbations sent more than their fair share, while a lower percentage came from the textile areas with their 'unusually supportive networks' of neighbours and relations. The important variables would appear to be migration patterns (three-fifths of the patients from Liverpool had come more than 30 miles), family structure and economy and the scale of urban living.[143] The asylum inexorably grew, but no one was really promoting it; ratepayers disliked its expense and families found it shameful. Insanity in the Victorian period, and indeed later, was primarily a problem of poverty; in the 1840s the poverty of the middle years of life rather than that of old age.[144] By the end of the century the pauper insane formed 90 per cent of the asylum population. Increasingly, they became a dumping ground for elderly women. According to the 1871 census, for every 1,000 male lunatics, there were 1,182 females; for every 1,000 male pauper lunatics, 1,242 females. By the end of the century 'women had decisively taken the lead in the career of psychiatric patient'. The tightening up of poor law administration increased stress on poor women; for others, the asylum offered a more tolerant

[139]   A. Scull, *Museums of Madness: The Social Organisation of Insanity in Nineteenth Century England* (1979).
[140]   K. Doerner, *Madness and the Bourgeoisie: A Social History of Insanity and Psychiatry* (Oxford, 1981), pp. 19–95.
[141]   M. Finnane, *Insanity and the Insane in Post Famine Ireland* (1981).
[142]   O. Anderson, *Suicide in Victorian and Edwardian England* (Oxford, 1987).
[143]   J. Walton, 'Lunacy and the Industrial Revolution: A Study of Asylum Admissions in Lancashire, 1848–50', *Journal of Social History*, 13 (1979), pp. 1–22.
[144]   *Ibid.*, pp. 12–13; M. A. Shepherd, 'Lunatic Asylum Patients in Warwickshire, 1841–1862', *Bull. SSHM*, 18 (1976), pp. 16–17.

and interesting life than they could expect outside. Notions of femininity and insanity were both culturally constructed; beliefs that women were naturally more emotional and unstable inspired medical theories – of puerperal and menopausal insanity, for example – postulating femininity as a kind of mental illness in itself.[145] Of what it meant to be an asylum patient – or to be mad – less is known.[146]

The demonstrated failure of the asylum did not lead to its abandonment – far from it, for in London, for example, the huge Metropolitan District asylums of Leavesden and Caterham were built as late as 1867 after enquiries into the metropolitan workhouses.[147] But, for financial reasons if nothing else, it became the policy by the 1870s to send the dangerously insane away and retain the harmless in the workhouse. From the 1860s, many workhouses, and all the larger urban ones, had begun to have separate insane wards.[148] The 1890 Lunacy Act was a reflection of this loss of faith. Asylums could only take certified patients – patients could not be certified until their illness was obvious to lay authorities. The work of the asylum was confirmed as largely custodial.

The early nineteenth-century theories of insanity had involved a crucial symbiosis between somatic and moral approaches. The 'moral regime' associated perhaps erroneously with the York Retreat (the Retreat never fully adopted its own moral regime, and physical restraint and medication were still in use) forced a medical reworking of the theoretical basis of insanity to encompass both medical and moral approaches.[149] Phrenology, a doctrine which had widespread support in progressive circles and which had particular connections with working-class radicalism and free thought, completely

---

[145] E. Showalter, 'Victorian Women and Insanity', *Victorian Studies*, 23 (1979), pp. 157–81, reprinted in A. Scull, ed., *Madhouses, Mad-Doctors and Madmen* (1981), pp. 313–36. See also E. Showalter, *The Female Malady: Women, Madness and English Culture, 1830–1980* (New York, 1985).

[146] MacDonald's study, *Mystical Bedlam*, shows what can be done with seventeenth-century material; see also R. Porter, *A Social History of Madness: Stories of the Insane* (1987). For the experiences of a contemporary mental patient, see R. Woods, 'From the Pit', *Oral History*, 7 (1979), pp. 59–62.

[147] Hodgkinson, 'Provision for Pauper Lunatics', pp. 138–54; D. J. Mellett, *The Prerogative of Asylumdom* (1982), p. 151.

[148] Mellett, *The Prerogative of Asylumdom*, p. 156, points out that by 1864, 104 of the 688 workhouses in England and Wales had separate lunatic wards.

[149] A. Digby, 'Moral Treatment at the York Retreat', in W. F. Bynum, R. Porter and M. Shepherd, eds., *The Anatomy of Madness*, 3 vols. (1985), vol. 2, pp. 52–72; A. Digby, *Madness, Morality and Medicine: A Study of the York Retreat 1796–1914* (Cambridge, 1985).

reorientated psychiatric theory.[150] The phrenological concept of the brain as the organ of the mind made possible an interpretation of mental illness related to the physiology of the brain. All mental functions were accompanied by physiological processes; mental derangements therefore had their corresponding structural malformation. Even moral insanity, the condition described in 1835 by the Bristol physician, James Cowles Prichard, could be explained as the derangement of the sections of the brain controlling the moral faculty. Medical theory could therefore encompass moral treatment while retaining a physical disease basis.[151] In ascribing to insanity a form of moral perversity it emphasised the values of self-help and self-control.

But the changes in theories of insanity which marked the last quarter of the century largely had their effect outside the asylum. The somatic–pathological approaches to psychological medicine exercised an ever stronger hold and there was a tendency to disparage any kind of psychological approach to problems of mental disorder.[152] New and broader concepts of disease – as, for instance, George Beard's 'discovery' of neurasthenia – asserted for whole realms of functional nervous disorders a common origin, and gave them respectable status as genuine disease entities with a somatic basis.[153] Such concepts – at least initially – were applied almost exclusively to the better-off classes, who in any case formed a relatively small proportion of the institutionalised insane population. Those in private madhouses and individual care had, in contrast to the pauper insane, hardly increased at all in the nineteenth century.[154] But other tendencies were also apparent. The writings of Henry Maudsley – *Responsibility in Mental Disease* (1874) for example – not only broadened the concept of insanity

[150]   See Cooter, *The Cultural Meaning of Popular Science*; also *idem*, 'Phrenology: Provocation of Progress', *History of Science*, 14 (1976), pp. 211–34; G. N. Cantor, 'The Edinburgh Phrenology Debate, 1803–28', *Annals of Science*, 32 (1975), pp. 195–218; Shapin, 'Phrenological Knowledge'; McLaren, 'Phrenology: Medium and Message'; D. de Guistino, *Conquest of the Mind: Phrenology and Victorian Social Thought* (1975).

[151]   E. T. Carlson and N. Dain, 'The Meaning of Moral Insanity', *Bulletin of the History of Medicine*, 36 (1962), pp. 130–40; P. McCandless, 'Liberty and Lunacy: The Victorians and Wrongful Confinement', *Journal of Social History*, 11 (1978) pp. 366–86, describes the appeal of a theory ascribing moral perversity to insanity.

[152]   M. J. Clark, 'The Rejection of Psychological Approaches to Mental Disorder in Late Nineteenth Century British Psychiatry', in Scull, ed., *Madhouses, Mad-Doctors and Madmen*, pp. 271–312.

[153]   B. Sickerman, 'The Use of a Diagnosis: Doctors, Patients and Neurasthenia', *Journal of the History of Medicine and Allied Sciences*, 32 (1977), pp. 33–54.

[154]   Scull, *Museums of Madness*, pp. 242–5; Parry-Jones, *Trade in Lunacy*, pp. 46–51, indicates how the movement of pauper lunatics into the county asylums left the private madhouses with relatively few patients.

to include the neuroses, but emphasised hereditary and 'constitutional predisposition' to insanity. This had a strong influence on theories of disease in allied areas such as homosexuality and alcohol.[155]

IV 1900–50

Many of the themes so richly investigated in the nineteenth-century social history of medicine await research in a twentieth-century context. The social history of health and medicine in England in the twentieth century has largely focussed on the development of health policy. Despite the undoubted change from public and preventive health to a focus on personal health and curative, clinical medicine at the end of the twentieth century, the development and creation of state collective action in health service provision was one of the outstanding features of the first half of the twentieth century. The nineteenth-century relationship between medicine and the state became a central feature of health policy development; and public expectations also swung towards government provision in health matters, probably from around the First World War. The main part of this section will therefore concentrate on that development. But we still know relatively little about other areas of health – about patterns of self-medication, for example, or the treatment of insanity or mental illness.

Health policy 1900–11: welfare liberalism and national health insurance

The welfare reforms of the 1900s in which health played an important part, and which were in particular associated with the Liberal government of 1905–15, have, in the traditional historiography, been seen as the beginnings of the welfare state, benevolent measures which were the first steps on the road to an all-encompassing system of social welfare. But this interpretation is inadequate. First, social reform in the health sphere had clear Victorian antecedents. Despite the curative emphasis of late nineteenth-century medicine, there was a longstanding tradition of state action in the public health sphere, underlined by Public Health Acts of 1875 and 1890. But the important immediate impetus came from concern about the economy and Britain's status as an imperial power; and the debate on national

---

[155] Weeks, '"Sins and Diseases"', pp. 211–19; also J. Weeks, *Coming Out* (1977), pp. 23–32, and J. Weeks, *Sex, Politics and Society* (1981), pp. 96–121. For drink, see P. McCandless, 'Curses of Civilisation: Insanity and Drunkenness in Victorian Britain', *British Journal of Addiction*, 79 (1984), pp. 49–58.

deterioration which also had its origins in the 1880s, but which became acute in the 1900s in particular because of the impact of the Boer War. During that war, which Britain won only with difficulty, large numbers of army volunteers were rejected because they were physically unfit to fight. The publication of Charles Booth's survey on the London poor and Seebohm Rowntree's study of York reinforced fears about national decline which were investigated in 1904 by an Inter-Departmental Committee on Physical Deterioration. There was a new urgency, fuelled also by the high infant mortality rate, of discussions of poverty and sickness. Fears of racial decline stimulated eugenic views which advocated measures of race hygiene such as the physical segregation, or even sterilisation, of the mentally and physically unfit. Eugenics, a doctrine with appeal to the professional middle classes and to some social reformers such as the Webbs, stimulated a debate between 'nature' and 'nurture'.[156] But it was 'positive' rather than 'negative' eugenics which had the most impact. Only the Mental Deficiency Act of 1913, which provided for the certification and confinement of mental defectives, expressed eugenic views unalloyed.[157] Most discussion in the 1900s concentrated on measures to improve the environment and numbers of the working class rather than removing the unfit. Lesley Doyal has called the welfare reforms an 'important element in the attempt to restructure British capitalism';[158] and J. R. Hay's research on employers' attitudes to state welfare has shown how employers, too, were in this period beginning to provide – or demanding from the state – pensions, sickness benefit and medical care, mostly not out of altruism, but in order to promote national (and business) efficiency.[159]

Welfare (and health) reforms were also stimulated by the growth of the labour movement and its increasing militancy after 1909. But the attitude of the labour movement to state welfare, even in health matters, was divided. A united labour movement demanding social welfare and health provision is also part of historical mythology. There was a strong distrust of state and bureaucratic intrusion in particular where, as with health visitors, for example, assessment of

---

[156]   For eugenics, see G. R. Searle, *Eugenics and Politics in Britain, 1900–1914* (Leyden, 1976).

[157]   H. G. Simmons, 'Explaining Social Policy: The English Mental Deficiency Act of 1913', *Journal of Social History*, 11 (1978), pp. 387–403; also *idem*, 'Mental Handicap and Education', *Oxford Review of Education*, 9 (1983), special issue.

[158]   L. Doyal and I. Pennell, *The Political Economy of Health* (1979), p. 160.

[159]   J. R. Hay, 'Employers' Attitudes to Social Policy and the Concept of Social Control, 1900–1920', in P. Thane, ed., *The Origins of British Social Policy* (1978), pp. 107–25.

working-class habits was involved.[160] Many working-class people felt that the need was for full employment and proper levels of pay to enable the working class to provide for their own needs. There was indeed a thriving independent tradition of working-class self-help in health matters before the 1911 act. Friendly societies and insurance companies underwrote medical care for those too poor to pay private medical fees but who were not eligible for poor law provisions. 'Contract' or 'club' practice under lay, not medical, control was part of the bewildering array of medical services, but also indicative of trends of local and grass-roots control which were abandoned in the moves towards municipal and state provision in health matters in the 1930s and 1940s.[161]

The demand for 'national efficiency' concentrated, in health matters, on children and young adults. For children, the argument still focussed on the role of inadequate and ignorant mothering, on working mothers and lack of breast-feeding or proper care, rather than environmental factors.[162] Sir Arthur Newsholme, Medical Officer to the Local Government Board, in three reports on infant mortality between 1909 and 1914, still placed most blame on women's work. Anna Davin has shown how such arguments represented shifts in belief about woman's role within the family as mother rather than wife and about the relation of the family to the state.[163] Most emphasis was thus placed on instruction for motherhood, clinics and health visitors, rather than the provision of material aid. The role of health visiting, which expanded just before the decline in the birth rate, has proved controversial. The movement did have some effect on the death rate although there is disagreement about how much.[164] The Education (Provision of Meals) Act of 1906 was a step towards recognition that mothers were not necessarily to blame for poor feeding. School medical inspection became law in 1907. The Midwives Act of 1902 and legislation on the registration of births were measures

---

[160] J. Lewis, *The Politics of Motherhood: Child and Maternal Welfare in England 1900–1939* (1980), p. 105.

[161] See D. Green, *Working Class Patients and the Medical Establishment: Self Help in Britain from the Mid-Nineteenth Century to 1948* (1986); also R. Earwicker, 'Miners' Health Services in the 1930s' (paper given to History Workshop Conference, Oxford, 1984).

[162] C. Dyhouse, 'Working-Class Mothers and Infant Mortality in England, 1895–1914', *Journal of Social History*, 12 (1978), pp. 248–67.

[163] A. Davin, 'Imperialism and Motherhood', *History Workshop*, 5 (1978), pp. 9–65.

[164] See, for example, D. Dwork, *Work is Good for Babies and Other Young Children: A History of the Infant and Child Welfare Movement in England, 1898–1918* (1987); also, I. M. Buchanan, 'Infant Mortality in British Coal Mining Communities, 1880–1911' (unpublished PhD thesis, London University, 1983).

intended to reduce the high rate of infant mortality. The childhood diseases were in decline; deaths from whooping cough and diarrhoea fell rapidly in the early 1900s. Jane Lewis concludes that 'the reasons for the decline in the infant mortality rate were as complex as the causes of infant death'. It is also salutary to remember that in England and Wales as a whole just before the First World War, infant mortality in unskilled labouring families was double that of families belonging to the upper two social classes.[165]

Adult males were dealt with by the 1911 National Health Insurance Act.[166] This provided a basic income during sickness (and for certain workers during unemployment) and a national scheme of primary medical care. It covered all workers earning below £160 a year (the limit for income tax) and all manual workers irrespective of their level of earnings. There was a disability pension and a 30s. maternity benefit paid to the wives of insured men. Contributions – 7d. week from male and 6d. from female employees, 3d. from the employer and 2d. from the state (although Lloyd George's slogan was 9d. for 4d.) – were administered by familiar organisations, the friendly societies, trade unions and commercial insurance companies, the 'approved societies'. Insured contributors had the right to medical treatment by a doctor on a local list or 'panel'. Free hospital treatment was available only for TB cases. The manoeuvring behind the 1911 act – analysed in detail by Bentley Gilbert – had less to do with the welfare of working people than might be expected. The medical elite wanted to stamp out competition; the Fabians wanted state socialism; and Lloyd George saw health insurance as a bulwark against pauperism, not sickness. For this reason the wives and children of insured men were almost entirely ignored. As Gilbert remarks, 'the aim of national insurance was to replace lost income not to cure sickness'.[167] It had other crucial effects on health care provision. The establishment of a Medical Research Committee (Medical Research Council after the 1914–18 war) was one of its more significant side-effects. One of its specific aims was to end the conflict between GPs and hospitals about the use of hospital out-patient departments as a form of primary health care.

The resultant availability of a GP service to manual workers may

---

[165]   Lewis, *Politics of Motherhood*; Wohl, *Endangered Lives*.
[166]   The most detailed account of national health insurance is in B. B. Gilbert, *The Evolution of National Insurance in Great Britain: The Origins of the Welfare State* (1966). See also J. L. Brand, *Doctors and the State: The British Medical Profession and Government Action in Health, 1870–1912* (Baltimore, 1965).
[167]   Gilbert, *Evolution of National Insurance*, p. 314.

have resulted in the undoubted decline in out-patient numbers in the second decade of the twentieth century. The principle of GP referral and other restrictive measures, together with the effects of the First World War, were also important. But the act also led to a much sharper division between the consultant-based hospital service and general practice and a lengthened chain of medical care. GPs, secure in their income from insured persons, were encouraged to send patients into hospital for treatment; out-patients conversely now had access to GP care. Separation had always existed between hospitals and GPs in urban areas but both had been providing almost complete medical care for different sections of the population. Now, care of the patient was divided between the GP and the hospital, with the hospital providing a specialist service at an out- as well as an in-patient level. This was of fundamental importance for the subsequent development of health policy and care.[168]

Health and the First World War

This system was barely in place before it was put to the test in the First World War. The debate on 'war and social change' which has animated twentieth-century historians includes a health dimension and has recently begun to focus on the First rather than the Second World War. The pre-revisionist view was that conditions in Britain during that war were detrimental to the health of the civilian population, in the main because of food shortages. Recently, however, this view has been modified. Jay Winter's work in particular has argued that the war years were a time of significant gains for civilian health, with the greatest improvements coming among the poorest sections of the community.[169] In his view, the improvement of life expectancy reduced class differentials in survival rates, and survival rates between different strata of the working class. Such improvements were maintained after the war.

So far as wartime standards of living are concerned, the evidence suggests a modest increase. During the war, many men and women were in regular employment for the first time with opportunities for

---

[168]   There is discussion of this development in Loudon, 'Outpatients', and Abel-Smith, *The Hospitals*, pp. 238–47.
[169]   J. M. Winter, *The Great War and the British People* (1986).

overtime working as well as higher rates of pay. But rising food prices and rents were the other side of the coin; and it is difficult to estimate whether earnings were actually rising faster than prices. A general improvement in living standards is suggested by the decline in mortality among adult male workers who did not enter the services. Life expectancy for men increased from forty-nine in 1911 to fifty-six in 1921. But these are national figures, and, clearly, regional, class and occupational variations were considerable. Also, the lack of available data on morbidity may disguise the continuing prevalence of poor health. The trend in female mortality was also a downward one during the war. There were increases in 1915 and 1918; the decline, according to Winter, occurred primarily in nutrition-related diseases, diarrhoea and complications in pregnancy and childbirth. But the risks of pregnancy and childbirth were in fact no worse, but not much better than either the prewar or postwar periods. In 1917, for example, total puerperal mortality rates were similar to those for 1911. Prewar trends were not significantly altered during the war. The decline in maternal mortality may even have been a result of the absence of many doctors on wartime service. There was a marked correlation between maternal mortality and medical intervention; unlike doctors, midwives rarely practised instrumental deliveries.

Medical services in general were less apparent during the war because of the diversion of doctors and services into the war effort. For the first time the government subsidised the voluntary hospitals so that they could deal with war casualties, but many closed their out-patient departments and certain wards. It is unclear how far this absence of medical care had anything to do with health developments. Winter's argument is that the medical community in Britain had a holding role preventing worse things from happening. But Linda Bryder has recently pointed out that it is difficult to see how medical services could have had any impact at all.[170] There were 8,000 doctors providing care for 14,200,000 people (a ratio of 1 to 1,777, with considerable local variation). And even in 1918, only 40 per cent of the population was covered by medical insurance.

The impact of the influenza epidemic of 1918–19 was so uniform throughout Europe and in all social classes that both Winter and his

---

[170]   L. Bryder, 'The First World War: Healthy or Hungry?', *History Workshop*, 24 (1987), pp. 141–55.

critics avoid the apparently commonsense conclusion that nutritional levels and epidemic mortality were associated. As Pat Thane remarks, 'it is difficult to ascribe the high death rate to any cause but the strength of the virus'.[171] But the rise in tuberculosis is a fact which ill-fits the optimistic point of view. There was a 25 per cent increase in deaths from the disease in England and Wales from 1913 to 1918 and a 35 per cent increase among women aged twenty to twenty-five. Winter has related these deaths to the concentration of population in large urban centres and in particular in munitions factories, and also to the deterioration in housing conditions during the war. He denies any association with nutritional factors, which might tend to under-mine the general optimistic thesis. But Linda Bryder's work on tuber-culosis has cast doubt on this explanation.[172] Contemporaries did stress nutrition as a factor in the rise in TB deaths. The high tubercu-losis death rate of Jarrow, for example, compared with the relatively low rates of neighbouring Blaydon, which had equally poor housing but better employment opportunities. And the disruption of TB ser-vices because of the conscription of TB officers was hardly important; for the service had barely got under way before the war broke out.

The case for tuberculosis is certainly not proven; and the increased death rate of elderly people during the war indicates that their stan-dards of living did not improve. It is also likely that the same was true for those not in full-time war work. Even those with such work may have suffered a deterioration in health; TNT poisoning in muni-tions factories – the yellow 'canary girls' – was one example.[173] Win-ter's conclusion that 'There is no basis for the claim that in the short-term or in the long-term, war conditions were damaging or injurious to the health of men who stayed at home or to their families' remains in dispute.[174]

Aspects of civilian health did improve during the war. The establish-ment in 1916 of the Central Control Board, control of pub opening

[171] P. Thane, *The Foundations of the Welfare State* (1982), p. 134; J. M. Winter, 'The Impact of the First World War on Civilian Health in Britain', *Economic History Review*, 2nd ser., 30 (1977), pp. 487–507.

[172] Bryder, 'The First World War', pp. 141–55; also *idem, Beyond the Magic Mountain: The Social History of Tuberculosis* (Oxford, 1988).

[173] A. Ineson and D. Thom, 'TNT poisoning and the Employment of Women Workers in the First World War', in Weindling ed., *Occupational Health*, pp. 89–107; also E. Hall, *Canary Girls and Stockpots* (Luton, 1977), pp. 10–14.

[174] Winter, 'The Impact of the First World War', p. 503.

hours and of 'treating' had a significant impact on an already declining level of alcohol consumption; it also affected directly alcohol-related deaths from cirrhosis of the liver.[175] Concern about the wartime rise in venereal disease led to the Venereal Disease Act of 1917, which controlled the advertising of worthless remedies. Infant mortality also continued to fall. Infant welfare continued its expansion during the war years and a whole battery of measures affecting child health passed into law. Comprehensive ante-natal and post-natal care pressed ahead under the auspices of the Local Government Board. From 1915 the Board of Education financed childcare classes for mothers, the Midwives Act was amended in 1916 to make training more rigorous; and in 1918 a Maternity and Child Welfare Act further enabled local authorities to establish ante-natal and child welfare clinics. The number of full-time health visitors in England and Wales rose from 600 in 1914 to 1,355 in 1918, many of them employed by voluntary organisations. But such an apparently impressive expansion should not disguise the fact that, as Jane Lewis has pointed out, the services offered were extremely limited. In particular, these infant welfare centres only offered diagnosis and advice, and not treatment. This was primarily because of the infant welfare movement's stress on the individual mother and self-help. The centres were educational, not nutritional or curative, centres.[176] Moreover, only 60,000 of the 700,000 babies born each year were under the care of health centres by 1918. The fall in mortality may also have been connected with improved standards of nutrition. There was a notable decline in mortality after the first months of life, and deaths from gastro-enteritis, in particular, were checked. The rationing of milk and the fixing of prices for it in 1917 may have had some impact, although, in fact many poor families could still not afford to buy it. It could have been shortage, and not plentiful supply of milk which determined the decline, since there is no evidence that the quality of milk supply improved during the war.[177]

[175]   M. E. Rose, 'The Success of Social Reform? The Central Control Board (Liquor Traffic) 1916–1922', in M. R. D. Foot, ed., *War and Society* (1973); J. Turner, 'State Purchase of the Liquor Trade in the First World War', *Historical Journal*, 23 (1980), pp. 589–616; R. Smart, 'The Effect of Licensing Restrictions during 1914–18 on Drunkenness and Liver Cirrhosis Deaths in Britain', *British Journal of Addiction*, 69 (1974), pp. 109–21.
[176]   Lewis, *Politics of Motherhood*.
[177]   Bryder, 'The First World War', pp. 141–55.

Interwar health and health policy

Health policy in the post First World War period resumed some of its prewar concerns. One of these was the establishment of a Ministry of Health. Fabians had long been interested in the establishment of such a ministry as a means to prevent sickness and consequently poverty. In 1907, when school medical inspection was established, a small group of social reformers hoping to create a comprehensive school medical service was already planning for an eventual Ministry of Health. They included the Webbs and the socialist Margaret McMillan, along with George Newman, head of the newly established Medical Department of the Board of Education, and Robert Morant, chief civil servant at the Board. Morant and Newman hoped to develop a comprehensive free health service for children as the basis of an eventual national free health service. Their belief in comprehensive health planning rested in particular on the Minority Report of the Royal Commission on the Poor Laws, which had pressed for the integration of public and poor law health services into a 'State Medical Service'. Opposition from the British Medical Association, then as later, was founded on a fear of local authority domination of medical care. The situation was complicated when Morant left the permanent secretaryship at the Board of Education and became chairman of the National Health Insurance Commission, where he set about building up a competing health service. Relations were also strained between George Newman and Dr Arthur Newsholme, from 1908 Chief Medical Officer for the Local Government Board. Newman objected to Newsholme's plans to centralise medical services under his own department.

The possibility of postwar reconstruction brought such tensions to a head. The idea of a Ministry of Health was supported by Christopher Addison, himself a doctor, and head of Lloyd George's Ministry of Reconstruction. But although the ministry was eventually established in 1919, the form it took was no victory for the advocates of an integrated health service.[178] When in 1916 Lord Rhondda became President of the Local Government Board, there began a move which led to the Ministry of Health. Rhondda supported the idea of such a Ministry; but the struggle hinged on who would control the new department, the Local Government Board with its established connections among the local authorities, or the newer National Health

---

[178] For the establishment of the Ministry of Health, see F. Honigsbaum, *The Struggle for the Ministry of Health, 1914–1919* (1970).

Insurance Commission. There was conflict between the Local Government Board and the National Health Insurance Commission which wished to avoid any association with the poor law. The approved societies feared for the safety of their monopoly of health insurance; and the poor law guardians guarded their health functions. Lloyd George's response was to move Lord Rhondda to the Food Ministry; his successor at the Local Government Board, Hayes Fisher, was determined to maintain the Board's power undisturbed. The Health Ministry was delayed for eighteen months. When it was established in 1919, with Addison as the first Minister of Health, it took over the health and poor law functions of the Local Government Board with the National Insurance Commission attached.

The new ministry was little improvement on its predecessor. Anne Crowther has pointed out how the last years of the Local Government Board had been active ones with institutional change, and a greater preparedness for reform on the part of the guardians.[179] But such activity did not survive the war and the depression; Ministry of Health reports in the 1920s urged economy in institutional relief. The struggle over the establishment of the ministry and its subsequent performance encapsulated a central issue in health policy in the interwar years – how an effective health service was to be integrated and run. Health care provision in the 1920s as in the 1890s was a patchwork of ramshackle and unco-ordinated services – the voluntary hospitals often limiting their admissions to specialised cases; the workhouse infirmaries coping with the mentally handicapped, senile, venereal and chronic and elderly cases; local authority ante-natal clinics, GP services under the NHI Commission catering for a minority of the population. The MacClean committee enquiring into the poor law and reporting in 1918, described the situation.[180] Services overlapped to a chaotic extent at the local level. Administrative districts did not coincide; seven different local authorities gave money in the home; six provided forms of medical care, all operating different forms of assessment. There was little or no co-ordination between services and relations were often openly hostile.

The interwar years have been seen as a time of stagnation in health reform, succeeded by the reforming spirit of the Second World War, culminating in the establishment of the National Health Service. But

---

[179]   M. A. Crowther, 'The Later Years of the Workhouse, 1890–1929', in Thane, ed., *The Origins of British Social Policy*, pp. 36–55; *idem, The Workhouse System*, pp. 182–4.
[180]   Thane, *Welfare State*.

there is an alternative interpretation which stresses the 1920s and 1930s as a time of increased expenditure on health care (the setting up of the NHS in 1948 resulted in only a small increase in the amount of GNP spent on state medical services).[181] Not only did the NHS have roots in developments in the 1920s and 1930s, but those years also provided models of health care provision which suggested alternatives to the administrative structure eventually settled upon in 1948. One such was the Dawson committee report of 1920. This Consultative Council on Medical and Allied Services, appointed by Addison, and chaired by Lord Dawson, recommended the 'close co-ordination' of preventive and curative services. It particularly recommended a two-tier network of health centres in which services would be concentrated and where GPs and specialists would work together. The Dawson committee recommendations are usually seen as the starting point for regional schemes for health services, and as a model of health service provision which stressed local, GP-based services and accessibility of specialist care. The Labour party's policy document, *Curative and Preventive Medical Services*, of 1919, had also advocated an integrated network of hospitals and health centres, but it went further than Dawson in advocating a free and comprehensive National Health Service.[182] Both were models which, if adopted, might have avoided some of the problems of the hospital-based undemocratic structure of the National Health Service. But as Sir George Godber has pointed out, in Britain in 1920, 'the local government units were no suitable base for health service administration and the differences in function, finance and management between public and voluntary hospitals were profound. The British did not really believe in the capacity of government at any level to run such human services in 1920.'[183] The Dawson committee's recommendations were pigeonholed and remained unimplemented in the interwar years in the cause of financial retrenchment. The Peckham Health Centre (operating between 1926 and 1930 and again between 1935 and 1950), although based on an understanding of the threat which specialism posed to general practice, had a different holistic rather than pathological philosophy of health; the most extensive local authority health centre was that

[181] C. Webster, 'Political Economy of the National Health Service' (seminar paper, Wellcome Unit, Oxford, 1988).

[182] R. Earwicker, 'The Emergence of a Medical Strategy in the Labour Movement, 1906–1919', *Bull. SSHM*, 29 (1981), pp. 6–9.

[183] G. Godber, 'The Domesday Book of British Hospitals', *Bull. SSHM*, 32 (1983), pp. 4–13.

built in Finsbury in 1938.[184] The health centre movement in general did not revive until the 1960s; and then in the context of hospital dominance.[185]

The 1920s and 1930s were years when the work of local authority public health departments grew significantly. They took over the poor law hospitals. Poor law medical facilities had improved since the early years of the century. The poor law medical service was increasingly used by large numbers of the non-destitute working class. Poor law medicine was emerging as a form of embryonic state medical service and an alternative to the widespread contract and club provision before 1911. This had been realised by the Webbs in their minority report of the Royal Commission on the Poor Laws in 1909.[186] Whereas the majority report sought to remedy problems by an increased measure of charity and an expanded poor law, the minority, led by Beatrice Webb, wanted to municipalise the functions of the poor law. Poor law medical services – hospitals, infirmaries and out-relief – together with other local health activities would be placed under committees of county and county borough councils. The minority report had become a powerful influence on Labour party thinking about health and the poor law. But it was not until Neville Chamberlain's Local Government Act of 1929 which disbanded Poor Law Unions and Boards of Guardians that some of its proposals became reality.[187] The act's aim was to separate the poor law's dual responsibility for the able-bodied, mainly the unemployed, and the sick. The medical services of the poor law were gradually dispersed to the health, education and other committees of the local authorities. The able-bodied were dealt with by Public Assistance Committees also appointed by local authorities. The poor law infirmaries were gradually appropriated by the health departments of the large local authorities. These were already responsible for mental and infectious disease hospitals and for TB sanatoria, under the Public Health (Tuberculosis) Act of 1921. Their other range of responsibilities included maternal and child welfare services, the school medical service, dentistry, school meals and milk, VD services and health centres. The Cancer Act of 1939 also

---

[184]   J. Lewis and B. Brookes, 'The Peckham Health Centre, "PEP" and the Concept of General Practice during the 1930s and 1940s', *Medical History*, 27 (1983), pp. 151–61.
[185]   M. Jefferys and H. Sacks, *Rethinking General Practice: Dilemmas in Primary Medical Care* (1983).
[186]   See Crowther, *The Workhouse System*; also J. E. Pater, *The Making of the National Health Service* (1981).
[187]   B. B. Gilbert, *British Social Policy, 1914–1939* (1970).

placed responsibility for the development of regional cancer schemes on them. By the end of the 1930s local authorities provided more extensive hospital accommodation than the voluntary sector. In the interwar years it looked as if any future state medical service would be based on public health services.

The administration of the health insurance scheme was an obstacle to the development of a unified health service. Benefits offered by the 'approved societies' (mainly industrial insurance and friendly societies) could vary markedly according to the levels of sickness among their members. The national health insurance scheme was investigated by a Royal Commission which reported in 1926. Its two reports both recognised the deficiencies of the lack of co-ordination among health services and the varying standards of provision among the approved societies. The minority report favoured municipalis-ation, with the local authorities taking over the functions of the approved societies; the majority wanted the less medical solution of redistributing the surplus of the societies to bring about a 'pooling of risks'. But in the event nothing was done. The 1926 Economy Act took national health insurance funds to help pay for the Contributory Pensions Act and ended current hopes of an extended medical service. The role of the approved societies in health insurance, however, remains a controversial one, in particular in the light of current debates on the financing of health care. Noel Whiteside has recently argued that criticism of the approved societies' determination to maximise profits at public expense is less than satisfactory. Their political power was not that great and they were a convenient scapegoat for poli-ticians. However, the bulk of income for medical services in the inter-war period came from public authorities; insurance contributions were not a major source of health service income either at this time or post Second World War.[188]

But national health insurance, despite its modest extension in the interwar period, still covered less than half the population by 1939. A major defect was the lack of access to specialist and hospital treat-ment. The hospital services were badly distributed; regionalisation 'remained a watchword'. The voluntary hospitals were in a state of financial crisis. In 1921, the Cave committee had recognised this and

[188] N. Whiteside, 'Private Agencies for Public Purposes: Some New Perspectives on Policy-Making in Health Insurance between the Wars', *Journal of Social Policy*, 12 (1983), pp. 165–94; also F. Honigsbaum, 'The Interwar Health Insurance Scheme: A Rejoinder', *Journal of Social Policy*, 12 (1983), pp. 515–24; Webster, 'Political Econ-omy'.

had proposed administrative machinery to co-ordinate both their work and their finances. It also recommended a £1 million state subsidy, but with no permanent commitment to support them.[189] It was clear that income from voluntary sources alone was no longer sufficient to support these hospitals in their original function of caring for the sick poor. To cope with the problem and to cater for the increasing number of lower middle-class people who, even though privately insured, could not afford private care, the hospitals increased their provision of fee-paying wards. The rise of hospital contributory systems in the late 1920s helped stave off disaster; by the early 1940s, these were supplying about 50 per cent of the total receipts of the voluntary hospitals; their subvention from local authority funds was also growing.[190] In 1937, the Sankey Report recommended regional planning for the voluntary hospitals, but nothing had been done before the war. The hospital surveys published during and after the Second World War showed what a 'crazy patchwork' the system was.

There was no co-ordination between the municipal and voluntary hospital sectors. What Anne Crowther has called the 'rudderless drifting towards the specialised institutions' continued.[191] Many local authorities were in fact slow to take over poor law hospitals after 1929. In 1937, 466 public hospitals remained under the Public Assistance committees compared with 111 under local councils. The London County Council was the most active authority. Between 1930 and 1931, it assumed responsibility for seventy-six institutions with over 43,000 beds from the London guardians and the Metropolitan Asylums Board. London in 1939 provided nearly three-fifths of total English municipal general hospital space. Morant had proposed that the voluntary hospitals be brought directly under local authority control. But a national hospital service with the local authorities taking the initiative in local planning of hospital services remained unrealised in the prewar period.

The nature of private practice, too, was changing with income from public assistance bodies and from work in local authority clinics growing. But the patchwork and unplanned state of GP and specialist services caused dissatisfaction. So, too, did the question of poverty and health in the interwar period. The reduction in death rates, in particular in the diseases of infants and children, appeared to indicate that

[189]   Pater, *National Health Service*, p. 12.
[190]   Webster, 'Political Economy'.
[191]   Crowther, 'Later Years of the Workhouse', p. 51.

general standards of health were improving. This was a position adopted in official reports at the time and which has become received opinion since. As John Burnett put it, 'No one could seriously doubt that the working class on the eve of the Second World War were better fed, better clothed, and better housed than their parents had been a generation earlier.'[192] This revisionist account of the 1930s as a decade of generally improved living standards, marred only by some undoubted pockets of deprivation exaggerated out of all proportion by socialist propaganda, has in its turn come under attack. Historians such as Charles Webster have pointed to the danger, long accepted in analysis of nineteenth-century health reports, of accepting official reports at face value, and have shown how health statistics themselves are not objective value-free 'scientific' evidence, but are open to interpretation.[193] In particular, national aggregate statistics – often cited to support the 'optimist' case – disguised a tremendous diversity of regional patterns of morbidity and mortality, with significant differences also for occupation, class and gender. The differentials between classes in particular were significant and increased rapidly after the first month of life. Jay Winter has suggested that this demographic gap was not widening, and that the trend was substantially reversed by 1939.[194] However, the statistics do not point to such clear-cut conclusions; even where the gap was narrowed, the percentage improvement was slight.

A particular focus of concern – and of recent debate – was the high level of maternal mortality. In 1933 and 1934, this reached a peak, surpassing levels at the turn of the century. In 1934 there were 4.6 deaths per 1,000 live births in England and Wales, but thereafter the rate fell rapidly. The mortality rates were unusual in being higher among the better off, a fact attributed to the later age of marriage and greater proportion of first births. But maternal mortality was also a considerable problem among poor women and here the relationship between national health and standards of nutrition began to be recognised. The distribution of free food by the National Birthday Trust in 1934 in the Special Areas had a significant effect on the death rate.

---

[192]   J. Burnett, *Plenty and Want: A Social History of Diet in England from 1815 to the Present Day* (1966), p. 319.
[193]   For the debate on the 1930s, see C. Webster, 'Healthy or Hungry Thirties?', *History Workshop*, 13 (1982), pp. 110–29; and *idem*, 'Health, Welfare and Unemployment during the Depression', *Past & Present*, 109 (1985), pp. 204–30.
[194]   J. M. Winter, 'Infant Mortality, Maternal Mortality and Public Health in Britain in the 1930s', *Journal of European Economic History*, 8 (1979), pp. 439–62.

But there was little assistance for this approach from the Ministry of Health, which preferred to avoid the issue of class and health and to place most blame, as in the Victorian and Edwardian years, on the ignorance of housewives for the production of properly balanced diets. But there were some moves to meet the demand for free or cheap milk; by the mid-1930s, most local authorities were supplying this to expectant and nursing mothers.

Better nutrition and economic revival in the second half of the 1930s accounted for the decline in maternal mortality. Important, too, was the discovery of the sulphonamides, antibiotics able to counteract puerperal sepsis, the major cause of maternal mortality.[195] How far the ostensible improvements in formal health care contributed is less certain. In 1936, the Midwives Act established a local authority based trained service in place of the previous mix of public and voluntary arrangements. The hospitalisation of childbirth, although supported by both working- and middle-class women, contributed little. Most births still took place at home (1946 was the first year in which there were more hospital than home births); skilled midwifery and improved hygiene in the home had more of an impact than the more technical and expensive management of childbirth in hospital.[196] The impact of abortion on the mortality rate is unknown. The experiences of childbirth and rearing among working women movingly detailed by the Women's Co-operative Guild in *Maternity: Letters from Working Women* in 1915 had changed little twenty years later.[197] However, the spread of birth-control knowledge and practice among working-class women did contribute to improved general health.[198]

The debate on health and malnutrition, both in the 1930s and more recently, meant that questions of diet and nutrition assumed high priority. The connection of malnutrition with variations in working-class income and with poverty was demonstrated by John Boyd Orr's study, *Food, Health and Income*, published in 1936. His findings showed that a tenth of the population, including a fifth of all children, were chronically ill-nourished, and a half of the population suffered from some sort of deficiency. His findings, although criticised, were supported by other surveys. Dr McGonigle in a survey in

---

[195]   I. S. L. Loudon, 'Deaths in Childbed from the Eighteenth Century to 1935', *Medical History*, 30 (1986), pp. 27–41.
[196]   For discussions of the hospitalisation of childbirth, see Lewis, *Politics of Motherhood*.
[197]   M. Llewelyn Davies, *Maternity: Letters from Working Women* (1915; republished 1978).
[198]   E. Roberts, *A Woman's Place: An Oral History of Working-Class Women, 1890–1940* (Oxford, 1984).

Stockton-on-Tees found that the death rate among the poorer section of the population spending only 3s. a head on food, was twice that of the most affluent, who spent 6s a head.[199] Nor was this simply a matter of blackspots concentrated in the depressed areas. The example of Oxford, a centre of new industry, where nearly 10 per cent of children were found malnourished by a 1939 survey, suggests that extensive malnutrition was not confined to those areas.[200] As John Welshman has shown, the impressive national totals for free school meals, and free milk, were insufficient to counteract problems of poverty and malnourishment among schoolchildren.[201] Work in the field of vitamin biochemistry which identified the micro-nutrients as the chief source of dietary deficiency redefined the understanding of factors underlying nutritional status itself. It was assumed that vitamin and mineral supplements alone would remedy conditions which were the result of poor quality diet. Celia Petty comments, 'Poverty was thus reduced to a "deficiency" disease, and the social and environmental deprivations experienced by the poor passed over.'[202] The debate on health and the depression, fuelled by contemporary divisions on the relation between health, class and unemployment, will continue, aided by the addition of new nutritional methodologies in historical assessment.[203] On present evidence, however, the 'optimistic' case must remain in serious doubt; a significant proportion of the population, and not only in the depressed areas, was condemned, through poverty, to ill-health in the interwar period.

There was a renewed concern for 'national efficiency' in the 1930s fuelled by concerns that levels of mortality, infant in particular, were still too high, and about the rapidly falling birth rate. Industrial and occupational health became a focus of concern; in 1938 a new Factories Act increased the staff of factory inspectors to include eleven medical inspectors.[204] Eugenic arguments were again popular in professional circles. A major problem among the hereditary 'unfit' were seen to

---

[199] Webster, 'Healthy or Hungry Thirties?'.
[200] E. Peretz, 'Infant and Child Welfare in Oxford, 1919–39' (unpublished conference paper, 1986).
[201] J. Welshman, 'School Meals and the Problem of Malnutrition in England and Wales, 1900–1939', *Bull. SSHM*, 40 (1987), pp. 33–6.
[202] C. Petty, 'Food, Poverty and Growth: The Application of Nutrition Science, 1918–1939', *Bull. SSHM*, 40 (1987), pp. 37–40.
[203] For the contemporary debate on health see D. Black, *Inequalities in Health: The Black Report*, ed., with an introd. by P. Townsend and N. Davidson (1982).
[204] H. Jones, 'An Inspector Calls: Health and Safety at Work in Inter-War Britain', in Weindling, ed., *Occupational Health*, pp. 223–39.

be the mental defectives; the Brock Committee on Sterilisation in 1934 recommended voluntary sterilisation and sterilisation of defectives did occur. So far as mental treatment in the asylums is concerned, it is probable that little changed between the end of the nineteenth century and before the movement to phase them out began in the 1950s. Certainly the image of the asylum remained unchanged, and average asylum size even increased.[205] Other developments in this area took place outside the asylum and helped confirm its eventual demise. Chief among them was the impact of psychology, aided by the discovery of 'shell-shock' during the First World War.[206] The use of psychological techniques and insights became common in mental health in the interwar years; they were based on moves by the psychiatric profession towards a middle-class clientele outside the asylum and towards out-patient treatment.[207] The Maudsley Hospital, founded in 1923, catered for voluntary patients only; and this emphasis was confirmed by the 1930 Mental Treatment Act. The insane asylum became a mental hospital; the lunatic, a person of unsound mind. The development of mental testing also demonstrated the impact of psychology.[208] Professional and political strategies lay behind the change in definitions.

Improvements in public health, in particular in the water supply, continued in the interwar years. But medical advances were more uncertain in their impact. The sulphonamides had a clear impact on puerperal sepsis and pneumonia. Insulin was used from the 1920s in the treatment of diabetes; and immunisation for diphtheria began in the 1930s. Salvarsan provided a safer more effective treatment for syphilis. Knowledge of orthopaedics expanded after the First World War. But little had been achieved in the cure of tuberculosis, which remained a major problem. The major effort went into the provision of sanatoria, another local authority responsibility after 1921; the BCG vaccine was not effective until 1945. As in the early 1900s, the extent of self-medication in the interwar period was considerable. More worthless remedies were controlled by the Cancer Act of 1939, which

[205] W. L. Jones, *Ministering to Minds Diseased: A History of Psychiatric Treatment* (1983).
[206] M. Stone, 'Shellshock and the Psychologists', in Bynum, Porter and Shepherd, eds., *Anatomy of Madness*, vol. 2, pp. 242–71.
[207] For discussion of these developments in a North American context, see S. E. D. Shortt, *Victorian Lunacy: Richard M. Burke and the Practice of Late Nineteenth-Century Psychiatry* (Cambridge, 1986).
[208] G. Sutherland and S. Sharp, *Ability, Merit and Measurement: Mental Testing and English Education 1880–1940* (Oxford, 1984); also N. Rose, *The Psychological Complex: Psychology, Politics and Society in England, 1869–1939* (1985).

forbade the advertising of cancer 'cures'. The Pharmacy and Medicines Act of 1941, which restricted channels of patent medicine distribution, underlined an increasing reliance on professional medical care.[209] The trend towards occupational monopoly in health care occupations continued and intensified. The success of nurses (1919) and dentists (1921) in securing state registration led smaller groups to seek similar status. But medical and Ministry of Health officials worked together in the interwar years to frustrate such aims. In 1936 a 'Board of Registration of Medical Auxiliaries' was set up under BMA control; the medical profession, despite an increasing numerical disadvantage, protected its control of the health care division of labour.[210]

The Second World War and the National Health Service

By the outbreak of war in 1939, there was no lack of knowledge of the chaotic and unco-ordinated nature of health services both in terms of distribution, access, financing and much else. In 1937 a Political and Economic Planning (PEP) report on *The British Health Services* underlined how 'a bewildering variety of agencies, official and un-official, have been created during the past two or three generations to work for health mainly by attacking specific diseases and disabilities as they occur'.[211] It was clear that neither the private and voluntary agencies, nor the public and local authority services as they were at that stage constituted, could satisfy the demand and need for health care. The free market was no solution to the provision of health services. Already before the war there was a growing demand for change. The Socialist Medical Association was pressing for a free national health service; more importantly, in 1930 and again in 1938, the British Medical Association issued its *Proposals for a General Medical Service for the Nation* which suggested a system of health insurance for nearly all adults and their dependents.

Change was certainly in the air before 1939; the question is, how much would have been achieved but for the impact of war, and in particular the advent of the Labour government in 1945. More recently,

---

[209] Matthews, *History of Pharmacy*, p. 366.
[210] G. Larkin, 'The Licensing of Health Professions: Medical or Ministry Control?', *Bull. SSHM*, 40 (1987) 51–3; also *idem, Occupational Monopoly*.
[211] Quoted in Pater, *National Health Service*, p. 19.

awareness of the deficiencies of current National Health Service organisation and ideology, its hospital-dominated, undemocratic structure based on curative, not preventive medicine, has led to historical examination of the type of structure established in 1946 and whether it should or could have been different. Discussion of the impact of war on health policy has started from Richard Titmuss's assertion that the war led to decisively new attitudes to social policy.[212] Bombing and evacuation, he argued, led to a high degree of social solidarity, an awareness for the first time of the extent of poverty, malnutrition and the maldistribution of health services. It impressed on central government the necessity of having a population which was fit and efficient.

The basis of a reformed health service was certainly under discussion before the war, and a broad band of opinion was already being converted to some form of 'socialised medicine'.[213] This continued during the war. In August 1940, the BMA, the Medical Officers of Health and the Royal Commission set up a commission to plan postwar health services which produced a draft interim report in 1942. (However, the radical nature of its proposals proved an embarrassment to the BMA and it was quickly buried.) In February 1941, the Ministry of Health received a delegation from the TUC requesting improved health benefit and the overhaul and integration of hospital services. This, because of war needs, was already under way. The Emergency Medical Service (EMS) had been planned before the war, but the full integration of hospital services announced in 1941 is usually seen as the beginning of a National Health Service. The hospitals were run by existing authorities, but within a regional framework and with the Ministry of Health deciding what role each should play. Doctors and nurses were salaried employees often at higher rates than they had received before.

A strong impetus to comprehensive proposals on the part of the Ministry of Health came with the publication of the famous Beveridge Report in 1942 on *Social Insurance and Allied Services* with its recommendation for a comprehensive free health service. In February 1943, the government announced its acceptance of the principle of a national health service and outlined a timetable for consultation and eventual

[212]   R. M. Titmuss, *Problems of Social Policy* (1950).
[213]   For discussion and criticism of aspects of the Titmuss thesis, see J. Harris, 'Some Aspects of Social Policy in Britain during the Second World War', in W. J. Mommsen, ed., *The Emergence of the Welfare State in Britain and Germany* (1981), pp. 247–62.

legislation.[214] This was followed, a year later, in February 1944, by the Willink White Paper (Willink was the new Conservative Minister of Health), which, at Labour insistence, included proposals for a salaried service and for health centres. But the White Paper was, because of Conservative and medical opposition, only a watered-down version of the original Labour party scheme. Separate general practice was to continue alongside the health centres; GPs in the health centres would not be salaried local employees but under contract to the central health authority. The voluntary hospitals were to remain independent, but were to be encouraged to co-operate with public hospitals in their area. The White Paper was a consultative document and stressed that it did not wish to establish an entirely new structure but to build on the pre-existing one of local authority control and health insurance.

It was becoming clear that one of the major planks of opposition to a national health service was the medical profession itself. The BMA in particular, retreating from the radicalism of its 1942 report, was opposed to the idea of a salaried service and of local authority control. It also wanted an enhanced role for the voluntary hospitals and their consultants. The profession itself was not united. The Medical Officers of Health who already worked within a local authority structure were most committed to a universal, free service, as were GPs with poorer patients and no substantial private practice. But the hospital consultants and GPs in wealthier areas were firmly opposed to state control. Discussions between Willink and the National Health Service Negotiating Committee, dominated by the BMA leaders, Dr Guy Dain, chairman of its Council and Dr Charles Hill, its secretary, had led to substantial concessions by 1945. Important elements of the 1944 White Paper had been abandoned, including controls on the distribution of doctors, the rapid development of health centres and the cardinal principle of combining planning and execution of the service in the same local hands. Private practice was to be allowed in health centres, which were to be run by GPs. Local authority control was to be diminished with overall control in the hands of regional

---

[214] A number of books deal with the wartime moves towards the National Health Service. See, e.g., Pater, *National Health Service*; A. Lindsey, *Socialised Medicine in England and Wales: The National Health Service, 1948–1961* (Chapel Hill, 1962), pp. 24–73; C. Webster, *The Health Services since the War*, vol. 1: *Problems of Health Care: The National Health Service before 1957* (1988). I have here also drawn on C. Webster, 'Labour and the Origins of the National Health Service', in N. Rupke, ed., *Science, Politics and the Public Good: essays in honour of Margaret Gowing* (1988), pp. 184–202.

planning bodies containing both local authority and voluntary hospital representatives. A new White Paper was being prepared on this basis, but the Labour party had never been fully informed of the extent of the concessions and it was abandoned before the 1945 general election on political grounds.

This was the position when the new Labour government assumed power in the summer of 1945. Aneurin Bevan, the new Minister of Health, was determined to achieve a universal free service, but was up against determined opposition both from the doctors and, in the latter half of 1945, from sections within the cabinet. The question of local authority control was the stumbling block there. Bevan's espousal of the principle of national ownership of all hospitals – both local authority and voluntary – under appointed local bodies with voluntary membership exercising powers delegated by central government – a compromise which found favour both with Ministry of Health civil servants and with influential consultants like Lord Moran, President of the Royal College of Physicians – was a clear departure from the Labour party's own policy.[215] The chief defender of the local authority or joint authority alternatives was Herbert Morrison who, as leader of the LCC, had responsibility for a substantial proportion of public hospitals. Morrison's opposition, whether strategic or tactical, placed emphasis on practical considerations; in particular, he argued that the move from a rate- to a tax-based service would lead to an increase in expenditure.[216] But Bevan, supported by Addison, now a member of a Labour cabinet, won the day. When the National Health Service Bill was published in March 1946 it, and its accompanying White Paper, proposed a service conducted through three main channels, hospital, GP and local authority services. Both the voluntary and local hospitals were to be nationalised and placed under the control of regional boards consisting of local authority and voluntary hospital representatives. The voluntary hospitals were to be allowed considerable independence within this structure, retaining their own endowments, and with their own boards of governors. Consultants could be whole or part time and private practice within the hospital was allowed as a more acceptable alternative to the proliferation of

[215]   For details of the move towards nationalisation of the hospitals, see Pater, *National Health Service*, pp. 106–26; Webster 'Labour and the Origins of the National Health Service'; M. Foot, *Aneurin Bevan*, vol. 2: *1945–1960* (1975), pp. 130–71.

[216]   Morrison's position is discussed by Webster, 'Labour and the Origins of the National Health Service'; and J. Rowett, 'Herbert Morrison Reappraised' (unpublished seminar paper, 1987).

separate private institutional care. Counties and county boroughs retained responsibility for health centres, clinics and other health services such as health visiting and ambulances. GP, dental and pharmacy services were to be administered by executive councils, half professional and half lay (with local authority and ministerial appointees). Health centres under local authority control were to be the main feature of GP services; the doctors were to be paid on a part-salary, part-capitation fee basis.

The struggles between Bevan and the medical profession between the passing of the act in 1946 and the 'appointed day' for the National Health Service on 5 July 1948 demonstrated that, although the consultants had been appeased by the arrangements for private practice and the voluntary hospitals (in particular after the Spens Report on consultants' pay had recommended the establishment of an awards system), the GPs were unhappy with the new system. Important sections of the scheme had to be modified to obtain their support. The National Health Service Amendment Act of 1949 prohibited a full-time salaried service and made capitation fees the basis of payment. A circular in December 1947 cancelled the requirement in the act for the submission of proposals for health centres and few were built or opened in the postwar period. The effective abandonment of the health centre, intended to combine GP, dental, ophthalmic and local authority services and to work in close co-operation with local hospitals, removed a key co-ordinating body in the new tripartite structure.

How far then can, first, the impact of war, and, secondly, the particular impact of Bevan and the Labour government be given credit for the National Health Service? Clearly health policy did not move in a decisively new direction during the war and many of the proposals under discussion followed along existing lines. The war undoubtedly speeded up both the need for the integration of health services and the popular demand for change, although it is doubtful if evacuation did indeed influence a mood for change; class antagonism and prejudice may have been promoted as much as solidarity.[217] Nor would it be correct to talk of a mood of wartime consensus about the form the health service should take; as Charles Webster has shown, the wartime preparations showed 'remarkably few concessions to the

---

[217] John MacNicol's researches on evacuation suggest this conclusion. See J. MacNicol, 'The Evacuation of Schoolchildren', in H. L. Smith, ed., *War and Social Change: British Society in the Second World War* (Manchester, 1986), pp. 3–31.

spirit of solidarity and altruism which is supposed to have taken precedence over self-interest'.[218] The war also presented Bevan and the
Labour party with an opportunity which would not have occurred
in peacetime. Had the Labour party lost the 1945 general election,
the Willink Bill would still have been there; but reform proceeded
farther and faster under the Labour Minister of Health. Revision of
the uncritical hagiography of Bevan in the labour movement should
not blind us to the very considerable achievement against determined
professional opposition.[219] 'He knew what he wanted and so did we'
commented Dr Guy Dain.[220]

Nonetheless, the structure established for the National Health Service perpetuated many of the anomalies and inequalities of the previous system. Major disadvantages were the fragmentation of the
service, the escalation of hospital costs and the lack of democracy.
Because of fragmentation, inequalities persisted in expenditure and
allocation of resources. The dominance of hospital-based medicine
(a point of similarity with contemporary American health policy)
ensured that hospital costs would escalate and would be subject to
cutbacks in national expenditure.[221] The regional hospital structure
was effectively handed over to the voluntary hospital interests. The
consultants and the voluntary hospitals had won; labour, trade-union
and worker representatives were largely excluded from participation.
The idea of giving the local authorities a role in primary care collapsed.
The expertise of the GP declined under the NHS and public health
services were, as Jane Lewis has noted, forced to search for a new
identity in a rigid and unreformed local government structure. The
alienation of the new discipline of social medicine from practical public
health emphasised its decline.[222] Awareness of the deficiencies of
health service structure has been increased by the two reorganisations
of 1974 and 1982. The demand for local authority and democratic control has found favour and Bevan's stock as an apparent advocate of

---

[218]   Webster, *Health Services*, pp. 392–3.
[219]   One uncritical biography is Foot, *Aneurin Bevan*. Recent revisionist accounts include
J. Campbell, *Nye Bevan and the Mirage of British Socialism* (1987), pp. 165–85.
[220]   Quoted in M. Foot, *Aneurin Bevan*, vol. 2, p. 120.
[221]   For a recent account which argues on the basis of essential similarity between
development in health policy in western nations in the mid-twentieth century,
see D. M. Fox, 'The National Health Service and the Second World War: The
Elaboration of Consensus', in H. L. Smith, ed., *War and Social Change: British Society
in the Second World War* (Manchester, 1986), pp. 32–57.
[222]   J. Lewis, *What Price Community Medicine? The Philosophy, Practice and Politics of Public
Health since 1919* (1986), p. 11.

bureaucratic centralism, consequently diminished.[223] The politics of recession have made clear the serious structural imbalance perpetrated by the 1948 reorganisation. But the difficulties of the situation in the 1940s made this then an impossible solution except under a reformed local government; and this was not undertaken by the 1945 government. Nationalisation of the hospitals was, as Rosemary Stevens comments, 'at the time the only viable solution to the hospital reorganisation problem'.[224] Bevan's rationale was that a universal health service needed the top doctors inside it; nationalisation of the hospitals and private practice were the carrot to attract them in. His belief was that the superiority of the NHS would cause private practice to wither away. To criticise the 1948 arrangements is also to ignore the real gains in health care made after 1948, in particular by women and their families, who had had very imperfect access to services in the interwar period.

Conclusion

The National Health Service as established on its tripartite basis in 1948 was recognisably the inheritor of nineteenth- and early twentieth-century relationships between medicine and the state. This remains one of the central themes of the social history of medicine; and the social history of twentieth-century medicine has been largely dominated by analysis of the development of health policy. Much valuable work has been done, and remains to be done, in this area.[225] Contemporary debates on the direction and function of health policy clearly need an historical dimension. As Charles Webster comments,

a review of seemingly remote history may reveal the source of later difficulties and therefore constitute a positive contribution to current thinking. It is indeed striking to note the degree to which seemingly unanticipated problems and apparently novel solutions turn out, on closer examination, to be reverberations from the past, even from the earliest history of the NHS.[226]

This is a vital historical function in the debate on the organisation

---

[223] See C. Webster, 'Democracy and the National Health Service' (paper given to conference on 'The NHS: Past, Present and Future', Oxford, 1984).

[224] R. Stevens, *Medical Practice in Modern England* (New Haven, 1966), p. 73.

[225] For example, little sustained analysis has been made of the development of drug and alcohol policies after the 1920s. See V. Berridge 'Drugs and Social Policy: The Establishment of Drug Control in Britain 1900–1930', *British Journal of Addiction*, 79 (1984), pp. 17–29.

[226] C. Webster, 'Origins of the NHS: Lessons from History', *Contemporary Record*, 2 (1988), pp. 33–6.

of health services. But there is also a need for research on twentieth-century health to expand from its administrative and high politics focus and to take up some of the themes which have been so richly investigated for the nineteenth century. The broader aspects of the relationship between health and social forces still, on the whole, need investigation. The role of oral history here is already an important one.[227] We need to know more, for example, about popular medicine and theories of illness and their relation to orthodox practice; about the treatment of insanity in the inter and post Second World War years; about reactions to disease; about para-medical professionalisation; about the roles of medical research and of public health; about the relation of health to questions of gender.[228] The impact of AIDS upon historians has suggested other new directions for research, in the 'contemporary social history' of health policy and the history of postwar science and medicine.[229] The twentieth century is by no means barren of such research, and the vitality of the social history of medicine will ensure further development.

[227]   See, for example, Roberts, A Woman's Place; and E. Peretz, 'Memories of Health and Caring' (conference report), History Workshop, 25 (1988), pp. 213–14.

[228]   For example, Bryder, Magic Mountain; Lewis, Community Medicine.

[229]   E. Fee and D. Fox, 'The Contemporary Historiography of AIDS', Journal of Social History (forthcoming, 1990); V. Berridge and P. Strong, 'AIDS Policies in the United Kingdom: A Preliminary Analysis', in E. Fee and D. Fox, eds., AIDS: Contemporary History (Princeton, 1990).

CHAPTER 5

Crime, authority and the policeman-state

V. A. C. GATRELL

Part 1   The policeman-state

I   INTRODUCTION

For centuries in Britain, stealing from and hurting other people have been pursuits as common and traditional as drinking and fornicating. All social classes have participated in them. Poorer and younger people have stolen to procure food or clothing, to demonstrate daring, or to relieve tedium. Affluent, older or upwardly mobile people have embezzled, evaded taxes, excise and currency regulations, defrauded each other and their clients under the guise of commercial or professional practice, and lifted from shops. They have done these things far more frequently than the courts have ever recognised, as self-report studies nowadays show. And in times past, for good measure, the rich no less than the poor used violence to assert prowess, relieve tension and settle disputes. 'Crime' in these many senses has been as much a part of our national heritage as has a taste for beer, politics and sex.

This makes the history of crime an unimaginably large subject. Commentators usually therefore take a short cut. They address themselves not to the ubiquity of law-breaking at all social levels, but to those actions, merely, which come to be labelled as crimes by the reactions of the law-enforcement and judicial systems. This in turn, however, puts them at the mercy of the prejudices and constraints which determine how the law selects some targets and ignores others. That is why no discussion of 'crime' can sensibly proceed which does not first discuss how, by whom and why attitudes and policies towards crime are formed, and what often covert purposes those policies serve.

The early sections of this chapter argue that in and after the later eighteenth century anxiety about the lawlessness of poorer people

243

was greatly intensified. This was part of a mounting disciplinary assault on those mainly proletarian classes who were assumed to threaten dominant and newly articulated definitions of order: those reluctant to enter a disciplined labour force, for example, or those who were excluded from, or who dissented from, the consensual society which the political nation was beginning to try to construct. In these years, also, 'crime' became (as it remains) the repository of fears which had little to do with its relatively trivial cost to the society and economy at large. It came to be invested with large significance because it provided a convenient vehicle for the expression of fears about social change itself. For a century and a half it has been next to impossible to perceive the meanings of crime except through these ideological filters. How and why those filters were constructed may be of greater interest even than the ubiquity of lawlessness itself.

One agency behind this reshaping of attitudes (as well as one effect of it) was what is here termed the 'policeman-state' (sections IV and V of this chapter). In the nineteenth century, the state assumed increasing control of the criminal justice system, as it did of the police who were put in the vanguard of the disciplinary enterprise. This process was not unchallenged, unqualified, or unresponsive to its critics. But it generated its own momentum, nonetheless, as 'experts' accumulated evidence that more and yet more bureaucratic control was needed to solve 'problems'. Politicians and public connived in this growth in the interests of reinforcing social discipline in an increasingly fissiparous society. Law was the means and order the primary objective of this enterprise, and the state became its necessary agent. In the rhetoric of the powerful, the direct Whiggish appeal to 'English liberties' became ever more qualified and muted.

The second part of the chapter examines how and why policemen collaborated in this disciplinary enterprise; how far poorer people consented to or resented it; how policing and other factors influenced the behaviour and organisation of those who were labelled as criminal; how the history of crime relates to theories of social and moral deterioration; whether or not we can talk of sub-cultures of professional crime; and what the relationship might have been between the lawlessness of these poorer people and their experiences of deprivation.

Major themes in the history of policing must be omitted from this discussion. These include the policing of industrial relations; of the nation's drunks, vagrants, paupers, prostitutes, homosexuals and aliens; of those who might service allegedly deviant cultures, like publicans and pawnbroker-receivers and sellers of pistols or of obscene publications; or of those whose practices subverted an increasingly rigid ideal of urban order, whether they be street-traders, traffic offenders, or those who merely beat carpets in the highway. The statutes, bye-laws and policing practices which were to enmesh all these groups were largely in place as early as 1914. They exemplify the developing range and potency of the policeman-state even in the nineteenth century, and they should not be forgotten. But there is one justification for their omission here. It would be vain to seek a public acknowledgment on the part of politicians or of policemen in 1900 or in 1950 (or today) that the major functions of policing – absorbing most man-hours and resources – were expressed in its attention to these non-criminal constituencies. To win their consent, the public has instead been enticed into the belief that the primary rationale of the policeman-state has been to contain and detect crimes against property and the person. This was and is a self-serving and convenient obfuscation; but it is such a large and pervasive obfuscation that this chapter is content to see how it came to pass and with what justifications and effects.

If this survey has any single objective, it is not to summarise recent research, still less to offer a bibliographical guide. It is, in a discursive vein, to reaffirm a framework of meanings within which the history of law-enforcement and law-breaking might be located. This is one reason why, for example, it stresses continuity rather than change. It is not denied that governments and moral panics come and go, or that the targets of their policies are endlessly redefined. Nor, come to that, is it denied that over the past couple of centuries Britain has been a *relatively* free society. But after every qualification has been adduced in support of those views, hard truths remain. Over the past couple of centuries, the policeman-state protected and still protects an unequal and fissiparous society; and it did so supported by the convenient and enduring belief that most criminals were likely to be found among poorer people. The history of crime, accordingly, is largely the history of how better-off people disciplined their inferiors; of how elites used selected law-breakers to sanction their own authority; or of how in modern times bureaucrats, experts and policemen used them to justify their own expanding functions and influences. The history of crime is also always about how public fears about change and disorder were displaced on to 'criminals', even when criminals were inappropriate objects of those fears. It can never be about the real extent of law-breaking which goes on at all social levels. In these senses, the history of crime is not always about legality – or about liberty, either. Certainly, the rhetoric of liberty, justice and impartiality has always been usefully turned against the pretensions of the great; but those values have been more frequently compromised before the more expediential, discretionary and prejudicial devices of law as they were wielded in practice by policemen, judges and politicians. Historians might profitably remind themselves that the history of crime is a grim subject, not because it is about crime, but because it is about power.

II   CHANGING RESPONSES TO CRIME, 1750–1850

Is there any meaningful watershed in the history of crime? Did it acquire new meanings and invite new responses in the early nineteenth century unprecedented in the eighteenth century?

Watersheds in history are always debatable: continuities have to be acknowledged. All elites have worried about lawlessness, and eighteenth-century elites were no exception. They deplored the thieving instincts of the poor, their unruly pastimes and secret economies, their vagrancy and fecklessness, and their turbulence at times of dearth and political excitement. These things subverted deference. They also caused inconvenience. 'One is forced to travel, even at noon', Horace Walpole lamented of the London streets, 'as if one were going to battle.'

Reactions were always harsh, too. The crimes which touched elite interest provoked spectacular displays of legal force. Even if eighteenth-century judges and hangmen enmeshed only a few offenders in their grisly rituals, they enmeshed enough to testify to the majesty of the law and the power of those who wielded it. Middling sorts of people used the law as well. Artisans, shopkeepers and farmers were fond of prosecuting their equals and fonder still of prosecuting their inferiors. Even labourers prosecuted each other (though rarely their betters) with surprising frequency. By European standards the British were a litigious people; they used their law as seriously as any later generation did.[1]

[1] D. Hay, 'Property, Authority and the Criminal Law', in D. Hay, P. Linebaugh and E. P. Thompson, eds., *Albion's Fatal Tree: Crime and Society in Eighteenth-Century*

Moreover, although most eighteenth-century law-enforcement agencies were locally controlled and staffed by amateurs, they were more effective than later generations liked to think. Parish policing and detective procedures were quite appropriate to the perceived needs of the time.[2] Even the state was taking an increasing if hesitant interest in the way law was enforced in the localities. There had been a great 'increase in governance' after 1625; eighteenth-century governments yet further extended their bureaucratic presence through the appointment of increasing numbers of active justices to deal with expanding business.[3] Central policy made itself increasingly felt, too, through pardons, judges' homilies at assizes in tense years, and through the granting of partial costs to some prosecutors from the 1750s. The criminal law was a palpable presence in the nation's life. It may only be a comparison with later developments which makes eighteenth-century attitudes and policies towards crime appear phlegmatic and unco-ordinated.

And yet when all is said and done, people who looked back on eighteenth-century law-enforcement a century later would have believed that they were contemplating an *ancien régime*. They would have been struck, for example, by the fact that eighteenth-century law remained for most people an expensive discipline of last resort; cheaper disciplines often did as well. Eighteenth-century society was cemented less by law than by the informal sanctions neighbour wielded against neighbour, landlords against tenants, employers against labourers. Control was exercised face-to-face, not bureaucratically. Few, moreover, wished law-enforcement to be better co-ordinated for fear of the centralised despotism which had been so bitterly resisted in the seventeenth century. Local autonomy was a bastion of liberty. Cheapness was a consideration too. Popular lawlessness

---

England (1975); P. King, 'Decision-Making and Decision-Makers in the English Criminal Law, 1750–1800', *Historical Journal*, 27 (1984), pp. 25–58. See J. A. Sharpe, *Crime in Early Modern England, 1550–1750* (1984), and J. M. Beattie, *Crime and the Courts in England, 1660–1800* (Oxford, 1986), for a general guide.

[2] D. Philips, *Crime and Authority in Victorian England: The Black Country, 1835–1860* (1977), chap. 3; J. Styles, 'Sir John Fielding and the Problem of Criminal Investigation in Eighteenth-Century England', *Transactions of the Royal Historical Society*, 33 (1983), pp. 127–50.

[3] K. Wrightson, 'Two Concepts of Order: Justices, Constables and Jurymen in Seventeenth-Century England', in J. Brewer and J. Styles, eds., *An Ungovernable People: The English and their Law in the Seventeenth and Eighteenth Centuries* (1980); N. Landau, *The Justices of the Peace, 1679–1760* (Berkeley, California, 1985).

cost eighteenth-century gentlemen little: it was farmers and tradesmen who bore the brunt of its costs – or the poor themselves. When it cost them so little, gentlemen were sensibly concerned that the business of curtailing it should cost less. And so (by later standards) the state kept a low profile. Detection and prosecution remained at the discretion and mainly at the expense of victims or of associations of local farmers and businessmen. Sentencing was discretionary also, and character testimony deeply influenced an offender's fate. Judges might process up to thirty felonies a day with a low regard for rules of evidence and without restraint of appeal.

Above all, Victorian observers would have been struck by their forefathers' relative indifference to crime as a 'problem', and by their relative satisfaction with the apparently arbitrary and capricious mechanisms which contained it. This was not because crime was infrequent then: it is not at all clear that there was less thieving and violence *per capita* in eighteenth-century cities than in nineteenth. But crime did not as yet appear to threaten hierarchy, and the terms in which crime might be debated as a 'problem' were not yet formed. Historians of early modern crime must realise not only that 'their subject was not known then by that name',[4] but that as a subject it did not exist. The word 'crime' when used at all before the 1780s, usually referred to a personal depravity. It lacked the problematic and aggregative resonance it was soon to acquire. Despite occasional panics about the ubiquity of thieving, crime in aggregate was not yet thought to be increasing as a necessary and potentially uncontrollable effect of social change. Similarly, the 'criminal' was not yet discerned as a social archetype, symbolic of the nation's collective ill-health.

It was in and after the 1780s that these attitudes began to alter. Sensibilities became softer, and pragmatic pressures for change came into play as well. Prosecutors, juries and even judges got queasier about visiting the full penalty of death on lesser offenders. The abolition of transportation to the American colonies after their revolution necessitated some hard thinking about alternative forms of punishment. Large intellectual currents, too, were making it difficult to regard crime in the old way as a simple function of individual depravity. Materialist psychology led Bentham and others to argue that criminals

---

[4]   G. R. Elton, 'Introduction', in J. S. Cockburn, ed., *Crime in England, 1550–1800* (1977).

were driven not by original sin but by their ignorance of how best to calculate the costs of their wrongdoing. And a few reformers were beginning to think about 'crime' aggregatively, as a social issue bred in the squalor of the back streets. Thus Paley and then Colquhoun denounced the growth of great cities for the 'refuge they afford to villainy, in means of concealment, and of subsisting in secrecy'. Colquhoun attributed the 'depraved habits and loose conduct of a great proportion of the lower classes' to 'the enlarged state of Society, the vast extent of moving property, and the unexampled growth of the Metropolis'. It was Colquhoun, too, who, in the light of French events and to justify his call for stronger policing, first equated the dangerous classes with the excesses of revolution. This intruded a new resonance into the debates on the increasing insubordination and presumed politicisation of the poor which was not to be lost for half a century.[5]

Responses to these pressures were hesitant because events in France dampened English zeal for reform. But slowly elites' relative tolerance of and indifference to the criminal poor (as of the riotous poor) were eroded. By the time Peel took up the challenge of penal, police and law reform in the 1820s, the political and cultural climate was quite transformed. Crime was fast becoming 'important'. In the postwar world, and on into the 1840s, the subject came to be cemented into an ideology about the Condition of England. Crime was becoming a vehicle for articulating mounting anxieties about issues which really had nothing to do with crime at all: social change and the stability of social hierarchy. These issues invested crime with new meanings, justified vastly accelerated action against it, and have determined attitudes to it ever since. These are the issues which determine that the history of crime from the early nineteenth century onwards is indeed a 'modern' history.

III CRIME AND ITS MODERN MEANINGS: 'CHANGE'

If, from the early nineteenth century onwards, crime has assumed a looming importance for modern sensibilities, it is not because of its real cost to society, which even today is relatively trivial. It is

---

[5] M. Ignatieff, *A Just Measure of Pain: The Penitentiary in the Industrial Revolution, 1750–1850* (1979); D. Philips, ' "A New Engine of Power and Authority": The Institutionalization of Law-Enforcement in England, 1780–1830', in V. A. C. Gatrell, B. Lenman and G. Parker, eds., *Crime and the Law: The Social History of Crime in Western Europe since 1500* (1980).

because it has come to bear an emblematic relationship to other, larger anxieties – first about 'change' and secondly about 'order'.

'Change' was not commonly, before the second quarter of the nineteenth century, identified as an independent force. By 1831, however, J. S. Mill was not alone in identifying it as 'the first of the leading peculiarities of the present age'. This, he wrote, is 'an age of transition', a fact 'obvious a few years ago only to the more discerning: at present it forces itself upon the most unobservant'.[6] For Mill the problem was that popular clamour for political rights exceeded the readiness of the populace to appreciate the obligations attached to those rights: 'the world of opinions' had become 'mere chaos'. For many others contemplating the costs of the economic, urban and demographic growth which later generations were to call the industrial revolution, what was at issue in urban and industrial society was 'the natural progress of barbarian habits', the 'explosive violence' of the poor, the decay of deference, the collapse of family life, the diffusion of pauperism. The criminal – always the working-class criminal – fast assumed a privileged position in this constellation of bogeys. Onto him were displaced fears about these other changes which were otherwise difficult to express, and must otherwise remain diffuse and without focus.

Why the criminal should be specially targeted in early nineteenth-century debates is no mystery. The judicial system since 1805 had been generating spurious evidence, through statistics, that crime was increasing alarmingly. There could be no more eloquent support for the notion that the moral condition of England was deteriorating and that crime was the emblem of that deterioration.

We know now that what was increasing in the first half of the nineteenth century was not crime but the prosecution rate, a very different matter. In the half-century after 1780, disciplinary responses to the poor and the workshy accelerated markedly. Partly this was because business activity was expanding. In pursuit of an economical and comprehensive way of disciplining recalcitrant workmen, manufacturers were among the loudest in their demand for less random and capricious law-enforcement. In many districts they added most to the mounting volume of summary prosecutions as they clamped down on the often custom-sanctioned and petty embezzlements of their

---

[6] J. S. Mill, 'The Spirit of the Age' (1931), in G. L. Williams, ed., *Mill on Politics and Society* (1976), p. 171.

workforces.[7] Partly these responses reflected anxieties about the Malthusian threat and, after 1815, the escalation of poor rates to support the idle able-bodied who should properly be harnessed to work. It was now being affirmed that both the pauper and the criminal shared cognate moral failing: both wilfully refused to enter the respectable community at work. Laziness, not hunger or environment, explained theft and pauperism alike, and why both were apparently increasing. In 1818 a select committee had already referred without irony to 'that class of persons who ordinarily commit crime, meaning the poor and indigent'. By 1839, the Royal Commission on the County Constabulary could insist that 'In scarcely any cases is [crime] attributable to the pressure of unavoidable want or destitution; ... it arises from the temptation of obtaining property with a less degree of labour than by regular industry.'[8] The association of criminality with the indigent underclasses was now axiomatic.

And so a good half-century before the Summary Jurisdiction Acts of 1847–55 at last statutorily sanctioned the device, urban magistrates were shovelling increasing numbers of petty (and poor) larcenists and workplace embezzlers through summary process and into prison. Thanks to increasing social anxieties and the lowering costs of prosecution, assizes and quarter sessions had mounting work on their hands too. Whereas a mere 3,267 males and 1,338 females were prosecuted in these courts in 1805, 25,740 and 5,569 were so prosecuted in the peak year of 1842, more than ever again before the twentieth century. (Summary courts took the load off thereafter.)[9]

When they analysed prosecution figures, early Victorians were no more critical of their meaning than many of us are today. From that day to this, questionable crime rates have always been used to inflame unreal fears and to give shape to imagined problems. Moreover, on to crime were projected anxieties about social changes which had nothing directly to do with crime itself. A critical displacement

---

[7] D. Hay, 'Manufacturers and the Criminal Law in the Later Eighteenth Century: Crime and ''Police'' in South Staffordshire' (unpublished paper, *Past & Present* colloquium, Oxford, 1983); J. Styles, 'Embezzlement, Industry and Law in England, 1550–1980', in M. Berg *et al.*, eds., *Manufacture in Town and Country before the Factory* (Cambridge, 1984).

[8] *SC on the State of the Police of the Metropolis*, 3rd Report, PP 1818, VIII, p. 34; *RC on the County Constabulary*, PP 1839, XIX, p. 181.

[9] V. A. C. Gatrell and T. B. Hadden, 'Nineteenth Century Criminal Statistics and their Interpretation', in E. A. Wrigley, ed., *Nineteenth-Century Society: Essays in the Use of Quantitative Methods for the Study of Social Data* (Cambridge, 1972), Table III, pp. 392–3.

occurred when 'change' became part of an *explanation* of crime, and embedded in a broad thesis of social deterioration. By the 1840s this motif was firmly in place. The growth of towns; working-class politicisation; the employment of women and the alleged erosion of the family resulting from it; industrial employment and the false values it induced in those who lived by it – fear of all these things was transferred to their emblem.

One typical example of this mode of argument was published in *Blackwood's Magazine* in 1844. It sounds a note with which many later generations were to become overfamiliar: 'Crime in England has increased 700 per cent: in Ireland about 800 per cent, and in Scotland above 3,500 per cent ... What is destined to be the ultimate fate of a country in which the progress of wickedness is so much more rapid than the increase in the number of the people?'

Crime was increasing, the author went on, because 'the restraints of character, relationship and vicinity are ... lost in the [urban] crowd'; because high wages 'flowed in upon' a workforce not yet 'civilised' enough to know how to spend or save them; because industrial workers were learning to go on strike, whence a crime-inducing 'confusion of moral principle, and habits of idleness and insubordination'; because the employment of women destroyed the familial bond, 'emancipating the young from parental control'. These conditions, he wrote, were at odds with those of past generations, or indeed with the enduring peace of rural society. They must generate a criminal class – a 'dismal substratum', a 'hideous black band of society', from which already 'nine-tenths of the crime, and nearly all the professional crime ... flows'.[10] Propaganda of this kind ever since has been less concerned to analyse crime rationally than to mobilise anxieties about change which in many instances had no *necessary* (or proven) criminogenic implications at all.

In the long term the displacements of meaning and anxiety which suffused all these explanations and judgments carried with them their own linguistic effects. 'Crime', as a word, acquired the aggregative and problematic meaning it had only dimly possessed in the eighteenth century and which it will never now discard. And as the nineteenth century progressed, the term became enshrouded in the metaphors of disease, cancer, contamination, contagion, the associations with which it also retains. Attention shifted from the iniquity

---

[10]   Anonymous, 'Causes of the Increase of Crime', *Blackwood's Edinburgh Magazine*, 56 (1844).

of the individual act, which eighteenth-century law had sought to penalise, to the symbolic meaning of the act and the pathological nature of the actor. So the 'criminal' was transformed by Victorian and subsequent policy and categorisation into a special and an afflicted type, even a dehumanised object. By the end of the century 'experts' like the chairman of the prison commission (Du Cane) had no doubt that men turned to crime because of physical and mental as well as moral defectiveness. The psychiatrist Dr Bevan Lewis agreed that habitual criminals were 'simply a degenerate offspring of a very degenerate stock; and if I may be allowed to express my opinion more freely, I would say that both insanity and crime are simply morbid branches of the same stock'.[11]

To be sure, the perceived problem in criminality, even if not the meanings ascribed to it or its social location, shifted many times in the nineteenth and twentieth centuries. The march of 'social science', and the increasing expertise of prison governors, doctors, civil servants, social investigators and 'criminologists' subjected those who broke the law and were foolish enough to be caught to ever sharper categorisation, the better to shape policy for their management. The collectivised image of the dangerous classes gave way after mid-century, in Mayhew and in the 1863 Royal Commission on Penal Servitude, for example, to an ever sharper discrimination between the opportunistic and the professional criminal; in debates on reformatories distinctions between the young offender and the hardened habitual were clarified; or in later nineteenth-century penology the necessitous thief was to be distinguished from the irremediable 'moral defective'. The image has been fragmented further ever since. The twentieth century introduced new archetypes: the motor-car bandit, the cat burglar, the black-marketeer, the gang-leader, down to the mugger, armed robber and drug-dealer today. These all had plausible and more or less unpleasant real-life representations. Most of them were worth catching and penalising. What was in question was the ideological burden these scapegoats continued to carry, and the cost in clear-sightedness paid by those who imposed it.

For the old core images in terms of which these archetypes were explained remained intact. Even in the interwar years, when eugenist

---

[11] *Report from the Departmental Committee on Prisons*, PP 1895, LVI, qq. 10,968–72, 9083. For a general introduction to Victorian ideologies of crime, see Sir L. Radzinowicz and R. Hood, *A History of English Criminal Law*, vol. 5: *The Emergence of Penal Policy* (1986), Part I.

theories of crime (though still current) yielded supremacy to new forms of criminological positivism, pundits were still identifying the criminal as an emblem of assumed social changes for the worse, as writers had a century before. H. Mannheim, for example, in his influential study of *Crime between the Wars* (1940), was still presenting crime as an effect on the working classes of deplored changes in communal and work relations, consumer expectations and affluence, the extension of welfarism to the undeserving, the economic and sexual freedoms of women and the young, and of urban alienation – in short, as an effect of 'the decay of moral values'. Thus 'crime' was still a metaphor for 'change'. It was still, as by axiom, located among the underclasses. Old issues still worried people. Only the language got fancier.

IV   CRIME AND ITS MODERN MEANINGS: 'ORDER'

Early nineteenth-century thinking about crime became entangled in a second set of associations, clustering around the ever more insistent social value of 'order'.[12] Established hierarchical relationships were perceived to be under chronic threat. The populace was expanding, increasingly insubordinate, unshackled from rural controls, and politically opinionated. Accordingly, in political and journalistic rhetoric, and in common usage too, the old Whig notion that the proper end of civil society was the defence of natural liberty against the despot was slowly eclipsed by the assumption that order was a sufficient social value in terms of which the legitimacy of policy might be assessed. It became less thinkable that the law-breaker should be pursued largely for the offence he delivered to his victim. However trivial in real terms his depredations might be, the law-breaker was now also to be pursued for the offence he delivered to 'society', as one of the 'enemies within' whom the mass society engendered, a threat to social order itself. This shift gave the nineteenth-century state the ideological sanction to take unambiguous charge of the law-breaker's containment.

Law-enforced order had been a component of the eighteenth-century moral universe. When has it not been? In the 1760s, the Whig

---

[12]   A. Silver, 'The Demand for Order in Civil Society: A Review of Some Themes in the History of Urban Crime, Police and Riot', in D. Bordua, ed., *The Police: Six Sociological Essays* (New York, 1967).

jurist William Blackstone had quoted Locke axiomatically: 'where there is no law, there is no freedom'. Nonetheless, liberty remained the primary value in mid-eighteenth-century Whig ideology, even if property was both its guarantor and justification. For Blackstone, liberty was rooted in natural rights: 'the principal aim of society is to protect individuals in the enjoyment of those absolute rights, which were vested in them by the immutable laws of nature ... The first and primary end of human law is to maintain and regulate these absolute rights of individuals.' Every man, on entering society, necessarily surrendered part of his natural liberty; but he retained political or civil liberty, which was 'coeval with our form of government'. It was, moreover, only to ensure the 'grand ends of civil society, the peace and security of individuals' that the legislature ensured that 'to everything capable of ownership a legal and determinate owner' was assigned.[13]

To lament the progressive dilution of this ideology would be to lament the passing of a bucolic idyll which never existed. In the eighteenth century, 'liberty' was not meant to accrue to those who lacked property. All that the language of liberty entailed was a defence against the threat to elite interests delivered by the despotic, central state; property was always the reference point. Property remained the reference point in the nineteenth century ('order', indeed, was only a Victorian euphemism for it). But in the nineteenth century there was a change: a greater threat to elites came to be discerned not in the state, as hitherto, but in the urban working classes. Against that plebeian threat, the state could now plausibly be represented as property's bastion and ally. The result was assured. The old language of liberty and natural rights had been anti-statist in its rationale. As that rationale became less self-evident, executive authority could be massively extended. The state itself gradually became the implicit source of rights, for it could fairly claim that rights were conditional on the order which it alone had the resources to protect.

One early indication of the shift – even in Whig discourse – was the lament of the Royal Commission on the Criminal Law in 1839 that rights were susceptible of wide and expediential definition; their 'natural' basis was, in short, no longer self-evident. The commissioners resorted instead to Beccarian and Benthamite certainties. 'A

---

[13]   William Blackstone, *Commentaries on the Laws of England* (1765–9), Book I, chap. 4.

scale of crimes may be found, of which the first degree should consist of those which immediately tend to the dissolution of society, and the last, of the smallest possible injustice done to a private member of society.' As its fifth report put it in 1840: 'It is manifest that all specific laws for the security of persons or property would be unavailing, unless the due operation of such laws were protected by imposing efficient restraints upon forcible violations of public order.' The protection not of natural rights but of social and political order – equated with the state itself – was elevated into law's primary objective.[14]

Police campaigners were also saying that the principle of liberty was a mere derivative of the principle of order: liberty was what was left over when order was guaranteed. In this spirit, Edwin Chadwick campaigned for a national and centralised police force by offering the public a fair exchange: liberty diminished, but security gained. After marshalling a highly alarmist case to establish the extent of contemporary disorders and criminality, the 1839 Royal Commission on the County Constabulary put it as follows. It admitted that centralised policing might diminish the liberty of the subject. It insisted nonetheless that 'the [criminal] evils we have found in existence in some districts, and the abject subjection of the population to fears [of crime] which might be termed a state of slavery ... form a condition much worse in all respects than any condition that could be imposed by any government that could exist in the present state of society in this country.'[15] Fears that the state might erode liberty were supernumerary when the greatest threat to liberty could now be defined as the criminal disorder of the plebeian mass.

In modern times the appeal of this formulation was and has remained a compelling one, for citizens and governments alike. By the later nineteenth century, indeed, 'new' liberal politicians and a managerial civil service were even beginning to make clear what in Chadwick's day could only be put circumspectly: that the primary source of rights was in fact the state itself. As Haldane put it in 1896, Liberals 'must be willing and desirous to assign *a new meaning to liberty*; it must no longer signify the absence of restraint, but the presence of opportunity'. The state, in short, should ever more actively intervene, extending rights (or opportunities) to the deserving or

[14]   *RC on the Criminal Law*, 4th Report, PP 1839, XIX, p. vii; 5th Report, PP 1840, XX, p. 90.
[15]   *RC County Constabulary*, 1839, pp. 184–5.

withholding them from the undeserving in the interests of stabilising society.[16] Mill's fear that 'a tendency towards over-government' would be at the cost of liberty was coming closer to fulfilment. And the ideological structures in which debate about crime had to be located were now irretrievably established.

V THE POLICEMAN-STATE

If Mill's fear about the political costs of the disciplinary state was not wholly fulfilled even in the twentieth century, it was no thanks to the law-and-order ideologues of the policeman-state – from Colquhoun in the 1790s, Chadwick in the 1830s, down to present-day home secretaries and chief constables. Debate was vigorous enough in Britain to ensure that they did not have all the running. We are not confronted with a ruling-class conspiracy.

From the late eighteenth century onwards even the apologists and agents of the centralising process usually disagreed vehemently with one another. They were in sublime innocence of their participation in anything as grand as a 'disciplinary discourse'. They vigorously debated the best sources of order, whether it be 'social policing', education, paternalism or the extension of political participation. And Chadwick's programme was never to be fulfilled in all its authoritarian and centralising rigour: the state still falls far short of omnipotence. Nor were libertarian principles eclipsed, even if they became more vulnerable as natural rights theory lost its older *raison d'être*. Together with large constituencies of public support all the way down to the humble ratepayer, the political nation placed subtly differing values on competing principles: efficiency and order on the one hand, and economy, liberty, local autonomy and tradition on the other. In contexts where the preservation of order was *not* at issue, they were likely to be suspicious of centralising and statist tendencies. When they did act, they invariably believed that they were responding pragmatically only to self-evident anomalies and exigencies, or simply as agents of self-evidently rational administration. In the history of policing and statutory innovation, accordingly, the dominant motifs remained those of delay, compromise and half-measure.

In the same mode it has to be acknowledged that the nascent

---

[16] *Progressive Review*, 1 (1896), p. 4, cited in R. Kamm, 'The Home Office, Public Order and Civil Liberties, 1880–1914' (unpublished PhD dissertation, Cambridge University, 1986), in which there is a full discussion of this general theme.

law-and-order bureaucracy often vigorously resisted external, public pressures for it to expand its surveillance over petty irregularity, domestic conduct, the abuse of health, traffic or educational regulation, and the like. Add to this the fact that social and political change does create new and real problems 'out there' (drugs or terrorism, for example) to which a new control initiative may be a rational response, and we are a long way from the notion that the disciplinary state was the only agent of its own expansion.

Despite these powerful reservations, however, important truths need to be affirmed. The first is that, even as they argued, all respectable people became increasingly committed to an often unspoken premise of social policy: that 'respect, deference and obedience' lay at 'the very foundation of social order and well-being'.[17] The second is that in the nineteenth century Britain, like other states, was fast acquiring the technical and economic resources to underpin an evolving archipelago of centralised regulatory power. The third is that, even as they quarrelled, the entrepreneurs of order and their critics acquired in common a dependent relationship to the institutional systems which were set up piecemeal to advance the disciplinary enterprise. These systems in time came to order 'the self-repression of the repressors themselves'[18] – if only because all bureaucracies take on a life of their own. For the point holds that with respect to what they conceived as their primary functions, Home Office officials, police chiefs and other entrepreneurs of law from the mid-nineteenth century onwards have repeatedly (and from within) assessed the shortcomings of the *systems* they operated, and this in terms of 'statist' criteria: efficiency and rationality. They have referred more or less cosmetically to an external threat, often only part real, sometimes invented, to justify the correction of those shortcomings through the bureaucracy's expansion and internal specialisation. They have generated data (like criminal statistics) which proved there was still a 'problem' to respond to, or indeed that the problem was getting worse. And so piecemeal, and without long-term premeditation, they have multiplied the

---

[17]   See, for example, A. P. Donajgrodzki, '"Social Police" and the Bureaucratic Elite: A Vision of Order in the Age of Reform', in A. P. Donajgrodzki, ed., *Social Control in Nineteenth-Century Britain* (1977). For the language of order in early modern England, see Wrightson, 'Two Concepts of Order', pp. 21–46.

[18]   M. Ignatieff, 'State, Civil Society and Total Institution: A Critique of Recent Social Histories of Punishment', in D. Sugarman, ed., *Legality, Ideology and the State* (1983), p. 199.

bureaucracy's personnel and refined its statutory powers and obligations with the connivance of Parliament and government.

Finally, it was in fact in its policeman guise rather than in its paternalistic guise that the Victorian state was first to demonstrate its power and its purposes. In 1863, even while the watchword in other fields of regulation was laissez-faire, the jurist J. F. Stephen could identify the state primarily through its function as law-enforcer: 'The administration of criminal justice is the commonest, the most striking, and the most interesting shape, in which the sovereign power of the state manifests itself to the great bulk of its subjects.'[19] The expansion and meaning of the modern state was first made palpable, in short, through its progressive erosion of the older discretionary procedures at law, and of the individual and communal sanctions, many of them extra-legal, which had sufficed to maintain order in Britain for centuries. And, indeed, the nineteenth-century poor knew this better than most. We shall see that the disciplinary state was not only an earlier but also a more powerful presence in working-class life than the more benign state which our blander textbooks approvingly emphasise (the state which began to take an interest in factories, sanitation or education, for example).

Observers first recognised the implications of this process in the 1870s. 'If anybody were called on to portray the advancing civilisation of England', the Conservative J. H. Scourfield observed in Parliament with admitted hyperbole, 'It might be fitly conveyed by the representation of a prison.' The *Pall Mall Gazette* complained of the threat to individual liberty from the prevailing compulsion 'to drill, discipline and dragoon us all into virtue'. The feminist Josephine Butler announced that 'police government . . . combines the evil of extreme centralisation with the activity, in every corner of the nation, of a vast and numerous agency of surveillance'.[20]

But the major concern by the 1880s was that in pursuit of order, the British had unwittingly sanctioned the growth, in bureaucracy, of a new social power, whose momentum was indeed self-generated. 'Every great public department', one jurist noted, had become 'a

---

[19] J. F. Stephen, *A General View of the Criminal Law of England* (1863), pp. 99–100, quoted by D. Hay, 'The Criminal Prosecution in England and its Historians', *Modern Law Review*, 47 (1984), p. 28.

[20] See P. Smith, *Disraelian Conservatism and Social Reform* (1967), p. 162; *Pall Mall Gazette*, 26 Aug. 1872; J. Butler, *Government by Police* (1879), p. 56. I owe these references and those in the next footnote to Stefan Petrow, 'Policing Morals: The Metropolitan Police and the Home Office in London, 1870–1914' (unpublished PhD thesis, Cambridge University, 1987), pp. 1–25.

centre of force and influence which may rival all the more desultory forces of public opinion.' The historian Ramsay Muir observed in 1910 that 'if all the legislation of the last half-century by which the daily routine of English life has been affected could be traced to its source, it would certainly be found that a very large proportion of this legislation is essentially bureaucratic in its origins'.[21] Bureaucracy fuelled its own expansion, and through legislation provided itself with work to do. The appetite for control was enlarged by what it fed on.

The development of the policeman-state was a process rather than an event. The process continues, and it can have no moment of completion. The history of policing was only one aspect of this story, though the most dramatic. Most familiarly, the establishment of Peel's Metropolitan Police in 1829 embodied a new conception of policing at odds with the discretionary and parochial procedures of eighteenth-century law-enforcement. Full-time, professional, hierarchically organised, they were intended to be the impersonal agents of central policy. But the 'new' police often turn out on closer examination to be akin to the old, in personnel, efficiency and tactics; so that in the long view 1829 may be of interest mainly for the trend it revealed towards an increasing subjection of law-enforcement in all its aspects to central direction.[22]

Ostensibly the forces multiplying in the boroughs and counties after 1835–9 remained under local watch committee control. But even in the nineteenth century the parochial principle was being fast eroded, in the interests of systematisation, collaboration and greater neutrality. In some boroughs like Liverpool, chief constables achieved a fair degree of autonomy from their watch committees as early as the 1850s. Elsewhere they gained their *de facto* independence during the 1870s, as central government increasingly dictated their duties.[23] The 1856 County and Borough Police Act made police forces mandatory in boroughs and counties alike, subjected them to central inspection and

21 S. Amos, *Fifty Years of the English Constitution, 1830–1880* (1880), p. 467; R. Muir, *Peers and Bureaucrats* (1910), pp. 18–19.

22 Most critical studies of policing stop, oddly, around 1870–80. See, notably, W. R. Miller, *Cops and Bobbies: Police Authority in New York and London, 1830–1870* (Chicago and London, 1977); C. Emsley, *Policing and its Context, 1750–1870* (1983); C. Steedman, *Policing the Victorian Community: The Formation of English Provincial Police Forces, 1856–1880* (1984). Later themes can be teased out of the uncritical narratives of T. A. Critchley, *A History of Police in England and Wales, 900–1966* (1967), or D. Ascoli, *The Queen's Peace: The Metropolitan Police, 1829–1979* (1979), and kindred works.

23 M. Brogden, *The Police: Autonomy and Consent* (1982); Steedman, *Policing the Victorian Community*, chap. 10.

sanctioned Exchequer grants to forces certified as 'efficient'. From the 1870s onwards Home Office rules helped to regulate pay, discipline and criteria for employment. The 1890 Police Act permitted mutual-aid agreements between forces to facilitate the borrowing of constables in times of severe – usually industrial – unrest.

Scotland Yard came to play an important part in the centralising process too. The Home Office's direct control of metropolitan policing from 1829 onwards was turned to powerful effect. Under Home Office direction, most new police policies and practices were first evolved in London. In this way Scotland Yard set the pace for an increasing specialisation and centralisation of police functions which Peel could never have foreseen. And all provincial police forces were gradually affected by it.

Detectives offer one example. In Peel's day, plainclothes spy systems of any kind had been held in the deepest suspicion. When the Home Office did establish a small detective force in 1842 it had done so surreptitiously. In the 1870s, however, detectives went public, as it were. The occasion was a major corruption scandal within the detective body: the conviction in 1877 of Chief Inspectors Druscovitch and Palmer and Inspector Meiklejohn for obstructing investigation into a major turf fraud. In the full glare of publicity, the Home Office seized the opportunity to overhaul the detective system and to establish, to public acclaim, a much augmented CID in 1878. The number of arrests by metropolitan detectives rose from 13,000 to 18,000 within five years.[24] This success alone ensured the continuing expansion of the CID and of detective work throughout the country thereafter. The legitimacy of secret detection was seldom again to be challenged.

Similarly, it was the Home Office and Scotland Yard which in 1869 instituted the criminal records system whose computerised descendant we live with today. Primitive and unwieldy in its early years, it got better with the increasing use of photography and after 1902 of fingerprinting. And even the regular circulation of simple information sheets to provincial forces brought satisfying results. Either way, the state was learning to keep closer tabs on the unrespectable citizenry. It was learning to keep tabs on political dissidents, too: in 1884 the Special Branch was established in response to Fenian bomb outrages.

Moreover, while Peel's first policemen had largely enforced the

---

[24] Ascoli, *Queen's Peace*, p. 150 n. 1.

common law, most proceedings on the part of their late Victorian successors were to be under statute or delegated statute as Parliament and Home Office alike extended police control over a bewildering array of social groups, from habitual criminals to abused children, from pornographers to inebriates. The state also assumed an increasing direction of the penal system (notably in the 1877 Prison Act), and, tentatively, of the ancient discretionary area of sentencing: the establishment of the Court of Criminal Appeal in 1907 was the critical moment here.[25] Most significantly of all, the police themselves after mid-century very gradually became the main agents of prosecution, while Whitehall's assumption of a central position in the process was symbolised by the establishment of the office of Director of Public Prosecutions in 1879.[26] By these means, by 1900, what policemen, magistrates and even judges had to do even in remote areas of the country was being effectively dictated from Westminster and Whitehall. The growth of the criminal department of the Home Office speaks eloquently for this expansion. Set up in 1870 by Cross and Lowe, by the 1880s the department exceeded the home department in importance, and by 1906 was dealing with a third of all Home Office business.[27]

Clearly, in respect of central control of the criminal justice system as in other spheres of government activity, the forty years after 1870 present themselves as a major period of innovation. What ensued in the twentieth century was an acceleration of trends already well under way. As regards policing, the parochial principle still remained more than merely cosmetic in 1914. Standards of pay, service and manpower still varied widely:[28] fifty forces had strengths of less than fifty men, and borough watch committees remained jealous of their independence if only to keep an eye on costs and the deployment of policing in their own interests. But the war and its aftermath brought large changes.[29] Home Office directives, committees and inter-force conferences multiplied, and chief constables increasingly responded to central direction. In response to the 1918–19 police strike and the

---

[25] Radzinowicz and Hood, *A History of English Criminal Law*, vol. 5, chap. 23.

[26] D. Hay, 'Controlling the English Prosecutor', *Osgoode Hall Law Journal*, 21 (1983), pp. 165–86.

[27] Jill Pellew, *The Home Office, 1848–1914: From Clerks to Bureaucrats* (1982).

[28] J. P. Martin and G. Wilson, *The Police: A Study in Manpower* (1969).

[29] For a valuable account of interwar developments in policing, still sadly neglected in the secondary literature, see J. B. Lopian, 'Crime, Police and Punishment, 1918–1929: Metropolitan Experiences, Perceptions and Policies' (unpublished PhD dissertation, Cambridge University, 1986).

ensuing Desborough committee, the 1919 Police Act outlawed any attempt to induce police to strike, standardised training, pay and conditions of service, placed half the cost of all policing on the Exchequer and, significantly, gave the Home Office a police department and an expanded inspectorate. To contain mounting industrial unrest, small borough forces were abolished or amalgamated, and co-operation between forces facilitated – with interesting results in the deployment of outside forces in areas affected by the 1926 General Strike. The 1929 Royal Commission on Police Powers went on to standardise arrest procedures; Trenchard's Hendon Police College (1934) aimed to generate 'officer material' to feed all the nation's forces; the 1938 Committee on Detective Work put paid at last to inter-force rivalries in this context too, and achieved a major rationalisation and integration of detective procedures across the country. Between the wars the British police were transformed into a federal rather than an independent structure of forces. In the later twentieth century the process of consolidation was to be carried very much further.

And what were the cost-benefits of this prodigious enterprise? They ought to have been substantial. The strength and cost of the policeman-state has risen continuously, faster than inflation. In 1861 there was one policemen for every 937 souls in England and Wales, by 1891 one for every 731, by 1951 one for every 661; and these figures say nothing about the even faster expansion of the personnel of the penal and judicial systems and of the technical services which supported them. National expenditure on policemen alone rose from £1.5 million in 1861 to over two-and-a-half times that amount in 1891 and nearly four-and-a-half times by 1911. It rose again from £7 million in 1914 to £18 million in 1920, across which time, similarly, the cost of the prison service quadrupled. Bureaucratic growth and the increasing demands of non-criminal business, and not only inflation, were to boost British expenditure on policing to £1.1 billion in 1978–9 and again to £2.8 billion by 1985–6.[30]

In seeming justification of all this, the perceived cost of theft, admittedly, rose too. But it is a truism which even the present-day Home Office has assimilated (though not widely publicised) that so long as the resources of law-enforcement increase, the perceived costs and incidence of 'crime' will increase, as hitherto concealed illegalities

---

[30] V. A. C. Gatrell, 'The Decline of Theft and Violence in Victorian and Edwardian England and Wales', in Gatrell, Lenman and Parker, eds., *Crime and the Law*, pp. 275–6; twentieth-century data from annual reports of inspectors of constabulary.

are brought into view.[31] Thus the cost of crime rose not because some atavistic urge to dishonesty increased among the British people, but because of increases in the value of stealable commodities and in the ease of their appropriation and disposal, in public readiness and ability to call in the police, in the facility of prosecution, but above all in the intensity of police action itself.

Even so, it comes as a shock to realise that when the cost of reported theft is compared against the mounting cost of the policeman-state, it has always been laughably small. According to Metropolitan Police statistics in 1848, reported break-ins and robberies in London cost then a mere £2,507, and all felonies against property £44,666. Even by 1899, when reporting was more reliable and extensive, reported burglary cost Londoners only £88,406 (3d. per head of the metropolitan population). By 1950 it still cost a mere £482,000, and in only 17 per cent of the cases reported did the value of the stolen property exceed £100. And today? The reported loss to burglars and robbers in England and Wales in 1980 was £201 million; another reported £350 million was lost to lesser kinds of theft. This is less than the £800 million which in 1984 the Controller of the Audit Commission for Local Authorities in England and Wales said could be saved if local councils were more prudent in their purchase of such necessities as envelopes, refuse sacks, exercise books and tennis balls.[32]

It goes without saying that the costs of theft (and of violence) would have been far higher had there been no police: these figures are in some degree the achievement of deterrence. Nonetheless, it is not surprising that the figures were and are little publicised. As they stand, they subvert the rationale of a good deal of law-and-order panicking in modern British history. The figures also subvert some of the larger meanings some historians have bestowed on crime. Historians who try to give the criminal a niche in the pantheon of major historical agents have to be of a romantic disposition. Most reported crimes have been banal, distressing for their immediate victims though they might be. It is difficult to ascribe to them any large social purposes.

---

[31]   P. Morris and K. Heal, *Crime Control and Police: A Review of Research* (Home Office Research Study No. 67, 1981).

[32]   Gatrell, 'Decline of Theft and Violence', p. 327; *Annual Criminal Statistics*, 1950 and 1980; *Guardian*, 29 Aug. 1984. The 1987 figures for the UK were: burglary £272 million, thefts from vehicles £120 million, thefts of vehicles £662 million. Meanwhile, policing cost £3.5 billion, prisons £698 million, courts £323 million, and probation services £200 million. Only 13 per cent of the loss to burglary and 6 per cent of property stolen from vehicles were recovered: Crime Prevention Unit, Home Office, *Costs of Crime* (1989).

Still less have criminals had a large effect upon the established order of things, other than by intensifying the authoritarian instincts of their enemies. The only social bandits modern Britain has had to cope with have been tax inspectors. For centuries, indeed, Britain's working-class thieves have found easier pickings among their social equals than among their superiors. Great robberies have been as infrequent as great murders. For every jewel stolen, Britons have suffered the theft of a million boots, a million sides of bacon and loaves of bread, and probably rather more pocket handkerchieves. Complex societies cannot be subverted by depredations of this order.

Disproportionate and growing expenditure on law-enforcement, then, has to be understood partly as an expression of bureaucratic imperatives, partly as a response to public expectation, orchestrated by officials, politicians and newspaper proprietors though it might be. The state did have its side of a bargain to fulfil, after all; and the deterrent effectiveness of policing meant that the bargain citizens struck with the state has not been an empty one for them. But the state also fulfilled and fulfils its obligation to the citizen with the greater alacrity because the cost-returns on the expenditure which supports the policeman-state reside elsewhere than in crime prevention. And on these returns the public has never quite so systematically (or has only recently) been invited to have much of an opinion. The reference must be to the regulation of industrial and political dissent, intelligence-gathering and surveillance, or the symbolic enunciation of social, economic or sexual norms which it is always one of the covert purposes of law-enforcement to achieve.

VI   POLICING PUBLIC ORDER

The construction of consent through more or less concealed forms of coercion remained an option with which the liberal state could no more dispense than could the totalitarian. For it was an inevitable corollary of consent-building that *dissent* should come to be invested in the liberal state with new, increasing and peculiar significance.

Even in the early nineteenth century it was apparent that the collaboration upon which the state might increasingly have to rest its legitimacy if a class-divided society was to hold together was not going to be willingly entered into at all social levels. Too many of the poor were incapable of entering into a working relationship with a free government, let alone with a free market, as elites conceived those things. A few refused to enter into either relationship while the market distributed its riches inequitably and while government expressed that inequality. Obstinately and annoyingly, these people seemed to reconstitute their numbers with each generation that passed.

From that day to this, therefore, the state's altruism and benevolence has been compromised by the need to deploy against these not necessarily criminal dissidents ever more efficient and economical forms of force to maintain the relationships upon which, elsewhere, a qualified consensus might depend. Those who dissented from prevailing norms had always been penalised. They had never before the nineteenth century, however, acquired the large meanings henceforth ascribed to them, or been subjected to so concerted a barrage of overt and coercive or covert and persuasive regulation. As disciplinary organisations grew stronger, around these 'enemies within' accreted an ever-richer cluster of stigmatic images and of restrictive legal rulings and policing practices which were to identify them as the enduring foci of law-and-order strategies down to our own day.

We can address here, briefly, only the example of political dissidents, who challenged the consensual principle even more explicitly than the 'criminal'. In two ways, the development of policing very early on affected the way of containing them. Thanks to policemen, first, the use of the military after the Chartist era tended to become confined to the regulation of industrial disputes. Troops were called out a dozen times between 1907 and 1914, it is true. They shot dead two miners at Featherstone in 1893 and two strikers in Llanelli and two more in Liverpool in 1911, and another protester in Liverpool in 1919. The military's utility was sanctioned by inter-departmental committees in 1895 and 1908. And the Emergency Powers Act of 1920 allowed their use to protect food or fuel supplies. Their readiness to hand in the battle with organised labour suffused all interwar industrial unrest, and even more after 1945.

Nonetheless, troops were not used in the regulation of non-industrial collective behaviour in mainland Britain after the 1840s. And here the second shift in the tactics of containment was major. Thanks to their growing skills in crowd control,[33] policemen enabled governments to discard the symbolic and rare sledgehammer assault on seditious *speaking* in favour of deploying a more economical but broader

---

[33]   D. Goodway, *London Chartism, 1838–1848* (Cambridge, 1982), Part 3; Phillip T. Smith, *Policing Victorian London: Political Policing, Public Order, and the London Metropolitan Police* (Westport, Conn., and London, 1985), chap. 5.

restrictive power at the point of dissident *meeting*. In 1790 you could peaceably assemble where you liked but not say what you liked; in 1890 you could say what you liked (if the libel laws permitted) but certainly could not assemble where you liked.

Trial indices indicate how the law was being realigned in this way. Trials for *sedition* in England and Wales dwindled from 1,725 in the Chartist decade to virtually nil by the time of the failure of the prosecution case in R v. Burns in 1888 (which put a virtual end to the utility of this charge at law). But conversely there were more trials for felonious *riot* in the 1860s than there had been even in the Chartist decade, even though popular turbulence by then was greatly diminished. By attacking the behaviour of the crowd rather than the opinions of the speaker public opinion was less affronted, and police were allowed more scope for initiative. At this level, too, policemen became more discriminating in their arrests and more adept at framing charges that would stick. The conviction-to-trial ratios for felonious riot rose from 41 per cent to 75 per cent between the 1840s and 1860s; for common law riot they rose from 59 per cent to 89 per cent by the 1890s.[34]

Policemen's increasing wisdom in resorting to lesser charges in more doubtful cases assisted in this achievement. Since it is still the presumption in law that the only right in general which the public can acquire is of passing and repassing on the highway, the charges of obstruction and breach of peace, easily processed in magistrates' courts, became and remain the favoured device for containing Britons' inexplicably naive delusion that they have a right of free assembly. 'The primary and over-riding object for which streets exist is passage', a judge ruled in 1913; 'There is no such thing as a right in the public to hold meetings as such in the streets; . . . streets are for passage, and passage is paramount to everything else.'[35] The Metropolitan Police Act of 1839 and the Town Police Causes Act of 1847, followed by innumerable local bye-laws, had made the point long before. The discretionary power of anticipatory prohibition which these permitted police to wield over would-be demonstrators was (and is) prodigious, for what constitutes the element of obstruction and breach of peace which police are entitled to anticipate in these cases is splendidly undefined. Duncan v. Jones (1936) was to make the point explicit (if it was not before) that there are no standards for assessing police

---

[34] All data computed from annual judicial statistics.
[35] M. Supperstone, *Brownlie's Law of Public Order and National Security* (2nd edn, 1981), p. 44, and *passim* for this paragraph.

resort to preventive justice of this kind other than their own view of its expedience. In the same spirit it was expedient that the wartime Defence of the Realm restrictions should be reshaped and cemented permanently into the 1920 Emergency Powers Act, to give legal sanction to the government's strike-breaking apparatus. Similarly the 1936 Public Order Act came to be applied not against fascist marchers for whom it was ostensibly designed but against collective disorder of any kind, for some forty years rendering the common law charge of riot all but redundant in the process (until the 1984–5 miners' strike brought it to life again).

'The common people of England have succeeded to the greatest heritage of all – the heritage of Freedom', Lord Denning opined in one of his fulsome pronouncements on this large subject. It would be more honest to admit to the contrary that 'the history of public order in the United Kingdom is essentially a history of restrictions':[36] a truism to which the history of trade unionism alone would testify, if it fell within our brief, as it did battle against that other conveniently comprehensive common law concept, conspiracy, from the days of the Combination Acts onwards.

Part 2   Policemen and criminals

VII   THE TARGETS OF LAW-ENFORCEMENT

The enforcers of law have never liked political dissidents. It has been the whole thrust of our argument so far to show why they have never trusted poorer people either. Numerically these were the law's major target, and it is time we proved it.

It was not that opportunities were neglected to bring to trial those of the propertied classes who stepped out of line. From the execution of Lord Ferrars in 1760 to the imprisonment of Oscar Wilde in 1895 and the prosecution of Noel Coward for currency offences in 1941, via a few thousand assorted middle-class charlatans and wife-poisoners, the law theatrically exhibited its capacity for impartiality. But with infinitely greater frequency, it demonstrated also its obedience to the law-and-order strategies we have outlined. The emphasis of these strategies was not on the equitable defence of property and person, but on their defence against those who had persons but no (or little) property. The emphasis was also on the potential insubordination

---

[36] Ibid., p. 25.

of such people, and on the future implications of their numbers and continuing enjoyment of liberty. Comparatively speaking, therefore, law was enduringly lax in its attention to the wrongdoings of its pay-masters.

Three kinds of index reveal the social identity of those who usually experienced legal disciplining.[37] As regards the identity of those arrested or summoned for *non-indictable* (petty) offences, first, the dis-tribution of the main groups of offences speaks for itself. In 1908, as representative a sample year as any, a trivial 1.1 per cent of the total of 689,100 summary proceedings in England and Wales were for offences against the laws protecting labour and sanitary and hous-ing conditions. Proceedings against other offences of the employing or landlord classes were insignificant. (The 9 per cent for offences against highway acts caught the drivers of carts etc. rather than their owners, and most were for obstruction.) Most proceedings were against poorer people whose offences were essentially street-offences: drunks (29 per cent), offenders against the regulation of marginal economies and street cultures through police acts and bye-laws (16 per cent), offenders against vagrancy statutes (10 per cent) and those accused of assault (7 per cent).

As regards the identity of those arrested for serious *indictable* crimes, secondly, the indices are multiform and more explicit. Two-thirds of Essex indictments in the second half of the eighteenth century were against labourers, servants, vagrants and paupers, and another quarter against artisans and lesser tradesmen.[38] In the Black Country in the mid-1850s unskilled manual workers comprised about half of the male population but about three-quarters of those committed to trial; skilled manual workers and shopkeepers provided another quarter; but clerical workers only 1.1. per cent, professionals 0.2 per cent, and farmers 0.2 per cent.[39] Throughout the period 1840 to 1890, similarly, never more than 0.4 per cent of prisoners in England and Wales were identified as having enjoyed 'superior instruction', and as late as 1890 one in five male prisoners was illiterate and three-quarters could only read, or read and write 'imperfectly'.[40] In the late 1890s, next, a trifling annual average of twenty-four out of some 40,000 people convicted of indictable offences possessed property

---

[37] Unless otherwise indicated, data from annual criminal statistics.
[38] P. King, 'Crime, Law and Society in Essex, 1740–1820' (unpublished PhD disser-tation, Cambridge University, 1984), p. 127.
[39] Philips, *Crime and Authority*, pp. 164–8.
[40] Gatrell and Hadden, 'Criminal Statistics', pp. 379–80.

sufficient to justify the appointment of administrators of prisoners' property under the 1870 Abolition of Forfeiture Act. Before that act, when the property of persons convicted of treason or felony escheated to the crown, the total value of property thus extracted from all those convicted ranged from a minimum of £253 in 1849 to a puny maximum of £1,318 in 1854.[41] Victorian prisoners were very poor people indeed.

Twentieth-century official sources are more coy about commenting on offenders' social status. Nonetheless, thirdly, confirmation of the enduring social bias of the law's vision resides in the low-profile 'middle-class' illegalities retained right up to 1950. Law-enforcers from 1914 to the present 'have been more consistent in trying to suppress the working-class crime of pilfering than they have the white-collar crime of tax-evasion ... Jail sentences have been imposed far more freely on working-class offenders than on businessmen and shop-keepers who broke the law.'[42]

There is no knowing the relationship between the real and the reported incidence of white-collar and commercial crime, because of the impossibility of defining the border-line between a clearly criminal act and a dubious but tolerated commercial practice. What is certain is that police and courts became only tardily sensitised to its probable extent. In 1850 there were a mere 948 trials in England and Wales for embezzlement, obtaining by false pretences, frauds and falsifying accounts; the transfer of some of these offences to summary jurisdiction raised the total to 2,948 by 1900. Even so, most of the offenders were very small fry indeed: it was clerks, for example, and not managers or directors who were caught falsifying accounts, and it was workmen, mainly, who accounted for the 1,378 embezzlement cases in 1900. Few big fish were attended to by policemen, and for good reasons. As a chief constable lamented in 1905, 'the intricacy of the facts and ... the technical nature of modern financial transactions' put the question beyond the expertise of most policemen. His call for stronger defences against fraud in criminal law had little immediate effect.[43] It was only in 1945 that the Metropolitan and City Police instituted their joint company fraud department. In 1950 this was to submit 793 cases for criminal action on behalf of government departments, the stock exchange and private business. Prosecutions for frauds by agents, trustees, directors etc. shot up accordingly from

---

[41]   Gatrell, 'Decline of Theft and Violence', p. 334 n. 199.
[42]   E. Smithies, *The Black Economy in England since 1914* (Dublin, 1984), p. 132.
[43]   Gatrell, 'Decline of Theft and Violence', pp. 323–4.

a paltry average of some 600 per annum in the 1920s and 1,000 in the 1930s to 3,777 in 1950. (This still trifling number invites comparison with the 428,000 'ordinary' thefts in that year.) That it bore no meaningful relationship to the likely scale of illegality and fraudulent practice in business and the professions is suggested by the fact that the 390 London fraud prosecutions in 1950 each involved an average sum of a mere £494.[44] The law's attention was as ever fixed on offenders who had breached the trust of their employers, not on the employing class itself.

VIII POLICING: OCCUPATIONAL ETHICS AND OPERATIONAL CONSTRAINTS

We have seen that this time-honoured fixation of law-enforcers on the less well-defended populace responded in part to a prophecy about the social location of crime which ideology affirmed from the early nineteenth century onwards. But there remains more to say about it than that. The ensuing direction of policing to that location could only gratifyingly fulfil the prophecy, and for reasons other than ideological. The technicalities of fraud might be beyond the policeman's comprehension. What was not beyond his comprehension was the behaviour he daily encountered on the streets, where poorer people conducted a good deal of their business with each other and often behaved illegally. Constrained as he was mainly to police the streets, the policeman fed back into the ideology of crime a confirmation of the premise that the bottom quarter or third of the urban population were indeed the most criminal. And that self-fulfilling prophecy policeman have never been in a position properly to gainsay. Poorer law-breakers were the only ones the policeman could usually see, or was even inclined to see.

The early constable was usually recruited from the agricultural labour force, paid an agricultural labourer's wage, and liable to leave the force with deplorable rapidity. In the larger forces by mid-century, however, a more stable career structure and command hierarchy was already beginning to enclose lesser officers within an occupational sub-culture with its own values and standards.[45] Sustained by this, Victorian policemen undertook the task of patrolling the poor with the unselfconscious alacrity their twentieth-century successors

---

[44] Judicial statistics, 1950.
[45] Steedman, *Policing the Victorian Community*, chap. 8.

brought to the task of patrolling aliens, blacks and street-corner delinquents. Isolated by uniform, discipline and function from the working-class community, and upholding 'order' in the face of chronic hostility and abuse from their targets (and at danger to themselves), the career policeman made (and makes) sense of his extraordinary situation only by internalising authoritarian values and deferring to conventional standards of respectability. At the same time, contradictorily, to establish a feasible negotiation with his targets, he had to generate his own operational standards on the streets – 'tacit, assumed, unwritten, and passed on via ''apprenticeship'' from officer to officer'. These standards were often less than respectable and often at odds with those of the rulebooks and the letter of the law.

In controlling this lower-rank ethic, the command hierarchy was in a difficult position. It was not in their interests or within their capability wholly to subvert it, but their connivance was reluctant. Some degree of tension between the command and the station-men was endemic in British policing.[46] It stemmed from grievances about service conditions (the 1918–19 police strike had significant precedents in abortive Metropolitan Police strikes in 1879 and 1890). It stemmed from the chronic remoteness of commissioners and chief constables (often, before the 1930s, trained in the military or colonial services) from lower-rank notions that 'good policing' signified detection rather than deterrence, action rather than service, physical engagement rather than administration. It stemmed above all from the command's greater accountability to public images of policing and to Whitehall's interest in keeping those images in good trim.

So pressure on the men to fulfil their service roles was unrelenting, and sporadic campaigns against their corruption and malpractices spatter as yet tactfully hidden pages of police history. These last usually surfaced only in circuitous ways: through public interest in the trials of Inspector Druscovitch in 1877 or Inspector White in 1880 or Sergeant Goddard in 1929, or in the public disquiet which resulted in the issuing of Judges' Rules on interrogation and arrest procedures in 1912. When, twice, police malpractices warranted investigation by a Royal Commission, it was usually because policemen had made the mistake of doing tactless things to articulate people who could fight back. The 1906–8 commission was initiated over the allegedly wrongful arrest for riotous and indecent conduct of Mme D'Angely,

[46]   R. Reiner, *The Blue-Coated Worker: A Sociological Study of Police Unionism* (Cambridge, 1977).

a lady of dubious reputation but a lady nonetheless. The 1928–9 commission arose from the ill-considered arrest of Sir Leo Chiozza Money for frolicking with Irene Savidge one May evening in Hyde Park, and for the lady's subsequent less than gentle interrogation. The aptly-named Sir Leo was a financier.

Not much that was unmitigatedly evil came to light in these investigations. The 1906–8 Commission, for example, thought only nineteen of the complaints it invited were worth examining, and few were satisfactorily proven. Perhaps the empires of corruption which were to come to light in the Metropolitan Police after 1969 could evolve only with the squad-specialisms and discrete organisational structures of big-city policing in the later twentieth century. But, equally, perhaps not. How much police corruption is perceived depends on the sensitivity of the beholder's eye. Before the 1960s (less so now) the affluent public that mattered had a sanguine view of the trustworthiness of its servants, and carpets were less diligently lifted. The impoverished public that did not matter but might know better about police malpractices did not speak out; when rarely it did, as to the 1906–8 commission, it was discredited by hostile questioning.

What nonetheless can be perceived in the evidence of the Royal Commission is the ice-berg tip of a long-standing system of wheeling and dealing between police and underworld which had its own unwritten rules and at which command officers had no choice but to connive. Blind eyes were turned, favours exacted and reciprocated, informers employed, bribes exchanged, some brutality was standard practice. In these relationships of power, continuities from past to present are more striking than change. Relations between police and law-breakers were necessarily close, and it would be surprising if, then as now, they were not also contaminating. Even a tame police historian admits that by the early 1920s 'the CID had become a thoroughly venal private army'.[47] Other sources confirm this. Witnesses before the 1878 confidential detective committee drew a thin veil over the implications of detectives' using 'a certain class of people among the criminal class from whom we get information by small payments and other means'.[48] In old age, the Edwardian East End gang leader Arthur Harding recalled what this might mean. In his world there were 'good' policemen and 'brutal' policemen; they could

---

[47] Ascoli, *The Queen's Peace*, p. 210.
[48] *Confidential Departmental Commission Report on the Metropolitan Detective Force*, 1878–9, §143: Public Record Office (hereafter PRO), HO 45/9442/66692.

be both brutal and good; but the worst were the crooked: 'The CID at Commercial Street were good policemen. They were brutal, but they were proper policemen. At Leman Street ... they were villains. There was money about and the police got their cut ... You had to be well in with the police if you were to make a living.'[49]

Police tolerance of Harding's gang exhibited an age-old rationale. They turned a blind eye when the gang raided Jewish clubs demanding protection money, once in the hope of flushing out the Houndsditch murderers of 1910, or for simpler purposes: 'We got friendly with the City police – they wanted to put a bit of fear into the Jewish flashboys at Aldgate.' Police responses to other difficulties and temptations of their job were timeless in character. In disturbances from Cold Bath Fields (1833) on through the Sunday trading riots (1855) to the General Strike, not to mention beyond, truncheons were wielded vigorously against innocent heads. A certain amount of knocking about was standard in street-policing and in interrogation: it was economical in its effects and never likely to come to light.

Officials recurrently compromised in their efforts to cleanse these stables. Some degree of acquiescence in the ethics of street-policing was necessary on the part of chief constables, Home Office and watch committees alike. Police practices were, after all, difficult to control. They also brought results. In particular, the discretionary powers police wielded, and from which abuses often arose, had to be protected at all costs. One way of protecting them was to deny their existence. The disingenuous but comforting notion was reinforced (as it was classically expressed by the 1929 commission) that 'a Policeman possesses few powers not enjoyed by the ordinary citizen', and that he was merely 'a person paid to perform, as a matter of duty, acts which if he were so minded he might have done voluntarily'. This was fiction.

There was another way of protecting these discretionary powers. When they were abused, secrecy enshrouded most disciplinary procedures and the evidence Royal Commissions heard was delicately censored. When in 1900–10 up to 11 per cent of the metropolitan force were being disciplined annually, the Home Office was determined that the import of the more serious cases should not sully the public print lest 'ventilation in public of details of cases of grave

---

[49] R. Samuel, ed., *East End Underworld: Chapters in the Life of Arthur Harding* (1981).

misconduct ... set up a feeling of mistrust ... which would greatly weaken the sense of security that now exists'.[50] In similar spirit the 1906–8 commissioners confidentially warned metropolitan magistrates 'not to reply in public to any questions the answers to which publicly made might be detrimental to the police service'.[51] The 1929 Commission admitted that police took bribes from bookmakers and prostitutes and abused discretionary powers; but it took the position adopted by every select committee or commission since the enquiry into the Cold Bath Fields fiasco a century earlier. It issued a qualified rebuke, if rebuke it can be called at all, and dressed it up in the exculpatory doctrine of the rotten apple. As the 1908 Commission had put it: 'no reasonable man would, in approaching the question of the efficacy of so large a body as the Metropolitan Police, expect that every one of them should on all occasions act with sufficient intelligence and be invariably courteous and good-tempered in the discharge of very difficult duties'.

Which again might or might not be true. What is not in doubt, as these evasions show, is that by the early twentieth century the ideological solidarity in the trade of law-enforcement which may nowadays be taken for granted was all but complete. At the top, as early as 1880, the judge presiding over the corruption trial against Inspector White could tell the Home Secretary (privately) that 'it is simply sickening to hear the Police abused, and every unworthy motive assigned to them, in the way that has now become almost a rule at the Old Bailey'.[52] At the bottom, ranks in big forces were ever more closely bonded in that authoritarian mind-set which regards its own values as 'decent' and 'sane' and any deviation from them as irrationally 'political' if not indicative merely of a lack of moral backbone. The head of the Special Branch in 1926, Sir Wyndham Childs, luxuriated in his belief, for example, that 'politically motivated agitation' could be the only cause of the General Strike: 'I have never been able to understand why the successive governments I served always refused to strike one overwhelming and fatal blow against the Communist organisation.' He had been anticipated by the *Police Chronicle* in 1921: 'There never was a time when public interests stood more in need of a police independent of and uninfluenced by party politics ... The

---

50   PRO, HO 45/10540/15630.
51   *Ibid.*, 45/10540/140292.
52   *Ibid.*, 45/9567/96206.

Bolshies in this country must be reckoned with and their defeat is assured only if we see to it . . . Every policeman should devote himself quietly to a hunt for Communists and other Extremists.'[53] There have always been sensible and nice policemen, but policemen of narrow political sympathy, wit and imagination have a long pedigree too.

Where 'extremists' were parodied, the poor could expect little more sympathy. Commissioner Warren, with a rare eye on public relations, had tried to appease a public critical of police conduct in the 1887 unemployment riots by opening a register of the unemployed in each of his districts. To this initiative the poor responded with the chilliness of the Trojans watching the Greeks bearing gifts.[54] Their instincts were sound. In 1904 metropolitan divisional inspectors and superintendents reported confidentially to Scotland Yard on the extent of hardship in the course of that bitter winter. These reports provide a rare glimpse of the uniformity of tone of an occupation not only out of sympathy with its primary targets but also ideologically at one with itself:

The so-called unemployed . . . have . . . the appearance of habitual loafers rather than unemployed workmen.

The poor and distressed appearance of numbers of persons met in the East End is due more to thriftlessness and intemperate habits than to absolute poverty.

Poverty is brought about by a want of thrift.

That more outdoor relief is being distributed is in my belief the consequence of the publicity given to the fact by the press and by the agitators.

[Local socialists] are almost all of an agnostical religious belief . . . and prejudice grows by their loudly proclaimed opinions and vituperations.

[The] so-called 'unemployed' [marching from Canning Town to Trafalgar Square] could not be in the starving condition they profess for they travelled at a pace that required considerable endurance.

It has become the vogue for journalists to dabble in philanthropy as a means of promoting circulation of the press, and it appears to me that the indiscriminate and unorganised almsgiving of the present day is to be deplored as likely to be productive of immense mischief . . . [No politician] will tell the working man that he is mainly responsible for his own condition, nor have

[53] B. Weinberger, 'Police Perceptions of Labour between the Wars' (unpublished paper, University of Warwick Conference on History of Crime and Law, 1983).
[54] PRO, Mepo 2/185.

the courage to point out how . . . industry is everywhere being ruined under the despotic power of Trade Unionism.[55]

Reflexes of this kind were not peculiar to policemen: they drew on a long tradition of working-class authoritarianism and on the platitudes of contemporary debate. Among policemen, however, they were an occupational hazard. They defended self-esteem in the negotiation of the social distance they had to put between themselves and target groups who spoke with the same accents. They also, no doubt, projected anger outwards on to those who daily abused and wounded them. The values of the stationmen were not merely or mainly emulative of their officers' values; they were forged in the streets where the law-and-order drama was daily enacted.

For it was through the operational exigencies of policing at street level that the modern image of crime was largely reaffirmed, if not initially constructed. From here it fed into and reinforced every existing presupposition about the real location of 'crime' which the great and the good already had their own reasons to possess.

The poor had always been the targets of the law, but systematised urban policing could only accentuate this bias. As one compelling elucidation has pointed out, all police forces are (in terms of the expectations placed upon them) financially constrained, thin on the ground, normally excluded from home and workplace, enduringly cautious about offending those whose rates or taxes financed them – cautious, even, about offending the people they policed. And yet they are obliged to maintain high arrest rates to prove their efficacy to their penny-pinching paymasters. Their own prejudices apart, they had no choice, operationally, but to be highly selective in their attack on the nation's illegalities; they had to concentrate on the regulation of public space. These spaces – the streets pre-eminently – were where the poor had to conduct a large part of their lives.[56]

The main statutory weapons with which police were provided to conceal their operational nakedness put poor people in their sightlines too. The 1824 Vagrancy Act, the 1839 Metropolitan Police Act, analogous police acts and bye-laws across the country, the habitual criminals legislation of 1869–71 and after – all combined to give police

[55] *Ibid.*, 2/742.
[56] Jennifer Davis, 'Law-Breaking and Law-Enforcement: The Creation of a Criminal Class in Mid-Victorian London' (unpublished PhD dissertation, Boston College, 1985), chap. 4.

immense discretionary powers of arrest on suspicion of intent to commit a felony. The substantive arrestable offence in these cases was nothing more interesting than 'loitering with intent'. After 1869 even intent could be dispensed with if it was an ex-convict who loitered; he could be found guilty on grounds of known character alone. The police had equal discretionary powers of defining obstruction, breach of peace, drunkenness, even the quality of 'reasonableness' which justified their suspicions and actions; they could decide *ad hoc* whether or not to arrest, whether to bring charges, and what charges. So the constable was armed with a weaponry against which poorer people had little defence.

In application this discretion was group-specific. It was meant to be. Early police orders told constables to desist from interfering with 'respectable' working people.[57] Stop-and-search powers resulted in the arrest of vagrants, suspicious characters and, with luck, a few burglars too. They fed these vulnerable and accessible people into the judicial process in droves. Magistrates convicted or committed them to trial on little evidence, often, other than police testimony as to character. These then became the 'criminal class'; and ideological stereotypes were thus fuelled and self-confirming. As has been well put, the police themselves came to be and still are convinced that the class they had a decisive hand in *making* were the group among whom crime was most prevalent and hence most in need of surveillance.[58] As ratepayers read the reports of court proceedings which the press fulsomely purveyed, they had no difficulty in acquiescing in this definition too. Some historians have had little difficulty, either.[59]

The scale of this enterprise should not be underestimated. In the nineteenth and twentieth centuries alike, very many more people had a direct experience of the disciplinary and coercive effects of policing and law than is widely appreciated. Post-1945 evidence was to be eloquent on this. For 1962, for example, it was calculated that 'the total risk of being convicted [for an indictable offence] during a life-span was ... 29.5 per cent for males and 7.1 per cent for females'; over a fifth of the male population alive in 1962 had probably been

---

[57] Miller, *Cops and Bobbies*, p. 55.
[58] Davis, 'Law-Breaking', p. 220.
[59] J. J. Tobias, *Crime and Industrial Society in the Nineteenth Century* (1967); K Chesney, *The Victorian Underworld* (1970).

so convicted.[60] When the reach of the policeman is assessed (however roughly) in terms of the experience not of convictions but of *arrests or summonses* for non-indictable *and* indictable offences in any one year, the results are even more startling. They are conveyed in relation to population for the years 1861, 1901, and 1951 in Table 5.1.

Of course, these ratios cannot be 'hard' ratios because many people were arrested or summoned a couple or several times a year (for drunkenness, for example), and this greatly narrowed the target area at risk. In practice, however, the ratios were also narrowed in another and more significant way – and this is why we dwell on them. The prodigious implications of the figures remain unsullied when it is recalled that these are diluted national and not urban ratios (in towns the experience of policing was more intensive); that the ratios accommodate all manner and classes of person (the poor were arrested much more frequently than the rich); and that they accommodate all ages of the population too (most arrests were concentrated in that quarter of the male population aged between fifteen and thirty; taking this into account would cut the ratios by a factor of four and by itself largely offset the number of multiple arrests among the young). Multiple arrests of individuals therefore cannot weaken the impression the figures give of the comprehensiveness with which urban, poorer, younger and male Britons were liable annually to an experience of police discipline.

The crude aggregate ratios were extraordinarily high as early as 1861. There was one male arrest or summons in that year for every twenty-nine of the whole male population, and one female for every one hundred and twenty of all females. As the policeman-state learnt to flex its increasingly efficient muscles thereafter, arrest policy became more comprehensive and aggressive.[61] And summary prosecutions expanded enormously. Thanks to the proliferation of licensing acts and statutes and bye-laws regulating street order etc., and to the increasing use of the summons (58 per cent of all proceedings by 1901), the number of summary prosecutions rose between 1861 and 1901 by 73 per cent. So even though this was a period when serious crime was reportedly declining, the crude statistical odds against being

---

[60] L. Radzinowicz, *Ideology and Crime* (1966), pp. 129–30.

[61] Between 1861 and 1901, for example, reported and prosecuted larcenies fell in number and in rate far more rapidly than arrests did; so the proportion of arrests to reported larcenies rose from 73 to 86 per cent. Gatrell, 'Decline of Theft and Violence', Appendix Table A4.

Table 5.1 *Arrests and summonses for indictable and non-indictable offences, England and Wales, 1861, 1901, 1951: numbers and ratios to population*

	(a) Indictable offences				(b) Non-indictable offences				(c) All offences (a + b)			
	Males		Females		Males		Females		Males		Females	
Year	Number	Ratio to population	Number	Ratio to population	Number	Ratio to population	Number	Ratio to population	Number	Ratio to population	Number	Ratio to population
1861	20,354	1 in 482	6,820	1 in 1,513	315,256	1 in 31	79,461	1 in 130	335,610	1 in 29	86,281	1 in 120
1901	50,253	1 in 314	12,179	1 in 1,383	612,409	1 in 26	124,741	1 in 135	662,662	1 in 24	136,920	1 in 123
1951	126,584	1 in 166	17,006	1 in 1,337	566,780	1 in 37	59,092	1 in 385	693,364	1 in 30	76,098	1 in 299

Source: annual criminal statistics.

subjected to legal discipline by arrest or summons actually worsened considerably. By 1901 males had a one in twenty-four chance of being arrested or summonsed, and more were liable to arrest for indictable crime, too, even though there was less of it to be reported or to result in trial and conviction.

By this rough measure the immediate threat the policeman offered to the social life of the poor had greatly increased in precisely those later nineteenth-century decades when the policeman-state, we have seen, was making its major bureaucratic advances. And perhaps the Edwardian working classes were in this sense more closely regulated not only than their mid-Victorian forebears, but also than their mid-twentieth-century descendants. For by 1951, in a period of admittedly relatively low crime rates, police action against male non-indictable offenders had receded (despite the multiplication of traffic regulations), and against women it had fallen away substantially. Only at the point of arrest against male indictable crime had it greatly intensified. Overall, there was now one male arrest or summons for every thirty males in England and Wales – still a remarkable ratio, however (Table 5.1).

In the course of their youth and young adulthood could many (or any) of the urban unskilled, the unemployed or the immigrant reasonably hope to evade a policeman's hand on the shoulder or a summons through the letter-box – in some cases many times more than once? This was a negative experience of policing of which most of the propertied classes were and remain ignorant. It expressed a profound social differentiation in the relationship between law and the people. It not only shaped public perceptions of the social location of law-breaking. It shaped popular attitudes to the law too.

IX   THE PROBLEM OF CONSENT

The question of how poorer people regarded the law and its enforcers – the question of consent itself – is central to all assessments of the legitimacy of the state. It is a question on which opinions divide.

Until recently the main advances in the social history of law involved the exposure of the cynical uses of law in defence of privilege, property and profit (against industrial and agrarian saboteurs, political dissidents, trade unionists, common land users, poachers, filchers from the workplace, streetfolk, as the case might be). These historians were also concerned to expose the vehemence of popular resistance to those usages.[62]

A growing orthodoxy, by contrast, now insists that an adversarial view of the relations between law and populace is one-dimensional and crude. It is not that bias in the law and some popular resistance to it is denied by this school. These things, rather, are simply down-graded in importance by being relegated to the taken-for-granted. The search is on, instead, we are told, for a depiction of reality that purports to be more 'complex' and 'pluralistic'.

The main effect of recent research has been to present law as a 'multiple-use right', accessible to the middling and poorer if not (signi-ficantly) very poorest sorts of people. We are reminded that most such people acquiesced in its legitimacy and, even in the eighteenth century and despite the high costs of prosecution, were those who used it most. Occasionally, they even turned it successfully against their betters to defend their own conceptions of justice, liberty and customary right.[63] By the mid-nineteenth century, we are told, more-over, 'there was a large measure of assent to the basic legitimacy of the legal order, based not on ideological manipulation, but on the use of its coercive aspects by working-class victims against offenders.' This assent remained intact until very recent times.[64]

The evidence supporting this depiction of free access to law is sub-stantial. In late eighteenth-century Essex, for example, a third of felony prosecutors were farmers or yeomen, another third tradesmen or arti-sans, and a fifth to a sixth labourers or husbandmen. In the early to mid-nineteenth-century Black Country, unskilled and skilled work-ing-class prosecutors at quarter sessions comprised never less than 28 per cent of all prosecutors and as many as 50 per cent in 1836. In mid- to late Victorian London, stipendiary magistrates spent much of their time processing the complaints of poor people against neigh-bours who stole from or abused them, and even learnt the wisdom of resolving disputes in terms of popular notions of social justice often at odds with those of the propertied classes. Down to the present, moreover, poorer people have looked to the law to protect their

---

[62]   See, classically, Hay et al., eds., Albion's Fatal Tree; R. Storch, '"The Plague of Blue Locusts": Police Reform and Popular Resistance in Northern England, 1840–57', International Review of Social History, 20 (1975); E. P. Thompson, Whigs and Hunters: The Origin of the Black Act (1975).

[63]   Brewer and Styles, eds., An Ungovernable People, p. 21, and Brewer's article in ibid.; King, 'Decision-Makers', pp. 57–8.

[64]   R. Reiner, The Politics of the Police (1985), p. 41.

persons, property and living space; most police prosecutions for petty theft and violence have been on behalf of working-class victims. The outcome of this long negotiation between populace and law enforcement is alleged to have been a heartening one. The opinion survey published in 1962 by the Royal Commission on the Police showed that 'while 85.2 per cent of the professional and managerial classes had "great respect" for the police, so too did 81.8 per cent of the skilled and 81.9 per cent of the semi- or unskilled working class'.[65]

Thanks to research of this kind, it is not now in question that the credibility of the rule of law and of the policemen enforcing it was constructed effectively through these devices and this accessibility. Nor is it in doubt that it was maintained by the inculcation of public respect for the service roles of policemen and for their occasional heroism, by (until recently) the relatively low political profile of British policing, or by the remorseless prosecution, now and then, of wealthy people who were caught doing unavoidably prosecutable things. Moreover, within the limits laid down by rulings of contempt, libel and official secrecy (large constraints, needless to say), libertarian lobbies were never silenced in their determination to criticise the uses of law in terms of its own professed values. Law protects as well as oppresses; the principles of equality and justice were never wholly lost sight of; and by global standards English law has, in its qualified ways, been open to public scrutiny.

This perspective would be unobjectionable were it not for its unduly comforting though perhaps unintended effects. It serves dominant mythologies well. It displaces from the *centre* of concern the harsher processes by which law mediates the inequalities of social power. And it marginalises the attitudes of that large minority who were already marginalised by social policy, and who never doubted that the policeman and the law were their enemies.

For still the problem persists: 'respect' for the police in many social consituencies consisted and consists in little more than a 'sullen acceptance of *de facto* power'. Even if all the foregoing is accepted, it would be unfortunate if it were forgotten that the well-publicised and benign aspects of law-enforcement camouflage its harsher meanings as they

---

[65] King, 'Crime, Law and Society', p. 180; Philips, *Crime and Authority*, pp. 123-9; J. Davis, '"A Poor Man's System of Justice"': Stipendiary Magistrates' Courts and the Working Class in London in the Later Nineteenth Century', *Historical Journal*, 27 (1984), pp. 309-36; Reiner, *Politics of the Police*, p. 49.

were experienced by a very large and not always silent minority across whose lips the phrase 'multiple-use right' would never pass.

Despite the readiness of some of them to depend on police protection and to use the courts, attitudes to law-enforcement among the poorer half of the urban working classes have always been more variable and sceptical than they have been among those (historians of crime included) who have never directly experienced its sanctions. Attitudes varied both regionally and within the same communities across time. They varied (and vary) within the same individual. They depend on whether he accepts the ascription of most criminality to other poorer people like him or perceives instead, with indignation, the relative immunity from prosecution of people with bank accounts. They depend on whether his neighbourhood is as well protected as he thinks it should be, or protected at all: all police have a nasty habit of patrolling St Giles to defend St James. They depend on the most recent of his experiences of policing, and on his episodic sensitisation to its political, strike-breaking or service functions, as the case might be. As has been well put, they depend on the tension between his conception of policing in the abstract ('necessary') and his possible experience of it in practice ('corrupt', 'coercive', 'brutal').[66]

Among the upwardly mobile, the skilled, the apprenticed, the politically organised and the mildly prospering, there were many reasons for siding conditionally with the law. When this happened, at stake was likely to be the individual's or community's investment in or aspiration towards status and respectability. The rise of new skills and occupational groups could modify a community's relation to the law within a generation. In the 1920s, for example, with the growth of print and railway employment and the decline of irregular street economies in Islington (north London), the chronic affrays with police which had beset the area since the 1880s declined dramatically. 'People started using flower pots to grow flowers in. When I was a lad there, they kept them empty to throw at the law.'[67] But elsewhere, in less prospering communities, hostility was endemic and enduring.

What the nineteenth-century and early twentieth-century urban poor experienced was the daily imposition upon them of disciplines which were both alien in origin and coercive in application. The law

---

[66]   M. Brogden, '"All Police is Conning Bastards"': Policing and the Problem of Consent', in B. Fine et al., eds., Capitalism and the Rule of Law (1979), pp. 118–36.

[67]   P. Cohen, 'Policing the Working-Class City', in Fine et al., eds., Capitalism and the Rule of Law, pp. 118–36.

aimed to subvert irregular street economies and cultures and the illegal economies of petty thieving by which more than a minority supplemented their irregular incomes. This was done by uniformed agents often drawn from their own class.[68] Resentment at this was inevitable. 'Nobody in our Northern slum', Robert Roberts wrote of Salford in the first quarter of the twentieth century, 'ever spoke in fond regard ... of the policeman as "social worker" and "handyman of the streets"':

> The poor in general looked upon him with fear and dislike ... One spoke to a 'rozzer' when one had to and told him the minimum ... The 'public' (meaning the middle and upper classes) ... held their 'bobby' in patronising 'affection and esteem', which he repaid with due respectfulness; but these sentiments were never shared by the undermass, nor in fact by the working class generally.[69]

In the second quarter of the nineteenth century, anti-police riots had expressed this frame of mind forcefully – here giving vent to outrage against interventions in customary pastimes and economies and elsewhere suspicion that policemen would be used to enforce the poor law.[70] These confrontations did, it is true, decline into insignificance after 1850, and except in the important case of industrial disputes, vanished until their re-emergence in the modern ghetto riot.

The significance of this decline can be misconstrued, however. It indicated less the 'growing acquiescence' of an incorporated working class than the isolation, marginalisation and defeat of its poorest and most turbulent sectors: of those 40 per cent of adult males, for example, who remained excluded from the franchise until 1918 and who were unionised only fitfully if they were in regular work at all. The decline in their collective opposition to police, like the decline of all riotous behaviour in the later nineteenth century, reflected in good measure the growing effectiveness of crowd control by policemen, and the obligation imposed on an increasingly marginalised residuum to come to terms with the permanence of the social order, even when they benefited little from it.

The much-quoted fact that recorded assaults against policemen also

[68]   R. Storch, 'The Policeman as Domestic Missionary: Urban Discipline and Popular Culture in Northern England, 1850–1880', *Journal of Social History*, 9 (1976), pp. 481–509.

[69]   R. Roberts, *The Classic Slum: Salford Life in the First Quarter of the Century* (Manchester, 1971), p. 77.

[70]   Storch, '"The Plague of Blue Locusts"'.

declined after 1850 does not qualify this view.[71] Policemen have always used this offence at their discretion to achieve quick and simple arrests, and its apparent decline might reflect nothing more than a progressive shift, with experience, to the use of more appropriate charges which would withstand the scrutiny of sceptical magistrates.

We may be sure, in fact, that violence against policemen did not greatly recede. Nor did police anxiety about it, as one example will show.[72] When in January 1905 a sober man struck a metropolitan constable on the head with a paving stone in a bid to rescue a prisoner, the commissioner and his solicitors were disturbed enough by the frequency of such incidents to initiate a little conspiracy. Pressure was to be put on magistrates who were handing down foolishly lenient sentences in cases of this kind. 'Every year', the commissioner wrote, 'over 2,000 [metropolitan] constables receive injuries more or less severe at the hands of prisoners; some are very grievously injured, crippled for life etc., and as there is no diminution in this class of offence, it would seem that the punishments are not sufficiently severe to be deterrent.' So in a nice foreshadowing of the improprieties of present-day media manipulation, statistics on police injuries were released to the press and (privily) to the sitting magistrate. The *Morning Advertiser* gave eight inches to the fact that in 1903 an astonishing 20 per cent of the whole metropolitan force had been assaulted in the course of their duties – 'generally single-handed in the midst of a hostile crowd'. The magistrate was intimidated enough to receive this information 'with much attention'. He duly gave the assailant a swingeing five months' hard labour. The police solicitors thought this 'very satisfactory as the sentence is probably two months more than the prisoner would have got at the Sessions'.

The conspirators missed the point, however, that the problem was not soluble through sentencing. It was structural. It would not go away. Only next day a 'normally respectable shoemaker', stopped for drunkenness, kicked a constable twice in the abdomen and put him on the sicklist for a month. 'I'm not', he shouted, 'going to be taken by a **** Constable: you're the scum of the earth.' A quarter century later the problem was still there. Between 1920 and 1927 inclusive an annual average of 2,421 metropolitan constables were injured in similar circumstances. Annually, this was 12 per cent of the whole

---

[71]   See Gatrell, 'Decline of Theft and Violence', for my own premature inferences from the data on assaults on police tabulated in *ibid.*, Appendix Table A5.

[72]   PRO. Mepo 2/752.

police strength.[73] If the problem has receded somewhat in postwar decades, it is not thanks to the disappearance of an alienated inner city underclass. It is thanks to the protection police receive from the radio and patrol-car.

X   THE INFLUENCE OF POLICING

One can envisage a history of law-enforcement dissociated from the history of crime but not a history of crime dissociated from the history of law-enforcement. It is to law-enforcement that the perceived criminal area owes its shape. But artificial construct though it is, it may still be appropriate to enquire whether and how the perceived criminal area changed with time. Much public discussion and policy is organised around this question, after all, on the not irrational premise that policy and social changes do affect the frequency and forms at least of that small amount of law-breaking that comes to the record.

Explanations of changes in criminal behaviour, we have seen, have become wedded to the notion that they are an index and function of changes in economic, social, cultural and moral relationships. Explanations have also been linked to the impact of policing, legal regulation and social policy. If there can be said to be an orthodox position on this matter, it might hold that socio-economic influences shaped the scale and nature of criminal behaviour far more than policing did. In its diversifying organisations and practices, lawlessness is assumed to respond most to the burgeoning opportunities and anonymity offered within a rapidly urbanising and economically dynamic society. Policing has had to be expanded in a desperate attempt to curb a more numerous and better camouflaged criminal populace; but it can do no more than dampen the escalation of crime rates which is inevitable in a society in which traditional social disciplines and norms are under chronic stress.[74] Relatively weak in its battle with the forces of darkness, always outpaced by them, the state is obliged perpetually to extend its authority, defensively, in the interests of civilised life.

By tacitly legitimising it, this formulation clearly serves the policeman-state well. But it does beg two questions. In the first instance, it betrays an interest in under-representing the very real disciplinary and coercive powers policing and law have successfully wielded over

---

[73] *RC on Police Powers and Procedure*, PP 1928–9, IX, para. 296.
[74] See L. Radzinowicz and J. King, *The Growth of Crime: The International Experience* (1977).

the populace in the past 200 years. In the second instance, the apocalyptic view that criminal history articulates a history of moral deterioration rests on an assumption that crime in 'modernising' society usually and necessarily increases, and that through some profound atavistic compulsion as well as in response to opportunity, criminal practices and organisations usually and necessarily get more sophisticated, dangerous and sinister.

Neither position is valid. First, the evidence that stealing from and hurting other people become more frequent with 'modernisation' is highly ambiguous. Secondly, the suggestion that with time 'crime' becomes more sophisticated not only ignores the enduring triviality of most recorded theft and violence, it also ignores long continuities in criminal organisation and motivation which have far-reaching implications. Granted that greed and aggression are present at all social levels, their expression in working-class criminality has always been shaped also by a common experience of inequality and relative deprivation deeply rooted in popular cultures past and present. In this respect present and past generations of law-breakers have far more in common than deteriorationist theses may care to accommodate.

Let us insist first on the potency of policemen. It is true that some confirmation of the view that police were relatively impotent agents in curtailing popular lawlessness can be mustered from many quarters. Present-day Home Office research argues for a start that 'the traditional strategies adopted by the police have but a limited impact on crime'; most offences are cleared up by the taking of past offences 'into consideration', and testify to the success only of stressful interrogation.[75] This is confirmed, historically, by the fact that what stationmen thought of as 'good policing', and what we now think of as 'traditional' policing, brought few results even in their target areas. In one sample of 144 metropolitan burglaries and robberies in 1856 and 1876, not one police arrest ensued from a scene-of-crime examination and standard detective procedures, and only three from police enquiries; in twenty-nine cases the offender's identity was already known to the victim, and in nineteen the victim could describe him; fourteen resulted from chance stop-and-search procedures.[76] And finally, to take a larger view, absolute success in policing (as with regard to any so-called social control) is logically a chimera. Those

---

[75]   Morris and Heal, *Crime Control and the Police*, p. 2.
[76]   Davis, 'Law-Breaking', p. 216.

controlled invariably adapt to and side-step the controls they are subjected to, and so merely redefine the problem to be controlled. Urban popular cultures have thus proved to be extraordinarily resilient over the past centuries in the face of the disciplines launched against them. Concerted and sustained campaigns against gambling, drinking, soliciting, workplace embezzlement, or picketline violence affected the locations and forms of those practices, but hardly affected their ubiquity and frequency. In each of these contexts British policing for a century and more had to accept the limits on its potency and go for containment rather than eradication.

But even these points embody a major concession. *Qualified effectiveness in law-enforcement is not to be discounted simply because it was less than total.* None of these objections can undermine the certainty that policing can affect behaviour or that (to take merely historical examples) it helped in a major way to curb the ancient marginal economies of the poor. The proliferation of regulatory statutes after 1870, for example, did not eradicate illegal drinking, betting, street-trading, or prize-fighting. But it did delineate the physical arenas in which those activities might be legally pursued and supervised. The effect of this was witnessed as much in the *breach* of regulation as in the observance. For the act of evading the law itself entails an adaptation in behaviour and perception. It demands of those who do the evading greater covertness and organisation; it also demands a subliminal or real recognition that what they are up to is 'wrong'.

The last effect was profound and far-reaching. By the later nineteenth century there were few who would confidently appeal to 'custom' to defend freshly criminalised illegalities of this order. Even the habitual drinker or street-gambler had had a subliminal message about a legally defined right and wrong firmly delivered to his consciousness, and had cause to register the ubiquity of law even in the process of outwitting it. An East End Edwardian gangster like Arthur Harding evaded the law many times, for example. When caught he won twenty-seven acquittals between 1901 and 1922. But 'success' in policing can be measured in the fact that he never doubted the ability of the police to interfere with his life; their presence haunted and influenced his every action. He knew he was a marked man and that blind eyes could become seeing again. By 1922, when give or take the odd fiddle or two he went straight, he had served two hard-labour sentences for larceny; five years' penal servitude for screwing a broken glass in the face of a rival, one Darky the Coon; and another five years in Dartmoor for what he claimed was a trumped-up charge of receiving.[77]

This cat-and-mouse relationship between police and their targets was by then of long-standing in British towns, and behavioural adaptations to it were widely observed. The vagrant thief who said in 1839 that he did not go to Manchester if he could help it because Diggles the detective knew him well was presumably expressing a sensible caution. Again, concerted police drives against notorious black spots around mid-century had to be selective in their targets: in Merthyr Tydfil the small force had to go for street disorders and violence at first and leave property to look after itself. But even in that 'frontier town' respectable citizens by the late 1860s could congratulate themselves that the messages of legality were beginning at last to be assimilated. Further, when Bracebridge Hemyng (Mayhew's reporter) was taken on a tour of St Giles in the early 1860s by Sergeant Bircher of the Met., that officer appeared to know its denizens personally, and Hemyng himself was persuaded that whereas 'fifteen or twenty years ago this locality was the scene of perpetual riot and disorder', 'the greatest order and decorum [now] reigned'. 'The burglars in our day', he added, 'are not in general such desperate men as those in former times: . . . They are better known to the police than formerly', so that crime 'has assumed more subtle forms . . . more of [a] secret, restless and deceitful character.'[78] In all Victorian sources testimony of this kind is easily and copiously quarried. It multiplied after the habitual criminals legislation of 1869/71 gave police yet greater supervisory powers over the labelled criminal class. And we have already noted in section VII the intensification and extraordinary frequency of police arrests as the nineteenth century wore on.

The best proof of the success of these multiplying regulations in later Victorian and Edwardian England lay just where all modern policemen would wish it to lie. Between the late 1850s and the prewar quinquennium indictable crime rates fell pretty steadily (and extraordinarily). The *reported* larceny rate (per 100,000 of the population) declined by 35 per cent, the common assault rate by 71 per cent, the wounding rate by 20 per cent and the homicide rate by 42 per cent. The rate of reported burglaries and breakings fell by 35 per cent

[77] Samuel, ed., *East End Underworld*.
[78] *County Constabulary*, 1839, pp. 27, 29; D. Jones, 'The Conquering of "China": Crime in an Industrial Community, 1842–64', in D. Jones, *Crime, Protest, Community and Police in Nineteenth-Century Britain* (1982), pp. 85–116; H. Mayhew, *London Labour and the London Poor*, 4 vols. (1861–2), vol. 4, pp. 237, 344–5.

between the early 1860s and late 1890s, though thereafter it regained (but did not exceed) mid-century levels. These figures carry a large incidental meaning. The fact that English society was certainly 'modernising' when indictable crime rates declined gives the lie to the notion that recorded crime *must* increase with the consequences of demographic, urban and economic growth – securely embedded in much twentieth-century criminology (and in all deteriorationist theories) though those assumptions might be.[79]

How far this achievement was attributable to the clearance of rookeries, to ameliorative social policies and to the diversifying disciplines delivered through poor laws, reformatories, asylums, charity and religiosity is an open question. The effect of education is also debatable. At least one Edwardian chief constable was observing that education taught the thief to avoid violence; another contemporary that the criminal is 'nowadays a milder, and more civilised person than his predecessor of thirty years ago'; and yet another that 'veneer . . . is very palpable today in the police-courts'. But it is not easy to demonstrate how these large social variables necessarily worked to curb 'crime'. None of them ceased to pertain between the wars, for example, and crime rates began to increase then. The implication is powerful that the long decline in indictable offences *c*. 1860–1914 expressed a peculiar if transient advantage which policing managed then to establish over ancient forms of popular lawlessness visible on the streets. Perhaps uniquely in this period, in other words, the perceived criminal area was ill-defended against and adapting too slowly to the attacks delivered upon it, and declining crime rates were the result.

The status of this argument depends of course on the credence that can be given to the statistical evidence that crime declined in that half-century. For many analytical purposes, crime rates are misleading if not useless: we shall see how dubious they may be when they point to *increases* in crime. When they point to *decreasing* crime, however, they seem to speak for something that really happened. The decline admittedly had no reliable relationship with the forever unverifiable movements in the huge scale of filching and bashing which went unrecorded at all social levels. But it must have borne some relationship to changes in the incidence of the kind of theft and violence with which police were habitually concerned.

Objections can be anticipated and dealt with. It could be objected

[79] This and following paragraphs are based on Gatrell, 'Decline of Theft and Violence'.

that crime rates fell only because the apparent defeat of the social evils of the early industrial age led to a softening of attitudes to, and hence less enthusiastic reporting and prosecution of, petty and juvenile crime. But softer attitudes were already being catered to in the mitigation of punishments and the extension of summary jurisdiction over juveniles and first offenders. In any case, reported homicide and wounding offences decreased too, and these were not susceptible to this attitudinal variable. It might be objected that crime rates fell because increasing police control of prosecution curbed the currency of vexatious and malicious prosecution which had helped swell rates in the 1840s. But it is not easy to prosecute maliciously for homicide, wounding or burglary, the rates for which fell or steadied anyway. It might be objected, thirdly, that crime rates fell because policemen always have an interest in under-recording reported crime in pursuit of better clear-up rates. But if this pushed rates down in 1850–1914, why did it not do so before and after that period, when rates unapologetically increased?

What is far more striking than these objections is the fact that, other things being equal, many pressures should have pushed recorded rates upwards in these decades. Policing was expanding, more people were acquiescing in and co-operating with it, prosecution was becoming easier, sentences shorter and imprisoned offenders were released into society more rapidly. That theft and violence rates in all these circumstances *declined* in the half-century or so before 1914 suggests that in terms of its own objectives against what it saw as the criminal area, the policeman-state really was enjoying an era of rare success.

XI VIOLENCE AND ORGANISED CRIME: CONTINUITY OR DETERIORATION?

The thesis that in modern times the history of crime is inevitably a history of deterioration, and that policemen are powerless to do more than check its growth in a modernising society, clearly does not fit the Victorian and Edwardian case. Since policing has never failed to extend its disciplines subsequently, there is no reason to doubt its actual or subliminal effects on social behaviour and feeling in the twentieth century either.

But what, secondly, of the main plank in the deteriorationist thesis? Did things really get worse, from a criminal point of view, in the twentieth century? Did criminals, as it were, get cleverer than police-men, better organised? Did they get more violent?

It has to be admitted that the argument in the preceding section encourages inferences of this kind. If the perceived criminal area con-tracted up to the First World War in part because it was weakly defended against the disciplines imposed upon it, its apparent increase in this century might indicate merely that the necessary defences were soon acquired. There is plenty of evidence that those targeted by controls learn to adjust to those controls and outwit them. As early as the 1850s it was noted that safe-breaking techniques were keeping pace with safe-breaking technology; and criminals' 'deceitful-ness' and 'veneer' no doubt spoke for the adoption of better social camouflages on the part of those whose criminality had once been predicted in their very manner of dress and walking. Other things are learnt, too. The rise of new industries and work practices, and of new forms of retailing and banking, have always generated new malpractices. The robbery of banks, rare in the early nineteenth cen-tury, has never ceased to multiply with their subsequent diffusion; the growth of a relatively ill-protected suburbia was deemed respon-sible for a perceived interwar increase in burglary; the motor-car brought new terrors, from the smash-and-grab raiders who grabbed press attention in the 1920s to the ubiquitous car-thief of the later twentieth century; wartime brought prosperity to black-marketeers.[80] Opportunities and adaptations of these kinds must across time affect the balance of advantage accruing to law-enforcement agents or to 'criminals' respectively.

If for half a century before 1914 policemen were in the ascendant, the argument might therefore go, twentieth-century law-breakers were better able to exploit the social camouflages, opportunities, tech-niques and forms of mobility which the modern environment has massively multiplied. Policing became more difficult, accordingly; 'success' was less easily registered; crime rates began to climb.

Some sociologists have sought to systematise this argument. In Vic-torian cities, they would say, most 'professional' thieves were 'craft' thieves, like their eighteenth-century predecessors. They were routin-ised and specialised in their practices, and worked as individuals or in fairly permanent groups of two or three, picking pockets, swindling

---

[80] Lopian, 'Crime, Police and Punishment', chap. 1; E. Smithies, *Crime in Wartime: A Social History of Crime in World War II* (1982).

the innocent, or housebreaking as the case might be. Their personnel were, however, easily identifiable through improving systems of criminal supervision and record, or to policemen who regularly patrolled the usually public territories in which they operated, and they were decimated with relative ease: crime rates declined accordingly. In the twentieth century, by contrast, it is proposed that the serious thief has learnt to turn himself into the so-called 'project' thief. He works for a criminal entrepreneur and planner who on agreed business terms assembles specialists for a long-planned one-off job which calls for resourceful and skilled execution, often in territories far from home. Some societies have developed the yet 'higher' form of criminal organisation-as-business, hierarchical in its command structure, disciplined by its own codes: in Britain the protection racket has been the classic case in point, and internationally the mafia. This developmental process is said to express a rational response to the evolving complexities of control and the larger opportunities of an economically dynamic society.[81] Policing has had immensely to increase its technologies and resources in an often vain attempt to keep pace with it. Rising crime rates testify to the difficulties they have encountered.

This beguiling formulation accords comfortably with that image of the manichean battle waged between crime and legality which serves authority so well but from which we have sought to maintain a critical distance. There were adaptations in some forms of criminal practice, of course; and some have made policing more difficult. Nonetheless, the reasons why this is not the most interesting thing to say about twentieth-century crime are multiple.

Not only does this argument attribute to modern policing a more defensive position than it has ever in fact enjoyed. It draws support also from an often wilful misreading of the evidence that suggests that crime in this century has spectacularly increased and become more dangerous. It generalises from particular and exceptional instances of highly professionalised crime and ignores the triviality of most twentieth-century theft and violence. It camouflages large continuities in professional criminal practice and organisation which give the lie to the notion that these are of a peculiarly twentieth-century provenance. And finally it attributes to professional crime, such as it was, a sub-cultural identity which conceals the intimate relationship

---

[81] M. McIntosh, *The Organisation of Crime* (1975).

of the 'criminal fraternity' to the working-class community with whom they shared a common experience of powerlessness and deprivation. Less that was fundamental and more that was superficial might have changed than might at first seem apparent.

Agnosticism is first recommended in contemplating the statistical basis for a deteriorationist thesis. It should be axiomatic that rates of recorded crime are inflated when policing expands or becomes more efficient, when public pressure to this end increases, when the public learn to co-operate with policemen more, when prosecution becomes cheaper and easier, when sensitivity to certain kinds of offence is heightened, when (as after 1918) the spread of household insurance increases public readiness to report theft. Even the Home Office nowadays has come privily to terms with the consequences of the most important of these variables. More policing, it acknowledges, leads to more reported crime; more reported crime results in the unfortunate statistical corollary of lower clear-up rates; these in turn unleash a call for additional police resources; more resources lead to more reported crime.[82]

When in these inflationary circumstances crime rates decrease, as in the later nineteenth and early twentieth centuries, we may be entitled to believe that they indicate a real decline at least in those forms of crime policemen concern themselves with. When, however, in these inflationary circumstances crime rates increase, all we are entitled to infer is that these administrative and attitudinal variables were operating positively – not necessarily that crime increased too. In real terms crime might well have been declining even as the rates of crime rose.

So it is neither here nor there that recorded rates of theft and violence rose from 1805 (when they were first published) to their peak in the middle of the nineteenth century, and rose again from the mid-1920s and ever onwards (bar a brief post-1945 interlude).[83] As far as aggregate figures are concerned, it is next to impossible to prove that they were pushed upwards by increases in criminal behaviour. It is always possible to prove that they were pushed upwards by the thrust of law-enforcement and other variables mentioned.

Agnosticism is recommended secondly in contemplating changes in the distribution pattern of crime. The criminal area expands and changes shape in modern society largely because it is a decision of

---

[82] Morris and Heal, *Crime Control and the Police*, chap. 4.
[83] F. H. McClintock and N. H. Avison, *Crime in England and Wales* (1968), chap. 2.

policy to put more and different kinds of people within it. New forms of crime were time and again 'discovered' in the course of passing moral panics or in the criminalisation of newly perceived problems: 'garotting' in the 1860s; child abuse, sexual assaults and homosexuality in the 1880s; juvenile hooliganism and 'professional' crime in the 1890s; cat-burglary in the 1920s; black-marketeering in the 1940s; down to mugging in the 1970s. Old offences were uprated in importance by this sensitisation, and often classified in new ways under the most serious headings that could be made to apply to them. All of these variables (and many more) are worth attending to and have been attended to: but the historians who attend to them will be historians of law-enforcement and not of crime.

None of this is to deny that there were some twentieth-century behavioural changes which justified new forms of control if order and security were to be maintained: drug-dealing and terrorism are modern cases in point. Rather, it is to question whether all of these changes could bear the ideological charge they were invested with, whether all of them were as substantial and real as the protagonists of order insisted, and whether they justified the homilies about moral decay to which those who wielded authority gave vent.

The problem of violence raises interesting questions in this connection. Press, politicians and policemen have orchestrated this into one of the looming problems of modern Britain. They provide evidence in plenty to fuel our alarm. Even in 1950 there were nineteen London robberies in which firearms were used, and fifteen in which they were thought to have been carried. In 1980 in all England and Wales, armed robbers caused twenty-four fatal injuries. Nonetheless, the case has still to be properly argued and demonstrated, and not merely asserted, that we live in an age of greater inter-personal violence than our Victorian forebears. What seems to have changed more is our sensitivity to inter-personal violence, and, even more, the political and cultural capital and media profit which can now be extracted from it.[84]

Violence in the nineteenth century was ubiquitous – in industrial disputes, in popular leisure arenas, in the streets, and certainly in the home. And there were, of course, passing panics about it: about Chartist violence in the 1840s, garotting and union 'outrages' in the 1860s, child abuse, hooliganism and armed burglary in the last quarter

[84]   S. Hall et al., Policing the Crisis: Mugging, the State, and Law and Order (1978).

of the century.[85] The main difference was that in the larger Victorian discourse on crime, violence was not identified as the *central* problem, as it is a century later. In the nineteenth century, an authoritarian consensus was far better mobilised around theft, property and order because two key variables were absent. The first was the pictorial representation in a mass media of the effects of violence. The second was the fact that those being invited into the consensus – the respectable and the enfranchised – all had some specialised interest in the security of property, but inhabited spaces from which violence was remote. Unlike today, those who lived in violent areas largely lacked both property and the vote, and their plight could be tacitly ignored.

In vain, therefore, magistrates were urged by one of their number in 1867 to 'teach the public to think that injury to the person is more serious than injury to the purse; that life is dearer than money'. In vain, in 1881 an MP could protest in the Commons that property was better defended in English law than the person, and that 'when a man was flogged for robbery with violence, he was flogged for the robbery and not for the violence'. Notwithstanding a panic in the 1880s about the physical abuse of women and children, violence, characteristically, was simply not the *perceived* problem in Victorian England, and Parliament's refusal to tinker with differentials in sentencing for men of violence and for thieves respectively proved the point that in the penal system it was the thieves who were required to suffer most.[86]

Yet Victorian violence was real enough. Whereas in the 1970s there were on average 467 classified homicides annually in England and Wales (and 315 in 1950), in the 1870s there were on average 389 a year and in the 1880s, 393. This, in relation to population, gives a higher Victorian homicide rate than the modern. Petty casual violence of the kind policemen attend to has apparently declined, too: prosecuted assaults were six times more numerous in the 1870s than a

---

[85] See R. Price, 'The Other Face of Respectability: Violence in the Manchester Brickmaking Trade, 1859–70', *Past & Present*, 66 (1975); N. Tomes, '"A Torrent of Abuse": Crimes of Violence between Working-Class Men and Women in London, 1840–1875', *Journal of Social History*, 11 (1978); J. Davis, 'The London Garotting Panic of 1862 : A Moral Panic and the Creation of a Criminal Class in Mid-Victorian England', in Gatrell, Lenman and Parker, eds., *Crime and the Law*; G. K. Behlmer, *Child Abuse and Moral Reform in England, 1870–1908* (Stanford, 1982); G. Pearson, *Hooligan: A History of Respectable Fears* (1983).

[86] Gatrell, 'Decline of Theft and Violence', p. 296 and section IV generally for discussion of sentencing differentials.

century later.[87] And as for armed robbery, that touchstone of present-day fears, the modern figures given above are not without their precedents. Between 1877 and 1886 London burglars carrying firearms killed two policemen and five householders, wounded another eleven policemen, and on eighteen occasions escaped arrest by the use of firearms and on fourteen more were found on arrest to be in possession of them. To cope with these dangers, metropolitan constables were first permitted to draw guns if they chose in 1883 (inspectors had been allowed pistols in exceptional cases since 1829), and on 931 occasions that year they did so choose. Pistol-licensing was tightened up by statute in 1903, but Edwardian gangsters still had no difficulty in buying guns for 4s. 6d., and in 1911 they were used in twenty-nine London cases and were known to have been carried in another eleven.[88] And to take an even longer view on this question, it has been calculated that 'medieval English society was twice as violence-prone as early modern English society, and early modern English society at least five times more violence-prone that contemporary English society. It also seems clear that most of this pre-modern violence was outside the family, rather than within it, as today.'[89] Long-term calculations of this kind can pretend to no hard statistical authority, of course, and their import has been strongly challenged.[90] It remains true, however, that available evidence simply cannot be bent to justify the panic about the *peculiar* ubiquity of modern violence against the person (technologically sophisticated and devastating though some of its expressions might be), in which our governors have their own reasons for inviting us to participate.

Take next the suggestion that with time crime has become more professionalised. This is also closely linked to a deteriorationist thesis, as we have seen. But here too the keynote of continuity is struck easily. The truth is that crime-as-business and crime-as-project have ancestries which thoroughly subvert sociologists' developmental models. The East End protection racket of the Kray twins in the 1950s or the black-market empire of Billy Hill, self-proclaimed boss of the underworld, had antecedents in the Sabini gang of Saffron Hill, said

[87]   *Ibid.*
[88]   PRO. HO 45/10595/18736; HO 45/9673/A46696B; HO 45/9605/A1842B; HO 45/9788/B3845A; HO 45/10636/202756; Mepo 2/163.
[89]   L. Stone, 'Interpersonal Violence in English Society, 1300–1980', *Past & Present*, 101 (1983), p. 2.
[90]   See J. A. Sharpe, 'The History of Violence in England: Some Observations' and L. Stone, 'A Rejoinder', both in *Past & Present*, 108 (1985), pp. 206–24; also A. Macfarlane, *Justice and the Mare's Ale* (1984).

to be earning £20,000 a year in 1926 in their racecourse protection business. That gang in turn originated in 1910 in the gangland Arthur Harding knew: 'manors', or territories, were handed on through the generations. Also, patterns of consumption and display linked twentieth-century villains with yet earlier forebears. 'What with all the villains in their genuine Savile Row suits and their wives and girl friends wearing straight furs and clothes by the best West End dressmakers', Billy Hill recalled of the 1930s, 'that club looked like the Ascot of the Underworld.' 'Most thieves at Clark's coffee shop', Harding recalled of Edwardian Bethnal Green, 'were small-time crooks ... Only one ... was a complete all-round criminal ... He used to dress magnificent and was called "The Count".' Mayhew's mid-Victorian swell-mob dressed themselves in the 'same elaborate fashion as a Jew on a Saturday', and earlier still, in 1839, the swell-mob were described as men 'who have received education, some respectably connected, all well dressed'. And perhaps there was continuity in practice and ambition too. As early as 1839, the governor of Cold Bath Fields prison observed that warehouse or bank robbery 'is only practised by "tip-top" men'. With specialist burglars consulted and commissioned,

a meeting is called, they agree as to the likelihood of success; an equal stake is put down by each party, say £50 to defray expenses; and this sum has oftentimes to be repeated ... In most cases, three or four months are required, and several entries are actually made into the premises before a fitting opportunity presents itself to complete the work.

If 'project-theft' is a twentieth-century phenomenon, what are we to make of a long-standing pedigree like this?[91]

Finally, the antiquity of a self-conscious and well-maintained hierarchy of criminal skill is also well attested. The internal economy of the most benighted area even of mid-nineteenth-century Merthyr Tydfil, for example, 'built on prostitution and female crime', was ruled by recognised leaders of the community known as the 'emperor' and 'empress'. London had its infinitely more complex hierarchies of specialism. Mayhew lists exhaustively a multiplicity of 'regular crafts, requiring almost the same apprenticeship as any other mode of life': swindlers, charley-pitchers, bouncers and besters, flatcatchers and bubble-men, jollies and magsmen, bonnets, cracksmen and

---

[91] Smithies, *Crime in Wartime* (1982), pp. 111–12, 124–5; Samuel, ed., *East End Underworld*; Mayhew, *London Labour*, vol 4. p. 32; *RC County Constabulary*, 1839, App. 6, 'Practices of Habitual Depredators', pp. 205–15.

rampsmen, bludgers and mobsmen, buzzers, sneaksmen, snoozers, starglazers, sawney-hunters, dead-lurkers, bluey-hunters, toshers and fences and smashers and many more. Most of these were 'professional' only in Mayhew's fanciful designation. Most referred to forms of opportunistic larceny – stealing lead from roofs, bacon from shops, clothes from hedges, lumps of coal and rope from riverside vessels – with which every poor Londoner was familiar. But some spoke for systematically won skill: the cheats, tricksters, pickpockets, window-smashers and grabbers. Others speak for hard-won status, with the swell-mob, the cracksmen (housebreakers), the shoful men (counterfeiters) and the fences at the top of the tree. 'The cracksman would no more think of associating with the sneaksman [sneak thief] than a barrister would dream of sitting down to dinner with an attorney', Mayhew noted.[92]

It is right to be suspicious of much in Mayhew's and other Victorians' commentaries on low life. But their testimony receives some lateral confirmations both in the antiquity of thieves' cant (or jargon) and in the survival of analogous hierarchies into this century. Mayhew might have been overdoing it when he identified Saxon origins for the shofulman and charley-pitcher (gaming cheat: 'charley' = 'ceorla' = countryman). But the fact that the criminal specialisms of Victorian London were not the products entirely of his perfervid imagination is suggested by the first recorded use of 'fence' in 1698, 'sneaksman' in 1725, 'swindler' in 1775, 'cracksman' in 1797, 'swell-mob' and 'mob' (gang) in 1830. The Elizabethan language of pocket-picking was in some variants still current in early twentieth-century America.[93] And the status system which helped shape this deprived and harum-scarum world was still alive and well in early twentieth-century London. The poverty in which Arthur Harding was conceived in Bethnal Green was as dire as it had ever been in that district, and the ways of living with it in Edwardian years were by no means new. They would have been familiar to the Artful Dodger. They would have been familiar to the assorted vandraggers, burglars and sneaksmen who for a small consideration had opened their souls to the governor of Cold Bath Fields in 1839. At the other end of the time scale, they

---

[92] Jones, 'The Conquering of "China"', p. 118; Mayhew, *London Labour*, vol. 4, p. 31.

[93] E. Partridge, *A Dictionary of the Underworld* (3rd edn, 1968); M. McIntosh, 'Changes in the Organisation of Thieving,' in S. Cohen, ed., *Images of Deviance* (1971), pp. 103–4.

would have been no less familiar to the Kray twins with whom the ageing Harding hobnobbed in the 1950s.

At the bottom of Harding's world was a bewildering array of sneak-thieves, con-men, pickpockets, forgers and musclemen whose status-insignia he could read at a glance. The free-lancers, the non-specialists, the pilferers, the sneaks, earn his contempt: 'half-mad loafers', he calls them – Spud Murphy, One-Eyed Charlie Walker, Cocky Flatnose. You had to be a specialist to be looked up to, or you had to have style, like Moishe the Gonoff, the most celebrated of the Jewish pick-pockets, from whose associate Harding as a boy had learnt the art 'just like the Artful Dodger in Dickens'. You had to be like Billy Holmes, 'a good all-round thief – vandragger, burglar, coiner'; like Emmanueal, the Jewish Al Capone of the East End; and like the Titanic mob of Hoxton, 'very well-dressed fellows . . . they used to straighten everybody up . . . Very specialist' – and certainly a cut above the Hoxton mob, who 'weren't such good-class thieves as the Titanics . . . more hooligans than thieves'. The pecking order was recognised universally. In Dartmoor, 'everyone wanted to be regarded as belonging to the highest rank of the criminal fraternity . . . the inmates have a tendency to only associate and talk to men of their own standards of professional behaviour'. In prison and in Bethnal Green alike Harding gained access to these elites by exploiting his reputation for violence: 'Burglars, as a rule, are not terrors . . . they kept to themselves as a rule. But [terrors] like me used to get in – they'd tell us all about what was going on.'[94]

Enough has been said to suggest that twentieth-century anxieties about the growth of lawlessness and violence are less soundly based than superficial statistical and newspaper evidence has encouraged most Britons to believe. Escalating crime rates can tell lies; inter-personal violence in many if not all of its forms has declined; 'professional' and 'organised' crime has a long pedigree. The deteriorationist thesis which underpins much of what passes for debate about crime today is vulnerable to very large doubts indeed.

XII   CRIME AND DEPRIVATION

But it remains now to be reminded of the ambiguity of all positivist arguments about crime such as those addressed in the last two sections. These arguments have lulled us into a tacit acquiescence in

[94] Samuel, ed., *East End Underworld, passim.*

categorisations of the 'criminal' which may say more about the minds of the categorisers than about the experiences of those so labelled. This stricture applies to the vexed identity of the 'professional and organised' criminal particularly. Since he remains one of the dominant bogeys in the demonology of law-and-order lobbies, it is fitting that in the rest of this chapter this archetype should now be approached from a more critical perspective.

The professional criminal has served a covert but useful social service. He has provided a major justification for an authoritarian response to the 'anti-social' indisciplines of the poor. But like the 'criminal class' itself, we shall see, he was in some degree a mythical construct, to which a prophetic ideology and police practice alike sought to give substance.

On the face of it, it would appear perverse and glib to deny 'professional' criminals the discrete identity they claimed for themselves. 'Villains' and 'terrors' after all did and do behave more villainously and terrifyingly than other people. Their hierarchies were self-attested; cant was their own language, and an ancient one. Can it really be said that when they deemed themselves to be 'professional' they were merely internalising the definitions of those who hunted them?

Up to a point, yes. The fact that such people have always been the targets of external definition cannot but have accentuated their sense of their own separateness. After the 1869 Habitual Criminals Act and the 1871 Prevention of Crime Act and its subsequent amendments, they became an especially well-defined target of law-enforcement – closely supervised on release from penal servitude, for example. It was a tactic of policing and penology increasingly to present them as a distinct species (as members of a sub-culture, we might say now). Police supervision, differential penal treatment, as well as insistent public moralising at their expense (and much speculation about their perverted psyches) served to segregate them from the universe of the respectable working class and from that of the casually criminal poor alike: the underclasses were differentiated the better to rule them. The denizens of this world were encouraged to think of themselves in terms of these differentiations too. Not always with good reason, men like Arthur Harding thought of themselves as cleverer than most, for example.

However, large implications attach to the fact that those labelled as 'professional' criminals were (and are) usually conceived within and sheltered by the urban poor. The label is not commonly attached to company directors. Denied access to the spheres of economic influence and power where egoism, ambition and acquisitiveness might be camouflaged or legitimised and knighthoods won, they reconstituted their numbers in rookeries, slums or council estates generation after generation. This enduring relationship they bore to the world of the deprived must prompt our main question – whether the historian should acquiesce in the labels of the law-enforcers and reach for the language of 'sub-culture' also. That language conceals more than it illuminates. It conceals in particular the relationship all forms of perceived working-class crime, 'professional' or not, have borne to deprivation and inequality. It conceals the truth that swells, terrors, cracksmen, sneaks and their latter-day counterparts have always had more in common than otherwise with the opportunistic larcenist, the juvenile thief, the vagrant, the drunk, the prostitute – as all of those have with the wider communities which sheltered them.

What they had in common with all who had only unskilled labour to sell (and in some cases a disinclination or inability to sell it), was a need to cope with deprivation, social irrelevance, and the unattainability of the goals of consumption and success an affluent society held out. Food and clothing had to be found, great swathes of unemployed time had to be filled, some fun had to be had, devices and rituals had to be invented in terms of which manhood could be tested and status established; and this under the supervision of a system of law-enforcement which was implacably hostile to these processes. Among the bottom third of the population, then, the 'professional' criminal, the casually, necessitously and opportunistically criminal, and the contingently law-abiding were all of them yoked within the same defensive relationship to law. They were also yoked within the same neighbourhoods, the same kinship networks, the same flux in life-cycle and employment-cycle; and they were subject to the same stigmatisations which policemen, magistrates and poor law guardians daily imposed. The boundaries between these under-groups, therefore, were ectoplasmic. They were visible to social analysts and other true believers, but were crossed again and again by the vast generality of the poor, as the exigencies of urban life dictated.

Even the black sheep, for example, invariably had respectable kin or associates in the lateral branch of the family or in the immediate neighbourhood. Harding's devastated family in the Old Nichol had its respectable branch living near Victoria Park ('very posh people'). He himself learnt pocket-picking from a mentor whose father, he finds it necessary to write, worked respectably for the Port of London Authority and whose mother had not even gone on the game. Similarly, terrors might go 'respectable' in middling life (as Harding did). By the same token, middling-aged 'respectables' were bonded into criminality if only because they might have lived on the wrong side of the law when young. All judicial evidence, eighteenth-century to modern, points to a peaking of lawless behaviour in pre-nuptial male adolescence and young adulthood. Thus the natural ageing of each generation ensured an endlessly repeated migration within the working-class community from a condition of more or less criminal fecklessness in youth to a condition of greater or less respectability in maturity. But the greatest solvent of the boundaries which observers sought vainly to draw between the 'criminal classes' and the rest was the collective experience of hardship. 'Want, horrid want', Cobbett wrote, is 'the parent of crime.'

Much ink has been spilled arguing for and against this causal connection. Political creeds have always somewhat turned on it. Chadwick insisted in 1839, as Prime Ministers insist a century and a half later, that crime results from the instinct not to work rather than from the unavailability of work. Nonetheless, this is not a debate that ought to detain us long because it is a silly debate. Poor people broke the law for all the diverse, intimate and unpleasant reasons rich people broke the law: they stole because they were as greedy or dishonest as we all may be, or because it was easier to make ends meet that way than to work. This is not inconsistent with the view, however, that they *also* stole because theft was a sensible way of dealing with deprivation and often the only way of dealing with it. And this was an imperative which suffused the world of the 'professional' and the casual thief alike.

We know that more people have always stolen more often in wintertime than in summer and that these seasonal fluctuations express in part the pressures of want. Ever since they were first published in 1857, the police had no particular interest in fabricating the statistics which prove it. Nights were longer then, making some kinds of theft easier; but seasonal unemployment was higher too, and the weather colder.

We also think that more people have always stolen more often in years of dearth. In all later eighteenth-century counties so far examined, theft indictments were usually higher in years of high food prices. Similarly, in the first half of the nineteenth century, the national larceny rates peaked in years of high food prices and high unemployment, and similar patterns are visible again before the First World War and in the 1930s.[95] The inference has been that short-term increases in unemployment and food prices drove many poor people across the boundaries of illegality who in better times were comfortable enough more or less to observe the law.

Arguments about the reliability of these correlations have been much laboured by historians, including this one in his time. But are they necessary? They are uncomfortably remote from the actual quality of working-class life where the best answers lie. For the relationship between theft and deprivation is not to be measured only in the impact of dearth. The truth which carries more significance, and which academic number-crunching obfuscates, is a simpler but glaring one. It is that the vast majority of the property-offenders to whom police and courts attended were – like all working people, and like 'professional criminals' too – *chronically* poor and socially powerless. By comparison with this fact the proposition that in bad years the more or less law-abiding might have been propelled into the criminal area is interesting but not deeply significant.

Thus it is chronic as much as episodic deprivation which year in and year out is encoded in the doleful catalogue of boots, shoes, loaves of bread, sides of bacon, lumps of lead, etc., which confronts any student of court records up to the 1930s at least. It is encoded in burglary records too: it was for thefts no less trivial and necessitous that most burglars were arrested in good years as well as bad.[96] Deprivation is encoded also in the innumerable depositions and letters begging for lenient sentences which again the historian soon accepts as a gloomy and unceasing refrain accompanying his research. This material fast makes the statistical debate on crime and poverty appear merely insensitive and perverse.

Here are three typical begging letters in the Middlesex quarter session records for 1910. Charles Cuthbert, aged twenty-two pleads guilty to the theft of a bicycle, and since he has had three previous convictions

---

[95] See D. Hay, 'War, Dearth and Theft in the Eighteenth Century', *Past & Present*, 95 (1982); Gatrell and Hadden, 'Criminal Statistics'; H. Mannheim, *Crime between the Wars* (1940); King, 'Crime, Law and Society', chap. 2; Gatrell, 'Decline of Theft and Violence', pp. 301–16, 325.

[96] Gatrell, 'Decline of Theft and Violence', p. 325, and below, section XIII.

for the theft of a watch, a doorknocker, and a ring, he gets eighteen months' hard labour at Wormwood Scrubs:

My lord, I have never stolen anything unless driven to do so by hunger ... I have not had anything to eat since half past five on saturday night untill given something at the police station monday morning. My lord I do not want to thieve I would sooner work as it is much easier but a man of my character is not able to get work ... For God's sake give me this chance.

Richard Probert, a twenty-two-year-old costermonger, had three previous convictions for the theft of a garden hose, some lead piping, and a copper; now he and two others plead guilty to stealing two iron hurdles by the roadside, and he duly writes from Brixton:

Please sir we did not know it was rong and we sed there is A bit of food now for our wife they had not food for free days was think of them at home Sir we was out of work for 8 week befor we went out doing this ... we are sorry now we took it sir.

And Frederick Shepherd, thirty-two, and six times convicted for stealing a garden frame, some bacon, twice some boots, and twice for being a suspected person loitering, now gets six months' hard labour in the Scrubs for being found by night in unlawful possession of a certain implement of housebreaking, to wit one screwdriver:

My lord and gentlemen of the jury, I am suffering from Morbis Cordis and Double Initial of the heart. I have got a deform foot as well ... well I never could do a hard days work and when the weather get a fine bit I has to give in my discharge from the Infirmary I have to go buying rags and bones.

Well-meaning policemen and magistrates sometimes did their best for tear-jerkers of this kind. The trouble was that well into the twentieth century, and still, these sad cases were not exceptional, and the emotional arteries of policemen and magistrates soon hardened.

XIII   THE INVENTION OF THE PROFESSIONAL CRIMINAL

So where (finally) do the 'big' criminals fit in this spectrum? Did they merit the significance policy-makers attached to them? The questions are pertinent because professional crime was first 'discovered' and dealt with in the late nineteenth and early twentieth centuries. But what was to be exposed in the anxious search for large-scale and systematic villainy says more about the orchestration of social fears and fantasies by experts and officials than it does about the existence of a distinct professional criminal sub-culture. The reason is simple. The 'professionals' whom a half-century-long campaign eventually brought to light turned out to differ little from the pathetic procession of the needful who took up most police and court time.

Sensible people might have anticipated this. Old Bailey burglary trials in this period refuse to concern booty much more spectacular than boots, clothes, food and occasional silver spoons and candle-sticks.[97] A sampling of Middlesex quarter session records addressed to the many-times convicted in 1900 and 1910 refuses to expose many who were as near to the peak of their profession as (say) William Condon. Aged twenty-four and a billiard marker, he was convicted in 1903 for stealing a watch, etc.; in 1904 for stealing a manicure set, etc.; in 1905 for stealing clothing; and in 1907 for stealing a bicycle. In 1910 he was convicted at last to two concurrent sentences of three years' penal servitude followed by five years' preventive detention under the 1908 Prevention of Crime Act for breaking and entering two dwelling houses to steal jewellery and clothing worth some £90, and for being a habitual criminal.[98] These men were nuisances. But if they were also professional, they were a far cry from fictional and Lombrosian stereotypes. They were only a little more systematic in the depredation than the opportunistic larcenist. The truth was to become clear that the sub-cultural boundaries of crime were so shadowy that they were impossible to patrol.

This fact, however, was no impediment to the ongoing disciplinary enterprise. If a criminal problem did not exist (and recall that this was an era of declining indictable crime rates), officials would have to find one. They proceeded to do so.

In the second half of the nineteenth century, several episodes had focussed official attention on the problem of the habitual-cum-pro-fessional criminal. The earliest had been the abolition of transportation in 1853 (this obliged the home country to accommodate its own convict detritus both in prison and after release) and the garotting panic of 1862.[99] A new panic was to be set in motion by the spate of armed burglaries which hit London between 1877 and 1886.[100] The state fed itself with its own justifications for concern as well, not least through the generation of fuller statistics on recidivism made possible by the developing record systems at Scotland Yard. Recidivism, the

---

[97]   *Ibid.*, p. 325.
[98]   Middlesex quarter session records, Greater London Record Office.
[99]   Davis, 'The London Garotting Panic of 1862'; P. Bartrip, 'Public Opinion and Law Enforcement: The Ticket-of-Leave Scares in Mid-Victorian Britain', in V. Bailey, ed., *Policing and Punishment in Nineteenth-Century Britain* (1981).
[100]   See n. 88 above.

Gladstone committee on prisons duly agreed in 1895, was now not only 'the most important of all prison questions' but, worse, 'a growing stain on our civilisation'. The committee proposed a solution. While it advocated shorter sentences for lesser offenders, it advocated a new form of preventive detention designed to segregate for long periods the many thieves convicted who 'live by robbery and thieving'. When he became Home Secretary, Herbert Gladstone envisaged that the sentence of preventive detention should be of indeterminate length. Another expert, Sir Robert Anderson (recently head of the CID) agreed, reminding those 'humanity-mongerers' who thought indeterminate sentences a bit much that 'the extermination of the unfit is one of the plainest of natural laws'. The time was ripe, he argued, to clamp down not only on the habitual thief but also on that aristocracy of professional criminals – a few hundred perhaps – who were holding the nation to ransom. After all, he added in a mode which the twentieth century was to make ever more familiar, 'never a night passes that some crime of this kind is not committed in the metropolis. No one can be certain, as he shuts his door and lies down to sleep, that the sanctity of his home will not be . . . outraged before morning.' Influential judges were cajoled into supporting these principles.[101] Where experts led, newspapers followed. The press filled with blood-curdling images of a London held to ransom by professional criminals with low foreheads and beatling brows and eyes that were suspiciously close together.

The outcome of this long campaign was one of the more extraordinary acts in British penal history, the 1908 Prevention of Crime Act. This had its benign face: it introduced borstals for young offenders in place of prison. And admittedly its sentence of preventive detention stopped short of a wholly effective extermination of the unfit. The offender sentenced to penal servitude after three or more past convictions and who led a 'persistently dishonest life' was to be liable (*after* completing his latest penal servitude) to between five and ten years' preventive detention. Nonetheless, it introduced a new principle in British penology. It sanctioned an anticipatory punishment, not for a crime actually committed but for one which might be committed in future. It accepted Ruggles-Brise's startling principle that a man

---

[101]   See report of the *Departmental Committee on Prisons*, 1895, p. 31; Sir E. Ruggles-Brise, memoranda, Dec. 1899 and Nov. 1911, PRO, P.Com. 7/286; H. Gladstone in *Hansard* debates on Prevention of Crime Bill, 27 May 1908; Sir R. Anderson, articles in *Nineteenth Century* (1901), reprinted in his *Criminals and Crime: Some Facts and Suggestions* (1907).

should be punished 'not for doing what he did, but for being what he was'.[102]

In the event, not surprisingly, the act never hit its target; the target was part-fantasy anyway. Professional criminals were hard to find. In its first seven months, 112 men and 1 woman were sentenced to preventive detention, and although all were 'habituals' not one was a professional in Anderson's or Gladstone's sense of the term. One had stolen a pair of boots, another 1s., another four dishes; like William Condon, most were small-time housebreakers and larcenists. When ten years' detention was imposed in 1910 on a man convicted for stealing 2s. from a church offertory on the grounds that he had nine previous such convictions, Churchill (as new Home Secretary) threatened to repeal the act if it were not properly restricted to those who were 'a danger to society'. It remained difficult to find criminals whom a jury would regard as any such thing. The number sentenced in 1911 slumped to 53, and declined thereafter until the 1908 act was finally supplanted by the detention clauses of the 1948 Criminal Justice Act. Even so, only 7 of the 325 committed between 1928 and 1945 were agreed to be men of real dangerousness. The 1932 committee on persistent offenders still found most of the rest 'men with little mental capacity ... whose frequent convictions testify as much to their clumsiness as to their persistence in crime'.

The significance of this story is twofold. First, like all such archetypes, the professional criminal might have been part-invention, but he served the bureaucratic state well. For all his elusiveness, he had helped to feed the kinds of fear that justified a wider legislative crackdown on all the derelicts, misfits, inebriates, mental defectives and paupers who remained stubbornly outside the consensual society the liberal state was busily trying to construct. A thinly-disguised Social Darwinism sanctioned this strategy in liberal thought, and the 1908 act accorded well with it. The act was conceived in a generation which was becoming conscious of mounting international competition; the nation's competitive fitness and efficiency were high on the agenda. The unfit and inefficient had (in Charles Booth's words) to be 'hounded out of existence'. It was inevitable, as ever, that the criminal should be obliged to bear the burden of anxieties which at base had nothing to do with the security of property and person at all. A problem was invented, a solution found, which in the interests of greater

---

[102]   Radzinowicz and Hood, *A History of English Criminal Law*, vol. 5, chap. 8, provides the main guide to this and the ensuing paragraph.

efficiency and order added yet another brick to the edifice of the disciplinary state.

Secondly, the unreality of the enterprise lay in the fact that both as regards unorganised labour and as regards 'crime' itself, this was not a time of justifiable fear. Booth had shown that the dangerous classes were few, 'a disgrace but not a danger'. Most indictable crime rates, in terms of which all modern generations ill-advisedly decipher their social health, had been tumbling since the 1860s. The Criminal Registrar in 1901 commented that his era had 'witnessed a great change in manners: the substitution of words . . . for blows . . . ; an approximation in the manners of different classes; a decline in the spirit of lawlessness'.[103] With 40 per cent of the adult male population still excluded from the franchise, the working classes were nonetheless pacified and in their places. The policeman-state was doing its work well enough.

The irony ultimately presents itself, then, that the professional criminal became an object of concern not because he was numerous, or even visible, but because there were few other targets left which experts could plausibly represent as dangerous. On the part of the pundits who allowed his phantom to haunt them, he was a vehicle for the expression of unreal anxieties, and above all, perhaps, of the subliminal need they felt to demonstrate their professional credentials and utility.

Moral panics of the kind that led to the Prevention of Crime Act, orchestrated by experts and media as they invariably are, litter the history of law and order. Displaced anxieties about social orderliness and moral decline, as well as bureaucratic self-interest, usually underpin them. Their effects have seldom been explicitly calculated; but they usually conspire to legitimise the growing authority of the state, and provide opportunities for its expansion as well. Perhaps these panics became – had to become – more frequent as public participation in the political process was extended. Either way, they have served the disciplinary state well. There is no reason in logic or in history to expect that the ongoing expansion, centralisation and specialisation of the policeman-state will ever now lose its momentum.

---

[103] *Judicial Statistics for England and Wales, 1899, Part I: Criminal Statistics*, PP 1901, LXXXIX, Introduction (Master of the Supreme Court), pp. 36–7.

CHAPTER 6

Religion

JAMES OBELKEVICH

If Britain was the first industrial and urban nation, it was also, for much of the period between 1750 and 1950, a remarkably religious one. During the first century of industrialisation the social relevance of religion actually increased, and the churches played a major role in both the public and the private spheres. Religion provides one of the keys to the history of the age.

Given Christianity's ancient origins, that may seem surprising: was not a traditional faith bound to wither away in a period of rapid modernisation? And since the two main churches, the Church of England and the Church of Scotland, had been integral parts of the pre-1832 'old regime', were they not also bound to decline in an age of liberal and democratic political reform?

Similar questions were posed about the churches in all the advanced European countries. But Britain's answers were different. For while the established churches in Britain were comparable to those in Europe, there was also, as in America, an array of competing independent denominations. The combination of European quasi-monopoly and American 'free market' gave British religious life much of its distinctive character.

In the event the churches thrived on competition and for much of the period responded to social and political change with considerable success. During the Victorian religious 'boom' their influence, for better or worse, was greater than it had been since the seventeenth century; like America in more recent times, Victorian Britain shows that a modernising society can be religious.

In the decades before 1914, however, it was apparent that the churches' long period of growth was coming to an end, and the first half of this century was one of decline. Religion retreated into the private sphere, gradually losing the broad political and social significance it had had in previous centuries.

THE ESTABLISHED CHURCHES AND THE EVANGELICAL
REVIVAL 1750–1830

The Church of England in 1750 was more secure and more confident
of itself than at any time since the Reformation. With the support,
active or passive, of all but a small minority, it had little to fear from
rival churches, and so close were its links with the state that contemporaries spoke of a unitary 'constitution in church and state'. In
principle, the church was the nation at prayer: attendance at Anglican
worship had a civic as well as religious meaning.

The state consequently protected the church and granted it important privileges. The monarch was required by the Act of Settlement
(1701) to be a member of the church; a promise to maintain it and its
privileges was part of his coronation oath. Though the clergy did not
receive their stipends from the state, the payment of tithes on which
their income depended was enforceable in the courts. Legal restrictions on non-Anglicans meant that central and local government, the
army, navy and the universities were virtually Anglican monopolies.

Yet a 'state church' was not only protected by the state but to a
large extent controlled by it. The crown appointed all the bishops
(who sat in the House of Lords as of right) and about a tenth of
the parish clergy; Parliament had the last word on matters of doctrine
and discipline. The church, moreover, was expected to serve the state
and uphold its authority. Every parish was to be provided with an
educated clergyman whose duty it was not only to supply his people's
religious needs but to teach and civilise them and, not least, to make
them obedient to their superiors and loyal to the state. In a period
in which the church still held its own courts, exercising jurisdiction
over marriage and inheritance, and when many schoolmasters and
all university dons were clergymen, Anglicanism's broad social and
political role was as striking as its specifically religious one.

But a church so subservient to the state and to the aristocracy paid
a price, and not surprisingly it was the religious role that suffered.
Bishops, seeking promotion in return for political services, spent as
much time in London, voting for the government of the day in the
House of Lords, as they did in their dioceses. And added to the evils
of the aristocracy-controlled patronage system were those of the
church's own ossified structure and lack of internal reform. One of
the worst was the gross disparities in clerical incomes: the Bishop
of Durham, for example, received £6,000 a year, but the Bishop of

Bristol only £450, and there were similar inequalities among the parish clergy; in 1810 nearly a quarter of parish livings were worth less than £100 a year.[1] The result was rampant pluralism, absenteeism and careerism, seriously reducing the church's effectiveness at the parish level. A fortunate clergyman with an aristocratic patron could expect to be appointed to several of the more lucrative livings, take the income from them, reside in the most attractive parish and pay curates a pittance to perform his duties in the rest. By 1830, when only 40 per cent of the parishes were served by resident incumbents, the church's creaking, unreformed machinery was both a handicap and a public scandal.

To some extent the problem was eased because more men were entering the priesthood with private incomes; and because parliamentary enclosure, exchanging tithes for land, left many a parson with a large rental income and an impressive new parsonage house to match. In the past many clergymen had been little more than servants of the squires; now, as their income and status rose, they were becoming gentlemen themselves. No doubt most were conscientious men doing their duty according to the standards of the time. But in their approach to their work and their style of life they were not so much religious specialists as gentlemen who happened to be ordained. And as their strictly clerical authority diminished, with the decline of church courts and excommunication, their growing interest in secular forms of social control aligned them still more closely with the landed classes. Many became magistrates – by the 1820s about a quarter of the bench were clergy, perhaps one clergyman in five – enforcing the game laws and repressing popular recreations. The danger was that in becoming landowners and magistrates they would grow more distant from their people and less likely to win their trust.

The Anglican message itself, and the way it was preached, was also losing touch with popular needs. The average Anglican sermon – dull, dignified and devoid of any trace of 'enthusiasm' – offered little to the poor, or the poor in spirit. Not that theological subtleties were the problem – most clergymen had not studied theology, and the universities no longer taught it. But there was little for thirsty souls in the insistent moralism and emphasis on doing one's duties

---

[1] G. F. A. Best, *Temporal Pillars: Queen Anne's Bounty, the Ecclesiastical Commissioners and the Church of England* (Cambridge, 1964), pp. 196, 204, 407 n. 2; D. R. Hirschberg, 'Episcopal Incomes and Expenses 1660–1760', in R. O'Day and F. Heal, eds., *Princes and Paupers of the English Church* (Leicester, 1981), pp. 213–16.

in Anglican preaching – even if those duties were 'not grievous' and the most important was simple benevolence. Preachers who spoke of Jesus as the 'best and happiest man that ever was' somehow missed the point. And when they described the advantages of Christian faith in terms of rewards and punishments in the after-life, they did so in a calculating, utilitarian spirit that might have been more appropriate to the selection of an insurance policy.

Distrust of mystery and emotion was also reflected in Anglican worship. The sermon rather than the sacrament provided the main attraction, and the pulpit, standing near the centre of the nave, overshadowed the altar. Yet if the parson was the principal figure in the service, he did not have everything his own way. The parish clerk, the choir, singing their own 'folk' anthems and psalm tunes (though not hymns until the 1820s) and the bands of instrumental players in the west gallery – all had a part in the proceedings and all had a will of their own.[2] Not till the Victorian age were the clergy strong enough to dictate the pattern of worship regardless of lay opposition.

By the early nineteenth century the Anglican church was less secure than it looked. It was losing touch with large sections of its flock in both town and countryside. Its links with the state were a mixed blessing. Its organisation, still largely medieval, was designed for stability, not change; the church seemed powerless to redeploy its clergy to the growing urban centres where they were needed most. Its failure to accommodate the Methodist movement meant the loss of its best chance of regaining mass support. Anglicanism all but stood still as its Methodist and Nonconformist rivals raced ahead.

Britain's second established church, the Church of Scotland, was in a more favourable position, partly because it was more independent of the state. Presbyterian in structure, with no deferential bishops in the House of Lords, it exercised far more control over its affairs than the Anglican church; there was no Anglican equivalent to the General Assembly of clergy and laity, electing its own Moderator and serving as a kind of Scottish national assembly. The Scottish church was also less elitist than the Anglican. A 'lad o' parts', intellectually able but from a humble background, could hope to make his way to university, enter the ministry and 'wag his head in the pulpit'.

---

[2] N. Temperley, *The Music of the English Parish Church*, 2 vols. (Cambridge, 1979), vol. 1, chap. 6.

If there was a truly national church in Britain in 1750 it was the Church of Scotland.

The parallels between the two established churches were nevertheless becoming as significant as the differences. The Patronage Act of 1712 revived lay patronage and put it in the hands of the landlords, as in England: the origin of a conflict between rival parties within the church which eventually led to the disastrous Disruption of 1843. In the second half of the century the dominant party was the aptly named Moderates, and under their leadership the church moved in much the same direction as the Anglican, allying itself with the landlord class, relaxing its moral discipline over the laity (which nevertheless remained far stricter than in England), and making a rapprochement with secular culture – the urbane, brilliant culture of the Scottish Enlightenment. But what pleased the Moderates dismayed the stern, unbending traditionalists. Successive groups of the disaffected left the establishment and founded new independent churches of their own, analogous to the Protestant nonconformist denominations south of the border; by 1830 presbyterian dissenters formed nearly a third of the population.[3] For all its advantages, the Church of Scotland had long since lost its near-monopoly and was under more numerical pressure than the Anglican church itself.

It was Anglicanism, however, that faced the more serious challenge from dissenters. In Scotland, where most of the Protestant denominations approved at least the principle of an established presbyterian church, they served as a kind of loyal opposition to a Church of Scotland from which they had only recently broken away. In England and Wales Protestant Dissent was older and more radical. It rejected not only bishops but the very principle of establishment, and it made it itself a rival to Anglicanism in the social and political realm as well as the ecclesiastical.

All the English minority churches were subject to legal disabilities which restricted worship and excluded members from political life. For in a period still haunted by the religious strife of the previous century, anyone rejecting the state church was liable to be regarded as a threat to the state itself; religious minorities suffered not just from legal disabilities but from outbursts of 'church and king' violence from loyalist mobs. By contemporary standards, however, Britain enjoyed a large measure of religious freedom. Minority churches were

[3] Callum Brown, *The Social History of Religion in Scotland since 1730* (1987), p. 31.

neither suppressed nor expelled, as still sometimes happened on the continent, and enforcement of the law was often lax. The pattern was one of grudging official toleration and social assimilation. Despite their disabilities, and the smallness of their numbers in 1750, the minorities grew rapidly in the next hundred years and challenged the predominance of the established church.

The largest of the religious minorities was the Protestant Dissenting churches – Independents (Congregationalists), Baptists, Presbyterians, Unitarians and Quakers. Having declined since their seventeenth-century heyday, their membership in 1750 amounted to about 6 per cent of the population of England and Wales.[4]

Their place in society was determined in the first instance by the legal disabilities which included the obligation to pay tithes and church rates and to have their marriages performed in Anglican churches. These and other grievances rankled; Dissenters felt themselves to be second-class citizens. But if they were willing to receive communion in the parish church ('occasional conformity') they were not entirely debarred from public life. Forty Dissenters were elected to Parliament in the eighteenth century, and in towns like Norwich and Coventry (but not where there were closed corporations) they were a force in local politics.

Dissent drew its membership largely from tradesmen and artisans, a narrower social range than in the past; no longer did village chapels look for support to the gentry. Though Dissent faltered, individual Dissenters often prospered – even if business success usually owed more to their reputation for honesty and their supportive networks of family and friends than to the 'Protestant ethic' or to the now-waning influence of Calvinism.

There was an air of high-mindedness, of dedication to principle, about Dissent and Dissenters. They refused to conform to the established church knowing full well the price they had to pay – the legal disabilities, the Anglican intolerance, the social disadvantages; they not only praised religious freedom but made sacrifices for it. And they did much to put it into effect within the dissenting denominations themselves. These were the loosest of structures, without bishops and mostly without hierarchy of any kind, each local congregation forming a self-governing community. The middle of the eighteenth century was not a happy period for Dissent. Prolonged theological

---

[4]   M. R. Watts, *The Dissenters*, vol. 1 (Oxford, 1978), p. 270.

controversy – carried on by a new breed of intellectuals, based in the Dissenting academies – ended in schism and disarray. For all its intellectual sparkle Dissent seemed in religious terms a spent force, with its 'landlocked emotions' and its indifference to making new converts. Only in the 1770s, when their fervour was rekindled by the Evangelical movement, did they emerge from their long decline.

The second largest religious minority was the Roman Catholics, perhaps 100,000 strong in 1750. Their position was an unenviable one, due not only to anti-Catholic prejudice but to legal disabilities (including double land tax) considerably worse than those of Protestant Dissenters; they also faced problems arising from tensions within the Catholic community itself.

In their traditional strongholds – Lancashire, the north east and the west Midlands – Catholics lived under the protection of local gentry families who had long been the dominant influence in the church. But the gentry, having abandoned Jacobite politics and become firm supporters of the Hanoverian dynasty, now fitted comfortably, perhaps too much so, in upper-class society; some abandoned Catholicism altogether. And with the gentry and their churches still absorbing the bulk of clerical effort – as in Anglicanism – the growing Irish Catholic population in the towns began to be neglected.

Catholic worship reflected both the anxiety not to disturb the Protestant majority and the church's affinities with Dissent. Catholic 'chapels', when they were not simply adjuncts to country houses, resembled those of Dissenters, unembelished by statues or incense. Priests dressed like Dissenting ministers, frowned on monasticism and 'superstition', played down their sacramental role and preached charity and benevolence.

What was unclear was the balance of power between the clergy, still without bishops since the Reformation, and the gentry. The gentry's own bid for supremacy came at the end of the century, in a reform programme calling not only for married priests but for a lay (i.e. gentry) role in appointments to higher clerical posts. The defeat of this programme was decisive. Control passed to the clergy, and by 1830, on the eve of mass Irish immigration, they dominated Catholic life as never before.[5]

[5] J. Bossy, *The English Catholic Community, 1570–1850* (1975), chaps. 8, 10, 13, 14; J. C. H. Aveling, *The Handle and the Axe: The Catholic Recusants in England from Reformation to Emancipation* (1976), chaps. 12–15.

Few Catholics could be unaware of the deep antagonism toward their church in a land where Protestantism was part of the national identity. Religious animosities, moreover, were intensified by fears of absolutism ('slavery'), impoverishment ('wooden shoes') and treachery (Guy Fawkes); Guy Fawkes day itself was officially celebrated as one of the 'state services' in every parish church. There were attacks both against the Catholic rich, as in the Gordon Riots of 1780, and against poor Irish immigrants in Liverpool or Glasgow. The Act of Union (1800), bringing Ireland and its large Catholic population into the United Kingdom, further deepened Protestant anxieties.

One of the smallest of the religious minorities, the Jews, numbered only about 8,000 in 1750 – 'desperately poor' immigrants, for the most part, with a sprinkling of prosperous City families.[6] Like other minorities they faced religious prejudice as well as legal disabilities. But neither the anti-Semitism (as elsewhere Christian in origin) nor the legal disabilities were severe, compared with those faced by Jews on the continent; and there was no need for such defensive measures as communal organisation (or reform Judaism). By contemporary standards Britain was a tolerant haven for its tiny Jewish population.

Religion was by no means confined to the churches. There was also a wide variety of unofficial religious phenomena, some nearly orthodox, others totally pagan. Though the churches had accomplished great things in Britain, they had never fully Christianised it.

Closest to the churches was a kind of popular Protestantism. There was always more to it than mere hatred of popery, and its most enduring expression, Bunyan's *Pilgrim's Progress*, was a people's classic. More distant from Christianity was 'folk' religion, the jumble of pagan and semi-Christian beliefs and practices which continued to flourish as for centuries past. At one end of the spectrum were beliefs (for example, that confirmation was a remedy for rheumatism) which drew upon Christian powers for non-Christian ends. At the other end, quite separate from Christianity, were the beliefs about such beings as witches and fairies, and the realms of astrology and magic. But given the absence of any overarching myth or high god, 'folk religiosity' should not be thought of as a distinct religion (let alone a counter-religion) but as an unsystematic collection of diverse religious phenomena – some of which people believed implicitly, others they

[6] T. M. Endelman, *The Jews of Georgian England 1714–1830* (Philadelphia, 1979), p. 31.

could pick and choose from as they saw fit. In practice they held folk beliefs and Christian beliefs side by side without any feeling of inconsistency.

Folk belief had many functions. It not only explained misfortune but provided remedies, such as 'wise men' who identified thieves or magical cures for illness. (Prayer, the churches' alternative, must have seemed passive and ineffective by comparison.) It interpreted dreams, following the rule that they 'go by contraries': a death, for example, signifying a wedding. It placed human life in the larger natural world and revealed correspondences between them which man could use to his advantage. It was not optimistic: it tended to see misfortune round every corner, and (like Christianity) it aroused a good deal of fear. It had little to say about the great questions of human existence but it stayed close to most people's everyday experience and helped them make sense of it.

Folk belief has usually been associated with the rural poor, but it could be found among farmers and tradesmen as well, and among the middle-class clients who consulted wise men and astrologers. The educated elite, however, including ministers and clergy, began to dismiss 'superstition' as obsolete, pre-scientific nonsense – a new development in the eighteenth century. But folk belief was no mere 'survival': it was alive and well and served real purposes in people's lives.

An ecclesiastical 'golden age', with 100 per cent church attendance, has never existed. In the second half of the eighteenth century, before the rise of modern industry and large towns, many people attended church infrequently at best, and religious practice was influenced by a wide variety of social circumstances.

In the case of the Church of England, attendances were often disappointing, even in the countryside which it regarded as its own preserve. Where conditions were favourable – in small parishes (chiefly in southern and eastern England) with arable agriculture, concentrated settlement, centrally sited churches and, above all, resident landlords and squires – Anglicanism flourished. Where the Anglican 'dependency system' of parson and squire was weak – notably in the north and west and in towns – attendance was a minority affair and there were openings for Nonconformity and for indifference.

Religious practice also varied by class. The landed gentry were overwhelmingly Anglican, supporting the established church out of habit and duty. A landlord attended church himself (to set an example, if for no other reason), ensured that tenants came to church and kept dissenters out of his parish. Where he was patron as well as squire, he might appoint a younger son or other relation to the living and use his influence to advance his clerical career. But there was also a minority of upper-class males among whom Anglicanism, and Christianity, did not go unchallenged. Some, under the spell of the Enlightenment, became sceptics and deists; those with a taste for sacrilege joined the Hell-Fire clubs, where mockery of religion and morality was part of the fun.

Much less is known about religious activity in the middle ranks of society. Church-going had long been part of their way of life and Nonconformity as well as Anglicanism was an option. But the assumption that church attendance was essential to a family's respectability was probably a new development in this period.

What would later be called the lower middle and the upper working classes played a more active role in religious life than might be supposed. From these groups came the majority of Methodist and Nonconformist converts, not to mention the parish clerks and musicians in the parish churches. The poorest families, though looking to the Anglican clergy for rites of passage and for charity, probably attended church infrequently and had only a loose grasp of Christian doctrine; few became Methodists or Dissenters. It was assumed that of all classes they were the most 'superstitious'.

The influence of gender on religious practice remains unexplored. It was commonly accepted, as in previous centuries, that women were more religious than men. (In upper-class church monuments women were shown in idealised form as exemplars of piety and virtue, while the male portraits were more secular and realistic.) Women provided a majority of the congregations (as well as a number of preachers) in Methodism. But in every church men held the positions of authority. They still took all the leading roles in Anglican worship; and there are suggestions that they were more frequent communicants than their wives, perhaps as 'representatives' of their families in a rite with civic as well as religious meaning. The effects of the Evangelical movement were ambiguous: while in its Anglican version it reinforced patriarchal authority within the family, it also opened up philanthropic and other activities for women outside the home, particularly in Methodism and Nonconformity. The importance of age is still more obscure. Though large numbers of young people received

Anglican confirmation (more girls than boys), few became communicants. But Methodism won many converts among those on the brink of adult life, in their late teens and early twenties. The main new development for younger (and sometimes older) children was Sunday schools, founded in the 1780s, mostly on a non-denominational basis, by Evangelicals and other middle-class philanthropists. They soon attracted large numbers of working-class children, who were taught to read (in order to read the Bible) and sometimes to write, even if they rarely took the religious instruction seriously enough to become church members when they grew older. Though Sunday schools were attacked by radicals for being too conservative and by Tories for confusing the children of the poor with ideas above their station, they were extremely popular in the working classes for whom they were intended.

What brought change and disturbance to the religious scene was the evangelical movement, a revitalisation of traditional Protestantism that left its mark not only in Britain but throughout the Protestant world. In its British form it first took root in the Anglican church and has continued to inspire a large Anglican minority down to the present day. It also created the Methodist movement which arose within Anglicanism but eventually broke away and became the established church's largest rival; and it soon became the dominant force in older Dissent and in Scottish Protestantism as well. Religion, for most people during the next 150 years, meant some variety of evangelicalism, and its influence was felt far beyond the strictly religious sphere.

The starting point for the early evangelicals was their alarm at the signs of decay and failure in the contemporary church – the idleness of the clergy, the semi-paganism of the labouring poor and, especially, the 'laxity' and 'nominal' Christianity of the middle and upper classes. The remedy they offered was in some ways a simple one. There was not much concern with ritual and sacraments, nor with church government – evangelicals liked to say that they allowed no one to intervene between God and man. Doctrines mattered more – the Bible as the Word of God, original sin, salvation by faith, the atoning sacrifice of Christ, God's forgiveness – even if they were neither new nor theologically sophisticated. But it was experience, and above all the experience of conversion – the 'big change' – that was at the heart of evangelicalism: evangelicals were born-again Christians. They were also intensely moralistic. Describing themselves as 'serious' they saw life as a perpetual battle between right and wrong, in which every action, no matter how small, was to be subjected to moral scrutiny. The result was a religion not only of prayer and Bible reading but of active good works – not because good works were of the slightest help to anyone seeking salvation, but because God required them, and because they might be taken as evidence of divine favour, and because they might help bring others to God. Evangelicals consequently were tireless do-gooders, organising and campaigning for a bewildering array of moral, philanthropic and missionary causes. Characteristically they supported the anti-slavery movement not only because slavery was wrong but because they believed free men would be easier to convert. The aims of the evangelicals could hardly have been more ambitious: to convert Britain, to roll back the Catholic Church (not least in Ireland) and ultimately to carry their version of Christianity to every nation on earth.

The 'Evangelicals' proper – those remaining in the Anglican church following the departure of the Methodists – formed a distinct 'party', socially and politically conservative, yet determined to win converts and influence. Initially they sought friends in the aristocracy but it was in the middle classes that they found the most support. For if Evangelical virtues were not simply a religious gloss on middle-class values, the two were remarkably similar. The Evangelicals' call for self-discipline, hard work and moral rectitude; their obsession with the use of time, their fetish of early rising and their strict accountability to God for every waking moment; their condemnation of idleness and frivolity: all these found a positive response in the middle classes. The 'moral entrepreneurship' which Evangelicals brought to their missionary and philanthropic work was to reappear in middle-class pressure groups like the Anti-Corn Law League; middle class too was the Evangelical religion of the home – critics called it 'parlour religion' – with the father leading prayers for the assembled servants and family. And when Evangelicals (most of whom were staunch Tories) spoke of wealth as a 'blessing' and of the social order itself as God-given they could hardly have done more to calm middle-class anxieties in times of social unrest.

They had much less appeal to the poor. Hannah More's *Cheap Repository Tracts*, widely distributed among the poor in the 1790s, told them to be grateful for what they had, not to envy the rich, and that it was better to starve than to sin. When Evangelicals won working-class support it would be in districts like south Lancashire with a large Irish population, where hatred of popery was their main attraction.

By 1800 Anglican Evangelicalism had emerged as a nationwide movement with both lay and clerical support. Perhaps a tenth of the clergy (largely from Cambridge) were Evangelicals; the 'Clapham Sect', a circle of rich businessmen and their families living near Clapham Common in London, provided the lay leadership. William Wilberforce, a Claphamite and a central figure in the anti-slavery campaign, gave them a spokesman in Parliament. Evangelicals, with their own organisations, periodicals, causes and catchwords, were mobilised to do battle with opponents inside and outside the church.

For opponents were numerous and highly critical. In their view Evangelicals were no more than puritanical humbugs, obsessed with their own souls, complacent about being 'saved', eager to suppress the pleasures of the poor while turning a blind eye to those of the rich. They were accused of being humourless, anti-intellectual (as in the typical boast that 'I know nothing worth knowing but Jesus Christ and Him crucified') and philistine, mistrusting the imagination whether in Shakespeare or in fairy tales. Radicals attacked them for telling the poor to 'starve without making a noise'. There was some truth in all these criticisms.

The Evangelicals, a rather beleaguered minority in the Anglican church, never found much support outside the respectable classes. Methodism, by contrast, evangelical through and through, was a new religious movement with unprecedented popular appeal.

John Wesley, the high church Anglican clergyman who founded Methodism, was converted in 1738 and started his long evangelistic preaching career the following year. Though always intending to keep his movement within the Anglican church, he led it inevitably into a separate life of its own, and after his death in 1791 it moved quickly towards independence. Yet his own role should not perhaps be exaggerated: Methodism made its greatest advances after Wesley's death, and it was always the movement that mattered.

For it was a religious movement of a new kind, with a single-minded dedication to making converts and a high degree of evangelistic 'aggression'. Unlike other churches Methodism relied not only on ministers but also on 'lay agency' – the lay men and women who did the bulk of the preaching, organising and pastoral care. Methodist itinerant preachers did not confine themselves to existing congregations, but took the gospel into neglected hamlets and villages and created new ones. Once converted, members attended not only the normal chapel services but also the 'class' meetings, conducted by a lay class leader, providing mutual support and pastoral care. Methodism combined in unique fashion ministerial authority at the top (which later provoked much discontent) with lay initiative and fervour at the grassroots.

The Methodist message – justification by faith, rejection of predestination, immediate assurance of salvation, sanctification – was both a powerful and a democratic one, holding out the prospect of salvation to all sinners and not only to the elect. Methodist services were urgent, emotional and unpredictable. There were extemporary prayers from the preachers and spontaneous participation from the congregation – cries of distress from sinners in the throes of conversion and praise and rejoicing from those who had 'found liberty'. To Anglicans, Methodist services were scandalous for their lack of order and decorum, their pandering to 'mere animal excitement'. But to Methodists themselves 'enthusiasm' was something positive, evidence of an outpouring of the spirit in those whom Anglicanism had stifled or neglected.

Methodism grew rapidly, its membership increasing from only 25,000 in 1770 to 94,000 in 1800 and 286,000 in 1830 – besides still larger numbers of 'hearers' and 'adherents' who attended regularly without becoming members. Mainly urban during Wesley's life time, it later expanded into rural and semi-urban districts of the west and north where both Anglicanism and older Dissent were weak – while making little headway in London, the south and south-east. Though winning few converts among the rich or the very poor, it was attractive to the cottagers, miners, artisans, small tradesmen and shopkeepers who were becoming more numerous in the early stages of industrial growth. Methodism had a strong appeal to late adolescents, vulnerable to sexual anxieties (including guilt over masturbation) and to women, who found opportunities to play an active role in the new movement that were denied them in the Anglican church. But perhaps the strongest motive of all was fear of death and damnation, a constant theme in Methodism and throughout the evangelical movement.[7]

Methodism grew fastest, significantly, in the period of heightened social strain in the first half of the nineteenth century. For those making the difficult transition from a traditional way of life to a more

---

[7] Watts, *Dissenters*, p. 418; A. D. Gilbert, *Religion and Society in Industrial England* (1976), pp. 59–68.

individualistic and competitive one, Methodism did much to ease the way. It subjected its members to strict moral discipline, rescuing them from what it saw as the irresponsibility and immorality of the traditional plebeian way of life. There was also an element of social protest. Methodism enabled the common people to declare their independence of squire and parson, to show that as far as fervour, morality and self-respect were concerned, they were the equal or superior of any gentleman. Yet if Methodists disapproved of the 'older, half-pagan' culture, their deep interest in such things as dreams and visions ensured that they did not break with it entirely. 'Modernisation' was not the whole story.

Like new religious movements in more recent times, Methodism aroused much opposition – down to 1780 more than 600 anti-Methodist tracts were published – on social as well as theological grounds. To employers, Methodism threatened a breakdown of work discipline; to young men, the danger that girl friends would turn their affections elsewhere; to husbands, loss of control over wives; to neighbours, division and disruption within the community. Persecution of Methodists, including mob attacks encouraged by parsons and magistrates, continued into the nineteenth century.[8]

The social and political consequences of Methodism have been much debated. One claim is that Methodism, by instilling the work ethic in the poorer classes, served to promote capitalist industrial discipline. But Methodists were no more insistent about this than, for example, the Anglican clergy, and their weeknight prayer meetings often left them unfit for work the next morning. Another suggestion has been that during the years of social unrest around 1800 Methodism prevented a possible revolution. Before 1800, however, there were too few Methodists to have made much difference; after 1800 the ministers indeed drove out the radicals, and Bunting, the Methodist 'pope', declared that 'Methodism hates democracy as much as it hates sin', but there was a good deal of liberal and reformist (if not revolutionary) sentiment among the ordinary members who remained. Methodism has been criticised for repressing or distorting normal sexual feeling: at the time, though, the usual charge was the opposite, that it encouraged sexual licence and debauchery. And if it was obsessed with sin and damnation, it probably differed little in this from other churches

[8] J. D. Walsh, 'Methodism and the Mob in the Eighteenth Century', in G. J. Cuming and D. Baker, eds., *Popular Belief and Practice* (Studies in Church History 8, Cambridge, 1972), pp. 216–24.

of the period. It may have had a narrowing effect but it also released energies and abilities long suppressed and can hardly be thought to have made people resigned or fatalistic.

By the 1770s the evangelical impulse was spreading to the older Dissenting denominations, and by 1830 the combined forces of Non-conformity and Methodism were making deep inroads into the Anglican majority. Methodists, however, did not at once identify with dissent: many continued to attend the parish church as well as their own 'means of grace'; in Wales they did not break away from Anglicanism until 1811. With the religious world increasingly polarised between Anglicans and Dissenters, Methodists stood ambiguously in the middle.

Between 1790 and 1815 the main influences on British religious life were the great events of revolution, war and reaction. In no church could there be business as usual while the fate of nations hung in the balance.

Among the Anglican Evangelicals the war years brought a dual response of social conservatism at home and apocalyptic optimism abroad. To Britain Evangelicals offered what has been called a 'new moral economy' of sobriety, self-control, sexual restraint and respectability; a challenge both to the hedonism of the aristocracy and to the levelling and violence of the Revolution, it inaugurated that 'Victorianism' which appeared decades before the accession of Queen Victoria herself. At the same time their imagination was powerfully stimulated by events abroad. The fall of the Catholic monarchy in France encouraged hopes that they might not have long to wait for the destruction of the Catholic church itself. Seeking clues in the prophetic books of the Bible, Evangelicals foresaw still mightier events in the immediate future – the conversion of the heathen, Christ's second coming, His rule for a thousand years, a new heaven and a new earth. In the 1790s, when Evangelicals (Dissenting as well as Anglican) launched the modern missionary movement, they expected nothing less than the rapid and imminent conversion of the entire world.[9]

But as far as actual growth in membership was concerned the largest gains were those of the Methodists. Against a background of political turmoil and economic and social dislocation, Methodism advanced into previously neglected rural and semi-industrial districts and won many

---

[9]   D. N. Hempton, 'Evangelicalism and Eschatology', *Journal of Ecclesiastical History*, 31 (1980), pp. 182–6.

converts among cottagers, craftsmen and the labouring poor. Most fervent and evangelistic of all were the Primitive Methodists, originally a movement within the Wesleyan connection, but whose open-air camp meetings and unrestrained revivalism led them to become independent in 1807; the success of the 'Ranters' among miners and farm workers made them the most plebeian religious movement before the Salvation Army. Their appeal was notably strong among women, anxious to affirm the 'sanctity of the household' against the threat of pauperisation and the break-up of families; 'cottage religion', with informal prayer and revival meetings often led by women, was at the heart of much of the Methodist rural expansion.[10]

For the older Dissenting churches, the period brought not only increases in membership but new political dangers. As early as 1791 their advanced political views – support for the Revolution in France as well as for reform at home – exposed them to the mob violence of the Priestley riots; during the wars, when they advocated a negotiated peace rather than outright victory, they were still more vulnerable.[11] To the Anglican majority, determined to crush the Revolution and to close ranks against dissent and reform of any kind, Nonconformists seemed disloyal and unpatriotic. Later, the Anglican-dominated Parliament even threatened their (and the Methodists') religious institutions – Sidmouth's bill of 1811 would have put tight restrictions on itinerant preaching, one of the keys to their success. The lesson drawn by Dissenters was that they were at odds not just with the established church but with the entire system of aristocratic rule and privilege.

Still more radical was the popular infidel movement which had its origins in this period. Previous attacks on Christianity, like those of Voltaire and the philosophes, had had a limited circulation within the educated elite. But after the publication of Thomas Paine's classic text, *The Age of Reason* (1795), infidelity began to reach the labouring classes, not only a larger audience but a more politically dangerous one. It was on moral and political grounds, significantly, that Paine argued his case against Christianity. The Bible was full of 'obscene stories' with 'cruel and torturous executions'; the church always tended to 'terrify and enslave mankind, and monopolize power and

---

[10] D. M. Valenze, *Prophetic Sons and Daughters: Female Preaching and Popular Religion in Industrial England* (Princeton, 1985).

[11] J. Cookson, *The Friends of Peace: Anti-War Liberalism in England, 1793–1815* (Cambridge, 1982), pp. 190–1, 240–1.

profit'; he particularly condemned the 'adulterous connection of church and state'. Paine's book was the inspiration for a popular infidel movement, founded in the 1790s, which campaigned against Christianity and the churches for more than a century; radical in politics as well as religion, it won support among artisans in London and elsewhere, and had an influence in the working class out of proportion to its small numbers.

After the wars the religious scene was dominated by the deepening crisis of the Anglican establishment. In the short run its links with the state were still strong: two large grants from Parliament, in 1818 and 1824, enabled it to build more than 600 new churches in the rapidly growing towns. But the new churches made little difference: Anglicanism appeared to be losing its hold on the middle classes as well as the poor, and with farmers refusing to pay tithes there was trouble even in its rural heartland. Radicals like Cobbett were not alone in denouncing Anglican abuses – the tithe system, Anglican 'bigotry' towards minority churches, clerical absenteeism and pluralism, the gross inequalities between 'bloated sinecurists' and the underpaid 'working clergy'; the sense of a malaise in the church was widespread among churchmen themselves. At the end of the 1820s came the long-delayed reforms which brought the crisis to a head in the state church and the confessional state alike: repeal of the Test and Corporation Acts in 1828 (allowing dissenters to hold public office); Catholic Emancipation, in 1829, seen by many Anglicans as a 'betrayal' of the 'Protestant constitution'; and finally the 1832 Reform Act, passed despite the opposition of the majority of bishops and clergy. When the new Parliament met, the church seemed certain to come in for long-overdue structural reform, for punishment (after its obstinacy in 1831–2), possibly even dismemberment. 'The church, as it now stands', wrote the Rev. Thomas Arnold in 1833, 'no human power can save.'

RELIGION IN VICTORIAN SOCIETY 1830–1914

The Victorian age was self-consciously religious. Britain's greatness, Victorians believed – its prosperity, social stability, political liberties, and Empire – was rooted in Christian (and Protestant) faith.

Yet if religion flourished, it did not bring harmony or good feeling. The transition from religious unity to pluralism brought with it conflict and controversy, with Protestant ranged against Catholic, Anglican against Dissenter, Evangelical against high churchman, Christian against unbeliever. Nor were the conflicts limited to the religious sphere. Both politics and social life were riven by the clashes of churches and creeds.

The churches' biggest problem, however, was not their disputes with one another but changes in the wider society – the continued spread of industry and large towns, and the deepening of class divisions. Characteristically the churches responded with energy and determination, making religion more relevant to British society in 1850 than it had been a century earlier. Yet despite their best efforts they largely failed to win the allegiance of the urban working classes, and by the end of the century they were losing their hold on the respectable middle classes as well. The portents of decline were apparent long before 1914.

Perhaps the most important, if least expected development in this period was the resurgence of the Church of England. After the crisis of the 1830s it belatedly reformed itself, fought back against the Nonconformists and regained much of the initiative it had lost.

The first round of reform was imposed from outside, by the Whig governments of the 1830s. Tithes were commuted, the rules of clerical non-residence were tightened and resources began to be shifted from cathedral foundations to needy urban parishes. The church also put its own house in order. A tough new breed of bishops cracked down on pluralism and non-residence, and warned parsons away from the hunting field and the magistrates' bench. In the towns, thousands of new churches were built – though the country parish remained the Anglican ideal – and by the end of the century the number of clergy had doubled.

The clergy played the central role in the Anglican revival. Gentlemen they still were, but they also began to receive professional training and to bring to their work a more energetic and even combative approach; in urban parishes they served not only as priests and pastors but as social organisers as well. They set up social and recreational activities, mobilised the laity (though keeping control in their own hands) and conducted the services with smooth professionalism. With the church now showing 'aggression' of its own, and using some of the weapons of Dissent against Dissent, it steadily improved its share of the religious market; the slow-moving establishment recast itself as a church militant.

It was also in the 1830s making a new departure in its spiritual life. As Evangelicalism had revived its Protestant and Puritan traditions, the Oxford Movement now revived its Catholic traditions, rescuing them from Protestant contempt and restoring them to the life of the church.

Spiritual renewal brought discord. Newman and his Oxford allies, in their widely read 'Tracts for the Times' (1833–41), caused offence not only by a provocative display of their Catholic sympathies, but by turning their irony and sarcasm against fellow-Anglicans and particularly (despite Newman's own Evangelical origins) against the Evangelicals, attacking them for their Protestant excesses, for subordinating church to state, and not least for their vulgarity and irreverence. Catholic-hating Evangelicals in turn assiled the new movement as a threat to the Protestant establishment from within; when Newman and some of his followers went over to Rome their worst suspicions were confirmed.

More trouble came in the 1850s when the younger Tractarian clergy began to introduce incense, vestments and other 'Catholic' ritual practices into their services. Outraged Protestants reacted with sermons, lawsuits, legislation and even mob violence in a long and futile campaign to halt the 'ritualist plague'. Disraeli, denouncing the 'mass in masquerade', passed the Public Worship Regulation Act (1874), under which five ritualist clergymen were convicted and sent to jail. To their opponents, the ritualists were suspect not only because they were not Protestant, but because they seemed not quite English and – with their celibacy, their peculiar dress and refined artistic tastes – not quite men.[12]

From the 1840s Anglicanism was torn by conflict between its rival 'parties'. (The broad churchmen, liberal in theology and politics, were caught in the middle.) The Anglo-Catholics, as they later came to call themselves, formed a virtual sect within the church, complete with heroes (but not heroines), martyrs, seminaries, organisations, periodicals and even travellers' guides. Anglo-Catholic priests tended to be courageous but 'spiky', men of extremist and rebellious temperament never afraid of defying their bishops. Though their best known efforts were in slum parishes, where they hoped to win over the poor with their colourful ritual and self-sacrificing pastoral work, it was eventually the middle classes, particularly in London and the southeast, who provided the bulk of their support. The Anglo-Catholics

[12]   D. Hilliard, 'Unenglish and Unmanly: Anglo-Catholicism and Homosexuality', *Victorian Studies*, 25 (1982), pp. 181–210.

nevertheless brought change to Anglicanism as a whole. Their insistence that communion was the central act of worship (and the badge
of active church membership) gradually came to be accepted in nearly
all sections of the church; the doubling of the number of communicants
in the decades before 1914, even as attendances declined, was a reflection of their influence.

No less significant than the changes within the church was its altered
relationship with state and society. In a period which saw Parliament
stripping away its privileges, minority churches openly competing
for congregations, and a large section of the nation attending no place
of worship at all (even if they came to the vicar for christenings or
weddings), Anglicanism's claim to be a national church was being
steadily undermined. Though it did not cease to make that claim,
it was also becoming just one denomination, albeit the largest and
most respectable, among many.

Nothing in the Anglican church, however, could match the upheaval
in the Church of Scotland, where the conflict between Moderates
(favouring choice of minister by the landlord) and Evangelicals (favouring choice by the congregation) reached its climax. In 1843 most of
the Evangelical party – nearly 40 per cent of the ministers and congregations – left the establishment and formed the Free Church. The
Disruption, the biggest crisis in the Scottish church since the seventeenth century, dominated its history in the Victorian period.

What lay behind the Disruption was not for the most part a clear
social divide between the two parties. If the Moderates were stronger
in the landlord class and in provincial market towns, and the Evangelicals in the middle classes in the larger urban centres, it was only
in the Highlands that either side came close to a clean sweep: there
the Free Church won overwhelming popular support in opposition
to a Church of Scotland still closely identified with the landlords responsible for the Clearances. Otherwise, cultural and ideological differences
mattered most. The Moderates were more content with the status
quo, both religious and political, and more at ease in secular culture;
the Evangelicals, with something of the drive and fervour of their
Anglican counterparts, were the more urgent about saving souls.[13]

Yet despite the upheaval caused by the Disruption, religious developments in Scotland continued to be broadly similar to those in the
rest of Britain. At first, to be sure, the Free Church regarded itself

[13]   Brown, *Social History of Religion in Scotland*, pp. 15–17, 32.

not as an English-style independent denomination but as the true national establishment, and built a complete duplicate set of churches (and schools) to challenge those of the parent church. But by the 1870s it rejected the very principle of an establishment – which now became the leading issue in Scottish politics – and moved closer to Nonconformity; the two main churches were divided, as in England, between the Conservatives and Liberals. There were also parallels between the two established churches. The Church of Scotland, even weaker in 1851 than its Anglican counterpart, also staged a vigorous recovery in the second half of the century; with only a very small 'Catholic' revival, and the General Assembly still playing a leading role in Scottish life, the Scottish establishment preserved its national status more successfully than the English. Religion altogether mattered more in Scotland than in England and, with a mixture of Calvinism and Evangelicalism as common ground for all the presbyterian churches, rested on a broader consensus.

Splits and secessions – notably in Wesleyan Methodism in the 1840s – were not unknown among the Nonconformists and Methodists in England and Wales. The Victorian period was nevertheless one of the high points in their history. They matched their Anglican rivals in numbers – in the middle 1880s their combined membership, excluding adherents, was probably about 1.4 million, much the same as the number of Anglican Easter communicants, while their huge Sunday school enrolments easily surpassed those of the Anglicans; they were largely successful, too, in their campaign to remove their disabilities. Only near the end of the period did it become clear that with the political gains had come a loss of evangelical fervour, and that the future of Dissent would be less happy than its past.

In the 1830s and 1840s, however, dissent was still expanding rapidly. Carefully planned yet intensely emotional revival meetings produced thousands of conversions and enabled Dissent more than to keep pace with the increase in population. But after 1850, as British society stabilised, religious revivals gradually ceased (the Welsh revival of 1904–5 was the last) and growth rates slackened. Recruitment was also affected by competition from the Anglicans and by the further spread of factory industry, which left fewer of the independent artisans who had flocked to the chapels in the past. As the supply of adult converts dwindled, Nonconformists were forced to recruit from within, concentrating on the children of existing members; the revival meeting was replaced by the Sunday school.[14] In the 1880s Dissent began to decline relative to the total population; in the decade before 1914 there was a fall in absolute numbers.

Dissent's social composition nevertheless changed little. The core of the membership was still drawn from the lower middle and upper working classes; not even Primitive Methodism, the most plebeian of the larger churches, made much headway with factory workers. But each of the main denominations could also boast its galaxy of rich businessmen – such figures as W. H. Lever (Congregationalist), Thomas Cook (Baptist), George Cadbury (Quaker), Jesse Boot (Wesleyan Methodist) and Samuel Courtauld (Unitarian) – and solid middle-class prosperity was well represented among the leading lights in the chapels. It was often said that such people eventually went over to the socially superior Church of England, that 'the carriage only stops for one generation at the chapel door'. Nevertheless, a significant minority of the provincial urban elite were Dissenters, and though socially untypical of chapel-goers as a whole, they did much to give Dissent its characteristic tone – its confidence, its energy and also its resentment towards the Establishment.

What it meant to be a Dissenter always involved more than accepting certain religious beliefs or attending a particular chapel. At the very least it meant a determination to uphold their faith regardless of legal disabilities or social snobbery. Dissenters were Dissenters by choice and principle, priding themselves on their independence and refusing to defer to the powers that be: 'Dare to be a Daniel, Dare to stand alone, Dare to have a purpose firm/And Dare to make it known' were lines from one of their favourite hymns. In most denominations they chose their own ministers, paid their stipends and managed chapel affairs with the minimum of interference from outside. Dissent also brought with it a social network and a public identity. Dissenters did business with one another, married into each other's families, and came to be known as Dissenters in the local community. And from their preachers and denominational press (and missionary societies) they gained a distinctive perspective on the wider world and its problems. In Wales, where the majority of the population were chapel-goers, dissent was virtually incorporated into the national identity. More than a religious commitment, Dissent involved a way of life and an outlook on life.

---

[14] Gilbert, *Religion and Society*, pp. 198–202.

At the centre of that outlook was the principle of religious freedom. Condemning Anglicanism as a 'state church' Dissenters argued that there should be 'free trade' in religion as there was in the economy. But they wanted more than just to be left alone. A free and fair competition in religion, they believed, was one they would expect to win, one that would confirm that they and not the Anglicans were the true national church. Increasingly they saw themselves as the nation's moral arbiters, bringing the 'nonconformist conscience' (a phrase first used in 1890 in connection with the Parnell case) to bear on all manner of public and private issues, and above all on the drink problem. Temperance, in the second half of the century, became not only their favourite moral reform but part of their identity and part of their claim to moral superiority. Most Dissenters became total abstainers and all new converts were expected to sign the pledge; even the wine in the communion service was replaced with unfermented grape juice. When their campaign against drink escalated from persuasion to restriction (through licensing laws) and to outright prohibition, they acted not like a beleaguered minority but like a would-be moral majority, ready to impose their will on society as a whole.

As Dissent prospered it became more settled and dignified. New chapels were larger and more expensive than the ones they replaced, and after the 1850s increasingly in the Gothic style – though characteristically a less expensive, more idiosyncratic and architecturally 'incorrect' Gothic than was favoured by Anglicans. Inside, cushioned pews reflected a taste for comfort and luxury which marked Nonconformity's 'mahogany age'. Ministers received academic training and were addressed as 'reverend'. The denominations themselves, previously calling themselves 'connections' and 'unions', now took the dignified title of 'church'; in the 1890s they adopted the collective name of Free Churches.

By this time much of their former rigour had been lost. Discipline over members relaxed; services became shorter and 'brighter'; auxiliary activities like literary societies and cricket clubs multiplied. The forbidding doctrines of Calvinism were watered down; 'devil' and 'worms' were removed from hymns; doctrines made fewer impositions on the sovereign individual conscience. The sacrament of communion itself was adapted to the individualist spirit (and to anxieties about hygiene): the grape juice was taken to communicants in the pews and served in tiny individual glasses, reminiscent, it was said, of a dolls' tea party. The punitive God of old gave way for the kind father who understood and made allowances; Christ became a Hero, Brother and Guide. Inward experience of sin and conversion faded; everyone had their spark of the divine spirit.

Outside its own ranks Dissent had few friends. Critics branded it as narrow, negative, moralistic, hypocritical, philistine, provincial, stiff-necked, envious of the establishment, perversely glorying in the 'dissidence of Dissent'. Anglicans still regarded it as socially inferior, sneering at the religious conceits of mere tradesmen. What the critics overlooked, however – few had any direct experience of Dissenting life – was Dissent's more positive achievements: helping many thousands of ordinary people lead lives of dignity and self-respect, giving them opportunities for self-improvement and responsibility in the life of their chapels; and contributing a religious cast, absent on the continent, to liberalism, the dominant political force of the age.

But neither the Anglican church nor its Protestant rivals changed as profoundly as Roman Catholicism. From the continent came the ultramontanism that transformed its devotional life. From Ireland came the immigrants who increased the Catholic population from only 100,000 in 1780 to 750,000 in 1851 and over 2 million in 1914; the great majority of Catholics (who in Scotland formed over 15 per cent of the population) now were urban, Irish and working class. From Anglicanism, finally, came a small but significant stream of converts, of whom Newman and Manning were the best known, bringing new blood into the clergy and the promise of further gains amongst the educated classes. As English Catholicism entered its 'second spring' some hoped for nothing less than the 'reconversion' of England to Rome.

The arrival of the Irish also posed problems. The 'folk' Catholicism that had served them well enough in rural Ireland did not hold up long in London or Liverpool, and a high proportion of the immigrants lost all contact with the church. Anxious to avert further 'leakage', priests carried out what amounted to a 'devotional revolution', abandoning the cool, restrained piety of the eighteenth century and adopting an unashamedly emotional, almost missionary approach. Their preaching matched the fervour of Protestant revivalists; their new chapels, with the candles, incense, plaster statues and other props of ultramontane piety, emulated those of Rome or Naples.[15]

Victorian Catholicism was dominated by the clergy. The role of the

---

[15]   S. Gilley, 'Vulgar Piety and the Brompton Oratory, 1850–1860', in R. Swift and S. Gilley, eds., *The Irish in the Victorian City* (1985), pp. 255–66.

old Catholic gentry, previously so influential, was now, according to one priest, 'to hunt, to shoot, to fish and on no account to interfere with the work of the Church'. Nor was there any challenge to the priests from the small Catholic middle class. In the poor, inner city parishes, the priests were dedicated, dominant, often paternalist figures, laying down the law to their parishioners as well as bringing them the faith and sacraments. 'Improvement' was not ignored – priests too pleaded for temperance – but this was a church of the unskilled, where (unlike most Protestant churches) it was no disgrace to be poor and stay poor. Whatever the church's dreams of reconverting England, the immediate strategy was realistic and defensive. Mixed marriages were condemned; great sacrifices were made to build a Catholic school system. The aim was to shield Catholics from all Protestant and secular influence, to keep them in self-enclosed communities where the church was the focus of social as well as religious identity.

What most Protestants knew of Catholicism, however, was the bold, triumphalist ultramontanism of its public stance; and its effect on them was to deepen alarm (triggered by the appearance of Catholic fellow-travellers in the Church of England) into panic. When bishops were restored to the Catholic church in 1850, Cardinal Wiseman provoked near-hysterical charges of 'papal aggression'; in the Stockport riots of 1852 anti-Catholic (and anti-Irish) feeling erupted into violence. Many Protestants regarded the pope as antichrist, the mass as 'idolatry', the Irish famine as just punishment for the rejection of Protestant truth. They surrounded Catholicism with a kind of religious pornography, dwelling especially on the horrors of the confessional, where priests insinuated 'impure' ideas into the minds of innocent girls and turned wives against their husbands. Good Protestant families felt shame and disgrace when one of their members 'perverted' to Rome. Anti-Catholic prejudice flowered in this period and was widespread in every social class.

Immigration also brought change to the Jewish community. By the 1830s there had emerged an Anglo-Jewish 'gentry', an elite of City and landed families who provided leadership for a community otherwise mainly consisting of small traders and pedlars. Political emancipation went through its final stages with the election of the first Jew, Lionel Rothschild, to the House of Commons in 1847 – though he was not allowed to take his seat until 1858 – and the opening of the universities in 1871. There was also a considerable degree of acculturation. The handsome synagogues and decorous services favoured by the Anglo-Jewish gentry followed obvious Anglican models. But after 1880 the arrival in Britain of over 120,000 refugees from anti-Semitic persecution in Russia brought not only a sharp increase in the Jewish population (rising to 300,000 in 1914), but also significant change to its religious life. Immigrant workers felt ill-at-ease in the existing synagogues, where the atmosphere seemed cold, formal and middle class; in their shuls, backroom meeting places for men only, they worshipped in an informal, emotional style which had certain parallels with that of the early Methodists and other working-class sects. And as with Catholic (and Protestant) workers, there were problems with leakage and loss of faith. Later, in the twentieth century, when the immigrants were more finally settled, the shuls declined, and the main focus of religious observance for most Jews shifted to the home, where it was now the women who had the most important roles, keeping a kosher kitchen and preparing for the Sabbath and for the holidays.[16] Jews came to practise their religion with the same degree of commitment, or lack of it, as gentiles in the same social class. Judaism had formerly encompassed an entire way of life: it now tended to be confined to a separate compartment in a way of life which was increasingly British and secular.

Religious practice, to most churchmen, was virtually synonymous with Sunday attendance. But when attendance was measured – notably in the religious census of 1851 – the results were disconcerting. In England and Wales total attendances on census Sunday (counting twice those who attended twice, a significant minority) amounted to 60 per cent of the total population; on another calculation, of those able to attend church only about half did so. A high proportion by late twentieth-century standards, this was regarded as worryingly low by contemporaries. Still more controversial, the census also indicated that the Church of England had lost its majority position, at least among church-goers: Nonconformists, Catholics and others together made up just over half of all attendances.

Church-going was influenced by a wide variety of social and geographical circumstances. Attendance was higher in Scotland than in England and highest of all in Wales. Within England it was higher in the countryside than in the towns, though this should not be

---

[16]   R. Burman, 'Women in Jewish Religious Life: Manchester 1880–1930', in J. Obelkevich, L. Roper and R. Samuel, eds., *Disciplines of Faith: Studies in Religion, Politics and Patriarchy* (1987).

exaggerated, as there were wide variations within both rural and urban areas. If attendance was poor in many of the northern industrial towns it was partly because they drew immigrants from the surrounding rural areas where church-going had been weak for generations. There was also considerable variation between regions. But undoubtedly the strongest influence was that of class.[17]

Not that religion simply reflected class divisions: none of the larger churches was the preserve of any single group or class; all cut across class lines. Nevertheless, class had a bearing not only on the mere fact of attendance but on what church (if any) people worshipped in, and more importantly on the content and character of their religiosity and on the place religion had in their lives. Among the gentry and aristocracy, for example, there was a sense that the Anglican church deserved support precisely because it was part of a social order in which they themselves had a privileged position. In country parishes the squire and his relations sat in the front of the church and were the first to receive communion; they attended partly to set an example to their inferiors – and sent the bailiff round if a tenant was absent. They gave large amounts of money to build and restore churches, working with the clergy to promote Anglican interests – and their own.

It was in the middle classes that the Victorian religious boom had the biggest impact. Religion was the opiate not of the masses but of the bourgeoisie, and their heavy involvement in church life was one of the distinctive features of the British religious scene; religion was thus allied with the forces of change and modernisation and not opposed to them, as on the continent. It was in these classes that religion was most strongly sustained by social pressure: regular church attendance and keeping of the Sabbath were felt to be essential for a family's respectability. Yet external motives were far from being the only ones, and the deep and genuine religious commitment evident in this and other classes in Victorian society should not be underestimated.

There was in any case a good deal of variation in church-going and religious attitudes within the middle classes. In London, at the end of the century, the upper middle class had the highest level of

---

[17] H. McLeod, 'Class, Community and Region: The Religious Geography of Nineteenth-Century England', in M. Hill, ed., *Sociological Yearbook of Religion in Britain*, 6 (1973), pp. 29–72; B. I. Coleman, *The Church of England in the Mid-Nineteenth Century: A Social Geography* (1980).

religious practice of all, while the lower middle class was closer to the working class: the difference was as great between these two groups as it was between the middle class as a whole and the working class.[18] Church and chapel gave rise to contrasting religious styles, as did the various church parties within Anglicanism.

Middle-class religiosity nevertheless reveals some common themes. One was that religion was treated as a family matter. Husband, wife and children formed a religious unit not only at church (Sunday school was mainly for the children of the working class) but at home, in family prayers and grace before meals. Middle-class people also tended to regard their church as a social centre, where they could meet others of similar outlook and join in the various recreational and philanthropic activities, and where young people could meet suitable partners of the opposite sex.

As for the urban working class, now the majority of the population, the common view was simply that they rarely attended church and that they were therefore 'spiritually destitute'. Though the denominations made great efforts to reach the workers (with special services, missions, central halls, etc.), the result, as churchmen were the first to admit, was on the whole a failure. Yet in their obsession with Sunday attendance they overlooked the fact that working-class people came into contact with the churches on a great many other occasions, and that they had religious notions of their own, however unorthodox.

To most working-class people the churches were alien, middle-class institutions where people like themselves, lacking good clothes and unable to afford pew rents, felt out of place. Church-goers they tended to regard as snobs and hypocrites; any working-class person going to church was liable to be condemned for putting on airs, setting himself above his neighbours. Social pressure did as much to deter church-going in the working class as it did to encourage it in the middle and upper classes.

There was, however, an important minority – to be found especially among artisans and miners, and among the Welsh and the Irish – who were deeply involved in the life of their church. Though working-class Anglicanism should not be underestimated, it was Methodism and Nonconformity (apart from Catholicism for the Irish) which had the most appeal. It was said of the Methodist chapel that it 'took

---

[18] H. McLeod, *Class and Religion in the Late Victorian City* (1974) pp. 144, 323.

nobodies and made somebodies out of them': converting them, teaching them to read and write (and to speak in public), helping them to conquer drink and to take responsibility for themselves and their families. Chapel men, many of them preachers and other officials, often played leading roles in trade unions and the labour movement. There were also many working-class people who attended church services occasionally or on the major holidays: attendances went up at Christmas, at the Methodist watch-night service, at harvest festivals and other special services.

The great majority of working-class people, neither regular attenders nor total strangers to the churches, considered themselves Christians. Most were married in church; many mothers insisted on being churched after giving birth; most had their babies christened – even if for good luck or for other reasons not approved by ministers or clergy. Most working-class children went to Sunday school – for the moral teaching, to have a good time, and not least to give the parents some rare privacy for sexual intercourse on Sunday afternoons. Children looked forward to the summer treat as one of the high points of the year; the Sunday school anniversary, particularly in Nonconformity, was a major festival, with the chapel packed with applauding parents many of whom never set foot in it on any other occasion. Many children received religious instruction in church day schools; those in board schools were given undenominational Protestantism – the Bible 'without note or comment' – and plenty of hymns. Working-class people also looked to the churches, and to Anglican parsons in particular, for charity; a constant stream of poor people came to the vicarage door asking for help and they rarely went away empty-handed. Most urban churches set up extensive welfare schemes, doling out food, blankets, money and Bibles, even if such charity was only a degree less shameful than going into the workhouse. Working people dealt with the churches on their own terms, taking what they wanted and ignoring the rest.

They picked and chose in a similar way among the churches' doctrines and moral teachings. Most working-class people believed in God (though a rather remote one) and in an after-life: but not in sin (they felt more sinned against than sinning), judgment or hell. Doctrine of any distinctive denominational kind they regarded as a waste of time. Where the churches were strong on puritanism and moral purpose, and as often as not on the evils of drink, working-class people preferred to 'take life as it comes' and believed that 'a little of what you fancy does you good'. Where churchmen dedicated their Sundays to worship and Sabbath observance, the working classes treated themselves to a late lie-in, followed by shopping, relaxing and drinking. (Some certainly benefited from sabbatarian efforts to limit Sunday work.) What Christianity meant to them was not belief or doctrine but kindness, 'decent behaviour' and doing as you would be done by. Few churchmen from other classes grasped that these virtues were part of a specifically working-class moral outlook in which 'generosity ranks far above justice, sympathy before truth'. The working-class indifference to the call for repentance caused alarm in the churches; in the long run, ironically, it was they who converted the majority of the middle classes to their own perfectly viable form of 'spiritual destitution'.

Much less is known about the links between religion and gender. Though women were the majority in most congregations, their actual rate of attendance was probably not greatly higher than that of men, and religion was much less 'feminised' (or demasculinsed) in Britain than in some Catholic districts on the continent, where no self-respecting man set foot in church. In the working classes the wife who attended chapel and the husband who went to the pub made a familiar pattern; when the parson called, the husband would excuse himself and ask his wife to speak to him. The gender gap was narrower in the middle and upper classes, where it was expected that husband and wife would attend church as a couple. But it still was the mother who taught the children to say their prayers, the father who led worship for the family as a whole.

Though men controlled the churches both nationally and locally, women's roles became more varied. In country parishes there was often a pastoral role – visiting the poor and dispensing charity – for the parson's wife or daughter. Besides the many women hymn writers, church choirs, especially in Nonconformity, included many women and girls, even if high church Anglicans insisted on male voices only and regarded the 'cock and hen' choirs of dissent with contempt. Women may well have outnumbered men among Sunday school teachers, and they played the major part in the churches' flourishing philanthropic activities. (Methodist women preachers, however, had become rare by the middle of the century.) Women's organisations were founded by all the larger churches and they soon grew to considerable size: the (Anglican) Mothers' Union, founded in 1876, had 200,000 members by 1900. Their membership was much larger than that of women's trade unions or feminist or suffragette groups.

Voluntary organisations for women were one thing, paid employment (apart from philanthropy) another. The number of women in Roman Catholic religious orders, mainly as teaching sisters, was small but growing. In the Church of England the sisterhoods revived by the Oxford Movement in the 1840s were never more than marginal; deaconesses, paid pastoral workers first appointed in 1861, were few in number and were not allowed to do anything regarded as the proper work of the clergy.[19] Opportunities for women were generally greatest in Nonconformity (Methodist deaconesses outnumbered Anglican); only among the Quakers and in the Salvation Army did women and men take part on anything like an equal basis.

The religious conflicts of the Victorian period were fought out not only in pulpits and pamphlets but also in the political arena – where such issues as social reform, considered more important by later generations, were often quite overshadowed by them. The churches during much of the period did more to mobilise political feeling than the political parties themselves.

The oldest antagonism of all, between Protestants and Catholics, was intensified in a period which saw heavy Irish immigration in Britain, the nationalist struggle in Ireland, and the adoption of aggressive tactics both by the Catholic church and by its Protestant opponents. It had its effect at national level on such issues as the Maynooth grant (1845) and Irish home rule; locally, in areas with large Irish Catholic populations, it led to party divisions along religious lines.

No less hard-fought were the battles over the established churches. Even the Church of Ireland, church of the tiny Anglican minority, was a leading issue in the election of 1868 (before being disestablished by Gladstone the following year). In Scotland, debates over the establishment dominated political life for most of the century. In Wales, disestablishment was the chief aim of the Liberal Nonconformist majority and the central political issue from the 1860s to the First World War. But it was England which saw the conflict between church and chapel in its classic form.

On one side were the Dissenters, allied with Whigs and Liberals,

---

[19] B. Heeney, 'Women's Struggle for Professional Work and Status in the Church of England, 1900–1930', *Historical Journal*, 26 (1983), pp. 333, 346–7.

seeking to remove their disabilities; on the other were the Anglicans, allied with the Conservatives, defending the privileges of the establishment. They clashed not only at national level (though there were few Dissenting MPs initially) but in the localities, where Dissenters now entered municipal politics in large numbers (as in Leicester, where the first seven mayors after 1835 were Unitarians). The struggle to turn a confessional state into a secular state was a long one. The Whig governments of the 1830s, with measures introducing civil registration and allowing Dissenters to perform their own marriages, did little more than whittle away at Anglican privilege; compulsory church rates remained in force despite bitter local struggles in which a number of Dissenters were sent to jail for refusing payment. In the 1850s the church courts lost their jurisdiction over divorce and wills and the 'state services' were abolished. The main breakthrough came with Gladstone's first government, which finally abolished compulsory church rates (1868) and opened up Oxford and Cambridge to Dissenters (1871); the last major disability was removed by the Burials Act of 1880 which allowed Nonconformist ministers to perform their own funeral service in parish churchyards. But the establishment itself remained a matter for dispute (during the 1885 general elections, for example), as did a variety of other issues, above all the closely related and bitterly contested question of education. Attempts by governments to channel public money into denominational schools (Roman Catholic as well as Anglican), or to give the Church of England a privileged place in state schools, provoked intense opposition from Dissenters; that England was late in creating a system of public education was mainly due to rivalry and mistrust between the churches. The 1902 Education Act, which favoured the Anglicans, spurred a large Nonconformist protest vote for the Liberals in the election of 1906. But by this time religious issues were being displaced by class issues – the 'social gospel' attracted little interest – and support grew for the notion that the churches should stay out of politics altogether.

Yet whether politically active or not, every church had its political preferences. In the case of the Anglican church, its reputation as 'the Conservative party at prayer' was not undeserved. There were exceptions – broad churchmen and Anglo-Catholics who broke ranks to support the Liberals (and Labour), and a considerable minority of laymen. But at the end of the period most clergymen were still as loyal to the party as their predecessors generations before.

What Nonconformists brought to politics was not only their

grievances and their Liberalism but a distinctive moralistic style.[20] For them, political questions were a straightforward matter of right and wrong; political action took the characteristic form of the single-issue moral crusade. And since 'what was morally wrong could not be politically right', they insisted that politicians must be good men: Gladstone, a high church Anglican who 'said his prayers every morning', was a leader to admire, but Parnell, when his private life fell foul of the 'nonconformist conscience', had to be repudiated, whatever the justice of his cause. Nonconformists believed themselves to be the 'backbone' of the Liberal party. That was an illusion – they lacked influence at the top (not till 1868 did John Bright become the first Nonconformist cabinet minister) and many Nonconformists, frightened by Home Rule (with the spectre of Catholic control) and by the rise of labour, deserted to the Liberal Unionists and the Conservatives. Though there were more Nonconformists in the Parliament of 1906 than in any other before or since, Nonconformist influence was already in decline.

For all the conflicts between the churches, there was also a Victorian religious culture which cut across denominational lines – and which in important respects tended to escape denominational control altogether.

The threat of eternal punishment, for example, was regarded as essential to Christian faith and morals, at least at the beginning of the period, by virtually all churchmen. Without the fear of hell, it was assumed, people would neither accept Christian belief nor even observe common morality. Fire and brimstone were the stock in trade of Catholic as well as Protestant preachers; horrific descriptions of the torments of the damned were written specially for children. Later, however, in the 1860s and 1870s, the 'religion of the torture chamber' began to seem inconsistent with God's love – and with current moral standards; and the churches, embarrassed by a doctrine previously indispensable, quietly pushed it into the background.[21] The churches had to adapt to a moral consensus they could no longer control.

There was also general agreement, among Protestants at least, about public worship. For what they expected from the Sunday service was above all a good sermon, and ministers were rated primarily on their preaching ability. Popular preachers became stars, printed sermons sold well, 'sermon tasters' went from church to church in quest of pulpit eloquence. Gradually, however, sermons got shorter – their

---

[20]   D. W. Bebbington, *The Nonconformist Conscience: Chapel and Politics, 1870–1914* (1982), pp. 10–17.

[21]   G. Rowell, *Hell and the Victorians* (Oxford, 1974), pp. 147–52, 171–3, 212–13.

average length shrank from an hour at the beginning of the century
to twenty-five minutes or less at the end – and lost their pre-eminence.
What took their place, in effect, was church music (or, in Anglo-
Catholic churches, music allied with ritual). Church music not only
grew longer but more expert (with trained choirs), more expressive
(with richer harmonies and powerful organs) and more elaborate;
it now took a more central role in worship than at any time in the
past. It was as though a religion of the unadorned word was being
replaced by a religion of mood and feeling. Hymns, long established
in Nonconformity, quickly caught on in Anglican churches (*Hymns
Ancient and Modern* appeared in 1861) and became the most popular
and widely accepted form of worship (though not in Scotland, where
older types of church music kept their appeal and the ban on musical
instruments was lifted as late as the 1860s). Not sermons or theologies
but hymns, however sentimental, were the truest expression of Victorian religion; ex-Congregationalist D. H. Lawrence recalled how they
'live and glisten in the depths of a man's consciousness'.[22] Like ornate
ritual, beautiful music rekindled the spirit of worship even when the
object of worship was becoming problematic.

'Efficient' churches in all denominations also worked hard to attract
congregations by providing a wide array of auxiliary activities; one
Anglican church in Reading had forty separate funds for its various
pieces of parish 'machinery'.[23] Sunday schools alone were a major
industry; in Dissent, where they were particularly strong, Sunday
scholars outnumbered adult members by a wide margin. Other church
activities included literary and debating societies, which helped Ernest
Bevin and many others along the path of self-improvement; recreation, including cricket and football teams (from which professional
clubs like Aston Villa and Everton later emerged); and philanthropy,
which probably did more for the poor, and more humanely, than
the poor law. Altogether these activities made an immeasurable contribution to social and cultural life. But they also carried with them a
danger, of diverting the church from its primary religious role, particularly as they became vulnerable to the expansion of commercial leisure
and to the growing provision of welfare by the state.

Most churches were anxious not only to convert the nation but to
reform its manners and morals. The temperance movement, though

---

[22] D. H. Lawrence, 'Hymns in a Man's Life', in Warren Roberts and Harry T. Moore,
eds., *Phoenix II* (1968), pp. 382–3.
[23] S. Yeo, *Religion and Voluntary Organisations in Crisis* (1976), p. 66.

non-denominational, drew strong support from Dissent and the Scottish churches (the Scottish Temperance Act of 1913 granted licensing restrictions by local option), if less from Anglicans and Roman Catholics. Sabbatarianism was the other Protestant shibboleth, with the Lord's Day Observance Society, founded by Anglican Evangelicals in 1831, acting as the main pressure group. Most of their attempts to impose their views by legislation were defeated when they too blatantly interfered with the habits of the poor while conniving at the private Sabbath-breaking of the rich. But in 1856 they scored a major success in ensuring Sunday closing for the British Museum and the National Gallery; in Scotland dismal Sundays became a national institution. The Welsh Sunday Closing Act (1881), the first legislation specifically for Wales, reflected the sabbatarian and temperance enthusiasms of evangelical Protestantism in the region where it was strongest – and most politicised.

The churches were less successful in keeping control of holidays and the holiday calendar. Christmas, in its modern form largely a Victorian invention, is the best example: new customs like Christmas trees (from the 1830s), greeting cards (mostly non-religious from the start) and the exchange of presents had less to do with the churches or with Christianity than with the middle-class cult of the family. The harvest festival, though introduced (in the 1840s) by high church Anglicans, was essentially pagan in spirit and became more popular in many churches than Christmas or Easter. National days of prayer and thanksgiving fell into disuse; the Bank Holidays, created in 1871, by-passed Christianity altogether.

In the arts, however, the influence of religion was still strong. British musical life was dominated not by the opera, as in the rest of Europe, but by a religious genre, the oratorio. The leading architectural style, the gothic, was primarily ecclesiastical, even if widely used for secular buildings as well. Novels on religious themes were written by, for and against evangelicals, Anglo-Catholics, broad churchmen, Roman Catholics, Nonconformists and agnostics. In poetry, religious themes are central in the work of such leading writers as Tennyson, the son of an Anglican country parson, Browning, a Congregationalist, and Hopkins, an Anglican convert to Roman Catholicism. Religion was still one of the components of the national culture.

In the 1870s the first signs appeared that the long period of growth was coming to an end. Though membership was still increasing, it failed to keep pace with the growth in population, and church-going actually began to decline: in middle-class districts in London attendances fell by more than a third between 1886 and 1902. Such hallmarks of Victorian religiosity as strict Sunday observance and family prayers were being abandoned; the churches condemned, but were unable to curb, the middle-class practice of birth control. Criticism of Christian doctrines was openly published; agnosticism and 'secular religions' won support. Behind the statistics of falling attendances lay a deeper disaffection from the churches and their message.[24]

The decline of the churches has had many explanations, no one of them sufficient by itself. The most general argument is simply that modern industrial society makes secularisation inevitable. But this says nothing about the specific causes and processes of decline – and ignores the continuing success of the churches in North America. The effect of scientific discoveries is difficult to estimate. There was less 'warfare' between science and religion than is often supposed (if only because most scientists themselves were Christians), and most British churches, unlike conservative Protestants in North America, did not find it difficult to accept Darwin's theory of evolution by natural selection (in *The Origin of Species*, 1859); but Christian faith was undoubtedly shaken by scientific advance. The higher criticism of the Bible also contributed to the mood of unease; though in Scotland, where it caused storms among the ministers and theologians, churchgoing itself appears to have been little affected. Commercial sport and entertainment probably had a greater impact on the working classes, already distant from the churches, than on the middle classes. A more persuasive suggestion is that the social pressures which had encouraged middle-class church-going earlier in the century were weakening: in an economy of large firms and professional qualifications attending church to demonstrate one's moral credentials no longer seemed so necessary. And at the level of ideas it was less the scientific than the moral critique of Christianity which did the most damage. Eternal punishment now seemed cruel and barbaric, the God responsible for it something of a monster; and if the everlasting fire burned no longer, what was the point of seeking salvation? There could be morality, people now believed, without the fear of hell and without religion altogether. More generally, Puritan self-denial was replaced by a new philosophy of life affirming the value of pleasure and the 'divine right of self-development'; late Victorian

[24] McLeod, *Class and Religion*, chap. 8.

optimism put its faith in 'science, reason, progress and character'. It was all these factors, social, ideological and cultural, which undermined Christian belief and practice in the church-going classes.

Yet the decline of the churches did not necessarily mean a decline of religion in a broader sense. Those who drifted away from orthodox belief (and many who did not) were sometimes attracted to successor faiths like nationalism which themselves had a religious quality. Queen Victoria's jubilees, the increasingly elaborate coronations and the cult of Empire were the rituals of a civil religion; like other nations in the heyday of nationalism, Britain worshipped itself. Socialism, when it revived in the 1880s, was attractive precisely because it took the form of a 'religion of socialism', with a high ethical ideal, a vision of human brotherhood and a faith to live by. There was also a religious cast to art and literature. Matthew Arnold noted that 'the strongest part of our religion is its unconscious poetry' and predicted that mankind would 'turn to poetry to interpret life for us, to console us, to sustain us'; reading the classics of English literature, one of their later advocates declared, was 'almost sacramental', 'not a routine by a religion'.[25] In this period, for the first time, religious impulses found expression on a large scale outside the churches and outside Christianity – though probably not enough to make up for the decline in the churches themselves.

THE DECLINE OF THE CHURCHES 1914–50

The period after 1914, with its wars, depression and increasingly secular way of life, brought further losses to the churches. From the mainstream of British society they withdrew to the margins, diminished not just in membership but in authority and influence. And yet the decline should not be exaggerated. The churches remained the largest voluntary organisations, at least as far as weekly attendance and participation were concerned, and their presence was still felt, even if indirectly, across wide areas of public and private life.

The outbreak of war in 1914 came as a shock to churchmen as it did to everyone else. Nearly all church leaders prayed for victory and supported the war effort; at the same time they hoped that the war would lead people back to church and thus work to religion's

---

[25]   M. Arnold, 'The Study of Poetry' (1880) in R. H. Super, ed., *Complete Prose Works of Matthew Arnold*, vol. 9 (Ann Arbor, Mich., 1973), p. 161; G. Sampson, *English for the English* (1921), p. 105.

benefit. But the long-awaited revival never materialised. At the front, the soldiers knew their hymns but were grossly ignorant of Christian doctrine; their swearing and their 'immorality' left the padres in dismay. If the men believed in anything, it was not God but fate: one chaplain remarked that 'the soldier has got religion, I am not sure that he has got Christianity'; another suggestion was that with their comradeship and their readiness to die for others they were 'Christians without knowing it'.[26] Demobbed, however, most simply reverted to the religious indifference of civilian life.

Christian faith inevitably emerged from the war weakened and discredited: how could a loving God allow death and destruction on such a scale? Yet religious responses of a less orthodox kind were actually stimulated by the war. Spiritualism is the best known example; another is the undenominational civil religion reflected in the official war memorials. The message conveyed by the war cemeteries, monuments and Armistice Day ceremonies – that life was sacred, and that to sacrifice one's life for one's country was sacred – was a religious one, but it was inspired less by the death of Christ than by the deaths of hundreds of thousands of ordinary citizens.

Over the period as a whole, most churches lost a large proportion of their membership and attendance. But the process was an uneven one. It was slower in Scotland (where 60 per cent of the adult population in 1951 still were church members, three times higher than in England); and Roman Catholic numbers, helped by a steady influx of Irish immigrants, actually grew. In the relatively prosperous 1920s, moreover, the churches largely held their own: only during the 1930s and the war years did the curve turn downward, with sharp falls in all the major Protestant denominations. Yet in 1950 prospects were brighter, and only in the 1960s did the churches again suffer major losses.

In 1950 probably more than three-quarters of the population in England and Wales claimed an allegiance, however vague, to a church: about 60 per cent to the Church of England, 10 per cent to the Free Churches and 8 per cent to Roman Catholicism. About 10 per cent attended church once a week; 6 per cent more often; 45 per cent attended intermittently, at least once or twice a year; 40 per cent went to church for weddings and funerals if at all.[27] These figures mark a sharp decline since the middle of the nineteenth century. Rites of

[26]   A. Wilkinson, *The Church of England and the First World War* (1978), pp. 156, 161.
[27]   G. Gorer, *Exploring English Character* (1955), p. 241.

passage were much less affected. Church weddings in Britain were still 71 per cent of the total in 1950, not much below the figure of 77 per cent in 1914. In England and Wales Anglican baptisms held steady at a little over two-thirds of live births. At funerals it was diffi-cult to avoid some form of religious ceremony. (New services were devised for cremation, which by 1950 was the method of disposal in 16 per cent of deaths.) At birth, marriage and death people insisted on their rites: on ordinary Sundays religion could be left to fend for itself.

The churches' problem was not so much the loss of existing members as difficulty in recruiting new ones; and given the failure of traditional evangelistic methods, church leaders looked to alternative strategies. One option was to reduce competition and overlap by reuniting churches previously divided: in Scotland all but a handful of Presby-terians rejoined the Church of Scotland in 1929, and the great majority of Methodists came together in 1932 to form the Methodist Church.

A second strategy, institutional reform, was tried in the Church of England. The Church Assembly, set up during the war, comprised not only bishops and clergy but also lay members elected by communi-cants; with powers under the Enabling Act of 1919 to present measures to Parliament, it gave the church for the first time a corporate and semi-democratic voice in its dealings with the state. Yet when the church submitted proposals for a new prayer book, they were twice (in 1927 and 1928) rejected, and by a Parliament with a large Conserva-tive majority. This humiliating rebuff, on an issue central to the life of the church, exposed the gap between church activists (largely Anglo-Catholic) and ordinary Protestant opinion, still fearful of an Anglican drift towards Rome.

Nor did the reforms make the church more attractive to the laity: active members (communicants on the electoral rolls) fell from 14 per cent of the adult population in 1924 to 9.6 per cent in 1950. But if the church was unable to halt the decline, it did the next best thing and managed it, scaling down its own ambitions while maintaining much of its traditional style. It brought under control the long and unseemingly squabbles between Anglo-Catholics and Evangelicals. It preserved its links with the social elite – most bishops had private means and came from public school and Oxbridge backgrounds. It continued to see itself as a national church, and undertook to speak as one – even though attendance figures were more suggestive of a denomination. With its ancient churches and cathedrals, it was part of the nation's history and heritage; with its ritual, more elaborate than ever, it played a leading role in the nation's ceremonial 'show'; it was coming to stand less for religion of any narrow or dogmatic sort than for a certain kind of Englishness. Indeed, what the church meant, and what people wanted it to mean, was becoming as important as what it did. Bishops, for example, had their ecclesiastical role but they were also figures in the social landscape and, as T. S. Eliot observed, 'part of English culture'; the nation's gallery of social types also included that revealing character the stage vicar. A church that was becoming all things to all men claimed the allegiance of people of every class, every shade of religious belief and every degree of devotion or lack of it – including a considerable number of ex-Nonconformists looking for a softer option. But since most people did not take religion very seriously, what they wanted was a religion of the lowest common denominator, with holidays and rites of passage and no duties or sectarian extremes. Asked what church they preferred, people could say 'C of E' without trepidation – a moderate, decent affair which (apart from the zealots) made few demands.

A dignified decline was less easy for the Free Churches. For the problem was one not only of numbers – membership fell from 1.8 million in 1914 to 1.6 million (5 per cent of the adult population) in 1950 and the large body of adherents dwindled away – but of purpose and direction. Disestablishment, one of the burning issues of the previous century, was now resolved: in Wales where the process was completed in 1920, in England where it was abandoned as a lost cause. The Free Churches' historic aim, equal legal status with Anglicanism, they had largely achieved; but what were they to do next? Everywhere the church–chapel distinction began to fade; if there was still a nonconformist conscience, it had less to be conscientious about. Worship, often criticised as drab and unrewarding, was another problem, a reflection of the narrow cultural horizons of groups like the Congregationalists whose outlook in 1950 was 'strictly Home Service'; some nonconformists, seeking a beauty and mystery (and superior social tone) they could not find in their own churches, ended by going over to Anglicanism. Worthy but old-fashioned, the Free Churches lost their disabilities but had not found a role.

For the Roman Catholic church, by contrast, this was a period of advance, with rising numbers of priests, people and chapels. The church claimed a total British Catholic population (including children and all who had been baptised) of 2.3 million in 1914 and 3.5 million in 1950.

Whatever the church's 'snob' image, most Catholics were still Irish and working class. Members of an inward-looking and rather marginal community – where converts were regarded by 'cradle Catholics' with a certain condescension – they were content to stay within the Catholic sub-culture. Being Catholic determined not only their place of worship but their schools and clubs and activities (every church had its network of auxiliary activities for all interests and age groups); it also often influenced where they lived, where they worked and where they drank. Catholics stood out because their families were noticeably larger than average, now that most Protestants practised birth control. Catholics believed that their church was superior to all others – the oldest, biggest and best; but they also had something of a ghetto mentality, a sense of being surrounded by a dominant and unfriendly majority population.

For if anti-Catholic riots had ceased, Catholics still faced prejudice and discrimination. No Catholic priest took part in Remembrance Day services at the Cenotaph until the 1960s. In the 1930s 'No Catholics need apply' signs appeared on factory gates, and in many workplaces like the Jarrow shipyards Protestants workers kept Irish Catholics out of the skilled, better paid jobs. In areas of Irish settlement the Protestant–Catholic divide was still significant, not merely in the rather ritualised scuffles between schoolboys but in the strong pressures, from both sides, against intermarriage. In Glasgow, where clashes between Celtic and Rangers supporters had a tribal flavour, it was the Protestants, with street songs vilifying the 'papes', who ordinarily were the more aggressive. Indeed, anti-Catholic feeling was probably strongest in Scotland, and was by no means limited to the poor and uneducated; freemasonry and the Orange Order attracted Protestants from all social classes. Though hostility eventually faded, and Irish Catholics assimilated to British ways, their sense of being a somewhat alien minority long remained.

The influence of the churches on political life was smaller than it had been before 1914. The limits of that influence were made clear in the General Strike. When the Archbishop of Canterbury, supported by leaders of the Catholic and Free Churches, wished to speak on the BBC to appeal for compromise, he was refused permission – by a Director General fearing retribution from the Conservative government. Rarely now did religious or ecclesiastical issues come before Parliament – a marked contrast with the previous century. Nor were there great controversies between the churches over foreign affairs:

nearly all churchmen supported the policy of appeasement, though only the Catholics, particularly during the Spanish civil war, showed any sympathy for fascist regimes. But religion was still a major determinant, second only to class, of party allegiance. Committed Anglicans – apart from a small minority of socialist Anglo-Catholics – were Conservative, often almost automatically so; support for Labour they regarded as 'political' and divisive, support for the Conservatives as mere common sense. The Free Churches still favoured the Liberal party and only gradually shifted towards Labour, despite the fact that many Labour leaders, like the Methodists Snowden and Henderson, were themselves active Nonconformists. (The Anglican minority included Lansbury, Cripps and Attlee.) Labour nevertheless owed much to Nonconformity. In opposing the Anglican and Conservative establishment Labour, like the Liberals before it, made itself the natural home, not only for Dissenters but for other religious minorities, including Catholics, Jews and unbelievers. The Catholic Irish, mainly unskilled workers, might have given their support to Labour in any case; but they were also encouraged by their priests, who saw Labour as a bulwark against Communism and, in Scotland, as a defender of state aid to Catholic schools. Outside Irish districts, however, Catholicism, or even an Irish name, could be a political handicap. In Liverpool, where local politics turned almost entirely on the religious issue, the Irish Catholics backing Labour were outnumbered by working-class Protestants loyal to the Conservatives, and not till 1956 did Labour win a council majority. There was, however, a growing feeling that the churches should stay out of politics, one probably shared by most of the clergy and ministers themselves.

The churches continued to be major providers, if on a smaller scale than in the past, of welfare, recreation and, especially, education. Both the Anglican and the Catholic churches maintained large school systems, and most people, including non-church-goers, still wanted religion taught in the state schools; the common view was that 'it makes you a better citizen, even if you don't believe in it'.[28] (Hence the favourable treatment of religion in the 1944 Education Act.) In the universities, however, the influence of religion was waning. At Oxford and Cambridge the Anglican grip loosened with the ending of compulsory chapel in the 1920s and the appointment of Nonconformists (but not Catholics or unbelievers) to previously Anglican

[28] Mass-Observation, *Puzzled People* (1947), p. 87.

chairs in theology. Most intellectuals were agnostics and scholarly enquiry rested on 'methodological atheism'.

Yet despite the decline of the churches as institutions, something of their moral teaching and their puritanism lived after them. Among men who had long since given up the kirk- or chapel-going habits of childhood it was not unusual to find a commitment to temperance, for example. And if most people did not attend worship on Sunday they still approved of sabbatarian restrictions. In Scotland and elsewhere children's swings in parks were still locked on Sunday, and while cinemas and concert halls were allowed to open (in 1932), theatres and professional sports grounds, as well as most shops, stayed closed.

On questions concerning sex and marriage, however, 'traditional morality' gradually lost its hold, and the Anglican church in particular lagged behind an increasingly liberal and tolerant Protestant lay opinion. The Anglican ban on birth control was ignored by most of the laity; the Nonconformists left the matter to be decided by the (usually approving) individual conscience. Not till 1958 did the Anglican bishops approve artificial methods and acknowledge that the role of sexuality was emotional as well as reproductive. On divorce, too, the church's policy was restrictive and increasingly unpopular. (In 1912 proposals to permit divorce on grounds of cruelty, incurable insanity or habitual drunkenness had been blocked by an Anglican-led minority.) The church's refusal to remarry even the innocent party in a divorce case, and its denial of the sacraments to those who remarried, caused much bad feeling; when Sir Anthony Eden remarried (in 1952) after his divorce there were references to his 'so-called marriage' by some Anglican hardliners. Even when churches and nation were broadly in agreement, church spokesmen could fail to strike the right note, as in Archbishop Lang's radio broadcast after Edward VIII's abdication, when Lang condemned the king's 'craving for private happiness'.

The social bases of religious practice in this period have not been examined in detail. The indications are that the upper and upper middle classes continued to be the most frequent church-goers, though less so than in the previous century. At the end of the period only about a third of middle-class adults attended regularly.

There was less change in the working classes. As before the war, few were regular church-goers, but many, especially young people, had contacts with the churches on other occasions – at holidays, rites of passage, Sunday schools, church clubs and activities. Attitudes changed little. Most working-class people felt that it was not necessary to go to church to be a Christian, that religion was primarily a matter of kindness and decent behaviour.

It remains unclear whether the religious life of women underwent any important change in this period. Women were somewhat more likely than men to attend services and to pray in private; at church, besides arranging the flowers, they still did most of the Sunday school teaching and more than their share of charitable work. But the churches were also responding to women and their needs in more positive ways, ranging from special services on Mothering Sunday to the big women's organisations like the Mothers' Union and the Catholic League of Mary; during the First World War the Free Churches ordained the first few women ministers. But in the Church of England, though women were elected to parochial church councils and to the Church Assembly, deaconesses met much opposition, based on feelings that menstruation made women 'ceremonially unclean' and that nothing should be done to open the way to women priests.[29]

The religious role of children attracted new interest in this period. In part this was because of the crisis in recruitment and the sharp drop in Sunday school enrolments, which fell by nearly a third between 1930 and 1950 – though at the end of the period about a third of all children were still on the books. It was also due to a new sentimental regard for the child as innately religious, in contrast with the evangelical view of the child as tainted with original sin. Anglican churches saw the introduction of Christmas cribs and the interwar fashion for children's corners, complete with tiny tables and chairs and religious pictures with 'plenty of rabbits and birds in the foreground'.[30] Another innovation was Anglican 'parish communion', a service beginning around 9 a.m. and intended to bring children back to worship alongside their parents in the adult congregation.

Most people in mid-twentieth-century Britain were neither devout nor anti-religious but indifferent; their beliefs were eclectic, questionably orthodox and often inconsistent. Most people believed in God, but only about half believed in an after-life; few accepted the churches'

[29]   Heeney, 'Women's Struggle for Professional Work and Status in the Church of England, 1900–1930', p. 343.

[30]   P. F. Anson, *Fashions in Church Furnishings 1840–1940* (1960), pp. 330–1.

doctrines of judgment, hell and the devil. Horoscopes were extremely popular, and Gorer estimated that about a quarter of the population held an essentially magical view of the universe. A reasonable conclusion was that 'most people nowadays don't think much about religion, don't set much conscious store by it, and have decidedly confused ideas about it'.[31]

The churches were confronted not by hostility but by a civilisation which despite its Christian roots was turning away from Christian concerns. To most people the world was not a vale of tears but a place where some measure of happiness was possible, and where the Christian call to repentance and self-denial no longer seemed relevant. Yet a more secular existence was not for many a vastly more rational or scientific one, and the need for some imaginative or emotional focus in their lives was still widely felt. That, however, could be found as readily outside the churches as within them. Not merely was there religious broadcasting on the radio (where the largest audiences, significantly, were for Sunday Half Hour, a programme of community hymn singing, rather than for broadcasts of formal services), quasi-religious satisfactions could also be found in the arts, in sport (the 'religion' of rugby football in South Wales was proverbial) and in political creeds like socialism and imperialism. The British Empire, for example, was regarded by many not just as a system of rule but as a calling with high moral purpose, something to be believed in; Empire Day, celebrated with church services and a national radio broadcast, had a religious as well as political significance. At a quite different, folkloric level, there was also an 'invisible' or 'implicit' religion in such things as the widespread belief in luck and the belief that misfortune was a punishment for sin. To some extent, then, the gaps left by the decline of the churches were filled by a variety of pre- and post-Christian alternatives. Christian influence on mid-century British society was still considerable, but it owed less to the contemporary churches than to their more vigorous predecessors in the Victorian age.

---

[31]   Gorer, *Exploring English Character*, p. 269; Mass-Observation, *Puzzled People*, p. 14.

This corrected version restores capitalisation to a number of important terms which were erroneously printed in lower case in the original hardback edition of 1990. The Press apologises unreservedly for any embarrassment or confusion caused by this earlier impression.

CHAPTER 7

Philanthropy

F. K. PROCHASKA

I

No country on earth can lay claim to a greater philanthropic tradition than Great Britain. Until the twentieth century philanthropy was widely believed to be the most wholesome and reliable remedy for the nation's ills, a view that is not without adherents today. For every affliction, individual or social, physical or spiritual, the charitable pharmacopoeia has a prescription or at least a palliative. Disease, old age and immorality are perennial problems. Others come and go with the elements or the trade cycle. Others still fall out of fashion or disappear because of medical or technological advance. Little is heard nowadays of cholera victims, chimney sweeps or thirsty horses in the metropolis, yet they all aroused public concern in the nineteenth century. Such causes have given way to those in tune with changed conditions, some of which would amaze, indeed alarm, past philanthropists. What would William Wilberforce or Lord Shaftesbury make of modern voluntary societies in aid of gay rights or family planning? Would they join the National Trust (1895), a charity in receipt of government grants, one of whose purposes is the preservation of country houses emptied of a paternalist aristocracy and gentry? Few subjects bring out so well the differences between ourselves and our ancestors.

As befits a nation in which philanthropists are ubiquitous, enormous sums have been contributed, representing a massive redistribution of wealth. But while financial records exist for many charities, it is impossible to measure the overall sums contributed to philanthropy in a single year or to compare the percentage of national income

I would like to thank Dr John Dinwiddy for his helpful comments.

redistributed at different periods.[1] Some individuals have given away millions of pounds. Eighteenth- and nineteenth-century families at almost every level of the social scale commonly tithed their incomes to charitable causes. A study of middle-class households in the 1890s established that on average they spent a larger share of their income on charity than on any item in their budget except food.[2] A survey of working-class and artisan families in the same decade showed that half of them subscribed weekly to charity and about a quarter of them also made donations to church or chapel.[3] Even after the beginning of this century the sums contributed each year, not including church and chapel collections and unremembered alms, far exceeded government expenditure on poor relief. Philanthropic receipts for London alone, observed *The Times* in 1885, were greater than the budgets of many European states.[4]

Few deny philanthropy's importance, but there have always been sharp disagreements over its character and effects. As Walter Bagehot put it, there is a melancholy doubt 'whether the benevolence of mankind does most harm or good'.[5] Philanthropy's defenders do not doubt its humane effects and say it reflects the nation's genius for the *ad hoc* and institutional, for self-help and personal sacrifice. Critics, on the other hand, judge philanthropy to be largely insensitive to the genuine needs of the poor and see it as a thinly disguised form

---

[1] The financial accounts of voluntary societies are incomplete for the past and remain unstandardised today. The records of charitable trusts – there were 110,000 of them in 1950 according to the Nathan committee – are chaotic and inaccessible. The financial picture is made the more impressionistic by the confusion over what constitutes a charity. Charitable status in law brings considerable tax advantages. Many voluntary societies which have a charitable dimension are not 'registered charities'; current estimates of the total income of voluntary organisations thus vary enormously depending on which bodies are being studied. To complicate the issue further philanthropic fashions and forms have changed over the centuries making comparisons between periods all the more difficult. Casual almsgiving, for example, came under increasing attack in the nineteenth century, but we will never know how much money passed from hand to hand in this way in 1750 or 1950. Charitable income fluctuates with economic conditions, but in just what way and by how much is not obvious. The Wolfenden committee detected a decline in voluntary contributions in Britain following the recession of 1974, but we should not jump to conclusions about the past. The history of philanthropy resists precise measurement.

[2] *Statistics of Middle-Class Expenditure*, British Library of Political and Economic Science, Pamphlet HD6/D267 (n.d.? 1896), Table IX.

[3] *Family Budgets: Being the Income and Expenses of Twenty-Eight British Households, 1891–1894* (1896), p. 75.

[4] *The Times*, 9 Jan. 1885, cited in David Owen, *English Philanthropy, 1660–1960* (1964), p. 469.

[5] Walter Bagehot, *Physics and Politics* (1872), pp. 188–9.

of self-interest. Past radicals and socialists and today's Marxists are inclined to treat it as essentially the preserve of the middle classes, perhaps forgetting the conviction of Engels and others that the poor were more charitable than the rich.[6] A recent trend among historians of Victorian Britain is to interpret charity as a means by which the dominant professional and commercial classes confirmed their power and status. Through philanthropic agencies they sought to 'control' the poor, in the hope of creating a subservient class of Mr Pooters, disciplined and independent, below them.[7] By such means they turned privilege into virtue without undermining existing institutions.

Despite conflicting interpretations, philanthropy has not been a favoured topic among scholars. Many historians shy away from studying practices redolent of hierarchical values and now unfashionable pieties. Existing scholarship focusses our attention on the powerful personalities and the great societies, such as Dr Barnardo's (1867) and the National Society for the Prevention of Cruelty to Children (1884) at the centre of the stage.[8] Humble workers and commonplace institutions and the successions of daily life in which charity played a prominent part remain largely a blur in the background. There has also been a detectable Whiggishness in the historiography, a tendency to see philanthropy primarily as a stage in the evolution of the welfare state. The changing relationship between private and public responsibility for relief is a compelling issue. But a preoccupation with it narrows our understanding of philanthropy and gives the distorted impression that it is a thing of the past.

[6] Friedrich Engels, *The Condition of the Working Class in England*, trans. and ed. W. O. Henderson and W. H. Chaloner (Stanford, 1958), p. 140.

[7] See, e.g., Gareth Stedman Jones, *Outcast London: A Study in the Relationship between Classes in Victorian Society* (Oxford, 1971); A. P. Donajgrodzki, ed., *Social Control in Nineteenth-Century Britain* (1977); R. J. Morris, 'Voluntary Societies and British Urban Elites, 1780–1850: An Analysis', *Historical Journal*, 26 (1983), pp. 95–118. Stedman Jones modified his position on social control. See 'From Historical Sociology to Theoretical History', *British Journal of Sociology*, 27 (1976), pp. 295–305, and 'Class Expression versus Social Control? A Critique of Recent Trends in the Social History of Leisure', *History Workshop*, 4 (1977), pp. 162–70.

[8] For an introduction see Owen, *English Philanthropy*. For Scotland, see Olive Checkland, *Philanthropy in Victorian Scotland: Social Welfare and the Voluntary Principle* (Edinburgh, 1980). See also Brian Harrison, *Peaceable Kingdom: Stability and Change in Modern Britain* (Oxford, 1982). Among recent works on specific institutions see George Behlmer, *Child Abuse and Moral Reform in England, 1870–1908* (Stanford, 1982); Patrick Joyce, *Patronage and Poverty in Merchant Society: The History of Morden College, Blackheath, 1695 to the Present* (Henley-on-Thames, 1982); Asa Briggs and Anne Macartney, *Toynbee Hall: The First Hundred Years* (1984). Among recent biographies see Stewart J. Brown, *Thomas Chalmers and the Godly Commonwealth in Scotland* (Oxford, 1982); G. B. A. M. Finlayson, *The Seventh Earl of Shaftesbury* (1981); and Gillian Wagner, *Barnardo* (1979). See also Frank Prochaska, *The Voluntary Impulse* (1988).

II

It is suggestive to think of the history of philanthropy broadly as the history of kindness. This conveys the importance of philanthropy at all social levels and reveals its implications for individuals, families and communities. The standard definition of philanthropy, or charity, is love of one's fellow man, an inclination or action which promotes the well-being of others.[9] It thus includes benevolence within classes as well as between them; it encompasses a neighbourly visit or a widow's mite as well as the momentous decisions of great charities with international connections and legislative programmes. Cast widely to include informal, domestic expressions of kindness, the philanthropic net catches virtually everyone at one time or another. Often the recipients themselves turned charitable in better days, for one of the striking things about kindness is its contagiousness. Many a workingman, for example, having had the hat passed round for his own emergency, gave generously to others in their time of trouble. It was customary. The springs of philanthropic action are deeply rooted in such customs, often little more than impulses, and in the needs and aspirations of people who respond to their difficulties and ·opportunities in a particular way, whether it be at home, in the pub or in some grander social setting.

'Charity', as the saying goes, 'begins at home'. And where better to launch an investigation, for the benevolent took it for granted that the family was the fundamental social unit of British society, its protection the cornerstone of philanthropic policy. The influential Scottish thinker Thomas Chalmers argued in the early nineteenth century that the best way to sanctify the home was to work through it, a view shared by virtually all philanthropists, from humble visitors dropping in on a neighbour to the directors of the Charity Organisation Society. The managers of institutions such as orphanages, asylums, refuges, and 'homes' saw them in terms of the family and sought to return their charges whenever possible to the domestic fold. Moral reformers and social purity workers from Hannah More to Mary Whitehouse have been at pains to elevate the family in their many and various activities. Abroad, missionaries held up to those they saw as benighted

---

[9] Some historians make a distinction between philanthropy and charity and argue that the former has a broader humanitarian aim, free of religious moralising. See Checkland, *Philanthropy in Victorian Scotland*, p. 2. This distinction may have its uses to the modern scholar, but it was not clear-cut in the past, when the words usually were used interchangeably.

heathens the model of the free and happy British family, ennobled by Christianity's domestic qualities. The home, the very fountain of the nation's life, was the most invigorating image in the philanthropic world and was commonly raised to metaphor. The state itself became the family fully extended, in need of moral regeneration based on familial virtue.

The image of home and family was all the more potent because so often charitable needs and motives had domestic origins. The great diversity of family experience and opinion created the specialised character of much philanthropy. Many an orphanage or lying-in charity owed its existence to the death of an infant or the desire of the childless to find a surrogate family. As Archbishop Tait said of his wife Catharine: 'It cannot be doubted that the ever-present thought of her own children whom she had lost was an incentive to her care for . . . destitute little girls.'[10] Medical charities, great and small, benefited substantially from familial loss due to illness. Domestic education and religious upbringing could be vital in determining philanthropic predilections – children followed in the charitable footpaths travelled by their parents. Class and occupation too influenced philanthropic choices. Ownership of estates brought with it certain charitable responsibilities, sometimes taken with political purposes in mind.[11] Family life among the respectable poor imposed its own distinctive obligations. Diversity and specialisation were then hallmarks of philanthropy stamped by family circumstances.

Whatever one's trouble, whatever one's station, the first place to turn was the family. Even with the state's increased role in social welfare and the expansion of institutional care, the family tie remains crucial. As one east London woman told a social investigator not long ago: 'If anything goes wrong and I'm in trouble I always go running round to Mum's.'[12] Large families were the norm until this century. They often extended to those who, while not blood relations, lived with or depended on the household for a livelihood: servants or employees in a family firm, for instance. Domestic life gave rise to a philanthropic buzz, humming recurrently in a world that was hazardous and unpredictable and, well into this century, relatively

---

[10] William Benham, ed., *Catharine and Craufurd Tait* (1879), p. 76.
[11] F. M. L. Thompson, *English Landed Society in the Nineteenth Century* (1971), pp. 207–8.
[12] Quoted in Peter Willmott and Michael Young, *Family and Class in a London Suburb* (1960), p. 39.

unadministered by the state. Having and raising children, the misfortunes of relatives and servants, sickness and death, required immediate familial assistance. And here, as elsewhere, altruism was rarely pure; it was typically given with an unspoken understanding of mutual obligation. Many of the traditional forms of domestic charity now seem archaic: lying-in and death-bed visiting, the distribution of 'mourning money' to servants on the death of an employer, or 'marriage settlements'. As signs of a distinctive domestic culture they should not be overlooked.[13]

III

The familial and immediate character of so much charitable work is never more striking than in the case of working-class philanthropy, the charity of the poor to the poor. The survey of working-class and artisan families already mentioned reveals that philanthropic subscriptions were not limited to the rich. To ignore this fact is to miss an important feature of working-class life and to encourage a narrow understanding of philanthropy which can reduce it simply to a reflection of class conflict. Historians, perhaps unconsciously, tend to perpetuate the view of many middle-class Victorians, who, according to the Chartist John Collins, had little idea 'that working men possessed any feeling or humanity'.[14] As he was aware, the sympathies of the poor were often expressed privately, and the relative dearth of written evidence of their kindness to one another helped to make its extent underestimated. But those with a first-hand knowledge of working-class life were well aware that egalitarian beneficence came naturally to the poor. Fellow feeling, remarked W. R. Greg in reviewing *Mary Barton*, 'can only exist in its fullest extent among persons of the same condition, surrounded by the same circumstances, inured to the same privations – who know that the distress they are called upon to mitigate was their own yesterday, and may be their own again to-morrow'.[15]

Charity in working-class families was essential in their domestic economy. Clannishness was a strong feeling in poor families, as in rich ones, and hardship brought it to the fore. For large numbers of migrants, such as those to the north-west in the mid-nineteenth

---

[13] Harrison, *Peaceable Kingdom*, p. 220.
[14] Quoted in Brian Harrison, 'Philanthropy and the Victorians', *Victorian Studies*, 9 (1966), p. 369.
[15] *Edinburgh Review*, 69 (1849), p. 410.

century, relatives were a critically important source of assistance.[16] Indeed, it was the likelihood of need that kept many working-class families in touch with each other. It was said that charity within poor families would have been even more pronounced had it not been for the fact that parents or children could be compelled by justices of the peace to maintain members of their immediate family unable to provide for themselves.[17] Once children supported a parent or grandparent they were more likely to be expected to go on doing so; thus the instinct for self-preservation moderated natural generosity. The customary duty of looking after one another was also threatened, as Chalmers warned, by the expectation of support from outside agencies, whether public or private.[18] Nonetheless, charitable practices within working-class families were extensive and poor law guardians were relieved to discover that aged parents, sick and orphaned children were kept off the rates by them. Running out of relatives was a short-cut to the workhouse.

The kindness of neighbours extended the boundaries of the protective familial world in working-class communities. Relatives would be expected to take in kin for long periods; neighbours often provided temporary relief in emergencies. They knew quickly enough when they were needed, for in the cramped conditions of slums and housing estates home life spilled over into public life. Much working-class benevolence of this type was casual, and, not untouched by self-interest, could be little more than the exchange of mutual favours. The part played in it by women was crucial, for their domestic experience and the distinctive world of female relationships established connections between families which contributed much to local welfare.[19] Among the most usual acts were visits to the sick and dying. Also a commonplace was the provision of Sunday dinner, that most

---

[16] M. Anderson, *Family Structure in Nineteenth-Century Lancashire* (Cambridge, 1971), p. 154. See also Standish Meacham, *A Life Apart: The English Working Class 1890–1914* (1977), chap. 2.

[17] See 43 Elizabeth c. 2. s. 7. When this act was passed it was not intended to apply to labourers, but JPs had absolute discretion in the matter.

[18] William Hanna, *Memoirs of the Life and Writings of Thomas Chalmers*, 4 vols. (Edinburgh and London, 1849–52), vol. 1, p. 306.

[19] See Ellen Ross, 'Survival Networks: Women's Neighbourhood Sharing in London before World War I', *History Workshop*, 15 (1983), pp. 4–27. Ross prefers the word 'sharing' to charity or philanthropy, perhaps because of the associations these words have in her mind with the middle classes. Yet 'sharing' tends to diminish the element of kindness and plays down the religious motive among working people, which was often pronounced.

important event among the poor, which meant much from the point of view of self-respect. Free lodging or a reduction in the rent was provided to those in debt. Sums, large and small, were collected by a 'whip round' in that working-class voluntary society, the pub. Friends were found work, holidays sacrificed so that someone else might get a change of air, washing taken in, cooking done, children looked after. The penurious Karl Marx pawned Jenny's coat to relieve a destitute friend.

The need in poor neighbourhoods was often such that it could not be satisfied by spontaneous, informal acts of kindness; thus the poor organised. Many of their societies came and went with the seasons, for example soup kitchens in which the labouring classes handled the operations entirely.[20] Servants set up their own charities to look after servants in distress.[21] Navvies, who had a marked sense of self-help, established sick clubs and visiting societies, complete with navvy officials.[22] Formal subscriptions were taken up, sometimes by trade unions, friendly societies or benefit clubs, often simply by neighbours with common needs and worries. Such donations served a great variety of purposes, from support for infant schools to assisting transported prisoners. At their best, working-class charities were preventive. In Seven Dials in the early nineteenth century a group of workingmen formed the West Street Chapel Benevolent Society in which a committee of twelve met weekly to inspect the books and plan the campaign of relief and religious conversion.[23] The well-run West Birmingham Relief Fund, established in 1892 by workingmen, gave advances to the disabled and paid rent for deserving cases.[24] Working-class philanthropy and self-help commonly merged in medical causes. Well over half of the income of several general hospitals outside London came from humble subscribers.[25]

In the nineteenth century, working-class philanthropists were sometimes singled out for mention, to encourage others and to show that no one class had a monopoly of good works. John Pounds (1766–1839),

[20] William Conybeare, *Charity of Poor to Poor, Facts Collected in South London at the Suggestion of the Bishop of Southwark* (1908), pp. 17–18. On working-class charity see also Harrison, 'Philanthropy and the Victorians', pp. 368–9.

[21] *The Servants' Institution* (1835); C. S. Dudley, *An Analysis of the System of the Bible Society throughout its Various Parts* (1821), p. 355.

[22] Elizabeth Garnett, *Our Navvies: A Dozen Years Ago and To-day* (1885), pp. 215–33.

[23] Anthony Highmore, *Pietas Londinensis* (1810), pp. 920–1.

[24] *RC on the Aged Poor*, PP 1895, XV, pp. 885, 888.

[25] Brian Abel-Smith, *The Hospitals, 1800–1948* (1964), p. 250.

shoemaker and founder of ragged schools, and Sarah Martin (1791–1843), seamstress and prison visitor, were perhaps the most celebrated examples. Only the occasional memoir or chance reference preserves the memory of others. Kitty Wilkinson of Liverpool, once dependent on poor relief, turned to sick visiting, supported orphans and founded public washhouses.[26] A former domestic servant, Eliza Plomer, worked for crippled children in Marylebone.[27] Lydia Reid, servant and Spitalfields silk winder, held adult reading classes and mothers' meetings, and took in to her home an orphan and her mother-in-law.[28] David 'Navvy' Smith became a missionary on the Great Central in the 1890s and ran the Good Samaritan Home outside Nottingham for tramp navvies.[29] Others could be identified, including many ragged school and Sunday school teachers, Bible women and Bible nurses, and humble Salvation Army workers. They represent the poor of respectability and quiet progress. In improving the conditions of life they made a contribution which, noted in the past, should not go unrecognised today.

Personal emergency, epidemic, trade depression or simply everyday experience in the slums brought out a resilience and personal sacrifice at which the outsider could only marvel. Engels reported in the Chartist years what socially conscious clerics knew in greater detail: that it was through working-class 'charitable' practices that 'large numbers of the surplus population manage to survive a crisis'.[30] Just before the First World War, the clergyman William Conybeare, who compiled a social survey of south London, was at first mystified by the thousands of unemployed who, untouched by agencies for relief, never became paupers or entered the workhouse. He concluded: 'The poor breathe an atmosphere of charity. They cannot understand life without it. And it is largely this kindness of the poor to the poor which stands between our civilization and revolution.'[31] He might have added that the poor law authority and the voluntary societies run by the well-to-do were saved much time and money by the customs of benevolence and self-help among the poor. If some social reformers had their way,

---

[26] Herbert R. Rathbone, ed., *Memoir of Kitty Wilkinson of Liverpool 1786–1860* (Liverpool, 1927).
[27] *Reformation and Refuge Journal* (March 1864), pp. 46–7.
[28] Mary Pryor Hack, *Self-Surrender* (1882), pp. 215–33.
[29] Dick Sullivan, *Navvyman* (1983), pp. 211–12.
[30] Engels, *The Condition of the Working Class in England*, p. 102.
[31] Conybeare, *Charity of Poor to Poor*, p. 6.

more public money would have been spent in propping up these traditions.[32]

IV

In many charities working-class men, women and children joined together with the higher classes in a common cause. The precise extent of this co-operative benevolence is impossible to measure, though the second half of the nineteenth century was probably the heyday of its institutional forms. It varied considerably from place to place, depending on, among other things, local philanthropic traditions and the existence of a resident middle class. The belief in material and spiritual improvement cut across class lines and acted as powerful incentives in bringing together volunteers from different backgrounds. Whatever one's station, contributions to philanthropic causes were a sign of that much sought after status, respectability. For those with social ambition, contact with better-off neighbours was essential. It acted as a spring-board for many working people who wished to integrate into the existing social and economic system.

Whether working in philanthropic causes with their social superiors or not, respectable working people wanted to promote good health, educational opportunity and family life free from dependence on alms or the workhouse. Undoubtedly philanthropy spread middle-class values up and down the social scale, but most people, however humble, did not need to be reminded that fitness, decency and independence were wholesome. Nor were those telling distinctions between the 'deserving' and 'undeserving' absent from the vocabulary of the poor. As philanthropists they did not wish to waste time and money on fraudulent cases, but sought to look after the genuine troubles of their communities. Assistance from well-wishers up the social hierarchy could provide them with added protection against adversity. Co-operative benevolence, often kindled and extended by the poor themselves, worked to unite the nation's aspirations, contributing to social stability and a common culture.

The forms of co-operative benevolence were diverse. Special collections for emergencies and disasters, not unknown before 1750, brought the classes into contact. The Mansion House Funds, which relieved unemployment and other calamities, often listed 'working

---

[32] See, e.g., Eleanor Rathbone, *The Disinherited Family* (1924).

men' and 'servants' among subscribers in the nineteenth century. But most charities in which the classes mixed were small, typically parish-based and sought to keep the immediate community's body and soul intact. The better-off assisted their poorer neighbours in setting up and running provident societies, savings banks, ragged and Sunday schools, mechanics' institutes, lying-in and visiting charities, mothers' meetings, missionary associations, clothing and boot clubs, temperance societies and village libraries. In port and garrison towns and in cities where there was a marked geographical divide between the classes, middle-class philanthropists gave financial assistance and advice. A working-man's pastoral aid society in Liverpool run along these lines had 2,000 subscribers.[33] On a larger scale was the White Cross Army, founded in 1883 by the moral reformer Ellice Hopkins and the Bishop of Durham. Excluding women from the ranks, it recruited thousands of workingmen to the cause of social purity. Volunteers pledged to mind their manners, to show a 'chivalrous respect for womanhood' and to support legal reform for women and children. The society, which had a particularly large following among Yorkshire miners and artisans, spread to other parts of the Empire and North America and may be seen as part of the nation's moral arsenal.[34]

Of all the long-standing charitable campaigns, the foreign missionary and Bible societies were probably the most adept at getting the co-operation of the poor. Some of them enjoyed incomes in excess of £100,000 a year in the nineteenth century; domestic missions, by contrast, were poor relations. This imbalance was a scandal to critics like Dickens, who believed that charitable resources were better spent in Holborn than in Borrioboola-Gha. But to many philanthropists, especially evangelicals, foreign and domestic missions were indivisible, part of a common crusade. Industrious penny-a-week subscribers, working side by side with their wealthier neighbours were essential to the success of mission work at home and abroad. They represented the heart of an idealised Christian community without frontiers. However impoverished the Briton might be, the African or Asian could be made to look more wretched. The *Bible Class Magazine* calculated in 1848 that 36,860,000,000 heathens had died during the

---

[33] A. Hume, *Analysis of the Subscribers to the Various Liverpool Charities* (Liverpool, 1855), p. 11.

[34] Ellice Hopkins, *The White Cross Army: A Statement of the Bishop of Durham's Movement* (1883); *White Cross League Church of England Society Twelfth Annual Report* (1895).

Christian era and that thirty-eight still died every minute. 'Reader, what influence should these facts have upon your mind.'[35]

With their idealism and their calculus of souls won and pennies lost the missionary and Bible societies set up thousands of associations in working-class parishes around the country. At headquarters these institutions were fundamentally middle class. But in the branches they took on the character of the community. As early as 1820 there were seventeen Bible associations among Liverpool mechanics attached to the Bible Society.[36] Among seamen, the same charity counted thousands of subscribers, a phenomenon not unconnected with the evangelical revival on the upper deck.[37] The Methodist Missionary Society received over £1 million from children alone in the nineteenth century, much of it from working-class juvenile associations and Sunday schools.[38] It is impossible to put a percentage on working-class subscriptions, but they were believed to be 'the most precious portion' by the missionary movement.[39] 'Poor contributions', announced the *Christian Mother's Magazine* in 1845, 'whether we consider the proportion which they bear to the whole wealth of the givers, or their aggregate amount are, in effect, beyond all comparison the most important.'[40] Self-respecting dispensers of charity, it might have added, were unlikely to become parochial charges.

Charitable co-operation between the classes could be imaginative in technique. Where humble volunteers were in short supply the use of paid working-class missioners or Bible women was widespread. In towns and villages the well-to-do sometimes took it upon themselves to hire working-class visitors to canvass poor neighbourhoods. In cities this innovation became highly organised in the mid-Victorian years and is perhaps best illustrated by Ellen Ranyard's Bible and Domestic Female Mission, founded in 1857. Her Bible women and later Bible nurses, drawn from the districts being visited, were given a three-month course in subjects ranging from scripture to the poor law and paid about £30 a year in the 1860s. Familiar figures in the slums, they worked closely with lady supervisors. As elsewhere, self-help was a priority and from the London poor alone Bible women

---

[35]   *Bible Class Magazine*, 1 (1848), p. 15.
[36]   Dudley, *An Analysis of the System of the Bible Society*, p. 265.
[37]   *Ibid.*, pp. 327–40.
[38]   F. K. Prochaska, *Women and Philanthropy in Nineteenth-Century England* (Oxford, 1980), pp. 82–3.
[39]   *Evangelical Magazine*, n.s., 29 (1851), p. 226.
[40]   *Christian Mother's Magazine*, 2 (1845), p. 640.

collected £44,000 in ten years to be put into provident schemes. An ingenious mixture of working-class and middle-class employees and volunteers, Mrs Ranyard's society pioneered social casework well before the Charity Organisation Society and the National Society for the Prevention of Cruelty to Children, the charities usually given credit for the innovation. By 1862 there were Bible women in virtually every city in England and the idea soon spread to other parts of the world.[41]

By the mid-nineteenth century, prevailing laissez-faire ideas strengthened the resolve of the middle classes to promote philanthropic co-operation with their poorer neighbours. Self-reliance and thrift were social gospel, and charities taken up by working people commonly fostered these traits. As charitable co-operation assisted in the social and political integration of the working classes, it represented an implied attack on aristocratic power.[42] To the commercial mind aristocratic philanthropy, widely associated with almsgiving and ancient endowments, led to indigence and servility. It was unbusinesslike. The benevolence of industrialists often merged with sound business practices. In their support for evening classes, Sunday schools and social improvements at 'the works' they expected a return. Such encouragement to working-class self-help is often described as paternalism (as so much of it was carried out by women, 'maternalism' might be more apt), but it was certainly a break with traditional aristocratic paternalism.[43] Yet, like the aristocracy, the middle classes used philanthropy to justify their social position and expected loyalty from their social inferiors. In the face-to-face immediate setting, philanthropy invigorated deferential behaviour, giving it the character of a moral relationship.

All was not smooth sailing, of course, between rich and poor in their joint philanthropic ventures. (There was often tension enough between middle-class and upper-class contributors in charities.) In line with their own traditions, large numbers of working people willingly joined philanthropic causes, but they often calculated the advantages and disadvantages of doing so. Like the higher classes, their charitable associations were a sign of status or, as has been suggested,

---

[41] Prochaska, *Women and Philanthropy in Nineteenth-Century England*, pp. 126–30. On the Ranyard nurses see F. K. Prochaska, 'Body and Soul: Bible Nurses and the Poor in Victorian London', *Historical Research*, 60 (1987), pp. 336–48.

[42] Harrison, *Peaceable Kingdom*, pp. 229–30.

[43] For a discussion of paternalism see David Roberts, *Paternalism in Early Victorian England* (New Brunswick, NJ, 1979), and Patrick Joyce, *Work, Society and Politics: The Culture of the Factory in Later Victorian England* (Brighton, 1980), chap. 4.

a means of advancement. They were frequently a way of keeping on the right side of an employer. Domestic servants and workers in family firms were particularly vulnerable to pressure from employers to make subscriptions or to support a school or mothers' meeting. They could only resist such pressure at some risk. As one critic complained in the early nineteenth century, the poor often gave to charity because of 'solicitations' from their employers and not out of compassion.[44] Those many seamen who subscribed to the Bible Society cannot all have been enthusiastic about joining in ship's prayers or paying for their own testaments. If so, the Society would not have had to ask pawnbrokers to refuse Bibles issued with its imprint.[45]

V

The ruling classes largely took it for granted that deference would flow from their philanthropy. But in times of particular social tension, most notably during the French Revolution and the Napoleonic Wars, they openly expressed a desire to subordinate the lower classes through charitable agencies, especially schools and visiting societies. At the end of the eighteenth century Mrs Sarah Trimmer, a founder of Sunday schools, recommended that the women of England visit the poor in their own homes as a means of averting social unrest.[46] And one of the objects of the Bible Society some years later was to evoke in the labouring population 'the duty of loyalty, and subordination to their superiors'.[47] Such views represented an explicit attack on working-class life, but how sinister was it when many causes were a reflection of shared values and willing co-operation? Moreover, it is easy to overplay the effects of pressure to conform to middle-class manners and morals, for it was possible for the recipients of charity to take what they wanted from philanthropic institutions without imbibing cultural values. There are many ways round philanthropists, and reactions to them ranged from gratitude and compliance, through disingenuousness and hypocrisy, to hostility and violence.

The concept of 'social control' which has been introduced to explain

---

[44] Bodleian Library, William Conybeare to Mrs Hodge, n.d., Montagu MSS, d. 12, fo. 131. See also *Bible Associations Exposed: Being a Review of the Fourth Annual Report of the Committee of the Henley Bible Society* (1818), p. 15.
[45] Richard Lloyd, *Strictures on a Recent Publication Entitled 'The Church her own Enemy'* (1819), p. 128.
[46] Sarah Trimmer, *The Oeconomy of Charity*, 2 vols. (1801), vol. 2, pp. 57–9.
[47] Dudley, *An Analysis of the System of the Bible Society*, p. 535.

charitable action is rather murky and reductionist, for the wish to make others conform to the same values and speak the same language is implicit in social relations generally, from family life to national politics.[48] When associated with concepts such as 'bourgeois hegemony' it may also be misleading, for it begs the question whether there was a revolutionary proletariat in need of control. Historians find it difficult to deal with 'social control' when it is implicit and unconscious. And as a conscious philanthropic motive it is easily over-played. Fear of social unrest cannot explain the persistence of chari-table subscriptions through changing political circumstances. Sunday schools, visiting charities and the Bible and tract societies did not lose support after 1815 or 1848. If fear of domestic revolution was a crucial consideration, the ruling classes could have done a more effective job of controlling their social inferiors by passing general statutes. To rely on the chaos of *ad hoc* charitable institutions, many of which were rivals and at cross-purposes, was not a very efficient form of subduing the disaffected.

Whether working in co-operation with their poor neighbours or setting out on their own, the philanthropic activities of the well-to-do were often a response to the complaints and aspirations of the needy, moderated by their own perceptions of what was required and the best way to proceed. It was far easier for the rich to fall into line with widely recognised needs and customs than to impose their will against the grain of the community. In areas where they lived or worked side by side with the poor this was particularly so. In manufac-turing districts they provided schools, refreshment rooms and sick nurses. In port towns they favoured missions for seamen, life boats and truss societies. The latter were of considerable importance, for it was estimated in 1818 that about one in five of the entire male population in ports and manufacturing districts had a hernia.[49] Con-ditions, then, commonly dictated the forms of benevolence; and the rich were usually willing to contribute to a cause if it did not contradict their principles or undermine their social position. Popular forms of

---

[48] See F. M. L. Thompson, 'Social Control in Victorian Britain', *Economic History Review*, 2nd ser., 34 (1981), pp. 189–208; Stedman Jones, 'Class Expression versus Social Control?', pp. 162–70. On the labour aristocracy and 'hegemony' see Geoffrey Cros-sick, *An Artisan Elite in Victorian Society: Kentish London, 1840–1880* (1978), pp. 20, 134.

[49] *City of London Truss Society for the Relief of the Ruptured Poor throughout the Kingdom* (1818), p. 3.

charity which brought them into contact with respectable working people enhanced it.

During much of our period local philanthropic institutions held out to the population the prospect of self-help and Christian community compatible with a rooted sense of social hierarchy. Popular forms of charity merged with daily life while tying families and employees to local and national charitable campaigns and, no less important, immediate business interests. If this world of give and take is described as a form of 'bourgeois hegemony' it was one which operated in an atmosphere of little overt conflict. The well-to-do would have been surprised, indeed upset, to see their charitable work challenged. Those below them, often unsure of their social position, tended to disguise their feelings and exaggerate respect. Much of what was on offer from their social superiors was broadly welcomed, particularly medical treatment, education and recreation.

The example of Carrow Works in Norwich, the manufacturing centre of Colman's mustard, was typical of the way in which provincial Victorian philanthropy encouraged local residents and employees to identify with their communities. Caroline Colman, wife of the wealthy manufacturer and Liberal MP for Norwich James Colman, set about her good works promptly upon her marriage in 1856. Guided by her religious conscience and a strong belief in self-help, she initiated various schools attached to the works. Technical classes were provided for up to 200 men and sewing and cooking classes for the women. She taught the children herself in the Sunday school until her daughters were old enough to carry on the tradition. Through such institutions, particularly the Sunday school, various national charities, including the Bible Society, the London Missionary Society and the RSPCA were supported. So too was the local hospital. This was typical of the way in which the provinces provided the financial base for the campaigns of large, often national institutions. Without the aggressive, ingenious money making of well-connected provincial women like Mrs Colman, the great societies would have dried up for want of funds.

No aspect of the employees' lives at Carrow Works was overlooked by Mrs Colman. With her husband's encouragement she hired sick visitors and nurses for them, provided a blanket and parcel distribution and at Christmas distributed hampers and works' almanacs of her own design. She established or oversaw a home for girls, a lending library, refreshment rooms at the factory, a milk scheme for children, mothers' meetings, a medical club, a sick benefit society with 500 members, a clothing club with 960 members and almshouses for pensioners. These and other charitable activities she fitted in to the demands of her household and the care of her six children, who were given a strong sense of community responsibility. Her sole complaint was that she did not have enough time to spend on civic life in Norwich and its numerous charities. But her concentration on Carrow proved a shrewd and effective combination of Christian charity and sound business. The aim was 'to raise the moral as well as the commercial standing of the firm'.[50] Most of her charities survived her; few people in Carrow were left untouched.

The degree to which charity saturated people's lives, both givers and recipients, is difficult to imagine for anyone who has grown up in the shadow of the welfare state. A glimpse of the Rothschild Buildings in the East End, themselves a part of late Victorian 'philanthropy at 4 per cent', is as telling as the life at Carrow Works. Apart from the extensive network of casual benevolence performed daily by the residents, organised societies luxuriated. Run mostly by women, often with the assistance of the poor of the tenements, they included: Sick Room Helps' Society, Jews' Lying-in Charity, Israelite Widows' Society, Jewish Soup Kitchen, Whitechapel Children's Care Committee, Boot Club, Clothing Club, Children's Penny Dinner Society, Ragged Schools' Union, Bare Foot Mission, Children's Country Holiday Fund, Jewish Ladies' Clothing Association and a Savings Bank run by St Jude's School. This concentration of 'charity, thrift, and paternalistic interference in the lives of the respectable working class', remarks the historian of the Buildings, 'was to steal its way into every pore' of the residents, particularly the children.[51] This would not have happened, it should be said, if the 'respectable working class' had not co-operated or had not reaped some benefit from the charitable world which engulfed them.

VI

The recipients of philanthropy were not invariably at the bottom of the social hierarchy. As firm believers in self-help and mutual aid the privileged classes looked after their own with an enthusiasm

[50] Laura E. Stuart, *In Memoriam Caroline Colman* (Norwich, 1896), p. 56 and *passim*. See also *Carrow Works Magazine*, 1 (1907).
[51] Jerry White, *Rothschild Buildings: Life in an East End Tenement Block 1887–1920* (1980), p. 148 and *passim*.

strongly tinged by self-interest. Indeed, here was the closest they would come as philanthropists to having their cake and giving it away. As with their social inferiors, familial visiting and general neighbourliness kept many gentlefolk from falling too far in station. But this assistance was insufficient for many in reduced circumstances or poor health who needed more permanent propping up: debtors for example, or orphans of professional men, aged widows of naval and military officers, and superannuated governesses. Thus members of the wealthier classes often found themselves dependent on charity. In time more and more of them found themselves in institutions.

Charity within the privileged classes represented one of the fastest growing forms of philanthropic endeavour from the late eighteenth century onwards. Many institutions made annual grants to applicants, focussing on particular professions and localities. Typical of these were the Society for Relief of Widows and Orphans of Medical Men in London and its Vicinity, the London Clergy Orphan Fund and the Royal Navy Benevolent Society. Some charities, like the National Benevolent Institution, founded in 1812, provided pensions to a wider range of applicant, including indigent gentry, decayed merchants and former tutors and governesses.[52] The growth of such institutions may have been connected with the reform of crown pensions, which began in the late eighteenth century and gradually reduced the number of well-connected pensioners on the government payroll. By the mid-nineteenth century scores of pension and benefit societies existed in London alone and catered to genteel applicants, from artists to old Etonians. Aged and incapacitated 'ladies' made a particularly powerful call on public sympathy; and by the First World War seventy convalescent and rest homes, many by the seaside, joined the long list of pension and benefit societies which specialised in their needs.[53]

Funds were plentiful but conditions of entry stringent in those residential charities associated with genteel distress. Like institutions which dealt with the lower classes, they were commonly run on an explicit system of patronage. Subscribers to orphanages, almshouses and homes of various descriptions had voting rights, and for a fixed contribution they could nominate and elect applicants for relief. As the selection of candidates gave publicity and power to subscribers, it was a clever method of extracting funds. But the system was inefficient and much abused, and it came under sharp attack in the second

[52]   Sampson Low, *The Charities of London* (1850), p. 236.
[53]   *Annual Charities Register and Digest* (1910), pp. 131–4, 149–50, 191–5.

half of the nineteenth century, though many charities continued the practice into the 1930s. As Florence Nightingale remarked, it was 'the best method for electing the least eligible'.[54] Elections resembled the casino or the race track as rival subscribers backed favoured candidates; and they were not above striking deals. Seeing an applicant home in a highly competitive field was no small achievement and success highlighted the influence of the sponsor and the indebtedness of the nominee.

Those familiar tags 'deserving' and 'undeserving' played their part in the proceedings of voting charities and perhaps had a special meaning for the genteel applicant, whose hardship and dependency had about them a whiff of failure. Such people were, after all, to be models of respectable independence. Their application to an almshouse or home was likely to be a last resort. The fall from familial grace resulted in a difficult adjustment and a degree of acquiescence to charitable authority. In their new surroundings they could be made to feel in need of moral reformation. Institutional regulations were often petty and demeaning, and the preoccupation with rectitude, which was pronounced in the nineteenth century, a source of friction. Here was a subtle form of social subordination within the middle classes which historians, even those given to theories of social control, have rather ignored.[55] In residential institutions the inmates must have felt something of the stigma that is usually associated with the poor in receipt of charity. Conditions were luxurious by comparison with what the poor might expect, but reactions were not dissimilar. The history of Morden College in Blackheath, for example, a residential home for necessitous merchants, shows that the tacit acceptance of charitable authority was punctuated by outbreaks of resistance, most notably in the form of drunken and disorderly conduct.[56]

VII

The response of those on the receiving end of charity was predictably various. As the numerous letters from beneficiaries will testify, the merits of much philanthropic work, particularly in health and education, are undeniable. The charity hospitals, most of which were absorbed by the National Health Service in 1948, were among the

[54] Quoted in Owen, *English Philanthropy* p. 48.
[55] An exception to this is Joyce, *Patronage and Poverty in Merchant Society*, chap. 4.
[56] *Ibid.*, p. 56.

glories of British life. Genteel or humble, many recipients were grateful for services rendered or found opportunities for self-improvement. Others, not least those in need of residential care, disliked the presumption of philanthropists and found the very act of applying for charity humiliating. Thousands of prostitutes voluntarily entered Magdalene homes in the late nineteenth century when rescue work became the rage, but they commonly resented the stringent rules and having their heads shaved as a symbol of guilt. One prostitute, who eventually returned to the streets, complained: 'I was so miserable always thinking about my sins.'[57] Discipline in remedial institutions was severe and the lavish use of scripture and soap sought to break down pride and scour the sinner in preparation for conversion. It was no accident that such a regime resembled that which obtained in evangelical families. Philanthropists moved between their immediate family and their extended family with relative ease.

When mixed with wormwood and gall, compassion sometimes led to a 'kindness that kills'. It produced embarrassment and conflict not only inside institutions but outside as well. As might be imagined, the man from the Vice Society or the RSPCA was an unwelcome guest at a cockfight. (What does today's fox-hunter think of the anti-blood sports activist who hounds him?) Philanthropists courted unpopularity, especially those moral reformers radiating self-righteousness. The door slammed in the face was a common form of deflection, as many tract distributors and district visitors discovered. Randy soldiers and sailors commonly resisted the tender mercies of rescue workers, who threatened to frustrate their favourite pastime, chasing whores. In the 1870s and 1880s, when the social purity movement reached a climax, interfering ladies scolded suspicious-looking couples on park benches or on public transport. The rebukes, rotten eggs and occasional assault meted out to them did little to dampen their enthusiasm. They believed the stakes were high, for as St Paul warned: 'If ye live by the flesh, ye shall die. . .'. Some of them, however, acted as though they were St Peter, but without his keys. They needed to be reminded that a fixation with sin could get in the way of a reputation for forgiveness.

If hostility to philanthropists was not uncommon, exploitation of them was rife. Charitable resources were often administered amateurishly and recipients could easily take advantage, particularly in those

---

[57]   Ellice Hopkins, *Notes on Penitentiary Work* (1879), p. 5.

cities where the wealthier classes lived apart and where it was difficult to distinguish between real and feigned distress. Begging-letter writers lived off the rich with reputations for benevolence. It was estimated in 1838 that in London alone about 1,000 such letters were written a day.[58] Dissembling parents scrubbed their children for the visiting lady in the hope of extracting a few bob. As one East End boy remembered about his father's reactions to the Ragged School Mission: 'They'll be round today . . . now mind, you behave yourself.'[59] Some, changing their religion from visitor to visitor, found themselves attending different church and chapel services several nights a week.[60] Artful mendicants roamed the neighbourhoods of the rich with fictitious tales of woe. As one Yorkshire beggar told a lady visitor when asked if he could read or write 'No Ma'am I can't, . . . and if I'd known as much when I was a child as I do now, I'd never have learnt to walk or talk.'[61] A skin-deep calculated deference which could end in pauperism was one unintended consequence of charitable action. It was a continual source of anxiety to the philanthropic world, a stimulus to rethinking aims and tactics, and a point of criticism.

VIII

Though increasingly on the defensive, the charitable were not easily reasoned out of their humanity by the likes of Harriet Martineau and the dismal scientists of the *Westminster Review*. Despite the criticism, often oblivious to it, they remained ready to do battle with sin and suffering. This was not simply because misfortune, irreligion or fear of social unrest called forth their works, or because the state was reluctant to intervene in the social sphere. There is a philanthropic *disposition*, Christian in character, geared to the giver as well as the recipient. Many a fervent Christian, having little regard to material need or social science, confused the family Bible for a pharmacopoeia. This led to pious self-indulgence and much of the arbitrary and inefficient philanthropy which critics laid at his door. But unmoved by such misconceived criticism, he produced a flurry of good works in the best of times as in the worst, disproportionate to the need of

[58] James Grant, *Sketches in London* (1838), p. 4.
[59] Raphael Samuel, ed., *East End Underworld: Chapters in the Life of Arthur Harding* (1981), p. 24.
[60] RC on the Aged Poor, PP 1895, XIV, p. 222.
[61] *Westminster Review*, 135 (1891), p. 373.

the recipients perhaps, but proportionate to his own. To religious enthusiasts, charitable motives may be independent of social and economic conditions, though they may accommodate to them. This helps to explain why the relatively prosperous mid-Victorian period was a philanthropic golden age. What would be the repercussions for charity and welfare in a time of Christian decline?

The philanthropic disposition was inseparable from religion in the Christian mind, the word charity itself synonymous with the conduct of Christ. As one writer put it 'uncharitableness is that which strikes at the heart of Christianity'.[62] This view was especially strong among evangelicals or Bible Christians, who set the pace and tone of philanthropy from the late eighteenth century onwards. There were, of course, many philanthropists who were not religious, or being religious were not Christian. Some Jewish charity may be seen as a defence of Judaism, a response to the raids made on it by evangelical institutions such as the formidable London Society for Promoting Christianity amongst the Jews (1809). Among Christians, some denominations gave greater prominence to good works; most had philanthropic emphases. Low church Anglicans favoured tract and Bible societies; Unitarians promoted educational causes; Congregationalists and Methodists, among other enthusiasms, were well represented in the temperance movement. For dissenters and Catholics (and women and the working classes) the choice of charitable emphasis was all the more important because they were excluded politically for much of our period. Philanthropy contributed to their integration.

In the late eighteenth and nineteenth centuries the character and intensity of religious belief was such that an outpouring of good works co-existed with the fatalistic attitude toward poverty which marked economic thinking after Malthus. With its individualistic ethic, British Protestantism was compatible with laissez-faire doctrine. Philanthropic enterprise was, in a sense, laissez-faire capitalism turned in on itself. Charities proliferated in a liberal society splintered by religious, class, local and occupational allegiances. They competed for converts and custom. But unlike liberal economists, philanthropists tended to look beyond material life to eternity. This was a source of their vitality and helps to explain their strength in a less than ideal intellectual climate. As the socialist Rachel McMillan argued, the religious temper is 'forged in red caverns of love and hate ... with seeing eyes and

---

[62]   A Lady, *The Whole Duty of Woman or, a Guide to the Female Sex, from the Age of Sixteen to Sixty* (Stourbridge, 1815), p. 23.

conscious choice'. By contrast 'liberalism happened along'.[63] Christianity, she might have added, is not simply a theory of past and future events, but something that actually happens to people. Sin, conversion, the ministry of works are experienced as real events, bringing with them a large measure of emotional turmoil.

In unsettling the emotions, religious experience proved a great spur to philanthropic activity, especially among Bible Christians, for whom heaven and hell were realities. By the end of the eighteenth century many evangelicals, including such influential figures as John Wesley and William Wilberforce, had rejected Calvinist predestination in favour of the view that salvation was conditional and provisional. In their daily lives this resulted in a preoccupation with sin, a fear of backsliding and the elevation of works, particularly those of a missionary character. Benevolence was not simply, as doctrine would have it, a natural result of conversion, the product of a true acceptance of the Gospel covenant. In religious diary after diary, good works follow closely upon spiritual vacillation, an immediate, deeply felt struggle with Satan. They were stored up against the Day of Judgment. Zealots commonly visited the poor, or worked for a tract society or charity school, not because of certainty of grace, but because of fear of damnation. Their 'heartburning', harangues and supplication suggest that their needs were as great as the needs of those they wished to serve. When they were looking into the souls of fellow-sinners, they were nursing their own souls and fortifying themselves against the terrors of self-examination.

IX

The Christian disposition to benevolence was forged in that ubiquitous 'cavern of love and hate', the home. British Christianity had a pronounced domestic character, and never more so than after the eighteenth-century religious revival. With the rise of class consciousness in the nineteenth century, families became more self-sufficient and cherished their religious privacy and independence.[64] In many homes family prayers and Scripture readings were as important as church

---

[63] Margaret McMillan, *The Life of Rachel McMillan* (1927), p. 89.
[64] James Obelkevich, *Religion and Rural Society: South Lindsey 1825–1875* (Oxford, 1976), p. 313.

attendance. In the development of domestic religious sentiment women played a most active part. They were quick to take advantage of any informality in church or chapel activities and happily brought religious practices into the home, where they had greater authority. This trend was marked among evangelicals, where religious experience was a question of individual conscience and where parish work was relatively open to women. As a faith which placed service above doctrine, evangelicalism had a special appeal to women. It suited their view of themselves as moral and compassionate, and they could turn it to their advantage, not least in the education of their children.

The home was the foremost school in society, and the rigorous religious education given there to countless children, particularly the girls, inculcated habits of benevolence from an early age. Among the pious and respectable, familial duty was clear, and before the rise of compulsory state education, there was more than a grain of truth in the view: 'yes, mother, that little child of yours is mainly what you choose to make it'.[65] It was on mother's knee that a child was first taught to fear the Lord and bear the burden of moral accountability. Parental watchfulness, 'intimidation' as one critic called it,[66] began in infancy; and one of the earliest lessons drummed into children was the need to be charitable. Many parents imposed the habit of giving before benevolent impulses had any chance to develop, thus giving children's good works a sometimes mechanical character. The explanation for parental anxiety lies partly in their fear, in a time of high child mortality, that a son or daughter might die before conversion. Acts of kindness were a hopeful sign that progress towards conversion was being made. The decision to contribute and distinguish between charitable objects was, moreover, part of a child's moral training and self-discipline. Children's memoirs themselves (a phenomenon of nineteenth-century publishing) are full of examples of small acts of mercy and the concern of parents to point their young down the straight and narrow, into what Hannah More called the 'right channel of Christian Benevolence'.[67]

Among the most common channels of indoctrination were working parties and Dorcas meetings, which combined compassion,

[65] [Eleanor C. Price], *Schoolboy Morality: An Address to Mothers* (1886), p. 5.
[66] *Westminster Review*, 135 (1891), p. 306.
[67] Hannah More, *Moral Sketches of Prevailing Opinions and Manners* (1819), p. 214. For a list of several children's memoirs see Prochaska, *Women and Philanthropy in Nineteenth-Century England*, p. 74.

needlework and prayer. Whether attached to a national charity or simply an informal domestic meeting, such gatherings were an integral part of middle-class religious life in the Victorian and Edwardian years. They provide us with one of the more enduring Victorian images: devoted mothers surrounded by their children stitching and praying. Run on a weekly basis, members spent hours in ritualised instruction and supplied goods to families, church or chapel, needy neighbours, the annual bazaar and mission stations. Here was the source of the clutter of needlework and baubles that we associate with the Victorian drawing room. Didactic in purpose, they inculcated patriotism and industry, made more palatable by gossip, refreshments and lantern lectures. One of the common denominators of philanthropic activity, they were schools of good works, in which benevolence merged with day-to-day pastimes and recreations.

Another local institution, which recruited vast numbers of working-class women and children, was the mothers' meeting. In it, maternalism and the Victorian ideal of parochial service neatly joined. By the 1880s, most organisations dealing with poor relief sponsored mothers' meetings, and commentators as diverse as Lord Shaftesbury and Charles Booth thought them to be among the most practical and successful forms of philanthropy.[68] Membership figures, although fragmentary, suggest that in the Edwardian years perhaps as many as a million women and children attended meetings each week. In Lambeth alone there were fifty-seven meetings run by Anglicans and nonconformists, with 3,600 members.[69] The Mothers' Union (1876) could boast over 9,000 branches and 435,000 members, many of them cottage wives, during the First World War (it has about the same number of members today).[70] Supervised by ladies, often with the assistance of working-class missioners, meetings typically had about fifty or sixty regular members, who listened to stories or lectures while bowed over their needles. The meetings offered cheap clothing to poor families, relief from domestic drudgery, a source of female comradeship, training for children, respectability and, for many, the consolation of religion. In time, the organisers gave more and more attention to social schemes, medical benefits, and infant welfare. Like the

---

[68] See F. K. Prochaska, 'A Mother's Country: Mothers' Meetings and Family Welfare in Britain, 1850–1950', *History*, 74 (1989).

[69] Jeffrey Cox, *The English Churches in a Secular Society: Lambeth 1870–1930* (Oxford, 1982), pp. 71–3.

[70] *Mothers' Union Official Handbook* (1917), p. xvii.

working party or Dorcas meeting, the mothers' meeting relieved the rigours of self-help with outings and teas.

Philanthropy was prominent as a recreation in the past, especially for children in communities cut off from the centres of culture. Among evangelicals generally and Quakers in particular, restrictions on entertainment and dress reduced the diversions available, highlighting charitable celebrations. Memoirs and devotional literature are rich in detail on entertainments with philanthropic purposes, some of which may seem quaint and comical, but which were widespread and avoided only with difficulty by the respectable, whatever their station. Among the commonplace were children's bazaars, ladies' sales and jumble sales, charity balls, dinners and concerts, preparations for Boxing Day, Sunday school marches and outings, and the festivities surrounding the opening of collection boxes for one of the great London societies. In such popular activities benevolence helped to erode the distinctions between labour and love, seriousness and fancy, and gave the extra satisfaction of the performance of a duty. Like mothers' meetings and working parties they contributed to the development of a sense of community and the disposition to kindness in children and adults.

Given the pronounced religious training of children, the many millions of pounds which they contributed to various charities since the early nineteenth century become more comprehensible. To the missionary and Bible societies, the RSPCA and the NSPCC, the temperance movement and other causes, their donations, channelled through domestic meetings, Sunday schools and juvenile associations, became an important, in some cases an indispensable, source of funds. As time passed charities paid more and more attention to their contributions and kept up to date with the creation of new organisations and fund-raising gimmicks. The League of Pity, founded in 1894 as the children's branch of the NSPCC, raised £290,000 in 1979 through such innovations as spell-ins.[71] The success of the campaign to lighten the child's purse ensured that parents and teachers were assiduous in overseeing the charitable impulses that their training aroused. Quite naturally they wished for their children to be like themselves. The future of their causes depended on a steady supply of subscribers and workers drawn from the ranks of youth. As the pennies dropped in the collection boxes, greater recognition was given to the child's

[71] *NSPCC Annual Report* (1979), pp. 12, ii.

personality and habits of benevolence passed from generation to generation.

x

Whatever one thinks of the aims of philanthropists, there is no denying their masterly money-making skills. As the children's pennies show, small donations produced enormous receipts when added together. Increasingly sophisticated, organised charity took every opportunity to extract even the smallest sums – few indigent widows or domestic servants were unaware that the privilege of giving was open to all. The subscription lists of the great London societies illustrate the importance of small sums from provincial auxiliaries, which began to appear around 1800 in the missionary and Bible societies. In the many national institutions using the auxiliary system, most of the money, by the mid-nineteenth century, came from the provinces, much of it from female and children's collections along the lines practised by Mrs Colman in Carrow. The grand London headquarters of the missionary societies and other charities were built largely on a pyramid of pounds, shillings and pence, underpinned by the customary predisposition of the British to join a cause even when they are ignorant of its aims.

Innovation was a hallmark of fund raising. The creator of the orphanage or the home for widows had compassion, to be sure; the inventor of the charity bazaar, Flag Day or the Deed of Covenant had genius. With increasing demands made on limited resources, the benevolent showed great ingenuity in extracting funds from unlikely places. As we have seen, the range of fundraising activity was phenomenal and often merged with recreations. (The charity walk, run, rock concert and sporting event extend the tradition.) Many forms, like the collection box or card, refinements of the hat, could be applied to any cause, informal or organised. Perhaps the most resilient was the bazaar or ladies' sale, established in the early nineteenth century. It raised tens of millions of pounds by the end of Victoria's reign for innumerable purposes, from the relief of individuals to the Anti-Corn Law League.[72] The secret of much charitable money-making was that it was admirably suited to human behaviour. The bazaar, jumble sale and charity store served the community, heightened self-esteem and provided a pleasure dear to the human heart, shopping. Such pastimes

[72] See Prochaska, *Women and Philanthropy in Nineteenth-Century England*, chap. 2.

made the practice of charity, in Robert Louis Stevenson's words, 'entertaining in itself'.[73]

Competitive and acquisitive, the charitable societies put the public under relentless pressure to contribute. Thriving on advertisement, they would form a large chapter in any history of publicity. Every effort was made to elicit favourable notice, to merge philanthropy and fashion. Thus institutions invited celebrities and public figures to be patrons and patronesses. As such people needed philanthropic attachments to give them respectability and opportunities for display, perhaps even a knighthood, such invitations were taken seriously. A 'royal' or an actress could be worth thousands of pounds a year to a society – a bishop or a Member of Parliament rather less. Parish charities, of course, had to make do with local worthies, the vicar's wife or a magistrate, perhaps. Patrons received backing from a host of administrators, writers, speakers and preachers (today from paid consultants as well) anxious to give publicity to their causes and geared to capitalise on it. The published subscription lists, the opulent offices and lavish dinners, the newspaper advertisements (*The Times* prospered on them) were all part of the marketing of philanthropy. At the doorstep were the countless charitable salesmen who invaded the nation's homes. In the Bible Society alone there were 15,000 agents, mostly women, raising funds from door to door by 1820.[74] At the end of the century the NSPCC had 6,000 female collectors, using methods learned from district visiting.[75] In recent years broadcasting and direct mail have reduced their numbers.

XI

As the number of publicists and fund raisers suggests, philanthropy looms large in any history of employment, though it has not been much studied in this context. Few occupations in the nineteenth century could match the labour force marshalled by the charitable societies. There were nearly twice as many paid workers in the 'domestic services' of the benevolent institutions and charity hospitals as there were employees in the poor law authority. Tellingly, there were more

---

[73] [Robert Louis Stevenson], *The Charity Bazaar: An Allegorical Dialogue* (no place of publication given [1868]), p. 2.
[74] Lloyd, *Strictures on a Recent Publication Entitled 'The Church her own Enemy'*, pp. 113–14.
[75] Behlmer, *Child Abuse and Moral Reform in England*, p. 144.

paid Scripture readers or missionaries than scientists.[76] For women, opportunities for salaried employment in philanthropy were good by the end of the century. It was estimated in 1893 that 20,000 women worked as full-time paid officials in charities, excluding nurses and women in religious orders, making it one of the leading female professions.[77] In the nineteenth century, of course, philanthropy was seen as the vocation for middle-class women, an outlet for their domestic skills and their much heralded characteristics of kindness and compassion. This helps to explain why roughly 500,000 women worked 'continuously and semi-professionally' as volunteers in philanthropic institutions by the end of the century.[78] Only domestic service recruited larger numbers of females. The notion of the 'idle' Victorian woman, which stems from the view that only paid employment matters, may be seen largely as a fiction when charitable work in introduced.

Few volunteers, however inexperienced, can be turned away from charitable campaigns; and they invariably leave their mark on the tone and policy of institutions. Philanthropy has been suggested recently as a solution to unemployment, a training ground for school leavers, which would also serve to keep them off the streets.[79] But many in the charitable establishment worry that their societies will be swamped by ill-trained and ill-bred youngsters, with a consequent distortion of objectives. Many of their nineteenth-century predecessors feared the effects of meddling and 'strong-minded' women, who joined charities in ever greater numbers as a cure for boredom and as a way in which they might extend female virtue. The fears were justified, for women did interfere, with telling effects. Through weight of numbers, imaginative fund raising, and a willingness to do work which men found disagreeable or for which they were ill-equipped, they changed the tenor of philanthropy.

The pronounced domestic quality of philanthropy in the nineteenth century was a sign of growing female authority, that 'flow of maternal love'[80] into an increasing number of campaigns. Wherever women worked, home influences became more conspicuous. As recognised guardians of the family they were its front line of defence. Often

---

[76]   *1891 Census of England and Wales*, III, p. xxx.
[77]   Louisa M. Hubbard, 'Statistics of Women's Work', in Baroness Burdett-Coutts, ed., *Woman's Mission* (1893), p. 364.
[78]   *Ibid*.
[79]   *The Times*, 27 Sept. 1983; *The Observer*, 15 Jan. 1984.
[80]   A Woman [Sarah Lewis], *Women's Mission* (1839), p. 128.

against considerable opposition and sometimes at risk to life and limb, women redirected charitable energies to the issues relating to their particular needs and aspirations. The welling up from below of female power produced, among other changes, the rapid growth of district visiting, with its emphasis on the moral and physical cleansing of the nation's homes; the prominence of institutions for servants, widows, and 'ladies'; the application of the 'family system' in orphanages, ragged schools and other institutions; and the expansion of children's charity. Various crusades on behalf of moral reform and social purity also owed much to women's influence. The nineteenth-century female suffrage societies, which may be seen as the political wing of moral reform, called for votes for women because they wished to spread the distinctive homely virtues of women into the wider world. Predictably, the charitable campaigns of women changed their own lives and expectations. Philanthropy both broadened their horizons and pointed out their limitations. It was the taproot of female emancipation in the nineteenth century.

XII

With so many philanthropists fighting their own corner or working out their own salvation, one may be excused for thinking that the charitable world was confusion tempered by self-interest. Muddle proliferated. The range of motive and opinion within individual societies made ordering priorities ticklish. Meetings could be tumultuous. As Arnold Bennett observed, the benevolent required the 'vocal rather than the meditative temperament'.[81] The battle between charitable aims and workers pulling in different directions made it essential to apply specific guidelines. But many volunteers bridled at being told what to do with their money and how best to utilise their spare time, so it was no easy matter to bring them into line with policy. Like some of the causes that they wished to espouse, they might be here today and gone tomorrow. Not uncommonly they broke away to form their own societies, where they were free to make their own decisions. Self-interest and sectarianism, petty jealousies and dislike of London rule triggered philanthropy's centrifugal tendencies.

Criticism of philanthropy's failings mounted in the late nineteenth century. Much of the comment centred on the arbitrary and inefficient

[81] *Anna of the Five Towns* (1902), p. 79.

use of charitable resources, which encouraged indigence and hypocrisy while threatening privacy and individual liberty. Certainly philanthropists laid themselves open to attack from economists and intellectuals. They were commonly untheoretical in approach and ignorant of the social process, particularly the women, whose charity tended to reflect the pragmatic, unanalytic mentality encouraged in the other spheres of their lives. They often raised money from those who could not afford it only to pass it on to those who did not need it. This could demoralise the giver as well as the recipient. Rivalry between institutions, slack procedures and administration, and the widespread use of untrained volunteers, often exploited child labour, further damaged the cause. Some critics argued that the system of charity simply shifted the duties of the whole community onto the shoulders of benevolent activists. Annual reports bear out the view that enthusiasts or those most easily imposed upon, women typically, did most of the dogsbody work. The fact that philanthropists were often narrowly sectarian and gullible played into the hands of their enemies.

In response to the failings of philanthropy the Victorians began to bring together various charitable institutions. (The National Council for Voluntary Organisations, formerly the National Council of Social Service (1919) is in the vanguard of this tradition today.) But finding common ground was difficult, as the Charity Organisation Society (COS) and other 'organising' societies discovered. What every philanthropist willingly supported were those age-old emphases on neighbourliness and the sanctity of family life, which were the essence of informal and local benevolence. No society dependent on volunteers could question these home truths, even if they wished to. Given them, the COS and other charities like the Liverpool Central Relief Society (1863) largely made do with the traditional remedies of friendly visiting and encouragements to providence and personal reformation. They brought to customary practice greater system and the principles of political economy. Family and community were to be propped up on 'scientific' lines, Christian kindness tempered by individual casework. Leading philanthropists took to social statistics when they became the fashion with a naive enthusiasm borne of former factual deprivation. The results for the elimination of pauperism were disappointing, but charitable contacts made with the poor law authorities and the emphasis on professional casework did result in a finer appreciation of the problems of poor relief. Philanthropic organisers did not worry overmuch that social statistics might one day provide the government with the background information necessary to take over a larger share of erstwhile charitable responsibility.

XIII

The attitude of philanthropists to the state in the nineteenth century has been likened to the feelings of the curly-haired boy in *Nicholas Nickleby*, as his mouth opened before Mrs Squeers's brimstone and treacle spoon.[82] This is too sweeping and severe, but many philanthropists had deep-seated views about the respective roles of government and charity which made accommodation difficult. Inclined to attribute the source of social problems to individual failings, they concluded that the remedy must be found in personal reformation, assisted by discretionary charity. Steeped in an individualist and familial ethic they believed that state action in the social sphere obstructed the free development of home and community life. Inspired by that central doctrine of the atonement, many Christians recoiled from Caesar. The individual, not as ratepayer but as fellow-sufferer, was responsible for the expiation of sin and the cares of the world. The law and the state were artificial contrivances, useful in punishing sinners, but incapable of redemptive action.

Such opinions were all too often reinforced by contact with government departments in the nineteenth century. Many civil servants and MPs were, of course, notable in the charitable establishment themselves and sympathetic to the idea of give and take between the state and philanthropy. Yet others looked upon volunteers as so many Mrs Pardiggles, ignorant busybodies who were best kept at arm's length. This was especially noticeable in their attitude to the women who wished to carve out a niche for charity in public institutions. With little enthusiasm for the 'family system', government officials worried that charitable activists would be incapable of prudent and discreet co-operation; and they feared that enquiries might expose abuses in their institutions which could be politically embarrassing and would lead to calls for reform for which there was little money. The Home Office severely restricted charitable activities in prisons after they took over full responsibility for them in 1877. Frustrated, philanthropists shifted their interest to the cause of discharged prisoners. Poor law officials too, particularly workhouse masters, made

---

[82] Hilda Jennings, *The Private Citizen in Public Social Work* (1930), p.18.

life difficult for volunteers who wished to visit workhouses. Affronted by prying ladies in their wards, they sometimes had them removed for meddling or sectarianism. Such experiences confirmed the worst fears of many philanthropists. With its unbending bureaucracy and standardisation, government could be a forbidding world.

For all their reservations about the state, more and more philanthropists came to recognise that on their own they were incapable of changing the conditions which bred many of the problems they sought to redress. In various nineteenth-century campaigns, such as anti-slavery and the protection of children, they lobbied for legislative action with striking results. As they probed more deeply into injustices, many started to think again about the causes of the central problem of destitution. In a society of 'unrestricted and unregulated capitalism and landlordism', to use the words of Beatrice Webb, those age-old remedies of self-help and personal reformation looked like palliatives.[83] Some philanthropists, including Canon Samuel Barnett and the Quaker Seebohm Rowntree, became forerunners of the state social services. Others, Octavia Hill among them, appear so only by the play of hindsight. The investigations of Charles Booth and Seebohm Rowntree and the evidence of the Royal Commission on the Poor Laws (1905–9) were seen by many as a powerful case for the extension of state assistance. Most philanthropists, even inveterate Christian individualists, eventually accepted it, particularly if there was the promise of fruitful co-operation between the state and charitable institutions.

Arguably the growth of government responsibility for welfare contributed to the devitalisation of Christian charity and by implication Christianity itself. As formal religion declined in the first half of the twentieth century the individualist opposition to state intervention probably diminished. Was there an erosion of charitable tithes which made a social tax more urgent? Without reliable statistics, we should not jump to conclusions about philanthropic resources on the evidence of falling church attendance. But as the state's activity in the social sphere tended to divorce material from spiritual welfare, philanthropy became more a question of personal choice for Christians. Many of them, of course, continued to contribute to established Christian charities, some of which have shown themselves to be remarkably resilient in difficult circumstances. For those reconsidering or losing faith, allegiances often shifted from church or chapel to charities thought

[83] Beatrice Webb, *My Apprenticeship* (1926), p. 207.

to be more relevant to social need and in tune with changing values. Here they would come into contact with philanthropy's temporal wing. In a relatively informal and secular age charitable institutions play a crucial role as repositories of moral and ethical values.

Despite the growing readiness to co-operate in certain causes, the relationship between philanthropy and the state in the first half of the twentieth century is perhaps best described as fitful. Against a background of the changing nature of social problems and the mounting concern over pauperism, ageing, and unemployment, there was no clear demarcation of authority. The *ad hoc* character of both government legislation and charitable activity added to the confusion. In the interwar years philanthropic bodies set the pace for government action in such areas as family planning and nursery schools. But as greater responsibility for social welfare shifted to the state, those charities which dealt with the social services had to forge a new relationship with government agencies. When the machinery of the welfare state rolled into action after the Second World War, many of them had no choice but to redefine themselves and their objectives. Their continuing importance should not be underestimated.

Charities have had to battle with Whitehall to be taken seriously and to work out a clearer perception of their respective spheres and responsibilities. The Nathan Report (1952), which made recommendations on charitable practice in the wake of postwar social legislation, assisted in this process. The growing number of government grants given to charities in recent years suggests that the much heralded 'partnership' between public and private welfare has real meaning. But in a society in which light houses are run by the state and life boats by philanthropists (the Royal National Lifeboat Institution was founded in 1824) the citizen may be excused for believing that much muddle persists. Attitudes about charity and welfare have been further confused in the 1980s by the political debate over 'privatisation'. On the right there is talk of reducing state services to a bare minimum. The left are up in arms about 'welfare on the cheap'. Caught in the middle, philanthropists are worried lest they be expected to fill the gaps created by welfare cuts, which would threaten their resources and flexibility.[84] Not since 1948 has there been such a challenge to the charitable establishment.

The controversial issue of what constitutes a 'charity' dogs the

---

[84] *Voluntary Action* 2, no.3 (1984), p. 3.

relationship between the state and organised philanthropy. Many voluntary societies do not have charitable status in law and consequently do not enjoy tax relief. But why, many ask, are Eton College and the British Goat Society registered charities while the National Council for Civil Liberties, Amnesty, and mutual aid societies are not? The Charity Commission was set up in 1853 to remedy the misapplication of endowed charities, but, since 1960, has had the additional responsibility of registering and regulating 'collecting' charities, whose incomes derive from subscriptions and grants rather than endowments. Cautious and understaffed, it resists attempts at widening the rather narrow and arbitrary definition of charity which it inherits from the courts. In this century the courts have gradually excluded political activity from the range of charitable purposes. If the British and Foreign Anti-Slavery Society, founded in 1839 and still active, were to apply for registration from the Charity Commissioners today, it could be rejected on the grounds that it seeks political solutions to fulfil its aims. Likewise the Lord's Day Observance Society (1831).

XIV

Philanthropy has lost its pre-eminence, but its decline can be easily exaggerated. A National Opinion Poll revealed in 1976 that about 5 million British adults participated in some form of charitable work during the course of that year and that in regard to the personal social services the voluntary sector provided more hours of manpower than did the state.[85] Impressed by the dimensions of neighbourly philanthropy, the Nathan committee argued that the informal actions of the good neighbour made 'satisfactory social relationships possible'.[86] On a more formal level, many long-established societies prosper and new ones are founded each week. More professional and in tune with planning than in the nineteenth century, they have unlimited scope for growth. Indeed, the welfare state has proved a blessing in disguise. Freed from many of their former thankless tasks, philanthropists have shown themselves able to build on local initiatives and to respond spontaneously to fresh challenges in a way that is all but impossible for government. The Penlee Life Boat Disaster Appeal of 1981 serves to remind us of this. In the give and take arrangements

---

[85] *The Future of Voluntary Organisations: Report of the Wolfenden Committee* (1978), pp. 35–6.
[86] *Committee on the Law and Practice Relating to Charitable Trusts*, PP 1952–3, VIII, para. 53.

that obtain between charities and the state, charities can pinpoint problems and pioneer solutions without imposing a burden on the taxpayer.

The defence of charitable action in the twentieth century is not without a touch of irony. Many liberal critics of philanthropy in the late nineteenth century, thinking largely of its effects on the recipient, alleged that it was so powerful as to pose a threat to individual liberty. If they were alive today they would be mortified by the ascendancy of the state. Suspicious of its intentions, they would probably hail philanthropists as champions of freedom. In recent decades, social commentators from all the main political parties have argued that charitable activity is a democratic safeguard, or as Stanley Baldwin remarked in 1933, 'a means of rescuing the citizen from the standardising pressure of the state's mechanism'.[87] For his part, William Beveridge, who gave much of his time and income to charitable causes, detected 'the distinguishing marks of a free society' in the independent decisions of the volunteer.[88] As a student of the history of philanthropy he took a spacious view. In search of a fruitful balance between welfare and self-help he believed that voluntary action should play a more effective and creative role alongside the state in the drive for social progress.

From their different political perspectives Baldwin and Beveridge would have much to criticise in current welfare arrangements, but they would both applaud the recent resurgence of interest in philanthropy and 'community action', which highlights the work of volunteers. Whether dropping in on a neighbour, running a play group or a feminist refuge,[89] or directing a leading society such as the Salvation Army (1865) or Band Aid (1986), the charitable are free to choose the objects of their concern and make decisions about them independent of external control. To use the language of the Nathan committee, their work may be said to constitute a 'nursery school of democracy'.[90] If so, the diversity and rivalry, the love of the *ad*

---

[87] *The Times*, 27 Oct. 1933, quoted in Elizabeth Macadam, *The New Philanthropy* (1934), p. 304.

[88] William Beveridge, *Voluntary Action: A Report on Methods of Social Advance* (1948), p. 10. Beveridge was Sub-Warden of Toynbee Hall early in the twentieth century, and from 1924 to 1936 he was an enthusiastic member of the propaganda committee of the King Edward's Hospital Fund for London. A purpose of the committee was to defend the voluntary hospitals from ministerial interference. See the annual reports of the King Edward's Hospital Fund for London.

[89] There are 150 or so of these refuges for battered wives attached to the Women's Aid Federation. See *Voluntary Action*, no. 13 (1982), pp. 22–3.

[90] *Committee on Charitable Trusts*, 1952–3, para. 53.

hoc remedy, the seemingly inefficient muddle that typified so much nineteenth-century charity, paid democratic benefits. They may be the most enduring legacy of those philanthropists of the past, rich or poor, misguided or wise, whose works radiated from the home into the wider world.

CHAPTER 8

Clubs, societies and associations

R. J. MORRIS

When in 1837, in the pages of his first periodical, *Master Humphrey's Clock*, Charles Dickens celebrated the doings of the Mudfog Association, with all its little formalities, its concern for rules, and its sense of importance and purpose, he was recording one of the most pervasive, diffuse and amorphous social developments of the past 200 years. The creation of formal voluntary associations was not new in his generation but what was new was the increase in their number, variety and public importance which took place, especially after 1780. That increase was to continue for many decades. The basis of that growth was in the adult male urban middle classes, but this adaptable and flexible form of social institution could never and was never limited to this group.

As society became more complex, those with power, those with no power and above all those with slender fragments of power which they sought to defend and extend began to organise themselves in a variety of specific ways. A whole new series of words came into common use in the English language, often changing or adding to their meaning – the association, the society, the chairman, the agenda, the membership, the rules and constitution and the annual report. After the mid-eighteenth century voluntary organisations appeared in increasing numbers. Their defining characteristics were minimal, a set of rules, a declared purpose and a membership defined by some formal act of joining. These organisations acted independently of the family, household, neighbourhood, firm or work group. They had none of the prescriptive power of the state or the contract. Civil society was becoming more complex. The number of social roles which each individual fulfilled increased in variety and number. The rate of change was increasing and its directions less predictable and familiar. The creation of voluntary associations was one major social response to the problems posed by change and complexity. Many informal groupings took on rules and titles. They emerged from the public house and the coffee house into purpose-built Halls, Institutes and Assembly Rooms.

BEFORE 1780

The associations of the eighteenth century took a number of social models as their basis. The club was derived from the informal drinking group of the tavern and mixed with this certain features of the household or family. The head of household became mine host became the chairman with power to lay down and interpret certain vague rules of conduct. The members like the family had a clearly identified central core but a vague periphery as individuals came and went, visitors, friends and supporters. The middle years of the eighteenth century were still those of the tavern and the coffee house. It was the world which Aiken described for Manchester in the 1720s:

About this period there was an evening club of the most opulent manufacturers, at which the expense of each person was fixed at fourpence for ale and a halfpenny for tobacco. At a much later period, however, a sixpennyworth of punch and a pipe or two were esteemed fully sufficient for the evening's tavern amusement of the principal inhabitants.[1]

It was a world in which an increasing number of these informal groupings began to gain a structure and the discipline of rules. They brought a little order to the exchange of ideas. It allowed more broadly based groups to meet and explore a variety of common interests. Clubs like the Shropshire Fraternity of the True Blue or the Friendly Association of Worcester Gentlemen were little more than a base for feasting and fox-hunting. In the organising urban world of Birmingham such clubs acted as a bridge between professional men, middling tradesmen and skilled artisans, the Bucks, the Freemasons, reading clubs and book clubs. Outstanding for its durability and influence was the Birmingham Bean Club, a loyalist dining club in which the gentlemen of the county and the principal inhabitants came together for food and confidential discussion.[2]

---

[1] Quoted by James Croston, *The History of the County Palatine and Duchy of Lancaster*, 5 vols. (1888–93), vol. 2, p.16.
[2] John Money, *Experience and Identity: Birmingham and the West Midlands, 1760–1800* (Manchester, 1977), pp. 98–152.

In 1769, the Bean Club held its dinners at the Swan Inn but its representation of the Birmingham interest was soon to shade into a party and Tory identity in the 1770s. The rival group was gathering around John Freeth's coffee house. There had been a book club with Unitarian links there since 1758. In 1774, it was the base for the Constitutional Society with its eyes firmly on the independent interest in the 1774 election. The Amicable Debating Society, the Free Debating Society, the Conversation Society discussed matters of grand general philosophy like the question, 'Whether Justice or Injustice depend upon the institutions of civil society or on Nature?' as well as more specific matters such as the morality of allowing the performance of plays in Birmingham and the justice of the game laws.

These societies gave discipline and structure to discussions. Chairmen were appointed. The Anacreontic Society formed by a group of tradesmen in Birmingham in 1793, 'for social enjoyment', told a member (rule three), that 'no compulsion is upon him further than good order and regularity at the meetings'.[3] The Free Debating Society fined its members 1s. if they swore. Ladies were admitted 'gratis' which prompted one critical observer to reflect 'cleanliness is a compliment due to the sex everywhere'. Women who were not content with such patronage formed their own societies. The annual festival of 'The Original Female Society' was held at Lichfield in 1775 with a hundred guests and a few lines of verse from one of the members.

> Long by the men's hand
> Has friendship's fair wand
> Been carried without opposition
> Till our sex has caught fire
> And to friendship aspire

There was a brief glimpse of collective female action in the public sphere before the flood tide of evangelicalism swept the gender frontier back into the private and the domestic.[4]

The changes in the formality of patterns of association were mirrored in the changing meaning of the word club. In the seventeenth century it had advanced little beyond its old meaning which signified the

---

[3] Benjamin Walker, 'The Anacreontic Society', *Transactions of the Birmingham Archaeological Society*, 63 (1939–40), pp. 76–80.
[4] *Ibid.*, p. 99; Catherine Hall, 'The Early Formation of Victorian Domestic Ideology', in Sandra Burman, ed., *Fit Work for Women* (1979), pp. 15–32.

division of the reckoning amongst guests at a dinner table. Addison's elegant pen had suggested that 'our modern celebrated clubs are founded upon eating and drinking, which are points wherein most men agree'.[5] The clubs of late seventeenth-century London had little more than a time and place of meeting and an identity. The best known were the political clubs like the Whig Green Ribbon Club which had a reputation for manipulating mobs and riots. They were followed by the Kit Kat Club and the Tory Loyal Brotherhood. The latter was a 'select if rowdy drinking club', with an initiation ceremony and elaborate rituals of drinking and toasts.[6] The increase in formality was reflected by the dictionary makers who attempted to batter the English language into order and uniformity in the eighteenth century. Dr Johnson defined clubs as 'an assembly of good fellows meeting under certain conditions', whilst by Todd's time they were 'an association of persons subjected to particular rules'.[7]

The aristocratic need for gambling in orderly, comfortable and well-fed conditions was one of the pressures for greater rule-making in the 1760s. Almacks was established in Pall Mall in 1764 by twenty-seven noblemen. Its rules were strict.

Rule 21 No gaming in the eating room. . .
Rule 40 That every person playing at the new guinea table do keep fifty guineas before him.

Fox, Gibbon and later Pitt and the young Wilberforce were attracted by an environment in which the fall of the cards might have been left to chance but nothing else was. By the start of the nineteenth century, the London club had become identified with the heavily capitalised establishment like the Athenaeum founded in 1824, which provided a wide range of services from dining to the library in an environment of strict rules and a membership selected not only by the high subscription but also by a careful procedure of proposal and blackballing. These nineteenth-century clubs were noted for a strict and obsessive exclusion of women, which would have puzzled the

---

[5] *The Spectator*, no. 9, Saturday, 10 March 1710–11.
[6] Linda J. Colley, 'The Loyal Brotherhood and the Cocoa Tree: The London Organization of the Tory Party', *Historical Journal*, 20 (1977), pp. 77–95; David Allen, 'Political Clubs in Restoration London', *Historical Journal*, 19 (1976), pp. 561–80.
[7] Samuel Johnson, A.M., *A Dictionary of the English Language . . .* (1755); Rev. Henry John Todd, *A Dictionary of the English Language by Samuel Johnson . . . with Numerous Corrections and Additions* (1818); John Timbs, *Clubs and Club Life in London* (1872).

mid-eighteenth century. Almacks opened Assembly Rooms in 1765 in which the balls were run by a committee of ladies of high rank. In 1770, a new gambling club associated with Almacks was based upon the principle that men could only be nominated and vetoed by women and women by men, a means of managing gender relationships that would have horrified a later generation. Mrs Boscowen recorded that 'Lord March and Brook Boothby were blackballed by the ladies to their great astonishment'.[8]

William Hutton was clearly wrong when he claimed that the clubs of Birmingham were only a matter for the lower orders, but his early history showed that the club principle of combining resources and dividing benefits was adaptable to a variety of needs and circumstances. In 1783, there were hundreds of clubs in Birmingham. The majority were for the support of their members in times of sickness. 'Each society is governed by a code of laws of its own making.' Many of them had accumulated considerable capital. They met once a fortnight. The publican was the key figure and was often the treasurer. Many clubs had some savings function, often with a specific purchase in mind. There were rent clubs, book clubs, watch clubs, building clubs and clock clubs. 'In the breeches club, every member ballots for a pair, value a guinea . . . this club dissolves when all the members are served.'[9]

These clubs were urban in origin but by the end of the eighteenth century were spreading into the countryside where some of them lasted well into the twentieth century often providing a focus for community identity and ritual. The Woodborough Male Friendly Society was founded in 1826 on models from Nottingham and Southwell. It provided sick pay and funeral benefit for members. By 1841 it had purchased land to let as allotments to members, a valuable alternative source of support during depression in the framework knitting trade. The club feast was celebrated by a walk from the club room to a church service. There was considerable spending upon mutton, cheese, lettuce, mustard, cabbage, bread, sugar and ale. A band was an important part of the event. By the 1920s, the walk was a splendid perambulation of the village public houses, starting at the Nags Head and finishing with a dance on the tennis courts. This essentially eighteenth-century form elaborated with the leisure technology of the next

[8] Timbs, *Clubs and Club Life*, p. 75.
[9] William Hutton, *An History of Birmingham*, 2nd edn (Birmingham, 1783), pp. 135–8.

150 years survived until the Second World War and the Beveridge welfare state destroyed both its rationale and its community.[10]

It was in Edinburgh that the full social development and implications of the eighteenth-century club became evident. Voluntary societies have an enormous potential for enabling a society experiencing rapid and disturbing change to adapt to that change, to experiment with and devise new values. Such societies are a means of asserting status for those outwith the established institutions and networks of state power. Scotland in the eighteenth century, and most critically Edinburgh, needed to adapt not only to the spread of capitalist and commercial relationships but also to the loss of government entailed by the Act of Union of 1707. Scotland was a nation within a nation. Edinburgh was a capital city without a government. The early eighteenth-century clubs would have had a familiar sound to the Londoner – the Sulphur Club, the Hell Fire Club, the Demireps – noted for hard drinking, free talk, ribald verses and blaspheming songs, an irritation but hardly an innovative threat to the establishment and its values.[11] The direction of change was evident by the 1720s, when Allan Ramsay was drinking and reciting his verses at the Easy Club and the gentlemen of the Lothians were forming the Society of Improvers of Knowledge of Agriculture. These changes culminated and were focussed in the formation of the Select Society in 1754. Here a generation of intellectuals mixed with a selection of the elite who either could not or would not afford the trip to London, landowners, controllers of patronage, leading professional and commercial men.[12] Here the developing code of polite learning and culture, of rational and secular discussion was perfected. There was a search for accuracy and precision in argument. Morals were to be based upon experience which led to an interest in history and social structure. Polite learning led to a search for social and cultural improvement. The members were influential and instrumental in the formation of a number of other societies. The most important were the Edinburgh Society for the Encouragement of Arts, Sciences, Manufactures and

[10] Julie O'Neill, 'Self Help in Nottinghamshire: The Woodborough Male Friendly Society, 1826–1954', *Transactions of the Thoroton Society of Nottinghamshire*, 90 (1986), pp. 57–63; J. D. Marshall, 'Nottinghamshire Labourers in the Early 19th Century', *Transactions of the Thoroton Society of Nottinghamshire*, 64 (1960), p. 64.

[11] Henry Grey Graham, *The Social Life of Eighteenth Century Scotland* (1906), p. 93.

[12] David Daiches, Peter Jones and Jean Jones, eds., *A Hotbed of Genius: The Scottish Enlightenment, 1730-1790* (Edinburgh, 1986); Roger L. Emerson, 'The Social Composition of Enlightened Scotland: The Select Society of Edinburgh, 1754–1764', *Studies on Voltaire and the Eighteenth Century*, 114 (1973), pp. 291–329.

Agriculture and the Select Society for Promoting the Reading and Speaking of the English Language in Scotland. These two were self-conscious responses to the problems posed by economic development and the need to relate in a dignified and effective manner to the power-ful and dominant partner of the Union of the two kingdoms.[13] These societies which were part of a wide and varied network provided an identity for the aristocratic and commercial society of Edinburgh and for an elite without a court which sought status and legitimacy.

One of the most successful forms of association of the eighteenth century was the Masonic Order. The modern 'speculative' form of masonry originated in England and Scotland in the late seventeenth century and spread rapidly. Its lodges provided a common fund of ritual, rhetoric and experience which grew and was elaborated. In its mythology the order drew upon its understanding of the guilds, especially the mysteries of the operative masons. By the time the Grand Lodge was formed in 1717, the order had developed a tradition of supportive male exclusiveness, mutual aid and fellowship sanc-tioned by its medieval roots. The Freemasons achieved their success and sustained growth in the eighteenth century against a background of political and religious divisions. The order insisted on tolerance and the exclusion of contention. The fourth Charge required that 'no private piques or quarrels' should be brought into the lodge, and 'we . . . are resolved against all Politicks, as what never yet conduced to the welfare of the Lodge, nor ever will'.[14] The Grand Lodge created a clear hierarchical structure and encouraged rules which eliminated some of the grosser forms of horseplay which had crept into initiation ceremonies. Since 1721, the Grand Master has always been a noble-man, seven of them royal princes. By that time the Grand Masters of the most important lodges were being drawn from the local gentry.[15] The order was much more public than in the twentieth century, frequently parading with its aprons and regalia and advertising meet-ings and ceremonies in the growing newspaper press. The order

[13] N. T. Phillipson, 'Culture and Society in the 18th Century Province: The Case of Edinburgh and the Scottish Enlightenment', in Lawrence Stone, ed., *The University in Society* (Princeton, 1974), pp. 407–48; D. McElroy, *Scotland's Age of Improvement: A Survey of 18th Century Literary Clubs and Societies* (Washington, 1969).

[14] J. M. Roberts, *The Mythology of Secret Societies* (1972), pp. 17–31; S. Pope, 'The Devel-opment of Freemasonry in England and Wales', *Ars Quator Coronatorum* (1956–8), pp. 68–79.

[15] Douglas Knoop and G. P. Jones, *The Genesis of Freemasonry* (Manchester, 1947), p. 296; Dudley Wright, *Gould's History of Freemasonry*, 5 vols. (1931–6), vol. 2 (1932), p. 213.

provided contact, sociability and the exchange of information and support in an increasingly open society, but it did this in a manner which recognised social hierarchy.[16] Above all, the order provided a model of semi-secret hierarchical lodge organisation which could be used in other ways. The ritual, initiation ceremonies and claims to ancient roots were used by the craft unions and friendly societies to bond together men divided by party, status and geography.

In addition to the club and the lodge, the eighteenth century adapted the semi-feudal forms of the great country house to the need to co-ordinate social action around growing urban centres and to accumulate collective social capital in those centres. This form of association was most evident in the assemblies and race meetings which were the focus of elite social life in most towns.[17] Later in the century subscription concerts were held in the same way. Despite the growth of commercialised leisure in this period, many important assemblies and race meetings were taken into the voluntary sector. The market was unable to supply the standard of social discipline which the elite required or perhaps, as with Edinburgh's New Town Assembly Rooms, the entrepreneur simply failed to raise the capital so that collective accumulation outside the market was necessary. The races and assemblies were organised by stewards, often the younger male members of the elite. They were sanctioned and given prestige by patrons, usually the senior male members of that elite. In mid-century, where the dancing and the social display and mixing of the Assembly Rooms were concerned, the details of control were often taken over by committees of women, again confirming the aristocratic household as the model.[18] When capital had to be accumulated, it was lodged with trustees, a legal form which was rapidly being developed by the courts of equity to handle delicate problems of family relationships and property. The gentry who came to Lincoln for the races decided in 1773 to subscribe for ground and a stand. This act of collective accumulation was prompted by the rapid spread of capitalist relationships regarding local land use, for the races were being driven from one site to another by enclosure.[19] At Lichfield, the clerk of the course, a local lawyer, operated under the watchful eye of two stewards elected by the

[16] J. M. Roberts, 'Freemasonry, Possibilities of a Neglected Topic', *English Historical Review*, 84 (1969), pp. 323–35.

[17] Peter Borsay, 'The English Urban Renaissance; The Development of Provincial Urban Culture, *c*. 1680–*c*. 1760', *Social History*, 5 (1977), pp. 581–603.

[18] Leonore Davidoff, *The Best Circles* (1973).

[19] Sir Francis Hill, *Georgian Lincoln* (Cambridge, 1966), p. 15.

subscribers to the races. So far were the races removed from capitalist relationships that the accounts were published to counter accusations that the clerk had been making a profit. The subscription for a stand, again in 1773, developed naturally from the subscriptions which had supported the races themselves. When profits were made they were used to pay for a new race cup and not distributed to 'shareholders'.[20]

Edinburgh saw the full range of the social forms which provided dancing assemblies. In the early years of the eighteenth century, the initial demand had been provided through the speculations of a few dancing masters, but in the 1720s this was rapidly taken over by a group of directors, advocates, merchants and gentry. They hired rooms off the High Street and handed over the details to a committee of lady directresses including Lady Panmure and Susanna, Countess of Eglinton.[21] These ladies 'agreed upon certain rules'.

1 No lady to be admitted in a night gown and no gentlemen in boots. . .
5 No dancing out of regular order but by leave from the Lady Directress of the night. . .
8 No misses in skirts and jackets, robe coats or stay bodied gowns, to be allowed to dance country dances but in a sett by themselves.[22]

Dancing and sexuality went together and not far behind were marriage and property. Such relationships were too important to be left to the market and the cash economy. Hence the need for control by the lady directors. By the 1750s, the Edinburgh Assembly Rooms were ruled by the formidable Miss Nicky Murray, sister of Lord Mansfield. The profits of many of the dances went to the Royal Infirmary. The directors were to keep account books which were to be 'open to the ladies at all times'. In 1781, a new subscription was open and the Assembly Rooms in the New Town were built. This time, regulation was placed in the hands of a male steward rather than the lady directresses. It was an early sign that the gender frontier was on the move out of public life. This time the rules *forbad* 'young ladies out of women's dress' and gentlemen with 'unpowdered hair'. The major elements of collective social provision were all there, rules, subscribers, committees and general meetings.

A fourth group was more directly related to the spread of capitalist

[20] Ann J. Kettle, 'Lichfield Races', *Transactions of the Lichfield and South Staffordshire Archaeological Society*, 6 (1964–5), pp. 39–44.
[21] Graham, *The Social Life of Eighteenth Century Scotland*, pp. 98–9.
[22] *Notes from the Records of the Assembly Rooms of Edinburgh* (Edinburgh, 1842).

relationships in the eighteenth century. Capitalism was not new and certainly not complete in its hold on social and economic relationships by 1750, but the power of its characteristic relationships was growing, the dominance of cash transactions, of the private and exclusive ownership of property and the motivation of profit as a guide to pro- duction and exchange. Now these primary characteristics of capital- istic relationships could not always sustain many of the secondary relationships that were essential for the dynamic and stability of pro- duction and distribution ordered in this way. Such an economic sys- tem needed to accumulate and maintain the value of capital, it needed stability, it needed predictability. A capitalist may be a risk-taker, but the wise capitalist prefers to reduce that risk to a minimum. A growing number of organisations were created to fill those needs of capitalism which capitalism itself could not provide through the profit motive. These were the collectivist agents of capitalist production. The Honourable Society of Improvers of the Knowledge of Agriculture was established in Edinburgh in 1723. It was the first of many in Britain. It was to serve members with general instruction on scientific agriculture and offer advice on specific problems.[23] Rich farming areas like the Lothians were amongst the first parts of the economy to feel the full effects of an unrestrained market in the use of property, and with it came the need to sustain economic growth through increased productivity. If the market was not going to supply the knowledge needed then the Society of Improvers made the attempt as Lothian agriculture smashed its way through the bankruptcy of several noted improvers to a massive and profitable reorganisation of production.

The general hospitals come into this group. The care of the sick and injured, the development of medical skills were benefits which it was hard to allocate through the cash system. The motivations of Christian charity were sharpened to provide the social capital needed. The social base on which so many infirmaries were founded after mid-century has been little explored. They were always located in major provincial centres with the support of the urban elite and the surrounding gentry. The motivation of the medical profession was clear as was the importance of these organisations for medical history. It was not so clear why the elite of mid-century should express itself in this way. The demonstration of Christian charity and the assertion of urban status and identity were part of it, but as many of them

[23] Phillipson, 'Edinburgh and the Scottish Enlightenment', p. 436.

excluded infectious disease, the motives of self-protection were not as evident as they were in the later Houses of Recovery. The hospitals were a primitive form of the type of association which was to become characteristic of the nineteenth century, having an open and published subscription list, a committee, trustees, treasurer, fundraising events and annual reports. The infirmary subscription lists had the eighteenth-century characteristic of linking the urban elite with the surrounding gentry.

Whatever their reputation for heroic individuality, the industrialists of the eighteenth century were not averse to the collective benefits of association. Their profits and liquidity were constantly set at risk by the fluctuations of prices in investment cycles and by the vagaries of government foreign and fiscal policy. In the seventeenth century when foreign trade had been dominated by London, the leading merchants had direct access to government. By the mid-eighteenth century this was no longer adequate. Difficulties were especially serious in the American war in the 1780s and a number of manufacturers' associations appeared. The Association of the Manufacturers of Earthenware appeared in 1784 and joined with other groups in the General Chamber of Manufacturers.[24] Their main business was to hold regular meetings and make collective representations to the government. The political divisions created by the American war had broken their old reliance upon local county MPs as an effective route through which to lobby government.[25] The ironmasters with their heavy fixed costs and exposure to the investment cycle held quarterly meetings from the 1780s. Their initial concern was with government policy. This was especially important for the ironmasters as the industry was uncompetitive right into the 1820s and only survived through tariff protection and military demand.[26] These quarterly meetings soon produced price agreements as well as good dinners. The effect was limited by the regional nature of most of the associations and the temptation to undersell during a slump but some temporary smoothing of the intense price fluctuations was usually achieved in the early part of a depression.[27]

[24] V. W. Bladen, 'The Association of the Manufacturers of Earthenware, 1784–86', *Economic History, a Supplement to the Economic Journal*, 1 (1926–7), pp. 356–67.
[25] Money, *Experience and Identity*, pp. 34–45.
[26] Charles Hyde, *Technological Change and the British Iron Industry, 1700–1870* (Princeton, 1977).
[27] T. S. Ashton, 'Early Price Associations in the British Iron Industry', *Economic Journal*, 30 (1920), pp. 331–9.

1780–1890

The century after 1780 brought massive changes in the number and the nature of voluntary associations. By the 1840s, two major groups stood out from the rest, the subscriber democracies of the middle classes and the network of neighbourhood societies favoured by the working classes and some of their middle-class allies. Each of these deserves separate treatment.

In the 1780s, there were a few indications of what was to come. Most towns of any size had a general infirmary organised with a public openness which was to become part of the nineteenth-century tradition.[28] The Leeds Infirmary was founded after a meeting at the New Inn in 1767. In Newcastle in 1751, the initiative came from the members of an elite convivial society for whom age and death had curbed meetings. They sponsored a public subscription and printed a sermon to raise money for the first building.[29] Sheffield delayed until 1792, when a meeting was called by the mayor at the Town Hall. This was characteristic of that town's imperfect development of an elite urban consciousness.[30] The second important group of elite institutions were the proprietary libraries. The model of the first such library in Liverpool was followed in Leeds. The Leeds Library was founded in 1767 under the influence of Joseph Priestley, the experimental scientist and dissenting minister who was leading his congregation at Mill Hill towards Unitarianism. The important feature of these libraries was the manner in which they were financed. Membership was limited; 500 in the case of Leeds. Entry was by the purchase of a proprietary share. This could be bought and sold like any item of real estate and entitled the holder to membership provided the 25s. annual subscription was paid.[31] The model of association here was that of the joint stock company. It was to appear again and again for items of social capital which varied from public baths to botanical and zoological gardens. These libraries were another instance of the manner in which collective voluntary action removed the provision of an important

---

[28]   Brian Abel-Smith, *The Hospitals, 1800–1948* (1964); S.T. Anning, *The General Infirmary at Leeds*, vol. 1: *The First 100 Years* (1963).

[29]   Eneas Mackenzie, *A Descriptive and Historical Account of the Town and County of Newcastle upon Tyne* (Newcastle, 1827), pp. 501–12.

[30]   Joseph Hunter, *Hallamshire: The History and Topography of the Parish of Sheffield*, new edn, ed. Rev. Alfred Gatty (1879), p. 323; Dennis Smith, *Conflict and Compromise: Class Formation in English Society, 1830–1914* (1982).

[31]   Thomas Kelly, *Early Public Libraries in Great Britain before 1850* (1966), pp. 125–30; Frank Beckwith, *The Leeds Library* (Leeds, 1950), p. 7; F. W. Gibbs, *Joseph Priestley* (1965), pp. 169–70.

service for the elite from the market economy in order to ensure control and permanence.

At the same time the world became more political. Consensus over prices, wages, ideology and the organisation of power became harder to achieve. What the American war had begun was completed during the 1790s with increasing social and physical violence. The major manufacturers, the merchants, the shopkeepers and their professional allies were faced with the double task of gaining and asserting authority in the new situations which urban and industrial growth were continually providing. Their social, economic and political power needed to be continually defended and extended against the threats of disease, food scarcity, crime, public disorder, labour organisation and radical ideological and political action. By 1830, it was clear that a growing network of voluntary societies was part of the response to this situation. They were listed in the front of trade directories and local guides. Their notices and meetings filled the local newspaper press. Their flysheets, pamphlets and annual reports found their way into many hundreds of homes. The nature of the need for authority and the challenge to authority changed with the development of the economy, so that the voluntary societies responded to this changing situation as well as to their own successes, failures and innovations.[32]

Amongst the early responses to this sense of instability was a series of voluntary organisations intended to achieve stability through co-ercion. Prosecution and propaganda were the major weapons against a series of threats which ranged from Sabbath-breaking to radical politics. The Proclamation Society, founded in 1787 under the inspiration of William Wilberforce, included the publisher of Tom Paine's *Age of Reason* amongst its targets. The Association Movement, a response to the political crisis of 1792, was country wide. The Society for the Suppression of Vice was a City of London middle-class version of the Proclamation Society.[33] At a more mundane level Watch and Ward Societies and Associations for the Prosecution of Felons were formed in many parts of the country in the last thirty years of the eighteenth century. They organised dinners, prosecutions and voluntary police

[32] David Owen, *English Philanthropy, 1660–1960* (1964); Margaret B. Simey, *Charitable Efforts in Liverpool in the Nineteenth Century* (Liverpool, 1951); B. H. Harrison, 'Philanthropy and the Victorians', *Victorian Studies*, 9 (1966), pp. 353–74, substantially revised as B. Harrison, *Peaceable Kingdom* (Oxford, 1982), chap. 5.

[33] M. J. D. Roberts, 'The Society for the Suppression of Vice and its Early Critics, 1802–1812', *Historical Journal*, 26 (1983), pp. 159–76; Austin Mitchell, 'The Association Movement of 1792–1793', *Historical Journal*, 4 (1961), pp. 56–77.

patrols. The most important of the coercive organisations were the troops of voluntary yeomanry which were created with government support and approval in the 1790s for the double purpose of countering French invasion and internal radical disorder.[34] These auxiliary military units proved an ideal way of channelling the growing self-awareness of the middling social classes in support of existing power structures. By the early 1820s, it was clear that the contemptuous and hostile ineffectiveness with which these troops managed the coercive aspects of class relationships was counter-productive. The Edinburgh troop was called out in 1820 to challenge the radical weavers who had begun to march upon Edinburgh with a mixture of political courage and naivety that met with early and easy defeat.[35] The derisive verses of one Private Tytler hardly suggest that the experience prepared the young lawyers and clerks of Edinburgh to make a contribution to stable and consensus-bound class relationships.

> Let us sing of the heroes that marched from yon town
> To keep liberty up, to put radicals down
> Lawyers flung by the fee book to furbish their pops
> And mettlesome merchants strode fierce from their shops
> ... Twas at Bathgate, this war might be said to commence
> To the tune, as was fitting of 'D-m the expense'.
> ... When one greasy disciple of Carlile and Hone
> Had surrendered his shuttle Te Deum was blown.[36]

The most disastrous episode in the history of these volunteer yeomanries was the 'Peterloo' massacre. In 1819, the Manchester yeomanry rode into a massive crowd gathered for a radical political meeting. As a result eleven were killed and over 500 injured. It was an act of class aggression and military incompetence by the 'shopkeepers on horseback'.[37] The protests which followed reflected a working-class anger which lasted many generations but also a middle-class recognition that brutal coercion was not the way in which they wanted to conduct class relationships. The search for ideological, cultural and moral dominance was to achieve prominence. Voluntary organisations were central to such an attempt.

The most important middle-class response to this acceleration of

---

[34] J. R. Western, 'The Volunteer Movement as an Anti Revolutionary Force, 1793–1801', *English Historical Review*, 71 (1956).

[35] P. Berresford Ellis and Seumas Mac A'Ghobhain, *The Scottish Insurrection of 1820* (1970).

[36] 'Western Campaign', from Patrick Fraser Tytler, *Songs of the Edinburgh Troop* (Edinburgh, 1825).

[37] Robert Walmsley, *Peterloo: The Case Re-Opened* (Manchester, 1969).

change and uncertainty was to turn in large numbers to the evangelical strands which had twisted their way under the calm surface of eighteenth-century religious life since mid-century. Evangelicalism was forged into a powerful weapon motivating public action and regulating private lives. Prayer and enthusiasm, the move from convivial drinking clubs to ordered family life were one side of the movement.[38] Practical public action involved the formation of a host of voluntary associations to fulfil the aims of the faithful. Sunday schools and missionary societies played a major part in this action. They were a massive act of collective cultural assertion as the middling classes projected themselves upon the Catholic French, their own lower orders, upon India and later on Africa and the West Indies. Voluntary organisation was used to seek status and identity and above all to find a means of co-ordinating class action within an emerging social group divided by religion and politics. The 1790s was the decade of chapel-wrecking in Birmingham, Manchester and Sheffield. These societies were national and metropolitan in form. They gave rise to new forms of political action. The Anti-Slavery Society created the characteristic forms of the modern pressure group, public meetings, petitions and reports in the growing newspaper press. They were to be developed by the Anti-Corn Law League and dozens of others. Their rhetoric was in heavy moral tone. Their assertive petitions were not just those of an interest group claiming its place in national policy but those of a platform party claiming the high moral ground in which God Almighty was the first signature on every petition.[39]

Thomas Chalmers, the charismatic Glasgow preacher, enthused for many pages on the virtues of the principle of locality. Each area of each city was to be organised into parishes in which the local middle classes would maintain contact with the lower orders through a network of voluntary associations. Household visiting was an important part of this supervision. In his parish of St John's in Glasgow where he had set this principle to work, he recognised the reality of 'the bustle and distraction of manifold societies' and the 'pacing away among dull committees', but claimed that from organisations like the Saltmarket Sabbath School Society 'a thousand nameless cordialities are constantly issuing out of the patriarchal relationship which

---

[38] Leonore Davidoff and Catherine Hall, *Family Fortunes, Men and Women of the English Middle Class, 1780-1850* (1987), pp. 76–148.

[39] Patricia Hollis, ed. *Pressure from Without in Early Victorian England* (1974).

has thus been formed between a man of worth and so many outcaste and neglected families'.[40]

This confident arrogant lunge for world cultural hegemony should not obscure other important trends amongst the middle classes in their search for identity. Indeed, part of the power of the voluntary association as a social form was the manner in which it could contain so many varied often contradictory trends within one social class group whilst limiting the clashes that must have occurred if those trends had been asserted by a contest for control or influence in the agencies of the state.

The first wave of literary and philosophical societies was created in the 1790s. Their spread was uneven. The major wave of formations did not come until the early 1820s.[41] In this case the urban elites used science as the basis for cultural assertion. In Sheffield they were a vehicle for marginal members of the middle classes, but evidence from Manchester and Leeds showed them to be an alliance between the local elite and the leaders of the professions. Science was built into middle-class and urban elite identity as part of a bid for legitimacy and power.[42] By the 1840s this stream of cultural production had divided into agencies of 'rational recreation' and vehicles for the creation of a variety of educational initiatives which were to be the basis of university education in the great provincial centres of England.

The timing of the formation of each individual society in specific places was influenced by two sorts of pressure. Many foundations were part of a response to a specific crisis. In the winter of 1799–1800, Leeds, like most of Britain, was affected by the typhus epidemic which followed the food scarcity of that winter. As a direct result of this epidemic, Dr Thorpe, a leading local physician, began a campaign which resulted in the opening of a fever hospital, the House of Recovery, on the north-east edge of the town in 1804. This was supported by annual subscriptions as 'affording a ready and safe asylum to the

---

[40]   Thomas Chalmers, *The Christian and Civic Economy of Large Towns*, 3 vols. (Glasgow, 1821), vol. 1, pp. 23–30 and 59.

[41]   Rev. A. Hume, *The Learned Societies and Printing Clubs of the United Kingdom* (1847); Edwin Kitson Clarke, *The History of 100 Years of the Life of the Leeds Philosophical and Literary Society* (Leeds, 1824); A. D. Orange, *Philosophers and Provincials: The Yorkshire Philosophical Society from 1822 to 1844* (Yorkshire Philosophical Society, 1973); Steven A. Shapin, 'The Pottery Philosophical Society, 1819–1835: An Examination of the Cultural Uses of Provincial Science', *Science Studies*, 2 (1972), pp. 311–36.

[42]   Ian Inkster and Jack Morrell, eds., *Metropolis and Province: Science in British Culture, 1780-1850* (1983), p. 41; Robert H. Kargon, *Science in Victorian Manchester* (Manchester, 1977).

poor, but also security to the more opulent, by the reception of their apprentices and servants when attacked by fever'.[43] In Edinburgh, the economic distress of 1812 resulted in an increase in street begging which led to the creation of the Edinburgh Society for the Suppression of Beggars.[44] In Leeds, the same crisis was followed by the formation of a Lancastrian or British and Foreign and a National School Society. These took up the ideas of Lancaster and Bell developed in London and applied them to the situation created by the 1812 crisis.

As the density of the network of societies increased in the 1820s society formation tended to be influenced by fashion and the example of innovations in other urban centres. A large number of Mechanics' Institutes were formed after the establishment of the London Institute in 1824.[45] Wilderspin's ideas on the education of young children brought a wave of Infant School Societies in 1825.[46] A different sort of influence was brought by the English tours of Scotsmen like John Dunlop in 1830–1 which left a rash of anti-spirits societies in their wake.[47] Although London was the most frequent direct source of fashion and influence in the formation of voluntary societies it was not always the source of innovation. Many of the crucial items in the network which the middle classes had established by 1840 originated in Scotland. The Mechanics' Institute movement was based upon the work of Anderson in Glasgow, but needed its journey to London before becoming a national movement. The trustee savings banks also had their origin in south-west Scotland before being taken up by London and spread through the influence of the legislation of 1818.[48]

The variety and profusion of societies need to be listed. Here are some of the Leeds societies which operated in the 1830s and 1840s. In addition to the missionary societies, the medical and poor relief societies, there were scientific societies, occupational associations, societies concerned with culture and education as well as the provision

[43] Dr Hunter, 'On Continued Fever in Leeds', *Edinburgh Medical and Surgical Journal*, 15 (1819), pp. 234–45.

[44] *First Report of the Edinburgh Society for the Suppression of Begging, Instituted 25 January 1813* (Edinburgh, 1814).

[45] J. F. C. Harrison, *Learning and Living, 1790-1960: A Study in the History of the English Adult Education Movement* (1961), pp. 59–61.

[46] Phillip McCann and Francis A. Young, *Samuel Wilderspin and the Infant School Movement* (1982).

[47] B. Harrison, *Drink and the Victorians: The Temperance Question in England, 1815–1872* (1971), p. 104.

[48] H. O. Horne, *The History of Savings Banks* (Oxford, 1847).

of amenities of all kinds. The Benevolent or Stranger's Friend Society was formed in 1789. It was joined by the Church District Visiting Society in 1833. The Leeds General Infirmary (1767) and the House of Recovery (1804) were joined by the Child Bed Relief Society (1823) and the Leeds Public Dispensary (1824). The National School Society and the British and Foreign School Society had come to Leeds in 1812 and 1813. They were joined by the Infant School Society in 1826, whilst the Leeds Ragged School Association in 1849 represented the next wave. The Phil. and Lit. was founded in 1819 and the Mechanics' Institute in 1824. They were joined by the Literary Institute in 1834. The Temperance Society arrived in 1830 and the Town Mission in 1837, whilst the Leeds Guardian Society had been seeking to care for and reform prostitutes since 1821. Gardening emerged from the public house in 1837 to form the Leeds Horticultural Society and the Leeds Horticultural and Floral Society. The Leeds Zoological and Botanical Gardens began their brief and financially insecure history in 1836. The Law Society (1828) and the Medical Society (1838) were formal organisations for two major professions. The Leeds Friendly Loan Society (1844) provided small loans to help working-class people avoid the money club and the pawnbroker, whilst the Leeds Tradesmen's Benevolent Association (1844) granted small annuities to 'decayed or distressed tradesmen and manufacturers', their widows and children.[49] The shopkeepers and tradesmen formed the West Riding Trades' Protection Society in 1848 to protect members against bad debts. This led to a Chamber of Commerce which appeared fairly late in Leeds compared to places like Manchester and Birmingham. The Leeds General Cemetery Company (1833) and the Leeds Public Baths Company (1826) were joint stock organisations with motives that included more than the profits. The Smoke Consumption Committee (1842) had modest success against the local manufacturers whilst the Footpath Association of 1849 had some part in resisting the enclosure of Woodhouse Moor.

The characteristic institutional form of this network of voluntary societies was the subscriber democracy. Money was collected from members. The funds were distributed and activities organised by a committee and officers elected by the subscribers at the annual general meeting. One subscription, one vote was the general rule and uncontested elections the normal practice. In general this led to rule by

---

[49] *Leeds Mercury*, 28 Oct. 1843.

an oligarchy selected from the higher-status members of the society. The president was a high-status local leader, often a local industrialist, the secretary usually a solicitor and the treasurer a local banker or merchant. The committee included a number of hard-working regular attenders. Such an arrangement was the perfect compromise between middle-class people striving for self-respect and independence, and the reality of hierarchical society with its massive inequalities of wealth and power, even within the middle classes.[50] In many societies this was acknowledged by elaborate hierarchies of patrons, vice presidents and trustees, as well as by grades of membership with different privileges and subscription levels. The Leeds Benefit Building and Investment Society was structured to secure trust as well as active participation from its membership. The patrons were local and regional notables such as councillors, JP's and MP's like Richard Cobden. They were expected to visit the offices of the society and inspect the accounts as well as add prestige to the annual meeting. The trustees held the assets of the society. Bankers, solicitors, a surveyor, a manager, treasurer and auditor were all named. Unpaid administration was provided by the president, stewards and the committee. Last but not least were the members.[51] In the Leeds Mechanics' Institute a division between members who elected the 'working man' section of the committee and the subscribers proved unacceptable to many members and potential members and had to be modified in the early 1840s to allow the expansion of the institution.[52]

In this period, the units of activity of the voluntary societies were based upon a local community, but most were related in various ways to national movements, groups or identities. Members, subscribers and money came from one town or district, and funds were usually spent on activities in that town or district. The link to national movements might be direct as in the case of the Bible and missionary societies, which were branches of the London-based organisation. They collected money, organised sermons, did some local evangelising and Bible distribution but sent most of the funds to London. In 1849, the Leeds Religious Tract Society met for its forty-ninth annual meeting to hear about the foreign operations of the parent society from Shanghai to Bechuanaland, and to congratulate itself on the

---

[50] R. J. Morris, 'Voluntary Societies and British Urban Elites, 1780–1850', *Historical Journal*, 26 (1983), pp. 95–118.
[51] *First Annual Report of the Leeds Benefit Building and Investment Society* (Leeds, 1850).
[52] Frederic Hill, *National Education: Its Present State and Prospects* (1836), p. 195.

distribution of 42,000 copies of the *Monthly Messenger* to inhabitants of Leeds who included 2,000 frequenters of the casino and 19,000 threatened by the cholera epidemic.[53] The National and the Lancastrian School Societies had more local independence but relied upon the national society to inspire policy and supply literature and teaching manuals. The Edinburgh Society looked to London to train and supply teachers; Lieutenant Fabian, RN, agent for the parent society attended as many annual general meetings as he could making much the same speech at each one.[54] Other societies lacked this formal national network, but were aware that they were following the example of others. The Edinburgh Society for the Suppression of Beggars referred to the example of Bath, whilst the Newcastle Society for the Suppression of Vagrancy and Mendicity, founded in 1831, quoted examples in Bristol, Cheltenham and Bath.[55] Wider national identities were often strengthened by a periodical literature, like the *Mechanics Magazine* or the *British and Foreign Temperance Intelligencer*, which grew around many voluntary societies and gave the local reader-subscriber the sense of being part of a national movement with interests in common. The readers of the Edinburgh *Missionary and Philanthropic Register* in Edinburgh learnt of the doings of the Glasgow City Mission, the Greenock Seaman's Friend Society as well as the itinerating libraries of Jamaica.[56] The voluntary societies were networks of people in similar situations solving similar problems and fulfilling like needs in an independent manner but conscious of each other's existence. This was one part of the process of creating those forms of social consciousness – class and status, sectarian, party, occupational and national loyalties – which competed for the attention of men and women in the nineteenth century. The structure of the voluntary society network served and exploited local community and urban identities and at the same time moulded them into national identities.

Voluntary associations can be used to adapt to new needs and relationships in situations where there was no relevant system of values or, even more confusing, inappropriate or contradictory sets of values. The great merit of the voluntary society for a social group unsure

[53]   *Leeds Mercury*, 24 Nov. 1849.
[54]   *Report of the Ordinary Directors of the Edinburgh Lancastrian School Society* (Edinburgh, 1813); *British and Foreign School Society, Manual of Teaching* (1816); 'Annual General Meeting of the British and Foreign School Society', Newcastle upon Tyne, Wilson Collection, vol. 4, fo. 866.
[55]   'Meeting for the Foundation of the Newcastle Society for the Suppression of Vagrancy and Mendicity' (27 Jan. 1831), Wilson Collection, vol. 3, fos. 689–90.
[56]   *Scottish Missionary and Philanthropic Register*, vol. 12 (Edinburgh, 1831).

of itself or divided is and was that joining entailed a very limited commitment, quite unlike, for example, supporting or accepting an item of legislation. The development of the poor law after the legislation of 1834 and 1843 was the result and cause of bitter disputes between social classes and within the middle classes.[57] The voluntary societies were able to experiment in a more tranquil manner with a variety of tactics. The Leeds Benevolent and Stranger's Friend Society was founded in 1789 after the model of an earlier society in London. It used a system of recommendations and household visiting to try and reconcile the conflict between the teaching of Malthus and the demand of Christian charity.[58] Edinburgh favoured a Society for the Suppression of Beggars founded in 1812 which added a coercive element. They asked the police to prosecute anyone caught begging in the streets rather than accept the attentions of the Society. As the work ethic became increasingly important for both the middle classes and a growing portion of the working classes, this was met by the provision of relief in return for labour on public works projects like the roads around Holyrood Park in Edinburgh, which were built by men working under the Association for the Relief of Industrious Labourers and Mechanics.[59] Those who wished to offer religious advice with their material relief could act through denominational groups. The avoidance of conflict through the formation of a multiplicity of voluntary societies was evident in education, temperance and other areas of activity.

Many societies adjusted and changed aims, tactics, constitution, membership and the content of their activities in the light of experience. The temperance people switched from a moderationist to a teetotal pledge. The Mechanics' Institutes moved away from practical education for artisans to day schools for teenage boys and entertaining lectures and library books for adult members.[60] This change was part

[57] J. R. Poynter, *Society and Pauperism: English Ideas on Poor Relief, 1795–1834* (1969); R. Mitchison, 'The Making of the Old Scottish Poor Law', *Past & Present*, 63 (1974), pp. 58–93; Audrey Patterson, 'The Poor Law in 19th Century Scotland', in D. Fraser, ed., *The New Poor Law in the Nineteenth Century* (1976), pp. 171–93.

[58] J. M. Gardiner, *History of the Leeds Benevolent or Stranger's Friend Society, 1789–1889* (Leeds, 1890).

[59] *First Report of the Edinburgh Society for the Suppression of Beggars; Seventeenth Annual Report of the Edinburgh Benevolent or Stranger's Friend Society* (Edinburgh, 1832); *Report of the Association for the Relief of Industrious Labourers and Mechanics* (Edinburgh, 1816).

[60] Harrison, *Drink and the Victorians*, p. 38; J. W. Hudson, *The History of Adult Education* (1951), pp. 92–5; Edward Royle, 'Mechanics Institutes and the Working Classes, 1840–1860', *Historical Journal*, 14 (1971), pp. 305–21; Mabel Tylecote, *The Mechanics Institutions of Lancashire and Yorkshire before 1851* (Manchester, 1957).

of the middle-class move from evangelical seriousness to mid-century rational recreation.

Although the leaders of many of these societies explicitly sought control and hegemony over the working classes, such dominance was unlikely ever to be complete. The societies offered a variety of areas of cultural bargaining between classes. There was a variety of means of disciplining; the recommendation system, house visiting, the endless rules and regulations, together with the offer of crucial cultural and material resources. Whatever middle-class ambitions, there were simply too many alternatives for any complete control of ideology, thought or social practice. Choice could never be directed. What this network did was to place a powerful set of conventions into class relationships. Within a generation of this formative period between 1820 and 1850, working-class people were organising in societies, associations and unions with the same traditions of chairmen, agendas, rules, members, subscriptions and rational orderly discussion which had begun a century earlier with groups like the Select Society in Edinburgh. A modern trade-union leader, who complains that normal 'procedures' have not been followed by the employers, pays an unwitting tribute to the traditions created by the middle-class network of societies long after words like respectability and self-help have lost their original meanings.

Alongside this, another very different group, a neighbourhood network, had been created by the skilled working class and the small masters and independent producers who identified with them in that social group which Paine called 'the people'. Samuel Smiles in his radical phase had many dealings with this group: 'The great power which seems yet destined to effect the social emancipation of the working classes, is the power of co-operation.'[61] The trade unions based upon local and community occupational groups, tied together by tramping networks and delegate conferences, Smiles regarded as a 'most imperfect form'.[62] More important for showing 'the mutual benefit, attained by the clubbing of small means together', were the friendly societies. These had grown in number at the end of the eighteenth century as local societies and box clubs. By 1815, they

---

[61] Samuel Smiles, 'What Is Doing for the People in Leeds', *The People's Journal*, 1 (1846), p. 136; R. J. Morris, 'Samuel Smiles and the Genesis of Self Help: The Retreat to a Petit Bourgeois Utopia', *Historical Journal*, 24 (1981), pp. 89–109.

[62] E. J. Hobsbawm, *Labouring Men* (1964), pp. 34–65; Richard Price, *Masters, Unions and Men: Work Control in Building and the Rise of Labour, 1830–1914* (Cambridge, 1980), pp. 55–90.

encompassed over 8 per cent of the population. Through their weekly meetings and subscriptions they offered members convivial and select companions, as well as sickness and burial benefit. The 1830s saw the growth of the affiliated orders. These were most important in the northern counties of England. The Manchester Unity of Odd-fellows was based upon that city whilst the Ancient Order of Foresters (Adam was the first, they said) had its headquarters in Leeds. The friendly societies always provided much more than insurance. One rule essential to most was that members should always follow the coffin at the funeral of another lodge member. The lodge provided not only weekly companionship but assurance against that primitive terror in a changing and geographically mobile world of a lonely death with no friends to ensure decent burial.[63] Friendly societies, building societies, trades clubs could all thrive in the neighbourhood or occupational context. They were a major target of government attempts at control and regulation through the Registrar General of Friendly Societies. They were offered the security of legal identity in return for allowing the inspection of their rules and accounts by a government agency.

By 1850 it was clear that many societies serving this group on the boundary of the middle and working classes had adopted a set of values often identified with the bourgeoisie, values of self-help, thrift, temperance and mutual improvement. The discussion of these activities has tangled with the debate over the place of a 'labour aristocracy' in the social peace of the 1850s and 1860s.[64] In practice, the organised activities of this social group provide unlikely evidence for any social 'collaboration' or 'manipulation'.[65] They dipped into the stream of culture offered by the middle-class network to select and transform items in that package to suit different interests. In some cases the societies themselves became objects of class contest. Temperance societies were created by middle-class evangelicals in the early 1830s, and then captured by a respectable working-class membership, which transformed them from cosy affirmations of middle-class superiority

---

[63] P. H. J. H. Gosden, *Self-Help: Voluntary Associations in Nineteenth Century Britain* (1973), pp. 11–75, and *idem, The Friendly Societies in England, 1815–1875* (Manchester, 1961). I am struck by the similarity of these societies with organisations created by African people to cope with the changes they faced in the 1950s: K. L. Little, *West African Urbanization: A Study of Voluntary Associations in Social Change* (Cambridge, 1965).

[64] E. J. Hobsbawm, 'Lenin and the "Aristocracy of Labour"', *Marxism Today*, 14 (1970), pp. 207–10; Henry Pelling, *Popular Politics and Society in Late Victorian Britain* (1968), pp. 35–61.

[65] Robert Q. Gray, *The Labour Aristocracy in Victorian Edinburgh* (Oxford, 1976).

to teetotal organisations which created a whole new life style around their pledge.[66] Adult education was no less contentious. The East Greenwich Mutual Improvement Society, like many others, was formed by artisans who resented the patronage involved in Mechanics' Institutes.[67] In the north of England, there was a formalising of the traditions of the weavers' libraries and the working-class botanical societies of Lancashire and Yorkshire. In some cases, like the new Volunteer Corps of the 1860s, the result was class control without any very obvious hegemony; in others like the Clubs and Institute Union, it was the working-class membership which took control.[68]

By the 1860s the working class had at once more leisure, more income and a greater exposure to urbanising influences. The rise of organised sport entailed its own class battles of organisation. The Amateur Athletic Association was a win for the gentlemen amateur, although the survival of professional handicaps like the Powderhall sprints in Edinburgh showed the strength of working-class traditions. The contest for class territory took place not only in great strikes and franchise reform campaigns, but in an accumulation of local events like the day in the 1870s when Christ Church Football Club walked out on the local vicar, crossed the road to the Gladstone Hotel and formed Blackburn Rovers Football Club.[69] Soccer was clear working-class victory with few of the limitations of the third Reform Act. The campaign began in 1883 with the defeat of the Old Etonians by Blackburn Olympic in the Football Association Cup Final. The FA responded by banning all forms of professionalism, money in the boot, broken time payments and the rest. The northern clubs, who now played the best football in the game formed their own British Association in 1884. The FA gave way with remarkable speed. The rule of the game by the gentlemen from London was no hegemony. It was an arena of class bargaining in which the working-class clubs of the north who had the top players and attracted the largest crowds had the upper hand.[70] The rugby code was score draw after the professional Rugby League broke away. What mattered was that the battle

---

[66]   Harrison, *Drink and the Victorians*, pp. 107–46.
[67]   Geoffrey Crossick, *An Artisan Elite in Victorian Society: Kentish London, 1840–1880* (1978), p. 138.
[68]   Hugh Cunningham, *The Volunteer Force* (1975); Richard Price, 'The Working Men's Club Movement and Victorian Social Reform Ideology', *Victorian Studies*, 15 (1976), pp. 301–28.
[69]   Peter Bailey, *Leisure and Class in Victorian England: Rational Recreation and the Contests for Control, 1830–1885* (1978), p. 139.
[70]   *Ibid.*, pp. 140–4.

did not take place in terms of legal action or public order campaigns against street football, bull running, dog fighting or prize fighting. It took place as a series of disputes within and between organisations vying with each other to control property, audiences and memberships. Conflict in sport as in many other spheres of life was organised.

The limited commitment and adaptive qualities of the voluntary societies made them ideal for carrying contradictory and conflicting values within and between classes. Thus the missionary societies and poor relief societies carried their differences over denominational practice and identity through the formation of several competing societies. This was especially suited to the urban environment in which a growing, massed population was able to support a wide variety of undertakings. The moral suasion temperance societies existed alongside the United Kingdom Alliance which sought state intervention. Each denomination had its missionary societies. The school societies competed for funds, enabling the middling classes to defuse one of the most divisive social policy debates of the century. Despite this division, the practice and social forms within each society were remarkably similar. The evangelical Baptists from the missionary society would have followed the conventions of the utilitarian Society for the Propagation of Useful Knowledge with ease even if they had disliked the content of the meeting. The voluntary society could also act as an integrative agency. In an important group of societies contentious items were excluded by the rules. Most literary and philosophical societies had rules which forbad the discussion of politics and religion. The middle-class members could then explore a wide range of topics on which they agreed and such societies could act as a base for class initiatives.[71] In the second half of the century many working-class trade unions and co-operative societies had the same rule to fulfil the same need to avoid fragmentation. They were the site of much class bargaining and class formation over culture and social action.

THE 1890S TO THE 1950S

By the 1890s, patterns of association were being established which were to last into the 1950s. A number of important long-run social and economic trends lay behind these changes. Increasing leisure,

---

[71]   R. J. Morris, 'Middle Class Culture, 1700–1914', in D. Fraser, ed., *A History of Modern Leeds* (Manchester, 1980), pp. 200–22.

rising incomes and hence consumption, secularisation and the growing power of the state, a growing working-class consciousness
expressed through the labour movement, women's struggle first to
achieve and then to respond to important gains in the public sphere,
were all added to existing factors such as the need to respond to
the instability of capitalist prosperity, the need to order and regulate
conflicts and to create new values and forms of social action in the
face of change. The Great War acted as a stimulus and trigger of
change. It interrupted and accelerated many trends but rarely
appeared as a major discontinuity. There was a cluster of initiatives
in 1919 and 1920 but almost all related to developments in the twenty
years before 1914.

If there was a high noon for religious activity in Britain it came
in the 1890s. It came not in terms of the proportion of adults attending
church but in the bustle and activity of dozens of clubs, societies,
associations and fellowships which gathered in the penumbra of the
churches and chapels as they spread into the new suburbs and as
the middle classes turned one more time to that compulsive leisure
activity, bringing the working classes to church. The aggressive evangelical activity which had originated in the early nineteenth century
reached its peak in the 1870s and 1880s with the street spectacular
of the Salvation Army. Already the churches were becoming leisure
centres with endless clusters of societies based upon sex, age, denomination and even occupation. In the biscuit-making town of Reading,
the Church of England Men's Society was matched by the dissenters'
Christian Endeavour Society. The Boys' Brigade was countered by
the Church Lads' Brigade. Book clubs and discussion societies came
and went. Each winter different groups turned towards the various
needs they perceived amongst the poor. Ladies' Visiting Associations,
Dorcas Societies, Soup Kitchens, Provident Funds, Coal and Clothing
Clubs, Penny Banks and Poor Stewards met around the Methodist
chapels. In many of the new suburbs, leisure and sociability was largely organised by the church. Indeed the wise developer always left
land for a church or in some cases provided one himself.[72] In Caver-
sham, a suburb of Reading, the cricket club, the choral society, the

[72] F. M. L. Thompson, *Hampstead: Building a Borough, 1650–1964* (1974), p. 284; J.
M. Rawcliffe, 'Bromley: Kentish Market Town to London Suburb, 1841–1881', in
F. M. L. Thompson, ed., *The Rise of Suburbia* (Leicester, 1982), p. 67.

horticultural society and the football clubs all had some link with the Anglican parish.[73] Church and chapel buildings, new and old, began to sprout halls for sports and dances, rooms for meetings and discussions. All this cost money. That required meetings to plan, meetings to sew and make, sales of work, subscriptions and appeals. The results still decorate the inner suburbs of British cities. Even organisations which came into being well before 1890 tended to change their nature. The Young Men's Christian Association had been formed in London in 1844 to protect young men newly arrived in that city to work as clerks or in retailing. The Association spread rapidly to commercial cities like Liverpool. Their aim was 'the improvement of the spiritual and mental condition of young men engaged in business'.[74] These aims were reflected in the rules of the Reading YMCA in 1900 which gave Bible study a central place, but it was clear that sport and recreation were the real focus of attention. The churches were competing for attention in a world which offered an increasing variety of leisure attractions. Sport, the music hall, commercial leisure of all kinds, homes which offered a little more comfort to many and the labour movement itself were all alternatives. The churches had to compete and did so by refining and specialising the product to serve a market divided by age, sex and occupation. St Mary's Free Church in Govan had Sunday schools, Bible classes, a Literary Society, male and female fellowships, the Boys' Brigade, Gospel Temperance and a Penny Savings Bank.[75] There were railwaymen's missions, mill girl prayer groups, the Glasgow Foundry Boys' Religious Society, the YMCA and the YWCA.[76] In London, the Home Mission Sunday School, the Mission to Coalies, the Navvy Mission, the Barmaids' Mission and the Midnight Meeting Movement sought the attention of their target groups.[77] Organisations sought to attract rather than convert or terrify. In Reading, the St Giles Church Lads' Brigade had a band, a football club, and a cricket club.[78] It was little wonder that clerics and ministers felt that 'many chapels are all but buried beneath their accumulated societies'.[79]

This great transformation of formal religious structures was running

[73] Stephen Yeo, *Religion and Voluntary Organisations in Crisis* (1976), pp. 58–60 and 204.
[74] Gregory Anderson, *Victorian Clerks* (Manchester, 1976), pp. 74–85.
[75] Callum Brown, *The Social History of Religion in Scotland since 1730* (1987), pp. 146–8.
[76] *Ibid.*, p. 145.
[77] R. Mudie Smith, *The Religious Life of London* (1904), p. 278.
[78] Yeo, *Religion and Voluntary Organisations in Crisis*, p. 164.
[79] *Ibid.*

out of steam by the mid-1900s.[80] The ministers of Reading reported that they were struggling to find officers and committee members for the organisations that clung to their chapels. The Great War accelerated this trend. In Rochdale an active social life around the churches and chapels revived briefly; 'weekly meetings in the "Band Room", friendly and informal with "tuppenny pies" and coffee to round off a pleasant half hour of games and discussions'. Within a few years of 1919, many organisations were dead and others a shadow of what they had been. Although the cinema did not reach its full potential until the 1930s, there were already five in Rochdale in 1922 playing to full houses.[81] The deaths, injuries and disorganisation caused by the war caused untold and long-term damage to the ability of many communities to sustain organisations. Many groups had prospered under the patronage of local manufacturers who had lived locally. As the structure of capital changed and traditional industries met the hostile economic conditions of the 1920s, many of these capitalist patrons withdrew. Like the Palmers in Reading they moved away from the community which was their productive base. In Kirkcaldy this process was added to by the family disaster of losing a son in the war. The linoleum-making Nairns left behind a memorial art gallery and library.[82]

The momentum of these clusters of associations and the social capital of the churches and chapels with which they were associated were too powerful to be stopped by the social changes of a generation. They were slowed but not destroyed. In York, the YMCA closed for lack of interest in 1938, but the YWCA was still an active girls' club with a large lounge, canteen, a study and rooms for games, social events and dramatics; 'The main activities are Bible study, keep fit classes, country dancing, singing, tap dancing and hockey.'[83] In its first year of publication in 1938, *Picture Post* found the Grandmothers' Club run by the Victoria Dock Mission operating much as it would have done in the 1890s. 'First a short service. Then tea and talk. Then some gramophone music and singing . . . community singing.' The

[80] Mudie Smith, *The Religious Life of London*, p. 274.
[81] Paul Wild, 'Recreation in Rochdale, 1900–40', in John Clarke, Chris Critcher and Richard Johnson, eds., *Working-Class Culture: Studies in History and Theory* (1979), pp. 140–5.
[82] Augustus Muir, *Nairn's of Kirkcaldy: A Short History, 1847–1956* (Cambridge, 1956).
[83] B. Seebohm Rowntree, *Poverty and Progress: A Second Social Survey of York* (1941), pp. 346–8.

ladies paid a penny per week and played draughts.[84] A few miles away in north London was a Grandfathers' Club run by Upper Holloway Baptist church, which had singing, draughts, chess, cards and dominoes with their hymns and Bible lesson.[85] In 1947, in prosperous High Wycombe, expanding in the orbit of London, there were thirty-five churches with organisations like those of the Methodist church which had a women's meeting, a men's institute, a youth club, a young people's fellowship, a cricket club, a sick and poor fund, a junior missionary society as well as the Sunday school.[86] Such a world was now only one margin of organised social life, but it was a world which survived well into the 1950s with the cautious sexuality of the many formal dances and socials which smoothed dozens of dusty worn boarded floors, to the accompaniment of endless games of table tennis, as participants graduated from Sunday school and the Band of Hope to flower-arranging classes at the Mothers' Union and earnest discussion in the Men's Fellowship.

An important section of the organisations which filled the church halls and chapel rooms were a new group of youth organisations which emerged in the generation before 1914. The Boys' Brigade emerged in the 1880s in the West of Scotland. Its founder, William Smith, came from the commercial and presbyterian world of Glasgow. He welded together his experience as a member of the YMCA and the volunteer Lanarkshire Rifles to form a brigade of boys, twelve and over, for 'The Advancement of Christ's Kingdom'. Military discipline and organisation, uniforms with dummy rifles for drill and summer camps were an immediate success. The boys liked playing at soldiers and joining marching bands even with the Sunday Bible class. The movement spread to England where it split in 1891 with the formation of the Church Lads' Brigade by the Anglican church. The formula was extended by Baden-Powell in 1908 with the dramatic success of *Scouting for Boys* and the formation of the Boy Scout movement which followed. Scouting wove together imperialism, the concern for national efficiency and the growing enthusiasm for the cleansing effects and moral regeneration of contact with the 'outdoors'. Baden-Powell's charismatic personality reinforced by the story of the siege of Mafeking was coupled with the publicity skills of Sir Arthur Pearson, publisher of the *Express* and the *Standard*. Uniforms, tests, badges,

---

[84] *Picture Post*, 22 Oct. 1938.
[85] *Ibid.*, 17 Dec. 1938.
[86] B. Seebohm Rowntree and G. R. Lavers, *English Life and Leisure* (1951), p. 406.

games, camping, the hierarchy of patrols and leaders, an atmosphere of rushing about free of immediate parental supervision were all part of the formula for success. Although there were church parades and the Scout Promise 'to do my duty to God and the King', the movement took another step away from the Sunday school and the YMCA. There was little religious or denominational identity. Some 34 per cent of males born between 1901 and 1920 claimed to have belonged to the Scouts. The movement gained this breadth of appeal and a durability which survived the Great War because Baden-Powell succeeded in creating an ideology which was more broadly based than its imperial and military origins. In *Citizenship* he showed a support for social reform and placed his movement as a counter to class antagonism: 'you must begin as boys, not to think of other classes of boys to be your enemies'.[87] Between 1911 and 1913, the leaders of the Scout movement took care to distance themselves from government attempts to draw them into military training and recruitment.[88] It was thus easier for the movement to identify itself in the 1920s with international fellowship and the League of Nations philosophy through well-publicised international jamborees.

This evolution of ideology and practice did not satisfy those who felt that one strand of the ideals which went into the Scout movement had been too heavily diluted by imperialism and citizenship. Baden-Powell had learnt a lot from Ernest Thompson Seton's idealism. Seton's Woodcraft movement in the USA sought 'the promotion of interest in out of doors life and woodcraft, the preservation of wild life and landscape and the promotion of good fellowship amongst its members'.[89] These ideas migrated to the fringes of the labour movement leading to the formation of the Woodcraft Folk in 1925 with a loose association with the Co-operative movement. Socialism, eugenics and pantheistic mysticism were part of a small but enthusiastic movement which set itself as a deliberate counter to scouting and the Boys' Brigades and made important contributions to the wider

[87] Paul Wilkinson, 'English Youth Movements, 1908-30', *Journal of Contemporary History*, 4 (1969), pp. 3–23.

[88] Allen Warren, 'Sir Robert Baden-Powell, the Scout Movement and Citizen Training in Great Britain, 1900–1920', *English Historical Review*, 101 (1986), pp. 376–98.

[89] Brian Morris, 'Ernest Thompson Seton and the Origins of the Woodcraft Movement', *Journal of Contemporary History*, 5 (1970), pp. 183–94.

labour movement, pacifism and working-class identity, notably in parts of London.[90]

By the 1920s, the Scout movement had acquired all the necessary age and gender specialisms. The foundation of the Girl Guides in 1916 as a segregated organisation was much more acceptable to parental concern for moral supervision than the Woodcraft Folk's refusal to segregate. The fact that the female side of the movement was founded and led by Baden-Powell's young wife was perhaps a vignette of the model of female citizenship which was to emerge after 1918. Taken together the uniformed youth organisations had attracted some 59 per cent of the adult males and 52 per cent of the adult females of the mid-1960s.[91] They were significant for avoiding the political extremism of some youth movements in Europe. They also provided an organised and socially acceptable transition from the Victorian suppression of adolescence to the consumer-based teenage identity which emerged in the late 1950s. The Scouts and Guides were brand leaders in an ideological supermarket of youth organisations.

In the 1890s, the remaking of the British working class took place around three social processes. There was a general acceptance of industrial capitalism and the need to come to terms with the power relationships which it entailed. Increasing real income for many sections of the working class meant a growing enjoyment of a commercialised leisure system of public houses, music halls, professional spectator sport, popular newspapers and for some seaside holidays. The most dynamic of these processes was the production of a vast infrastructure of socialism, fragments of organisation within which groups and individuals not only began to question the subordinations and poverty they experienced but sought to puzzle out ways of reorganising social and economic relationships which seemed so unsatisfactory. The alliance between the Labour party and the trade unions was to become the focus of this movement, hence it is natural that most attention should be given to those small groups which buzzed like gadflies upon the body politic. One of the earliest was the Scottish Labour Party formed in Glasgow in 1888 which carried a theoretical syndicalism into many workplaces and a conviction that the working

---

[90] David Prynn, 'The Woodcraft Folk and the Labour Movement, 1925–70', *Journal of Contemporary History*, 8 (1983), pp. 79–95.

[91] The figures come from a Mass-Observation sample survey. Wilkinson, 'English Youth Movements'.

class needed to be educated before any major change could take place. The Independent Labour Party which had originated in West Yorkshire was the most pragmatic in its search for power, operating on the belief that it was important for working people to be elected to as many representative bodies as possible from the poor law authorities to Parliament. The Socialist Democratic Federation which became the British Socialist party in 1911 was a more thoroughgoing Marxist organisation and provided a home for people like Willie Gallacher and John MacLean. Gallacher found the Sunday school atmosphere of his ILP branch in Paisley too much for him and 'discovered a small group of Marxists who met in a cobbler's shop ... soon a branch of the Social Democratic Federation was in full swing'.[92] The enormous variety of these groups was significant. John Wheatley formed a Catholic Socialist Society in 1906. He had been victimised by the priests and needed a base from which to show that his religion and his socialism were compatible.[93] A Scottish Socialist Teachers' Society was formed around 1908 by James Maxton and John MacLean, the 'fighting dominie'. School Boards and school managers were dominated by religious and liberal influence deeply antagonistic to the materialism and radicalism of the socialists.[94]

The infrastructure of socialism was much more than the ideological writings of intellectuals, the doings of heroes and charismatic leaders or even the day-to-day political campaigning of the members of these fragments each bearing their own vision of the socialist future. This infrastructure extended into many areas of social life. Harry McShane has set out the record for Glasgow. The movements which gathered around Blatchford's *Clarion* newspaper were amongst the most important. In Glasgow there were Clarion cycling clubs, Clarion scouts, Clarion choirs and the Clarion vans which toured with speakers and literature.[95] The Clarion clubs were especially strong in Lancashire and Yorkshire. Together with the cycling craze, they were a release from domesticity and factory labour for many women. Alice Foley cycling out of Bolton wrote, 'Rules and riding disciplines were few and simple, no passing the captain; obedience to his whistle; cycling in pairs on busy roads, and all hands to the pump in case

[92]   William Gallacher, *Revolt on the Clyde* (1936), p. 6.
[93]   Joan Smith, 'Class, Skill and Sectarianism in Glasgow and Liverpool', in R. J. Morris, ed., *Class, Power and Social Structure in British Nineteenth Century Towns* (Leicester, 1986), p. 199.
[94]   Nan Milton, *John MacLean* (1973), p. 42.
[95]   Harry McShane and Joan Smith, *No Mean Fighter* (1978), pp. 30–1.

of punctures, breakdowns or accidents.'[96] By the late 1890s, the first Clarion huts were being established as a base for cheap weekend holidays for members. 'It was an outing – you took your own food and made your own tea.'[97] Such activities mixed recreation, sociability and politics. They could become intensely political in themselves. The Sheffield Clarion Ramblers established in 1900 introduced their members to the enjoyment of the nearby Peak District. Their frustration with the rights of property which barred walkers from many areas of moorland because of shooting rights culminated in the mass trespasses of the 1930s and pitched battles with police and gamekeepers. The whole principle of the National Parks embodied in legislation in 1949 was one of the quieter and less celebrated victories of this socialism.[98]

For others the labour churches and socialist Sunday schools formed an important bridge between the world of dissenting chapels and that of the labour movement.[99] They had their own hymns and the Socialist Ten Commandments, 'Remember that all good things of the earth are produced by labour. Whoever enjoys them without working for them is stealing the bread of the workers.'[100] Harry McShane described the many socialist Sunday schools in Glasgow:

Instead of the children being baptized as they were in church, there was a naming ceremony where a big crowd sang socialist songs. When I first saw it I was quite shocked, as I could not quite rid myself of Catholicism. Four little girls put flowers on the baby for purity and then a red rose was put on for the revolution.[101]

In Nelson in textile-mill Lancashire, Mary Cooper took her *Socialist Sunday School Hymn Book* to the ILP Hall. The baptisms were often accompanied by the visit of some prominent Labour politician, leaving behind children called Keir Hardie Clegg or whose middle names were Bruce Glasier. A generation brought up in the Primitive Methodist chapels of the Pennine valleys took much of that practice into their socialist movement. They treated their labour heroes like a new

---

[96] Jill Liddington and Jill Norris, *One Hand Tied Behind Us: The Rise of the Women's Suffrage Movement* (1978), p. 123.
[97] *Ibid.*
[98] David Prynn, 'The Clarion Clubs, Rambling and the Holiday Associations in Britain since the 1890s', *Journal of Contemporary History*, 11 (1976), pp. 65–77.
[99] Hugh McLeod, *Class and Religion in the Late Victorian City* (1974), p. 64.
[100] Liddington and Norris, *One Hand Tied Behind Us*, p. 118.
[101] McShane and Smith, *No Mean Fighter*, p. 31.

band of Old Testament prophets.[102] Other people were involved in educational organisations like the Plebs' League and the Central Labour College in London. John MacLean's economics classes in Glasgow and his contribution to the Scottish Labour College became legends in their own time. They were additions to the dozens of classes, meetings, addresses and libraries organised by bodies like Kinning Park Co-operative Education Committee.[103] Marxist economics and socialist versions of history were all part of this movement, but in a world where working-class education was limited to the elementary school system and continually interrupted by poverty and sickness, it must be remembered that simply to lay claim to study and re-interpret the high culture identified with the upper and middle classes was an act of class aggression which was part of the wider movement.

In terms of numbers and geographical extent the retail Co-operative Societies were one of the most important elements of this network. The political importance of the Co-ops was considerably sharpened in the 1890s. The move from communitarian to retail co-operation in the 1840s might seem to be reformism, but attention should be paid to the attacks made in the 1890s by shopkeepers who saw them as a threat to profits.[104] If the Co-operative movement's reluctance to be involved in politics seems odd, then it must be remembered that in a world divided between Liberals and Tories, an abjuration of politics might be a necessary if temporary aspect of class formation. Even in Reading where the SDF and any independent working-class educational organisation found it hard to survive, the Co-operative Society survived in cautious deference to the paternalism of the biscuit-making capitalists of the Palmer family.[105] It was in Yorkshire, Lancashire, London, the west of Scotland and mining areas like the north-east of England that the movement made its greatest impact.[106] In the mining village of Ashington in Northumberland, the Co-op store was run, as it was run in hundreds of other places by a committee of men elected by the annual meeting of shareholders. They were

---

[102] Jill Liddington, *The Life and Times of a Respectable Rebel, Selina Cooper, 1864–1946* (1984), p. 136.
[103] Milton, *John MacLean*, pp. 118–20.
[104] Sidney Pollard, 'Nineteenth Century Co-operation: From Community Building to Shopkeeping', in Asa Briggs and John Saville, eds., *Essays in Labour History* (1960), pp. 74–112; Geoffrey Crossick and Heinz-Gerhard Haupt, eds., *Shopkeepers and Master Artisans in Nineteenth Century Europe* (1984), pp. 62–94 and 239–69.
[105] Yeo, *Religion and Voluntary Organisations in Crisis*, pp. 253–92.
[106] John Langton and R. J. Morris, *Atlas of Industrializing Britain, 1780–1914* (1986), pp. 180–4 and 194–7.

men elected because of their standing in the working-class community and their belief in co-operative ideals. One or two of them would attend the annual conference of the Co-operative Union and as store managers they would often purchase from the Co-operative Wholesale Society. The Co-op was more than this. The work of the education committee was to push the Society into the community. In Ashington, it arranged classes, lectures, concerts, choirs, orchestras and the library. Co-operative summer school scholarships provided a much prized means of escape. The Society had a ball room in the Arcade. There were dances and dancing classes every Wednesday and Saturday.[107] Within the mining communities of Northumberland and Durham the Co-op was only one part of a network of institutions which included the Durham Miners' Union's lodge, the working men's club and the dominant local Methodist chapel.[108]

One of the most important of the organisations which clustered around the Co-operative movement was the Women's Co-operative Guild founded in 1883. Its founder, Margaret Llewelyn Davies, a university-educated rector's daughter, was secretary until 1921 and provided a remarkable example of successful middle-class leadership of a dynamic working-class organisation.[109] The labour movement was dominated by the assertive pride of the skilled adult male wage earner, confident that his demand for a family wage and rigid control of the gender structure of work and home was the best defence against the uncertainties of capitalist production. The Guild was one of the few organisations which could provide a focus and a release for women's political and social energies.[110] The Guild provided early training for women who took an important part in the suffrage movement and in many cases entered public life as local councillors, School Board members and magistrates.[111] It was a lever by which women edged their way into the public life of the labour movement. When the Kinning Park Co-operative laid the foundation stone of their new building in 1891, the committee decided 'it was not considered good

[107] Linda McCullough Thew, *The Pit Village and the Store* (1985), pp. 115–19, 165–7 and 178–81.
[108] K. Brown, 'The Lodges of the Durham Miners' Association, 1869–1926', *Northern History*, 23 (1987), pp. 138–52.
[109] Margaret Llewelyn Davies, *Maternity: Letters from Working Women*, with introduction by Gloden Dallas (1978).
[110] J. Gaffin and D. Thomas, *Caring and Sharing: The Centenary History of the Co-operative Women's Guild* (1983); see also review by Gillian Scott in *Bulletin of the Society for the Study of Labour History*, 50 (1985), pp. 37–8.
[111] Jill Liddington, *Respectable Rebel: Hannah Mitchell, the Hard Way Up* (1968), p. 226.

form for women to appear on the platform at Co-operative or other working class meetings'. By the time the building was opened, protests from the Guildswomen ensured that they had representatives on the platform.[112] The Guild brought a wide range of issues relating directly to women's experience into the public sphere of labour and national debate: birth control, legal abortion, family allowances, nursery schools, maternity clinics, school dinners and free school meals. They took a central place in the co-operative and pacifist movements of the 1920s and 1930s.[113] This pattern of claiming citizenship whilst bringing domestic issues firmly into the public sphere was something which characterised many women's organisations in the period after the franchise reforms of 1918.

THE GENDER FRONTIER AND 'OUT-GROUPS'

The networks of all three periods reflected the ebb and flow of the gender frontier. The turning points were different in different social classes but the pattern was very much the same. Many middle-class women entered the nineteenth century with a sense of class responsibility and evangelical enthusiasm upon them. A Ladies' Charity was formed in Liverpool in 1796, run and administered by women to visit the sick poor.[114] The Society for Bettering the Condition of the Poor reported in 1803 that the ladies of Leeds had established five schools of industry to teach reading, knitting and sewing to fifty poor girls. They were visited weekly by committee members and 'supplied the neighbourhood with some good female servants'.[115] Such independent and public initiatives by women met early opposition. The members of a visiting society in Glasgow were warned of those 'whose characters are such as to preclude the possibility of their being regularly visited by members of the society personally, without a violation of the feeling of propriety'.[116] In mid-century, sentiments like these

---

[112]   Joe Melling, *Rent Strikes: People's Struggle for Housing in West Scotland, 1890–1916* (Edinburgh, 1983), p. 25.

[113]   Gill Scott, 'The Women's Co-operative Guild', *Bulletin of the Society for the Study of Labour History*, 48 (1984), p. 19.

[114]   Simey, *Charitable Efforts in Liverpool in the Nineteenth Century*, p. 21.

[115]   Thomas Bernard, 'An Account of the Ladies' Schools and Some Other Charities at Leeds', *Report of the Society for Bettering the Condition of the Poor*, 4 (25 Dec. 1803).

[116]   *Glasgow Herald*, 20 Feb. 1810, quoted in Stana Nenadich, 'The Structure, Values and Influence of the Scottish Urban Middle Class: Glasgow, 1800–1870' (unpublished PhD thesis, Glasgow University, 1986).

were summed up by John Angell James, the charismatic nonconformist Birmingham preacher:

Nothing could be more repugnant to my sense of propriety than for young women to be sent out with what are called collecting cards, to wander over a town knocking on the doors of anybody and everybody for the purpose of begging money, and sometimes entering into counting houses and assailing even young men with their importunities.[117]

By the 1830s women had been assigned a number of distinctive and limited roles in the middle-class network of societies. They sat on balconies, attended lectures by visiting missionaries and prepared for eternal fundraising bazaars and sales of work for hospitals, missionary societies, chapel-building funds or campaigns like the Anti-Corn Law League. Through the auxiliary system of the Bible and missionary societies they performed a limited number of tasks. Their main business was to collect subscriptions from friends and neighbours. They proved to be a feared and formidable force.[118] Those who went further than this earned the censure of a John Angell James or satirical derision in the style of Charles Dickens and his accounts of Mrs Pardiggle in *Bleak House*. The wives of leading philanthropic committee men were placed in positions which men found morally uncomfortable, like ladies' committees to inspect homes for the care of prostitutes.[119] By the 1840s women were returning as guests to lectures and conversaziones at the Mechanics' Institute and the Literary and Philosophical Society. In general, these limited roles reproduced aspects of domesticity in the public sphere. This was much more restricted than the active and independent intervention in matters of religion, missionary and welfare work, or the control of social interaction in assemblies and balls which had been curbed in the late eighteenth and early nineteenth centuries. The suggestion that the gender frontier was swept back does not imply that there was no subordination in the earlier period. It does imply that the nature of that subordination changed and that this left women less freedom in that public sphere in which policy, opinion and values were created and negotiated.

Working-class women, especially amongst the artisans, survived a generation longer with an active if subordinate place in public life. The friendly societies included a variety of female lodges which have attracted little attention from historians or contemporaries. The Loyal

---

[117]   Davidoff and Hall, *Family Fortunes*, p. 430.

[118]   F. K. Prochaska, *Women and Philanthropy in Nineteenth-Century England* (Oxford, 1980), pp. 5–27.

[119]   *Annual Reports of the Leeds Guardian Society* (Leeds, 1820–51).

Order of Shepherdesses met at the Reindeer in Quarry Hill, Leeds, in 1835. Seventy women sang hymns and took tea. Their aim was to provide for members in sickness and for their families at death.[120] After 1815, a network of female reform societies emerged. Women's support groups, like the Gorbals Female Universal Suffrage Association and the Female Political Union of Newcastle upon Tyne, were an active if small and little noticed part of the Chartist movement.[121] Their declared aim was to 'help our fathers, husbands, and brothers to free themselves and us'.[122] There was an especially powerful strand of Owenism, which advocated equal access by men and women to the public world of the platform and the control of production. It was a long hard look at an alternative form of gender relationships for working-class people before the great tide of skilled adult male authority and its accompanying ideologies finally engulfed the new organisations of the working class.[123] After 1850, the 'respectable' organised working class found fewer and fewer places for women in public life.

By the 1860s, this limited and limiting redefinition of gender roles was beginning to unravel. It was to do so with a slow and sometimes explosive force which has rumbled on into the late twentieth century. By the 1830s and 1840s, great stresses had been built up by a gender frontier which left women such narrow roles. Novels like *David Copperfield* presented to their readers the varied cruelties which men and women imposed upon each other as they twisted and turned in the trap of such tensions and contradictions. Such tight disciplines clashed not only with the increasing demands for companionate marriage, but with the individuality embedded in the evangelical movement and, above all, with the celebration of the individual provided by the romantic movement. If, as Wordsworth claimed, 'the child was father to the man', then by mid-century, others were realising that being mother to the woman implied more than etiquette and domestic manuals.

The breakout from domesticity occurred in three major areas. Two, education and health and welfare, reproduced domestic roles in the

---

[120]   *Leeds Mercury*, 11 April 1835.
[121]   Barbara Taylor, *Eve and the New Jerusalem: Socialism and Feminism in the Nineteenth Century* (1983), p. 80; Elspeth King, *The Scottish Women's Suffrage Movement* (Glasgow, 1978), p. 9; Dorothy Thompson, ed., *The Early Chartists* (1971), p. 128.
[122]   Thompson, ed., *The Early Chartists*, p. 128.
[123]   Taylor, *Eve and the New Jerusalem*.

public sphere, and then went on to extend those roles. The third, and potentially most serious, was a claim to the right to discuss and comment upon a wide range of public issues, a claim which ultimately led to the demand for the vote. The first sign of a break came in the anti-slavery societies of the 1840s, in which women played a part as fund raisers, audience and occasionally as speakers. Some clearly started to apply the language of 'bondage' and 'emancipation' to their own situation. The movement split over the issue of the admission of women as delegates to the major conventions. The Glasgow Ladies' Auxiliary Emancipation Society broke away like many others. It became the Glasgow Female Anti-Slavery Society. There was a long way to go to make sustained and successful claims for the vote. Some of this path was traced out by the history of the Ladies' Edinburgh Debating Society. For two generations they were a self-conscious 'training ground for women to fit them for public speaking'.[124] They wished 'to step on and off platforms as naturally as we enter a drawing room'. Week after week they debated 'questions of the day' in a manner which would be thought 'presumptuous' in those drawing rooms. They discussed the presbyterian Sunday, free will, Alsace Lorraine, George Eliot and decided that whatever their mothers said it was in order for women to go unchaperoned to canvass votes for the female candidates to the Edinburgh School Board in 1872. Like women in many other urban centres they used the caring and educating role of the women of the 1840s as a base from which to move naturally into a public role in education. The Ladies' Edinburgh Educational Association prepared women for the Local Examinations of the Scottish Universities, opening the way for the eventual admission of women to Scottish universities in 1892. Women like Flora Stephenson who founded the Edinburgh School of Cookery first established status for a female-specific activity by calling it 'domestic science' and then went on to become 'chairman' of Edinburgh School Board.[125] The Yorkshire Ladies' Council of Education was especially concerned with teaching hygiene and health care along with morality. They ran 'babies

---

[124] Lettice Milne Rae, *Ladies in Debate, Being a History of the Ladies Edinburgh Debating Society, 1865–1935* (Edinburgh, 1936).
[125] Helen Corr, 'The Schoolgirl's Curriculum and the Ideology of the Home, 1870–1914', in Glasgow Women's Studies Group, *Uncharted Lives: Extracts from Scottish Women's Experiences, 1850–1982* (Glasgow, 1983); Sheila Hamilton, 'The First Generations of University Women', in Gordon Donaldson, ed., *Four Centuries. Edinburgh University Life, 1583–1983* (Edinburgh, 1983).

welcomes', where 'thrift is taught and babies are weighed'.[126] In London, the Ladies' National Association for the Diffusion of Sanitary Knowledge produced a series of didactic pamphlets. They were loosely linked through Bessie Parkes to the *Englishwoman's Journal*, a periodical which laid claim to women's right to discuss public issues from infant mortality to the Italian Risorgimento.[127] Many of these pamphlets took the consensus female role of caring for children and health into the public role of class relationships and then pushed that role just a little beyond the expected. *Health of Mothers*, price 1d., discussed pregnancy, clothing, suckling, weaning and sore nipples in direct, unfussy language, recommended the Bible as 'a working day guide' but queried 'must women always suffer so much more than men'. *A Model Wife* (1874) was instructed on early rising, washing, healthy homes and cookery. *Why Do Not Women Swim?* was not just encouragement to 'so rational and necessary a means of exercise' but also an incitement to depart from passivity, 'So you dear reader, when you swim, do not go about like a floating coffin, but be cheerful, enjoy yourself.' If this together with a reading of *The Cheap Doctor: A Word about Fresh Air* and *The Evils of Wet Nursing: A Warning to Mothers* was not enough then there were the *Verses on Health and Happiness*,[128]

> Of poor folks how she tries
> To give them good advice
> And teach them clever thrifty ways
> To have things done up nice

In the Ladies' Sanitary Association and its urban provincial equivalents the ladies of the upper middle class used all their social superiority to instruct the working classes, but beneath the loud tones of class talking to class was the voice of women talking to women.

The discussions of the Ladies' Edinburgh Debating Society, gathered around the mahogany dining table of the Mair family in Moray Place, like those of the Ladies' Discussion Society formed in faraway Kensington in 1865, were redolent of the tension between the superiority of class and the subordinations of gender. That tension was

---

[126] L. V. Shairp, 'Leeds', in Mrs Bernard (Helen) Bosanquet, ed., *Social Conditions in Provincial Towns* (1912); Anne Summers, 'A Home from Home – Women's Philanthropic Work in the Nineteenth Century', in Burman, ed., *Fit Work for Women*.

[127] *Englishwoman's Journal*, 7 (1861).

[128] All these titles were published in the late 1860s and the 1870s by the Ladies' Sanitary Association. Most of them had no date but can be dated by context.

resolved as one group after another laid claim to the vote. The Edinburgh ladies debated and defeated a women's suffrage motion by a decreasing margin in 1866 and 1872. The motion was carried in 1884 and 1891. The freedom and flexibility of the voluntary association gave women the chance they needed to debate the suffrage issue amongst themselves before carrying the campaign *en masse* into the public sphere. Between 1870 and 1890, a network of regional suffrage societies was formed. They came together as the National Union of Women's Suffrage Societies in 1897. The flexibility of the voluntary association enabled these groups to form links with many working-class women and to contain within the broader movement the spectacular aggression of the Pankhursts and their followers in the Women's Social and Political Union. The basic tactics were those inherited from the Chartists and the Anti-Corn Law League. They organised meetings, marched and demonstrated, lobbied politicians, made speeches, wrote pamphlets and published journals.[129]

Once the vote had been gained, there followed a pause as if British society needed time to assess the meaning of a step which had been contested with such violence, bitterness and abuse and then granted so quietly. Many women explored the meaning of their new relationship with civil society through a variety of voluntary societies. The Towns Women's Guild and the Women's Institute were the most widespread, but it was two London groups which exemplified the solution which most women found to the question of a new identity. The Forum Club had been founded in 1919. Its founders deliberately refused to become simply a women's version of the gentlemen's clubs which had excluded them during the nineteenth century. Gentlemen were allowed as guests into most rooms and children were admitted for tea. Like the British Federation of Professional and Business Women they discussed world issues. The latter society discussed 'The Role of Women in Modern Statecraft' just before war broke out in 1939. But during the 1930s as the number of women at university declined and increasing resistance to female employment was met in a wide variety of jobs, women used their voluntary societies to create a double role of domesticity and citizenship: 'all this does not mean that the ladies of the Forum Club have forgotten the original province of women – the home. They meet also to exchange their

---

[129] Liddington and Norris, *One Hand Tied Behind Us*, pp. 64–83.

experiences with unusual vegetables or to take part in a movement which aims to revise the art of British Cookery.'[130] These women chose to show that domesticity and citizenship could both run together. The result was a proud and assertive duality which lasted into the 1950s.

One major contribution which the voluntary society has made to ordering the complexities of urban and industrial society has been its contribution to the history of 'out-groups', groups which were excluded from a significant share in the legitimate structure of power. The middle classes, women and the working people of the labour movement all used voluntary societies, at different times and in different ways, to formulate new identities and values, to experiment with new forms of social action and relationships and to provide support and help for each other. They all went on to make and sustain a claim for a share in that legitimate power that goes with recognition and status within a dominant ideology, with an easy and uncontested place in public life and open access to the power and resources of the state.

This ability of voluntary organisations to provide for out-groups was especially important for those who were divided from the dominant groups in British society by language, culture, religion and race. Many such groups from the Gaelic-speaking Highlanders of Glasgow to the African seamen of Cardiff and Liverpool were characterised not only by cultural features of language and race but by their place in the labour market and the organisation of production. By far the largest proportion were unskilled labour, casual, migrant and mobile labour or servants. Hence they lacked the resources for extensive formal organisation because of their poverty and their geographical mobility and fragmentation. Moves towards organisation came from several directions. Religious organisations were central. By the mid-eighteenth century there were Gaelic churches in Glasgow and Edinburgh.[131] The Catholic church made heroic efforts to retain the loyalty and one particular identity for the Irish populations of the great British cities through the spiritual and material content of their missions.[132] The synagogue was the centre of many Jewish communities just as

---

[130]   *Picture Post*, 25 Feb. and 25 March 1939.
[131]   Charles W. J. Withers, 'Kirk, Club and Cultural Change: Gaelic Chapels, Highland Societies and the Urban Gaelic Sub-Culture in Eighteenth Century Scotland', *Social History*, 10 (1985), pp. 171–92.
[132]   Sheridan Gilley, 'Catholic Faith of the Irish Slums, London, 1840–70', in H. J. Dyos and Michael Wolff, eds., *The Victorian City*, 2 vols. (1973), vol. 2, pp. 837–53.

the Calvinist chapels were for many of the Liverpool Welsh.[133] Despite the savage constraints of prejudice and limited access to capital and the labour market these social groups were not static. Individuals were able to make important contributions to many forms of organised activity. Olaudah Equiano, who came from the Ibo area of West Africa, took a leading part in the early movement against the slave trade, after a mixture of good fortune and his own ability to learn and use the English language enabled him to work his way out of the slavery into which he had been sold around 1750 and survive in the world of overseas shipping, commerce and evangelical activists in the London of the 1780s.[134] John Doherty entered the world of production as a child worker in the cotton industry of Buncrana in County Donegal. The Irish community in Manchester was the base from which he became a major trade union leader and radical publisher.[135]

Religious structures and upwardly mobile groups within these cultures became the basis for networks of voluntary societies which provided some framework of organisation. The Glasgow Highland Society started in 1727 amongst those who had been successful in business and the professions. Its aim was not just sociability for its members but to provide a fund for 'educating boys at school, or putting them to trades'. The boys were to be from the Highlands or Highland families. 'The Society should pay the expense of teaching the boys English, Writing and Arithmetic; and book-keeping to such as shew superior genius.' The Gaelic Club of Gentlemen was formed in 1780. They met at the Black Bull Inn 'to converse in Gaelic'.[136] The desire for congenial company and support in a strange and sometimes hostile environment has always been a powerful motive for organisation. During the 1830s and 1840s, the Ancient Order of Hibernians grew as a friendly society amongst those Irish people who gained a stable enough place in the system of production to pay the regular dues.[137] The Jewish faith was the basis for a complex culture which contained within itself all the tensions of class and status from the

---

[133] V. D. Lipman, *A Social History of the Jews in England, 1850–1950* (1954); Colin G. Pooley, 'The Residential Segregation of Migrant Communities in Mid Victorian Liverpool', *Transactions of the Institute of British Geographers*, n.s., 2 (1977), pp. 364–82.

[134] Paul Edwards, ed., *Equianos Travels* (1967).

[135] R. G. Kirby and A. E. Musson, *The Voice of the People: John Doherty, 1798–1854, Trades Unionist, Radical and Factory Reformer* (Manchester, 1975).

[136] Withers, 'Kirk, Club and Cultural Change'.

[137] John Denvir, *The Irish in Britain from the Earliest Times to the Fall of Parnell* (1892), pp. 127–36.

wider society plus others added by waves of migrants escaping pogroms in Eastern Europe. A growing network of formal organisations reflected this. Some affirmed and sustained the culture like the Manchester Hebrew Association (1838) and the Manchester Jewish School (1842). Others reproduced the middle-class concern for the welfare and control of the poor. The Manchester Hebrew Philanthropic Society was founded in 1826, whilst the Liverpool Hebrew Mendicity Society (1846) was one of the first to show a concern for protecting Jews from adverse criticism by ensuring that as few as possible of their faith had recourse to the poor law. The London Jewish Board of Guardians (1859) was designed to organise all these groups so as to prevent 'indiscriminate charity'. The increase in Jewish migration and the hostility this aroused only increased the urgency of the work of these formal organisations.[138]

All the social groups discussed gained a dynamic identity from political movements concerned with the fate of the societies from which they had come. From the late 1820s, the Repeal Association was as important for the Irish as the Catholic church. Later in the century the United Irish League played the same role. The politics of the Scottish Land and Labour League were taken into Liberal, then Labour politics by Highlanders in the lowland cities and played an important part in securing land rights for the crofters.[139] The first attempt to form a Pan-African 'Native African Association' in London came in 1859. By 1900, Pan-African movements and organisations were an important focus for black intellectuals and radicals in Britain.[140] In the twentieth century the density of formal organisation grew for each of these groups. *Picture Post* visited the 'coloured people of the Cardiff dock area (Tiger Bay)' and described organisations which must stand as an example for the rest. Prejudice, rioting and the legal provision of the Aliens Order, 1920, and the Special Restriction (Coloured Alien Seamen) Order, 1925, restricted their freedom in both the labour and housing market. Organised response represented cultural divisions, like the Sons of Africa and the Islamic Society, economic positions

---

[138]   Bill Williams, *The Making of Manchester Jewry, 1740–1875* (Manchester, 1976); L. P. Gartner, *The Jewish Immigrant in England, 1870–1914* (1960).

[139]   Smith, 'Class, Skill and Sectarianism'; Tom Gallagher, 'Catholics in Scottish Politics', *Bulletin of Scottish Politics*, 2 (1981), pp. 21–43.

[140]   Paul Edwards, Ian Duffield *et al.*, 'Blacks in Britain', *History Today*, 31 (1981), pp. 33–51; Michael Banton, *The Coloured Quarter: Negro Immigrants in an English City* (1955), pp. 18–40; K. L. Little, *Negroes in Britain: A Study of Racial Relations in English Society* (1947), pp. 52–83, 168–94; Immanuel Geiss, *The Pan African Movement*, trans. Ann Keep (1974), pp. 98–9, 166–98.

like the Crewmen's Association, the results of several generations' participation in British society like the Wesleyan church and Salvation Army, as well as that collective identity created by dealings with the rest of British society, the Colonial Defence Association.[141]

THE ROAD TO THE 1950s

The principle characteristic of the twentieth century was a simple increase in the density of organisation. There was a focus on organised leisure, on the world of clubs and hobbies. The Millwall Poultry Club was a group of dockworkers, lorry drivers, steeplejacks, metal workers and casual labourers who met in the LCC Men's Evening Institute in the 1930s for discussions, lectures and even collective autopsies on dead birds.[142] Every possible manner of occupational and interest group was organised. Professional organisations had grown in size, number and importance since the mid-nineteenth century.[143] The twentieth century brought an increase in number, in specialisation and in national integration for groups based upon economic position. The National Federation of Plumbers and Domestic Engineers (Employers) was formed just after the Great War. Local associations discussed conditions of trade and the problems brought by workmen's compensation and the wages councils. Their journal supplied members with advice technical and financial and the motto, 'Life, to be worth while, must always be a struggle'.[144] The *Textile Journal* was the official organ of the National Federation of Textile Workers' Managers' Association, the Guild of Calico Printers', Bleachers', Dyers' and Finishers' Foremen, and the National Federation of Cotton Mill Officials. It supplied them with yarn prices, technical articles, details of new products and news of the Ashton-under-Lyne and District Mill Managers' Association annual dinner at the Highland Laddie Hotel.[145] Their worries might now concern current wage rates as set out in 'Statutory Rules and Orders, no 602', but a good dinner was still an important bond for their common interest and co-operation as it had been for the clubs of the eighteenth century.

The relationship of the state to all this became closer. The corporatist

---

[141]   *Picture Post*, 18 March 1939.
[142]   *Ibid.*, 5 Aug. 1939.
[143]   G. Millerson, *The Qualifying Associations: A Study in Professionalisation* (1964); Terence J. Johnson, *Professions and Power* (1972).
[144]   *Plumbing Trade Journal*, 16 (Manchester, 1936–7).
[145]   *Textile Weekly*, 18 (1936).

state of unions, industry and government had its origins in the post-1918 period. Incorporation was more than this. The state now deliberately set out to organise society through the backstairs creation of the National Council of Social Service.[146] Formal 'voluntary organisations' were now promoted by the government as a means of communicating with the civil population. Organisations had an ability to mediate, both as opposition and conciliator. The state needed associations to relate to, to mediate with the mosaic of groups that make up civil society. This trend has continued with great power. Recent urban riots were experienced as major break-down of order and structure, with alienation and anomie crashing through every shop window. By morning, government and press were interviewing community spokesmen and beginning to mediate and bargain. Without formal voluntary organisations this would not have been possible. In a corporatist state the first thing a wise volunteer will do is to seek a grant from the local or national state, and a wise state will look for organisations to subsidise.

The pre-1850 state had been the target for many petitions and lobbies from formal voluntary associations, demanding legislation or action to protect trade. Most of the pre-1850 associations, from the Mechanics' Institutes to the Affiliated Order of Friendly Societies, sought to achieve their aims by avoiding the state, which in any case they distrusted as being aristocracy-dominated. Even the Royal Society for the Prevention of Cruelty to Animals which needed legislative action from the state then went on to enforce that legislation through its own inspectors.[147] In mid-century one area of voluntary action after another turned to the state. The most dramatic change was in education where deeply committed protagonists of voluntaryism admitted that they needed the financial and legal power of the state to carry out 'the duty of the wealthier classes to assist in the education of the humbler'.[148] By the 1920s, an increasing number of groups could only envisage carrying out their aims with the help of the state. Indeed, in some cases their very existence as a self-aware group was the result of state action. The National Spinsters' Pensions Association was started in 1935 by Miss Florence White who ran a confectionery shop in Bradford. 'On voluntary work and an annual subscription of only

[146]   *The Future of Voluntary Organization: Report of the Wolfenden Committee* (1978).
[147]   B. Harrison, 'Animals and the State in 19th Century England', *English Historical Review*, 88 (1973), pp. 786–820.
[148]   Edward Baines, *National Education: An Address as Chairman of a Breakfast of the Congregational Union of England and Wales at Manchester, Friday 11 October 1867* (1867).

1/-, it maintains a vast network of organization.' They wanted 'Equity with widows', in other words they wanted a pension without having to work until they were sixty-five. Their sense of injustice derived from the Great War. They included the 'sweethearts of 1914–1918' and reminded the government that 'there were war spinsters as well as war widows'.[149] The mass unemployment of the interwar period brought its own voluntary organisations. The National Unemployed Workers' Movement was based upon the energies of the local labour movement, but more significant for future trends were bodies like the National Council of Social Service and the Land Settlement Association which sponsored a variety of initiatives by co-ordinating voluntary activity and finance with limited amounts of government aid.[150]

In many areas of activity the trends begun in the 1890s were consolidated. The labour movement developed a variety and range of organisations which covered almost all social and economic life. Note, that it was the labour movement that operated here, not the Labour 'party' as such, indeed in a strict sense there was no 'Labour' party until 1918. At the centre were the political and workplace organisations, the Labour party and the trade-unions branch. Alongside these and linked in a vast network were bodies like the Co-operative Societies, holiday fellowships and cycling clubs. The Labour party ran its trips and dances. The Co-op movement had its retirement homes. This provision of a total social package was characteristic of the period after 1890. It was mirrored in other organisations like the churches. By the 1930s, some of the big companies were following this pattern with sports and social clubs. Irish and Jewish communities extended their networks and activities on the basis of associations founded in the 1890s. Very often the overlap of function of these networks like that of the Catholics and that of the labour movement in Glasgow offered a valuable freedom of choice for individuals.

These networks were to come apart and lose their influence in the 1950s. There were several reasons for this. First, working-class people gained greater spending power. They no longer needed the collectivist power of the Labour party dance, the holiday camp, the Clarion Club or the pea and pie supper. They could purchase and choose in the capitalist market. This was especially true of the fourteen to

---

[149] *Picture Post*, 8 Oct. 1938.
[150] Ralph H. C. Hayburn, 'The Voluntary Occupational Centre Movement, 1932–39', *Journal of Contemporary History*, 6 (1971), pp. 156–71; *Annual Report of the Land Settlement Association for the Year Ending 31 December 1937* (1938).

twenty-five age group. Youth culture recreated itself around consumption rather than any characteristic set of associations, either self-generated or provided by others. For older people, homes became more spacious, better furnished. Radio and the gramophone (record player), then television provided for more privatised, more home-based ways of spending leisure.

Secondly, the 1945–51 Labour government based its welfare socialism on the bureaucracy of the national and local state, rather than upon the labour movement or the wider range of working-class organisations. Little use was made of the Co-operative movement, the holiday fellowships or the friendly societies. In the long term the result was the break-up of this infrastructure of socialism. Within twenty years, innovative working-class associations were to be single-issue campaigns very often directed against the local state with which Labour party power was identified: the anti-dampness campaigns and tenants' and residents' associations took over from the Labour party branch, which was left to deal with 'Politics'. The churches found that they were to deal with religion and were rarely at the centre of a network of social activities affecting a whole town or suburb. A dwindling core of activists and professionals were left to seek innovations which would reverse this trend.

Other influences can be sought in the changing geography of British towns. The urban working-class areas of the 1930s combined housing, workplace and shopping and leisure space in a closely confined area. Thus one movement or network could organise them all. The planning legislation of the 1950s and 1960s, with the massive urban clearances of the 1960s house-building booms, purposefully separated these activities. Thus the spatial pressures which had created these networks of associations were broken up. The middle classes had experienced some of this separation with the slow move to the suburbs between the 1860s and the 1930s. In the 1950s, the motor car and telephone strengthened personal communication but further broke up the geographical space of the suburb with its church, tennis club, 'Little Theatre' and golf course.[151] These pressures all encouraged the move to single-issue, single-function organisations.

The theorists of urban and industrial society expected that the social processes of anomie and alienation would threaten a break-down of social order and individual integration in the face of rapidly changing

---

[151]   John Braine, *Room at the Top* (1957).

and disorientating social and economic conditions.[152] It was an event which never happened. One reason was the will and ability of individuals and groups to react to the threats of disorganisation through some of the wide variety of formal voluntary organisations, a tithe of which have been described here. Isolation and the break-down of civil cohesion was a choice for industrial society, not a necessity. Many perceived the threat. Formal organisation was a means of countering this threat. It was a means which came easiest for those with economic and cultural resources, namely the male middle class, and this social group probably still finds access to formal organisation easier than others. But formal organisation was adopted and extended by other groups, until by the 1950s there were very few who did not have access to some form of organisation, often with state help and blessing. The increasing density of organisation in Britain enabled the people of a changing and complex society to keep one step ahead of the theorists and their warnings of the break-down of social and personal order.

[152] Karl Marx, *Early Writings*, with introd. by Lucio Colletti (Penguin edn, 1975), pp. 322–4; Emile Durkheim, *The Division of Labour in Society* (New York, 1964), pp. 357–62; Emile Durkheim, *Suicide: A Study in Sociology* (1952), pp. 254–76; Anthony Giddens, *Capitalism and Modern Social Theory: An Analysis of the Writings of Marx, Durkheim and Max Weber* (Cambridge, 1971), pp. 10–17 and 79–84; Louis Wirth, 'Urbanism as a Way of Life', in Louis Wirth, *On Cities and Social Life*, ed. Albert J. Reiss (Chicago, 1964), p. 82.

Bibliographies

Place of publication is London, unless otherwise stated

1 GOVERNMENT AND SOCIETY IN ENGLAND AND WALES, 1750–1914

Anderson, O., *A Liberal State at War* (1967)

Brewer, J., *The Sinews of Power* (1989)

Brewer, J., and Styles, J., eds., *An Ungovernable People: The English and their Law in the Seventeenth and Eighteenth Centuries* (1980)

Burnett, J., *Plenty and Want: a Social History of Diet from 1815 to the Present Day* (Harmondsworth, 1968)

Clark, J. C. D., *English Society, 1688–1832* (Cambridge, 1985)

Clegg, H. A., Fox, Alan, and Thompson, A. F., *A History of British Trade Unions since 1889*, vol. 1: *1889–1910* (Oxford, 1964)

Colley, Linda, 'The Politics of Eighteenth-Century British History', *Journal of British Studies*, 25 (1986)

Cowling, M., *The Impact of Labour 1920–1924* (Cambridge, 1971)

Davidson, Roger, 'The Board of Trade and Industrial Relations, 1896–1914', *Historical Journal*, 21 (1978)

Davis, John, *Reforming London: The London Government Problem 1855–1900* (Oxford, 1988)

Dunbabin, J., 'The Politics of the Establishment of County Councils', *Historical Journal*, 5 (1963)

Elliot, A., 'Municipal Government in Bradford in the Mid-Nineteenth Century', in D. Fraser, ed., *Municipal Reform and the Industrial City* (Leicester, 1982)

Fraser, D., *Urban Politics in Victorian England* (1976)

Greenleaf, W. H., *The British Political Tradition*, vol. 2: *The Ideological Heritage* (1983)

Harris, José, *Unemployment and Politics: A Study of English Social Policy, 1886–1914* (Oxford, 1972)

Hennock, E. P., *Fit and Proper Persons: Ideal and Reality in Nineteenth Century Urban Government* (1973)

'The Creation of an Urban Local Government System in England and Wales', in Helmut Naunin, ed., *Stadteordnungen des 19 Jahrhunderts* (Köln, 1984)

British Social Reform and German Precedents (Oxford, 1986)

Henriques, U. R. Q., *Before the Welfare State: Social Administration in Early*

Victorian England (1979)

Hilton, Boyd, 'The Role of Providence in Evangelical Social Thought', in D. Beales and G. Best, eds., *History, Society and the Churches* (Cambridge, 1985)

The Age of Atonement: The Influence of Evangelicalism on Social and Economic Thought (Oxford, 1988)

Hollis, P., *Ladies Elect: Women in English Local Government 1865–1914* (Oxford, 1987)

Holton, S., *Feminism and Democracy: Women's Suffrage and Reform Politics in Britain, 1900–1918* (1986)

Johnson, R., 'Administrators in Education before 1870: Patronage, Social Position and Role', in G. Sutherland, ed., *Studies in the Growth of Nineteenth Century Government* (1972)

Lambert, R., 'Central and Local Relations in Mid-Victorian England: The Local Government Act Office, 1853–1871', *Victorian Studies*, 6 (1962)

Macdonagh, O., 'The Nineteenth-Century Revolution in Government: A Reappraisal', *Historical Journal*, 1 (1958)

A Pattern of Government Growth, 1800–1960: The Passenger Acts and their Enforcement (1961)

Early Victorian Government (1977)

McLeod, R., *Treasury Control and Social Administration* (1968)

Mandler, P., 'Cain and Abel: Two Aristocrats and the Early Victorian Factory Acts', *Historical Journal*, 27 (1984)

'The Making of the New Poor Law *Redivivus*', *Past & Present*, 117 (1987)

Aristocratic Government in the Age of Reform: Whigs and Liberals, 1830–52 (Oxford, 1989)

Mathias, P., and O'Brien, P., 'Taxation in Britain and France, 1715–1810: A Comparison of the Social and Economic Incidence of Taxes Collected for the Central Government', *Journal of European Economic History*, 5 (1976)

Matthew, H. C. G., 'Disraeli, Gladstone and the Politics of Mid-Victorian Budgets', *Historical Journal*, 22 (1979)

Gladstone, 1809–1874 (Oxford, 1986)

O'Gorman, F., *British Conservatism: Conservative Thought from Burke to Thatcher* (1986)

Owen, D., *English Philanthropy, 1660–1960* (1964)

Pellew, Jill, *The Home Office, 1848–1914: From Clerks to Bureaucrats* (1982)

Pelling, H., 'The Working Class and the Welfare State', in H. Pelling, *Popular Politics and Society in Late Victorian Britain* (1968)

Prochaska, F. K., *Women and Philanthropy in Nineteenth-Century England* (Oxford, 1980)

Rose, M. E., 'The Crisis of Poor Relief in England, 1860–1880', in W. J. Mommsen, ed., *The Emergence of the Welfare State in Britain and Germany* (1981)

Saville, J., *1848: The British State and the Chartist Movement* (Cambridge, 1987)

Searle, G., *The Quest for National Efficiency* (Oxford, 1971)

Smith, D., *Conflict and Compromise: Class Formation in English Society, 1830–1914* (1982)

Stedman Jones, G., 'Rethinking Chartism', in G. Stedman Jones, *Languages of Class* (Cambridge, 1983)

Storch, R. D., ed., *Popular Culture and Custom in Nineteenth-Century England* (1982)

Thane, P., 'Contributory vs Non-Contributory Old Age Pensions, 1878–1908', in P. Thane, ed., *The Origins of British Social Policy* (1978)

'The Working Class and State "Welfare" in Britain, 1880–1914', *Historical Journal*, 27 (1984)
Trebilcock, C., 'War and the Failure of Industrial Mobilization: 1899 and 1914', in J. M. Winter, ed., *War and Economic Development* (Cambridge, 1975)
Vincent, J., *The Formation of the Liberal Party, 1857–68* (1966)

2 SOCIETY AND THE STATE IN TWENTIETH-CENTURY BRITAIN

Abel-Smith, B., 'Public Expenditure on the Social Services', *Social Trends*, 1 (1970)
Addison, P., *The Road to 1945: British Politics and the Second World War* (1975)
Almond, G., and Verba, S., eds., *The Civic Culture: Political Attitudes and Democracy in Five Nations* (Princeton, 1963)
  The Civic Culture Revisited (Boston, Mass., 1980)
Amery, L. S., *The Framework of the Future* (Oxford, 1944)
Anderson, M., *Family Structure in Nineteenth-Century Lancashire* (Cambridge, 1971)
Beer, S. H., *Modern British Politics: A Study of Parties and Pressure Groups* (1965)
  Britain against Itself: The Political Contradictions of Collectivism (1982)
Beloff, M., 'The Whitehall Factor: The Role of the Higher Civil Service 1919–39', in Gillian Peele and C. Cook, eds., *The Politics of Reappraisal 1918–1939* (1975)
Bevan, Aneurin, *In Place of Fear* (1952; Quartet Books edn, 1978)
Beveridge, William, 'Soviet Communism', *Political Quarterly*, 2 (1936)
  Voluntary Action: A Report on Methods of Social Advance (1948)
Boyd, F., *British Politics in Transition* (1964)
Briggs, A., and Saville, J., eds., *Essays in Labour History 1918–1939*, 3 vols. (1960–77)
Brown, H. Phelps, *The Origins of Trade Union Power* (Oxford, 1983)
Burk, Kathleen, *Britain, America and the Sinews of War* (1985)
  ed., *War and the State: The Transformation of British Government 1914–19* (1982)
Butler, D., and Sloman, A., *British Political Facts 1900–1975* (4th edn, 1975)
Cartwright, Ann., and Anderson, R., *General Practice Revisited: A Second Study of Patients and their Doctors* (1981)
Chapman, B., *British Government Observed: Some European Reflections* (1963)
Chester, D. N., ed., *Lessons of the British War Economy* (Cambridge, 1951)
Cole, G. D. H., *Self-Government in Industry* (1917)
Cook, C., and Ramsden, J., eds., *Trends in British Politics since 1945* (1978)
Cowling, M., *1867: Disraeli, Gladstone and Revolution. The Passing of the Second Reform Bill* (Cambridge, 1967)
  The Impact of Labour 1920–1924 (Cambridge, 1971)
  The Impact of Hitler: British Politics and British Policy 1933–1940 (Cambridge, 1975)
Currie, R., *Industrial Politics* (Oxford, 1979)
Dangerfield, G., *The Strange Death of Liberal England* (1936)
Davidson, R., and Lowe, R., 'Bureaucracy and Innovation in British Welfare Policy 1870–1945', in W. J. Mommsen, ed., *The Emergence of the Welfare State in Britain and Germany 1850–1950* (1981)
Deacon, A., *In Search of the Scrounger* (Occasional Papers in Social Administration, No. 60, 1976)
Dicey, A. V., *Law and Public Opinion in England during the Nineteenth Century* (2nd edn, 1914)

Introduction to the Study of the Law of the Constitution (8th edn, 1924)

Donald, G. W., and Gospel, H. F., 'The Mond–Turner Talks 1927–1933: A Study in Industrial Cooperation', *Historical Journal*, 16 (1973)

Drummond, I., *Imperial Economic Policy 1917–1939* (1974)

Dunleavy, P., *The Politics of Mass Housing in Britain 1945–1975: A Study of Corporate Power and Professional Influence in the Welfare State* (Oxford, 1981)

Eatwell, R., *The 1945–1951 Labour Governments* (1979)

Emy, H., *Liberals, Radicals and Social Politics* (Cambridge, 1973)

Feinstein, C., ed., *The Managed Economy: Essays in British Economic Policy and Performance since 1939* (Oxford, 1983)

Flora, P., *State, Economy and Society in Western Europe 1815–1975*, vol. 1 (Frankfurt, 1983)

Floud, R., and McCloskey, D., eds., *The Economic History of Britain since 1700*, 2 vols. (Cambridge, 1981)

Franks, Sir Oliver, *Central Planning and Control in War and Peace* (1947)

George, V. N., *Social Security: Beveridge and After* (1968)

Gilbert, B. B., *British Social Policy, 1914–39* (1970)

Glass, D. V., ed., *Social Mobility in Britain* (1954)

Gosden, P. H. J. H., *Education in the Second World War: A Study in Policy and Administration* (1976)

Gowing, Margaret, 'The Organisation of Manpower in Britain during the Second World War', *Journal of Contemporary History*, 7 (1972)

Greenleaf, W., *The British Political Tradition*, vol. 1: *The Rise of Collectivism*; vol. 2: *The Ideological Heritage* (1983)

Hall, Phoebe, *et al.*, *Change, Choice and Conflict in Social Policy* (1975)

Halsey, A. H., ed., *Trends in British Society since 1900* (1972)

Halsey, A. H., Floud, Jean, and Arnold, C. Arnold, *Education, Economy and Society* (1965 edn)

Harris, José, *William Beveridge: A Biography* (Oxford, 1977)

   'Some Aspects of Social Policy in Britain during the Second World War', in W. J. Mommsen, ed., *The Emergence of the Welfare State in Britain and Germany* (1981)

   'Bureaucrats and Businessmen in British Food Control', in Kathleen Burk, ed., *War and the State: The Transformation of British Government 1914–19* (1982)

   'Did British Workers Want the Welfare State? G. D. H. Cole's Survey of 1942', in J. Winter, ed., *The Working Class in Modern British History: Essays in Honour of Henry Pelling* (Cambridge, 1983)

   'Political Ideas and the Debate on State Welfare 1940–45', in H. L. Smith, ed., *War and Social Change: British Society in the Second World War* (Manchester, 1986)

Harris, K., *Attlee* (1982)

Harrison, R., 'Labour Government: Then and Now', *Political Quarterly*, 41 (1970)

Hazlehurst, C., *Politicians at War July 1914 to May 1915* (1971)

Henderson, A., *The Government's Attack on Trade Union Law* (Trade Union Defence Committee, 1927)

Hewart, Lord, *The New Despotism* (1929)

Hinton, J., *The First Shop Stewards' Movement* (1973)

Hirsch, F., and Goldthorpe, J., eds., *The Political Economy of Inflation* (1978)

Howson, Susan, 'The Origins of Dear Money, 1919–20', *Economic History Review*, 2nd ser., 27 (1974)

Domestic Monetary Management in Britain 1919–1938 (Cambridge, 1975)

Hughes, M. V., *A London Family between the Wars* (Oxford, 1940)

Hunter, D. J., 'Back to Black', *Public Administration*, 61 (1983)

James, E., and Laurent, A., 'Social Security: The European Experience', *Social Trends*, 5 (1974)

Jay, D., *The Socialist Case* (1948 edn)

Jewkes, J., *Ordeal by Planning* (1948)

Judge, D., 'Specialists and Generalists in British Central Government: A Political Debate', *Public Administration*, 59 (1981)

Kavanagh, D., 'Political Culture in Britain: The Decline of the Civic Culture', in G. Almond and S. Verba, eds., *The Civic Culture Revisited* (Boston, Mass., 1980)

Kelsall, R. K., *Higher Civil Servants in Britain from 1870 to the Present Day* (1955)

Keynes, J. M., *The General Theory of Employment, Interest and Money* (1936)
How to Pay for the War (1940)

King, A., ed., *Why is Britain Becoming Harder to Govern?* (1976)

Kirby, M. W., *The British Coalmining Industry 1870–1946* (1977)

Laski, H. J., *The State in Theory and Practice* (1935)

Lee, J. M., *Reviewing the Machinery of Government 1942–1952: An Essay on the Anderson Committee and its Successors* (SSRC Report, 1977)

Lovell, J., 'The TUC Special Industrial Committe January–April 1926', in A. Briggs and J. Saville, eds., *Essays in Labour History 1918–1939*, 3 vols. (1960–77), vol. 3

Lowe, R., 'The Failure of Consensus in Britain: The National Industrial Conference 1919–21', *Historical Journal*, 21 (1978)
Adjusting to Democracy: The Role of the Ministry of Labour in British Politics 1916–1939 (Oxford, 1986)

Lowell, A. L., *The Government of England*, 2 vols. (New York, 1908)

McCallum, R. B., and Readman, Alison, *The British General Election of 1945* (Oxford, 1947)

McCrone, G., *Regional Policy in Britain* (1969)

McKibbin, R., 'The Economic Policy of the Second Labour Government 1929–1931', *Past & Present*, 68 (1975)
'Why Was there no Marxism in Britain?' *English Historical Review*, 99 (1984)

Mackintosh, J. P., 'The Declining Respect for the Law', in A. King, ed., *Why is Britain Becoming Harder to Govern?* (1976)

Macmillan, H., *Reconstruction: A Plea for a National Policy* (1933)

Marsh, A., *Protest and Political Consciousness* (Beverly Hills and London, 1977)

Marshall, T. H., *Citizenship and Social Class and Other Essays* (1950)

Martlew, C., 'The State and Local Government Finance', *Public Administration*, 61 (1983)

Mass-Observation, *The First Year's Work, 1937–38* (1938)

Matthew, H. C. G., ed., *The Gladstone Diaries*, vol. 7 (Oxford, 1982)

Matthews, R. C. O., 'Why Has Britain Had Full Employment since the War?', *Economic Journal*, 78 (1968)

Middlemas, R. K., *Politics in Industrial Society: The Experience of the British System since 1911* (1979)

Middleton, R., 'The Treasury in the 1930s: Political and Administrative Constraints to the Acceptance of the "New" Economics', *Oxford Economic Papers*, 34 (1982)
'The Treasury and Public Investment: A Perspective on Interwar Economic Management', *Public Administration*, 61 (1983)

450   *Bibliographies*

Miliband, R., *The State in Capitalist Society* (1969)
Milward, A. S., *War, Economy and Society 1939–1945* (1977)
Mitchell, B. R., *European Historical Statistics, 1750–1970* (1975)
Mitchell, B. R., and Deane, Phyllis, *Abstract of British Historical Statistics* (Cambridge, 1962)
Mommsen, W. J., ed., *The Emergence of the Welfare State in Britain and Germany* (1981)
Morgan, Janet, ed., *The Backbench Diaries of Richard Crossman* (1981)
Morgan, K. O., *Consensus and Disunity: The Lloyd George Coalition Government, 1918–22* (Oxford, 1979)
　Labour in Power (Oxford, 1984)
Newton, C. C. S., 'The Sterling Crisis of 1947 and the British Response to the Marshall Plan', *Economic History Review*, 2nd ser., 37 (1984)
Oakeshott, M., *Rationalism in Politics and Other Essays* (1962)
Parker, R. A. C., 'British Rearmament 1936–9: Treasury, Trade Unions and Skilled Labour', *English Historical Review*, 96 (1981)
Peacock, A. T., and Ricketts, M., 'The Growth of the Public Sector and Inflation', in F. Hirsch and J. H. Goldthorpe, eds., *The Political Economy of Inflation* (1978)
Peacock, A. T., and Wiseman, J., *The Growth of Public Expenditure in the United Kingdom* (2nd edn, 1967)
Peden, G., *British Rearmament and the Treasury* (Edinburgh, 1979)
　'Keynes, the Treasury and Unemployment in the Later 1930s', *Oxford Economic Papers*, n.s., 32 (1980)
　'Sir Richard Hopkins and the "Keynesian Revolution" in Employment Policy', *Economic History Review*, 2nd ser., 36 (1983)
Peele, Gillian, 'The Developing Constitution', in C. Cook and J. Ramsden, eds., *Trends in British Politics since 1945* (1978)
Peele, Gillian, and Cook, C., eds., *The Politics of Reappraisal 1918–1939* (1975)
Pelling, H., *Britain and the Second World War* (1970)
　'The 1945 Election Reconsidered', *Historical Journal*, 23 (1980)
Polanyi, M., *The Logic of Liberty* (1951)
Political and Economic Planning, *Report on the British Health Services* (1937)
　Report on the British Social Services (1937)
Prest, A. R., and Adams, A. A., *Consumers' Expenditure in the United Kingdom 1900–1919* (Cambridge, 1954)
Pugh, M., *The Making of Modern British Politics* (Oxford, 1982)
Ramsden, J., 'The Changing Basis of British Conservatism', in C. Cook and J. Ramsden, eds., *Trends in British Politics since 1945* (1978)
Rimlinger, G., *Welfare Policy and Industrialization in Europe, America and Russia* (New York, 1971)
Robinson, E. A. G., 'The Overall Allocation of Resources', in D. N. Chester, ed., *Lessons of the British War Economy* (Cambridge, 1951)
Roskill, S., *Hankey: Man of Secrets*, vol. 1: *1877–1918* (1970)
Royle, T., *The Best Years of their Lives: The National Service Experience 1945–63* (1986)
Salter, A., *Recovery* (1933 edn)
Sayers, R. S., '1941 – The First Keynesian Budget', in C. Feinstein, ed., *The Managed Economy: Essays in British Economic Policy and Performance since 1939* (Oxford, 1983)
Sidgwick, H., *The Principles of Political Economy* (3rd edn, 1901)
Skidelsky, R., *Politicians and the Slump* (1970 edn)

Smith, H. L., ed., *War and Social Change: British Society in the Second World War* (Manchester, 1986)

Smith, T., *The Politics of the Corporate Economy* (Oxford, 1979)

Smithies, E., *The Black Economy in Britain since 1914* (Dublin, 1984)

Stamp, J., 'Recent Tendencies towards the Devolution of Legislative Functions to the Administration', *Public Administration*, 2 (1924)

Stevenson, J., 'The Politics of Violence', in Gillian Peele and C. Cook, eds., *The Politics of Reappraisal 1918–1939* (1975)

Tawney, R. H., 'The Abolition of Economic Controls 1918–21', *Economic History Review*, 1st ser., 13 (1943)

Taylor, A. J. P., *English History 1914–45* (Oxford, 1965)

Thomas, Rosamund M., *The British Philosophy of Administration 1900–39: A Comparison of British and American Ideas* (1978)

Thomas, T., 'Aggregate Demand in the United Kingdom 1918–45', in R. Floud and D. McCloskey, eds., *The Economic History of Britain since 1700*, 2 vols. (Cambridge, 1981), vol. 2.

Titmuss, R. M., *Problems of Social Policy* (1950)

   The Gift Relationship: From Human Blood to Social Policy (1973)

Turner, J., 'Cabinets, Committees and Secretariats: The Higher Direction of War', in Kathleen Burk, ed., *War and the State: The Transformation of British Government 1914–19* (1982)

   ed., *Businessmen and Politics: Studies in Business Activity in British Politics, 1900–1945* (1984)

Wass, D., 'The Public Service in Modern Society', *Public Administration*, 61 (1983)

Webb, Sidney, 'Social Movements', in *Cambridge Modern History*, vol. 12: *The Latest Age* (Cambridge, 1910)

Whiteside, Noelle, 'Private Agencies for Public Purposes: Some New Perspectives on Policy-Making in Health Insurance between the Wars', *Journal of Social Policy*, 12 (1983)

Williams, D. G. T., 'The Donoughmore Report in Perspective', *Public Administration*, 60 (1982)

Williams, P. M., *Hugh Gaitskell* (Oxford, 1982 edn)

Winch, D., 'Britain in the Thirties: A Managed Economy?', in C. Feinstein, ed., *The Managed Economy: Essays in British Economic Policy and Performance since 1939* (Oxford, 1983)

Winter, J., ed., *The Working Class in Modern British History: Essays in Honour of Henry Pelling* (Cambridge, 1983)

3 EDUCATION

Anderson, R. D., *Education and Opportunity in Victorian Scotland* (Oxford, 1983)

   'Education and the State in Nineteenth-Century Scotland', *Economic History Review*, 2nd ser., 36 (1983)

Armytage, W. H. G., *Civic Universities: Aspects of a British Tradition* (1955)

Arnold, Matthew, *Complete Prose Works of*, ed. R. H. Super, 11 vols. (Ann Arbor, Mich., 1960–77)

Aston, T. S., gen. ed., *The History of the University of Oxford*, vol. 5: *The Eighteenth Century*, ed. L. S. Sutherland and L. G. Mitchell (Oxford, 1986)

Bamford, Samuel, *Passages in the Life of a Radical*, and *Early Days*, ed. Henry Dunckley, 2 vols. (1893)

Bamford, T. W., *The Rise of the Public Schools* (1967)

Berdahl, R. O. *British Universities and the State* (Berkeley, 1959)

Bone, T. R., *School Inspection in Scotland 1840-1966* (Scottish Council for Research in Education Publications, No. 57, Edinburgh, 1968)

Bryant, Margaret, *The London Experience of Secondary Education* (1986)

Burnett, John, ed., *Destiny Obscure: Autobiographies of Childhood, Education and Family from the 1820s to the 1920s* (1982)

Carswell, John, *Government and the Universities in Britain: Programme and Performance 1960-1980* (Cambridge, 1985)

Checkland, S. G., *The Gladstones: A Family Biography 1764-1851* (Cambridge, 1971)

Davie, George, *The Democratic Intellect: Scotland and her Universities in the Nineteenth Century* (Edinburgh, 1961)

Davis, Natalie Zemon, 'Printing and the People: Early Modern France', in Harvey J. Graff, ed., *Literacy and Social Development in the West* (Cambridge, 1981)

Dunlop, Jocelyn, and Denman, R. D., *English Apprenticeship and Child Labour: A History* (1912)

Durkheim, Émile, *Education and Sociology*, trans. Sherwood D. Fox (Glencoe, Ill., 1956)

Ellis, E. L., *The University College of Wales, Aberystwyth, 1872-1972* (Cardiff, 1972)

Engel, A. J., *From Clergyman to Don: The Rise of the Academic Profession in Nineteenth-Century Oxford* (Oxford, 1983)

Fletcher, Sheila, *Feminists and Bureaucrats: A Study in the Development of Girls' Education in the Nineteenth Century* (Cambridge, 1980)

Floud, J., 'The Educational Experience of the Adult Population of England and Wales as at July 1949', in D. V. Glass, ed., *Mobility in Britain* (1954)

Gardner, Phil, *The Lost Elementary Schools of Victorian England* (1984)

Garland, M. M., *Cambridge before Darwin: The Ideal of a Liberal Education 1800-1860* (Cambridge, 1980)

Glass, D. V., ed., *Social Mobility in Britain* (1954)

Godber, Joyce, *The Harpur Trust 1551-1973* (Bedford, 1973)

Graff, Harvey J., ed., *Literacy and Social Development in the West: A Reader* (Cambridge, 1981)

Harrison, J. F. C., *Learning and Living, 1790-1960: A Study in the History of the English Adult Education Movement* (1961)

Harte, Negley, *The University of London, 1836-1986* (1986)

Heron, Liz, ed., *Truth, Dare or Promise: Girls Growing Up in the Fifties* (1985)

Hoggart, Richard, *The Uses of Literacy* (1957; paperback edn, 1968)

Hollis, Patricia, *The Pauper Press* (Oxford, 1970)

Hope, Keith, *As Others See Us: Schooling and Social Mobility in Scotland and the United States* (Cambridge, 1984)

Houston, R. A., *Scottish Literacy and the Scottish Identity* (Cambridge, 1985)

Howarth, Janet, and Curthoys, Mark, 'The Political Economy of Women's Higher Education in Late-Nineteenth and Early-Twentieth Century Britain', *Historical Research*, 60 (1987)

Hurt, J. S., 'Professor West on Early Nineteenth-Century Education', *Economic History Review*, 2nd ser., 24 (1971)

Johnson, Richard, 'Educational Policy and Social Control in Early Victorian England', *Past & Present*, 49 (1970)

'"Really Useful Knowledge": Radical Education and Working-Class Culture, 1790-1848', in John Clarke, Chris Critcher and Richard Johnson, eds., *Working Class Culture: Studies in History and Theory* (1979)

Jones, M. G., *The Charity School Movement: A Study of Eighteenth Century Puritanism in Action* (Cambridge, 1938)
Kamm, Josephine, *Indicative Past: A Hundred Years of the Girls' Public Day School Trust* (1971)
Kiesling, H. J., 'Nineteenth-Century Education According to West: A Comment', *Economic History Review*, 2nd ser., 36 (1983)
Laqueur, T. W., *Religion and Respectability: Sunday Schools and Working Class Culture 1780–1850* (New Haven, 1976)
Life and Struggles of William Lovett (1876; 1967 edn)
Mueller, Detlef K., Ringer, Fritz, and Simon, Brian (eds.), *The Rise of the Modern Educational System* (Cambridge, 1987)
Murphy, James, *Church, State and Schools in Britain, 1800–1970* (1971)
Newson, John and Elizabeth, *Seven Years Old in the Home Environment* (1976)
Newson, John and Elizabeth, and Barnes, Peter, *Perspectives on School at Seven Years Old* (1977)
O'Day, Rosemary, *Education and Society 1500–1800* (1982)
Philpott, Hugh B., *London at School: The Story of the London School Board 1870–1904* (1904)
Prest, John, *Lord John Russell* (1972)
Roach, John, *A History of Secondary Education in England 1800–1870* (1986)
Robinson, Eric, ed., *John Clare's Autobiographical Writings* (Oxford, 1983)
Sheldon, Rothblatt, *The Revolution of the Dons: Cambridge and Society in Victorian England* (1968)
Sanderson, Michael, *The Universities and British Industry 1850–1970* (1972)
   Educational Opportunity and Social Change in England (1987)
Scotland, James, *A History of Scottish Education*, 2 vols. (1969)
Sherington, Geoffrey, *English Education, Social Change and War 1911–20* (Manchester, 1981)
Silver, Harold, *The Concept of Popular Education* (1965)
Slee, P. R. H., *Learning and a Liberal Education: The Study of Modern History in the Universities of Oxford, Cambridge and Manchester 1800–1914* (Manchester, 1986)
Springhall, John, *Youth, Empire and Society: British Youth Movements, 1883–1940* (1977)
Spufford, Margaret, 'First Steps in Literacy: The Reading and Writing Experiences of the Humblest Seventeenth-Century Autobiographers', *Social History*, 4 (1979)
Steedman, H., 'Defining Institutions: The Endowed Grammar Schools and the Systematisation of English Secondary Education', in D. K. Mueller, F. Ringer and B. Simon, eds., *The Rise of the Modern Educational System* (Cambridge, 1987)
Stone, Lawrence, ed., *The University in Society*, 2 vols. (Princeton, 1975)
Sutherland, Gillian, *Policy-Making in Elementary Education 1870–1895* (Oxford, 1973)
   Ability, Merit and Measurement: Mental Testing and English Education 1880–1940 (Oxford, 1984)
      ed., *Government and Society in Nineteenth-Century Britain: Commentaries on British Parliamentary Papers: Education* (Shannon, 1977)
Thompson, Flora, *Lark Rise* (1939; World Classics edn, 1954)
Thomson, Thea, ed., *Edwardian Childhoods* (1981)
Tompson, Richard S., *Classics or Charity? The Dilemma of the Eighteenth-Century Grammar School* (Manchester, 1971)
Tropp, A., *The School Teachers* (1957)

Vincent, David, *Bread, Knowledge and Freedom: A Study of Nineteenth-Century Working Class Autobiography* (1981)
  Literacy and Popular Culture in England 1750–1914 (Cambridge, 1990)
West, E. G., 'Resource Allocation and Growth in Early Nineteenth-Century British Education', *Economic History Review*, 2nd ser., 23 (1970)
  'The Interpretation of Early Nineteenth-Century Education Statistics', *Economic History Review*, 2nd ser., 24 (1971)
  'Nineteenth-Century Educational History: The Kiesling Critique', *Economic History Review*, 2nd ser., 36 (1983)

4 HEALTH AND MEDICINE

Abel-Smith, B., *A History of the Nursing Profession* (1960)
  The Hospitals, 1800–1948 (1964)
Ackernecht, E. H., 'Anticontagionism between 1821 and 1867', *Bulletin of the History of Medicine*, 22 (1948)
  Medicine at the Paris Hospital, 1794–1848 (Baltimore, 1967)
Anderson, O., *Suicide in Victorian and Edwardian England* (Oxford, 1987)
Baly, M., *Florence Nightingale and the Nursing Legacy* (1986)
Banks, J. A., *Prosperity and Parenthood: A Study of Family Planning among the Victorian Middle Classes* (1954)
  Victorian Values: Secularism and the Size of Families (1981)
Banks, J. A. and O., *Feminism and Family Planning in Victorian England* (Liverpool, 1964)
Barrow, L., 'Democratic Epistemology: Mid Nineteenth-Century Plebeian Medicine', *Bulletin of the Society for the Social History of Medicine*, 29 (1981)
Barry, J., 'Publicity and the Public Good: Presenting Medicine in Eighteenth-Century Bristol', in W. Bynum and R. Porter, eds., *Medical Fringe and Medical Orthodoxy* (1987)
Bartley, M., 'Coronary Heart Disease: A Disease of Affluence or a Disease of Industry?', in P. Weindling, ed., *The Social History of Occupational Health* (1985)
Bennett, T., 'Popular Culture: Divided Territory', *Social History Society Newsletter*, 6 (1981)
Berridge, V., 'Drugs and Social Policy: The Establishment of Drug Control in Britain 1900–1930', *British Journal of Addiction*, 79 (1984)
Berridge, V., and Edwards, J. G., *Opium and the People: Opiate Use in Nineteenth-Century England* (1981)
Berridge, V., and Strong, P., 'AIDS Policies in the United Kingdom: A Preliminary Analysis', in Fee, E., and Fox, D., eds., *AIDS: Contemporary History* (Princeton, 1990)
Black, D., *Inequalities in Health: The Black Report*, ed. with an introd. by P. Townsend and N. Davidson (1982)
Blackman, J., 'Popular Theories of Generation: The Evolution of *Aristotle's Works*. The Study of an Anachronism', in J. Woodward and D. Richards, eds., *Health Care and Popular Medicine: Essays on the Social History of Medicine* (1977)
Brand, J. L., *Doctors and the State: The British Medical Profession and Government Action in Health, 1870–1912* (Baltimore, 1965)
British Medical Association, *Secret Remedies, What they Cost and What they Contain* (1909)
  More Secret Remedies, What they Cost and What they Contain (1912)

Bryder, L., 'The First World War: Healthy or Hungry?', *History Workshop*, 24 (1987)

Beyond the Magic Mountain: The Social History of Tuberculosis (Oxford, 1988)

Burnett, J., *Plenty and Want: A Social History of Diet in England from 1815 to the Present Day* (1966)

Busfield, J., *Managing Madness* (1986)

Bynum, W. F., 'Health, Disease and Medical Care', in G. S. Rousseau and R. Porter, eds., *The Ferment of Knowledge* (Cambridge, 1980)

Bynum, W. F., and Porter, R., eds., *William Hunter and the Eighteenth-Century Medical World* (Cambridge, 1985)

Medical Fringe and Medical Orthodoxy (1987)

Bynum, W. F., Porter, R., and Shepherd, M., eds., *The Anatomy of Madness*, 3 vols. (1985)

Campbell, J., *Nye Bevan and the Mirage of British Socialism* (1987)

Cantor, G. N., 'The Edinburgh Phrenology Debate, 1803–28', *Annals of Science*, 32 (1975)

Carlson, E. T., and Dain, N., 'The Meaning of Moral Insanity', *Bulletin of the History of Medicine*, 36 (1962)

Chamberlain, M., *Old Wives' Tales: Their History, Remedies and Spells* (1981)

Chapman, S., *Jesse Boot of Boots the Chemists* (1974)

Cherry, S., 'The Role of a Provincial Hospital: The Norfolk and Norwich Hospital, 1771–1880', *Population Studies*, 26 (1972)

Clark, G. N., *A History of the Royal College of Physicians of London*, vol. 2 (Oxford, 1966)

Clark, M. J., 'The Rejection of Psychological Approaches to Mental Disorder in Late Nineteenth Century British Psychiatry', in A. Scull, ed., *Madhouses, Mad-Doctors and Madmen* (1981)

Clarke, B., *Mental Disorder in Earlier Britain* (Cardiff, 1975)

Cooter, R., 'Phrenology: Provocation of Progress', *History of Science*, 14 (1976)

'Interpreting the Fringe', *Bulletin of the Society for the Social History of Medicine*, 29 (1981)

The Cultural Meaning of Popular Science (Cambridge, 1985)

Corsi, P., and Weindling, P., eds., *Information Sources in the History of Science and Medicine* (1983)

Crellin, J. K., 'The Growth of Professionalism in Nineteenth Century British Pharmacy', *Medical History*, 11 (1967)

Crowther, M. A., 'The Later Years of the Workhouse, 1890–1929', in P. Thane, ed., *The Origins of British Social Policy* (1978)

The Workhouse System, 1834–1929 (1981)

Daunton, M. J., *House and Home in the Victorian City* (1983)

Davies, C., ed., *Rewriting Nursing History* (1980)

Davin, A., 'Imperialism and Motherhood', *History Workshop*, 5 (1978)

Digby, A., *Madness, Morality and Medicine: A Study of the York Retreat 1796–1914* (Cambridge, 1985)

'Moral Treatment at the York Retreat', in W. F. Bynum, R. Porter and M. Shepherd, eds., *The Anatomy of Madness*, 3 vols. (1985), vol. 2

Dingle, A. E., 'Drink and Working Class Living Standards in Britain, 1870–1914', in D. J. Oddy and D. Miller, eds., *The Making of the Modern British Diet* (1975)

Dingwall, R., Rafferty, A.-M., and Webster, C., *An Introduction to the Social History of Nursing* (1988)

Doerner, K., *Madness and Bourgeoisie: A Social History of Insanity and Psychiatry* (Oxford, 1981)

Donnison, J., *Midwives and Medical Men: A History of Inter-Professional Rivalries and Women's Rights* (New York, 1977)

Doyal, L., and Pennell, I., *The Political Economy of Health* (1979)

Durey, M. J., 'Bodysnatchers and Benthamites: The "Dead Body Bill" and the Provision of Bodies to the London Anatomy Schools, 1820–42', *Bulletin of the Society for the Social History of Medicine*, 19 (1976)

Dwork, D., *War is Good for Babies and Other Young Children: A History of the Infant and Child Welfare Movement in England, 1898–1918* (1987)

Dyhouse, C., 'Working-Class Mothers and Infant Mortality in England, 1895–1914', *Journal of Social History*, 12 (1978)

Earwicker, R., 'The Emergence of a Medical Strategy in the Labour Movement, 1906–1919', *Bulletin of the Society for the Social History of Medicine*, 29 (1981)

Ehrenreich, B., and English, D., *Witches, Midwives and Nurses: A History of Women Healers* (1974)

Eyler, J., *Victorian Social Medicine: The Ideas and Methods of William Farr* (Baltimore and London, 1979)

Fee, E., and Fox, D., 'The Contemporary Historiography of AIDS', *Journal of Social History* (forthcoming, 1990)

Figlio, K., 'Chlorosis and Chronic Disease in Nineteenth Century Britain: The Social Construction of Somatic Illness in a Capitalist Society', *Social History*, 3 (1978)

Finer, S. E., *The Life and Times of Sir Edwin Chadwick* (1952)

Finnane, M., *Insanity and the Insane in Post Famine Ireland* (1981)

Flinn, M. W., 'Introduction', to E. Chadwick, *Report on the Sanitary Condition of the Labouring Population of Great Britain* (Edinburgh, 1965)

Foot, M., *Aneurin Bevan*, vol. 2: *1945–1960* (1975)

Forbes, T. R., 'The Regulation of English Midwives in the Eighteenth and Nineteenth Centuries', *Medical History*, 15 (1971)

Foucault, M., *Madness and Civilisation: A History of Insanity in the Age of Reason* (1967)
  The Birth of the Clinic: An Archaeology of Medical Perception (1975)

Fox, D. M., 'The National Health Service and the Second World War: The Elaboration of Consensus', in H. L. Smith, ed., *War and Social Change: British Society in the Second World War* (Manchester, 1986)

Fraser Brockington, C., *Public Health in the Nineteenth Century* (London and Edinburgh, 1965)

Frazer, W. M., *History of English Public Health, 1834–1939* (1950)

Gaskell, E., *Mary Barton* (1848; Penguin edn, 1970)
  'The Coffinites', *Bulletin of the Society for the Social History of Medicine*, 8 (1972)

Gay, P., 'The Enlightenment as Medicine and as Cure', in W. H. Barber *et al.*, eds., *The Age of the Enlightenment: Studies Presented to Theodore Besterman* (Edinburgh, 1967)

Gelfand, T., 'The Decline of the Ordinary Practitioner and the Rise of the Modern Medical Profession', in S. Statum and D. E. Larson, eds., *Doctors, Patients and Society: Power and Authority in Medical Care* (Ontario, 1981)

Gilbert, B. B., *The Evolution of National Insurance in Great Britain: The Origins of the Welfare State* (1966)
  British Social Policy, 1914–1939 (1970)

Gillis, J., *For Better, for Worse: British Marriages 1600 to the Present* (Oxford, 1986)

Godber, G., 'The Domesday Book of British Hospitals', *Bulletin of the Society for the Social History of Medicine*, 32 (1983)

Granshaw, L., *St Mark's Hospital, London: A Social History of a Specialist Hospital* (1985)

Green, D., *Working Class Patients and the Medical Establishment: Self Help in Britain from the Mid-Nineteenth Century to 1948* (1986)

Guistino, D. de, *Conquest of the Mind: Phrenology and Victorial Social Thought* (1975)

Guthrie, D., 'Whither Medical History?', *Medical History*, 1 (1957)

Hall, E., *Canary Girls and Stockpots* (Luton, 1977)

Hamilton, D., and Lamb, M., 'Surgeons and Surgery', in D. Checkland and M. Lamb, eds., *Health Care as Social History: The Glasgow Case* (Aberdeen, 1982)

Hardy, A., 'Smallpox in London: Factors in the Decline of Disease in the Nineteenth Century', *Medical History*, 27 (1983)

Harris, J., 'Some Aspects of Social Policy in Britain during the Second World War', in W. J. Mommsen, ed., *The Emergence of the Welfare State in Britain and Germany* (1981)

Harrison, B., *Drink and the Victorians: The Temperance Question in England, 1815–1872* (1971)

Hartston, W., 'Medical Dispensaries in Eighteenth Century London', *Proceedings of the Royal Society of Medicine*, 56 (1963)

Hay, J. R., 'Employers' Attitudes to Social Policy and the Concept of Social Control, 1900–1920', in P. Thane, ed., *The Origins of British Social Policy* (1978)

Helleiner, K., 'The Vital Revolution Reconsidered', in D. Glass and D. Eversley, eds., *Population in History* (1965)

Hillam, C., 'The Financial Attractions of Being a Dentist in the Early Nineteenth Century', *Bulletin of the Society for the Social History of Medicine*, 41 (1987)

Hodgkinson, R. G., 'Provision for Pauper Lunatics, 1834–71', *Medical History*, 10 (1966)

  The Origins of the National Health Service: The Medical Services of the New Poor Law, 1834–1871 (1967)

Holloway, S. W. F., 'The All Saints' Sisterhood at University College Hospital, 1862–1899', *Medical History*, 3 (1959)

  'Medical Education in England, 1830–58: A Sociological Analysis', *History*, 49 (1964)

  'The Apothecaries Act, 1815: A Reinterpretation', *Medical History*, 10 (1966)

  'The Orthodox Fringe: The Origins of the Pharmaceutical Society of Great Britain', in W. F. Bynum and R. Porter, eds., *Medical Fringe and Medical Orthodoxy* (1987)

Holmes, G., *Augustan England: Professions, State and Society, 1680–1730* (1982)

Honigsbaum, F., *The Struggle for the Ministry of Health, 1914–1919* (1970)

  'The Interwar Health Insurance Scheme: A Rejoinder', *Journal of Social Policy*, 12 (1983)

Howie, W. B., 'The Administration of an Eighteenth Century Provincial Hospital: The Royal Salop Infirmary 1747–1830', *Medical History*, 5 (1961)

  'Finance and Supply in an Eighteenth Century Hospital', *Medical History*, 7 (1963)

Hunter, R., and MacAlpine, I., *Three Hundred Years of Psychiatry, 1535–1860* (Oxford, 1963)
  Psychiatry for the Poor, 1851. Colney Hatch Asylum, Friern Hospital, 1973: A Medical and Social History (1974)
Illich, I., *Medical Nemesis: The Expropriation of Health* (1975)
Ineson, A., and Thom, D., 'TNT Poisoning and the Employment of Women Workers in the First World War', in P. Weindling, ed., *The Social History of Occupational Health* (1985)
Inglis, B., *Fringe Medicine* (1964)
Inkster, I., 'Marginal Men: Aspects of the Social Role of the Medical Community in Sheffield, 1790–1850', in J. Woodward and D. Richards, eds., *Health Care and Popular Medicine: Essays on the Social History of Medicine* (1977)
Jefferys, M., and Sacks, H., *Rethinking General Practice: Dilemmas in Primary Medical Care* (1983)
Jewson, N. D., 'Medical Knowledge and the Patronage System in Eighteenth Century England', *Sociology*, 8 (1974)
Jones, H., 'An Inspector Calls: Health and Safety at Work in Inter-War Britain', in P. Weindling, ed., *The Social History of Occupational Health* (1985)
Jones, K., *Lunacy, Law and Conscience, 1744–1845* (1955)
  A History of the Mental Health Services (1972)
Jones, W. L., *Ministering to Minds Diseased: A History of Psychiatric Treatment* (1983)
Jordanova, L. J., 'The Social Sciences and History of Science and Medicine', in P. Corsi and P. Weindling, eds., *Information Sources in the History of Science and Medicine* (1983)
Kellett, J. R., *The Impact of Railways on Victorian Cities* (1969)
Kennedy, I., *The Unmasking of Medicine* (1981)
King, A., 'Hospital Planning: Revised Thoughts on the Origin of the Pavilion Principle in England', *Medical History*, 10 (1966)
King, L. S., *The Medical World of the Eighteenth Century* (New York, 1971)
Knight, P., 'Women and Abortion in Victorian and Edwardian England', *History Workshop*, 4 (1977)
Lambert, R., *Sir John Simon 1816–1904 and English Social Administration* (1963)
Lane, J., 'The Medical Practitioners of Provincial England in 1783', *Medical History*, 28 (1984)
Larkin, G., *Occupational Monopoly and Modern Medicine* (1983)
  'The Licensing of Health Professions: Medical or Ministry Control?', *Bulletin of the Society for the Social History of Medicine*, 40 (1987)
Leigh, D., *The Historical Development of Psychiatry* (Oxford, 1961)
Lewis, J., *The Politics of Motherhood: Child and Maternal Welfare in England 1900–1939* (1980)
  'The Social History of Social Policy: Infant Welfare in Edwardian England', *Journal of Social Policy*, 9 (1980)
  What Price Community Medicine? The Philosophy, Practice and Politics of Public Health since 1919 (1986)
Lewis, J., and Brookes, B., 'The Peckham Health Centre, "PEP" and the Concept of General Practice during the 1930s and 1940s', *Medical History*, 27 (1983)
Lindsey, A., *Socialised Medicine in England and Wales: The National Health Service, 1948–1961* (Chapel Hill, 1962)
Linebaugh, P., 'The Tyburn Riot against the Surgeons', in D. Hay, P.

Linebaugh and E. P. Thompson, eds., *Albion's Fatal Tree: Crime and Society in Eighteenth-Century England* (1975)

Llewelyn Davies, M., *Maternity: Letters from Working Women* (1915; republished 1978)

Loudon, I. S. L., 'Historical Importance of Outpatients', *British Medical Journal*, 1 (1978)

'The Origins and Growth of the Dispensary Movement in England', *Bulletin of the History of Medicine*, 55 (1981)

'Deaths in Childbed from the Eighteenth Century to 1935', *Medical History*, 30 (1986)

Medical Care and the General Practitioner, 1750–1850 (Oxford, 1987)

'The Vile Race of Quacks with which this Country is Infested', in W. F. Bynum and R. Porter, eds., *Medical Fringe and Medical Orthodoxy* (1987)

Luckin, W., 'Evaluating the Sanitary Revolution: Typhus and Typhoid in London, 1851–1900', in R. Woods and J. Woodward, eds., *Urban Disease and Mortality in Nineteenth Century England* (1954)

McCandless, P., 'Liberty and Lunacy: The Victorians and Wrongful Confinement', *Journal of Social History*, 11 (1978)

'Curses of Civilisation: Insanity and Drunkenness in Victorian Britain', *British Journal of Addiction*, 79 (1984)

MacDonald, M., *Mystical Bedlam: Madness, Anxiety and Healing in Seventeenth Century England* (Cambridge, 1982)

'Anthropological Perspectives on the History of Science and Medicine', in P. Corsi and P. Weindling, eds., *Information Sources in the History of Science and Medicine* (1983)

McHugh, P., *Prostitution and Victorian Social Reform* (1982)

McKeown, T., 'A Sociological Approach to the History of Medicine', *Medical History*, 14 (1970)

The Modern Rise of Population (1976)

McKeown, T., and Brown, R., 'Medical Evidence Related to English Population Change in the Eighteenth Century', *Population Studies*, 9 (1955–6)

McKeown, T., Brown, R. G., and Record, R. G., 'An Interpretation of the Rise of Population in Europe', *Population Studies*, 26 (1972)

McKeown, T., and Record, R. G., 'Reasons for the Decline in Mortality in England and Wales during the Nineteenth Century', in M. W. Flinn and T. C. Smout, eds., *Essays in Social History* (Oxford, 1974)

McLachlan, G., and McKeown, T., *Medical History and Medical Care* (1971)

McLaren, A., 'Phrenology: Medium and Message', *Journal of Modern History*, 46 (1974)

'Women's Work and Regulation of Family Size: The Question of Abortion in the Nineteenth Century', *History Workshop*, 4 (1977)

Birth Control in Nineteenth-Century England (1978)

MacLeod, R. M., 'The Edge of Hope: Social Policy and Chronic Alcoholism 1870–1900', *Journal of the History of Medicine and Allied Sciences*, 22 (1967)

'The Frustration of State Medicine', *Medical History*, 11 (1967)

'Law, Medicine and Public Opinion: The Resistance to Compulsory Health Legislation, 1870–1907', *Public Law*, 107 (1967)

'The Anatomy of State Medicine, Concept and Application', in F. N. L. Poynter, ed., *Medicine and Science in the 1860s* (1968)

McLoughlin, G., *A Short History of the First Liverpool Infirmary, 1749–1824* (Chichester, 1978)

McMenemy, W. H., 'The Hospital Movement of the Eighteenth Century and its Development', in F. N. L. Poynter, ed., *The Evolution of Hospitals in Britain* (1964)

MacNicol, J., 'The Evacuation of Schoolchildren', in H. L. Smith, ed., *War and Social Change: British Society in the Second World War* (Manchester, 1986)

Maggs, C., 'Nurse Recruitment to Four Provincial Hospitals, 1881–1921', in C. Davies, ed., *Rewriting Nursing History* (1980)

The Origins of General Nursing (1983)

Nursing History: The State of the Art (1986)

Matthews, L. G., *History of Pharmacy in Britain* (Edinburgh and London, 1962)

Mellett, D. J., *The Prerogative of Asylumdom* (1982)

Millman, M., 'The Influence of the Social Science Association on Hospital Planning in Victorian England', *Medical History*, 18 (1974)

Morris, R. J., *Cholera, 1832* (1976)

Newman, C., *The Evolution of Medical Education in the Nineteenth Century* (1957)

Oddy, D. J., 'Working Class Diets in Late Nineteenth Century Britain', *Economic History Review*, 2nd ser., 23 (1970)

'A Nutritional Analysis of Historical Evidence: The Working Class Diet 1880–1914', in D. J. Oddy and D. Miller, eds., *The Making of the Modern British Diet* (1975)

Parry-Jones, W. L., *The Trade in Lunacy: A Study of Private Madhouses in England and Wales in the Eighteenth and Nineteenth Centuries* (1971)

Pater, J. E., *The Making of the National Health Service* (1981)

Pelling, M., 'The Reality of Anticontagionism – Theories of Epidemic Disease in the Nineteenth Century', *Bulletin of the Society for the Social History of Medicine*, 17 (1976)

Cholera, Fever and English Medicine (Oxford, 1978)

'Medical Practice in the Early Modern Period: Trade or Profession?' in W. Prest, ed., *The Professions in Early Modern England* (1987)

Pelling, M., and Webster, C., 'Medical Practitioners', in C. Webster, ed., *Health, Medicine and Mortality in the Sixteenth Century* (Cambridge, 1979)

Peretz, E., 'Memories of Health and Caring' (conference report), *History Workshop*, 25 (1988)

Peterson, M. J., *The Medical Profession in Mid-Victorian London* (Berkeley, 1978)

'Gentlemen and Medical Men: The Problem of Professional Recruitment', *Bulletin of the History of Medicine*, 58 (1984)

Petty, C., 'Food, Poverty and Growth: The Application of Nutrition Science, 1918–1939', *Bulletin of the Society for the Social History of Medicine*, 40 (1987)

Pickstone, J. V., 'Medical Botany (Self-Help Medicine in Victorian England)', *Memoirs of the Manchester Literary and Philosophical Society*, 119 (1976–7)

'Comparative Studies of the Development of Medical Services in Lancashire Towns', in J. V. Pickstone, ed., *Health, Disease and Medicine in Lancashire, 1750–1950* (Manchester, 1980)

Medicine and Industrial Society: A History of Hospital Development in Manchester and its Region, 1752–1946 (Manchester, 1985)

ed., *Health, Disease and Medicine in Lancashire, 1750–1950* (Manchester, 1980)

Pinchbeck, I., and Hewitt, M., *Children in English Society*, vol. 2 (1973)

Porter, R., *English Society in the Eighteenth Century* (1982)

'Was there a Medical Enlightenment in Eighteenth Century England?' *British Journal of Eighteenth Century Studies*, 5 (1982)

'Lay Medical Knowledge in the Eighteenth Century: The Evidence of the *Gentleman's Magazine*', *Medical History*, 29 (1985)

Disease, Medicine and Society in England, 1550–1860 (1987)

Mind Forg'd Manacles: Madness and Psychiatry in England from the Restoration to the Regency (1987)

A Social History of Madness: Stories of the Insane (1987)

ed., *Patients and Practitioners: Lay Perceptions of Medicine in Pre-Industrial Society* (Cambridge, 1985)

Porter, R., and Wear, A., eds., *Problems and Methods in the History of Medicine* (1987)

Pound, R., *Harley Street* (1967)

Price, R., 'Hydropathy in England, 1840–70', *Medical History*, 25 (1981)

Razzell, P. E., 'Edward Jenner: The History of a Medical Myth', *Medical History*, 9 (1965)

'Population Change in Eighteenth Century England: A Reappraisal', *Economic History Review*, 2nd ser., 18 (1965)

Reiser, S. J., *Medicine and the Reign of Technology* (Cambridge, 1978)

Richards, D., 'Dentistry in England in the 1840s: The First Indications of a Movement towards Professionalisation', *Medical History*, 12 (1968)

'Final Chapters in the Campaign to Effect Dental Registration', *Bulletin of the Society for the Social History of Medicine*, 23 (1978)

Richardson, R., *Death, Dissection and the Destitute* (1987)

Riley, J. C., *The Eighteenth-Century Campaign to Avoid Disease* (1986)

Roberts, C., 'Oral History Investigations of Disease and its Management in the Lancashire Working Class, 1890–1939', in J. V. Pickstone, ed., *Health, Disease and Medicine in Lancashire, 1750–1950* (Manchester, 1980)

Roberts, E., *A Woman's Place: An Oral History of Working-Class Women, 1890–1940* (Oxford, 1984)

Roberts, R., *The Classic Slum: Salford Life in the First Quarter of the Century* (Manchester, 1971)

Rose, M. E., 'The Success of Social Reform? The Central Control Board (Liquor Traffic) 1916–1922', in M. R. D. Foot, ed., *War and Society* (1973)

Rose, N., *The Psychological Complex: Psychology, Politics and Society in England, 1869–1939* (1985)

Rosen, G., 'The New History of Medicine: A Review', *Journal of the History of Medicine and Allied Sciences*, 6 (1951)

A History of Public Health (New York, 1958)

From Medical Police to Social Medicine (New York, 1974)

Rosenberg, C. E., 'Inward Vision and Outward Glance: The Shaping of the American Hospital, 1880–1914', *Bulletin of the History of Medicine*, 53 (1979)

Schoeneman, T. J., 'The Role of Mental Illness in the European Witch Hunts of the Sixteenth and Seventeenth Centuries: An Assessment', *Journal of the History of the Behavioral Sciences*, 13 (1977)

Schofield, E. M., *Medical Care of the Working Class about 1900* (Lancaster, 1979)

Scull, A., *Decarceration: Community Treatment and the Deviant: A Radical View* (Englewood Cliffs, 1977)

Museums of Madness: The Social Organisation of Insanity in Nineteenth Century England (1979)

Searle, G. R., *Eugenics and Politics in Britain, 1900–1914* (Leyden, 1976)

Sedgwick, P., *Psycho-Politics* (1982)

Shapin, S., 'Phrenological Knowledge and the Social Structure of Early Nineteenth Century Edinburgh', *Annals of Science*, 32 (1975)

Shepherd, M. A., 'Lunatic Asylum Patients in Warwickshire, 1841–1862', *Bulletin of the Society for the Social History of Medicine*, 18 (1976)

Shortt, S. E. D., *Victorian Lunacy: Richard M. Burke and the Practice of late Nineteenth-Century Psychiatry* (Cambridge, 1986)

Showalter, E., 'Victorian Women and Insanity', *Victorian Studies*, 23 (1979), reprinted in A. Scull, ed., *Madhouses, Mad-Doctors and Madmen* (1981)

The Female Malady: Women, Madness and English Culture, 1830–1980 (New York, 1985)

Shryock, R., *The Development of Modern Medicine* (Philadelphia, 1936; London, 1948)

Sickerman, B., 'The Use of a Diagnosis: Doctors, Patients and Neurasthenia', *Journal of the History of Medicine and Allied Sciences*, 32 (1977)

Sigerist, H. E., *Civilisation and Disease* (Ithaca, 1943)

Sigsworth, E., 'Gateways to Death? Medicine, Hospitals and Mortality, 1700–1850', in P. Mathias, ed., *Science and Society, 1600–1900* (Cambridge, 1972)

Sigsworth, E., and Swan, P., 'Para-Medical Provision in the West Riding', *Bulletin of the Society for the Social History of Medicine*, 29 (1981)

Simmons, H. G., 'Explaining Social Policy: The English Mental Deficiency Act of 1913', *Journal of Social History*, 11 (1978)

'Mental Handicap and Education', *Oxford Review of Education*, 9 (1983)

Skultans, V., *English Madness, Ideas on Insanity, 1580–1890* (1979)

Smart, R., 'The Effect of Licensing Restrictions during 1914–18 on Drunkenness and Liver Cirrhosis Deaths in Britain', *British Journal of Addiction*, 69 (1974)

Smith, F. B., *The People's Health, 1830–1910* (1979)

Florence Nightingale: Reputation and Power (1982)

Soloway, R. A., *Birth Control and the Population Question in England, 1877–1930* (Chapel Hill, 1982)

Stevens, R., *Medical Practice in Modern England* (New Haven, 1966)

Stone, M., 'Shellshock and the Psychologists', in W. F. Bynum, R. Porter and M. Shepherd, *The Anatomy of Madness*, 3 vols. (1985), vol. 2

Summers, A., 'Pride and Prejudice: Ladies and Nurses in the Crimean War', *History Workshop*, 16 (1983)

Angels and Citizens: British Women as Military Nurses, 1854–1914 (1988)

Sutherland, G., and Sharp, S., *Ability, Merit and Measurement: Mental Testing and English Education 1880–1940* (Oxford, 1984)

Szasz, T., *The Manufacture of Madness: a Comparative Study of the Inquisition and the Mental Health Movement* (New York, 1970)

The Myth of Mental Illness (1972)

Szreter, S., 'The Importance of Social Intervention in Britain's Mortality Decline, *c.* 1850–1914: A Reinterpretation of the Role of Public Health', *Social History of Medicine*, 1 (1988)

Thane, P., *The Foundations of the Welfare State* (1982)

Thompson, J., and Goldin, G., *The Hospital, a Social and Architectural History* (New Haven and London, 1975)

Titmuss, R. M., *Problems of Social Policy* (1950)

Trease, G., 'Introduction', in F. N. L. Poynter, ed., *The Evolution of Pharmacy in Britain* (1965)

Turner, E. S., *The Shocking History of Advertising* (1952)

Turner, J., 'State Purchase of the Liquor Trade in the First World War', *Historical Journal*, 23 (1980)

Varlaam, C., 'The 1858 Medical Act: The Origins and the Aftermath', *Bulletin of the Society for the Social History of Medicine*, 21 (1977)

Versluysen, M., 'Old Wives Tales?: Women Healers in English History', in

C. Davies, ed., *Rewriting Nursing History* (1980)

Waddington, I., 'General Practitioners and Consultants in Early Nineteenth Century England: The Sociology of an Intra-Professional Conflict', in J. Woodward and D. Richards, eds., *Health Care and Popular Medicine: Essays on the Social History of Medicine* (1977)

The Medical Profession in the Industrial Revolution (Dublin, 1984)

Walkowitz, J., *Prostitution and Victorian Society: Women, Class and the State* (Cambridge, 1980)

Walton, J., 'Lunacy and the Industrial Revolution: A Study of Asylum Admissions in Lancashire, 1848–50', *Journal of Social History*, 13 (1979)

Webster, C., 'Social History and Medical Science', *Bulletin of the Society for the Social History of Medicine*, 19 (1976)

'The Crisis of the Hospitals during the Industrial Revolution', in E. G. Forbes, ed., *Human Implications of Scientific Advance: Proceedings of the Fifteenth International Congress of the History of Science* (Edinburgh, 1978)

'Healthy or Hungry Thirties?' *History Workshop*, 13 (1982)

'The Historiography of Medicine', in P. Corsi and P. Weindling, eds., *Information Sources in the History of Science and Medicine* (1983)

'Health, Welfare and Unemployment during the Depression', *Past & Present*, 109 (1985)

The Health Services since the War, vol. 1: *Problems of Health Care: The National Health Service before 1957* (1988)

'Labour and the Origins of the National Health Service', in N. Rupke, ed., *Science, Politics and the Public Good: Essays in Honour of Margaret Gowing* (1988)

'Origins of the NHS: Lessons from History', *Contemporary Record*, 2 (1988)

Weeks, J., ' "Sins and Diseases": Some Notes on Homosexuality in the Nineteenth Century', *History Workshop*, 1 (1976)

Coming Out (1977)

Sex, Politics and Society (1981)

Weindling, P., 'Linking Self Help and Medical Science: The Social History of Occupational Health', in P. Weindling, ed., *The Social History of Occupational Health* (1985)

'Patients and Practitioners: Virtues and Vices of the New Social History of Medicine', *History Workshop*, 24 (1987)

Welshman, J., 'School Meals and the Problem of Malnutrition in England and Wales, 1900–1939', *Bulletin of the Society for the Social History of Medicine*, 40 (1987)

West, J. L., *The Taylors of Lancashire: Bonesetters and Doctors, 1750–1890* (Eccles, 1977)

White, R., *Social Change and the Development of the Nursing Profession: A Study of the Poor Law Nursing Service, 1848–1948* (1978)

Whiteside, N., 'Private Agencies for Public Purposes: Some New Perspectives on Policy-Making in Health Insurance between the Wars', *Journal of Social Policy*, 12 (1983)

Wilson, A., 'William Hunter and the Varieties of Man Midwifery', in W. F. Bynum and R. Porter, eds., *William Hunter and the Eighteenth-Century Medical World* (Cambridge, 1985)

Winter, J. M., 'The Impact of the First World War on Civilian Health in Britain', *Economic History Review*, 2nd ser., 30 (1977)

'Infant Mortality, Maternal Mortality and Public Health in Britain in the 1930s', *Journal of European Economic History*, 8 (1979)

The Great War and the British People (1986)

Wohl, A., *The Eternal Slum* (1977)

Endangered Lives: Public Health in Victorian Britain (1983)

Woods, R., 'From the Pit', *Oral History*, 7 (1979)

Woodward, J., *To Do the Sick No Harm: A Study of the British Voluntary Hospital System to 1875* (1974)

Wright, P., and Treacher, A., 'Introduction', in P. Wright and A. Treacher, eds., *The Problem of Medical Knowledge: Examining the Social Construction of Medicine* (Edinburgh, 1982)

Wrigley, E. A., and Schofield, R. S., *The Population History of England, 1541–1871: A Reconstruction* (1981)

Youngson, A. J., *The scientific Revolution in Victorian Medicine* (1979)

5 CRIME, AUTHORITY AND THE POLICEMAN-STATE

Amos, S., *Fifty Years of the English Constitution, 1830–1880* (1880)

Anderson, R., *Criminals and Crime: Some Facts and Suggestions* (1907)

Ascoli, D., *The Queen's Peace: The Metropolitan Police, 1829–1979* (1979)

Bailey, V., ed., *Policing and Punishment in Nineteenth-Century Britain* (1981)

Bartrip, P., 'Public Opinion and Law Enforcement: The Ticket-of-Leave Scares in Mid-Victorian Britain', in V. Bailey, ed., *Policing and Punishment in Nineteenth-Century Britain* (1981)

Beattie, J. M., *Crime and the Courts in England, 1660–1800* (Oxford, 1986)

Behlmer, G. K., *Child Abuse and Moral Reform in England, 1870–1908* (Stanford, 1982)

Blackstone, William, *Commentaries on the Laws of England* (1765–9)

Brewer, J., and Styles, J., eds., *An Ungovernable People: The English and their Law in the Seventeenth and Eighteenth Centuries* (1980)

Brogden, M., '"All Police is Conning Bastards": Policing and the Problem of Consent', in B. Fine *et al.*, eds., *Capitalism and the Rule of Law* (1979)

The Police: Autonomy and Consent (1982)

Butler, J., *Government by Police* (1879)

Chesney, K., *The Victorian Underworld* (1970)

Cockburn, J. S., ed., *Crime in England, 1550–1800* (1977)

Cohen, P., 'Policing the Working-Class City', in B. Fine *et al.*, eds., *Capitalism and the Rule of Law* (1979)

Critchley, T. A., *A History of Police in England and Wales, 900–1966* (1967)

Davis, J., 'The London Garotting Panic of 1862: A Moral Panic and the Creation of a Criminal Class in Mid-Victorian England', in V. A. C. Gatrell, B. Lenman and G. Parker, eds., *Crime and the Law: The Social History of Crime in Western Europe since 1500* (1980)

'"A Poor Man's System of Justice": Stipendiary Magistrates' Courts and the Working Class in London in the Later Nineteenth Century', *Historical Journal*, 27 (1984)

Donajgrodzki, A. P., '"Social Police" and the Bureaucratic Elite: A Vision of Order in the Age of Reform', in A. P. Donajgrodzki, ed., *Social Control in Nineteenth-Century Britain* (1977)

Emsley, C., *Policing and its Context, 1750–1870* (1983)

Gatrell, V. A. C., 'The Decline of Theft and Violence in Victorian and Edwardian England and Wales', in V. A. C. Gatrell, B. Lenman and G. Parker, eds., *Crime and the Law: The Social History of Crime in Western Europe since 1500* (1980)

Gatrell, V. A. C., and Hadden, T. B., 'Nineteenth Century Criminal Statistics and their Interpretation', in E. A. Wrigley, ed., *Nineteenth-Century Society: Essays in the Use of Quantitative Methods for the Study of Social Data* (Cambridge, 1972)

Gatrell, V. A. C., Lenman, B., and Parker, G., eds., *Crime and the Law: The Social History of Crime in Western Europe since 1500* (1980)

Goodway, D., *London Chartism, 1838–1848* (Cambridge, 1982)

Hall, S., et al., *Policing the Crisis: Mugging, the State, and Law and Order* (1978)

Hay, D., 'Property, Authority and the Criminal Law', in D. Hay et al., eds., *Albion's Fatal Tree: Crime and Society in Eighteenth-Century England* (1975)

'War, Dearth and Theft in the Eighteenth Century', *Past & Present*, 95 (1982)

'Controlling the English Prosecutor', *Osgoode Hall Law Journal*, 21 (1983)

'The Criminal Prosecution in England and its Historians', *Modern Law Review*, 47 (1984)

Hay, D., Linebaugh, P., and Thompson, E. P., eds., *Albion's Fatal Tree: Crime and Society in Eighteenth-Century England* (1975)

Ignatieff, M., *A Just Measure of Pain: The Penitentiary in the Industrial Revolution, 1750–1850* (1979)

'State, Civil Society and Total Institution: A Critique of Recent Social Histories of Punishment', in D. Sugarman, ed., *Legality, Ideology and the State* (1983)

Jones, D., 'The Conquering of "China": Crime in an Industrial Community, 1842–1864' in D. Jones, *Crime, Protest, Community and Police in Nineteenth-Century Britain* (1982)

Crime, Protest, Community and Police in Nineteenth-Century Britain (1982)

King, P., 'Decision-Making and Decision-Makers in the English Criminal Law, 1750–1800', *Historical Journal*, 27 (1984)

Landau, N., *The Justices of the Peace, 1679–1760* (Berkeley, California, 1985)

McClintock, F. H., and Avison, N. H., *Crime in England and Wales* (1968)

Macfarlane, A., *Justice and the Mare's Ale* (1984)

McIntosh, M., 'Changes in the Organisation of Thieving', in S. Cohen, ed., *Images of Deviance* (1971)

The Organisation of Crime (1975)

Mannheim, H., *Crime between the Wars* (1940)

Martin, J. P., and Wilson, G., *The Police: A Study in Manpower* (1969)

Mayhew, H., *London Labour and the London Poor*, 4 vols. (1861–2)

Miller, W. R., *Cops and Bobbies: Police Authority in New York and London, 1830–1870* (Chicago and London, 1977)

Morris, P., and Heal, K., *Crime Control and the Police: A Review of Research* (Home Office Research Study No. 67, 1981)

Muir, R., *Peers and Bureaucrats* (1910)

Partridge, E., *A Dictionary of the Underworld* (3rd edn, 1968)

Pearson, G., *Hooligan: A History of Respectable Fears* (1983)

Pellew, Jill, *The Home Office, 1848–1914: From Clerks to Bureaucrats* (1982)

Philips, D., *Crime and Authority in Victorian England: The Black Country, 1835–1860* (1977)

'"A New Engine of Power and Authority": The Institutionalization of Law-Enforcement in England, 1780–1830', in V. A. C. Gatrell, B. Lenman and G. Parker, eds., *Crime and the Law: The Social History of Crime in Western Europe since 1500* (1980)

Price, R., 'The Other Face of Respectability: Violence in the Manchester Brickmaking Trade, 1859–70', *Past & Present*, 66 (1975)

Radzinowicz, L., *Ideology and Crime* (1966)

Radzinowicz, L., and Hood, R., *A History of English Criminal Law*, vol. 5: *The Emergence of Penal Policy* (1986)

Reiner, R., *The Blue-Coated Worker: A Sociological Study of Police Unionism* (Cambridge, 1977)

The Politics of the Police (1985)

Roberts, R., *The Classic Slum: Salford Life in the First Quarter of the Century* (Manchester, 1971)

Samuel, R., ed., *East End Underworld: Chapters in the Life of Arthur Harding* (1981)

Sharpe, J. A., *Crime in Early Modern England, 1550–1750* (1984)

'The History of Violence in England: Some Observations' (and L. Stone's 'Rejoinder'), *Past & Present*, 108 (1985)

Silver, A., 'The Demand for Order in Civil Society: A Review of Some Themes in the History of Urban Crime, Police and Riot', in D. Bordua, ed., *The Police: Six Sociological Essays* (New York, 1967)

Smith, P., *Disraelian Conservatism and Social Reform* (1967)

Smith, P. T., *Policing Victorian London: Political Policing, Public Order, and the London Metropolitan Police* (Westport, Conn., and London, 1985)

Smithies, E., *Crime in Wartime: A Social History of Crime in World War II* (1982)

The Black Economy in England since 1914 (Dublin, 1984)

Steedman, C., *Policing the Victorian Community: The Formation of English Provincial Police Forces, 1856–1880* (1984)

Stephen, J. F., *A General View of the Criminal Law of England* (1863)

Stone, L., 'Interpersonal Violence in English Society, 1300–1980', *Past & Present*, 101 (1983)

Storch, R., ' "The Plague of Blue Locusts": Police Reform and Popular Resistance in Northern England, 1840–57', *International Review of Social History*, 20 (1975)

'The Policeman as Domestic Missionary: Urban Discipline and Popular Culture in Northern England, 1850–1880', *Journal of Social History*, 9 (1976)

Styles, J., 'Sir John Fielding and the Problem of Criminal Investigation in Eighteenth-Century England', *Transactions of the Royal Historical Society*, 33 (1983)

'Embezzlement, Industry and Law in England, 1550–1980', in M. Berg *et al.*, eds., *Manufacture in Town and Country before the Factory* (Cambridge, 1984)

Supperstone, M., *Brownlie's Law of Public Order and National Security* (2nd edn, 1981)

Thompson, E. P., *Whigs and Hunters: The Origin of the Black Act* (1975)

Tobias, J. J., *Crime and Industrial Society in the Nineteenth Century* (1967)

Tomes, N., ' "A Torrent of Abuse": Crimes of Violence between Working-Class Men and Women in London, 1840–1875', *Journal of Social History*, 11 (1978)

Wrightson, K., 'Two Concepts of Order: Justices, Constables and Jurymen in Seventeenth-Century England', in J. Brewer and J. Styles, eds., *An Ungovernable People: The English and their Law in the Seventeenth and Eighteenth Centuries* (1980)

6 RELIGION

Anson, P. F., *Fashions in Church Furnishings 1840–1940* (1960)

Arnold, M., 'The Study of Poetry' (1880) in R. H. Super, ed., *Complete Prose*

Works of Matthew Arnold, vol. 9 (Ann Arbor, Mich., 1973)

Aveling, J. C. H., *The Handle and the Axe: The Catholic Recusants in England from Reformation to Emancipation* (1976)

Bebbington, D. W., *The Nonconformist Conscience: Chapel and Politics, 1870–1914* (1982)

Best, G. F. A., *Temporal Pillars: Queen Anne's Bounty, the Ecclesiastical Commissioners and the Church of England* (Cambridge, 1964)

Binfield, C., *So Down to Prayers: Studies in English Nonconformity 1780–1920* (1977)

Bossy, J., *The English Catholic Community, 1570–1850* (1975)

Bradley, I., *The Call to Seriousness: The Evangelical Impact on the Victorians* (1976)

Brown, Callum, *The Social History of Religion in Scotland since 1730* (1987)

Brown, K. D., *A Social History of the Nonconformist Ministry in England and Wales 1800–1930* (Oxford, 1988)

Burman, R., 'Women in Jewish Religious Life: Manchester 1880–1930', in J. Obelkevich, L. Roper, and R. Samuel, eds., *Disciplines of Faith: Studies in Religion, Politics and Patriarchy* (1987)

Chadwick, O., *The Victorian Church*, 2 vols. (2nd edn, 1970–2)

Coleman, B. I., *The Church of England in the Mid-Nineteenth Century: A Social Geography* (1980)

Cookson, J., *The Friends of Peace: Anti-War Liberalism in England, 1793–1815* (Cambridge, 1982)

Cox, J., *The English Churches in a Secular Society: Lambeth 1870–1930* (Oxford, 1982)

Currie, R., Gilbert, A., and Horsley, J., *Churches and Churchgoers: Patterns of Church Growth in the British Isles since 1700* (Oxford, 1977)

Davies, Rupert, *et al.*, eds., *A History of the Methodist Church in Great Britain*, 4 vols. (1965–88)

Endelman, T. M., *The Jews of Georgian England 1714–1850* (Philadelphia, 1979)

Gilbert, A. D., *Religion and Society in Industrial England* (1976)

Gilley, S., 'Vulgar Piety and the Brompton Oratory, 1850–1860', in R. Swift and S. Gilley, eds., *The Irish in the Victorian City* (1985)

Gorer, G., *Exploring English Character* (1955)

Haig, A., *The Victorian Clergy* (1984)

Hastings, A., *A History of English Christianity 1920–1985* (1986)

Heeney, B., 'Women's Struggle for Professional Work and Status in the Church of England, 1900–1930', *Historical Journal*, 26 (1983)

The Women's Movement in the Church of England 1850–1930 (Oxford, 1988)

Hempton, D. N., 'Evangelicalism and Eschatology', *Journal of Ecclesiastical History*, 31 (1980)

Methodism and Politics in British Society 1750–1850 (1984)

Hilliard, D., 'Unenglish and Unmanly: Anglo-Catholicism and Homosexuality', *Victorian Studies*, 25 (1982)

Hirschberg, D. R., 'Episcopal Incomes and Expenses 1660–1760', in R. O'Day and F. Heal, eds., *Princes and Paupers of the English Church* (Leicester, 1981)

Lawrence, D. H., 'Hymns in a Man's Life', in Warren Roberts and Harry T. Moore, eds., *Phoenix II* (1968)

Lovegrove, D. W., *Established Church, Sectarian People: Itinerancy and the Transformation of English Dissent, 1780–1830* (Cambridge, 1988)

Machin, G. I. T., *Politics and the Churches in Great Britain, 1832–68* (Oxford, 1977)

McLeod, H., 'Class, Community and Region: The Religious Geography of Nineteenth-Century England', in M. Hill, ed., *Sociological Yearbook of Religion in Britain*, 6 (1973)
  Class and Religion in the Late Victorian City (1974)
  Religion and the Working Class in Nineteenth-Century Britain (1984)
  'New Perspectives on Victorian Working Class Religion: The Oral Evidence', *Oral History*, 14 (1986)
Maison, M. M., *Search your Soul, Eustace: A Survey of the Religious Novel in the Victorian Age* (1961)
Malmgreen, G., ed., *Religion in the Lives of English Women 1760–1930* (1986)
Mass-Observation, *Puzzled People* (1947)
Obelkevich, J., *Religion and Rural Society: South Lindsey 1825–1875* (Oxford, 1976)
Obelkevich, J., Roper, L., and Samuel, R., eds., *Disciplines of Faith: Studies in Religion, Politics and Patriarchy* (1987)
Prochaska, F. K., *Women and Philanthropy in Nineteenth-Century England* (Oxford, 1980)
Rowell, G., *Hell and the Victorians* (Oxford, 1974)
Sampson, G., *English for the English* (1921)
Swift, R., and Gilley, S., eds., *The Irish in the Victorian City* (1985)
Sykes, N., *Church and State in England in the XVIIIth Century* (Cambridge, 1934)
Temperley, N., *The Music of the English Parish Church*, 2 vols. (Cambridge, 1979)
Thompson, D. M., 'The Religious Census of 1851', in R. Lawton, ed., *The Census and Social Structure* (1978)
Valenze, D. M., 'Prophecy and Popular Literature in Eighteenth-Century England', *Journal of Ecclesiastical History*, 29 (1978)
  Prophetic Sons and Daughters: Females Preaching and Popular Religion in Industrial England (Princeton, 1985)
Walsh, J. D., 'Origins of the Evangelical Revival', in G. V. Bennett and J. D. Walsh, eds., *Essays in Modern English Church History* (1966)
  'Methodism and the Mob in the Eighteenth Century', in G. J. Cuming and D. Baker, eds., *Popular Belief and Practice* (Studies in Church History, 8, Cambridge, 1972)
Watts, M. R., *The Dissenters*, vol. 1 (Oxford, 1978)
Wilkinson, A., *The Church of England and the First World War* (1978)
Yeo, S., *Religion and Voluntary Organisations in Crisis* (1976)
  '"A New Life": The Religion of Socialism in Britain, 1883–1896', *History Workshop Journal*, 4 (1977)

7 PHILANTHROPY

Abel-Smith, B., *The Hospitals, 1800–1948* (1964)
Anderson, M., *Family Structure in Nineteenth-Century Lancashire* (Cambridge, 1971)
Bagehot, W., *Physics and Politics* (1872)
Behlmer, G., *Child Abuse and Moral Reform in England, 1870–1908* (Stanford, 1982)
Benham, W., ed., *Catharine and Craufurd Tait* (1879)
Best, G., *Mid-Victorian Britain, 1851–1875* (1971)
Beveridge, W., *Voluntary Action: A Report on Methods of Social Advance* (1948)
Bradley, I., *The Call to Seriousness: The Evangelical Impact on the Victorians* (1976)

Briggs, A., and Macartney, Anne, *Toynbee Hall: The First Hundred Years* (1984)

Brown, F. K., *Fathers of the Victorians* (Cambridge, 1961)

Brown, S. J., *Thomas Chalmers and the Godly Commonwealth in Scotland* (Oxford, 1982)

Burn, W. L., *The Age of Equipoise* (1964)

Checkland, Olive, *Philanthropy in Victorian Scotland: Social Welfare and the Voluntary Principle* (Edinburgh, 1980)

Conybeare, W., *Charity of Poor to Poor, Facts Collected in South London at the Suggestion of the Bishop of Southwark* (1908)

Cox, J., *The English Churches in a Secular Society: Lambeth 1870–1930* (Oxford, 1982)

Crossick, G., *An Artisan Elite in Victorian Society: Kentish London, 1840–1880* (1978)

Donajgrodzki, A. P., ed., *Social Control in Nineteenth-Century Britain* (1977)

Dudley, C. S., *An Analysis of the System of the Bible Society throughout its Various Parts* (1821)

Engels, F., *The Condition of the Working Class in England*, trans. and ed. W. O. Henderson and W. H. Chaloner (Stanford, 1958)

Finlayson, G. B. A. M., *The Seventh Earl of Shaftesbury* (1981)

Garnett, Elizabeth, *Our Navvies: A Dozen Years Ago and To-day* (1885)

Grant, J., *Sketches in London* (1838)

Hanna, W., *Memoirs of the Life and Writings of Thomas Chalmers*, 4 vols. (Edinburgh and London, 1849–52)

Harrison, B., 'Philanthropy and the Victorians', *Victorian Studies*, 9 (1966)

   Drink and the Victorians: The Temperance Question in England, 1815–1872 (1971)

   'For Church, Queen and Family: The Girls' Friendly Society 1874–1920', *Past & Present*, 61 (1973)

   Peaceable Kingdom: Stability and Change in Modern Britain (Oxford, 1982)

Heasman, K., *Evangelicals in Action* (1962)

Highmore, Anthony, *Pietas Londinensis* (1810)

Hopkins, Ellice, *Notes on Penitentiary Work* (1879)

   The White Cross Army: A Statement of the Bishop of Durham's Movement (1883)

Hubbard, Louisa M., 'Statistics of Women's Work', in Baroness Burdett-Coutts, ed., *Woman's Mission* (1893)

Hume, A., *Analysis of the Subscribers to the Various Liverpool Charities* (Liverpool, 1855)

Jennings, Hilda, *The Private Citizen in Public Social Work* (1930)

Joyce, P., *Work, Society and Politics: The Culture of the Factory in Later Victorian England* (Brighton, 1980)

   Patronage and Poverty in Merchant Society: The History of Morden College, Blackheath, 1695 to the Present (Henley-on-Thames, 1982)

Lloyd, R., *Strictures on a Recent Publication Entitled 'The Church her own Enemy'* (1819)

Low, S., *The Charities of London* (1850)

Macadam, Elizabeth, *The New Philanthropy* (1934)

McMillan, Margaret, *The Life of Rachel McMillan* (1927)

Meacham, S., *A Life Apart: The English Working Class 1890–1914* (1977)

More, Hannah, *Moral Sketches of Prevailing Opinions and Manners* (1819)

Morris, R. J., 'Voluntary Societies and British Urban Elites, 1780–1850: An Analysis', *Historical Journal*, 26 (1983)

Obelkevich, J., *Religion and Rural Society: South Lindsey 1825–1875* (Oxford, 1976)

Owen, D., *English Philanthropy, 1660–1960* (1964)

[Price, Eleanor C.], *Schoolboy Morality: An Address to Mothers* (1886)

Prochaska, F. K., *Women and Philanthropy in Nineteenth-Century England* (Oxford, 1980)

   'Female Philanthropy and Domestic Service in Victorian England', *Bulletin of the Institute of Historical Research*, 54 (1981)

   'Body and Soul: Bible Nurses and the Poor in Victorian London', *Historical Research*, 60 (1987)

   The Voluntary Impulse (1988)

   'A Mother's Country: Mothers' Meetings and Family Welfare in Britain, 1850–1950', *History*, 74 (1989)

Pryor Hack, Mary, *Self-Surrender* (1882)

Rathbone, Eleanor, *The Disinherited Family* (1924)

Rathbone, H. R., ed., *Memoir of Kitty Wilkinson of Liverpool 1786–1860* (Liverpool, 1927)

Roberts, D., *Paternalism in Early Victorian England* (New Brunswick, NJ, 1979)

Ross, Ellen, 'Survival Networks: Women's Neighbourhood Sharing in London before World War I', *History Workshop*, 15 (1983)

Samuel, R., ed., *East End Underworld: Chapters in the Life of Arthur Harding* (1981)

Semmel, B., *The Methodist Revolution* (1974)

Simey, M. B., *Charitable Efforts in Liverpool in the Nineteenth Century* (Liverpool, 1951)

Stedman Jones, G., *Outcast London: A Study in the Relationship between Classes in Victorian Society* (Oxford, 1971)

   'From Historical Sociology to Theoretical History', *British Journal of Sociology*, 27 (1976)

   'Class Expression versus Social Control? A Critique of Recent Trends in the Social History of Leisure', *History Workshop*, 4 (1977)

Stuart, Laura E., *In Memoriam Caroline Colman* (Norwich, 1896)

Sullivan, Dick, *Navvyman* (1983)

Summers, A., 'A Home from Home – Women's Philanthropic Work in the Nineteenth Century', in S. Burman, ed., *Fit Work for Women* (1979)

Thompson, F. M. L., *English Landed Society in the Nineteenth Century* (1971)

   'Social Control in Victorian Britain', *Economic History Review*, 2nd ser., 34 (1981)

Trimmer, Sarah, *The Oeconomy of Charity*, 2 vols. (1801)

Wagner, Gillian, *Barnardo* (1979)

Webb, Beatrice, *My Apprenticeship* (1926)

White, J., *Rothschild Buildings: Life in an East End Tenement Block 1887–1920* (1980)

Willmott, P., and Young, M., *Family and Class in a London Suburb* (1960)

Young, G. M., *Portrait of an Age: Victorian England* (1936)

8 CLUBS, SOCIETIES AND ASSOCIATIONS

Abel-Smith, B., *The Hospitals, 1800–1948* (1964)

Allen, D., 'Political Clubs in Restoration London', *Historical Journal*, 19 (1976)

Anderson, G., *Victorian Clerks* (Manchester, 1976)

Anning, S. T., *The General Infirmary at Leeds*, vol. 1: *The First 100 Years* (1963)

Ashton, T. S., 'Early Price Associations in the British Iron Industry', *Economic Journal*, 30 (1920)

Bailey, P., *Leisure and Class in Victorian England: Rational Recreation and the Contests for Control, 1830–1885* (1978)

Banton, M., *The Coloured Quarter: Negro Immigrants in an English City* (1955)

Beckwith, F., *The Leeds Library* (Leeds, 1950)

Berresford Ellis, P., and Mac A'Ghobhain, S., *The Scottish Insurrection of 1820* (1970)

Bladen, V. W., 'The Association of the Manufacturers of Earthenware, 1784–86', *Economic History, a Supplement to the Economic Journal*, 1 (1926–7)

Borsay, P., 'The English Urban Renaissance: The Development of Provincial Urban Culture, *c.* 1680–*c.* 1760', *Social History*, 5 (1977)

Brown, C., *The Social History of Religion in Scotland since 1730* (1987)

Brown, K., 'The Lodges of the Durham Miners' Association, 1869–1926', *Northern History*, 23 (1987)

Chalmers, T., *The Christian and Civic Economy of Large Towns*, 3 vols. (Glasgow, 1821)

Colley, Linda J., 'The Loyal Brotherhood and the Cocoa Tree: The London Organization of the Tory Party', *Historical Journal*, 20 (1977)

Corr, Helen, 'The Schoolgirl's Curriculum and the Ideology of the Home, 1870–1914', in Glasgow Women's Studies Group, *Uncharted Lives: Extracts from Scottish Women's Experiences, 1850–1982* (Glasgow, 1983)

Crossick, G., *An Artisan Elite in Victorian Society: Kentish London, 1840–1880* (1978)

Crossick, G., and Haupt, H.-G., eds., *Shopkeepers and Master Artisans in Nineteenth Century Europe* (1984)

Cunningham, H., *The Volunteer Force* (1975)

Daiches, D., Jones, P., and Jones, J., eds., *A Hotbed of Genius: The Scottish Enlightenment, 1730–1790* (Edinburgh, 1986)

Davidoff, Leonore, *The Best Circles* (1973)

Davidoff, Leonore, and Hall, Catherine, *Family Fortunes, Men and Women of the English Middle Class, 1780–1850* (1987)

Davies, M. L., *Maternity: Letters from Working Women*, with introduction by G. Dallas (1978)

Denvir, J., *The Irish in Britain from the Earliest Times to the Fall of Parnell* (1892)

Durkheim, E., *Suicide, A Study in Sociology* (1952)

   The Division of Labour in Society (New York, 1964)

Edwards, P., ed., *Equianos Travels* (1967)

Edwards, P., Duffield, I., *et al.*, 'Blacks in Britain', *History Today*, 31 (1981)

Emerson, R. L., 'The Social Composition of Enlightened Scotland: The Select Society of Edinburgh, 1754–1764', *Studies on Voltaire and the Eighteenth Century*, 114 (1973)

Gaffin, J., and Thomas, D., *Caring and Sharing: The Centenary History of the Co-operative Women's Guild* (1983)

Gallacher, T., 'Catholics in Scottish Politics', *Bulletin of Scottish Politics*, 2 (1981)

Gallacher, W., *Revolt on the Clyde* (1936)

Gartner, L. P., *The Jewish Immigrant in England, 1870–1914* (1960)

Geiss, I., *The Pan African Movement*, trans. A. Keep (1974)

Gibbs, F. W., *Joseph Priestley* (1965)

Giddens, A., *Capitalism and Modern Social Theory: An Analysis of the Writings of Marx, Durkheim and Max Weber* (Cambridge, 1971)

Gilley, S., 'Catholic Faith of the Irish Slums, London, 1840–70', in H. J. Dyos and M. Wolff, eds., *The Victorian City*, 2 vols. (1973), vol. 2

Gosden, P. H. J. H., *Self-Help: Voluntary Associations in Nineteenth Century Britain* (1973)

Graham, H. G., *The Social Life of Eighteenth Century Scotland* (1906)

Gray, R. Q., *The Labour Aristocracy in Victorian Edinburgh* (Oxford, 1976)

Hall, Catherine, 'The Early Formation of Victorian Domestic Ideology', in Sandra Burman, ed., *Fit Work for Women* (1979)

Hamilton, Sheila, 'The First Generations of University Women', in G. Donaldson, ed., *Four Centuries. Edinburgh University Life, 1583–1983* (Edinburgh, 1983)

Harrison, B., *Drink and the Victorians: The Temperance Question in England, 1815–1872* (1971)

   'Animals and the State in 19th Century England', *English Historical Review*, 88 (1973)

   'Philanthropy and the Victorians', in B. Harrison, *Peaceable Kingdom* (Oxford, 1982)

Harrison, J. F. C., *Learning and Living, 1790–1960: A Study in the History of the English Adult Education Movement* (1961)

Hayburn, R. H. C., 'The Voluntary Occupational Centre Movement, 1932–39', *Journal of Contemporary History*, 6 (1971)

Hill, Sir Francis, *Georgian Lincoln* (Cambridge, 1966)

Hollis, Patricia, ed., *Pressure from Without in Early Victorian England* (1974)

Hobsbawm, E. J., *Labouring Men* (1964)

Horne, H. O., *The History of Savings Banks* (Oxford, 1847)

Hudson, J. W., *The History of Adult Education* (1951)

Hume, A., *The Learned Societies and Printing Clubs of the United Kingdom* (1847)

Hunter, J., *Hallamshire: The History and Topography of the Parish of Sheffield*, new edn, ed. A. Gatty (1879)

Hutton, W., *An History of Birmingham* (2nd edn, Birmingham, 1783)

Hyde, C., *Technological Change and the British Iron Industry, 1700–1870* (Princeton, 1977)

Inkster, I., and Morrell, J., eds., *Metropolis and Province: Science in British Culture, 1780–1850* (1983)

Johnson, T. J., *Professions and Power* (1972)

Kargon, R. H., *Science in Victorian Manchester* (Manchester, 1977)

Kelly, T., *Early Public Libraries in Great Britain before 1850* (1966)

Kettle, Ann J., 'Lichfield Races', *Transactions of the Lichfield and South Staffordshire Archaeological Society*, 6 (1964–5)

King, Elspeth, *The Scottish Women's Suffrage Movement* (Glasgow, 1978)

Kirby, R. G., and Musson, A. E., *The Voice of the People: John Doherty, 1798–1854, Trades Unionist, Radical and Factory Reformer* (Manchester, 1975)

Knoop, D., and Jones, G. P., *The Genesis of Freemasonry* (Manchester, 1947)

Langton, J., and Morris, R. J., *Atlas of Industrializing Britain, 1780–1914* (1986)

Liddington, Jill, *Respectable Rebel: Hannah Mitchell, the Hard Way Up* (1968)

   The Life and Times of a Respectable Rebel, Selina Cooper, 1864–1946 (1984)

Liddington, Jill, and Norris, Jill, *One Hand Tied Behind Us: The Rise of the Women's Suffrage Movement* (1978)

Lipman, V. D., *A Social History of the Jews in England, 1850–1950* (1954)

Little, K. L., *Negroes in Britain: A Study of Racial Relations in English Society* (1947)

   West African Urbanization: A Study of Voluntary Associations in Social Change (Cambridge, 1965)

McCann, P., and Young, F. A., *Samuel Wilderspin and the Infant School Movement* (1982)

McCullough Thew, Linda, *The Pit Village and the Store* (1985)

McElroy, D., *Scotland's Age of Improvement: A Survey of 18th Century Literary Clubs and Societies* (Washington, 1969)

Mackenzie, E., *A Descriptive and Historical Account of the Town and County of Newcastle upon Tyne* (Newcastle, 1827)

McLeod, H., *Class and Religion in the Late Victorian City* (1974)

McShane, H., and Smith, Joan, *No Mean Fighter* (1978)

Marshall, J. D., 'Nottinghamshire Labourers in the Early 19th Century', *Transactions of the Thoroton Society of Nottingham*, 64 (1960)

Melling, J., *Rent Strikes: People's Struggle for Housing in West Scotland, 1890–1916* (Edinburgh, 1983)

Millerson, G., *The Qualifying Associations: A Study in Professionalisation* (1964)

Milne Rae, Lettice, *Ladies in Debate, Being a History of the Ladies Edinburgh Debating Society, 1865–1935* (Edinburgh, 1936)

Milton, N., *John MacLean* (1973)

Mitchell, A., 'The Association Movement of 1792–1793', *Historical Journal*, 4 (1961)

Mitchison, R., 'The Making of the Old Scottish Poor Law', *Past & Present*, 63 (1974)

Money, J., *Experience and Identity: Birmingham and the West Midlands, 1760–1800* (Manchester, 1977)

Morris, B., 'Ernest Thompson Seton and the Origins of the Woodcraft Movement', *Journal of Contemporary History*, 5 (1970)

Morris, R. J., 'Middle Class Culture, 1700–1914', in D. Fraser, ed., *A History of Modern Leeds* (Manchester, 1980)

'Samuel Smiles and the Genesis of Self Help: The Retreat to a Petit Bourgeois Utopia', *Historical Journal*, 24 (1981)

'Voluntary Societies and British Urban Elites, 1780–1950', *Historical Journal*, 26 (1983)

Mudie Smith, R., *The Religious Life of London* (1904)

Muir, A., *Nair's of Kirkcaldy: A Short History, 1847–1956* (Cambridge, 1956)

O'Neill, Julie, 'Self Help in Nottinghamshire: The Woodborough Male Friendly Society, 1826–1954', *Transactions of the Thoroton Society of Nottingham*, 90 (1986)

Orange, A. D., *Philosophers and Provincials: The Yorkshire Philosophical Society from 1822 to 1844* (Yorkshire Philosophical Society, 1973)

Owen, D., *English Philanthropy, 1660–1960* (1964)

Patterson, Audrey, 'The Poor Law in 19th Century Scotland', in D. Fraser, ed., *The New Poor Law in the Nineteenth Century* (1976)

Pelling, H., *Popular Politics and Society in Late Victorian Britain* (1968)

Phillipson, N. T., 'Culture and Society in the 18th Century Province: The Case of Edinburgh and the Scottish Enlightenment', in Lawrence Stone, ed., *The University in Society* (Princeton, 1974)

Pollard, S., 'Nineteenth Century Co-operation: From Community Building to Shopkeeping', in A. Briggs and J. Saville, eds., *Essays in Labour History* (1960)

Pooley, C. G., 'The Residential Segregation of Migrant Communities in Mid Victorian Liverpool', *Transactions of the Institute of British Geographers*, n.s., 2 (1977)

Pope, S., 'The Development of Freemasonry in England and Wales', *Ars Quator Coronatorum* (1956–8)

Poynter, J. R., *Society and Pauperism: English Ideas on Poor Relief, 1795–1834* (1969)

Price, R., 'The Working Men's Club Movement and Victorian Social Reform Ideology', *Victorian Studies*, 15 (1976)

    Masters, Unions and Men: Work Control in Building and the Rise of Labour, 1830–1914 (Cambridge, 1980)

Prochaska, F. K., *Women and Philanthropy in Nineteenth-Century England* (Oxford, 1980)

Prynn, D., 'The Clarion Clubs, Rambling and the Holiday Associations in Britain since the 1890s', *Journal of Contemporary History*, 11 (1976)

    'The Woodcraft Folk and the Labour Movement, 1925–70', *Journal of Contemporary History*, 8 (1983)

Rawcliffe, J. M., 'Bromley: Kentish Market Town to London Suburb, 1841–1881', in F. M. L. Thompson, ed., *The Rise of Suburbia* (Leicester, 1982)

Roberts, J. M., 'Freemasonry, Possibilities of a Neglected Topic', *English Historical Review*, 84 (1969)

    The Mythology of Secret Societies (1972)

Roberts, M. J. D., 'The Society for the Suppression of Vice and its Early Critics, 1802–1812', *Historical Journal*, 26 (1983)

Rowntree, B. S., *Poverty and Progress: A Second Social Survey of York* (1941)

Rowntree, B. S., and Lavers, G. R., *English Life and Leisure* (1951)

Royle, E., 'Mechanics Institutes and the Working Classes, 1840–1860', *Historical Journal*, 14 (1971)

Scott, Gill, 'The Women's Co-operative Guild', *Bulletin of the Society for the Study of Labour History*, 48 (1984)

Shapin, S. A., 'The Pottery Philosophical Society, 1819–1835: An Examination of the Cultural Uses of Provincial Science', *Science Studies*, 2 (1972)

Simey, Margaret B., *Charitable Efforts in Liverpool in the Nineteenth Century* (Liverpool, 1951)

Smith, D., *Conflict and Compromise: Class Formation in English Society, 1830–1914* (1982)

Smith, Joan, 'Class, Skill and Sectarianism in Glasgow and Liverpool', in R. J. Morris, ed., *Class, Power and Social Structure in British Nineteenth Century Towns* (Leicester, 1986)

Summers, Anne, 'A Home from Home – Women's Philanthropic Work in the Nineteenth Century', in Sandra Burman, ed., *Fit Work for Women* (1979)

Taylor, Barbara, *Eve and the New Jerusalem: Socialism and Feminism in the Nineteenth Century* (1983)

Thompson, F. M. L., *Hampstead: Building a Borough, 1650–1964* (1974)

Timbs, J., *Clubs and Club Life in London* (1872)

Tylecote, Mabel, *The Mechanics Institutions of Lancashire and Yorkshire before 1851* (Manchester, 1957)

Walker, B., 'The Anacreontic Society', *Transactions of the Birmingham Archaeological Society*, 63 (1939–40)

Walmsley, R., *Peterloo: The Case Re-Opened* (Manchester, 1969)

Warren, A., 'Sir Robert Baden-Powell, the Scout Movement and Citizen Training in Great Britain, 1900–1920', *English Historical Review*, 101 (1986)

Western, J. R., 'The Volunteer Movement as an Anti Revolutionary Force, 1793–1801', *English Historical Review*, 71 (1956)

Wild, P., 'Recreation in Rochdale, 1900–40', in J. Clarke, C. Critcher and R. Johnson, eds., *Working-Class Culture: Studies in History and Theory* (1979)

Wilkinson, P., 'English Youth Movements, 1908–30', *Journal of Contemporary History*, 4 (1969)

Williams, B., *The Making of Manchester Jewry, 1740–1875* (Manchester, 1976)
Wirth, L., 'Urbanism as a Way of Life', in L. Wirth, *On Cities and Social Life*, ed. Albert J. Reiss (Chicago, 1964)
Withers, C. W. J., 'Kirk, Club and Cultural Change: Gaelic Chapels, Highland Societies and the Urban Gaelic Sub-Culture in Eighteenth Century Scotland', *Social History*, 10 (1985)
The Future of Voluntary Organization: Report of the Wolfenden Committee (1978)
Wright, D., *Gould's History of Freemasonry*, 5 vols. (1931–6)
Yeo, S., *Religion and Voluntary Organisations in Crisis* (1976)

Index